Social Information Retrieval Systems:
Emerging Technologies and Applications for Searching the Web Effectively

Dion Goh
Nanyang Technological University, Singapore

Schubert Foo
Nanyang Technological University, Singapore

INFORMATION SCIENCE REFERENCE

Hershey · New York

Acquisitions Editor:	Kristin Klinger
Development Editor:	Kristin Roth
Senior Managing Editor:	Jennifer Neidig
Managing Editor:	Sara Reed
Copy Editor:	Maria Boyer
Typesetter:	Cindy Consonery
Cover Design:	Lisa Tosheff
Printed at:	Yurchak Printing Inc.

Published in the United States of America by
Information Science Reference (an imprint of IGI Global)
701 E. Chocolate Avenue, Suite 200
Hershey PA 17033
Tel: 717-533-8845
Fax: 717-533-8661
E-mail: cust@igi-global.com
Web site: http://www.igi-global.com/reference

and in the United Kingdom by
Information Science Reference (an imprint of IGI Global)
3 Henrietta Street
Covent Garden
London WC2E 8LU
Tel: 44 20 7240 0856
Fax: 44 20 7379 0609
Web site: http://www.eurospanonline.com

Library of Congress Cataloging-in-Publication Data

Social information retrieval systems : emerging technologies and applications for searching the Web effectively / Dion Goh & Schubert Foo, editors.

    p. cm.

  Summary: "This book provides relevant content in the areas of information retrieval systems, services, and research; covering topics such as social tagging, collaborative querying, social network analysis, subjective relevance judgments, and collaborative filtering. Answering the increasing demand for authoritative resources on Internet technologies, this will make an indispensable addition to any library collection"-- Provided by publisher.

  Includes bibliographical references and index.

  ISBN-13: 978-1-59904-543-6 (hardcover)

  ISBN-13: 978-1-59904-545-0 (ebook)

  1. Internet searching. 2. Web search engines. 3. World Wide Web--Subject access. 4. Information storage and retrieval systems. 5. Information retrieval. I. Goh, Dion. II. Foo, Schubert.

  ZA4230.S63 2008

  025.04--dc22

                              2007023437

British Cataloguing in Publication Data
A Cataloguing in Publication record for this book is available from the British Library.

Table of Contents

Section VI
Applications and Case Studies in Social Information Retrieval

Detailed Table of Contents

Section I
Collaborative Querying

Chapter I

Searchers generally have difficulty searching into knowledge repositories because of the quantity of data involved and because searcher mechanisms are not tailored to their differing needs at different points in time. Also, every searcher generally searches alone without taking into account other users with similar search needs or experience. While the Internet may have contributed to information overload, the connectivity it has provides the potential to different searchers to collaborate when looking for information. In this chapter the authors: (1) review concepts related to social information retrieval and existing collaborative mechanisms; (2) discuss two collaborative mechanisms—cues and specialty search; and (3) see cues and specialty search in the context of the changing needs of a searcher in one of four modes. A case study of an online portal for the Singapore education community is used to show how collaboration could enhance learning and search efficacy.

Chapter II

Collaborative querying is a technique that makes use of past users' search experiences in order to help the current user formulate an appropriate query. In this technique, related queries are extracted from query logs and clustered. Queries from these clusters that are related to the user's query are then recommended to the user. This work uses a combination of query terms as well as result documents returned by queries for clustering queries. For the latter, it extracts features such as titles, URLs, and snippets from the result documents. It also proposes an extended K-means clustering algorithm for clustering queries over a simple measure of overlap. Experimental results reveal that the best clusters are obtained by using a combination of these sources rather than using only query terms or only result URLs alone.

Section II
Collaborative Classification and Organization

In this chapter the authors examine the use of collaborative classification to support social information retrieval by organizing search results. It subscribes to the view that the activity of collaborative classification can be characterized by top-down and bottom-up approaches, both in terms of the nature of concept classification and the process of classification development. Two approaches, collaborative indexing and search result classification based on shared classification schemes, are described and compared. It suggests that by allowing open access to classification development tools to generate shared classification schemes, which in turn become collaborative artifacts, cooperating user groups will generate their own coordination mechanisms that are not dependent on the system itself.

In this chapter the author argues the case that there is a mismatch between current metadata standards for the description of archival holdings and what many users actually want to know about a collection. Standard archival descriptions objectively describe what is in a collection, whereas users wish to know what they can do with a collection. It is argued that matching users' research questions to library resources that could help answer those questions is a crucial social role played by librarians, archivists, and other frontline staff. However placing descriptions of what is in a collection online for users to search directly risks disintermediating the users from library staff. "Use-centered descriptions" are proposed as a way of systematically describing what can be done with a collection, and are, in effect, an encoding of library staff's knowledge about what can be done with a collection. It is therefore argued that use-centered descriptions repair some of disintermediation gaps caused by putting collection descriptions online. A theoretical motivation for use-centered descriptions is presented by showing how Heaney's (1999) analytic model of collections, which underlies the Research Support Libraries Program (RSLP) collection description standard, only addresses finding and identifying resources. The author augments this model to address selecting resources from a range of possibilities and show how use-centered descriptions stem from this augmentation. A case study is presented demonstrating the experience of developing a set of use-centered descriptions for the University of London as part of a project to encourage wider access to their archival holdings. The project had necessarily limited aims, and therefore conclusions are drawn about the viability of use-centered descriptions in wider domains.

Social information retrieval systems, such as recommender systems, can benefit greatly from sharable and reusable evaluations of online resources. For example, in distributed repositories with rich collections of learning resources, users can benefit from evaluations, ratings, reviews, annotations, and so forth that previous users have provided. Furthermore, sharing these evaluations and annotations can help attain the critical mass of data required for social information retrieval systems to be effective and efficient. This kind of interoperability requires a common framework that can be used to describe in a reusable manner the evaluation approach, as well as the results of the evaluation. The authors discuss this concept, focusing on the rationale for a reusable and interoperable framework, that can be used to facilitate the representation, management, and reuse of results from the evaluation of learning resources. For this purpose, the authors review a variety of evaluation approaches for learning resources and study ways in which evaluation results may be characterized, so as to draw requirements for sharable and reusable evaluation metadata. Usage scenarios illustrate how evaluation metadata can be useful in the context of recommender systems for learning resources.

Section III
Using Social Networks for Information Retrieval

In this chapter the authors discuss the integration of information retrieval information from two sources—a social network and a document reference network—for enhancing reference-based search engine rankings. In particular, current models of information retrieval are blind to the social context that surrounds information resources, thus they do not consider the trustworthiness of their authors when they present the query results to the users. Following this point the authors elaborate on the basic intuitions that highlight the contribution of the social context—as can be mined from social network positions for instance—into the improvement of the rankings provided in reference-based search engines. A review on ranking models in Web search engine retrieval along with social network metrics of importance such as prestige and centrality are provided as background. Then a presentation of recent research models that utilize both contexts is provided, along with a case study in the Internet-based encyclopedia Wikipedia, based on the social network metrics.

Social information spaces are characterized by the presence of a social network between participants. The authors of this chapter present methods for utilizing social networks for information retrieval, by applying graph authority measures to the social network. The authors show how to integrate authority measures in an information retrieval algorithm. In order to determine the suitability of the described algorithms, they examine the structure and statistical properties of social networks, and present examples of social networks as well as evaluation results.

Chapter VIII

In this chapter the authors propose a collaborative peer network application called *6Search (6S)* to address the scalability limitations of centralized search engines. Each peer crawls the Web in a focused way, guided by its user's information context. Through this approach, better (distributed) coverage can be achieved. Each peer also acts as a search "servent" (server + client) by submitting and responding to queries to/from its neighbors. This search process has no centralized bottleneck. Peers depend on a local adaptive routing algorithm to dynamically change the topology of the peer network and search for the best neighbors to answer their queries. The authors present and evaluate learning techniques to improve local query routing. They validate prototypes of the 6S network via simulations with 70–500 model users based on actual Web crawls, and find that the network topology rapidly converges from a random network to a small-world network, with clusters emerging from user communities with shared interests. Finally, the authors compare the quality of the results with those obtained by centralized search engines such as Google.

Section IV
Social Issues

In this chapter the authors discuss some of the social and ethical issues associated with social information retrieval. Using the work of Habermas, they argue that social networking is likely to exacerbate already disturbing trends towards the fragmentation of society and a corresponding decline reduction in social diversity. Such a situation is not conducive to developing a healthy, democratic society. Following the tradition of critical theorists of technology, the authors conclude with a call for responsible and aware technological design with more attention paid to the values embedded in new technological systems.

Information and knowledge have become a crucial resource in our knowledge-based, computer-mediated economy. But knowledge is primarily a social phenomenon, on which computer processing has had only a limited impact so far, in spite of impressive advances. In this context have recently appeared various collaborative systems that promise to give access to socially situated information. The author argues that a prior analysis of the social context is necessary for a better understanding of the whole domain of collaborative software. The author will examine the variety and functions of information in modern society, where collaborative information management is now the dominant type of occupation. In fact, real information is much more complex than its usual technical sense: one should distinguish between information and knowledge, as well as between explicit and tacit knowledge. Because of the notable importance of tacit knowledge, social networks are indispensable in practice for locating relevant information. The author then proposes a typology of collaborative software, distinguishing between explicit communities supported by groupware systems, task-oriented communities organized around a common data structure, and implicit links exploited by collaborative filtering and social information retrieval. The latter approach is usually implemented by virtually grouping similar users, but there exist many possible variants. Yet much remains to be done by extracting, formalizing, and exploiting implicit social links.

Section IV
Social Information Seeking Models

In this chapter the authors demonstrate a number of contrasting uses of the social aspects of information seeking, and through those propose, demonstrate, and realize social models of information seeking that complement existing information seeking models and technologies. These include: information sharing among humanities researchers; creation of profiles for continuous, ongoing searching of medical material; and the capture of models of user behaviors in an interactive, mobile tourist information system. From the human perspective the authors illustrate differing social techniques and issues including: explicit and implicit sharing; seeking facilitated by subject (medical, academic) experts and search experts (librarians); and anonymized and attributed social environments.

In this chapter the author uses a study of human assessments of relevance to demonstrate how individual relevance judgments and retrieval practices embody collaborative elements that contribute to the overall progress of that person's individual work. After discussing key themes of the conceptual framework, the author will discuss two case studies that serve as powerful illustrations of these themes for researchers and practitioners alike. These case studies—outcomes of a two-year ethnographic exploration of research practices—illustrate the theoretical position presented in part one of the chapter, providing lessons for the ways that people work with information systems to generate knowledge and the conditions that will support these practices. The author shows that collaboration does not have to be explicit to influence searcher behavior. It seeks to present both a theoretical framework and case studies that can be applied to the design, development, and evaluation of collaborative information retrieval systems.

Chapter XIII

In this chapter the author presents an overview of citation analysis, emphasizing its formal aspects as applied social network theory. As such, citation linking can be considered a tool for information retrieval based on social interaction. It is indeed well known that following citation links is an efficient method of information retrieval. Relations with Web linking are highlighted. Yet, also social aspects related to the act of citing, such as the occurrence of invisible colleges, are discussed. The author presents some recent developments and presents his opinion on some future developments. In this way, he hopes the reader will realize how the fields of citation analysis and Webometrics can be helpful in building social information retrieval systems.

Section VI
Applications and Case Studies in Social Information Retrieval

Chapter XIV

Active learning is the ability of learners to carry out learning activities in such a way that they will be able effectively and efficiently to construct knowledge from information sources. Personalized and customizable access on digital materials collected from the Web according to one's own personal requirements and interests is an example of active learning. Moreover, it is also necessary to provide techniques to locate suitable materials. In this chapter, the authors introduce a personalized learning environment providing intelligent support to achieve the expectations of active learning. The system exploits collaborative and semantic approaches to extract concepts from documents and maintain user and resource profiles based on domain ontologies. In such a way, the retrieval phase takes advantage of the common knowledge base used to extract useful knowledge and produce personalized views of the learning system.

Chapter XV

In this chapter the authors propose the architecture of the multi-agent tourism system (MATS). Tourism information on the World Wide Web is dynamic and constantly changing. It is not easy to obtain relevant and updated information for individual user needs. A multi-agent system is defined as a collection of agents that work in conjunction with each other. The objective of MATS is to provide the most relevant and updated information according to the user's interests. It consists of multiple agents with three main tiers such as the interface module, information management module, and domain-related module. The authors propose the Rule-based Personalization with Collaborative Filtering technique for effective personalization in MATS which can address the limitations of pure collaborative filtering such as the scalability, sparsity, and cold-start problems.

Recommendation systems have been used in e-commerce sites to make product recommendations and to provide customers with information that helps them decide which products to buy. The recommendations are based on different methods and techniques for suggesting products, with the most well known being collaborative and content-based filtering. Recently, several recommendation systems adopted hybrid approaches by combining collaborative and content-based features as well as other techniques in order to avoid their limitations. In this chapter the authors investigate hybrid recommendations systems and especially the way they support movie e-shops in their attempt to suggest movies to customers. Specifically, the authors introduce an approach where the knowledge about customers and movies is extracted from usage mining and ontological data in conjunction with customer movie ratings and matching techniques between customers. This integration provides additional knowledge about customers' preferences and allows the production of successful recommendations. Even in the case of the cold-start problem where no initial behavioral information is available, the approach can provide logical and relevant recommendations to the customers. The provided recommendations are expected to have higher accuracy in matching customers' preferences and thus higher acceptance by them. Finally, the authors describe future trends and challenges and discuss the open issues in the field.

Preface

The popularity of the Web has led to a tremendous growth in the volume of available online information. The result is that people have now come to depend on the Web to meet their information needs via search engines, portals, digital libraries, and other information retrieval systems. However, the amount of information and its growth is a double-edged sword due to the problem of information overload, exacerbated by the fact that not all content on the Web is relevant or of acceptable quality to information seekers. Information overload has led to a situation where users are swamped with too much information and have to sift through the materials in search of relevant content.

A variety of techniques have been adopted on the Web to address these problems inherent in information search, drawing from the fields of information retrieval, information filtering, human computer interaction, and the study of information seeking behavior. Work in these areas has yielded many novel and useful algorithmic and user interface techniques. Research in information seeking behavior suggests yet an alternative promising approach in helping users meet their information needs. Many studies have found that interaction and collaboration with other people is an important part in the process of information seeking and use. It is not uncommon that in searching for information, we tap on our social networks—friends, colleagues, librarians—to help locate what we need.

Social information retrieval refers to a family of techniques that assist users in meeting their information needs by harnessing the collective intelligence of other users—their expert knowledge or search experience. Elements of social information retrieval may be found on the Web through the hyperlinks that connect different Web sites (e.g., bookmark lists), subject directories (e.g., Yahoo, Open Directory Project), Google's PageRank algorithm, and user annotations of resources (e.g., Amazon.com's book reviews and ratings). More contemporary techniques include social tagging, collaborative querying, social network analysis, subjective relevance judgments, and collaborative filtering.

Social information retrieval is an emerging area and a promising avenue for the design and implementation of a new generation of information retrieval systems. It has drawn interest in academia as well as in industry. This book introduces readers to this area as well as discusses the state-of-the-art techniques in social information retrieval. It serves as a resource for those dealing with information retrieval systems, services, and research, and is written for academics, researchers, information retrieval product managers and software developers, librarians, and students.

ORGANIZATION

The book's chapters are organized into six sections with the following themes:

- Collaborative Querying
- Collaborative Classification and Organization
- Using Social Networks for Information Retrieval
- Social Issues
- Social Information Seeking Models
- Applications and Case Studies in Social Information Retrieval

Section I deals with collaborative querying, discussing various techniques that support searching by harnessing other users' search experiences. This section consists of two chapters.

Chapter I, "Collaborating to Search Effectively in Different Searcher Modes Through Cues and Specialty Search" by Naresh Kumar Agarwal and Danny C.C. Poo, argues that searchers generally have difficulty searching in knowledge repositories because of the quantity of data involved and because searcher mechanisms are not tailored to their differing needs. Collaboration among searchers is one possible solution. They review concepts related to social information retrieval and other collaborative mechanisms, and discuss two collaborative searching mechanisms—cues and specialty search. A case study of an online educational portal is also presented to show how collaboration could enhance learning and search efficacy.

Chapter II, "Collaborative Querying Using a Hybrid Content and Results-Based Approach" by Ray Chandrani Sinha, Dion Hoe-Lian Goh, Schubert Foo, Nyein Chan Soe Win, and Khasfariyati Razikin, describes the concept of collaborative querying, a technique that makes use of past users' search experiences in order to help the current user formulate an appropriate query. Here, related queries are extracted from query logs, clustered, and used as candidates for recommendations. Query similarity is determined using a combination of query terms as well as search result documents. For the latter, features such as titles, URLs, and snippets from the result documents are used. Experimental results reveal that the best clusters are obtained by using a combination of these sources rather than using only query terms or only result URLs alone.

Collaborative classification and organization is covered in Section II. Chapters in this section examine how classification schemes and metadata can be constructed collaboratively. The section consists of three chapters.

Chapter III, "Collaborative Classification for Group-Oriented Organization of Search Results" by Kei-ichi Nakata and Amrish Singh, begins this section by examining the use of collaborative classification to support social information retrieval by organizing search results. Two approaches, collaborative indexing and search result classification based on shared classification schemes, are described and compared.

Chapter IV, "A Case Study of Use-Centered Descriptions: Archival Descriptions of What Can Be Done with a Collection" by Richard Butterworth, argues that there is a mismatch between current metadata standards for the description of archival holdings and what many users actually want to know about a collection. Use-centered descriptions are proposed as a way of systematically describing what can be done with a collection, and are, in effect, an encoding of library staff's knowledge about what can be done with a collection. An example of its use by the University of London to encourage wider access to their archival holdings is presented.

Chapter V, "Metadata for Social Recommendations: Storing, Sharing, and Reusing Evaluations of Learning Resources" by Riina Vuorikari, Nikos Manouselis, and Erik Duval, discusses how social information retrieval systems can benefit greatly from sharable and reusable evaluations of online resources in the form of metadata. To achieve interoperability among various systems, a common framework to describe the evaluation of such resources is required. Through a review of various approaches, they present an evaluation framework and apply it to learning resources.

Section III focuses on using social networks for information retrieval. Although the idea of using social networks to find information is not new, it has gained popularity since the introduction of the Google search engine and therefore warrants an in-depth examination of the techniques involved. There are three chapters in this section:

Chapter VI, "Social Network Models for Enhancing Reference-Based Search Engine Rankings" by Nikolaos Korfiatis, Miguel-Ángel Sicilia, Claudia Hess, Klaus Stein, and Christoph Schlieder, begins this section by discussing the integration of information retrieval information from two sources—a social network and a document reference network—for enhancing reference-based search engine rankings. The authors elaborate on the basic intuitions that highlight the contribution of the social context, which can be mined from social networks, into the improvement of the rankings provided in reference-based search engines. A case study on the Web-based encyclopedia Wikipedia is presented as an illustration of the ideas introduced in this chapter.

Chapter VII, "From PageRank to Social Rank: Authority-Based Retrieval in Social Information Spaces" by Sebastian Marius Kirsch, Melanie Gnasa, Markus Won, and Armin B. Cremers, presents methods for utilizing social networks for information retrieval by applying graph authority measures to the social network. The authors present techniques for integrating authority measures in an information retrieval algorithm. To demonstrate the applicability of their algorithm, the authors examine the structure and statistical properties of social networks, and present examples of social networks as well as evaluation results.

Chapter VIII, "Adaptive Peer-to-Peer Social Networks for Distributed Content-Based Web Search" by Le-Shin Wu, Ruj Akavipat, Ana Gabriela Maguitman, and Filippo Menczer, employs social networks in information retrieval from the perspective of collaborative peer-to-peer networks. Their system, called 6Search (6S), aims to address the scalability limitations of centralized search engines. Each peer crawls the Web in a focused way, guided by its user's information context. Each peers also acts as a search "servent" by submitting and responding to queries to/from its neighbors. Prototypes of the 6S system are evaluated via simulations that model users based on actual Web crawls. The quality of the results obtained is also compared against centralized search engines such as Google.

Section IV shifts its attention to examine social issues pertaining to social information retrieval systems. This section consists of two chapters.

Chapter IX, "The Ethics of Social Information Retrieval" by Brendan Luyt and Chu Keong Lee, attempts to examine social networking and social information retrieval in the context of Habermas's concepts of public sphere and communication actions against the problem of homophily (where a contact between similar people occurs at a higher rate than among dissimilar people), and posits that such activity is likely to increase the fragmentation of society and a reduction in social diversity as groups become more homogenous and isolated from rest of society who also have important roles to play towards learning, among others. The authors conclude with a call for more responsible and aware technological designs with an emphasis on values so that the effects of homophily are addressed.

Chapter X, "The Social Context of Knowledge" by Daniel Memmi, demonstrates that collaborative information management is now the dominant type of occupation with human information processing predominately taking place in a large social context. Interactions are supported by a range of collaborative information tools and systems that are designed to support the seeking, diffusion, and management of explicit and tacit knowledge. While some of these systems are virtually grouping similar users together (thereby promoting the problem of homophily, as discussed in Chapter IX), there is also a need to find new solutions by better understanding and modeling human cognitive processes in information processing from diverse heterogeneous sources to enable the creation of new design ideas for future systems.

Section V on social information seeking models presents a set of different information seeking models in different contexts and highlights the wide ranging applicability of this new emerging field of social information retrieval. This section consists of three chapters.

Chapter XI, "Social Information Seeking in Digital Libraries" by George Buchanan and Annika Hinze, first showed a number of contrasting uses of the social aspects of information seeking and abstracts a number of different approaches to present underlying principles, architectures, and models. Using digital library as a technological platform, the authors propose the provision of social context by the addition and integration of recommendation, alerting, and communication services into the architecture. They suggest that effective social information seeking pivots on closing the gap between human communication and the digital library.

Chapter XII, "Relevant Intra-Actions in Networked Environments" by Theresa Dirndorfer Anderson, provides a conceptual framework for relevance as a socially situated phenomenon, and goes on to describe an ethnographic study of academics engaged in research projects making relevant judgments of information when working with networked information systems. Relevance assessment when theorized as *intra-action* shows such judgments as emergent constructions that arose as a result of interplay between social and personal, technical and human elements in such a networked environment. The understanding of such a perspective can enable better collaborative systems to be designed, such as the facilitation for creating collaborative metadata schemes to enable alternative representations of content and to cater for different information seeking behaviors in different contexts.

Chapter XIII, "Publication and Citation Analysis as a Tool for Information Retrieval" by Ronald Rousseau, defines citation analysis in the context of applied social network theory, and highlights the relationship between citation linking as a source for information retrieval based on social interaction where authors cite and co-cite each other's publications. Relations between citation analysis and Web links in the emerging field of Webometrics are also distinguished. The author takes a peek into the future where he envisages: the integration of local and regional citation indexes into a virtual world citation atlas, the spot translation of existing scientific non-English literature on the Web to increase the knowledge base and visibility and citation levels of such authors, and the establishment of global repositories for research and others.

Section VI concludes this book by presenting applications and case studies in social information retrieval. The focus of this section is to examine where and how social information retrieval systems have been applied. There are three chapters in this section.

Chapter XIV, "Personalized Information Retrieval in a Semantic-Based Learning Environment" by Antonella Carbonaro and Rodolfo Ferrini, applies social information retrieval techniques to the education domain. The authors introduce a personalized learning environment providing intelligent support to achieve the expectations of active learning. The system exploits collaborative and semantic approaches to extract concepts from documents, and maintain user and resources profiles based on domain ontologies. With this approach, the information retrieval process is able to produce personalized views of the learning environment.

Chapter XV, "Multi-Agent Tourism System (MATS)" by Soe Yu Maw and Myo-Myo Naing, addresses the tourism domain. The authors argue that tourism information on the Web is dynamic, and it is not easy to obtain relevant and updated information to meet an individual's needs. To address this issue, they developed the multi-agent tourism system (MATS) with the goal of providing relevant and updated information tailored to the user's interests. Key to the system is the rule-based personalization with collaborative filtering technique for personalization in MATS. The technique is able to address the limitations of pure collaborative filtering, including scalability, sparsity, and cold-start problems.

Chapter XVI, "Hybrid Recommendation Systems: A Case Study on the Movies Domain" by Konstantinos Markellos, Penelope Markellou, Aristotelis Mertis, Ioanna Mousourouli, Angeliki Panayiotaki, and Athanasios Tsakalidis, examines how social information retrieval can applied to e-commerce sites, focusing in particular on recommendation systems. The authors investigate hybrid recommendation systems and the way they can support movie e-shops to suggest movies to customers. Specifically, the authors introduce a recommendation approach where knowledge about customers and movies is extracted from usage mining and ontological data in conjunction with customer-movie ratings and matching techniques between customers.

Acknowledgment

This book would not have been possible without the authors for their excellent chapters and the reviewers who have given invaluable comments, and the editors are grateful for all their hard work. We would also like to thank IGI Global for the opportunity to publish this book on social information retrieval systems, and for their assistance and support, which has made this process an enjoyable one.

Dion Goh and Schubert Foo
May 2007

Section I
Collaborative Querying

Chapter I
Collaborating to Search Effectively in Different Searcher Modes Through Cues and Specialty Search

Naresh Kumar Agarwal
National University of Singapore, Singapore

Danny C.C. Poo
National University of Singapore, Singapore

ABSTRACT

Searchers generally have difficulty searching into knowledge repositories because of the quantity of data involved and because search mechanisms are not tailored to the differing needs of the searcher at different points in time. Also, every searcher generally searches alone without taking into account other users with similar search needs or experience. While the Internet may have contributed to information overload, the connectivity it has provides the potential to different searchers to collaborate when looking for information. In this chapter, we: (1) review concepts related to social information retrieval and existing collaborative mechanisms, (2) discuss two collaborative mechanisms—cues and specialty search, and (3) see cues and specialty search in the context of the changing needs of a searcher in one of four modes. A case study of an online portal for the Singapore education community is used to show how collaboration could enhance learning and search efficacy.

INTRODUCTION

Knowledge repositories are increasingly a part of any enterprise. Masses of documents, e-mails, databases, images, and audio/video recordings form vast repositories of information assets to be tapped by employees, partners, customers, and other stakeholders (Papadopoullos, 2004). The content provided in such repositories is large, diverse, and huge in quantity. Searchers generally have difficulty searching into such kinds of repositories because of the quantity of data involved and because searcher mechanisms are not tailored to their differing needs at different points in time. Also, every searcher generally searches alone, without taking into account other users who would have conducted similar searches or have a similar work role as the searcher.

A searcher typically does not just access organization-level repositories, but has access to vast amounts of information from the Internet. The growth of the Internet has brought information access to individuals from all walks of life and has connected the world like never before. According to the Berkeley study "How Much Information" (Swearingen et al., 2003), print, film, magnetic, and optical storage media produced about 5 exabytes of new information in 2002 (1 gigabyte = 10^9 bytes; 1 terabyte = 10^{12} bytes; 1 exabyte = 10^{18} bytes; 5 exabytes are equivalent to all words ever spoken by human beings). The study estimated that the amount of new information stored in these media had doubled between 1999 and 2002, and grew about 30% each year. While there is no dearth of information, there is a long and meandering path before this information translates to knowledge and understanding. Sieving the important from the unimportant, the relevant from the non-relevant, getting answers to the questions, and making sense of all the data available are some of the challenges faced by searchers of information. The World Wide Web, while providing increased connectivity and accessibility to information, has also increased the amount of information a person must read and digest each day—a problem commonly referred to as *information overload*. Compared to the growth of the World Wide Web, "development of the human brain has been tardy: it has grown *only linearly* from 400 to 1400 cubic centimeters in the last 3.5 million years" (Chakrabarti et al., 1999).

To help retrieve information from this huge maze, search engines come in handy and serve as catalogs of the Web. They index the Web pages by using computer programs called 'spiders' or 'robots', which crawl from site to site and create a database that stores indices of Web pages on the Web. Users can enter search terms to query against the index database. The search engine processes the query and returns a list of Web pages, along with short descriptions of each page (Fang, Chen, & Chen, 2005). The search engines' critical role in helping people find information online makes them the gatekeepers to online information (Morahan-Martin & Anderson, 2000).

However, "search engines do not index sites equally, may not index new pages for months, and no engine indexes more than about 16% of the Web" (Lawrence & Giles, 2000, p. 33). This was in 2000, and the coverage of search engines has increased since then (but the size of the Web has also increased, along with the non-indexable 'deep Web'). Problems due to synonymy and polysemy plague the current information searches (Deerwester, Dumais, Furnas, Landauer, & Harshman, 1990; Morahan-Martin & Anderson, 2000). Synonymy is the semantic relation that holds between two words that can, in a given context, express the same meaning. Polysemy is the ambiguity of an individual word or phrase that can be used, in different contexts, to express two or more different meanings (WordNet 2.0, 2003). For example, the keywords "female sibling" and "sister" might mean the same thing but give different results on searching (the problem of synonymy). On the other hand, searching for the keyword 'apple' may give you a page full of links to 'Apple Computers', while you might be searching for information related to the fruit. Similarly, searching for 'Java' may give you top links about the Java programming language, while you might be interested in coffee or the Indonesian island of Java. This is the problem of polysemy. Search engines suffer from another major drawback—they make an underlying presumption that the user can formulate on-point queries to effectively narrow down the volume of information available (Narayanan, Koppaka, Edala, Loritz, & Daley, 2004).

Effective query formulation is possible only when the users are already familiar with the topic of research and they indeed can see the subtle differences in vocabulary of the search topic (Belkin, 2000). Yet another problem in using the search engines of today is that the interests of the users vary with time and cannot be represented by a fixed set (Narayanan et al., 2004) or a 'one-size-fits-all' model widely prevalent in the search engines of today. Thus, there is a lack of fit between the information systems available for search and the task needs of different searchers or of the same searcher at different times. Also, "most Web search engines in use fail to take advantage of the intentions, interests and preferences of their users" (Pujol, Sanguesa, & Bermudez, 2003). Every searcher is also expected to *reinvent the wheel* each time he or she searches, while there might be other searchers with similar needs or those who are experts in the area of the searcher's needs, whose expertise is not tapped in a useful manner.

The emphasis should hence be on addressing questions posed by users, through facilitating information search and knowledge discovery (Marchionini, 1997; Fayyad, Piatetsky-Shapiro, Smyth, & Uthurusamy, 1996). To facilitate this process of knowledge discovery, information providers should attempt to understand the context surrounding each search task rather than simply presenting searchers with a series of links.

People are very impressed with Web searches today but it's really quite poor compared to what it should be...a bunch of links that sort of start a treasure hunt that on average takes about 11 minutes. Bill Gates, Microsoft Chairman (Live! Forum, Singapore, July 1, 2005)

Knowledge discovery can happen if information systems are designed to store the search patterns of users and facilitate a new searcher by comparing his search behavior with records of prior searches. Once a pattern of similarity is found, tools and information may be extended to the new searcher that had served the needs of an existing searcher. If earlier searchers with similar needs had been satisfied with the information, there is the likelihood that the information is useful to a new searcher too. While the Internet may have contributed to information overload, the connectivity it has brought provides the potential to different searchers of information to *collaborate* and work together when looking for information. Collaborative or *social* approaches to searching harness voluntary efforts of several people that relate to each other through networked information systems. Social information discovery and filtering systems rely on the existence of other people who locate and evaluate relevant sources and are willing to share the discovered information (Karamuftuoglu, 1998; Hill, Stead, Rosenstein, & Furnas, 1995; Starr, Ackerman, & Pazzani, 1996).

For collaboration to be successful, the *similarity of information needs* between that of the searcher with those of previous searchers must be effectively established. The collaborator or collaborative mechanisms must be able to help the searcher either through expertise or experience, or similarity of needs. While providing collaborative mechanisms, an information provider must also take into account the different modes a searcher is in at different points in time (based on the characteristics of the task at the hand, or the qualities/expertise of the searcher), and provide technology features that match the task and searcher characteristics reflected from the searcher mode.

The objectives of this chapter are three-fold:

- To review concepts related to social information retrieval and some existing collaborative mechanisms.
- To discuss two collaborative mechanisms: *cues* and *specialty search*. These could be built in a system and will allow a searcher to retrieve information collaboratively with other like-minded searchers.

- To see cues and specialty search in the context of the changing needs of the information searcher at different points in time who could be in one of four modes—*novice, data gatherer, known-item searcher,* or *focused searcher.*

A case study of an online portal for the Singapore Education Community will be used for illustration. An outcome of the project is to demonstrate how students, teachers, and other users could collaborate among themselves to enhance learning and the efficacy of search.

In the next section, we seek to provide a basic background of concepts related to social information retrieval, and discuss collaboration and existing collaborative mechanisms in greater detail. We then look at two collaborative mechanisms, contextual cues and specialty search, followed by a discussion of the concept of searcher modes—the differing needs of a searcher at different points in time. We examine cues and specialty search in the context of these modes. Next, we provide an illustration using a case study on collaborating for education-related search. This is followed by a section on future trends. Finally, the conclusion highlights some key points and concludes the chapter.

BACKGROUND: COLLABORATION AND COLLABORATIVE MECHANISMS

Concepts Related to Social Information Retrieval/ Collaborative Search

Before delving deeper into collaboration and existing collaborative mechanisms, let us examine a few related concepts.

A commonly held view with sundry minor variants is that *data* is raw numbers and facts; *information* is processed data or "a construct on a continuum somewhere between data and knowledge" (North, North, & Benade, 2004; see Figure 1), while *knowledge* is authenticated information (Machlup, 1980; Dretske, 1981; Vance, 1997).

Yet the presumption of hierarchy from data to information to knowledge with each varying along some dimension, such as context, usefulness, or interpretability, rarely survives scrupulous evaluation (Alavi & Leidner, 2001). According to North et al. (2004), "information is determined or defined by its use...information has value when it is relevant to the task at hand, it is available in the right format at the right place, and is considered fairly accurate and recent." The goal of collaborative mechanisms espoused

Figure 1. Continuum of data, information, and knowledge

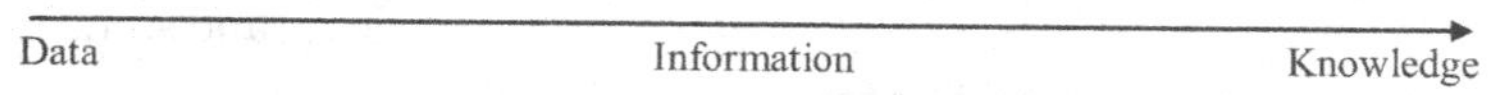

Data   Information   Knowledge

in this chapter is to ensure that the searcher gets access to the right information at the right time, using the help of other like-minded searchers or collaborative mechanisms.

Information need is the recognition that our knowledge is inadequate to satisfy a goal that we have (Case, 2002). "Need for information consists of the process of perceiving a difference between an ideal state of knowledge and the actual state of knowledge" (van de Wijngaert, 1999, p. 463). Search for information is based on some need, task, or problem at hand. Our propositions in this chapter are based on the premise that there are other people out there with needs similar to ours or those who have had similar needs in the past. We investigate ways and means to best collaborate with those with similar needs.

An *information retrieval* (IR) system has the goal of "leading the user to those documents that will best enable him/her to satisfy his/her need for information" (Robertson, 1981) or "for the user to obtain information from the knowledge resource which helps her/him in problem management" (Belkin, 1984). Information retrieval implies searching for information using a computer or information system.

Figure 2 shows the components of a basic information retrieval system. Based on the task at hand and the search context, the user tries to express his/her need in a few *keywords* and enters it into the information retrieval system. Depending on the information retrieval algorithm implemented, the system returns the information (typically a set

of links pointing to the information) that has words matching with the search keywords. In the classical IR sense, "an information retrieval system does not inform (i.e., change the knowledge of) the user on the subject of his inquiry. It merely informs on the existence (or non-existence) and whereabouts of documents relating to his request" (Lancaster, 1968).

The classic information retrieval research tradition commenced with the Cranfield tests in the 1950s and 1960s, and continued with the MEDLARS evaluation, research on relevance judgment (1970s), automated systems, theoretical work by Van Rijsbergen and Robertson (late 1970s), empirical work on relevance feedback, and comparisons of Boolean and best match searching (1980s). Statistical as well as cognitive approaches have been researched over the years (Ellis, Allen, & Wilson, 1999). Apart from the classical 'system-oriented' approach (where an IR system is an integral part), studies have also been done from the perspective of the user and his needs (person-oriented studies), under the umbrella of 'information seeking'. Here, the process of searching may not necessarily involve searching from an information retrieval system. See Case (2002) for a complete review.

Moving from classical information retrieval to social or collaborative information retrieval is the onus of the builders of information retrieval systems, that is, the information providers, who can provide mechanisms to help searchers collaborate amongst each other. We posit that the

Figure 2. Information retrieval system

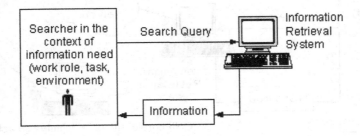

mechanisms provided must also take into account the differing modes of the searcher at different pints in time (see the subsection 'Changing Needs of the Searcher: Four Searcher Modes' later in the chapter).

Social information retrieval refers to a family of information retrieval techniques that assist users in obtaining information to meet their information needs by harnessing other users' expert knowledge or search experience. Users are linked through networked information systems such as the Internet. Such systems rely on other people who have found relevant information and are willing to share it (Karamuftuoglu, 1998; Hill et al., 1995; Starr et al., 1996). While classical IR deals with the interaction of an individual with an information system when looking for information (other users do not come into the picture), social or collaborative approaches to information retrieval makes use of the expertise of *other* users when searching for information. While the former can be likened to an *individual effort,* the latter is more of a *team effort* to search.

Collaborative search "exploits repetition and regularity within the query-space of a community of like-minded individuals in order to improve the quality of search results. In short, search results that have been judged to be relevant for past queries are promoted in response to similar queries that occur in the future" (Smyth et al., 2005, p. 1419). It relies on searchers willing to collaborate over network systems such as the Internet to contribute information to be used by other needy searchers with similar needs. Collaborative Web search combines "techniques for exploiting knowledge of the query-space with ideas from social networking to develop a Web search platform capable of adapting to the needs of (ad-hoc) communities of users. In brief, the queries submitted and the results selected by a community of users are recorded and reused in order to influence the results of future searches for similar queries. Results that have been reliably selected for similar queries in the past are promoted" (Smyth et al., 2005, p. 1419; Freyne, Smyth, Coyle, Balfe, & Briggs, 2004; Smyth, Balfe, Briggs, Coyle, & Freyne, 2003).

Figure 3 shows an IR system that facilitates collaboration. As shown in the figure, a searcher situated in a unique search context (a particular task at hand, work role, or surrounding environment) has a particular need for information. Based

Figure 3. Social information retrieval/collaborative search

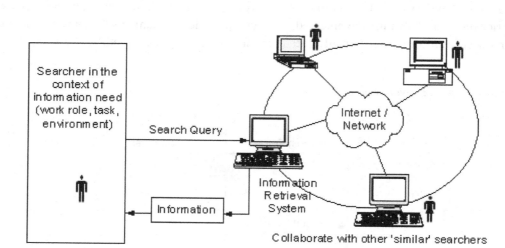

on his understanding of the topic or domain under search, he keys in a search query in an information retrieval system, hoping for results. Instead of simply doing a straightforward keyword search and spitting out results (classic information retrieval), the system enables the searcher to collaborate with other searchers who have conducted similar searches before or are experts in the domain of search. This would require matching the searcher with other similar searchers who could be of help to him. Specific collaborative mechanisms may be provided by the system. The information provided may be more useful to the searcher than without collaboration.

Apart from simple collaboration, we also posit that the information retrieval system understands the unique mode the searcher is in (based on his search context) and provides mechanisms that take the searcher mode into account. Let us delve deeper into the idea behind collaborative search.

Why Collaborative Search?

The idea is simple. Behind every search for information, there is an information need. This need is always *instrumental* (Green, 1990) in that it involves reaching a desired goal. The searcher wants to accomplish a certain goal with the retrieved information. This goal might be solving a problem, answering a question, accomplishing a work task, satisfying one's curiosity, or even entertainment. Knowing the information will put the searcher at or closer to an end state he/she wants to achieve (Case, 2002). In our world of 6 billion people, it is very likely that someone, somewhere would have encountered similar situations or contexts of information need as we have—that is, this person could have solved or is solving a similar problem, have looked for answers to a similar question, is in a similar work role, or is as curious as we are in looking for celebrity gossip. In an earlier era, locating such people with similar needs or who have had similar needs in the past could have been limited by physical or

geographical boundaries. The exercise would have been expensive and infeasible. The expansion of the World Wide Web, which continues to grow continuously and exponentially, has opened up opportunities like never before. Locating people with similar interests, experiences, work roles, and more importantly, with similar needs for information has been made as simple as a click of a mouse, making collaboration easy and natural.

For instance, vocabulary mismatch is a deep-rooted problem in information retrieval as users often use different or too few words to describe concepts in their queries as compared to the words used by authors to describe similar concepts. This leads to inadequate search results (Komarjaya, Poo, & Kan, 2004). Query expansion (or query reformulation), the process of expanding/disambiguating a user's query with additional related words and phrases, has been suggested to address the problem (Komarjaya et al., 2004). However, finding and using appropriate related words remains an open problem. Collaborative querying is an approach whereby related queries (the query clusters) may be calculated based on the similarities of the queries with past search experiences (as documented in the query logs) and either recommended to users or used as expansion terms (Fu, Goh, Foo, & Supangat, 2004). However, as pointed out by Fu et al. (2004), calculating the similarity between different queries and clustering them automatically (query clustering) are crucial steps here.

Not just query reformulation, search engines, in many ways and in their very implementation, make use of the similar experiences of past searchers to arrive at results. For instance, Google's PageRank "relies on the uniquely democratic nature of the Web by using its vast link structure as an indicator of an individual page's value. In essence, Google interprets a link from page A to page B as a vote, by page A, for page B." Google also analyzes the page that casts the vote. If it considers the page that casts the vote more important, the votes cast by it will weigh more heavily and help to make other pages important (Google Technology, 2004). Thus, if more and more pages link to a particular page, it becomes more and more important. This emphasis on *social role* in Web page ranking, compared to basic keyword/frequency matching, has found phenomenal success, with Google emerging as one of the most favorite search engines (Sherman, 2006).

There is huge potential for collaboration to extend beyond page linking/ranking to the very manner of looking for information in the World Wide Web. The motivation is compelling. The search engines of today, though good and ever improving, are not perfect. Users are still swamped with huge amounts of non-relevant data. Information gathering could easily extend from minutes to hours to days. In addition, the information needs of a searcher vary with time, the task at hand, and the ever-changing context or environment in which the information need arises.

In such a scenario, "…support for communication and collaboration is as important as support for information-seeking activities, and…indeed, support for the former is needed to support the latter" (Levy & Marshall, 1994). Virtual communities such as Weblogs (or blogs), online groups, and discussion forums are all aimed at supporting information sharing, and their success implies their effectiveness (Chi & Pirolli, 2006). "Cooperation may yield more benefits than simply making search more parallel and making it less prone to failure. Membership in a group provides actual or potential resources that can be utilized or mobilized to achieve individual goals. This is known as *social capital*" (Chi & Pirolli, 2006). Many informal group memberships are visible in the form of *communities of practice* or CoPs. While the term CoP is widely used (see Cox, 2005, for a review of different definitions), it comes from theories based on the idea of learning as social participation (Wenger, 1998). Wenger, McDermott, and Snyder (2002) define CoPs as "groups of people who share a concern, a set of problems, or a passion about a topic, and who

deep their knowledge and expertise in this area by interacting on an ongoing basis" (p. 7). Cox (2005, p. 531) lists Wenger's (1998, pp. 125-126) indicators of communities of practice:

1) sustained mutual relationships—harmonious or conflictual; 2) shared ways of engaging in doing things together; 3) the rapid flow of information and propagation of innovation; 4) absence of introductory preambles, as if conversations and interactions were merely the continuation of an ongoing process; 5) very quick setup of a problem to be discussed; 6) substantial overlap in participants' descriptions of who belongs; 7) knowing what others know, what they can do, and how they can contribute to an enterprise; 8) mutually defining identities; 9) the ability to assess the appropriateness of actions and products; 10) specific tools, representations, and other artifacts; 11) local lore, shared stories, inside jokes, knowing laughter; 12) jargon and shortcuts to communication as well as the ease of producing new ones; 13) certain styles recognized as displaying membership; 14) a shared discourse reflecting a certain perspective on the world.

Such indicators of CoPs and the way they work are important in understanding the efficacy of many existing social and collaborative approaches to searching such as social bookmarking, social networking, folksonomies, and so forth.

Existing Collaborative Mechanisms

By tapping into the resources and expertise of those more knowledgeable or experienced, there is huge potential to improve the efficacy of information search. Searchers could collaborate in a number of ways in order to retrieve information effectively. Techniques could include sharing of search queries, social bookmarking and tagging, folksonomies, social network analysis, subjective relevance judgments, and collaborative filtering.

Social Bookmarking and Tagging

Collaborative tagging "describes the process by which many users add metadata in the form of keywords to shared content" (Golder & Huberman, 2005). Users can collaboratively tag various content such as bookmarks, documents, photographs, blog entries, and so forth. Bookmarking is the activity when a Web user makes note of a favorite site or hyperlink on his browser. A user can manage, tag, comment upon, and publish his bookmarks on the Web, which represent a user's personal library being placed on the Web. When aggregated with other personal libraries, it allows for rich, social networking opportunities (Hammond, Hanny, Lund, & Scott, 2005). This is primarily the idea of social bookmarking and tagging. Hammond and his colleagues review various available tools to help achieve the same. Social bookmark services like del.icio.us (*http://del.icio.us/*) allow users to freely choose category names and tags without any a priori dictionary, taxonomy, or ontology to conform to. Such services may be seen as "social annotations" of the Web (Wu, Zhang, & Yu, 2006). However, "without a shared taxonomy or ontology, social annotations suffer the usual problem of ambiguity of semantics. The same annotation may mean different things for different people and two seemingly different annotations may bear the same meaning" (Wu et al., 2006, p. 418). Wu et al. suggest a method to group synonymous tags together and to identify and separate highly ambiguous tags. Social bookmarking is only as reliable as the people doing the tagging and provides a subjective, rather than an objective, opinion of the people tagging. You trust a stranger's recommendations for a topic. The positive part is that you may find better resources through somebody else's time and effort spent on research. Another downside is that there is no common language, so somebody else's bookmarked sites may not be related to what you are looking for. There is also the risk of spam being tagged, which could result in undesirable clutter (Asmus, Bonner, Esterhay, Lechner, & Rentfrow, 2005).

Folksonomies

A taxonomy is a structured way to categorize information and provides a subject-based classification that arranges the terms in a controlled vocabulary into a hierarchy. By relating word relationships (synonyms, broader terms, and narrower terms) and gathering the results in a common bucket, taxonomies can be used to bring common or similar material together. Humans can rapidly navigate taxonomies to find high concentrations of topic-specific, related information (Lederman, 2005; Papadopoullos, 2004). When such a taxonomy is generated by Internet users (instead of by professionals or content creators/authors) for their own individual use that is also shared throughout a community, using an open-ended labeling system to categorize various types of content, we get a novel combination of *folk* (not formal or professional) and *taxonomy,* that is, *folksonomy.* However, unlike a taxonomy, a folksonomy comprises terms in a flat namespace, where there is no hierarchy between terms. It is simply the set of terms that a group of users tagged content with, and not a predetermined set of classification terms or labels. Flickr (*www.flickr.com*) provides a collaborative way of tagging and categorizing photographs; del.icio.us (*http://del.icio.us/*) is a collection of bookmarks of various users; You Tube (*www.youtube.com*) allows tagging, sharing, and hosting of short video clips; CiteULike (*www.citeulike.org*) tags scientific publications; while 43Things (*www.43things.com*) allows users to annotate their goals and plans with keywords, and connects users with similar pursuits (Mathes, 2004; Golder & Huberman, 2005; Hammond et al., 2005; Mika, 2005). On the downside, there is absence of polysemy and synonymy management in folksonomies. For example, a goal to stop procrastinating has been tagged variously in 43Things as "stop procrastinating," "stop procrastination," "procrastinate less," "stop procrastinate," "stop procrastinating and do things asap," "do less of procrastination," and so forth. Thus, synonyms, ambiguity, and improper use of case sensitivity and punctuation marks is commonplace. However, the imperfections of tagging are nonetheless acceptable so far, and users can instantly link to other relevant, timely, socially ranked objects (Mika, 2005).

Social Network Analysis

"One of the most consistent findings in the social science literature is that who you know often has a great deal to do with what you come to know. Yet both practical experience and scholarly research indicate significant difficulty in getting people with different expertise, backgrounds and problem solving styles to effectively integrate their unique perspectives" (Cross, Borgatti, & Parker, 2002). From the view of social network analysis, the social environment can be expressed as patterns or regularities in relationships (referred to as 'structure') among interacting units, where structure is measured using quantities called structural variables (Wasserman & Faust, 1994, p. 3). According to Wasserman and Faust, a social network consists of a finite set or sets of actors and the relation or relations defined on them. Actors are discrete individual, corporate, or collective social units (Wasserman & Faust, 1994, p. 17). The presence of relational information is a critical and defining feature of a social network. According to Scott (2000), relational data are the contacts, ties and connections, the group attachments and meetings, which relate one agent [actor] to another and so cannot be reduced to the properties of the individual agents themselves. Relations are not the properties of agents, but of systems of agents; these relations connect pairs of agents into larger relational systems. The methods appropriate to relational data are those of network analysis, whereby the relations are treated as expressing the linkages that run between agents (p. 3).

In addition to the use of relational concepts, the central principles of the network perspective are (Wasserman & Faust, 1994, p. 4):

- Actors and their actions are viewed as interdependent rather than independent, autonomous units.
- Relational ties (linkages) between actors are channels for transfer or "flow" of resources (either material or nonmaterial).
- Network models focusing on individuals view the network structural environment as providing opportunities for or constraints on individual action.
- Network models conceptualize structure (social, economic, political, and so forth) as lasting patterns of relations among actors.

Wasserman and Faust also present Freeman's mathematical definition for a social network $Y = \langle S, G_d, X \rangle$, where the triple consisting of the algebraic structure S, the directed graph or sociogram G_d, and the adjacency matrix or sociomatrix X is viewed as a social network. These three notations S, G_d, and X are usually viewed together as providing the three essential components of the simplest form of a social network (Wasserman & Faust, 1994, p. 40).

- The algebraic structure S is a set of nodes and a set of arcs (from graph theoretic notations).
- A sociogram (notation G_d above) is a graph produced from the sets of nodes and arcs. 'Invented' by Jacob L. Moreno in 1933, a sociogram is a picture in which people (or more generally, any social units) are represented as points in two-dimensional space, and relationships among pairs of people are represented by lines linking the corresponding pairs (Wasserman & Faust, 1994, pp. 11-12; Scott, 2000, pp. 9-10). For Moreno, social configurations had definite and discernible structures, and the mapping of these structures into a sociogram allowed a researcher

to visualize the channels through which, for example, information could flow from one person to another, and through which one individual could influence another (Wasserman and Faust, 1994, p. 10).

- A sociomatrix (notation X above) is a two-way matrix used to present the data for each relation, where the rows and columns refer to the actors making up the pairs.

Social network analysis is an effective tool for collaborative search and social information retrieval. This is highlighted by Morville (2002), who points to the reciprocal relationship between people and content (we use *people* to find content ↔ we use *content* to find people). Using people to find content requires knowing what/who other people know. Using content to find people demands good search, navigation, and content management systems. Morville (2002) points out that with the way document surrogates such as *abstracts* are often used in information retrieval to represent the knowledge contained within that content, documents themselves may be considered as "human surrogates" representing the knowledge and interests of authors, while humans also serve as surrogates for one another. This suggests a need for metadata schema, tools, people directories, and incentives to enable and encourage explicit connections between documents and authors (Morville, 2002). There are a number of Internet social networks such as Orkut (*www.orkut.com*), Hi5 (*www.hi5.com*), Yahoo 360° (*http://360.yahoo.com*), Classmates (*www.classmates.com*), Friendster (*www.friendster.com*), MySpace (*www.myspace.com*), and LinkedIn (*www.linkedin.com*) (links business contacts), which are highly popular. By looking at the profile of a person in Orkut or Hi5 and the communities/ groups he/she is part of, one can get a pretty good idea about the personality of the person in question. However, privacy and safety may be a matter of concern here, including revealing information such as profiles clicked at. But since everybody is

free to look at each other's networks, most users do not seem to mind revealing certain aspects of themselves in such social networks.

Collaborative Filtering and Recommender Systems

Recommender systems use the opinions of a community of users to help individuals in that community more effectively identify content of interest from a potentially overwhelming set of choices (Resnick & Varian, 1997; Herlocker, Konstan, Terveen, & Riedl, 2004). Collaborative filtering is a technology for recommender systems that includes a wide variety of algorithms for generating recommendations (Herlocker et al., 2004). While 'collaborative filtering' is a specific technique/algorithm for implementing recommender systems—a term widely used along with or synonymously with recommender systems—one should note that 'recommender systems' is the more general term. This is because recommenders may not explicitly collaborate with recipients who may be unknown to each other. Also, recommendations may suggest particularly interesting items, in addition to indicating those that should be filtered out (Resnick & Varian, 1997).

The central idea of collaborative or social filtering is to base personalized recommendations for users on information obtained from other, ideally like-minded users (Billsus & Pazzani, 1998), the underlying assumption being *'those who agreed in the past will agree again in the future'*. Collaborative filtering systems "propose a similarity measure that expresses the relevance between an item (the content) and the preference of a user. Current collaborative filtering analyzes a rating database of user profiles for similarities between users (user-based) or items (item-based)" (Wang, Pouwelse, Lagendijk, & Reinders, 2006). For example, Amazon.com has popularized item-based collaborative filtering by recommending other related books/items ("Users who bought this item also bought…"). A problem with collaborative filtering is that recommendations do not exactly correspond to how recommendations are made in social settings, where people like to refer to "experts" to look for recommendations in an area. For example, when looking for a cooking recipe of a specific community, you would want a recommendation from that community, and not from your own peers or the population as a whole (Tkatchenko, 2005). Tkatchenko also mentions the issue of privacy, the question of how to hide individual ratings and still obtain good recommendations. Recommender systems also suffer from the *cold-start problem,* that is, the problem that systems based purely on collaborative filtering cannot provide much value to their early users, and indeed cannot provide much value to new users until after they have populated their profiles (Konstan, 2004).

We have seen a number of existing collaborative mechanisms—social bookmarking and tagging, folksonomies, social network analysis, and collaborative filtering/recommender systems. Other techniques can include sharing of search queries/collaborative querying, subjective relevance judgments, collaborative digital reference services, cooperative software agents for information retrieval, and so forth. Most prior research on collaborative IR has looked at collaboration from the perspective of the user with an information need collaborating with an experienced searcher to address the former's need (e.g., Fowell & Levy, 1995; Blake & Pratt, 2002). Systems have been developed (e.g., Procter, Goldenberg, Davenport, & McKinlay, 1998) that focus on collaboration among equally experienced members (as opposed to a novice collaborating with an expert). Work has also been done on collaborative browsing by allowing collaborators to see a trace of all the documents that users visited (e.g., Nichols et al., 2000; Twidale & Nichols, 1998; Blake & Pratt, 2002). Blake and Pratt (2002) propose a tool to support the collaborative information synthesis process used by public health and biomedical scientists.

USING CUES AND SPECIALTY SEARCH TO COLLABORATE EFFECTIVELY

Now that we have seen the reasons for collaborating and some of the existing collaborative mechanisms available, let us discuss two specific collaborative mechanisms—cues and specialty search. We will also see how these mechanisms must be placed in the context of the changing needs of the information searcher (different searcher modes) at different points in time.

Contextual Cues

One way of collaborating for search is through the usage of contextual cues. The notion of context has been introduced to enhance search tools and refers to a diverse range of ideas from specialty-search engines to personalization. Contextual information can be information related to the user's task, the problem at hand, what the user knows, his/her domain knowledge, his/her environment, the system capabilities, his/her familiarity with the system, and so forth. There could be several instances of the term 'context' outside information retrieval as well. For example, in ubiquitous computing research, *context-aware computing* may be defined as any attempt to use knowledge of a user's physical, social, informational, and even emotional state as input to adapt the behavior of one or more computational services (Abowd, Dey, Abowd, Orr, & Brotherton, 1997). Ingwersen and Jarvelin (2004) say that the searcher's need is a complex context consisting of the perceived work task or interest, as well as perceptions and interpretations of knowledge gap and relevance, uncertainty and other emotional states, the potential sources for the solution (if any) of the work task or interest, the intentionality (i.e., goals, purposes, motivation, etc.), information preferences, strategies, pressures (costs, time), self (i.e., own capabilities, health, experiences), systematic and interactive features, and information objects.

If the search system knows such attributes of the searcher, it can greatly enhance the relevance of search results and lead to a more satisfied searcher. Search would be more effective because the set of relevant results would increase, while the set of non-relevant results would decrease. However, "typically, the cost of acquiring full context is simply too high, compared to the benefits, let alone possible privacy issues" (Hawking, Paris, Wilkinson, & Wu, 2005).

Goh, Poo, and Chang (2004) propose a framework that helps to incorporate contextual cues in information systems. The framework draws on existing studies in user profiling and information filtering to suggest four sources of contextual information. User profiling is the ability to represent and reason about the interests or preferences of a user (Goh et al., 2004). Information filtering refers to tools/techniques to remove irrelevant data and present only the adequate and relevant information to the user that will satisfy his or her information requirements (Belkin & Croft, 1992). The four sources suggested by Goh et al. (2004) are *static content sources, dynamic content sources, static collaborative sources,* and *dynamic collaborative sources.* Static content sources are contextual cues derived from the information that changes rarely such as the demographic information of the user

and his/her interests. Dynamic content sources are cues derived from the dynamic changes in the behavior of users, such as the user's actions, history, and preferences.

As the focus of this chapter is collaborative search, we will look at the two collaborative sources of cues—static and dynamic, in some detail.

Automated collaborative filtering systems predict a person's affinity for items or information by connecting that person's recorded interests with the recorded interests of a community of people and sharing ratings between like-minded persons. Unlike a traditional content-based information filtering system, filtering decisions are based on human and not machine analysis of content. Thus, such systems are less error prone. Each user rates items that he or she has experienced, in order to establish a profile of interests. The system then matches the user together with people of similar interests. Then ratings for those similar people are used to generate recommendations for the user. Examples of automated collaborative filtering systems are GroupLens (Konstan et al., 1997; Resnick, Iacovou, Suchak, Bergstrom, & Riedl, 1994), Ringo (Shardanand & Maes, 1995), Video Recommender (Hill et al., 1995), and MovieLens (Dahlen et al., 1998; Herlocker, Konstan, & Riedl,

Figure 4. Static and dynamic collaborative sources

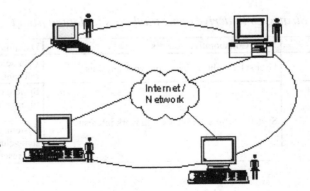

Static collaborative sources: Collect 'static' information (which changes rarely e.g. demographic information, interests, etc.) from other 'similar' users

Dynamic collaborative sources: Derive cues by organizing users with similar 'dynamic' behavior (user actions, history and preferences)

2000). As collaborative filtering relies heavily on user clusters, its effectiveness depends highly on how well the clustering of profiles correlates with those of users (Goh et al., 2004).

Static and dynamic collaborative sources draw on such automated collaborative filtering systems.

Static collaborative sources are contextual cues derived from the information that changes rarely (static content sources) after organizing users with similar profiles into peer groups. These cues may either be obtained automatically (implicitly by the system) or via a user's explicit request. Every time a new user is added to the system, the system collects information about the user and constructs a user's profile that will aid the system to serve the user's needs. Terveen, McMackin, Amento, and Hill (2002) observed that users wanted novel recommendations that closely related to what they were interested in. Thus, gathering of user profile information must be supported by collaborative filtering so that users receive support in finding like-minded users.

In order to cluster static sources, users are grouped according to the static content sources such as the information the user provided during registration. Such clustering can be performed by the system using some supervised machine learning or clustering algorithm. Based on the algorithm, the system will recommend groups that the user may be interested in joining. Cues can be derived from static collaborative sources

in two ways—explicit or implicit. Individuals can explicitly provide feedback on items, which can be shared with other users exhibiting similar behavior. The system can also automatically or implicitly adjust the similarity rating of a user with other users based on the matching of certain terms in the profiles of the users.

The notion of static collaborative sources can be expanded to include dynamic sources.

Dynamic collaborative sources are contextual cues derived from organizing users with similar actions and behavior into peer groups, and filtering information pertaining to the group's interest. The technique is similar to that used in static sources, but the difference is that the system performs clustering based on dynamic sources (i.e., via the user's behavior or actions), instead of simply relying on the user's profile. This could also be done in two ways—explicit or implicit. For introducing dynamic collaborative cues explicitly in the system, the system can automatically cluster a user's click stream data, recommend items of interest to the user, and allow him/her to indicate his/her interest. The system could also implicitly introduce dynamic collaborative sources by automatically adjusting the relevance of results presented to the user when the user issues a search query. Here, the relevance scores are derived from the actions and behaviors of other 'similar' users. Terveen et al.'s (2002) observation supports the use of dynamic collaborative cues for personalization in information systems.

Table 1. Strategies to derive contextual cues (Adapted from Goh et al., 2004, p. 480)

	Static Collaborative Sources	Dynamic Collaborative Sources
Explicit	User selects cluster based on work interests.	User selects search query suggested by system based on relevant items of other like-minded users.
Implicit	System clusters users based on work interests.	System clusters users' profiles based on loans and reservations. System assigns higher relevance score to items found in same cluster derived from like-minded individuals' loans and reservations.

Goh et al. (2004) identified the sources of contextual cues in an electronic repository of a library system. Static collaborative sources were identified as clustering *demographic information* of users. Dynamic collaborative sources were identified as clustering *loans and reservations information* of users. They also considered the means to incorporate these sources (see Table 1).

Goh et al. (2004) conducted an experiment with 20 subjects where they had to assess the pages returned by an electronic repository with a search engine with or without incorporating contextual cues. The results showed an improvement for a majority of users in relative search precision (improved percentage of relevant records) and an average reduction of total relevant records, or both, by incorporating cues.

In the subsection "Cues and Specialty Search in the Context of Searcher Modes," we will see how cues can be applied to a searcher with changing needs at different points in time, depending on his/her context of search. For now, let us look at another collaborative mechanism.

Specialty Search

Specialty search is another mechanism that could facilitate collaboration. Also referred to as topical search, "vertical" search, or "vortal" (Sullivan, 2000), specialty search helps provide information specific to an area or domain—for example (add dash instead of comma to break the long sentence), a search engine to be used exclusively by doctors or the medical community, saving them from having to weed out basic health/fitness information meant for the lay man and helping them focus on specific issues like the latest advances in medical science or medical job opportunities.

As highlighted by Lawrence and Giles (2000), the coverage of a general-purpose search engine is limited. Bharat and Broder's (1998) study saw the largest search engines covering just 50% of all Web pages, with a maximum overlap of 30%. Mori and Yamada (2000) also contend that a user cannot search well based on a single general search engine. If the big search engines are unable to deliver comprehensive access to the entire Web, perhaps the time has come for more focused sites to offer near comprehensiveness in their own chosen fields (Kawin, 2003; Khoussainov & Kushmerick, 2003; Battelle, 2004; Sullivan, 2000).

Specialty search can be considered an extension of an important Internet phenomenon—virtual communities, where groups of people communicate, interact, and collaborate with each other, often with a commonality of interest or intent (see discussion on communities of practice in the subsection "Why Collaborative Search?"). It is now much easier to build such virtual communities without much technological know-how, and a lot of these spring forth binding informal groups together. Examples of systems catering to such virtual communities are online groups, discussion forums, and the newly coined Weblogs or blogs. Online groups and discussion forums usually evolve from a need to share knowledge on a common platform. Blogs, on the other hand, usually cater to a group of readers, with the 'bloggers' deciding on the subjects of interest and contributing most of the content. Online groups, discussion forums, and blogs are not information retrieval systems or specialty search engines as such, but they do help bring a diverse group of people together to collaborate in different ways to share information. A lot of the information retrieved is through answers from *human* sources to queries put across on a forum or newsgroup.

Specialty search engines, on the other hand, could be considered as more formal and perhaps better organized than a lot of informal virtual communities. There are a large number of specialty search engines today. Gordon and Pathak (1999) say that of the 1,800 or so search engines estimated in 1997, most of those were specialty search engines that only cover a specific subject like automobiles or sports. Table 2 lists a small number of specialty search engines where different sets of individuals can collaborate socially for

Table 2. Specialty search engines

Specialty	Collaborators	Specialty Search Engines
Science	Individuals, students, teachers interested in science	Scirus (*www.scirus.com/srsapp/*); Sciseek (*www.sciseek.com*); Search4science (*www.search4science.com*)
Medical	Doctors, medical students, healthcare workers	HONMedhunt (*www.hon.ch/MedHunt*); MedicineNet (*www.medicinenet.com/script/main/hp.asp*); MedlinePlus (*http://medlineplus.gov/*); WebMD (*www.webmd.com/*)
Biology	Biology students, teachers, professionals	Biocrawler (*www.biocrawler.com*)
Chemistry	Chemistry students, teachers, specialists	Chemie.DE (*www.chemie.de/*)
Mathematics	Mathematicians, students, teachers interested in math	IntegerSequences (*www.research.att.com/~njas/sequences/*)
Civil Engineering	Civil Engineers	iCivilEngineer (*www.icivilengineer.com*)
Law	Lawyers, advocates, those involved in court cases	FindLaw (*http://lawcrawler.findlaw.com*); Law.com (*www.law.com*)
Art	Artists, art lovers, gallery managers, art sellers	Art-Bridge (*www.art-bridge.com/directory/abdir.htm*); Artcyclopedia (*www.artcyclopedia.com*); MuseumStuff [specific to museums] (*www.museumstuff.com*)
Finance	Financial analysts, brokers, businessmen	Business.com (*www.business.com*); Inomics (*www.inomics.com*); DailyStocks (*www.dailystocks.com*); TradingDay (*www.tradingday.com*); EarningsBase (*www.earningsbase.com*); MoneyWeb (*www.moneywebsearch.com*)
Research Papers	Academia, researchers, PhD candidates	GoogleScholar (*http://scholar.google.com*); CiteSeer (*http://citeseer.ist.psu.edu*)
Journalism	Journalists, reporters	Journalist's Toolbox (*www.americanpressinstitute.org/pages/toolbox/*)
Maps/Atlas	Geography teachers, students, individuals looking for maps	MapsArea (*www.mapsarea.com*)
Books	Students, professors, researchers	The Online Books Page (*http://digital.library.upenn.edu/books/*); AddALL (*www.addall.com*)
Jobs/Employment	Job Seekers, Employers	Monster (*www.monster.com*); JobWeb (*www.jobweb.com*); CareerBuilder (*www.careerbuilder.com*); JobsDB (*www.jobsdb.com*) (Singapore); BioView [specific to Biotechnology/Life Sciences] (*www.bioview.com/bv/servlet/BVHome*)
Origin	Genealogists	TheOriginsNetwork (*www.originsnetwork.com*)
Alumni	Alumni of a school, university, or institution; former school friends	Classmates (*www.classmates.com*); FriendsReunited [specific to UK] (*www.friendsreunited.co.uk*)

continued on following page

Table 2. continued

Specialty	Collaborators	Specialty Search Engines
Research Papers	Academia, researchers, PhD candidates	GoogleScholar (*http://scholar.google.com*); CiteSeer (*http://citeseer.ist.psu.edu*)
Journalism	Journalists, reporters	Journalist's Toolbox (*www.americanpressinstitute. org/pages/toolbox/*)
Maps/Atlas	Geography teachers, students, individuals looking for maps	MapsArea (*www.mapsarea.com*)
Books	Students, professors, researchers	The Online Books Page (*http://digital.library.upenn.edu/books/*); AddALL (*www.addall.com*)
Jobs/Employment	Job Seekers, Employers	Monster (*www.monster.com*); JobWeb (*www.jobweb.com*); CareerBuilder (*www.careerbuilder.com*); JobsDB (*www.jobsdb.com*) (Singapore); BioView [specific to Biotechnology/Life Sciences] (*www.bioview.com/bv/servlet/BVHome*)
Origin	Genealogists	TheOriginsNetwork (*www.originsnetwork.com*)
Alumni	Alumni of a school, university, or institution; former school friends	Classmates (*www.classmates.com*); FriendsReunited [specific to UK] (*www.friendsreunited.co.uk*)
Weather	Travelers, weather forecasters, individuals	WeatherBug (*www.weatherbug.com*)
Mobile	Mobile phone users	SomewhereNear [specific to UK] (*http:// somewherenear.com*); Waply (*www.waply.com*)
Travel	Travelers, hoteliers, travel agents, airline companies	Kayak (*www.kayak.com*); Mobissimo (*www.mobissimo.com*); SideStep (*www.sidestep.com*); Orbitz (*www.orbitz.com*); Expedia (*www.expedia.com*); Travelocity (*www.travelocity.com*); DoHop (*www.dohop.com*); IGoUGo (*http://igougo.com*); Travelazer (*www.travelazer.com*)
Dogs	Dog lovers/sellers	Doginfo (*www.doginfo.com*)
Shopping	Shoppers, sellers	BizRate (*www.bizrate.com*); Kelkoo (*www.kelkoo.co.uk*); NexTag (*www.nextag.com*); PriceGrabber (*www.pricegrabber.com*); PriceSCAN (*www.pricescan.com*)

Figure 5. Cues and specialty search

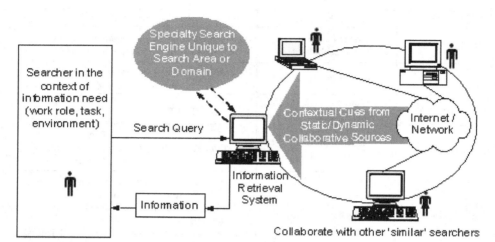

information retrieval in their specialties of interest (Sullivan, 2002; Meyer, 2006; VanFossen, 2005; ISEdb, 2005; Hofstede, 2000).

Figure 5 shows the concepts of cues and specialty search incorporated to Figure 3 discussed earlier. While contextual cues are derived from various collaborative sources *similar* to the user and his/her needs in order to make search results more relevant, specialty search engines serve as repositories/search interfaces specific to a particular domain which a searcher can utilize when searching for something in that particular area or domain.

So far, we have discussed aspects related to the *system,* that is, existing social information retrieval mechanisms, including two specific types of collaborative search mechanisms—cues and specialty search. Let us now look at search from the point of view of the *searcher* or the *user.* An aspect basic to any searcher of information is his or her changing needs.

Changing Needs of the Searcher: Four Searcher Modes

It is extremely important for a search service provider to understand the reasons and circum-

stances surrounding a search in order to truly satisfy the user. Not only are the goals behind a user's search query (requirement of specific information) important, the user's prior domain knowledge in the area of search must also be taken into account to carry out an effective search and output of results.

Agarwal and Poo (2006) refer to Papadopoullos (2004), who states that search and classification results must satisfy four basic categories of users. We term these four categories of users (searcher modes) as: (a) novice, (b) data gatherer, (c) known-item searcher, and (d) focused searcher. Depending on the context of data one is searching for and the domain knowledge the person has in the field of search, the same person may be in one of the four modes (see Table 3). The surfer is not looking for anything in particular and is just entertaining himself, so we do not count him in our typology of searcher modes. We are interested in addressing the needs of users performing goal-oriented search. For example, a student would be in novice mode when searching for course-related information, a medical doctor searching for latest advances in medicine would be in the data-gathering mode, and a researcher locating a research paper based on the author's name, publication,

Table 3. Four modes/activities of information searchers

No.	Searcher mode during a particular search	Searcher need during a particular search	Prior domain knowledge	Requirement of specific information
1	Novice	Needs information about a topic he is not familiar with in preparation for starting a new project	0 (no)	0 (not yet)
2	Data Gatherer	Needs information about a topic he *is* knowledgeable about and is therefore in data-gathering mode	1 (yes)	1 (yes)
3	Known-Item Searcher	Has a good idea what he is looking for, knows that a given document or piece of data exists, and simply needs to locate it	X (do not care)	1 (yes)
4	Focused Searcher	Needs a very specific answer to a specific question	X (do not care)	1 (yes)
-	Surfer	Does not need anything in particular; searching purely for entertainment	X (do not care)	0 (no)

Table 4. Searcher modes based on domain knowledge and requirement of specific information

Prior domain knowledge	Requirement of specific information	Searcher mode
0 (no)	0 (no)	Novice or Surfer
0 (no)	1 (yes)	Known-Item Searcher or Focused Searcher
1 (yes)	0 (no)	Surfer
1 (yes)	1 (yes)	Data Gatherer, Known-Item Searcher, or Focused Searcher

Table 5. Searcher modes based on five factors

Goal-oriented search	Prior-domain knowledge	Requirement of specific information	Focused search	Known-item search	Searcher mode
0	X	0	X	X	Surfer
1	0	0	X	X	Novice
1	X	1	1	0	Focused searcher
1	X	1	0	1	Known-Item searcher
1	1	1	0	0	Data Gatherer

and year would be in the known-item searching mode. A focused search would require a specific answer to a question, for example, "What are the differences between qualitative and quantitative data in information systems research?" A bored teenager searching for celebrity gossip would be in the surfer mode.

An understanding of the different searcher modes is extremely important to understand the differing needs of searchers at different points in time. Such an understanding will facilitate users in different searcher modes to collaborate effectively for search.

Table 4 below shows the searcher modes based on domain knowledge and requirement of specific information. Again (also in Table 5), the surfer is included for completeness but is outside the scope of this study.

From Table 4, we notice that there is ambiguity between novice or surfer modes (case 00); between known-item searcher and focused searcher modes (case 01); and between data gatherer, known-item searcher, and focused searcher modes (case 11). To resolve this, we add three more factors:

- Looking for anything in particular? *(goal-oriented search)*
- Looking for something you have seen before and know that it exists? *(known-item search)*
- Need a specific answer to a specific question? *(focused search)*

From Table 5, we can see that a surfer mode implies casual search, which is not goal oriented. Within goal-oriented searches, absence of (or insignificant in the view of the searcher) prior domain knowledge and non-requirement of specific information determines the novice mode. A focused search must be goal oriented, requires specific information, and has a specific question needing a specific answer. A known-item search is goal oriented, requires specific information, and is a case where the item has been encountered before and

simply needs locating. The data-gathering mode is goal-oriented where the searcher has prior domain knowledge and requires specific information.

Cues and Specialty Search in the Context of Searcher Modes

As mentioned, when we talk about collaborative mechanisms such as specialty search engines and contextual cues, these are mostly provided by the information retrieval system and are from a system perspective. There is a need to understand these mechanisms from a searcher perspective, based on his or her differing needs at different points in time.

Incorporating contextual cues from static/dynamic content or collaborative sources should benefit all the four searcher modes by increasing the set of relevant results and decreasing the set of non-relevant results. Usefulness to the searcher in data-gathering mode may range from medium to high depending on the cues obtained from dynamic collaborative sources by matching the actions of the data gatherer with those of others with similar domain knowledge.

Specialty search would be extremely useful to the searcher in data-gathering mode, as he would be able to access the search engine directly relevant to his prior domain knowledge and the domain of search. It would greatly benefit the focused searcher too, perhaps by pulling out answers from the FAQ (Frequently Asked Questions) section of a specialized portal. It might have medium to high utility for the novice depending on whether the specialty search engine provides background or basic information that could be understood by a novice. Specialization would have low utility for the known-item searcher, unless the known-item he is seeking resides within the specialty search engine.

We can also try to map the other collaborative mechanisms discussed with the four searcher modes. Collaborative tagging and folksonomies should be highly useful to the novice who can

Table 6. Usefulness of collaborative mechanisms to the different searcher modes

Usefulness: ↓ Low ~ Medium ↑ High	Searcher Modes			
Collaborative Search Mechanisms	Novice	Data Gatherer	Known-Item Searcher	Focused Searcher
Contextual Cues/Recommendation Systems	↑	~ ↑	↑	↑
Specialty Search	~ ↑	↑	↓	↑
Other Collaborative Mechanisms				
Collaborative Tagging/Folksonomies	↑	↑	↓	↓
Social Bookmarking	↑	↑	~ ↑	↓
Social Networking	↑	↑	↓	↓

search based on tags put by other expert users. A focused searcher can help to tag content but may find limited use of folksonomies, unless there is content that has been tagged by other focused searchers and can help answer the focused searcher's question. It should also be useful to a data gatherer who can gather data based on tags put forth by other users. It should have limited applicability for the known-item searcher.

Social bookmarking should greatly benefit the novice as well as the data gatherer, who can access relevant links based on bookmarks by other expert searchers. The known-item searcher should find medium to high usefulness for social bookmarking in tracking down content that he/she

has encountered before. It could be less useful for the focused searcher who needs a specific answer to his/her question, which may not be provided by social bookmarks.

Lastly, social networking should greatly interest the novice, who can get the profiles of other searchers with similar needs or who are experts in the area of search. It should help a data gatherer by linking him/her with someone else within his/her domain of search. It should have low utility for the known-item searcher, unless the specific item he/she is looking for is part of the social network. It may not be very useful for the focused searcher as well, unless he is linked to a person who can answer his/her question.

Figure 6. Snapshot of ETaP: Education Taxonomy Portal (http://etap.comp.nus.edu.sg)

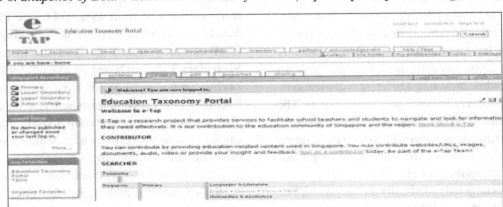

Let us now look at a case study to illustrate the collaborative mechanisms we have seen, as well as the four searcher modes, in the context of education.

COLLABORATING FOR EDUCATION-RELATED SEARCH: A CASE STUDY

The Education Taxonomy Portal (ETaP) is an online digital repository being developed for the Singapore Education community; it is still in its infancy. Accessible from http://etap.comp.nus.edu.sg (see Figure 6), ETaP provides services to facilitate schoolteachers and students to collaborate in contributing, searching, navigating, and retrieving education-related content effectively. Information retrieved is specific to users' local needs while enabling them to contribute and share their contents. Apart from search, a taxonomy based on the prescribed education curriculum helps provide browsing facilities.

Singapore teachers looking on the Internet for teaching materials and information relevant to their courses are almost always presented with a huge amount of data. Gathering required information is a time-consuming process, which may take hours. Students who want to search for information for project work or to supplement their course materials are similarly presented with a huge array of non-relevant data.

There are many education-related professionals, teachers, and schools that, in the past couple of years, have compiled their own frequently used education material as well as useful links gathered while browsing. Different organizations/individuals have their own small repositories. The project aims to provide a countrywide repository for gathering such material (Web sites, images, audio, video, journals, etc.) and classifying it into different categories for effective search.

ETaP is targeted specifically for Singapore. The scope will subsequently be expanded to include other countries in the ASEAN region. The portal aims to help teachers, students, parents, and all associated with the education community in Singapore to collaborate and perform quality search to be better satisfied with their search results. ETaP is available free for everyone's use.

The four searcher modes will be built into ETaP. A searcher will be able to specify whether he or she is a novice, data gatherer, known-item searcher, or focused searcher, depending on the context of search.

We intend to apply the different types of *contextual cues* in ETaP. Static content sources can be added by utilizing a database from participating schools containing users' information (name/majors). Dynamic content sources can be captured using a system that logs the users' actions. Users of the system can create a record of users whom they know so as to utilize the contextual cues that can be obtained from static collaborative sources. With such information, dynamic collaborative sources can also be obtained by matching the actions of the users with those of users with similar interests.

ETaP could implement collaborative filtering and serve as a recommender system. Educational resources found useful and recommended by students of a particular batch are likely to be useful to the next batch of students the following year. Similarity between users can be based on the grade of the student when the recommendation was made. For example, a Secondary 3 student recommends a Web site as useful for the Physics exam paper of Secondary 3. The following year, ETaP can recommend the Web site to another Secondary 3 student based on its usefulness, and having Secondary 3 as the similarity measure. Recommendation could also be based on expertise. A teacher recommending a study material can be viewed as useful by a student looking for material on a certain area.

ETaP provides *specialization* by focusing on the education domain. All the information is specific to the needs of students, teachers, as well as other stakeholders such as parents and tutors, owners of tutoring agencies, and so forth. Anybody who has an interest in an educational aspect can come to ETaP and get specific results, instead of searching a general-purpose search engine. The portal will eventually be expanded to gather relevant education-related material from major search engines and combine the result set based on user needs (specialty search).

Other collaborative mechanisms could also be implemented in ETaP.

With *collaborative tagging* and *folksonomies* implemented in ETaP, students could tag various resources, Web sites, and educational materials based on their specific needs. For example, a specific Algebra tutorial could be variously tagged as 'Algebra', 'Good tutorial on Algebra', 'Important for exams', and so forth. Teachers could tag the resources depending on how relevant they are to the subjects they teach. Teachers could also learn about the way students perceive educational resources from the way they tag them. This could help them in their own teaching. A study of the folksonomy of educational content tagged by students and teachers might provide useful insights into education from a student perspective, and help in evolving educational curriculum, method, and techniques. Implementation of collaborative tagging in ETaP will also require it to be able to group synonymous tags together and to moderate for spam.

The storing and categorizing of Web page links (pointing to educational resources), along with other content such as documents, images, tutorials, and so forth, can be likened to *social bookmarking*. Tools can be developed for the browser that allows a student to automatically bookmark a relevant educational site in ETaP and suggest categories under which the bookmark can be stored.

Social networking would also find useful application in ETaP. A student's profile could contain links to the profiles of other students in the school, as well as to teachers he/she has been taught by. The system could allow students to participate in communities of specific subjects and projects. By looking at a student profile, a new visitor will be able to know the subjects the student has taken in the past. Those willing (and not having privacy concerns) may also share their grades on the subjects to reflect level of expertise (or perhaps only those with high grades may choose to share their grades, as they are less likely to have inhibitions in sharing their grades). This will help connect new students not just to content and resources, but also to those students who have taken certain subjects in the past, and have received good grades. This will help enhance the support network among students. Peers could collaborate to form study groups. There could be sections and communities on previous-year exam papers related to specific subjects that students can try to solve and which can be overseen by teachers. Schools utilizing such social networks for education can allocate a small percentage of marks towards the level of participation and collaboration displayed by students in the educational network. This will help foster a sense of sharing among students.

With its focus on collaborative searching and retrieval, ETaP aims to bring together a diverse range of people (teachers, students, parents, etc.) to collaborate effectively for knowledge sharing.

While a novice would provide more questions than answers, he or she could contribute by bringing in new insights and different ways of looking at a topic or problem. A data gatherer in any educational topic (e.g., a student embarking on a new school project) would benefit from the repository of past experience in doing such projects, and from teachers or seniors more experienced in the area. Focused searchers and known-item searchers are also likely to be experienced in the different areas of the educational domain, and thus are useful to the novice searcher in providing answers and ways of approaching a problem at hand.

ETaP, we hope, will serve as an example to show how collaborative searching is enhanced when the needs of the searcher in different modes are matched with the right collaborative mechanism that allows collaborating with like-minded searchers.

FUTURE TRENDS

The world is at a phase where countries are coming together and collaborating, drawn by the power of economics and common goals, rather than traditional political and military agendas. ASEAN, European Union, and Free Trade Agreements among countries are a case in point. An unprecedented binding factor to bringing diverse thoughts and ideas together has been the connectivity provided by the Internet. Social approaches to information searching seeks to harness the most important phenomenon arising out of the growth of the Internet—bringing people of diverse nationalities, temperaments, personalities, and needs together in one common network. However, the Internet has also brought in 'info-glut', where too much information puts a huge cost on time and money, leaving individuals to sieve the important from the unimportant, the wanted from the unwanted, and the relevant from the non-relevant.

By harnessing the power of social networks, collaborative search mechanisms will make information comprehension easier and help reduce associated costs. The future will only see more and more collaborative mechanisms built into information retrieval systems.

The next generation of search engines will not just provide personalized searches, which will take into account the user's prior domain knowledge, experience in the area of search, experience with the search technology or search engine, and the searcher's task at hand; the user's interests and social affiliations will play a major role too. Virtual experts will be at hand to solve the problems faced by the majority. Already there are initiatives such as the Knowledge-Community

(K-Comm) project (*http://kcomm.redirectme.net*) at the National University of Singapore and About-Experts (*http://experts.about.com*). K-Comm is an initiative by the authors of this chapter to harness the tacit knowledge residing in different individuals. By recognizing that every individual is good at and has experience in some area or the other, K-Comm seeks to harness the latent expertise hidden in every individual and brings out a feeling of self-worth in everyone. This feeling is enhanced as users share more and more of their knowledge with others and collaborate to seek, as well as contribute to knowledge.

The experiments and approaches so far hold a lot of promise for collaborative search. The tremendous success of communities of practice shows how collaboration comes across naturally in the virtual world and can easily be extended to search. Active research and implementation will see the benefits reach all seekers of information.

As highlighted in this chapter, future search engines and information retrieval systems must also take into account the varying needs of the searcher at different points in time, and build collaborative mechanisms to serve that need.

From the perspective of this chapter, more research is needed into static and dynamic sources of collaborative cues, as well as the phenomenon of specialty search, to align them with different searcher modes and to best search the varying needs of the searcher. This alignment with searcher modes could also be explored further for the other collaborative mechanisms discussed.

CONCLUSION

In this chapter, we have seen how the search engines and search mechanisms of today are good but not the ideal. Information overload and difficulties in query formulation remain a major problem, and an average search still takes about

11 minutes. We posit that collaborative approaches to searching will provide an important way to help a user connect the dots and make sense of information.

For collaboration to be successful, the collaborator or collaborative mechanisms must be able to help the searcher either through expertise or experience, or similarity of needs. While providing collaborative mechanisms, an information provider must also take into account the different modes a searcher is in at different points in time (based on the characteristics of the task at hand or the qualities/expertise of the searcher), and provide technology features that match the task and searcher characteristics reflected from the user mode.

In this chapter, we reviewed concepts related to collaboration, as well as existing collaborative mechanisms that are finding a high level of success and are being widely adopted. We also discussed two collaborative mechanisms—cues and specialty search. These can be built into a system and will allow a searcher to retrieve information collaboratively with other like-minded searchers. However, simply building collaborative mechanisms is not enough. These mechanisms must also be viewed in the context of the different modes a searcher is in at different points in time.

An illustration was provided using a case study of an educational taxonomy portal.

It is our sincere hope that the world will see collaboration in more and more spheres, including the common, but ubiquitous activity of looking for information.

REFERENCES

Abowd, G.D., Dey, A.K., Abowd, G., Orr, R., & Brotherton, J. (1997). *Context-awareness in wearable and ubiquitous computing.* GVU Technical Report GIT-GVU-97-11. Retrieved September 2, 2006, from http://www-static.cc.gatech.edu/fce/pubs/iswc97/wear.html

Agarwal, N.K., & Poo, D.C.C. (2006). Meeting knowledge management challenges through effective search. *International Journal of Business Information Systems, 1*(3), 292-309.

Alavi, M., & Leidner, D.E. (2001). Review: Knowledge management and knowledge management systems: Conceptual foundations and research issues. *MIS Quarterly, 25*(1), 107-136.

Asmus, J., Bonner, C., Esterhay, D., Lechner, A., & Rentfrow, C. (2005, December 6). *Instructional design technology trend analysis.* Denver: University of Colorado. Retrieved September 1, 2006, from http://elgg.net/collinb/files/1136/2967/TrendAnalysisWeb.pdf

Battelle, J. (2004). GlobalSpec: Domain specific search and the semantic Web. *John Battelle's Searchblog.* Retrieved May 24, 2006, from http://battellemedia.com/archives/000519.php

Belkin, N.J. (1984). Cognitive models and information transfer. *Social Science Information Studies, 4*(2-3), 111-129.

Belkin, N.J. (2000). Helping people find what they don't know. *Communications of the ACM, 43*(8), 58-61.

Belkin, N.J., & Croft, B.W. (1992). Information filtering and information retrieval: Two sides of the same coin? *Communications of the ACM, 35*(12), 29-36.

Bharat, K., & Broder, A.Z. (1998). A technique for measuring the relative size and overlap of Web search engines. *Proceedings of the 7th International World Wide Web Conference (WWW7)* (pp. 379-388).

Billsus, D., & Pazzani, M. (1998). Learning collaborative information filters. *Proceedings of the 15th International Conference on Machine Learning* (pp. 46-54). San Francisco: Morgan Kaufmann. Retrieved May 28, 2006, from http://www.ics.uci.edu/~pazzani/Publications/MLC98.pdf

Blake, C., & Pratt, W. (2002, November 18-21). Collaborative information synthesis. *Proceedings of ASIST 2002* (pp. 44-56), Philadelphia.

Case, D.O. (2002). *Looking for information: A survey of research on information seeking, needs, and behavior.* San Diego: Academic Press, Elsevier.

Chi, E.H., & Pirolli, P. (2006, February). Social information foraging and collaborative search. *Proceedings of the HCIC Workshop,* Fraser, CO.

Cox, A. (2005). What are communities of practice? A comparative review of four seminal works. *Journal of Information Science, 31*(6), 527-540.

Cross, R., Borgatti, S.P., & Parker, A. (2002). Making invisible work visible: Using social network analysis to support strategic collaboration. *California Management Review, 44*(2), 25-46.

Dahlen, B.J., Konstan, J.A., Herlocker, J.L., Good, N., Borchers, A., & Riedl, J. (1998). *Jump-starting movielens: User benefits of starting a collaborative filtering system with 'dead data'.* University of Minnesota TR 98-017.

Deerwester, S., Dumais, S.T., Furnas, G.W., Landauer, T.K., & Harshman, R. (1990). Indexing by latent semantic analysis. *Journal of the Society for Information Science, 41*(6), 391-407.

Dretske, F. (1981). *Knowledge and the flow of information.* Cambridge, MA: MIT Press

Ellis, D., Allen, D., & Wilson, T.D. (1999). Information science and information systems: Conjunct subjects, disjunct disciplines. *Journal of the American Society for Information Science, 50*(12), 1095-1107.

Fang, X., Chen, P., & Chen, B. (2005). User search strategies and search engine interface design. In R.W. Proctor & K.-P.L. Vu (Eds.), *Handbook of human factors in Web design* (pp. 193-210). Mahwah, NJ: Lawrence Erlbaum.

Fayyad, U.M., Piatetsky-Shapiro, G., Smyth, P., & Uthurusamy, R. (Eds.). (1996). *Advances in knowledge discovery and data mining.* Menlo Park, CA: AAAI Press.

Fowell, S., & Levy, P. (1995). Developing a new professional practice: A model for networked learner support in higher education. *Journal of Documentation, 51*(3), 271-280.

Freyne, J., Smyth, B., Coyle, M., Balfe, E., & Briggs, P. (2004). Further experiments on collaborative ranking in community-based Web search. *Artificial Intelligence Review, 21*(3-4), 229-252.

Fu, L., Goh, D.H.-L., Foo, S.S.-B., & Supangat, Y. (2004, September 12-17). Collaborative querying for enhanced information retrieval. *Proceedings of ECDL 2004* (pp; 378-388), Bath, UK.

Goh, J.M., Poo, D.C.C., & Chang, K.T.T (2004, July 8-11). Incorporating contextual cues into electronic repositories. *Proceedings of the 8th Pacific-Asia Conference on Information Systems* (pp. 472-484), Shanghai, China.

Golder, S., & Huberman, B.A. (2005). *The structure of collaborative tagging systems.* Retrieved May 28, 2006, from http://www.hpl.hp.com/research/idl/papers/tags/tags.pdf

Google Technology. (2004). Our search: Google technology. *About Google.* Retrieved May 27, 2006, from *http://www.google.com/technology/*

Gordon, M., & Pathak, P. (1999). Finding information on the World Wide Web: The retrieval effectiveness of search engines. *Information Processing and Management, 35,* 141-180.

Green, A. (1990). What do we mean by user needs? *British Journal of Academic Librarianship, 5,* 65-78.

Hammond, T., Hanny, T., Lund, B., & Scott, J. (2005). Social bookmarking tools (I). *D-Lib Magazine, 11*(4). Retrieved May 28, 2006, from http://www.dlib.org/dlib/april05/hammond/04hammond.html

Hawking, D., Paris, C., Wilkinson, R., & Wu, M. (2005, August 9). Context in enterprise search and delivery. *Proceedings of the ACM SIGIR 2005 Workshop on Information Retrieval in Context (IRiX)* (pp. 14-16), Salvador, Brazil.

Herlocker, J.L., Konstan, J.A., & Riedl, J. (2000, December 2-6). Explaining collaborative filtering recommendations. *Proceedings of the 2000 ACM Conference on Computer Supported Cooperative Work (CSCW'00)* (pp. 241-250). Philadelphia.

Herlocker, J.L., Konstan, J.A., Terveen, L.G., & Riedl, J.T. (2004). Evaluating collaborative filtering recommender systems. *ACM Transactions on Information Systems, 22*(1), 5-53.

Hill, W., Stead, L., Rosenstein, M., & Furnas, G. (1995a). Recommending and evaluating choices in a virtual community of use. *Proceedings of the Human Factors in Computing Systems (CHI '95) Conference* (vol. 1, pp.194-201). New York: ACM.

Hill, W., Stead, L., Rosenstein, M., & Furnas, G.W. (1995b). Recommending and evaluating choices in a virtual community of use. *Proceedings of the Conference on Human Factors in Computing Systems* (CHI'95) (pp. 194-201). Denver, CO.

Hofstede, M. (2000). A collection of special search engines. *Universiteitsbibliotheek.* Retrieved May 28, 2006, from http://www.leidenuniv.nl/ub/biv/specials.htm

Ingwersen, P., & Jarvelin, K. (2004, July 29). Information retrieval in contexts. *Proceedings of the ACM SIGIR 2004 Workshop on Information Retrieval in Context* (pp. 6-9), Sheffield, UK.

ISEdb (Internet Search Engine Database). (2005). *Specialty search engines.* Retrieved May 28, 2006, from http://www.isedb.com/html/Internet_Search_Engines/Specialty_Search_Engines/

Karamuftuoglu, M. (1998). Collaborative information retrieval: Toward a social informatics view of IR interaction. *Journal of the American Society for Information Science, 49*(12), 1070-1080.

Kawin Interactive. (2003, January 1). *Kawin Vortalbuilding.com: Your gateway to the universe.* Retrieved May 24, 2006, from http://elibrary.line56.com/detail/RES/1098686731_907.html

Khoussainov, R., & Kushmerick, N. (2003). Learning to compete in heterogeneous Web search environments. *Proceedings of the 18th International Joint Conference on Artificial Intelligence (IJCAI-03).*

Komarjaya, J., Poo, D.C.C., & Kan, M.-Y. (2004, September 12-17). Corpus-based query expansion in online public access catalogs. *Proceedings of ECDL 2004* (pp. 221-231). Bath, UK.

Konstan, J. (2004). Introduction to recommender systems: Algorithms and evaluation. *ACM Transactions on Information Systems, 22*(1), 1-4.

Konstan, J.A., Miller, B.N., Maltz, D., Herlocker, J.L., Gordon, L.R., & Riedl, J. (1997). GroupLens: Applying collaborative filtering to Usenet news. *Communications of the ACM, 40*(3), 77-87.

Lancaster, F.W. (1968). *Information retrieval systems: Characteristics, testing and evaluation.* New York: John Wiley & Sons.

Lawrence, S., & Giles, C.L. (2000). Accessibility of information on the Web. *Intelligence, 11*(1), 32-39.

Lederman, P. (2005). Implementing a taxonomy solution. *AIIM E-Doc, 19*(2), 25-26.

Levy, D.M., & Marshall, C.C. (1994). What color was George Washington's white horse? A look at assumptions underlying digital libraries. *Proceedings of Digital Libraries '94* (pp. 163-169). College Station, TX.

Machlup, F. (1980). *Knowledge: It's creation, distribution, and economic significance* (vol. 1). Princeton, NJ: Princeton University Press.

Marchionini, G. (1997). *Information seeking in electronic environments*. Cambridge, UK: Cambridge University Press (Cambridge Series on Human-Computer Interaction).

Mathes, A. (2004, December). Folksonomies: Cooperative classification and communication through shared metadata. *Proceedings of the Computer Mediated Communication Doctoral Seminar* (LIS590CMC), Urbana-Champaign, IL. Retrieved September 2, 2006, from http://www.adammathes.com/academic/computer-mediated-communication/folksonomies.html

Meyer, H.A. (2006). *Topic search engines*. Retrieved May 28, 2006, from http://www.all-searchengines.com/

Mika, P. (2005, November 6-10) Ontologies are us: A unified model of social networks and semantics. *Proceedings of the 4th International Semantic Web Conference* (ISWC 2005), Galway, Ireland. Retrieved September 2, 2006, from http://www.cs.vu.nl/~pmika/research/papers/ISWC-folksonomy.pdf

Mitchell, J.C. (1969). The concept and use of social networks. In J.C. Mitchell (Ed.), *Social networks in urban situations* (pp. 1-50). Manchester, UK: University of Manchester Press.

Morahan-Martin, J., & Anderson, C.D. (2000). Information and misinformation online: Recommendations for facilitating accurate mental health information retrieval and evaluation. *CyberPsychology & Behavior, 3*(5), 731-746.

Mori, M., & Yamada, S. (2000, October 30-November 4). Adjusting to specialties of search engines using Meta Weaver. *Proceedings of the World Conference on the WWW and Internet (WebNet 2000)* (pp. 408-412). San Antonio, TX.

Morville, P. (2002, February 21). *Social network analysis*. Retrieved August 30, 2006, from http://semanticstudios.com/publications/semantics/000006.php

Narayanan, S., Koppaka, L., Edala, N., Loritz, D., & Daley, R. (2004). Adaptive interface for personalizing information seeking. *CyberPsychology & Behavior, 7*(6), 683-688.

Nichols, D.M., Pemberton, D., Dalhoumi, S., Larouk, O., Belisle, C., & Twidale, M.B. (2000, September 18-20). DEBORA: Developing an interface to support collaboration in a digital library. *Proceedings of ECDL 2000* (pp. 239-248). Lisbon, Portugal.

North, E.J., North, J., & Benade, S. (2004). Information management and enterprise architecture planning—a juxtaposition, *Problems and Perspectives in Management, 4,* 166-179.

Papadopoullos, A. (2004). Answering the right questions about search. *EContent leadership series: Strategies for...search, taxonomy & classification* (supplement to July/August 2004 *EContent and Information Today,* pp. S6-S7). Retrieved May 29, 2006, from http://www.procom-strasser.com/docs/Convera_Right_Questions.pdf

Procter, R., Goldenberg, A., Davenport, E., & McKinlay, A. (1998). Genres in support of collaborative information retrieval in the virtual library. *Interacting with Computers, 10*(2), 157-175.

Pujol, J.M., Sanguesa, R., & Bermudez, J. (2003, May 20-24). Porqpine: A distributive and collaborative search engine. *Proceedings of the 12th International World Wide Web Conference* (WWW2003, p. S25), Budapest, Hungary. Retrieved May 27, 2006, from *http://www2003.org/cdrom/papers/poster/p341/p341-pujol.html.html*

Resnick, P., & Varian, H.R. (1997). Recommender systems. *Communications of the ACM, 40*(3), 56-58.

Resnick, P., Iacovou, N., Suchak, M., Bergstrom, P., & Riedl, J. (1994). GroupLens: An open architecture for collaborative filtering of Netnews. *Proceedings of the 1994 Conference on Computer*

Supported Collaborative Work (CSCW'94) (pp. 175-186).

Robertson, S.E. (1981). The methodology of information retrieval experiment. In K. SparckJones (Ed.), *Information retrieval experiment* (pp. 9-31). Butterworths.

Scott, J. (2000). *Social network analysis: A handbook* (2nd ed.). London/Thousand Oaks, CA: Sage.

Shardanand, U., & Maes, P. (1995). Social information filtering: Algorithms for automating 'word of mouth'. *Proceedings of the Conference on Human Factors in Computing Systems (ACM CHI'95)* (pp. 210-217). Denver, CO.

Sherman, C. (2006, January 19). *Survey: Google, Yahoo still favorites in North America.* Retrieved May 29, 2006, from http://searchenginewatch. com/searchday/article.php/3578491

Smyth, B., Balfe, E., Boydell, O., Bradley, K., Briggs, P., Coyle, M., & Freyne, J. (2005, July 31-August 5). A live-user evaluation of collaborative Web search. *Proceedings of the 19th International Joint Conference on Artificial Intelligence (IJCAI-05)* (pp. 1419-1424). Edinburgh, Scotland.

Smyth, B., Balfe, E., Briggs, P., Coyle, M., & Freyne, J. (2003). Collaborative Web search. *Proceedings of the 18th International Joint Conference on Artificial Intelligence* (IJCAI-03) (pp. 1417-1419). San Francisco: Morgan Kaufmann.

Starr, B., Ackerman, M.S., & Pazzani, M. (1996). Do-I-Care: A collaborative Web agent. *Proceedings of the Human Factors in Computing Systems Conference (CHI '96)* (pp. 273-274). New York: ACM.

Sullivan, D. (2000, April 4). The vortals are coming! The vortals are coming! Retrieved May 24, 2006, from http://searchenginewatch.com/sereport/article.php/2162541

Sullivan, D. (2002, February 20). *Specialty search engines.* Retrieved March 23 and May 28, 2006, from http://searchenginewatch.com/links/article. php/2156351

Swearingen, K., Lyman, P., Varian, H.R., Charles, P., Good, N., Jordan, L.L., & Pal, J. (2003). *How much information?* Berkeley: University of California School of Information Management and Systems. Retrieved May 30, 2006, from http:// www.sims.berkeley.edu/research/projects/how-much-info-2003/

Terveen, L., McMackin, J., Amento, B., & Hill, W. (2002). Specifying preferences based on user history. *Proceedings of the Conference on Human Factors in Computing Systems* (CHI'02). Minneapolis, MN.

Tkatchenko, M. (2005). *Combining reputation and collaborative filtering systems.* Retrieved September 1, 2006, from http://www.cs.ubc. ca/~kevinlb/teaching/cs532a%20-%202005/ Class%20projects/Maria.pdf

Twidale, M., & Nichols, D. (1998). Designing interfaces to support collaboration in information retrieval. *Interacting with Computers, 10*(2), 177-193.

van de Wijngaert, L. (1999, August 13-15). A policy capturing study of media choice: The effect information [sic] of needs and user characteristics on media choice. In T.D. Wilson & D.K. Allen (Eds.), *Information Behavior: Proceedings of the 2nd International Conference on Research in Information Needs, Seeking and Use in Different Contexts* (pp. 463-478). Sheffield, UK: Taylor Graham.

Vance, D.M. (1997, August). Information, knowledge and wisdom: The epistemic hierarchy and computer-based information system. In B. Perkins & I. Vessey (Eds.), *Proceedings of the 3rd Americas Conference on Information Systems,* Indianapolis, IN.

VanFossen, L. (2005). *Top specialty search engines list.* Retrieved May 28, 2006, from http://www.cameraontheroad.com/index.php?p=196

Wang, J., Pouwelse, J., Lagendijk, R.L., & Reinders, M.J.T. (2006, April 23-27). Distributed collaborative filtering for peer-to-peer file sharing systems. *Proceedings of the 21st Annual ACM Symposium on Applied Computing (SAC'06),* Dijon, France.

Wasserman, S., & Faust, K. (1994). *Social network analysis: Methods and applications.* New York: Cambridge University Press.

Wenger, E. (1998). *Communities of practice: Learning, meaning and identity.* Cambridge: Cambridge University Press.

Wenger, E., McDermott, R.A., & Snyder, W. (2002). *Cultivating communities of practice: A guide to managing knowledge.* Boston: Harvard Business School Press.

Wu, X., Zhang, L., & Yu, Y. (2006, May 23-26). Exploring social annotations for the semantic Web. *Proceedings of the 15th International World Wide Web Conference* (WWW 2006), Edinburgh, Scotland.

Chapter II
Collaborative Querying Using a Hybrid Content and Results–Based Approach

Chandrani Sinha Ray
Nanyang Technological University, Singapore

Dion Hoe-Lian Goh
Nanyang Technological University, Singapore

Schubert Foo
Nanyang Technological University, Singapore

Nyein Chan Soe Win
Nanyang Technological University, Singapore

Khasfariyati Razikin
Nanyang Technological University, Singapore

ABSTRACT

Collaborative querying is a technique that makes use of past users' search experiences in order to help the current user formulate an appropriate query. In this technique, related queries are extracted from query logs and clustered. Queries from these clusters that are related to the user's query are then recommended to the user. This work uses a combination of query terms as well as results documents returned by queries for clustering queries. For the latter, it extracts features such as titles, URLs, and snippets from the results documents. It also proposes an extended K-means clustering algorithm for clustering queries over a simple measure of overlap. Experimental results reveal that the best clusters are obtained by using a combination of these sources rather than using only query terms or only results URLs alone.

INTRODUCTION

Web search engines play a vital role retrieving information from the Internet, but there are several challenges faced by users of information retrieval (IR) systems in general. Users are often overwhelmed by the number of documents returned by an IR system or fail to express their information needs in terms compatible to those used in the system. While new IR techniques can potentially alleviate these problems, specifying information needs properly in the form of a query is still a fundamental problem with users. Borgman (1996) attributed this to the lack of conceptual knowledge of the information retrieval process. Put differently, users need to know how to translate their information needs into searchable queries.

Research in information seeking behavior suggests an alternative approach in helping users meet their information needs. Studies have found that collaboration among searchers is an important step in the process of information seeking and use. For example, Taylor (1968) highlights the importance of the interaction between the inquirer and the librarian, while Ellis (1993) argues that communication with colleagues is a key component in the initial search for information. We use the term *collaborative IR* to refer to a family of techniques that facilitate collaboration among users while conducting searches. These techniques can be categorized based on the way people search for information into: collaborative filtering (Cohen & Fan, 2000), collaborative browsing (Lieberman, 1995), and collaborative querying (Setten & Hadidy, n.d.). In particular, collaborative querying helps searchers in query formulation by harnessing other users' search experience or expert knowledge (Goh, Fu, & Foo, 2005).

Queries, being expressions of information needs, have the potential to provide a wealth of information that could be used to guide other searchers with similar information needs, helping them with query reformulation. If large quantities of queries are collected, they may be mined for emerging patterns and relationships that could be used to define communities of interest (e.g., Lycos 50), and even help users explore not only their current information needs but related ones as well. One can imagine a network of queries amassed from the collective expertise of numerous searchers, representing what people think as helping them meet their information needs. Query formulation and reformulation will then be a matter of exploring the query network, executing relevant queries, and retrieving the resulting documents.

There are many techniques for uncovering related queries to support collaborative querying, one of which is query clustering (Wen, Nie, & Zhang, 2001). Here, query logs of IR systems are mined, and similar queries are grouped and used as recommendations. Different query clustering approaches are distinguished based on the measure of the similarity between queries. Traditional term-based similarity measures borrowed from classical IR (Setten & Hadidy, n.d.) represent one example. However, the short lengths of queries (e.g., Silverstein, Henzinger, Marais, & Moricz, 1998) limit the usefulness of this approach. An alternative is based on the overlap of the top N results (such as URLs) returned from an IR system (Raghavan & Sever, 1995; Glance, 2001). This approach however might not be effective for queries with different semantic meanings, but leading to similar search results since terms are not considered during clustering. Hence, a hybrid approach was proposed by Fu, Goh, Foo, and Na (2003) which is a linear combination of the content-based and results-based approaches. Experiments showed that this approach produces better query clusters in terms of precision, recall, and coverage than using either the content-based or results-based method alone. Although these results show potential, there is still room for improvement by using additional information for measuring similarity. Examples include titles, snippets (document excerpts), or other metadata in the search results listings. Such information is commonly returned by IR systems and is used by searchers to judge whether the results satisfy their information needs. These can therefore be used to complement query terms and results URLs as criteria to measure the similarity between queries.

In this chapter we extend existing work in query clustering by Fu et al. (2003) in two ways. First, the type of features used for calculating similarity between queries is expanded to include titles and snippets from search results documents in addition to query terms and results URLs. Secondly, a new algorithm, a variation of K-means, known as extended K-Means clustering algorithm is proposed for clustering queries. The results obtained are then compared with previous work to see if the addition of metadata from listings of search results produces any improvement in query clustering.

RELATED WORK

Query logs maintained by IR systems contain information related to users' queries including search sessions, query terms submitted, documents selected, and so on. Hence, query logs provide valuable indications for understanding the types of documents users intend to retrieve when formulating a query (Cui, Wen, Nie, & Ma, 2002). One of the common techniques for collaborative querying through the reuse of previously submitted queries obtained from query logs is via query clustering (Fu et al., 2003). Queries within the clusters are then used as candidates for query reformulation. For example, Goh et al. (2005) developed a collaborative IR system that recommended related queries extracted and clustered from query logs. Both query terms and results returned were utilized in their hybrid query clustering approach.

Query clustering approaches can be categorized into content-based, results-based, feed-back-based, and a hybrid of these approaches, depending on the type of information used to determine the similarity between queries. The content-based approach borrows from classical term-based techniques of traditional IR. Here, features are constructed from the query keywords. A major drawback is that, on average, queries submitted to a Web search engine are very short (Silverstein et al., 1998), comprising two to three words, in contrast to documents that are rich in content. Since the information content in queries is sparse (Chuang & Chien, 2002), it is difficult to deduce the semantics behind queries, which in turn makes it difficult to establish similarity between queries (Wen et al., 2001).

An alternative is to use click-through data (feedback approach), which uses documents selected by users returned in response to a query. The idea behind this approach is that two queries are similar if they lead to the same selection of documents by searchers (Cui et al., 2002). Work by Wen et al. (2001) demonstrated that a combination of the content-based and feedback-based approaches performed better in terms of the F-measure than the individual approaches. The disadvantage however is that the quality of query clusters may suffer if users select too many irrelevant documents.

In a results-based approach, documents returned in response to a query are used to measure similarity between queries. Here, document identifiers (e.g., URLs) as well as other metadata such as the document title, snippet, or even the entire document are used. The latter was used by Raghavan and Sever (1995) to determine the similarity between queries by calculating the overlap in document content, but this method is time consuming to execute. Glance (2001) therefore determined query similarity by the amount of overlap in the respective top-50 search results listings. Finally, Sahami and Heilman (2006) use the results documents containing the query terms to extract other terms which often occur in context with the original query terms, and use them to establish similarity between queries.

Our work differs from previous work in that it uses not only content and results URLs, but also the titles and snippets from search results documents since they are considered good descriptors of a query (Zamir, Etzioni, Madani, & Karp, 1997). Also, since the entire results document is not used as a feature set, it reduces the processing time, which is important in a Web search scenario. Moreover, our work uses the extended K-means algorithm (Wang & Kitsuregawa, 2002) to define the similarity between queries rather than a simple measure of overlap, as in Fu et al. (2003). The K-means algorithm is effective in computing the distances between objects in very large data sets which is appropriate due to the size of typical query logs.

QUERY CLUSTERING ALGORITHM

As discussed, this chapter adopts a hybrid query clustering approach that explores the use of search results titles and snippets, in addition to query terms and results URLs, to measure similarity between queries. Let W denote a collection of queries to be clustered. We represent each query Q_i in W with composite unit vectors:

$$Q_i = (D_i, E_i, F_i) \qquad (1)$$

where

- Q_i is the composite unit vector representing i-th query in the query set W, $1 \le i \le n$ (n is the total number of queries in the dataset);
- D_i is the component unit vector representing keywords in Q_i;
- E_i is the component unit vector representing the terms from the snippets and the title of the documents returned in response to Q_i ; and

- F_i is the component unit vector representing the results URLs returned in response to Q_i.

Content-Based Similarity Measure

A query is considered a "document" and query terms are vectors representing the query (Setten & Hadidy, n.d.). All terms are extracted after which stop words are removed and the remainder are stemmed. Terms that appear in less than two documents are eliminated, as they do not contribute in defining the relationship between two or more queries. The extracted terms are used to represent each query (Q_i) in the query set W as the content-based component vector (D_i) in Equation 1. Specifically, D_i is a weight vector obtained using the standard TFIDF formula:

$$w_{nQj} = tf_{nQj} * idf_n \qquad (2)$$

$$idf_n = \log\left(\frac{N}{df_n}\right) \qquad (3)$$

where w_{nQi} is the weight of the n-th term in query Q_j, tf_{nQi} is the query term frequency, N is the number of queries in the query set W, df_n is the number of queries containing the n-th term, and idf_n is the inverted term frequency for the n-th term.

The content-based similarity between query Q_i and Q_j is then measured using the cosine similarity function as defined as in Equation 4:

$$sim\_content(Q_i, Q_j) = \frac{\sum_{n=1}^{N} w_{nQi} \times w_{nQj}}{\sqrt{\sum_{n=1}^{N} w_{nQi}^2 \times \sum_{n=1}^{N} w_{nQj}^2}} \qquad (4)$$

where w_{nQi} and w_{nQj} are weights of the common n-th term in query Q_i and Q_j respectively obtained using Equation 2.

Results-Based Similarity Measure

As discussed, limitations exist when using only query terms for clustering. Fu et al. (2003) notes that the results lists returned in response to queries are readily accessible sources of rich information for measuring similarity. Such listings typically contain a variety of information such as the URLs of the results documents, the titles, and snippets. The titles and snippets in the results listings can be considered good descriptors of a query (Zamir et al., 1997) and are used by searchers to judge whether the results satisfy an information need. In our work, the results URLs as well as results terms (titles plus snippets) are used to represent each query as a results-based component vector (E) in Equation 1. For the results URLs component of E, let $U(Q_j)$ be a set of query results URLs to a query Qj, and $U(Q_j) = \{u_1, u_2, ..., u_n\}$ where u_i represents the i-th result URL for Q_j. We then define R_{ij} as the overlap between two results URLs vectors between two queries Qi and Qj:

$$R_{ij} = \{u : u \in U(Q_i) \cap U(Q_j)\} \qquad (5)$$

The similarity measure based on results URLs (adopted from Fu et al., 2002) is defined as:

$$sim\_results_{URLs}(Q_i, Q_j) = \frac{|R_{ij}|}{Max(|Q_i|, |Q_j|)}$$

$$(6)$$

where |Qi| and |Qj| represent the number of the results URLs in queries Qi and Qj respectively, and $|R_{ij}|$ is the number of common results URLs between Qi and Qj.

For the results terms component of E, we employ the cosine similarity measure as presented in Equation 4:

$$sim\_results_{terms}(Q_i, Q_j) = \frac{\sum_{n=1}^{N} w_{nQi} \times w_{nQj}}{\sqrt{\sum_{n=1}^{N} w_{nQi}^2 \times \sum_{n=1}^{N} w_{nQj}^2}}$$

$$(7)$$

where w_{nQi} and w_{nQj} are weights of the common n-th term in query Q_i and Q_j extracted from the results titles and snippets, using the TFIDF formula in Equations 2 and 3.

Finally, the complete results-based similarity measure is a linear combination of both URLs and terms and is defined as:

$$sim\_results(Q_i, Q_j) =$$
$$\omega_k * sim\_results_{URLs} + \omega_l * sim\_results_{terms}$$

$$(8)$$

where ω_k is the weight assigned to $sim\_results_{URLs}$, ω_l is the weight assigned to $sim\_results_{terms}$, and ω_k and ω_l are non-negative numbers such that $\omega_k + \omega_l = 1$.

The Hybrid Similarity Measure

Similar to Fu et al. (2003), the hybrid approach adopted in the present work is a linear combination of the content-based and results-based approaches, and is expected to overcome the disadvantages of using either approach alone:

$$sim\_hybrid(Q_i, Q_j) =$$
$$\alpha * sim\_results + \beta * sim\_content \qquad (9)$$

where α and β are non-negative weights and α + β = 1.

The Extended K-Means Algorithm

The extended K-means algorithm introduced by Wang and Kitsuregawa (2002) was used in our experiment. The algorithm draws from the concepts of the standard K-means and Leader algorithms. Thus, it inherits the advantages of

Figure 1. K-means clustering algorithm

1. Define a similarity threshold, t where $0 \leq t \leq 1$.
2. Randomly select a query as a cluster centroid.
3. Assign the remaining queries to the existing cluster if the similarity between the new query and the cluster centroid exceeds the defined threshold.
4. The query becomes a cluster by itself if condition in step 3 is not satisfied.
5. The centroids of the clusters are recomputed if its cluster members are changed.
6. Repeat steps 3 to 5 until all queries are assigned and cluster centroids do not change any more.

K-means in efficient computing of the distances between objects in very large data sets (Zhao & Karypis, 2003). It is also similar to the Leader algorithm, in that the number of clusters need not be pre-determined, which is an advantage since the number of query clusters are not known in advance.

Figure 1 summarizes the extended K-means algorithm (Wang & Kitsuregawa, 2002), an iterative partitioning algorithm which tries to overcome some of the limitations of the standard K-means. It uses similarity thresholds instead of pre-defined k centroids. This is the major advantage as the number of query clusters are not known in advance.

METHODOLOGY

Six months worth of query logs obtained from the Nanyang Technological University (NTU, Singapore) digital library was used in this work. The queries belong to various domains including engineering disciplines, business, and the arts. Each entry in a query log contains a timestamp indicating when the query was submitted, the submitted query, session ID, and the number of records returned. In the preprocessing stage, only the queries from the logs were extracted, as the remainder of the content did not contribute to the query clustering technique used in this work.

From the logs, approximately 12,700 queries were randomly sampled for use. Each query was then submitted to the Google search engine using the Google Web API. From the ensuing results listing, the top 10 URLs, titles, and snippets were extracted for use in the results-based component of the hybrid similarity measure.

Computing Similarity

Recall from Equation 9 that hybrid similarity is a linear combination of the content and results-based similarity. In our experiments, five pairs of values for (α, β) were used to vary the levels of contribution of each of these similarity measures:

- Content-based similarity (*sim_content*) – $\alpha = 0.0$, $\beta = 1.0$
- Results-based similarity (*sim_result*) – $\alpha = 1.0$, $\beta = 0.0$
- Hybrid similarity (*sim_hybrid1*) – $\alpha = 0.75$, $\beta = 0.25$
- Hybrid similarity (*sim_hybrid2*) – $\alpha = 0.50$, $\beta = 0.50$
- Hybrid similarity (*sim_hybrid3*) – $\alpha = 0.25$, $\beta = 0.75$

Note also that the results-based component of Equation 9, defined in Equation 8, is a linear combination of results terms and URLs. Here, three pairs of values ($\omega_k = 1.0$, $\omega_l = 0.0$), ($\omega_k = 0.5$, $\omega_l = 0.5$), and ($\omega_k = 0.0$ and $\omega_l = 1.0$) were used to represent the varying levels of contribution of results terms and URLs. In order to manage the number of experiments to be carried out to facilitate easier comparison, the following technique was used.

We first set $\omega_k = 1.0$ and $\omega_l = 0.0$ to observe the results-based method using results URLs alone. These similarity measures are denoting with a subscript "basic-link" and defined as follows:

1. Content-based similarity (*sim_content*) – α =0.0, β =1.0
2. Results-based similarity (*sim_result_{basic-link}*) – α =1.0, β =0.0
3. Hybrid similarity (*sim_hybrid1_{basic-link}*) – α =0.75, β =0.25
4. Hybrid similarity (*sim_hybrid2_{basic-link}*) – α =0.50, β =0.50
5. Hybrid similarity (*sim_hybrid3_{basic-link}*) – α =0.25, β =0.75

These measures are the same ones defined in Fu et al. (2003). Using these similarity measures, we carried out our query clustering experiments using the extended K-Means algorithm at two different similarity thresholds (0.5 and 0.9) to determine which threshold will provide better query clustering results in terms of the F-measure. That threshold would then be used for the remainder of the experiments.

Given the selected similarity threshold, we next set $\omega_k = \omega_l = 0.5$ so that the results-based method considered both the results URLs and terms equally during clustering. These similarity measures are denoted by the subscript "extended" and are defined as follows:

1. Results-based similarity (*sim_result_{extended}*) – α =1.0, β =0.0
2. Hybrid similarity (*sim_hybrid_{extended}*) – α =0.75, β =0.25
3. Hybrid similarity (*sim_hybrid_{extended}*) – α =0.50, β =0.50
4. Hybrid similarity (*sim_hybrid_{extended}*) – α =0.25, β =0.75

Finally, we considered results terms alone by setting ω_k =0.0 and ω_l =1.0. These similarity measures are denoted by the subscript "basic-term" and are defined as follows:

1. Results-based similarity (*sim_result_{basic-term}*) – α =1.0, β =0.0
2. Hybrid similarity (*sim_hybrid_{basic-term}*) – α =0.75, β =0.25
3. Hybrid similarity (*sim_hybrid_{basic-term}*) – α =0.50, β =0.50
4. Hybrid similarity (*sim_hybrid_{basic-term}*) – α =0.25, β =0.75

Note that the content-based similarity measure remains unchanged in the hybrid equation, although the results-based component has been changed by the three combinations of results URLs and terms. In total, 13 separate experiments were run.

Comparison Criteria

The quality of the query clusters generated from the 13 approaches was compared using average cluster size, coverage, precision, recall, and F-measures similar to Fu et al. (2003) and others. Average cluster size is the average of all the cluster sizes. Coverage is the percentage of queries in which the similarity measure is able to provide a cluster. Precision is the ratio of the number of similar queries to the total number of queries in a cluster. Recall is the ratio of the number of similar queries to the total number of all similar queries in the dataset (those in the current cluster and others). It is difficult to calculate recall directly because no standard clusters are available in our dataset. Therefore, an alternative *normalized recall* (Wen et al., 2001) was used instead (explained later). For measuring precision and recall, 100 sample clusters were selected. Finally, F-measure is used to generate a single measure by combining recall and precision.

For every similarity measure, 100 clusters were randomly selected from the results of the extended K-means clustering process. For each cluster, precision was determined manually by two human evaluators. The evaluators were told to take into account both query terms and results URLs. They were also asked to look up unfamiliar terms using search engines, dictionaries, and other information sources. The average precision was then computed using these 100 clusters. To ensure some degree of reliability between the evaluators, Cronbach's (1951) alpha was also computed.

FINDINGS AND ANALYSES

Measuring Quality of Query Clusters

Recall that two similarity thresholds 0.5 and 0.9 were used for the "basic-link" approach to determine which threshold provided the best result in terms of F-measure. It was found that the threshold 0.5 was the consistent best performer and hence this value was used in our experiments.

Average cluster size indicates the ability of the clustering algorithm to recommend queries for a user's query. Figure 2 shows a plot of the average cluster size against different values of α and β (see Equation 9). Average cluster size exhibits an increasing trend along with the increase in β, the weight for the content-based component. The average cluster size of *sim_content* at similarity threshold 0.5 ranks highest at 6.93, indicating that users have a higher likelihood of finding more

queries from a given query using the content-based approach. This is because different queries share a number of identical terms. Conversely, the average cluster size of $sim\_result_{basic-link}$ is the smallest (2.18), meaning that users will have the fewest number of recommended queries per issued query. This may be due to the fact that the number of distinct URLs is usually large and thus many similar queries cannot be clustered together for lack of common URLs [2]. Figure 2 also shows that the "basic-term" approaches have consistently higher average cluster sizes than those of other approaches. Thus when result terms were used, these similarity measures provided more recommended queries than those without using results terms.

Coverage (Salton & McGill, 1983) indicates the probability a user can obtain recommended queries from his/her issued query. The content-based approach *sim_content* ranks highest in coverage (82.40%) followed by the hybrid approaches $sim\_hybrid3_{basic-term}$ (78.55%) and $sim\_hybrid3_{extended}$ (76.99%), indicating that the content-based approach is better able to find similar queries for a given query than other approaches. The coverage of $sim\_result_{basic-link}$ is the

Figure 2. Average cluster size for different similarity measures

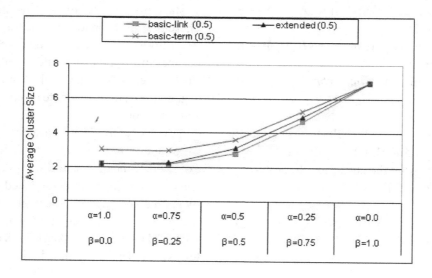

lowest (12.51%), which means that users will be less likely to receive recommended queries from an issued query. This reason may be the same for average cluster size in that the number of distinct URLs is usually large and many similar queries cannot be clustered for lack of common URLs (Chuang & Chien, 2002).

Figure 3 shows that like average cluster size, coverage exhibits an increasing trend along with the increase in β. In addition, the coverage of the

"basic-term" approaches is consistently higher than that of the other approaches, suggesting the importance of the use of results terms. Hence, users have a higher likelihood of receiving recommendations from a given query by using result terms during clustering than not using them.

In terms of precision, the hybrid approach *sim_hybrid1$_{basic-link}$* performs best (99.73%) followed by *sim_hybrid1$_{extended}$* (99.50%) and *sim_result$_{extended}$* (99.00%). The worst performer was *sim_content*

Figure 3. Coverage for different similarity measures

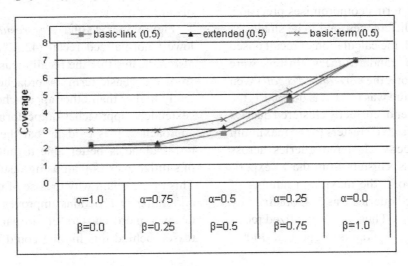

Figure 4. Precision for different similarity measures

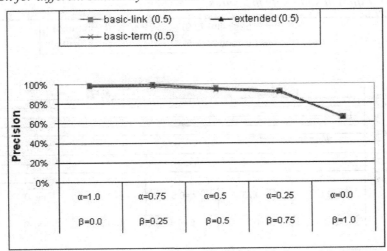

(65.92%), suggesting that the use of query terms alone is not sufficient for producing good quality clusters. Figure 4 shows that precision decreases with the increase in α while it increases with a corresponding increase in β, the weight for the results-based component. In general, *sim_hybrid1* generally performs better; this is attributed to the fact that the search engine used in our experiments (Google) tends to return results URLs that are the same for semantically related queries. It is also interesting to observe that the precision of the "basic-term" approaches are consistently lower than those of other approaches, indicating that the use of results terms compromises precision. However, these differences tend to be small.

As mentioned, the calculation of recall posed a problem as no standard query clusters were available. Therefore, the *normalized recall* (Wen et al., 2001) measure was used. It is defined as the ratio of the number of correctly clustered queries within the 100 selected clusters to the maximum number of correctly clustered queries across the dataset (that is, clusters from the 13 experiments). In our work, the maximum number of correctly clustered queries was 514, obtained by $sim\_hybrid3_{basic-term}$. Thus, the normalized recall of $sim\_hybrid3_{basic-term}$ ranks highest at 100%,

followed by $sim\_hybrid3_{extended}$ (96.03%) and *sim_content* (95%). This indicates that $sim\_hybrid3_{basic-term}$ is better able to uncover clusters of similar queries generated by different similarity functions on the given query set used in this experiment. At the similarity threshold of 0.5, the recall of $sim\_result_{basic-link}$ is the lowest (42.03%), meaning that users have the lowest likelihood of finding more query clusters. This could be because the number of distinct URLs is usually large and similar queries cannot be clustered together for lack of common URLs (Chuang & Chien, 2002), thus lowering the performance to uncover clusters of similar queries.

Figure 5 shows that $sim\_result_{extended}$ has the lowest normalized recall (42.35%). The figure also indicates that the recall measures resulting from the "basic-term" approaches are consistently higher than other approaches, though the "extended" approaches outperform "basic-link" approaches. It is evident that the use of result terms alone is better able to uncover clusters of similar queries than using result links alone. This may explain why the use of result terms in all similarity functions improves the ability to uncover more clusters of similar queries. The reason behind this finding could be that as the

Figure 5. Recall for different similarity measures

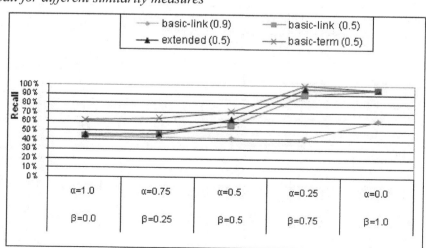

number of common terms increases due to the contribution of result terms used, the chances of finding related queries increase.

To measure the global quality of the clusters, the F-measure is used (Wen et al., 2001). Table 1 shows that the F-measures returned from "basic-link" experiments at threshold 0.5 were consistently better than those at threshold 0.9. Hence similarity threshold 0.5 was used in the other approaches to generate query clusters. It was observed that the use of result terms consistently improved the F-measure compared to the approaches that did not use them. The reasons for this are similar to those cited for precision and recall since the F-measure itself is the harmonic mean of precision and recall.

Computation of the Degree of Agreement Between Evaluators

The quality of the result query clusters on different criteria was evaluated from a sample of 100 clusters by two human evaluators. Since the evaluation of the quality of results clusters relied totally on the judgment of the human evaluators, the reliability of the evaluation is required to be assessed. The reliability of their judgments may be assessed from the degree of agreement between the two evaluators. A higher degree of agreement indicates a consistent response about the accuracy of clusters, while a lower degree of agreement indicates an inconsistent response about the accuracy of clusters or they have "low" reliability.

The degree of agreement can be assessed using Cronbach's alpha. Cronbach's alpha is an index of reliability associated with the variation accounted for by the true score of the "underlying construct." Construct is the hypothetical variable that is being measured (Hatcher, 1994). The alpha coefficient ranges in value from 0 to 1 and may be used to describe the reliability of factors extracted from dichotomous (that is, questions with two possible answers) and/or multi-point formatted questionnaires or scales (i.e., rating scale: 1 = poor, 5 = excellent). The higher the score, the more reliable the generated scale is. Nunnaly (1978) has indicated 0.7 to be an acceptable reliability coefficient, but lower thresholds are sometimes used in the literature. George and Mallery (2003) provide the following rules of thumb: " > 0.9–Excellent, >0.8–Good, > 0.7–Acceptable, > 0.6–Questionable, _ > 0.5–Poor, and < 0.5–Unacceptable."

Cronbach's alpha can be written as a function of the number of test items and the average inter-correlation among the items. For conceptual purposes, we show the formula for the standardized Cronbach's alpha below:

$$\alpha = \frac{N\bar{r}}{1+(N-1).\bar{r}} \qquad (10)$$

Here N is equal to the number of items and $\bar{r}$ is the average inter-item correlation among the items.

Table 2 summarizes average, minimum, and maximum measures of Cronbach's alpha obtained for five similarity measures.

Table 1. F-measure comparison

Similarity Function	basic-link (threshold = 0.9)	basic-link (0.5)	basic-term (0.5)	extended (0.5)
sim_result	0.60	0.62	0.76	0.62
sim_hybrid1	0.60	0.62	0.77	0.64
sim_hybrid2	0.59	0.71	0.81	0.76
sim_hybrid3	0.59	0.91	0.95	0.94
sim_content	0.75	0.78	0.78	0.78

Table 2. Degree of agreement (Cronbach's alpha)

	Extended Similarity Functions				
	sim_content	sim_result	sim_hybrid1	sim_hybrid2	sim_hybrid3
Alpha	0.70	0.73	0.88	0.72	0.71
Standardized Item Alpha	0.73	0.78	0.89	0.76	0.71
p	<0.005	<0.005	<0.005	<0.005	<0.005

The degree of agreement between two evaluators for all approaches exceeded 0.7. Hence, according to Nunnaly (1978) and George and Mallery (2003), this indicates that all evaluation results are acceptable.

DISCUSSION

We have observed that the "basic-term" approach performs better than the other approaches in terms of all the performance criteria except precision. As there are five similarity functions used in the "basic-term" approach, the comparison between the qualities of results for each is presented in Table 3. Only F-measures are reported in place of recall and precision. As can be seen in the table, the average cluster sizes of the results-based approach $sim\_result_{basic\text{-}term}$ and hybrid approaches $sim\_hybrid1_{basic\text{-}term}$ and $sim\_hybrid2_{basic\text{-}term}$ are low. However $sim\_hybrid3_{basic\text{-}term}$ and $sim\_content_{basic\text{-}term}$ provide 5.27 and 6.93 queries per cluster respectively on average. Since users are already burdened with a number of search results, too many query suggestions to the original queries will not be of much benefit to users. Hence, the average of five to seven suggestions per query is quite reasonable. Table 4 shows sample query clusters resulted from $sim\_hybrid3_{basic\text{-}term}$.

Table 3. Summary of evaluation results

	Best	Worst
Avg. Cluster Size	sim_hybrid3$_{basic\text{-}term}$	sim_result$_{basic\text{-}link}$
Coverage	*sim_content$_{basic\text{-}term}$*	sim_result$_{basic\text{-}link}$
Precision	sim_hybrid1$_{basic\text{-}link}$	*sim_content$_{basic\text{-}term}$*
Recall	sim_hybrid3$_{basic\text{-}term}$	sim_result$_{basic\text{-}link}$

Table 4. Two query clusters from sim_hybrid3 $_{basic\text{-}term}$

Similarity Functions (similarity threshold = 0.5)	Average Cluster Size	Range of Cluster Size	Coverage	F-Measure
sim_result$_{basic\text{-}term}$	3.04	2~7	17.89%	0.76
sim_hybrid1$_{basic\text{-}term}$	2.98	2~8	34.38%	0.77
sim_hybrid2$_{basic\text{-}term}$	3.60	2~33	63.39%	0.81
sim_hybrid3$_{basic\text{-}term}$	5.27	2~87	78.55%	0.95
sim_content$_{basic\text{-}term}$	6.93	2~181	82.40%	0.78

Table 5. Comparison of query clustering approaches

A wavelet tour of signal processing, wavelet processing, wavelet tool signal processing
Strains stresses, handbook formulas stress strain, aluminum stress-strain curve, strain material, stress transformation, distribution curve, engineering stress, failure curve

Moreover, *sim_content$_{basic-term}$* provides the highest coverage at 82.40% while *sim_hybrid-3$_{basic-term}$* ranks second highest at 78.55%. Stated differently, a user is more likely to receive recommendations to his original query using *sim_content$_{basic-term}$* and *sim_hybrid3$_{basic-term}$*. In terms of F-measure, *sim_hybrid3$_{basic-term}$* ranks highest at 0.95, which suggests that the recommended queries will be useful to the searcher. Also, *sim_hybrid3$_{extended}$* achieved the second highest score at 0.94, while *sim_hybrid3$_{basic-link}$* ranks third at 0.91 (refer to Table 1). It is observed that although *sim_content$_{basic-term}$* achieved the largest average cluster size (6.93) among other approaches and the highest coverage (82.40%), it has a lower F-measure (0.78) compared to *sim_hybrid3$_{basic-term}$* (0.95) (from Table 1).

It can thus be deduced that *sim_hybrid3$_{basic-term}$* provides the most balanced results for query clusters followed by *sim_hybrid3$_{extended}$* and *sim_hybrid3$_{basic-link}$*. Table 5 gives an alternative view by comparing the performances of all approaches at similarity threshold 0.5. Although there is no single best performer, the table shows that the combination of the content-based and results-based approaches outperforms the use of either approach alone. Further, the hybrid clustering approach *sim_hybrid3$_{basic-term}$* yields the best performance in terms of average cluster size, recall, and F-measure.

CONCLUSION

Collaborative querying is inspired from research in information seeking behavior, which shows that collaboration among searchers is important in the process of information seeking and use. In our work, we use query clustering to discover similar queries to assist in query formulation and reformulation. We compared the content-based approach, results-based approach, and a hybrid approach of both measures to cluster similar queries from query logs using the extended K-means algorithm. Our experiments also explored whether the use of more features (terms from title and snippets from the search results lists), in addition to the query terms and results URL, produces better clusters. Results showed that the use of either content-based or results-based approaches alone was inadequate. Instead, the hybrid content and results-based approach (*sim_hybrid3$_{basic-term}$*), considering query terms, title terms, and snippet terms, produced better query clustering results than approaches that do not consider terms from titles and snippets. The reason could be due to the increased number of common terms between two queries extracted from titles and snippets. With this increased number, term weights play a more important role in finding related queries.

Our proposed hybrid clustering approach will allow IR systems to identify high-quality clusters to help users reformulate queries to meet their information needs by sharing queries issued by other users. High-quality query clusters can also be used in automatic query expansion.

We propose to extend our work in the following directions. Firstly, phrases could be used in the calculation of query similarity since they are less sensitive to noise due to the lower probability of finding matching phrases in non-related queries (Hammouda & Kamel, 2002). Hence, this technique could increase precision. Further, lexical knowledge through resources such as Wordnet could be used to improve the recall of the clusters. Similar to Chuang and Chien (2002), the use of lexical knowledge can be used to create a query hierarchy representing broader or specialized queries and allow users to modify their queries by either broadening or narrowing their searches.

ACKNOWLEDGMENT

This project is partially supported by NTU research grant number RG25/05.

REFERENCES

Borgman, C.L. (1996). Why are online catalogs still hard to use? *Journal of the American Society for Information Science, 47*(7), 493-503.

Chuang, S.L., & Chien, L.F. (2002). Towards automatic generation of query taxonomy: A hierarchical query clustering approach. In V. Kumar, S. Tsumoto, P.S. Yu, & N. Zhong (Eds.), *Proceedings of IEEE 2002 International Conference on Data Mining* (pp. 75-82). Los Alamitos, CA: IEEE Computer Society.

Cohen, W., & Fan, W. (2000). Web-collaborative filtering: Recommending music by crawling the Web. In I. Herman & A. Vezza (Eds.), *Proceedings of the 9th International World Wide Web Conference on Computer Networks: The International Journal of Computer and Telecommunications Networking* (pp. 685-698). Amsterdam, The Netherlands: North-Holland.

Cronbach, L.J. (1951). Coefficient alpha and the internal structure of tests. *Psychometrika, 16*(3), 297-334.

Cui, H., Wen, J., Nie, J., & Ma, W. (2002). Probabilistic query expansion using query logs. In D. Lassner, D.D. Roure, & A. Iyengar (Eds.), *Proceedings of the 11th International Conference on World Wide Web* (pp. 325-332). New York: ACM Press.

Ellis, D. (1993). A comparison of the information seeking patterns of researchers in the physical and social sciences. *Journal of Documentation, 49*(4), 356-369.

Fu, L., Goh, D.H., Foo, S., & Na, J.C. (2003). Collaborative querying through a hybrid query clustering approach. In T.M.T. Sembok, H.B. Zaman, H. Chen, S.R. Urs, & S.H. Myaeng (Eds.), *Digital libraries: Technology and management of indigenous knowledge for global access* (pp. 111-122). Berlin: Springer-Verlag (LNCS 2911).

Glance, N. (2001). Community search assistant. In C. Cidner & J. Moore (Eds.), *Proceedings of the 6th International Conference on Intelligent User Interfaces* (pp. 91-96). New York: ACM Press.

Goh, D.H., Fu, L., & Foo, S. (2005). Collaborative querying using the query graph visualizer. *Online Information Review, 29*(3), 266-282.

Hammouda, K.M., & Kamel, M.S. (2004). Efficient phrase-based document indexing for Web document. *IEEE Transactions on Knowledge and Data Engineering 16*(10), 1279- 1296. Washington, DC: IEEE Computer Society Press.

Hatcher, L. (1994). *A step-by-step approach to using the SAS(R) system for factor analysis and structural equation modeling.* Cary, NC: SAS Institute.

Lieberman, H. (1995). Letizia: An agent that assists Web browsing. In C.S. Mellish (Ed.), *Proceedings of the 14th International Joint Conference on Artificial Intelligence* (pp. 924-929). Montréal, Canada: Morgan Kaufmann.

Nunnaly, J. (1978). *Psychometric theory.* New York: McGraw-Hill.

Raghavan, V., & Sever, H. (1995). On the reuse of past optimal queries. In E.A. Fox, P. Ingwersen,

& R. Fidel (Eds.), *Proceedings of the 18th International ACM-SIGIR Conference on Research and Development of Information Retrieval* (pp. 344-350). New York: ACM Press.

Sahami, M., & Heilman, T.D. (2006). A Web-based kernel function for measuring the similarity of short text snippets. *Proceedings of the 15th international Conference on the World Wide Web* (pp. 377-386). New York: ACM Press.

Setten, M.V., & Hadidy, F.M. (n.d.). *Collaborative search and retrieval: Finding information together.* Retrieved February 20, 2004, from *https://doc.telin.nl/dscgi/ds.py/Get/File-8269/ GigaCE-Collaborative_Search_and_ Retrieval Finding_Information_Together.pdf*

Silverstein, C., Henzinger, M., Marais, H., & Moricz, M. (1998). Analysis of a very large Alta-Vista query log. *Technical Report 1998-014.* Palo Alto, CA: Digital Systems Research Center.

Taylor, R. (1968). Question-negotiation and information seeking in libraries. *College and Research Libraries, 29*(3), 178-194.

Wang, Y., & Kitsuregawa, M. (2001). Link based clustering of Web search results. In C. Claramunt, W. Winiwarter, Y. Kambayashi & Y. Zhang (Eds.), *Proceedings of the 2nd International Conference on Web Information Systems Engineering* (vol. 1, p. 115). Washington, DC: IEEE Computer Society.

Wen, J.R., Nie, J.Y., & Zhang, H.J. (2001). Query clustering using content words and user feedback. In W.B. Croft, D.J. Harper, D.H. Kraft, & J. Zobel (Eds.), *Proceedings of the 24th Annual International ACM SIGIR Conference on Research and Development in Information Retrieval* (pp. 442-443). New York: ACM Press.

Zamir, O., Etzioni, O., Madani, O., & Karp, R.M. (1997). Fast and intuitive clustering of Web documents. In D. Heckerman, H. Mannila, D. Pregibon, & R. Uthurusamy (Eds.), *Proceedings of the 3rd International Conference on Knowledge Discovery and Data Mining* (KDD'97) (pp. 287-290). Menlo Park, CA: AAAI Press.

Zhao, Y., & Karypis, G. (2003). Prediction of contact maps using support vector machines. In H. Jamil, & V. Magalooikonomou (Eds.), *Proceedings of the 3rd IEEE Symposium on Bioinformatics and Bioengineering* (pp. 26-33). Washington, DC: IEEE Computer Society.

Section II
Collaborative Classification and Organization

Chapter III
Collaborative Classification for Group–Oriented Organization of Search Results

Keiichi Nakata
International University in Germany, Germany

Amrish Singh
International University in Germany, Germany

ABSTRACT

In this chapter the authors examine the use of collaborative classification to support social information retrieval by organizing search results. It subscribes to the view that the activity of collaborative classification can be characterized by top-down and bottom-up approaches, both in terms of the nature of concept classification and the process of classification development. Two approaches, collaborative indexing and search result classification based on shared classification schemes, are described and compared. It suggests that by allowing open access to classification development tools to generate shared classification schemes, which in turn become collaborative artifacts, cooperating user groups will generate their own coordination mechanisms that are not dependent on the system itself.

INTRODUCTION

It is widely understood that the task of information retrieval involves representation, storage, organization of, and access to information items (Baeza-Yates & Ribeiro-Neto, 1999). Moreover, the retrieved information should satisfy the user's information needs. As such, the user carries the task of translating his or her information needs into a representation or language provided by a retrieval system. This in itself is often problematic; users may not be able to express their information needs adequately, or the results may not be satisfactory due to limitations in the expressivity of the query language in articulating the information needs. Such problems that occur in individual information retrieval tasks are compounded when carried out in a group. The articulation of information needs of a group is far more complex than that of the individual.

The information retrieval task in the World Wide Web (WWW) is primarily assumed to be an individual task. This is reflected in the interaction design of most commercial search engines, in which users either enter search terms or browse through the categorized information space, often referred to as directories. Web-based search engines are engineered to provide links to pages that satisfy users' information needs. Most search engines return search results in a ranked ordered list. The ranks of the documents are determined by their relevance to the corresponding query. This relevance measure depends predominantly on the user's ability to suitably describe his or her information need as a query text. Since most queries are short, unconscious assumptions are made regarding the context of query terms, making the query less precise. This leads to a low precision in the retrieved results, and users are forced to manually sift through the list of returned pages to find relevant documents. This would be unproblematic if the users could easily separate irrelevant documents from the relevant ones. However, the presentation style of ranked lists used by most search engines does not make it easy to do so. Document ranking becomes virtually obsolete when documents lower in the list are more relevant to the user's information needs than the ones with higher ranks. Therefore, a major challenge for efficient Web search is to make search results helpful to the user even if the query is poorly formulated.

An argument in favor of the collaborative approach such as social information retrieval is that with the ever-increasing amount of electronically retrievable information, such as on the Internet, collaboration might be one of few ways to practically manage the complexity of information retrieval and management. To deal with the rate of growth in the information pool, which is in some cases already unmanageable by an individual, joining efforts in a group or community would enable us to manage the complexity of information retrieval such as indexing, organization, and storage, while maintaining reasonable coverage. Tools such as search engines and browsers enable users to engage in the exploration of a large information pool; there should also be effective tools for collaborative work that encourage such a participatory mode of information exploration and management.

One of the approaches to leverage groups' collaborative efforts in information retrieval is collaborative filtering, also referred to as social filtering. Essentially, collaborative filtering is an adaptation of relevance feedback by multiple members of a group. Relevance feedback can be seen as a form of query expansion through user feedback without the necessity to reformulate the query to improve the precision of the result. Being a query expansion implies that this applies effectively to single query. However, in the group context, the information retrieval task is often not carried out in isolation and the time scope is wider to allow for contributions from multiple members. When queries are made over time, the likelihood that the nature and context of query change also becomes higher. For such a situation, the model based on relevance feedback, such as collaborative filtering, may be too static, or not dynamic enough to capture such changes.

Instead, what we focus on here is the use of classifications based on conceptual structures. Such classifications can be shared and developed collaboratively by a group. They can be used to index documents or classify documents such as search results. If classifications can be dynamically restructured, the dynamic nature of group information needs may be dealt with more effectively.

A number of questions immediately arise from such an approach, especially for group scenarios.

They include:

- How are common conceptual structures generated?
- How would people share conceptual structures?
- Does personalization in information retrieval and organization help improve the satisfaction of information needs?

In this chapter we consider the approaches in using collaborative classification to address the problem stated above. Collaborative classification involves the development of a *shared* classification of information. In particular, we compare two approaches: the first is developing and using a shared taxonomy to index documents; the second is developing and using a shared classification to categorize documents. In both cases, it is intended that the group information needs be captured by the development and use of shared classifications.

BACKGROUND

Collaborative Classification of Concepts

Nakata (2001) argues that there are *top-down* and *bottom-up* approaches in information management that involves concept classification. The top-down approach refers to the classification of *a priori* concepts that are shared by the group. A typical top-down approach attempts to develop a shared conceptual hierarchy, in the form of ontology or category, and classify the information accordingly. Here, the information need is captured by a conceptual node, and users are expected to find required information in one or more of such nodes. The bottom-up approach refers to the formation of information needs through a process of identifying concepts that best represent them. A typical case of this approach is the collection

of common terms and vocabulary from which a classification can be constructed based on the documents available. Here, each concept should appear in the documents and is therefore *grounded* to the information. In this case, the information need is often captured by the combination of common terms.

The distinction between top-down and bottom-up concept classifications can be seen analogously to the issue of document-oriented and request-oriented indexing (Fidel, 1994). The former, while not entirely excluding contexts or users, focuses more on what the document is about. In another words, it would emphasize the conceptual domain in which the document would be classified. The latter is more user centered since it would take into account the context of the information request. Since request-oriented indexing requires the information regarding information seekers' conceptual model in their information seeking activity, the overhead will be high. However, if the information seeking activity takes place over a certain period of time, or as a part of collaborative efforts, such information could be captured through an interactive process. Moreover, there are issues on inter- and intra-indexer consistency (Lancaster, 2003). The consistency of indexing between indexers (inter-indexer) and by the same indexer (intra-indexer) can be more complex if the "indexer" is a group rather than an individual. In such a social information management situation, the process of concept classification and indexing requires further attention.

Collaborative Classification as a Social Process

The two approaches in concept classification also extend to a more top-down or a more bottom-up approach in the process of collaborative classification. This refers to the way the collaborative activity of classification is carried out (Table 1). In the top-down process, selected members of a group ("editorial board") take an initiative or coordinate the development of the classification. In the bottom-up process, the classification development is open to free participation, and its result is dependent on evolutionary and group dynamics. There are pros and cons in each of these approaches. For example, the top-down approach would inevitably impose a particular view which may not be acceptable to some members within a group. The bottom-up approach might lead to many inconsistencies or a "free-rider" problem which would not enable an effective development of the classification.

The four styles of classification scheme development process as summarized in Table 1 occur not exclusively, but may be combined to cater for the nature of group process and requirements at various phases of development. The editorial board seldom works in isolation without any user evaluation and feedback; the concepts to be included are judged by the editorial board through their expertise and knowledge. However, we can observe that many of the existing tools and systems support primarily top-down approaches.

Application of Collaborative Indexing and Classification for Social Information Retrieval

The bottom-up approach in concept classification is useful when the group collectively gathers relevant terms and concepts for their collective information needs to express relevance. This is effectively generating an index of terms that the group is interested in, which in turn defines the domain and focus of interest of the group. The conceptual hierarchy generated bottom-up from these terms reflects the manner in which the concepts are grouped and labeled. When the terms are indexed—that is, associated with the actual occurrences in the collection of documents, it provides a means to retrieve required documents effectively.

The conceptual hierarchy generated top-down constructs a set of categories according to which a document can be classified. This can be done statically such as in library classification, or more dynamically based on the nature of the document collection. The latter can be seen in approaches such as search result clustering that organizes documents often based on automatically generated clusters. Systems such as vivisimo.com and kartoo.com present search results by contextually organizing similar Web documents into groups (or clusters), and labeling each group with a characteristic word or phrase. This alleviates the problem with ranked ordering by enabling users to find relevant documents easier. Existing online clustering engines, however, still suffer from two basic drawbacks. First, the document clustering generated is very objective in nature and does

Table 1. A matrix of top-down and bottom-up approaches (Nakata, 2001)

		Concept Classification	
		Top-Down	Bottom-Up
Classification Development	Top-Down	Development of classification schemes for pre-conceived (*a priori*) concepts by an editorial board	Development of classification schemes for *grounded* concepts by an editorial board
	Bottom-Up	Development of classification schemes for pre-conceived (*a priori*) concepts through individual participation	Development of classification schemes for *grounded* concepts through individual participation

not consider the user's perspective. This forces users to look at the set of results from different perspectives (e.g., a technical perspective vs. a business perspective), which sometimes causes difficulty or may not make any sense to the user. Second, the automated keywords or key phrases created for each cluster often tend to be vague, ambiguous, and unrepresentative of the documents in the cluster.

A more effective way is to organize retrieved results in a structure which makes sense to the users. A classical way is to use a hierarchical structure such as classification schemes. As evident from the history of knowledge representation emphasizing inheritance hierarchies, a classification scheme can be considered to represent the way the information space (or "the world") is viewed by a person or group that shares a common view. Shared classification schemes, such as directories, are a product of social process; they represent not only the structure through which an information space should be interpreted ("made sense"), but also the scope of interest of those who employ them.

In the following, we describe two systems, Concept Index and WebClusters, that exemplify the two approaches, collaborative indexing and collaborative classification, aimed at enabling social information retrieval based on these paradigms.

COLLABORATIVE INDEXING

Concept Index (Voss, Nakata, & Juhnke, 2000) is an example of an index that provides cross-referencing among documents based on concepts. The motivation for a Concept Index is to capture relations between documents as relations between the concepts described, referred to or discussed in these documents. Its primary aim is to capture the group's interests scattered as conceptual terms in these documents, and it has the potential to support the emergence of group-oriented domain

vocabulary by identifying concept relations, making these explicit and enabling users to inspect and edit these concept relations.

A document typically can be associated with different contexts with several other documents. This implies that a document can belong to several collections of documents, depending on the context in which the document is created or retrieved. For example, documents can be collected for the following contexts:

- user group (documents produced by a defined group of users);
- task (documents produced for a particular task);
- location (documents organized under the same folder, stored at the same site, etc.); and
- neighborhood of hyperlinked documents (documents referenced by hyperlinks from a document).

These are explicit relations in terms of user affiliation, purpose, organizational context, and content-related information, respectively. In Concept Index, an index or a conceptual structure of terms may be generated for any arbitrary collection of documents, called a document pool. Such a document pool can be seen as the context in which documents belong. A document may be included in one or more of these document pools, reflecting the feature that one document can be seen from different perspectives.

As described below, a Concept Index encompasses lexical, semantic, and pragmatic levels. These levels progressively provide richer concept models as well as increased user involvement in the development. It is important to note that users can use and edit Concept Indexes at any level: indeed the generation of a Concept Index itself can be a collaborative task.

Term Identification

Given a pool of documents specified by the user group, Concept Index supports the group to generate an index that provides through indexed term cross-references between documents. The author or the reader of a document specifies occurrences of terms in the document that are to be included in the index (vocabulary) in terms of keyword tags. To ease the process of term identification, this can be performed by simply highlighting those words in the document; this is analogous to underlining or using a highlighter pen to mark printed documents. This process of term identification is an active behavior on the side of the author, the information provider, and the reader, the information recommender, with the intention of providing a set of concepts which is to be included in his or her contribution to the shared information base. A keyword tag can be assigned to a term (a word or a phrase), or a URL. At this stage, keywords are "exported" from documents to an index, producing a lexical index for the registered documents. Since the terms are processed lexically, this can be considered to be at the lexical level.

The set of index terms is the union of the sets of keywords exported from all the documents in the document pool. These documents are cross-referenced through these terms which appear as tags in every document that includes these terms. This means that it is possible that the words and phrases that a user did not originally mark as keywords are tagged, as a result of cross-referencing based on the lexical index that includes exported keywords from other members of the group for the same document, and those from other documents in the pool. We refer to the type of keywords that are introduced in this way as of the type "imported." Therefore, when the user reads the same document next time, he will see the keywords he highlighted together with those marked as important by others. Since these imported keywords may have been introduced

from other registered documents via the index, by following these tags, readers can jump from one document to another, or view several documents side by side regarding the parts of those documents that refer to a particular term. This provides support for the reuse of documents, consistent use of terms, identifying relations between documents, and automatic enhancement of documents through meta-information on these terms.

Although Concept Index presupposes that group members carry out term identification, there are alternative methods. This can be substituted by methods such as automatic term extraction (Green, 1998). The use of an index is not only useful for users to navigate through the space of registered documents, but also extends to the examination of external documents through this group-oriented set of terms. Given any document, a user would be able to identify and import keywords defined in a selected index that appear in that document. For example, when an arbitrary Web page is viewed with an index that inserts tags for the terms in the index, the user would able to see how relevant that page is according to the view represented in the chosen index. In this manner, such an index can be seen as a tool for document exploration.

Associations of Terms

If a term has synonyms, the procedure above can be extended to include synonyms for an indexed term. For example, if *university* and *higher education* both appear in the lexical index, these words could be cross-referenced between documents since they are synonymous. Specifying relationships between terms enriches the semantics of the index. In contrast to the lexical level, we refer to the process here as the semantic level. The vocabulary is therefore first extended by synonyms of the terms at this level. Through this process the terms may be considered to represent concepts: in the same way Miller, Beckwith, Fellbaum, Gross, and Miller (1990) characterize concepts. Here a concept is described, not defined, by a set of synonyms, or in the terminology used by WordNet (Miller et al., 1990), by a *synset.* A synset can be understood as a representation of a concept through a set of words that together exemplify the concept.

The introduction of synonyms is not only useful for enriching the vocabulary, but it can also help distinguish between different senses of words. For example, for the same word *particle,* there could be two synsets {*particle, molecule*} and {*particle, function word*}, which describe different concepts.

Furthermore, to provide a conceptual structure to the terms in the index, hierarchical relations between concepts, both in terms of generalization (super/subclasses) and mereological relations (part-of/has-part), can be defined. In this way the vocabulary is extended to include the concepts in hierarchical and compositional relations, facilitating the construction of a classification of terms.

Synonyms and word relations can be obtained from existing terminology databases such as WordNet, but users may also suggest these relations. To emphasize the collaborative aspect of the evolution of Concept Indexes, users are expected to participate actively in the generation of indexes. Therefore, automatic disambiguation of polysems (words that belong to several concepts) and treatment of synonymy (concepts described by several words) are not considered in Concept Index, since these should be identified interactively by users.

Concept Enhancement

A Concept Index can be further enhanced by identifying related concepts. This can be performed by specifying that two or more concepts are related, or mechanically by identifying co-occurring words in a document, applying, for example, text mining techniques. Text mining is based on statistical methods and is capable of identifying words that co-occur frequently in a given collection of texts. It can potentially identify concepts that are strongly associated, that is, those that may not be related in the sense of conceptual relations, but are related in a specific context, thereby generating contextually related concepts.

For example, as the result of text mining on a document pool, a strong co-occurrence between the term "university" and "community" may be found. These two terms would have no conceptual relation that can be found, for example, by WordNet. However, anyone who inspects the result within the context of the document pool may find it acceptable to relate these, acknowledging that there is indeed a relation between these concepts. This type of relation has been also captured by knowledge representation schemes in artificial intelligence such as semantic nets and conceptual graphs, and has been developed further by efforts in building ontologies (Gruber, 1993a). Taking this view further, inputs from ontology databases such as Ontosaurus (Loom Ontosaurus, 1998) can be exploited.

Relations between concepts identified in such a way is rather arbitrary and domain specific. Therefore we refer to this as the pragmatic level. The relation type for these cases is simply "related." Such arbitrary relations are often sufficient for identifying related documents.

Interactions with a Concept Index

It is an important requirement of a representation of a social information retrieval effort that group members would be able to edit the index and remove/add words at each level. To cater for this requirement, one of the external representations of Concept Indexes should be in the form of a document, which is controlled under a collaborative work environment. Since a Concept Index is essentially a semantic net (Quillian, 1968), it can be represented in terms of nodes (concepts) and arcs (connections between concepts). In this view, we can have two ways of interacting with the Concept Index. One is indirect interaction, through storing and updating documents that contain keywords identified by the user, who would directly interact with the documents, but indirectly with the index. The other is direct interaction, in which users would view and edit the index itself as a document via an editor that acts as a front-end to the index database.

In indirect interaction, Concept Indexes act as a mediator between documents. This means there is no direct, hard-coded reference from a keyword in a document to that in another document, but only through a lookup mechanism on a Concept Index, with the exception of explicit hyperlinks from one document to the other. For events concerning storing and viewing of documents, the cross-referencing operations are invoked as follows:

1. **Add a document to a document pool that has an associated Concept Index:** This can be done implicitly by placing the document in a specific document collection for which the index is maintained, or explicitly by registering it with a certain index.

2. **Identify or "export" terms from the document:** If the term already exists in the Concept Index as an entry of a concept, generate a link between the occurrence of the term in the document and the concept. Otherwise, a new concept is created and its occurrences in other documents in the pool is identified. The document is then scanned to find terms that describe the concepts that appear in the Concept Index. If any exists, add the occurrence of term in the document to the concept. This operation is referred to as "importing" keywords.

3. **Viewing (or loading) a document:** Insert actual cross-references to enable document space navigation (see #5 below). If the document has not been indexed before (e.g., a document before being added to the pool, viewing external documents), then terms need to be imported.

4. **Update/save document:** Update reference links between the Concept Index and the document. This may include deletion of a document (i.e., removal of links to the document).

5. **Navigate through the document pool:** This can be performed by traversing links through following relevant tags via the Concept Index.

In this scenario, the Concept Index serves as the data storage for links between term occurrences in documents.

Enhancing Indexes

The direct form of interaction with an index is necessary for the enhancement of Concept Indexes. While tools such as WordNet and Ontosaurus, and the application of text mining can be used to automate some of the semantic and ontological level enhancements, the most important input would come from the group of users themselves. For instance, WordNet can suggest different senses (meanings) of a word, but it will not be able to decide whether the same term from different documents means the same. Furthermore, terms in this context include phrases or longer sequences of words which cannot be dealt with by WordNet. Taking the viewpoint that Concept Index itself can be a document on its own right, those who use the index should have means to edit it, annotate it, and resolve any disagreements, for example whether two concepts should remain separate or be considered to be merged as a single concept. This process in fact captures collaborative construction of conceptual structures, making explicit common understandings and disagreements over how concepts are interpreted and terms are used.

Merging Indexes

Since a Concept Index is generated for a specified pool of documents, it reflects the conceptual relations between documents and the relations between concepts themselves as seen in that particular group of users sharing the index. This implies that a Concept Index provides a particular point of view concerning how documents are read or interpreted. In some cases, this feature can be exploited to look at the same documents from different perspectives using multiple indexes. In other cases, users might feel that two groups should agree on the common understanding of concepts for better collaboration. These alternatives are reflected in two possible ways of merging indexes. The first is to create a single index from two or more indexes. In this case, each concept is checked to see if there are any inconsistencies, and if so they should be indicated to the user to be resolved. The second is to keep the indexes separate, but to allow users to inspect a document by multiple indexes. In this case, users should be kept aware which index is being used when following a link. Both of these would have their advantages and disadvantages, and should be selected according to the needs.

Collaboration Through a Concept Index

Concept Indexes can be interpreted to represent the information needs of a particular group of people. In other words, they represent shared information needs in terms of concepts which are shared among a group, and relations between these concepts. From what is obtained we can view this process as concept modeling. The well-known problem of the knowledge acquisition bottleneck in concept modeling has been addressed by building up the index based on terms identified by the contributors of information, and through enhancement. The previous section described how the users would interact with Concept Indexes. Here we list their possible usage, particularly in the context of collaborative work.

- Document space navigation by concepts: since cross-references between documents based on related concepts are automatically maintained

Figure 1. A screenshot from the Concept Index prototype

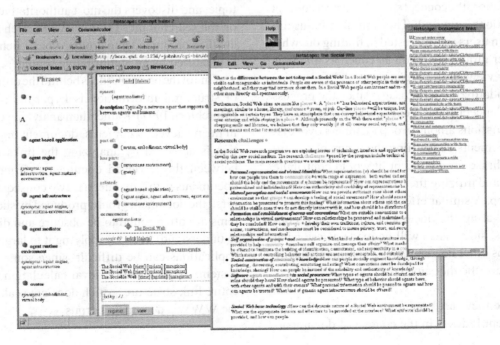

by the Concept Index via hyperlinks, it will be simple to navigate through the document pool, and the users are freed from the overhead of manually creating links.

- Since existing concepts are "tagged" into the documents upon browsing and indicated by different colors or symbols, readers of a new document are provided with visual cues concerning terms which are likely to reflect relevant issues. This feature is useful when browsing a document fetched by a search engine and deciding whether it is actually relevant.

- Using multiple Concept Indexes can offer different viewpoints in inspecting the same document. This would help one understand how other members from a different background or interest would view the document, and identify areas that might require discussions or negotiations.

- Since a Concept Index can be viewed as a shared information needs representation of the community of users building up the document pool through collaborative information retrieval and sharing interests, it can be used to explore the concept space to inspect concept relations acquired. This can also be useful when users are interested in finding out what other groups maintain as concepts and how they view concept relations.

- Standardizing term usage: since the process of Concept Index generation might involve discussions among group members over disagreements concerning the usage of a word or phrase for a concept, it would contribute to standardizing the usage of terms within a group. A similar effect could be obtained by navigating the document space using concepts, since users will be made aware what terms other documents are commonly using to describe the same concept.

While these are potential benefits in the use of Concept Indexes in the context of document-based collaborative work and social information retrieval, issues such as term standardization can be seen as a beneficial feature of constructing a shared community knowledge source.

In the following section, we examine an alternative approach to social information retrieval based on collaborative classification.

COLLABORATIVE CLASSIFICATION OF SEARCH RESULTS

Dumais and Chen highlight use of structural information, document clustering, and document classification as the three general techniques employed in organizing documents into thematic categories (Chen & Dumais, 2000; Dumais & Chen, 2000). Structural information refers to the special properties or metadata associated with each document. Structural information for example can be gathered by analyzing the link structure of the retrieved Web search results (Chen, Hearst, Hong, & Lin, 1999). Kleinberg (1999) exploits the link structure of Web pages by analyzing the collection of pages relevant to a broad search topic, and discovers the most authoritative pages on the search topic. The retrieved search results are then organized into groups where each group is identified by an authoritative source.

One of the principle ideas behind the utilization of structural information is hyper-information (Marchiori, 1997). Rather than analyzing the text in the retrieved documents, document organization is achieved by analyzing the links in and between the retrieved documents. Organizing documents in this manner has two consequences. First, the document groups produced by such systems are often found to be obscure and difficult to understand. Second, applying it to large-scale applications can be difficult, since some of the systems require pre-retrieval calculation of the entire link structure, which does not scale up to the WWW's document corpus.

The second approach, document clustering, organizes documents by placing documents into groups based on their overall similarity to one another. It is typically an unsupervised learning task where unlabeled documents are categorized into unknown and unpredicted categories automatically—that is, neither the documents nor the labels of each cluster (or group) are known prior to the clustering task. This premise makes document clustering an ideal approach to organizing search results. In contrast to using structural information, similarity measures in document clustering systems are based on the text of the provided documents. Usually, a document is represented as a collection of words (both ordered and unordered collections have been used), and the similarity between two documents is determined by comparing their word collections. These similarity measures coupled with the clustering algorithms form the basis of any document clustering system. To generate hierarchical clusters, Agglomerative Hierarchical Clustering (AHC) algorithms are often used (Zamir & Etzioni, 1998, 1999). These algorithms follow a bottom-up approach to organize documents into hierarchical clusters. Although such clustering systems have proved to be quite useful, current online clustering engines—which label clusters with shared phrases—are often unable to produce meaningful phrases, leaving the user to discern the contents of the cluster.

The third approach to document organization is classification. Contrary to clustering, document classification is a technique of assigning documents into predefined categories or classes. It is usually performed in two stages: (1) the training phase and (2) the testing phase. During the training phase, sample documents are provided to the document classifier for each predefined category. The classifier uses machine learning algorithms to learn a class prediction model based on these labeled documents. In the testing phase, unlabeled documents are provided to the classifier, which applies its classification model to determine the categories or classes of the unseen documents. This training-testing approach makes the process of document classification a supervised learning task where unlabeled documents are categorized into known categories. Therefore, document classification can only be used when the domain of the retrieved documents is already known or the set of predefined categories can effectively cover most domains. In this context, it is also important to note that document classification algorithms focus on the text of the documents (like document clustering) rather than the hyper-information (like structural information) available in them. They usually represent a document as a collection (ordered or unordered) of words.

A number of machine learning techniques have been applied for document classification. The naïve Bayes classifier, support vector machines, k-nearest neighbor, and decision tree algorithms are the most common algorithms used for document classification. Among the four, the naïve Bayes classifier is the most frequently used algorithm for real-time classification systems (Lewis, 1998). This is because naïve Bayes is a linear time algorithm and is easy to implement. However, it has been found to perform lower than several other classification algorithms (Yang & Liu, 1999; Rennie, Shih, Teevan, & Karger, 2003) with support vector machines receiving good reviews (Joachims, 1997; Shih, Chang, Rennie, & Karger, 2002). However, the quadratic complexities of other algorithms make them unsuitable for speed critical systems.

Hierarchical Classification

Document classification is normally considered as a flat classification technique, that is, documents are classified into predefined categories where there is no relationship specified between the categories. This approach is suitable when a small number of categories are defined. However, in areas such as search result classification, where the retrieved documents can belong to several different categories, flat classification becomes inefficient, and hierarchical classification is preferred. Hierarchical classification is the process of classifying documents into a hierarchical organization of classes. The assumption behind the hierarchical structure is that each class node in the hierarchy is a special type of its parent class node and a general type of its child nodes, thereby implying a hierarchical relationship. Web directories like *Yahoo!* directory or *dmoz* are good examples of such class hierarchies. In fact most online hierarchical classification systems utilize existing Web directories as their predefined class hierarchies.

Literature on hierarchical classification reports two basic approaches: (1) the big bang approach and (2) the top-down approach. In the big bang approach, documents are classified in one single step to internal nodes or leaf nodes in the hierarchy. In the top-down approach, flat classifiers are created at each node of the hierarchy. A document is classified by traversing it down the tree hierarchy and applying a sequence of classifiers, from the root node to the leaf node. Dumais and Chen (2000) used the linear support vector machine classifier to automatically classify search results from MSN's search engine into a hierarchical structure. An interesting usability study showed that users preferred their approach to the usual ranked presentation. Mladenic (1998) used the naïve Bayes classifier along with the *Yahoo! Science* hierarchy to classify text documents. Dhillon, Mallela, and Kumar (2002) used a combination of word clustering measures and naïve Bayes classification along with the *dmoz* Web directory for top-down hierarchical classification.

Ontologies, Personalization, and Group Orientation

Gruber (1993b) defined an ontology as an explicit specification of a shared conceptualization. Simply put, an ontology is a formal way of representing concepts and their relationships.

Taxonomical class hierarchies like Web directories are an example of how ontologies can be used in the context of the WWW. In terms of semantic annotation of Web pages, SHOE (Simple HTML Ontology Extensions) can be used to provide semantic metadata corresponding to concepts in predefined ontologies. This allows automated software agents to understand Web site content on a more semantic level. An example of using ontologies to represent user profiles is OBIWAN (Chaffee & Gauch, 2000), which facilitates personalized Web navigation. Users build their profiles by creating a hierarchical organization of concepts (personalized ontologies) which were then mapped to a core reference ontology. Software agents used this information to categorize Web sites into the user's personal hierarchy of concepts.

Although personalization of search results has been explored, most research does not focus on the explicit use of ontologies in this context. *Google Personalized* allows users to rank search results according to a collection of topics. The *Profusion* search engine also provides this facility of organizing search results into topics. Several other companies like AltaVista (with geotracking services), Yahoo! (*MyYahoo!*), and MSN are looking into tapping the personalized search market. An interesting addition to the idea of personalized search is the Stuff I've Seen (SIS) project (Dumais et al., 2003). SIS collects information on files or other text data which the user sees while working on his computer. The search interface allows users to search for these text documents at a later time.

Approaches in personalized search could be extended to groups to support social information retrieval through a shared object. Collaborative activities contain the following elements: cooperative work arrangement, common field of work, and articulation work (Schmidt & Simone, 2000). If we apply this to social information retrieval, we can identify the following:

- **Cooperative work arrangement:** The actors (users) who are engaged in common information seeking efforts, and the environment in which they work.

- **Common field of work:** The (partial) result of information retrieval.
- **Articulation work:** Formal and informal exchange of information, and sense-making activities.

In fact, the objective of collaborative information seeking is not only the result of information retrieval, but also the process of shared understanding and sense-making of the collaborative efforts. In order to align oneself to the collaborative activity, there should be a shared object that captures the state of a common field of work. An approach we examine here is to use a classification structure as such a shared object, making is available as a Web service to which group members can subscribe and access.

WebClusters System

We have brought the ontology-based hierarchical classification algorithm and the personalized search result organization paradigm together in a proof-of-concept demonstration system called WebClusters. WebClusters is designed to interface with existing search engines to retrieve search results for keyword queries and organize them into user-defined topic hierarchies. WebClusters consists of two main components: (1) a search interface, which allows users to specify search queries along with personalized ontologies to classify search results; and (2) an ontology editor called WOE (WebClusters Ontology Editor), which facilities creation of a user's personal or group ontologies. Simply put, given a list of search results, WebClusters imposes a selected classification scheme to organize the result. In a sense, it presents the search results through an ontological view.

A WebClusters session starts when the user enters a search query and chooses the user perspective (ontology) to be used for the search-and-classify process. The search query is typically a word or a set of words that succinctly describes the user's information need. The user ontology is either a generic ontology like the *dmoz* "Computers" or a personal ontology created using WOE. Once the user submits the query, the system queries a search engine to retrieve approximately 30-100 search results. This variance in the number of search results is based on the search engine chosen. After the search results are returned from the search engine, they are classified into the user ontology and presented on the user's browser (see Figure 2).

WOE is a browser-based application which allows users to construct personalized ontologies

Figure 2. WebClusters demonstrator

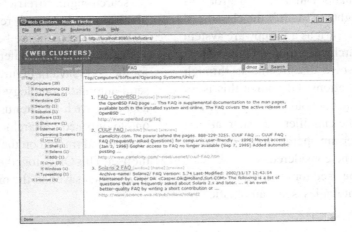

Figure 3. WebClusters ontology editor

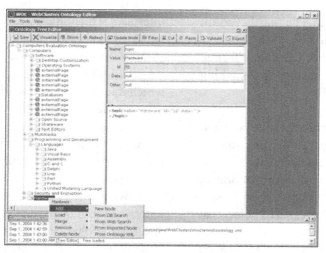

and save them to our ontology database. Figure 3 shows an ontology created using WOE's visual tree editor. By using WOE, users create ontologies by defining the concept hierarchy and assigning Web pages relevant to each topic. The hierarchy is shown as a tree in the pane on the left. The toolbar at the top and the localized popup menu provide most of the ontology editing functionality. The properties pane in the top right-hand corner, and the XML pane below that, show contextual information for the node selected. All of these features have been designed to make the process of constructing ontologies easy and intuitive.

WOE can be made available to a group of users with equal rights to modify the classifiers. This is in the same spirit as a groupware system whereby non-hierarchical group members trust each other and resolve disagreements through side-channel negotiations. Of course this is an assumption that may not hold in every case. The point here is that the classifiers are shareable; a feature to restrict certain operations for each user or limit access can be considered.

WOE can also be used for creating classifiers for concepts in ontologies semi-automatically.

This semi-automatic process is required when the user has defined the concept hierarchy but does not want to spend time specifying sample pages for each concept used for training. This feature in WOE can be used to automatically assign Web pages for each leaf-concept in the hierarchy. The system adds sample pages for each node in the hierarchy by using the node's path (from the root to the node) as a query term to a search engine and the retrieved search results as the training data for the classifier associated with this concept. This is illustrated in Figure 4.

This semi-automatic process relies heavily on the search engine to retrieve relevant results. High precision in the search results can be expected from the search engine because the queries are quite detailed ("Computers Programming Java" for the node Java in Figure 4). Once a manual or semi-automatic ontology has been created, the user can save it for later use. At this stage, a new ontology-based hierarchical classifier (OHC) is created and trained on the ontology provided by the user. This OHC, together with the user's ontology, is then saved to the ontology database.

Figure 4. Using search engines to obtain sample pages for ontology nodes

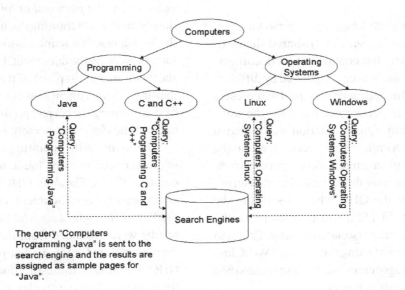

The query "Computers Programming Java" is sent to the search engine and the results are assigned as sample pages for "Java".

Classification of Search Results

In this section we discuss the empirical techniques used to evaluate the classification performance of our system. The purpose of our experiments was to address three key questions: (1) What is the accuracy of an OHC trained on a large ontology like *dmoz* where a large number of training samples are available? (2) How does OHC perform when a user-defined ontology is created where training samples are limited? (3) And what is the accuracy of (1) and (2) when only the summaries of each document are used for classification, rather than the entire text?

Datasets

We used the *Yahoo! Computers and Internet* (YCI) ontology as a reference for defining our testing ontology dataset. A total of 175 topics were selected from YCI to represent our ontology's class hierarchy. Textual samples for each class were also taken from the corresponding leaf classes in the YCI ontology. Table 2 shows the top-level classes in the testing dataset.

Table 2. Top-level categories of the Yahoo! computers and Internet testing dataset

Category Name	Test Pages
Programming and Development	1,434
Software	1,926
Multimedia	603
Security and Encryption	758
Hardware	687
Total	5,408

For our experiments, we also needed to create two OHCs: one trained on an ontology where a large number of Web pages are available for each topic in the hierarchy, and another representing a personalized user-defined ontology where training documents are limited. We used the default *dmoz* classifier from WebClusters as the former. The latter (personalized ontology) was created by using only the topic hierarchy of the YCI testing dataset and populating it with Web pages using the semi-automatic population feature of the WOE and some manual editing. In this ontology each topic was only assigned about 10 training Web pages.

Methodology

The two training sets (*dmoz* and a personal ontology) and the testing set (YCI) shared the same concept hierarchy but contained text documents from different data sources organized by different sets of users. This approach was used to represent the different perspectives of users for the same concept hierarchy. Our evaluation was aimed at measuring the correlation between views on the same hierarchy given three different perspectives. This correlation was determined by measuring the accuracy of the OHC when classifying the Web pages from YCI first into the *dmoz* hierarchy and second into the personal hierarchy. This also reflects the real-world usage scenario of WebClusters where heterogeneous documents are classified based on the user's perspective.

An OHC uses flat Multinomial Naïve Bayes (MNB) classifiers at each non-leaf node in the hierarchy to classify documents to the lower child nodes. A document is classified by traversing it down the tree hierarchy and applying a series of MNB classification tests at each internal node until a leaf node is reached. To test if a document has been classified correctly, we cross-checked the predicted class in *dmoz* and the personal ontology with the document's actual class in YCI. To measure the performance of the approach, we used the following definition of accuracy: the accuracy of a classification algorithm is defined as the ratio of documents which are correctly classified (correct class prediction) to the total number of test documents which are classified (correct and incorrect predictions).

Experiment Results

Four separate experiments were conducted to address the questions described in the beginning of this section. Experiment 1 tested the WebClusters *dmoz* Ontology on the YCI dataset using the entire text of the test documents. Experiment 2 did the same but used the short summaries available for

each document instead of the entire text. Experiment 3 used the *personal ontology* (which had a limited number of training documents) to classify the YCI dataset's documents using the entire text for representing the document. Experiment 4 used short summaries in place of the entire text to do the same as experiment 3. Accuracy was calculated by determining the correct predictions at each leaf node of the *dmoz* and personal ontology.

The *dmoz* OHC operating on the actual text of a text document was found to be the most accurate at 78.9%. The *dmoz* OHC working on small summaries of each document was less accurate in predicting the right classes (at 69.9%). Interesting results were produced from the experiments on the personalized ontology. The personal ontology OHC operating on the testing document's text was the second most accurate classifier at 74.6%. Even though very limited training Web pages were assigned, the model was able to predict unlabeled documents with acceptable accuracy. The personal OHC operating on the testing document's summaries was found to be least accurate at 67.6%. This showed that the OHC can be quite accurate in predicting the right classes even if a limited number of training samples are provided. Using these results we can argue that in a real-world scenario where the testing documents are quite heterogeneous in nature, the WebClusters system is able to classify search results into the user-specified hierarchy with a reasonable amount of accuracy. Accuracy is at a maximum when a large number of training documents are supplied for each concept and the entire text is used for classification.

DISCUSSION

Both Concept Index and WebClusters support collaborative classification of concepts. They enable a group of users to share the common understanding of how to "view" the information space in the same way ontologies describe a domain or the world. The primary difference is that conceptual hierarchies generated are more term-based, in the case of Concept Index, and in WebClusters resemble categories or directories. From that point of view, we may assume that Concept Index deals with taxonomies, while WebClusters deals with ontologies. Moreover, in Concept Index, terms belong to documents, while in WebClusters, documents belong to a category. We may argue that this is a natural consequence of the difference between the top-down and the bottom-up approaches in classification.

When grounded concepts are emphasized, they inevitably become term centric, that is, terms and their synsets *form* a concept. Therefore the resulting concept classification resembles a thesaurus. What is shared when the conceptual hierarchy is collaboratively constructed is the vocabulary or a set of terms in a shared domain of interest. From this perspective, such a conceptual hierarchy represents the shared focus of interest and context in social information retrieval. When a priori concepts are emphasized, they can relate more strongly to the shared view of how the information domain can be organized and structured in terms of categories. In social information retrieval this would support, as demonstrated in the WebClusters example, the construction of a shared directory. In this sense, while WebClusters can also be seen as an example of system-mediated information access (Muresan & Harper, 2001) which would improve the retrieval performance as a result of mediation through organization of conceptual terms, the emphasis here is the capability of generating a shared understanding of the conceptual space as a group activity, rather than personalizing the formulation of information needs.

The observation above also implies that these two types of concept classifications generated respectively by Concept Index and WebClusters do not mix well. There are two possibilities as to how these can be combined: (a) to treat terms in the index as leaf nodes of a classification, and (b) to interleave terms into classifications by defining a set of terms for each category. The combination (a) assumes a single conceptual hierarchy with categories as upper-level nodes and index terms as lower-level or instantiations of a node. In (b), categories and index terms are almost orthogonal. In both cases, however, the confusion of categories and terms would lead to misinterpretations and reduction in usability. There are, however, approaches that use multiple nodes in a conceptual hierarchy to characterize documents as in Ogure, Nakata, and Furuta (2001). This uses categories as handles to documents.

In both approaches, just as there is a possibility to generate shared conceptual hierarchies, there are also scenarios in which an individual member may generate his or her own scheme or adapt shared schemes to better suit individual viewpoints. Therefore, a further support in the alignment and combination of classifications would be useful.

One of the limitations of this study is the restricted scope in the evaluation of systems developed. The development of Concept Index and WebClusters was based on identified requirements to support collaborative concept classifications and document retrieval based on them. The evaluation of the systems regarding effectiveness of supporting actual collaborative information retrieval is very complex, in particular in determining the match between groups' information needs and the retrieval result. Such an approach to take the evaluation further to the task context (Järvelin & Ingwersen, 2004) is important; however, it would not only require the evaluation of information retrieval performance but also the group activity. This is a challenging task and would be among the next steps in this research direction.

CONCLUSION

In this chapter we examined the use of collaborative classification to support social information retrieval by organizing search results. We subscribed to the view that the activity of collaborative classification can be characterized by top-down and bottom-up approaches, both in terms of the nature of concept classification and the process of classification development.

To this end, two approaches, namely collaborative indexing and search result classification based on shared classification schemes, were described and compared. The former is a more bottom-up approach to concept classification, while the latter supports a more top-down classification development. Both approaches address and utilize the potential of social information retrieval by capturing group vocabulary or classification schemes. Two systems, Concept Index and WebClusters, were introduced to demonstrate how these activities could be supported. Both systems are Web-based tools that allow multiple people or collaborative groups to access, modify, and review the concept classification development and retrieval results.

It is fair to state that there is no purely top-down or bottom-up approaches in concept classification and its process of development. These approaches are seamlessly mixed in the process. While the two systems focused on these differences in concept classification itself, neither of the systems clearly focused on the differences in the group activity of classification development. It was assumed that by allowing open access to classification development tools to generate shared classification schemes, which in turn become collaborative objects, cooperating user groups will generate their own coordination mechanisms that are not dependent on the system itself. Instances of collaborative classification activity need to be studied further to better understand what kind of system features would be necessary to better support it. Further work that addresses the effective sharing of classifications and leveraging the group efforts to make effective the social aspects of information retrieval in these applications would contribute to the better understanding and support of social information retrieval.

ACKNOWLEDGMENT

We would like to thank the anonymous reviewers for valuable comments towards the earlier version of this chapter.

REFERENCES

Baeza-Yates, R., & Ribeiro-Neto, B. (1999). *Modern information retrieval*. New York: ACM Press.

Chaffee, J., & Gauch, S. (2000). Personal ontologies for Web navigation. *Proceedings of the 9th International Conference on Information and Knowledge Management* (CIKM'00) (pp. 227-234).

Chen, H., & Dumais, S.T. (2000). Bringing order to the Web: Automatically categorizing search results. *Proceedings of CHI'00, Human Factors in Computing Systems* (pp. 145-152).

Chen, M., Hearst, M., Hong, J., & Lin, J. (1999). Cha-Cha: A system for organizing intranet search results. *Proceedings of the 2nd USENIX Symposium on Internet Technologies and SYSTEMS* (USITS), pp. 47-58.

Dhillon, I.S., Mallela, S., & Kumar, R. (2002). Enhanced word clustering for hierarchical text classification. *Proceedings of the 8th ACM SIG-KDD International Conference on Knowledge Discovery and Data Mining* (pp. 191-200).

Dumais, S.T., & Chen, H. (2000). Hierarchical classification of Web content. *Proceedings of SI-GIR-00, the 23rd ACM International Conference on Research and Development in Information Retrieval* (pp. 256-263).

Fidel, R. (1994). User-centered indexing. *Journal of the American Society for Information Science, 45*(8), 572-576.

Green, S.J. (1998). Automated link generation: Can we do better than term repetition? *Computer Networks and ISDN Systems, 30,* 75-84.

Gruber, T. (1993a). *Toward principles for the design of ontologies used for knowledge sharing.* Technical Report KSL 93-04, Stanford University Knowledge Systems Laboratory, USA.

Gruber, T.R. (1993b). *A translation approach to portable ontology specifications.* Tech Report Logic-92-1, Department of Computer Science, Stanford University, USA.

Järvelin, K., & Ingwersen, P. (2004). Information seeking research needs extension towards tasks and technology. *Information Research, 10*(1), paper 212. Retrieved from *http://InformationR. net/ir/10-1/paper212.html*

Joachims, T. (1997). Text categorization with support vector machines: Learning with many relevant features. *Proceedings of ECML-98, the 10th European Conference on Machine Learning* (pp. 137-142).

Kleinberg, J.M. (1999). Authoritative sources in a hyperlinked environment. *Journal of the ACM, 46*(5), 604-632.

Lancaster, F.W. (2003). *Indexing and abstracting in theory and practice.* London: Facet.

Lewis, D.D. (1998). Naive (Bayes) at forty: The independence assumption in information retrieval. *Proceedings of ECML-98, the 10th European Conference on Machine Learning* (pp. 4-15). Berlin: Springer-Verlag (LNCS 1398).

Loom Ontosaurus. (1998). *Loom Web browser.* Intelligent Systems Division, Information Sciences Institute, University of Southern California, USA.

Marchiori, M. (1997). The quest for correct information on the Web: Hyper search engines. *Proceedings of WWW6, the 6th International World Wide Web Conference* (pp. 265-276).

Miller, G.A., Beckwith, R., Fellbaum, C., Gross, D., & Miller, K. (1990). Introduction to WordNet: An online lexical database. *International Journal of Lexicography, 3*(4), 235-244.

Mladenic, D. (1998). *Machine learning on non-homogeneous, distributed text data.* PhD Thesis, Faculty of Computer and Information Science, University of Ljubljana, Slovenia.

Muresan, G., & Harper, D.J. (2001). Document clustering and language models for system-mediated information access. *Proceedings of the 5th European Conference on Research and Advanced Technology for Digital Libraries* (pp. 438-449).

Nakata, K. (2001). A grounded and participatory approach to collaborative information exploration and management. *Proceedings of the 34th Annual Hawaii International Conference on System Sciences* (HICSS-34), Maui, HI.

Ogure, T., Nakata, K., & Furuta, K. (2001). Ontology processing for technical information retrieval. *Proceedings of the 1st International Conference on Universal Access in Human-Computer Interaction* (pp. 1503-1507), New Orleans, LA.

Quillian, M.R. (1968). Semantic memory. In M. Minsky (Ed.), *Semantic information processing.* Boston: MIT Press.

Rennie, J.D.M., Shih, L., Teevan, J., & Karger, D.R. (2003). Tackling the poor assumptions of naive Bayes text classifiers. *Proceedings of the 20th International Conference on Machine Learning* (pp. 616-623).

Schmidt, K., & Simone, C. (2000). Mind the gap! Towards a unified view of CSCW. *Proceedings of the 4th International Conference on the Design of Cooperative Systems* (COOP2000), Sophia Antipolis, France.

Shih, L., Chang, Y., Rennie, J., & Karger, D. (2002). Not too hot, not too cold: The bundled-SVM is just right! *Proceedings of the ICML-2002 Workshop on Text Learning.*

Voss, A., Nakata, K., & Juhnke, M. (2000). Concept indexes: Sharing knowledge from documents. In M. Divitini, T. Brasethvik, & D. Schwartz (Eds.), *Internet-based organizational memory and knowledge management* (pp. 123-146). Hershey, PA: Idea Group.

Yang, Y., & Liu, X. (1999). A re-examination of text categorization methods. *Proceedings of SIGIR-99, the 22nd ACM International Conference on Research and Development in Information Retrieval* (pp. 42-49).

Zamir, O., & Etzioni, O. (1998). Web document clustering: A feasibility demonstration. *Proceedings of the 19th International ACM SIGIR Conference on Research and Development in Information Retrieval* (SIGIR'98) (pp. 46-54).

Zamir, O., & Etzioni, O. (1999). Grouper: A dynamic clustering interface to Web search results. *Computer Networks,* 1361-1374.

Chapter IV
A Case Study of
Use–Centered Descriptions:
Archival Descriptions of What
Can Be Done with a Collection

Richard Butterworth
The Bridgeman Art Library, UK

ABSTRACT

In this chapter the author argues the case that there is a mismatch between current metadata standards for the description of archival holdings and what many users actually want to know about a collection. Standard archival descriptions objectively describe what is in a collection, whereas users wish to know what they can do with a collection. It is argued that matching users' research questions to library resources that could help answer those questions is a crucial social role played by librarians, archivists, and other front-line staff. However placing descriptions of what is in a collection online for users to search directly risks disintermediating the users from library staff. 'Use-centered descriptions' are proposed as a way of systematically describing what can be done with a collection, and are, in effect, an encoding of library staff's knowledge about what can be done with a collection. It is therefore argued that use-centered descriptions repair some of disintermediation gaps caused by putting collection descriptions online. A theoretical motivation for use-centered descriptions is presented by showing how Heaney's (1999) analytic model of collections, which underlies the Research Support Libraries Program (RSLP) collection description standard, only addresses finding and identifying resources. We augment this model to address selecting resources from a range of possibilities and show how use-centered descriptions stem from this augmentation. A case study is presented demonstrating the experience of developing a set of use-centered descriptions for the University of London as part of a project to encourage wider access to their archival holdings. The project had necessarily limited aims, and therefore conclusions are drawn about the viability of use-centered descriptions in wider domains.

INTRODUCTION

The author looks at archival holdings, the way that they are described online, and the social role that archivists play in matching users' research questions with archival resources. The central theme of the chapter is fairly simple: that there is a role for metadata descriptions of archival holdings which describe *what can be done* with an archival collection, as well as the more traditional schemas for metadata which set out to describe *what is in* a collection. We discuss how making descriptions of what can be done with a collection available online has the effect of surrogating some of the social roles that archivists play for their users.

In recent years there have been several well-funded efforts to place metadata descriptions of archival, library and museum holdings online, such that users can have direct access to them. The effect of doing so has been to raise the profile and accessibility of many collections that have been hidden away in libraries and record offices, and have only really been accessible to professional researchers and experts.

Substantial amounts of governmental records have been put online (e.g., the UK National Archives, *http://www.nationalarchives.gov.uk/*; the U.S. National Archives, *http://aad.archives.gov/aad/*; and the Japan Center for Asian Historical Records, National Archives of Japan, *http://www.jacar.go.jp/*), and there have been projects to develop centralized databases of archival holdings (e.g., the UK Access to Archives project, *http://www.a2a.org.uk/*), as well as projects by educational establishments to electronically catalogue and publish their holdings (e.g., AIM25, *http://www.aim25.ac.uk/*, is a searchable database of archival holdings of London universities). They constitute a plethora of sites, which must host data about millions of collections.

In a few cases collection custodians have produced item-level descriptions of their collections (where individual items in the collections are described), but in most cases the expense of doing so is prohibitive and so collection-level descriptions (where general descriptions of the contents of a collection are made) have been produced and published. These collection-level descriptions are highly standardized, objective descriptions of a collection using rigorous, controlled vocabularies. Typically a collection-level description contains a general description of the contents of a collection, some biographical notes about the collector, and some custodial details, such as access conditions and housing details.

In this chapter we question the value of publishing such descriptions online without archivists and other experts offering intermediation between such descriptions and users. From an information seeking perspective, we need to question how well these descriptions allow users to identify archival collections that contain materials that will help address their research questions. The relationship between a research question and archival resources is often not clear and is sometimes downright abstruse.

As an example consider the following research question and a description of an archival holding, and see if you can judge how the archive would be useful in addressing the research question. The research question is: "How has the climate altered in Africa in the past two centuries?" The archive is a collection of materials related to Christian missionary groups, including detailed records of society meetings, correspondence, and so on, held by the School of Oriental and African Studies, University of London (Porter, 1999). At first look one would think that the archive would certainly be useful to theologians and social historians, but it is difficult to see how it would be useful to climatologists. However the link exists: in their correspondence the missionaries would often write home and describe the local weather conditions, in enough detail that a modern researcher has been able to build up a detailed climate map.

We argue that the role for traditional archival collection-level descriptions is not directly to inform users of the contents of a given archive, but is to inform an archivist or other information professional about the contents of a collection who can then liaise with users to make judgments about whether the collections would be useful to the users in addressing their research questions. Making a judgment about the possible value of a collection to a given research question is not straightforward (as the above example makes clear) and is likely to require intermediation by information professionals. Placing traditional collection-level descriptions online allows the users direct access to them and runs the risk of disintermediation.

Given this risk, the author proposes a novel form of collection level-description which aims to augment (not replace) existing descriptions with descriptions of the uses that collections can be put to. The philosophy is simple: we propose 'use-centered' metadata descriptions of archival holdings which describe *what can be done* with a collection, as opposed to traditional archival descriptions which describe *what is in* a collection. These use-centered descriptions are in effect an encoding of front-line library staff's knowledge about what uses a given collection has been or could be put to, and so make this knowledge available to users even though they are not in direct contact with library staff. This may therefore go some way to surrogating online the important social roles that front-line library staff play.

Chapter Objectives

The central hypothesis of this chapter is therefore that publishing traditional collection-level metadata descriptions online runs the risk of breaking down an important channel of communication between users and library staff. Furthermore, use-centered descriptions are one way of repairing some of that breakdown.

In this chapter we outline use-centered descriptions, their rationale, and the practical issues we encountered in developing a set of such descrip-

tions for the University of London. We critically examine use-centered descriptions both as a concept and in implementation. Use-centered descriptions are intended to be an augmentation (not a replacement) of existing metadata descriptions, and so we review one of the primary models of collections (Heaney, 1999) which underlie the Research Support Libraries Program (RSLP) collection description schema, extend that model to include research questions and users, and show how use-centered descriptions implement this extended model.

So far use-centered descriptions have been compiled and published for a limited domain of archival collections and a limited domain of user groups. We conclude the chapter by discussing the prospects of broadening these domains in the future.

BACKGROUND

Several writers (e.g., Nardi & O'Day, 2000; Adams & Blandford, 2002) have demonstrated that 'disintermediation': the effect caused by putting information online and allowing users access to it via search engines is detrimental to the users' experience. In traditional research libraries, front-line staff act as intermediaries between users and information, using reference interviews to help the users better understand their own information needs and to identify resources that help meet those needs. Some of the early digital library advocates proposed that disintermediation was a benefit to users, as removing library staff from the information seeking cycle allowed the users to be 'closer' to the information authors. This is broadly made on the simplistic assumption that the intermediation role that front-line library staff play adds no or little value to the users. This is clearly false: intermediation adds considerable value to the users' information seeking processes, both in terms of the users having a better understanding of their information needs and having a better understanding of which resources will help fulfill those needs.

Non-Professional Information Use

Given that there are strong arguments that disintermediation is detrimental in the general case, we now look at the characteristics of the users that we set out to build digital library resources for in the project reported in this chapter and present a case that disintermediation is particularly detrimental to them.

The Accessing our Archival and Manuscript Heritage (AAMH) project took place at Senate House Library, University of London between 2004 and 2005 (Butterworth, 2006a). Its remit was very broad: to use Internet technology to help broaden access to the University of London's archive holdings to users not in higher education (HE). (It should be noted that the University of London is an umbrella organization covering approximately 30 independent colleges and institutes, which act as largely independent universities and research centers, most of which have their own autonomous libraries and archive collections.)

At first we delimited our area of concern to local and family history researchers (who we collectively refer to as 'personal history' researchers), as we knew that there were significant resources held in the University of London's libraries that were valuable to them. Personal history researchers are hobbyist researchers who research their family tree or (for example) the history of the house or town they live in.

Personal history research can be characterized a 'strongly social, but weakly collaborative' activity. The results of the research are typically produced for an audience of the researcher's friends and family (hence 'strongly social'), but personal history researchers tend to work individually or in very small groups (hence 'weakly collaborative'): their work is typically not collaborative in the sense described by Hydlegård (2006).

There were significant difficulties in building a model of user characteristics for such user groups, but in fact, it was the difficulties that told us a lot about the group.

Firstly, based on Wellman's (1997) definition the user groups are "sparse, ill defined" user networks. They have no formal boundaries: they are not bounded by being a member of an organization or profession, or by a homogeneous need. Personal history research is undertaken as a hobby activity, and therefore boundaries (if they exist at all) are defined by social groupings such as friends and families. We saw that many personal history researchers had organized or joined local and family history groups, but membership of these groups was sporadic, informal, and variable, and therefore membership of a local or family history group could not be used as a defining boundary. Furthermore the individuals in a sparse network of users have few relationships between each other.

The problem for the AAMH project was that most of the suggested ways of surveying user needs given in the digital library (and software engineering) literature are based on the assumption that the users are a well-defined, dense group. For example, assume that you are designing a digital library system to support the e-learning of a group of students. You know who the students are and how many of them there are. You could therefore interview, for example, 10% of them to get a reasonably accurate picture of the requirements of the whole group. But the same techniques cannot be applied to sparse, ill-defined networks of users. Being ill defined, you cannot tell exactly (or even approximately) how many people are in the network, so you cannot know how many people 10% is. Even if you could, the sparsity of the network means that the homogeneity assumption in a dense group cannot hold: you cannot tell that the users that have been interviewed so far are in any way representative of the whole.

Furthermore the sporadic nature of personal history research also posed serious problems for our efforts in building a coherent model of user characteristics. Typically a personal history researcher will engage in some research once or twice a month at the most, and will visit a library less than three times a year. If we were observing the information behavior of information professionals, observations for a week or two would provide substantial data for analysis, but observing a personal history researcher over the same period would possibly not gather any data at all.

Precisely how the project attempted to overcome these problems with data collection is not the emphasis of this chapter (see Butterworth, 2006b). However we have presented the above sketch of the characteristics of personal history research to demonstrate that human intermediation in any information system to support such users is even more important than for professional information users.

The typically reported role for information intermediaries is to help users better understand their information needs, identify information resources to fulfill those needs, and help the users to make best use of those resources. In the case of academics, students, and information professionals, this intermediation is easily available to them, but the same cannot be said to be true for personal history researchers who may not have subscriptions to libraries and access to library staff.

However, intermediation between users and information sources is not the only intermediation role that is important for personal history researchers. Butterworth and Davis Perkins (2005) showed that the role played by librarians outside the academic or commercial domain not only included an intermediation role between users and information sources typically described in the literature (e.g., Nardi & O'Day, 2000, ch. 7), but also included a strong social intermediation role whereby the librarians were responsible for putting researchers in contact with one another or with research groups. In this sense the most important and valuable thing about the libraries was the social system that they developed and supported, this social aspect being perhaps more important that the documentary holdings of the library.

This social role can have a very dramatic improvement on the quality of information seeking and retrieval by users characterized as a sparse network. The effect of an intermediator in a sparse network is to theoretically render all users in the network at most two relationships away from each other. A real possibility in a sparse network is sub-networks or individuals that have no connection with the others in the network. A social intermediator has the effect of linking up all these individuals. Compare this to the small effect that intermediation has on a dense network: its density means that most individuals in the network are closely linked anyway, and therefore adding an intermediator does not have the dramatic effect in increasing the amount of interconnectedness that it does for a sparse network.

As an example of the effect of social intermediation, recall the example of the missionary archives being used to develop a climate map of Africa. As we argued, this use is not immediately obvious, but in a dense network of users, once the possible use has been identified, then knowledge about the possible use can travel around the other researchers in the group through word of mouth or research meetings and so on. However, in a sparse group if a researcher identifies a novel way of using an archival collection, then that knowledge may only flow to the few other researchers that she is in contact with and may not get to many isolated researchers in the network. However the archivist responsible for the collection will be aware of the use that their collections can be put to and will be able to present that knowledge to other users, even if those users are not directly in contact with one another. This social construction and sharing of skills has been addressed in other research (e.g., Wenger, 1998) and forms a central plank of much computer-supported collaborative work analysis (e.g., Vicente, 1999; Baeker, 1992).

However much of this work is based around the notion of sharing skills between workers who in effect form dense social networks. As far as we are aware, there is no research specifically addressing the way that skills are shared in sparse social networks.

Technical Solutions to Intermediation

Given a recognition that librarians and information intermediaries have very positive effects on information systems, there have been several systems developed and reported which allow for interactions between librarians and end users.

There already exist plenty of computer-supported collaborative work (CSCW) (e.g., Baeker, 1992) systems that would seem to fit the bill, and there exist plenty of technical ways of allowing people to communicate (e-mail, discussion groups, chat rooms, etc.) which are not expensive to develop.

For example, there are several 'ask a librarian' systems (e.g., the Library of Congress Ask a Librarian service: *http://www.loc.gov/rr/askalib/,* or the People's Network Enquire service: *http://www.peoplesnetwork.gov.uk/enquire/index.html*) which connect users to a distributed group of public librarians who will endeavor to answer the users' questions, either by e-mail or in a chat room.

A more involved approach to intermediation is exemplified by 'learning spaces' in the ADEPT project (Coleman, Smith, Buchel, & Mayer, 2001). A learning space is a combination of a virtual learning environment and digital library system for HE students. The learning spaces reported are aimed at helping students develop deep conceptual skills and understanding of geographic reasoning. Crucially, a learning space allows for collaboration between students and teachers: the teachers provide a set of online resources, and the students can personalize and modify the space to suit their own learning styles. In this case the teachers take the role of information intermediaries to the students and can control (to a certain extent) the information that the students have access to.

The role of intermediation is also surrogated by recommender systems (e.g., Soboroff, Nicholas, & Pazzani, 1999), which draw out a profile of a given user's needs based on his or her previous requests and then matches that profile up to other documents or resources. Automatic recommender systems have shown considerable value in shopping sites, but their value in information systems is less clear. However DaeEun and Sea Woo (2001) demonstrate the value of a recommender system which includes the capability for a collection of human experts to add authoritative recommendations to the system. Interestingly, their system also allows the users to submit feedback on the quality of the recommendations made by the experts and therefore develop their own personalized collection of experts whose domain expertise most closely match the users' interests.

This very brief overview gives examples of implemented systems which:

- Directly surrogate the role of intermediation by supplying chat rooms and so forth with librarians on one end and users on the other,
- By more indirect means allow tutors and experts to control a user's view of the information in the digital library, or
- Add metadata in the form of recommendations to the system.

In most cases however, although the technology is cheap, the cost of staff time to sustain it once implemented is not. All the technical solutions outlined above rely on tutors, librarians, and teams of experts to provide human involvement with the systems over a long period of time, and that costs money. On the AAMH project if we had decided to implement (for example) a discussion group to allow users contact and discussion with archivist staff, then we would have had to guarantee that at least one archivist would have been available to respond to queries on a fairly permanent basis. The project, in common with most other digital library projects, was funded over a fixed period of time to deliver a working artifact that would work, more or less, without needing intervention beyond the lifetime of the project. There was not money in the project budget to fund staff time to deal with extensive user queries indefinitely.

Existing Archival Description Standards

Two prominent archive description standards used are General International Standard Archival Description (ISAD(G)) (International Council on Archives, 1999) and the Research Support Libraries Program (RSLP) collection description schema (Powell, Heaney, & Dempsey, 2000).

We focus on these two description standards because ISAD(G) is close to being an international standard, and other hierarchical description standards in use share the same broad structure and aims of ISAD(G). RSLP standards are similar to ISAD(G): they are hierarchical, allowing descriptions of collections to be made from collection to item level within a single framework. The RSLP schema is more generic in that it is aimed at 'collections' (including library, museum, and archival collections) whereas ISAD(G) is specifically aimed at describing archival collections. We look at RSLP in detail here because the underlying models which informed the development of the standard have been published (Heaney, 1999) and it is these models we wish to analyze. There are non-hierarchical standards (e.g., Dublin Core, *http://dublincore.org/*) which describe individual items, but not whole collections. Our focus is on what can be done with whole collections, and therefore item-level standards do not concern us.

An example of a ISAD(G) collection-level description of an archive is shown in Figure 1. The description is divided into four main areas: Identity Area, Context Area, Content Area, and

Figure 1. The ISAD(G) collection-level description of the archival collection of Sir Patrick Manson, held at the London School of Hygiene and Tropical Medicine. The description has been slightly edited for size.

IDENTITY STATEMENT AREA

Reference Code(s): GB 0809 Manson

Title: MANSON, Sir Patrick (1844-1922)

Date(s): 1865-1964

Level of Description: Collection (fonds)

Extent and Medium of the Unit of Description: 2 boxes

CONTEXT AREA

Name of Creator(s): Manson | Sir | Patrick | 1844-1922 | Knight | physician, parasitologist, tropical medicine specialist

Administrative/Biographical History: Patrick Manson was born in 1844 and studied medicine at Aberdeen University, passing M.B. and C.M. in 1865. In 1866 he became medical officer of Formosa for the Chinese imperial maritime customs, moving to Amoy in 1871. Here, while working on elephantoid diseases, he discovered in the tissues of blood-sucking mosquitoes the developmental phase of filaria worms. From 1883 to 1889 he was based in Hong Kong, where he set up a school of medicine that developed into the university and medical school of Hong Kong. Returning to London, he became physician to the Seaman's Hospital in 1892. He played a central role in the development of tropical medicine as a distinct discipline, publishing on tropical diseases, being instrumental in the setting up of the London School of Tropical Medicine in 1899, and becoming physician and advisor to the Colonial Office in 1897. He propounded the theory that malaria was propagated by mosquitoes, a theory to be proved by Sir Ronald Ross (1857-1932). He was elected Fellow of the Royal Society in 1900 and awarded CMG, 1900, KCMG in 1903, and GCMG, 1912; he died in 1922.
Immediate Source of Acquisition or Transfer: Donated by the family, c1963.

---

continued on following page

Figure 1. continued

CONTENT AND STRUCTURE AREA
Scope and Content: Papers of Sir Patrick Manson, 1865-1964, including Manson's diaries, 1865-1879, containing notes on the discovery of mosquitoes as carriers of malaria and patient case notes; bound manuscript notes of his discovery of filaria, 1877; original drawings of eggs of bilharzias and embryos of guinea worms, 1893; drawings by Manson of filarial embryos, 1891; correspondence with Charles Wilberforce Daniels, Herbert Edward Durham, and James Michelli on tropical medical matters, 1900-1914; photographs, including Manson's birthplace and the Manse (Manson's parents' house), Manson in 1864 and 1875, Manson lecturing in the original laboratory, original building and laboratory of LSHTM, Manson's grave; certificates and medals awarded to Manson; correspondence between Mary Rose Hossack (Manson's daughter) and the London School of Hygiene and Tropical Medicine over his papers, including a memorandum on Manson's will, 1963-1964; certificates of election as Fellow of the Royal Society 1900, and awards of CMG, KCMG, and GCMG; medals including Fothergill Medal, 1902, Bisset Hawkins Medal, 1905, Mary Kingsley Medal, 1905, and Jenner Medal, 1912.

CONDITIONS OF ACCESS AND USE AREA
Conditions Governing Access: Researchers are required to give prior notice (at least seven days), and complete a Rare Books Collection Form. Access is not available to these materials during the weekend.
Conditions Governing Reproduction: Material to be copied by Library Staff only.
Language/Scripts of Material: English.
Finding Aids: General index for each box available in hard copy at the school.

Access Area. The totality of these areas should provide an objective and unambiguous description of the contents and form of the collection, the people or organizations that produced it, and the access arrangements for it. Though not structured in exactly the same way with the same headings, an RSLP collection description essentially encodes the same sort of objective information about the content, form, and history of a collection.

The RSLP schema is derived from an underlying analytic model (Heaney, 1999), which also has its roots in the analysis performed for the Functional Requirements for Bibliographic

Records (FRBR) report (Plassard, 1998). According to the FRBR report, there are four tasks in the process of resource discovery for which metadata is needed:

- Fnding resources that correspond to the users' information need,
- Identifying a resource as being the resource that is actually required,
- Selecting a resource from a group of possibilities that is the most appropriate, and
- Obtaining access to the resource.

Heaney's (1999) analytical model captures the metadata needed to address at least the first two of these tasks: finding and identifying. As such it builds an entity-relationship model showing the relationships between collections, collection descriptions, items, locations, owners, and creators. A simplified version of Heaney's (1999) model is shown in Figure 2. (The simplification is for readability. All the main entities and relationships we are interested in the context of

Figure 2. A simplified version of the Analytical Model of Collections and their Catalogs from Heaney (1999)

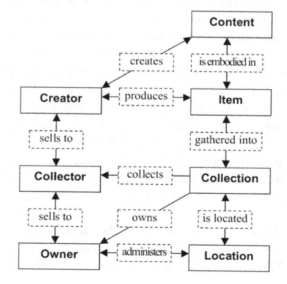

this work are included.) This analytical model is intended to be a general statement of the entities and relationships that characterize a collection, and based on this model a set of data fields has been derived which forms the RSLP collection description schema.

Note that all the entities in Heaney's (1999) model are 'internal' to the collection or the institution or individuals that hold the collection: they do not describe the uses and users of the collections. This is intentional, as the model intends to give a description of a collection that is useful for users in finding and identifying collections, and to do this a description is required which tells users unambiguously what is in the collection, who collected it, where it is kept, and by whom.

However in both Heaney's (1999) report and the FRBR report, precisely who the users are is never made explicit. The assumption that we worked on in the AAMH project is that there are at least two types of users: 'end users' who have an information need that they wish to be resolved, and users who act as information intermediaries between the end users and the collections descriptions. The users referred by Heaney (1999) are the latter. In other words the archival descriptions are not really meant to be used by end users (unless they are very highly skilled ones). They exist as descriptions to be used by information professionals to give them an unambiguous understanding of the content of a collection and allow the professional to find and identify resources, such that they can liaise with an end user to help make selection decisions about which resources best meet their needs. Archival metadata descriptions can be caricatured as being written by information professionals for use by other information professionals.

Summary

In this section we have discussed a class of information users who are interested in information seeking and retrieval as a hobby activity. This class of users is different in several crucial respects to the information professionals typically discussed in the information seeking and retrieval and digital library literature. A consequence of the characteristics of this group is that intermediation, while being important to information professionals, is imperative in an information system to support hobbyist researchers. We looked at other technical approaches to introducing intermediation to online information systems, but concluded that they require staff to supply this intermediation over an extended period of time and that there was not funding in the AAMH project to provide this. Finally we looked at archival description standards and the models and assumptions underlying them. Our conclusion is that archival metadata needs to be interpreted by information professionals as part of a collaborative process between the professional and an end user.

All in all this adds up to a system being required that in some way replicates the actions of an intermediary in helping make the selection decisions about which collections are useful for end users, but that existing systems do not really meet our needs. In the next section we describe how we developed a system that does.

USE-CENTERED DESCRIPTIONS

In this section we develop a schema for 'use-centered' descriptions.

The Motivation for Use-Centered Descriptions

As part of the AAMH project, we interviewed several archivists working in the colleges and institutions of the University of London about what (if any) materials they held that were of value to personal history researchers. In the ensuing discussions it became clear that how the archivists described their holdings verbally and how the collections were described in print or online were very different.

This distinction is made very clear by the Sir Patrick Manson archive held at the London School of Hygiene and Tropical Medicine. Its ISAD(G) description is shown in Figure 1. Sir Patrick was a founder of the school and was instrumental in showing that malaria was transmitted by mosquitoes. His working papers form the basis of his archival collection. However, if you are a family history researcher, there is no indication in the ISAD(G) description that the collection would be of any use to you.

However, the archivist showed that part of the collection was a set of medical records of people who emigrated to the British colonies between 1898 and 1919. As well as containing medical data, these records also detailed where the subjects were going in the colonies to work and their immediate family. This information could be vital to family historians.

The difference between the verbal and published descriptions of the archival collections is explained by the fact that when talking to users, the archivists naturally assume the role of intermediary and describe what can be done with their collections. Based on the interviews it became clear that the main intermediation service that the archivists could supply to personal history researchers was to identify and explain the collections they held that could be used in personal history research, particularly if (as was often the case) that use was not apparent from the published collection-level description. Furthermore we believed that we could define a systematic way of describing the uses that a collection could be put to, encode the archivists' knowledge about the uses that their collections could be put to, and publish these descriptions online as an augmentation to the existing ISAD(G) or RSLP descriptions.

We therefore believed that we had solved some of the problems set out in the Background section: we could develop an online system which gives the users the same sort of information they would get from an information intermediary, but the system could run without needing the intermediaries themselves to be available online to answer questions or make recommendations.

Figure 3. The augmented analytical model of collections and their catalogs

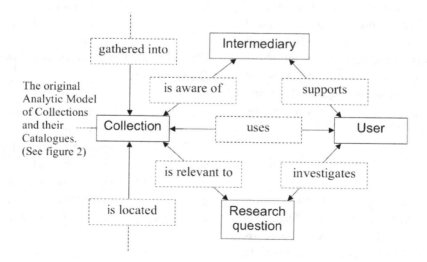

Augmenting the Analytical Model of Collections and Their Catalogs

Our augmentation to the Analytical Model of Collections and their Catalogs is shown in Figure 3. The augmentation adds users, research questions, and intermediaries to the model, and relates them to collections. The relationships between these entities is quite straightforward: users investigate research questions and use collections, collections are relevant to research questions, and intermediaries support users and are aware of collections.

The effect of disintermediation is to remove from the process the intermediaries' support of the users and awareness of the collections. Our aim is to develop collection descriptions that reintroduce this support and awareness, so we need to look at these two relationships in more detail.

As discussed in the Background section, the support offered by intermediaries to users can be broadly characterized in four ways:

1. Supporting users to better understand their research questions,
2. Identifying collections that are relevant to their research questions,
3. Informing the users how to use those collections, and
4. Putting users with similar research interests in touch with one another.

Improving users' understanding of their research questions (1) is about the relationship between users and their research questions, not about the relationship between users and collections, and therefore it is not something we can address as part of a description of a collection.

The identification of relevant collections (2) can be captured, broadly speaking, in a selection decision as to which collections we chose to describe as being relevant to personal history research, and those we do not. The first question we asked of archivists was: "What collections do

you have that are, or could be, useful to local and family historians?" The answers to that question were effectively encoded as decisions to describe certain collections.

The support offered in informing users how to use the collections (3) is typically about explaining what finding aids exist for a collection, and either showing the user how to use the finding aid or using it for them. There are a wide variety of finding aids available for different collections in different institutions, and how to use them may not be particularly intuitive. Therefore an important part of the description should be about the finding aids and how to make the best use of them.

Figure 4. The detailed usage description for the International Law Association Membership Records

The International Law Association (ILA) was established in 1873 to promote the harmonization of laws that crossed international boundaries. Its membership consisted mostly of those in legal professions, but also politicians and economists. This collection holds the complete membership details until 1938.

Name, occupation, and address are recorded. Unfortunately the address given for each member may be only specific to their town; this is particularly true for the earlier membership lists. In some cases other administrative details are recorded such as when fees were due, whether the individuals were honorary members, or in some cases their decease date.

Therefore this collection is only likely to be of use in breaking a research dead end: if you have very little information about a relative you know to have been in the legal profession then this collection may point you to an address or decease date which will allow you to move your research on. That said, the 1920s and 1930s membership lists include many members from mainland Europe with accurate addresses, and with the destruction of many of these sorts of records during the Second World War, this collection may contain one of the few remaining records of your relatives.

The support offered in putting researchers in contact with one another (4) cannot be directly surrogated by collection descriptions, but one of the benefits of researchers being in contact is that they can share knowledge about the uses that collections can be put to. The publishing of descriptions has the effect of surrogating this knowledge sharing.

The Structure of Use-Centered Descriptions

Based on the model and the analysis of it presented above, we can now lay out the fields that go together to make up a use-centered description, with their justifications.

Detailed Usage Description

The detailed usage description was the main part of a use-centered description, describing what can be done with the collection and giving examples of the sort of research questions that the collection could be used for. Typically it was divided into two halves: the first giving a very brief précis of what is in the collection, in the same way that an ISAD(G) collection-level description does, and the second half then explaining what can be done with the artifacts in the collection. The first half just gave enough information to put the second half in context: it was not simply be a repeat of the scope and content section of the ISAD(G) description.

See an example of a detailed usage description in Figure 4. Note how the actual usage description is the final paragraph, the first two paragraphs giving the context necessary to understand it. Also note that as well as stating what can be done with a collection, this description also suggests what *cannot* be done with it. Also note how the description flags the fact that the collection contains pre-Second World War addresses from mainland Europe, this being a category of information that can be particularly useful to family historians.

The Name of the Collection

Typically standard archival descriptions use very formal descriptions and reference numbers to name the collection. If possible it was attempted to give a more informal and less intimidating name for the collection. The formal name and its reference numbers were put in the More Information field.

The Holding Institution

The name of the holding institution was given, typically including a hyperlink to the institution's home Web page.

How to Tell if the Collection Is Useful

Most collections have finding aids; this section explained what those finding aids were, how to access them, and how to make best use of them. In many cases there were not finding aids available online, but archivists were happy to answer e-mails about their collections. This section also gave contact details for the archivists and suggested the information a user should give in an e-mail to help the archivist answer the query.

Because most of the archivists we spoke to had very similar stories about the sort of e-mails they received from researchers (particularly the difficult, badly expressed, or vague ones), we developed a general-purpose guide to e-mailing archivists, and when published this section also give a link to this guide. If specific information about how to compose a query was needed over and above that given in this guide, then it was included here.

Access Arrangements

This section described whether the collections were freely available to the public and how much will need to be paid if they were not. Most institutions had detailed access arrangements published on their Web pages; this section gave a précis of these instructions with emphasis on arrangements for non-HE researchers and then gave links to the institution's pages.

Examples of the Holdings

This section gave specific examples of the sorts of documents held in the collections. If the holding institution had examples online as part of their own Web sites, then this section provided links to them. Otherwise this section included one or two scans of representative documents, with annotations describing what information they held.

More Information

This section aimed to link a use-centered description to its more traditional metadata description. It gave the full formal title of the collection along with the ISAD(G) standard reference numbers. In most cases ISAD(G)-compliant descriptions had been published on other online databases (either AIM25 at *http://www.aim25.ac.uk/* or Access to Archives at *http://www.a2a.org.uk/*), and links to the records on these databases were given.

The More Information section was important as it allowed users to employ use-centered descriptions as an entry point into using archives in their research, but then offered a link from use-centered descriptions into the more traditional archival descriptions.

Abstracting Sections

These sections allowed for easier searching and browsing of the descriptions:

- **Overview:** A brief (50 words or so) summary of the whole description. The overview was shown in search results, and therefore had to give a good enough introduction to the collection that the user could make a decision as

to whether the collection would be useful to him or her without having to read the whole description.
- **Usage:** Whether the collection was good for local or family history (or both).
- **Themes:** A limited set of keywords to categorize the sort of research that the collection may be useful for. One collection could be described by several of these themes. The set of themes included:
  - *Correspondence:* A collection that is mostly letters, these are valuable to family history researchers because they can give very in-depth descriptions of the social context of the writers.
  - *Occupations:* A collection that gives details about people's work lives.
  - *Women's history:* A collection that is rich in information about women's lives, this was important to flag as many historic collections are male-centric and therefore it is difficult to research female ancestors.
  - *Pre-1750:* Most census and public records do not record information earlier than 1750, and therefore collections with information from before 1750 are particularly valuable.
  - *Contextualizing information:* A collection that is rich in information about people's social context; it is not just a list of names, addresses, and dates.
  - *Genealogical data:* In contrast to a collection with contextualizing information, this marks a collection that is primarily a list of names, addresses, and dates.
  - *Mobility:* A collection that is rich in information about migration.

Figure 5. A use-centered description of the Sir Patrick Manson archive

Title: Medical Examinations in connection with the Colonies and Protectorates

Holding Institution: London School of Hygiene & Tropical Medicine

Overview: Medical records of people who emigrated to the colonies between 1898 and 1919. If you have a relative you can't trace during this period, then this archive may show where they went. The records also hold a small amount of information about the interviewees' immediate relatives.

Detailed Usage Description: The London School of Hygiene and Tropical Medicine holds an archive of the medical exami nations of people who emigrated to the British colonies and protectorates between 1898 and 1919. As well as giving a detailed account of the subject's health, each record gives a small amount of family history: parents, children, and siblings) as well as some details about their current job, the job that they were intending to take up in the colonies, and its location.

If you have a relative who apparently 'disappeared' at the end of the 19th century, e.g., they're in the 1891 census, but not in the 1901 census, they may have emigrated, and this collection may give you a clue as to where and when they went. Also, although the family history on the record is brief, it could be useful to give supporting evidence to clarify ambiguities in your family history.

How to Tell If the Collection Is Useful: If you know that a family member emigrated between 1898 and 1919 then this collection is clearly useful. If you don't know for sure, but suspect that you may have an ancestor who emigrated, you may e-mail a query to LSHTM's archivist, giving as much detail as possible.

The minimum details you'll need to supply are:

• best guess at your ancestor's name (bearing in mind that they may be in the archive under their maiden name)
• best guess at when your ancestor emigrated
• what evidence you have that leads you to believe that your ancestor emigrated

Over half of the volumes are indexed by name, and approximately one-third of records have been added to an Access database which is available to use at the LSHTM archive.

Access Arrangements: The LSHTM archive is open to the public (see the LSHTM Web site for detailed access information). If you are planning to make use of the medical examinations archive, please make an appointment with the Archivist beforehand.

More Information: The records are part of the Sir Patrick Manson archive (Sir Patrick founded the school and was a pioneer in the study of malaria). A collection-level description is available on AIM25 and the LSHTM Web site.

Example(s) of the Holdings: Figure 5a shows a scan of a typical document from the medical records. The interviewee's name, age, marital status, and occupation are given on the top line, and the results of the examination are on the bottom half of the document. Of most interest to family historians would be the information on the top half: it details where the interviewee immigrating to, and what job they would be doing when they got there. Section 5 gives family details: the age of parent, number of siblings and children, etc.

Abstracting Information

Usage: Family history

Themes: Mobility, Genealogical data

Geographic Area Covered: International (shows where British subjects immigrated to within the British empire and colonies).

Size of Collection: The archive holds information about approximately 12,000 people.

Dates: 1898-1919

- **Geographic area covered:** Gave a detailed description of the areas referred to in the collection.
- **Size of collection:** Described how many people/artifacts are covered in the collection to give readers some idea of how likely they are to find information in the collection. This is in contrast to 'extent', the usual way of measuring the size of an archival collection, which is expressed in number of boxes or shelf space. A collection may have an enormous extent and be just about one person (and therefore be of little use to a family history researcher) or may be one piece of paper and yet contain a list of hundreds of people.
- **Dates:** Gave a range of dates for the materials in the collection.

Comparing Use-Centered Descriptions with Traditional Descriptions

A use-centered description drawn up for the AAMH project is shown in Figure 5. This is the use-centered description of the Sir Patrick Manson archive, the ISAD(G) description for which is shown in Figure 1. To show the real contribution of this work, it is important to compare the two.

Firstly note the difference in style of language: the ISAD(G) description is passive and terse, whereas the use-centered description is written discursively as if it is advising the reader in the second person ("if you have a relative…").

The use-centered description concentrates on only one part of the Manson collection, the part that is useful to personal history researchers, whereas the ISAD(G) description describes the whole collection. Also note the difference between the description of the size of the collection given in the ISAD(G) description ("2 boxes") and in the use-centered description ("The archive holds information about approximately 12,000 people"). This shows very clearly the difference between the two descriptions: the ISAD(G) description

describes the size of the collection in terms valuable to archivists (who need to know how many shelves are needed to hold the collection) whereas the use-centered description describes the size in a way that is relevant to users.

Relating Use-Centered Descriptions to the Augmented Analytical Model

Recall from the augmented model we proposed that there were two types of support that intermediaries supply that could be surrogated by use-centered descriptions: identifying collections that are relevant to their research questions and informing users how to use those collections. Use-centered descriptions need also to address the processes of finding and identifying resources that traditional descriptions do.

The Name of the Collection, the Holding Institution, the first part of the Detailed Usage Description, and More Information sections all address the process of finding and identifying resources, and are in effect a repeat of information held in ISAD(G) descriptions. However they are needed in a use-centered description to put the other sections in context or to allow the users to move on from a use-centered description to a more traditional description.

The second half of the Detailed Usage Description and Examples of the Holdings sections address the issues of identifying collections that are relevant to research questions.

The How to Tell If a Collection Is Useful and Access Arrangements sections address the issue of informing users of how to use the collections.

The Abstracting sections are a repeat of the information in the other sections structured to make it easy to search or browse the descriptions.

Methodology for Creating Use-Centered Descriptions

Several methods were employed to draw up use-centered descriptions which differed depending on the institutions involved. Firstly head librarians or archivists in all of the University of London's constituent colleges and institutions (there are approximately 30) were contacted by phone or e-mail to see if they had any holdings that were of interest to personal history researchers, and whether they were interested in contributing to the project.

Where responses were positive, workers on the project went to interview the archivists in question and to look at the collections that may be of interest. At the same time the project hired a personal history expert as a consultant. He trawled through the extensive archival holdings of Senate House Library, the central University of London library, picking out collections that were of interest and writing brief reports as to why they were of interest. The project workers used these brief reports as well as the findings of the interviews to draw up a project document describing what to look for in a collection that makes it interesting to personal historians (e.g., it has extensive information about women's historical roles, or has names and addresses of people from mainland Europe in the 1930s, etc.).

In several cases the archivists spoken to gave rich enough descriptions of their collections that the project workers could draw up draft use-centered descriptions without seeing the collections themselves. However, in most cases the archivists would point the project workers to collections that they believed to be interesting and the project workers would investigate the collections to draw up the descriptions. In one case an archivist expressed interest in developing the use-centered descriptions of their collections themselves, so the guide for developing use-centered descriptions was sent to them and they drafted a description and sent it to the project team.

Once a description had been drafted, it was published on a private area of the project Web site with a URL only known to the project workers. This URL was then sent to the archivist responsible for the collection so that they see the description as it would appear once published and could approve it. Once approved, the description was moved to the public area of the site.

This methodology and indeed the structure of the use-centered descriptions evolved through the process of interviewing the archivists. The hiring of the personal history consultant was key to the process as he validated many of the decisions that the project team had already made and made it very clear what were valuable personal history resources.

Implementing the 'Helpers' Site

The main outcome of the AAMH project was the 'Helpers' (Higher Education Libraries in your PERsonal history reSearch—*http://helpers.shl.lon.ac.uk/*) Web site, which featured a searchable and browsable database of approximately 60 use-centered descriptions of University of London archival holdings. The technology underlying the site is not in any way novel: the use-centered descriptions are generated as XML files in a dedicated editor, uploaded onto the server, where they are parsed into a database and queried by a collection of Web-based CGI scripts.

As well as the use-centered descriptions, the site also hosts a collection of tutorials relating to how to use university library resources, as well as a collection of links to other sites relevant to personal history research.

Care was taken with the site, as with the use-centered descriptions themselves, to ensure that non-technical language was used. Where technical language could not be avoided, an interactive glossary of terms was provided.

DISCUSSION

Our proposal of use-centered descriptions and their implementation in the 'Helpers' site has raised many questions, both theoretical and practical. These are discussed below.

Subjectivity

A key feature that distinguishes use-centered descriptions from more traditional descriptions is that use-centered descriptions are necessarily subjective, whereas one of the main benefits of traditional descriptions is their rigor and objectivity. While many of the archivists we spoke to as part of this project were positive about the work we undertook, others were uncomfortable with the emphasis we placed on subjectivity and the informal use of language we employed in the descriptions. Our intention was to use plain, discursive language in our use-centered descriptions so as not to intimidate readers, and the lack of a controlled vocabulary has caused some consternation by some in the archival community.

It is not possible to describe the uses that a collection can be put to either completely (someone can always think up another use that a collection could be put to) or objectively (different researchers are likely to find different values in the same collection). Also note that the use-centered descriptions describe not only the uses that a collection *has been* put to, but also the uses that it *might be* put to. It is possible to be fairly objective about the uses a collection has been put to, but if we were only to describe those uses, then we would run the risk of not encouraging users to explore the possibilities of a collection.

Overall, so long as use-centered descriptions are not used as a replacement for traditional descriptions, we see no reason why the two cannot complement one another. However the AAMH project was small scale, with only two workers compiling the use-centered descriptions, and therefore consistency in style could be easily maintained. In any larger future project with more workers compiling descriptions, ways of controlling vocabulary to achieve consistent descriptions would need to be investigated.

Implementation Cost

The implementation of use-centered descriptions can be simply a few extra fields in an archival description, and therefore, technology-wise, is not an expensive solution, unlike the other approaches to repairing disintermediation gaps (described in the Background section) which rely on chat technologies and so forth or sustained interactions with information intermediaries.

However, drawing up the descriptions is not cheap; each description on the Helpers site constitutes between one and two man days' work. Furthermore the project only looked at uses relating to personal history research. If we were to expand into other research domains, then it would be necessary to produce different descriptions of the same collection for different user groups.

Quantity and Quality

The AAMH project made the specific decision to pick out archival holdings that are judged to be particularly useful to personal historians and to describe them in detail. The Helpers site therefore does not in any way give a comprehensive picture of the holdings of University of London libraries: it is not intended to, in the way that the AIM25 site does aim to be comprehensive, but the problem is how to make that intention clear to the users. There are several assumptions that users need to understand in order to make best use of the descriptions: what use-centered descriptions are, the fact that the site is not intended to be used by beginners, and so forth. There are plenty of guides, both on the site itself, and printed guides which the project sent to local and family history groups, but of course there is no guarantee that the users will actually read any of them before using the site.

A long-term solution to the problem would be to combine use-centered descriptions with traditional descriptions and host all the information collectively in one site. In this case we would be able to provide comprehensive coverage, along with descriptions specifically aimed at personal history researchers. Such an endeavor is well beyond the scope of the AAMH project however.

User-Developed Use-Centered Descriptions

In an early version of the Helpers Web site, we experimented with allowing users to add comments to the descriptions, so that the descriptions would evolve in light of the user experience. However the comment facility has now been disabled because of the problems in moderating the comments made. Much of the comment traffic was simply inappropriate junk advertising, and the genuine comments that were added did not add significantly to the value of the descriptions: they were comments like 'nice site!' and so on.

One of the important design considerations was that the site should run without needing significant maintenance or intervention, and the effort of deleting the inappropriate comments became problematic. This became apparent after the completion of the development of the site and it was therefore too late to put in technical barriers to prevent inappropriate use of the comment system, and so it was decided to simply disable the comments.

However we still consider that there is a prospect for users contributing to use-centered descriptions even though it has proved pragmatically unviable on this project. As well as technical solutions allowing users to add comments online, we feel that there may be a lot of value in organizing focus groups of users to discuss and refine particular descriptions.

We also feel that there is scope for automatically collecting information from archivists about the uses that their collections are put to. Most queries from users about collection are now answered by e-mails, and many libraries have systems for documenting queries that are dealt with by phone. We see there would be value in a system that al-

lows archivists to annotate the e-mails they send and receive as being about certain collections or research questions and then store these annotations in some form of database. Periodically this database could be queried to see what collections are used for what research questions, and this would allow the development of use-centered descriptions on a very firm evidential base.

Further Work

The AAMH project had a very limited set of goals which are embodied in the resulting Helpers site. The project remit and the decisions that the project subsequently made to make the remit tractable within the project timeframe specifically limited our area of concern to personal history researchers based in the South East of England, and archival resources held in the various colleges and institutes that make up the University of London. We believe that the concept of use-centered descriptions is sound in theory, and the Helpers site is in effect a proof of concept showing they can be implemented practically.

However, the observations we made of the information seeking and retrieval behavior of personal history researchers were made informally and anecdotally. This was because we only had limited resources on the project, and making methodologically sound observations of user behavior would not have been cost effective. Informal interviews and meetings with personal history researchers, and discussions with archivists about their observations of the behavior of personal history researchers gave us good enough data to base our design efforts on.

We have started work (Butterworth, 2006c) on developing a general model of the information seeking behavior of personal history researchers and other researchers outside the academic and commercial domains, and the augmentation to Heaney's (1999) model presented in this work is a contribution to that model. However we are aware that we need to conduct much more formal studies of user behavior to make these models scientifically sound.

We believe that there is no reason why use-centered descriptions cannot be applied to collections other than archives. In particular most museums now have specific policies to broaden access to the collections they hold, and the development and publishing of use-centered descriptions would assist that agenda.

There are also plenty of other user groups that would benefit from use-centered descriptions: in our discussions with archivists, it became clear that fiction authors make extensive use of archival materials, and there is clearly scope for developing descriptions for them as a user group. Also throughout this work we have made the assumption that use-centered descriptions are particularly valuable for researchers outside the academic or commercial domain, but we have not addressed the issue of whether such descriptions would be valuable to academics. We believe that there is scope for developing such descriptions, particularly for undergraduates, as a tool in learning how to use archives and the standard archival metadata.

CONCLUSION

In this chapter we have argued that placing metadata descriptions online can cause the breakdown of the social intermediation role that library staff play, and that this can be particularly detrimental to researchers outside the academic or commercial domain. We have analyzed the nature of the intermediation roles and proposed that use-centered descriptions replace some (not all) of the information flows between researchers and information intermediaries that can be lost; further, compared to other approaches to online intermediation, use-centered description are very cost effective. We have described the implementation and publishing of a collection of use-centered descriptions, discussed its limitations, and proposed an agenda for further work.

REFERENCES

Adams, A., & Blandford, A. (2002). Acceptability of medical digital libraries. *Health Informatics Journal, 8*(2), 58-66.

Baecker, R.M. (Ed.). (1992). *Readings in groupware and CSCW.* San Francisco: Morgan Kaufmann.

Bates, M. (1989). The design of browsing and berrypicking techniques for the online search interface. *Online Review, 13*(5), 407-424.

Butterworth, R. (2006a). *The Accessing our Archival and Manuscript Heritage project and the development of the 'Helpers' Web site.* Middlesex University Interaction Design Centre Technical Report IDC-TR-2006-001. Retrieved June 8, 2006, from http://www.cs.mdx.ac.uk/research/idc/tech_reports.html

Butterworth, R. (2006b). Designing digital library resources for users in sparse, unbounded social networks. In Gonzalo et al. (Eds.), *Proceedings of the 10th European Conference on Research and Advanced Technology for Digital Libraries* (pp. 184-195). Berlin: Springer-Verlag (LNCS 4172).

Butterworth, R. (2006c). Information seeking and retrieval as a leisure activity." In Blandford & Gow (Eds.), *Proceedings of the 1st International Workshop on Digital Libraries in the Context of Users' Broader Activities.* Retrieved June 8, 2006, from http://www.uclic.ucl.ac.uk/events/dl-cuba2006/dl-cuba.pdf

Butterworth, R., & Davis Perkins, V. (2005). Assessing the roles that a small specialist library plays to guide the development of a hybrid digital library. In F. Crestani & I. Ruthven (Eds.), *Information Context: Nature, Impact, and Role: Proceedings of the 5th International Conference on Conceptions of Library and Information Sciences* (pp. 200-211). Berlin: Springer-Verlag (LNCS 3507).

Coleman, A.S., Smith, T.R., Buchel, O.A., & Mayer, R.E. (2001). Learning spaces in digital libraries. In Constantopoulos & Sølvberg (Eds.), *Proceedings of the Conference on Research and Advanced Technology for Digital Libraries* (ECDL 2001) (pp. 251-262). Berlin: Springer-Verlag.

DaeEun, K., & Sea Woo, K. (2001). Dynamics of expert groups to recommend Web documents. In Constantopoulos & Sølvberg (Eds.), *Proceedings of the Conference on Research and Advanced Technology for Digital Libraries* (ECDL 2001) (pp. 275-286). Berlin: Springer-Verlag.

Heaney, M. (1999). *An Analytical Model of Collections and their Catalogs.* Retrieved June 8, 2006, from http://www.ukoln.ac.uk/metadata/rslp/model/amcc-v31.pdf

Hydlegärd, J. (2006). Collaborative information behavior—exploring Kuhlthau's information search process model in a group-based educational setting. *Information Processing and Management, 42,* 276-298.

International Council on Archives. (1999*). ISAD(G): General international standard archival description* (2nd ed.). Retrieved June 8, 2006, from *http://www.icacds.org.uk/eng/ISAD(G).pdf*

Nardi, B.A., & O'Day, V. (2000). *Information ecologies.* Boston: MIT Press.

Plassard, M.-F. (Ed). (1998). *Functional requirements for bibliographic records: Final report of the IFLA study group on functional requirements for bibliographic records.* UBCIM. Retrieved June 8, 2006, from http://www.ifla.org/VII/s13/frbr/frbr.pdf

Porter, A.N. (1999). *The council for world mission and its archival legacy.* London: SOAS.

Powell, A., Heaney, M., & Dempsey, L. (2000). RSLP collection description. *D-Lib Magazine, 6*(9). Retrieved January 5, 2007, from http://www.dlib.org/dlib/september00/powell/09powell.html

Soboroff, I., Nicholas, C., & Pazzani, M. (Eds.). (1999). *Proceedings of the SIGIR-99 Workshop on Recommender Systems,* Berkley, CA.

Vicente, K.J. (1999). *Cognitive work analysis: Towards safe, productive and healthy computer-based work.* Mahwah, NJ: Lawrence Erlbaum.

Wellman, B. (1997). An electronic group is virtually a social network. In S. Kiesler (Ed.), *Culture of the Internet* (pp. 179-205). Mahwah, NJ: Lawrence Erlbaum.

Wenger, E. (1998). *Communities of practice: Learning, meaning and identity.* Cambridge: Cambridge University Press.

Chapter V
Metadata for
Social Recommendations:
Storing, Sharing, and Reusing
Evaluations of Learning Resources

Riina Vuorikari
Katholieke Universiteit Leuven, Belgium

Nikos Manouselis
Agricultural University of Athens, Greece

Erik Duval
Katholieke Universiteit Leuven, Belgium

ABSTRACT

Social information retrieval systems, such as recommender systems, can benefit greatly from sharable and reusable evaluations of online resources. For example, in distributed repositories with rich collections of learning resources, users can benefit from evaluations, ratings, reviews, annotations, and so forth that previous users have provided. Furthermore, sharing such evaluation feedback can help attain the critical mass of data required for social information retrieval systems to be effective and efficient. This kind of interoperability requires a common framework that can be used to describe the evaluation approach and its results in a preusable manner. In this chapter we discuss this concept, focusing on the rationale for a reusable and interoperable framework, that can be used to facilitate the representation, management, and reuse of results from the evaluation of learning resources. For this purpose, we review a variety of evaluation approaches for learning resources and study ways in which evaluation results may be characterized, so as to draw requirements for sharable and reusable evaluation metadata. Usage scenarios illustrate how evaluation metadata can be useful in the context of recommender systems for learning resources.

INTRODUCTION

Internet users are often times overwhelmed by the flow of online information, hence the need for adequate systems that help them manage such situations (Hanani, Shapira, & Shoval, 2001). Recommender systems attempt to guide the user in a personalized way to interesting and useful items in a large space of possible options, by producing individualized recommendations as output (Burke, 2002). They are usually classified into two basic types, according to how recommendations are produced (Adomavicius & Tuzhilin, 2005): content-based recommendation, where a user is recommended items similar to the ones that she preferred in the past; and collaborative recommendation (or collaborative filtering), where a user is recommended items that people with similar tastes and preferences liked in the past. To produce recommendations, these systems require a description of user preferences either in the form of preferred resources' characteristics (for content-based recommendation) or in the form of evaluations or ratings of resources (for collaborative recommendation).

There is an abundance of real-life applications of recommender systems on the Web that provide users with personalized recommendations regarding online content and services (Miller, Konstan, & Riedl, 2004). In some application domains the information used as input for recommendation (e.g., the characteristics of resources or the evaluations provided by users) may be reused between different user communities or different recommender systems. For example, for content-based systems this can be achieved when standardized descriptions of the resources are used as input. Following that idea, e-commerce recommender systems could potentially be built upon existing standardized ways to describe recommended items, such as the UN/CEFACT UNSPSC catalog of product and services classification (*http://www. unspsc.org/*). In e-learning recommender systems, interoperability of content-based recommender systems could be facilitated by existing technologies as well. For example, characteristics of digital learning resources could be described by using metadata standards such as the IEEE Learning Object Metadata standard (IEEE LOM, 2002).

However, reuse and shareability of user feedback (such as user opinions, ratings, evaluations, and reviews) has not been the focus of discussion for recommender systems. More specifically, in the case of collaborative recommendation, there are currently no proposals of frameworks or schemas for storing, sharing, and reusing evaluations of resources in a common data format. Such a framework could work to facilitate the reuse and interoperability in several domains, as well as the learning technologies' one. In this chapter we focus on the case of evaluation approaches for digital learning resources and aims to point out that there is an opportunity to reuse evaluation metadata for recommendation purposes. We attempt to carry out an initial discussion of relevant issues and to describe possible leads to solve this problem in the future.

The structure of this chapter is as follows: First we provide the background to previous work that introduces the use of metadata for digital learning resources and for storing information about the evaluation/quality of digital learning resources. Then, a review of a sample of current approaches used for evaluation of learning resources is carried out. In addition, a tentative classification of evaluation approaches is performed, and their produced evaluation results are studied. Furthermore, we propose a rationale and need for defining a reusable and interoperable metadata framework to store approaches and their results in evaluative metadata, and discusses the benefits of reusing evaluation results in the context of recommender systems. Characteristic scenarios of potential applications in supporting interoperable social recommendation of digital learning resources are given. Finally, the conclusions of this study and the directions of future work are provided.

RELATED WORK

Metadata

Metadata is defined as structured information that describes, explains, locates, or otherwise helps in retrieving, using, or managing a resource. It is often called 'data about data' or 'information about information' (NISO, 2004; Steinacker, Ghavam, & Steinmetz, 2001; Duval, Hodgins, Sutton, & Weibel, 2002). Metadata contains data items that can be added to or attached to a resource. Much of the more "traditional" work focuses on direct human interaction with metadata, listing the creator, subject, title, and other data needed to find and manage the resource. However, we believe that the focus should be more on less direct approaches that "hide everything but the benefits" (Duval & Hodgins, 2004).

Shreeves, Riley, and Milewicz (2006) discuss the qualities of sharable metadata in the context of digital libraries. They argue that metadata should not only be useful in its local context, but also usable to services outside of the local context in order to support search interoperability, that is, being sharable. It would be reasonable to apply this not only to the metadata that describe the object (descriptive metadata), but to the metadata that is generated by users in the format of annotations such as evaluations, reviews, and ratings. Some early standardization work already took place in this area in 1997; for example, the World Wide Web Consortium PICS-specification was created to enable first- and third-party rating of content. The attempt was to give users maximum control over the content they receive, without requiring new restrictions on content providers. This application of content rating further motivated the development of RDF and served to inspire the work on the "semantic Web" and its many tools (Oram, 2001).

Quality and Evaluation Metadata

Quality has become of primary importance in the agenda of metadata research. Manouselis and Costopoulou (2006) identified two separate strands of research related with this topic. The first one concerns finding ways to evaluate and ensure the quality of the metadata records, and has been termed the "quality *of* metadata." This strand has already received an important degree of research attention (e.g., Moen, Stewart, & McClure, 1998; Guy, Powell, & Day, 2004; Duval et al., 2002; Currier, Barton, O'Beirne, & Ryan, 2004; Hillman, Dusshay, & Phipps, 2004; Robertson, 2005; Ochoa & Duval, 2006). The second strand concerns finding ways to represent information about the quality of the resource in its metadata. It has been termed the "quality *in* metadata." It is related to the study of metadata elements or schemas that describe the quality characteristics of a resource and/or results from its evaluation.

In the latter strand several studies have implicitly or explicitly outlined the need for metadata that store quality and evaluation information regarding a resource. Examples come from the domains of statistical data and reports (Yamada, 2004), geospatial data (Devillers, Gervais, Bedard, & Jeansoulin, 2002; Wayne, 2004; IVOA, 2004; INSPIRE, 2005), geographical and marine data sets (Beard, 1996; NDN, 2004), medical resources and ontologies (Shon & Musen, 1999; MedCIRCLE, 2002; Supekar, Patel, & Lee, 2004; Supekar, 2005), e-commerce (Manouselis & Costopoulou, 2006), and other domains as well (Butler, 2001). Apart from outlining the general need, some of these studies also proposed metadata elements that allow storing quality-related information about the described resources (e.g., MedCIRCLE, 2002) or storing evaluation results (e.g., Manouselis & Costopoulou, 2006). Nevertheless, existing approaches are rather application oriented and cannot be applied in other domains without significant revisions. Thus, an overall framework of evaluation metadata, which could be used across application domains, does not exist, nor is there one that could over-arch across the domain of learning technologies.

Digital Learning Resources and Evaluation Metadata

In the field of learning technologies, the learning object (LO) concept has emerged. A learning object, also commonly called learning resource, is considered to be any type of digital resource that can be reused to support learning (Wiley, 2002; Downes, 2003). Metadata is used to describe a learning object. The most popular metadata schemas used for this purpose are the IEEE Learning Object Metadata (IEEE LOM, 2002) and the Dublin Core (ISO 15836, 2003) standards. Learning objects and/or their associated metadata are typically organized, classified, and stored in online databases, which are termed as learning object repositories (LORs). In this way, their offering to learners, teachers, and tutors is facilitated through a rich variety of different LORs that are currently operating online (Ternier, Olmedilla, & Duval, 2005; Tzikopoulos, Manouselis, & Vuorikari, in press).

Time and effort is invested by the users or operators of LORs in producing and collecting evaluations, reviews, ratings, and other annotations about learning resources. Thus, in addition to storing descriptive metadata about learning objects in repositories, evaluation metadata such as annotations, ratings, and other comments regarding the usage may be employed. The notion of evaluation metadata is similar to the notions of "third-party metadata" (Downes 2003), "third-party annotation" (Bartlett, 2001), "non-authoritative metadata" (Recker & Wiley, 2001), or "third-party labeling" (Eysenback, 2001). In this direction, many researchers have focused on how the quality of learning resources can be represented, stored, and shared with other users (Sutton, 1999; GESTALT, 1999; Recker & Wiley,

2001; ETB, 2002; Dron, Boyne, & Mitchell, 2002; EQO, 2004). To distinguish evaluation metadata from descriptive data, it is useful to think that evaluation metadata has a cumulative nature, meaning that annotations from different users accumulate over time, as opposed to having one single authoritative description, as is the case of metadata records in libraries and repositories.

A plethora of evaluation approaches for digital learning resources exist (e.g., Nesbit & Li, 2002; Muirhead & Haughey, 2003). As *an evaluation approach* (EA), we consider any procedure, method, set of criteria, tool, checklist, or any other evaluation/verification instrument and mechanism which has the purpose of evaluating the quality of a learning resource (EQO, 2004). In some cases approaches rely on national educational requirements, whereas in some other cases the repository has its own quality requirements that serve the needs of its user base. As many of the evaluation approaches only serve local (e.g., only in the context of a particular LOR) and national educational needs, little conformity or consensus has taken place in designing quality measures and evaluation approaches that would serve larger scope, for example when a federation of LORs is in question. There exist, however, many commonalities and overlaps in a number of cases, as the study in this chapter will illustrate.

It is reasonable to argue that evaluation approaches and their results—that is, evaluation metadata about digital learning resources and their usage—could be of interest to other users and repositories. Several uses may be envisaged for such kind of evaluation metadata, including sharing them among different repositories to allow communities of users to benefit from the collected knowledge. Leveraging the use of this type of data is a current challenge for the field. In this chapter we aim to point out that there is an opportunity to share evaluation metadata if it were interoperable and reusable. Moreover, it could be applied for different purposes, such as social information retrieval. As there is no commonly accepted framework that allows the description of the evaluation method applied on a learning resource, as well as the reusable and interoperable storage of the evaluation results, we aim to investigate the problem base and thus hopes to set the stage for a future solution.

EVALUATION APPROACHES FOR LEARNING RESOURCES

In this section we review a characteristic sample of evaluation approaches (EAs) and introduce the general problems related with the evaluation of resources. These EAs are applied for evaluating digital learning resources either within LORs or used as general guidelines when producing digital material for learning purposes. The goal of this section is to derive an overall set of requirements for a framework that could be applied for the description of EAs and for the representation of their results.

General Problems

A diversity of evaluation approaches for learning resources exists, such as models, methods, criteria, and instruments that are applied to assure the quality of the learning resources and their collections. Each approach represents the goals and ambitions of a particular context, for example, a given repository, a country, or a community of users. A recent survey by Tzikopoulos et al. (2007) indicates that 64% of LORs that were surveyed follow some quality control policy, whereas 43% have some resource evaluation/rating or review policy. It may become an increasingly impossible task for end users to follow which EA has been applied for a particular learning resource, to know the goals and focus of those approaches, and most importantly, to know what the results and their semantics actually mean. Moreover, the comparison of the results from different EAs is nearly impossible because of their different semantics.

A common framework for the description and categorization of existing EAs could be found useful for several practical reasons, especially in the context of social recommendation systems.

Describing and Classifying EAs

In order to identify the main dimensions upon which an EA for learning resources can be described and meaningfully distinguished among others, we reviewed a sample of EAs consisting of 13 approaches. They were collected through different means: based on a learning repository survey (Tzikopoulos et al., 2007), related literature (Muirhead & Haughey, 2003; Nesbit & Li, 2004), as well as by following the recent work in the field (Insight, 2005). Some of the EAs are currently applied in LORs in the world, whereas some are used as general quality guidelines for digital learning resources. These EAs are listed in Table 1 along with a short description. Each EA has been carefully studied and analyzed using the generic EQO model for quality approaches (EQO, 2004). The interested reader may find the detailed analysis of these EAs stored in the European Quality Observatory repository (*http://www.eqo.info*), searchable by the term "teaching material."

It has therefore been possible to produce a tentative set of classification dimensions that can be used for describing EAs for learning resources. The following characteristics are considered: process, stage of the learning resources lifecycle, focus, methods, intended audiences, criteria or metrics, evaluation results, and environment.

Process vs. Product

First of all, EAs may be distinguished according to a number of methodological characteristics. To start with, an important characteristic is the *process* on which the EA focuses. It can have different methodological properties. For example, it may focus on the process or a result of a process. From the reviewed EAs, some focus on the process

Table 1. EAs that have been identified as applicable for evaluating learning resources in LORs

No.	Title and URL	Acronym	Country of Origin	Description
1.	**Becta Quality Principles for Digital Learning Resources** (EQO ID[1]: 680) [1]ID in the EQO repository (*http://www.eqo.info*)	**Becta**	**UK**	The principles are part of Becta's work in support of the DfES e-strategy 'Harnessing Technology' which aims to maximize the benefit of the considerable investment in ICT in education use. The consultation document (which was used for this documentation) presents the 19 principles divided into two groups: (i) core pedagogic principles, and (ii) principles on aspects of the design and interoperability of digital learning resources.
2.	**BIOME—Factors Affecting the Quality of an Information Source** (EQO ID: 602)	**BIOME**	**UK**	The purpose is to explain the factors affecting the quality of an information source within the context of the BIOME service and repository of learning material.
3.	**Digital Library for Earth System Education: Community Review System** (EQO ID: 619)	**DLESE**	**USA**	The Digital Library for Earth System Education (DLESE) is an information system dedicated to the collection, enhancement, and distribution of materials that facilitate learning about the earth at all educational levels. All resources are reviewed. The Community Review System is a hybrid review system that combines two types of information: (a) feedback from educators and learners who have used the resource, delivered via a Web-based recommendation engine; and (b) formal reviews by specialists recruited by an Editorial Review Board.
4.	**Evaluation Criteria for Peer Reviews of MERLOT Learning Resources** (EQO ID: 579)	**MERLOT**	**USA**	MERLOT conducts structured peer reviews of online learning materials. The emphasis on the user's perspective is the reason peer reviews are performed by peer users of instructional technology and not necessarily peer authors of instructional technology. Peer reviews are performed by evaluation standards that divide the review into three dimensions: Quality of Content, Potential Effectiveness as a Teaching Tool, and Ease of Use. Each of these dimensions is evaluated separately. In addition to the written findings (review) by the reviewers, there is a rating for each of the three dimensions (1-5 stars, 5 being the highest). A review must average three stars (or textual equivalent) to be posted to the MERLOT site. Additionally, also regular MERLOT community members can post "member comments" on resources.
5.	**Interactive Dialog with Educators from Across the (United) State** (EQO ID: 581)	**IDEAS**	**USA**	Selected PK-16 educators from Wisconsin work in teams to identify, evaluate, catalog, and align to the state education standards resources that are already on the Internet such as lesson plans and reference materials. These resources are then made available from the IDEAS search engine. Teachers can leave reviews on a scale of 5 to 1 for five criteria. Other users can read about the resources and see exactly which state standards they address, but they cannot use the ratings for search criteria.

continued on following page

Table 1. continued

6.	**La marque "Reconnu d'Intérêt Pédagogique"** (EQO ID: 639)	**RIP**	**FR**	The mark "Reconnu d'Intérêt Pédagogique par le Ministère de l'Éducation Nationale" (RIP, Recognized Pedagogical Interests by the National Education) is there to guide teachers to find pedagogically sound multimedia material for their educational needs. The RIP logo facilitates recognition of the multimedia material that fulfills the needs and expectations of the national school system. The RIP multimedia material has been approved by a group of experienced teachers in the given domain and by a committee group.
7.	**LearnAlberta.ca: Content Development Technical Specifications for Developers** (EQO ID: 623)	**CDTS**	**CA**	This document defines the specifications that must be used when creating online learning resources for LearnAlberta. ca. There is no instrument to verify whether these guidelines were respected. LearnAlberta.ca supports lifelong learning by providing quality online resources to the kindergarten to grade 12 (K-12) community in Alberta. Students, teachers, and parents can use the site to find multimedia learning resources that are correlated to the Alberta programs of study.
8.	**Learning Object Evaluation Instrument for K-12** (EQO ID: 624)	**LOEI**	**CA**	Learning Object Evaluation Instrument (LOEI) was developed to examine school-level content. The criteria for evaluating learning objects were drawn from four sources: (a) the CLOE draft guidelines, (b) the Le@rning Federation Soundness Specification, (c) the rating scale previously used by Vargo et al. (2003) in their Learning Object Review Instrument (LORI), and (d) criteria developed with respect to the special concerns of the K-12 environment.
9.	**Learning Resources Exchange, User Evaluation of LOs** (EQO ID: 719)	**LRE**	**EU**	This evaluation is based on user experiences of learning objects (LOs) that users have used through the Learning Resources Exchange portal. Users can give a rating on the usability of the LO, as well as access the age of learners that the LO is feasible. An average value is computed that is available for users as they search for learning resources on the portal.
10.	**Peer Review Process for Collaborative Learning Object Exchange** (EQO ID: 621)	**CLOE**	**CA**	The CLOE peer review process requires the involvement of two kinds of reviewers: instructional design experts and subject matter experts. Instructional designers will be identified by CLOE members. Subject matter experts will be identified by the institutional contacts who will work with those involved in the design of the learning object (LO) to identify those best able to review the subject matter embedded in the LO. Before LOs are submitted to peer review, there is "initial functionality testing " by the CLOE gatekeeper which will include checking to ensure that links work, plug-ins are available, platform and browser compatibility are identified, and so forth.

continued on following page

Table 1. continued

11.	**Quality Criteria for E-Learning Material (Verkko-Oppimateriaalin Laatukriteerit)** (EQO ID: 659)	**EDU.FI**	**FI**	As part of the implementation of the Information Society Program for Education, Training, and Research 2004-2006, the Finnish National Board of Education appointed a working group that threw together quality criteria for e-learning materials used in elementary and upper-secondary education. The criteria has four sections: pedagogical quality, usability, accessibility, and production quality. Each section comprises main criteria with sub-criteria and examples. Criteria are meant to be used flexibly and selectively, rather to be a guideline than a strict criteria to follow step by step.
12.	**TEEM: Teachers Evaluating Educational Multimedia** (EQO ID: 699)	**TEEM**	**UK**	TEEM provides teachers with reliable and objective evaluations of educational multimedia on two main categories, the content and classroom usage. TEEM trains classroom teachers to become evaluators of curriculum-rich CD-ROMs, tools, and Web sites. Materials are used in the classroom, before evaluations are written using clear frameworks. Once edited, the results are published on the TEEM Web site, where there are currently (April 2006) 809 titles of UK Key Stage 1-4 materials available.
13.	**The Learning Object Review Instrument** (EQO ID: 599)	**LORI**	**CA**	The Learning Object Review Instrument (LORI) is used to evaluate the quality of e-learning resources. LORI is an online form consisting of rubrics, rating scales, and comment fields. Reviews help users to select learning resources for quality and fit. Review instruments like LORI make it easier to compare resources by providing a structured evaluation format. LORI may be used for individual or panel reviews. When a panel is available to evaluate a set of learning objects, we advocate the use of the convergent participation model described by Nesbit, Belfer, and Vargo (2002).

of creating resources, whereas others only focus on ready products and their evaluation. Becta [1] (the numbering in brackets "[]" refers to Table 1) and EDU.FI [11] are two characteristic examples of EAs that focus on the process. For example, Becta is an approach that focuses on 19 principles divided into two groups—(i) core pedagogic principles, and (ii) principles on aspects of the design and interoperability of digital learning resources—thus acting as a guideline for designers, producers, and teachers. Examples of EAs that focus on products are BIOME [2], CLOE [10], and LORI [13]. For example, LORI is an evaluation instrument, an online form of rubrics, rating scales, and comment fields that evaluates the final, ready-for-use LO to help users to select learning resources for quality and fit. LORI, which may be used by individual or panel reviews, claims that an instrument like this one makes it easier to compare resources by providing a structured evaluation format.

Stage of Lifecycle

Another characteristic is the *stage of the learning resource lifecycle* to which the EA is applied (Van Assche & Vuorikari, 2006). This is relevant when an EA is applied at a particular stage of the lifecycle of a learning resource, for example, *a priori* is a publication in an LOR or after it is added to a collection of learning resources (*a posteriori*). Often times *a priori* ones rely on subject experts and educational professionals, whereas those that seek end user contributions for evaluations are done *a posteriori*. For example, the CDTS [7] focuses only on development guidelines such as "instructional design guidelines" during the development stage, whereas the TEEM [12] evaluation is done by trained evaluators on a piece of learning material before it is added into the collection. This evaluation includes an overview, content evaluation, classroom evaluation, and product details sheet.

On the other hand, there are EAs that are applied only after the resource is in the collection,

(i.e., *a posteriori*); these characteristically include end user evaluations such as LRE [9] done by the users after the usage of a given resource. Some EAs like Becta [1] and EDU.FI [11] focus on both the development and educational guidelines for the production (*a priori*) as well as for the usage (*a posteriori*). EDU.FI, for example, guides that assessing the quality of learning material separately from the production process and circumstances of use only gives a narrow picture of quality. Thus, it comprises four modular sections—pedagogical quality, usability, accessibility, and production quality—which can be used separately in different situations by designers, by producers, as well as by teachers.

Focus

Furthermore, EAs can have different *focuses*. They can focus on evaluating educational processes related to the conception/design, development/production, implementation, or evaluation/optimization part of the lifecycle, as proposed in an ISO vocabulary (Pawlowski, 2006). From the sample of evaluation approaches, we can identify ones that focus clearly on development/production, for example CDTS [7]. On the other hand, some focus on the implementation process; TEEM [12] has a clear interest on classroom evaluation, whereas IDEAS [5] focuses on the suitability to attain targeted academic standards and on whether the resource contains sound educational practices that were effective with students.

Methods

Also, different *methods* of evaluation approaches can be differentiated: MERLOT [4], IDEAS [5], TEEM [12], and LORI [13] are evaluation instruments; they can be a questionnaire, a list of criteria, or concrete quality benchmarks, whereas RIP [6] is a certification instrument as it is awarded by an authoritative body, the French Ministry of Education, after a committee inspection.

Intended Audience

Different *intended audiences* can be one of the characteristics of EAs. They could be evaluators, subject experts, developers, content providers, teachers, and educators. For example, many of the approaches target more than one audience. The Becta [1] and EDU.FI [11] criteria target all of these groups, whereas the LORI [13] and MERLOT [4] models are mainly only used by evaluators and subject experts. MERLOT, for example, has a selected faculty who performs the peer review of learning resources following the model of the peer review of scholarship. It is led by editors and a discipline-specific editorial board. Additionally, a number of EAs target end users with questions after the usage of the resource; for example, LRE [9] and IDEAS [5] offer evaluation sheets for users. Moreover, the number of evaluation instances is distinguishing for EAs. Some may use a single evaluation instance whereas others may require/allow multiple evaluations by different actors. LRE [9], for instance, allows users to rate resources using one single form, whereas LORI [13], as implemented in the E-Learning Research and Assessment network (*http://www.elera.net*), requires a convergent participation model (Nesbit, Belfer, & Vargo, 2002), that is, many evaluation instances. Similarly, the CLOE [10] peer review process involves an instructional designer and two subject matter experts reviewing the resource in different instances.

Criteria or Metrics

In addition, EAs may be described in terms of the *criteria or metrics* they engage. For instance, EAs may result in qualitative evaluations such as reviews by TEEM [12]; in quantitative evaluation such as ratings MERLOT [4], IDEAS [5], and LRE [9]; in certificates, such as the quality logo by RIP [6]; and in admission to a collection of resources such as BIOME [2]. Moreover, EAs may be evaluated in a qualitative or quantitative

manner. For example, EAs such as TEEM [12] provide textual reviews of learning resources upon a number of evaluation dimensions, and DLESE [3] uses a rubric in its community review system. On the other hand, EAs such as MERLOT [4] require both evaluative and measurable evaluations—that is, ratings upon the evaluation dimensions. Indicative examples of these are given in Table 2 and explained in the next section.

Evaluation Results

Moreover, characteristic to the *evaluation results* is that EAs may engage a single dimension for the evaluation or multiple dimensions (e.g., several quality criteria or metrics). Examples of EAs that focus on a single dimension are LRE [9] on usefulness of the resource and IDEAS [5], with a single "smiley" representing three different facial expressions such as :-) , :-| , and :-(. Examples of EAs that focus on multiple criteria are MER-LOT [4] and CLOE [10], both with three criteria (Quality of Content, Potential Effectiveness as a Teaching Tool, Ease of Use) and LORI with its list of nine criteria (Content of Quality, Learning Goal Alignment, Feedback and Adaptation, Motivation, Presentation Design, Interaction Usability, Accessibility, Reusability, and Standards Compliance).

Environment and Context

Finally, EAs may be described according to the characteristics of the *environment* in which they are expected to be applied (e.g., by the creator of the EA). A distinguished characteristic of this type is the geographical area (e.g., country or region) for which an EA applies. For instance, DELSE [3] has been developed for the learning resources in the United States, whereas IDEAS [5] provides evaluative information on how the given resource complies to the U.S. curriculum at certain educational levels. RIP [6] has a more

European geographical focus, namely that of France.

Another *contextual* characteristic is related to particular topics or domains for which the EA applies. For example, EAs such as that of MediCIRCLE particularly focus on learning resources of the medical domain. Moreover, other contextual characteristics are related to the educational environment in which the learning resources are expected to be used (e.g., school, higher education, training). For example, IDEAS [5] focuses on learning resources to be used in the K-16 context, whereas LOEI [8] is only for K-12.

Storing the Results of EAs

As indicated earlier, social information retrieval systems such as collaborative recommender systems could be facilitated by the existence of a way to represent and store the results of different EAs in a reusable and interoperable format. However, the set of EAs analyzed shows that not all of them result in measurable results. First of all, there are EAs that act more like guidelines for production and use of learning resources, thus they have no evaluation instrument attached to them, for example, Becta [1] and EDU.FI [11]. Moreover, there are several EAs that are used to evaluate learning resources in order to allow their publication in an LOR, but do not produce any evaluation results (apart from a mark "Approved for Publication"). Examples from our study sample include BIOME [2].

On the other hand, several EAs produce evaluation results which may vary in various aspects:

- Some EAs produce qualitative evaluation results, such as textual reviews. Examples include TEEM [12] and DELSE [3], which have structured textual reviews with no measurable results.
- Other EAs produce quantitative results such as ratings. EAs such as LRE [9] produce single-attribute evaluations. EAs such as MERLOT [4] and LORI [13] produce multi-attribute evaluations. Some, like IDEAS [5], have both single- and multi-attribute evaluations.
- The scales used for the evaluation ratings can also be different. EAs such as LRE [9], MERLOT [4], IDEAS [5], and LORI [13] collect measurable evaluations upon a '1' to '5' scale, whereas IDEAS [5] has a scale of '0-2' (in the form of a smiley).
- There are also EAs that combine more than one way to represent evaluation results. MERLOT [4] is a characteristic example of an EA that collects both a measurable evaluation (rating) and a textual review upon three criteria, whereas LRE [9] combines the quantitative rating with a comment box.
- Finally, some EAs do not result in any type of qualitative or quantitative result, but only to addition of the resource into a collection BIOME [2] or formal national approval such as RIP [6]. This could be interpreted as a binary scale vote of '0-1'.

In Table 2 we list the EAs that produce evaluation results that maybe stored and potentially shared or reused. More specifically, we describe whether each EA produces qualitative or quantitative results, the number of evaluation dimensions it engages, the format in which evaluations are provided (e.g., textual or measurable), and (if applicable) the evaluation scale used.

RATIONALE FOR AN EVALUATION METADATA FRAMEWORK

From the classification of the sample of existing EAs, it has been demonstrated that a large diversity of approaches is applied in evaluating learning resources with different scopes and methods. Moreover, a wide variety of characteristics should be taken into account, in order for these evaluation

Table 2. Dimensions that may be used for the classification of EAs according to the results they produce

Name of the EA	Textual: Qualitative Evaluation			Measurable: Quantitative Evaluation		
	one dimension	*multiple dimensions*	*outcome*	*one dimension*	*multiple dimensions*	*scale*
Digital Library for Earth System Education: Community Review System (DLESE)		x				
Evaluation Criteria for Peer Reviews of MERLOT Learning Resources (MERLOT)		x			x	1-5 stars
Interactive Dialog with Educators from Across the (United) State (IDEAS) has two evaluations: one with a smiley (0-2) and the other one with an evaluation form from 1-5				x	x	0-2 smiley, 1-poor to 5- excellent
La Marque "Reconnu d'Intérêt Pédagogique" (RIP)		x	Approval "stamp"			
Learning Object Evaluation Instrument for K-12 (LOEI)		x				
Learning Resources Exchange, User Evaluation of LOs (LRE)	x			x		1-5 stars
Peer Review Process for Collaborative Learning Object Exchange (CLOE)					x	Not at all, somewhat, definitely
Teachers Evaluating Educational Multimedia (TEEM)		x				
The Learning Object Review Instrument (LORI)					x	1-5 stars

results to be reused in another context. It can be argued that to reuse and share the results of an evaluation in another context, it is not sufficient only to have the evaluation results as a stand-alone unit of information, but it is also beneficial to access a description of the evaluation approach itself to fully understand the semantics of the results. For example, an EA may use multiple criteria that vary from pedagogical to technical aspects and also bear cultural connotations. Thus, using an existing specification such as PICS, for example, is not sufficient, but would benefit from revisiting the concept to allow better description of EA, its results, and information about the context in which it is used.

Elaborating on the tentative classification dimensions identified in the previous section, it would be possible to conceptually design a metadata framework for describing EAs for learning resources. Such a framework of evaluation metadata could be used to support the following tasks:

- To describe which EA has been used for the evaluation of a learning resource, also identifying its main methodological and contextual characteristics. Reflecting upon the methodological properties can facilitate the mapping, matching, or merging evaluation results from different EAs with similar methodological properties. The contextual properties can allow relating one set of results with the results of other EAs that are aimed to be applied in similar contexts.
- To store the variety of evaluation results that the identified EAs utilize. For this purpose, an appropriate data structure could be included that would represent and store the collected results for numerous resources and from a variety of evaluators or users.

Evaluation Metadata for Describing EAs

An evaluation metadata framework would have a number of potential applications. First of all, evaluation metadata (including both the description and the results) that is stored in an interoperable way could be used for the description, collection, and categorization of EAs that are applicable to learning resources. For instance, it could be the basis for creating an online collection of EAs (that is, a metadata repository of EAs), similar to the way the EQO model is used for building a collection of e-learning quality approaches (*http://www.eqo.info*). In this way, online information services that will facilitate interested users when searching for appropriate evaluation approaches can be deployed. In addition, such a metadata framework could support applications related to the use of the results themselves. This type of evaluation metadata may be stored either together with the metadata description of the learning resource or in a separate repository of evaluations. In this way, results from different evaluation instances can be stored, shared, and reused in the future.

The rationale for introducing a new interoperable framework for evaluation metadata follows the work carried out in EQO, where a similar schema was created to describe different quality approaches for e-learning. It also builds upon the experience of developing a schema of evaluation metadata that has been previously proposed for e-commerce resources (Manouselis & Costopoulou, 2006). The strength of this approach is that it allows for describing a variety of individual EAs that are based on institutional and cultural needs, but still maintain a common reference framework to describe them and their results. This facilitates the comparison of EAs and allows identifying their similarities and differences in scope and methods. Also, this approach enhances the transparency, transferability, and possible usefulness of evaluation results, as users would not only be made aware of end results such as an individual rating or evaluation, but also have the possibility to find out what evaluation approach has been used to arrive at these results. In the context of LORs, for instance, the evaluative metadata of LOs and their results from one repository could also be made available for users in another repository, in the same manner as learning resources metadata, but with additional information indicating the evaluation approach used.

Evaluation Metadata for Social Recommendation Systems

In the field of learning technologies, a number of recommender systems have been introduced in order to recommend online learning resources to interested users (e.g., Recker & Walker, 2003; Recker, Walker, & Lawless, 2003; Anderson et al., 2003; Walker, Recker, Lawless, & Wiley, 2004; Rafaeli, Dan-Gur, & Barak, 2005; Lemire, Boley, McGrath, & Ball, 2005). Such systems, most of them based on collaborative recommending, could potentially play an important role for learning technologies, considering the variety of learning resources that are published online (Tzikopoulos et al., 2007) and the benefits of collaboration between tutors and learners (Recker & Wiley, 2000, 2001; Nesbit et al., 2002; Kumar, Nesbit, & Han, 2005).

As Adomavicius and Tuzhilin (2005) discuss, a limitation of current recommender systems is that new extensions and sources for data input are needed to satisfy users. This remark is also valid for recommender systems to be used to enhance retrieval in the domain of learning technologies. Much of the previous literature has proposed the use of evaluation metadata as input to process recommendations (Recker & Wiley, 2001; Downes, 2004; Lemire et al., 2005; Duval, 2006). However, the question of reusability and interoperability of this evaluation data has not been addressed so far. An interoperable model for evaluation metadata could be used to support such implementations.

More specifically, content-based recommender systems may be enhanced by evaluation metadata that will include some of the contextual characteristics of an EA. Knowing the properties of the environment in which an EA is intended to be applied, a content-based recommender may propose appropriate EAs based on the description of their contextual characteristics. For example, coverage characteristics could be used to recommend EAs appropriate for users in a particular geographical area or educational environment. Furthermore, evaluation results stored in a textual format (e.g., reviews or annotations) could be used to enhance content-based recommendation of learning resources (Dron et al., 2002). In a similar manner, storing quantitative evaluations of learning resources (e.g., single- or multi-attribute ratings) can facilitate the development of collaborative filtering systems that may share, combine, and reuse evaluation results.

Requirements for an Evaluation Metadata Framework

The above tentative classification of EAs identifies that an evaluation metadata schema would have to accommodate a variety of characteristics including general, methodological, and contextual ones such as resource lifecycle, focus, intended audience, instance of evaluation, criteria or metric, dimension, geographical, and the domain.

The general characteristics are useful for several practical reasons related to search and retrieval, such as identifying the EA from others in a collection or locating it online. Such elements could include the EA title, version, description, source, creator, date, as well as any associated copyrights or costs.

Furthermore, reflecting on the methodological properties of an EA schema, this part should allow the mapping, matching, or merging of evaluation results from different EAs with similar methodological properties. Example elements could include the process on which the EA focuses, the evaluation methods engaged, the metrics/criteria used, and the actors/evaluators involved.

As for the contextual properties, they should be able to relate the results with other EA results that are aimed to be applied in similar contexts. For instance, the evaluation metadata may store the geographical and regional coverage of an EA, its subject, language, the LO lifecycle, and educational processes on which it is expected to be applied, its audience, and its relation to other evaluation approaches.

Lastly, the schema will have to store the produced results when a given EA is applied on learning resources. For this purpose, appropriate elements have to be included which represent and store the collected results for numerous resources and from a variety of evaluators. For example, the relevant elements of the ECEM model could be appropriately adopted and used (Manouselis & Costopoulou, 2006). In the following section, we focus on the particular class of social recommendation systems, discussing a number of characteristic scenarios that illustrate the applicability of evaluation metadata.

CHARACTERISTIC SCENARIOS OF USE

In this section, we present some scenarios that demonstrate the value that shareable evaluation metadata can add to social recommendation.

Scenario A: Deploying a Social Recommendation for a Federation of Repositories

This scenario focuses on a (fictional) collaborative filtering system that uses as an input multi-attribute ratings by users on the learning resources in the GLOBE distributed network of learning repositories. For simplicity reasons, let us consider here only two GLOBE repositories, MERLOT

(*http://www.merlot.org*) and ARIADNE (*http://ariadne.cs.kuleuven.be*). MERLOT's EA [4], as presented in Table 1, uses three evaluation criteria, upon which both experts and users evaluate the learning objects in the repository. ARIADNE decides to use the LORI evaluation approach [13] as its evaluation instrument, collecting ratings along the multiple dimensions of LORI. The collaborative filtering system will use as input the multi-attribute evaluations stored in both repositories, in order to recommend suitable LOs to a user that initiates a federated search in ARIADNE.

The problem in this scenario is that the two repositories use different EAs and produce results in a different format. A solution would be to develop a system that will apply a hard-coded transformation to the collected ratings. That is, it will take as input the evaluations from those two particular repositories, create a mapping between their evaluation dimensions, appropriately normalize the values of collected ratings, and then use the combined transformed ratings in order to produce a prediction. The main drawback of such a solution is that for each new repository joining the federation, the recommender system software has to be revised in order to include the EA of the new repository in a hard-coded manner.

A schema of evaluation metadata could facilitate the development of such a system. First of all, the EA of each repository can be described in a structured manner, allowing for pre-defining the mapping between the different EAs' results. Knowing which EA is used in a new repository joining the federation, the recommender system can directly apply the appropriate mapping between the results (e.g., to a reference EA) and allow for the collection of comparable ratings. Each time a new EA is engaged, only the mapping between this EA and the reference EA will be required by the system. The transformation of the ratings can then be performed automatically. This can lower development and maintenance costs, allowing for further extendibility of the system. Also, repositories in the federation may change the EA they are using without losing the ratings collected so far.

Scenario B: Personal Portfolio of Learning Resources' Evaluations Within a Federation of LORs

In this scenario, the user of the LRE-portal (*http://lre.eun.org*) has access to an external service that allows her to evaluate digital learning resources that she finds on an educational portal or a repository. She can make evaluations by rating a resource or by adding textual evaluations; she can bookmark her own collections of resources and annotate learning resources by adding her own keywords, that is, tags, user comments, or pedagogical descriptions of usage.

These evaluation data, gathered over time, are saved on a server with her search history. She finds this service—called "portfolio of evaluations"—helpful; it seems to help her pick up good resources and proactively brings good suggestions on the use. On the LRE portal a multi-agent collaborative filtering service makes use of the portfolio of evaluation to offer better results on her searches. It uses three denominators—similar search histories, bookmarks, and ratings profiles—and looks for similarity of user profiles (i.e., similar personal agents).

Additionally, she really likes the fact that she can use the service also with other repositories. Thus, when she logs onto her national educational portal in Austria (*http://bildung.at/*), which offers only resources in German, she can, through single sign on, also use her portfolio of evaluations for recommendation purposes on the Austrian educational portal. A collaborative filtering algorithm based on nearest-neighbor technique recommends resources based on the German resources that she has rated previously. Thanks to the common schema for evaluation metadata and the appropriate mappings, similarity between bookmarks and ratings from her "portfolio of evaluations"

can be taken advantage of also by this recommender system.

Scenario C: Importing Previous Evaluations to an Interoperable Recommender System

In this scenario, an LOR that already uses some EA, and collects evaluations from experts and users, aims to enhance its services by adding a multi-attribute collaborative filtering service. Normally, a new recommender system would have to be developed ad-hoc for this specific repository, appropriately specialized to read evaluation results in its format. On the other hand, if an existing recommender system may already read evaluation results stored using the common evaluation metadata schema, then it can be adopted by a repository with minor further development. The evaluation metadata from this repository can be transformed to the format of this evaluation metadata schema as well, and the recommender system may use this structured information as its input. If the evaluation metadata in this system are in a different format than the one used by the existing recommender system (e.g., users rate LOs using an evaluation scale of '1' to '5', whereas the system receives as input binary ratings of 'dislike' or 'like'), then an appropriate mapping of the repository schema to the recommender schema can be defined (e.g., ratings below '2.5' can be considered as corresponding to 'dislike', whereas ratings over '2.5' can be considered as corresponding to 'like'). Then a simple transformation/mapping of the results from the one format of evaluation metadata to the other can be applied, in order for the recommender system to properly operate.

Generalization over the Fictional Scenarios

In conclusion of the above scenarios, we can derive a number of advantages that a common framework for evaluation metadata could offer:

- A common framework could facilitate the mappings between different evaluation approaches (EAs) and their results that use a variety of methods and semantics: only n mappings for n systems, rather than n^2, if we need to map between each pair of systems.
- Moreover, a common framework to describe EAs can make it easier to integrate heterogeneous tools that process evaluation metadata.
- Finally, a common EA framework can enable transfers of evaluation data for a particular user between different schemas.

CONCLUSION

In this chapter we introduced the need for a reusable and interoperable metadata framework for sharing and reusing evaluation metadata of learning resources. Such metadata are highly relevant to facilitate social recommendation purposes. There have already been studies in the field of learning technologies (e.g., Recker & Wiley, 2001; Downes, 2004; Lemire et al., 2005) that indicated the potential of evaluation metadata for describing learning resources. Nevertheless, reusability and interoperability have not been thoroughly addressed so far. In this chapter we focused on the rationale for a framework that can be used to facilitate the representation, management, and reuse of evaluation results of learning resources. We also discussed how evaluation metadata can support recommender systems, and we presented several scenarios of how such metadata can benefit end user interactions.

Future directions of work include consensus building around a common framework for evaluation metadata of learning resources, so that such data can be shared between LORs. Such a schema could be based on the tentative classification in the third section of this chapter, further elaborating on the general, methodological, and contextual

characteristics of EAs. Moreover, evaluation metadata can be integrated with a generic attention metadata framework, such as Contextualized Attention Metadata (Najjar, Wolpers, & Duval, 2006). In the long run, an evaluation metadata schema can be used alongside existing metadata standards for learning resources, such as IEEE LTSC LOM, or more generic metadata standards, such as Dublin Core or MPEG-7.

REFERENCES

Adomavicius, G., & Tuzhilin, A. (2005). Towards the next generation of recommender systems: A survey of the state-of-the-art and possible extensions. *IEEE Transactions on Knowledge and Data Engineering, 17*(6), 734-749.

Anderson, M., Ball, M., Boley, H., Greene, S., Howse, N., Lemire, D., & McGrath, S. (2003). RACOFI: A rule-applying collaborative filtering system. *Proceedings of IEEE/WIC COLA'03,* Halifax, Canada (NRC 46507).

Bartlett, K. (2001, June 15). *Backlash vs. third-party annotations from MS smart tags.* Retrieved August 26, 2006, from http://lists.w3.org/Archives/Public/www-annotation/2001JanJun/0115.html

Beard, K. (1996). A structure for organizing metadata collection. *Proceedings of the 3rd International Conference/Workshop on Integrating GIS and Environmental Modeling,* Santa Fe, NM.

Burke, R. (2002). Hybrid recommender systems: Survey and experiments. *User Modeling and User-Adapted Interaction, 12,* 331-370.

Butler, B. (2001). KnowBit reference information: A knowledge base specification. *Proceedings of the NISO Standards Review Meeting.*

Currier, S., Barton, J., O'Beirne, R., & Ryan, B. (2004). Quality assurance for digital learning object repositories: Issues for the metadata creation process. *ALT-J Research in Learning Technology, 12*(1), 5-20.

Devillers, R., Gervais, M., Bedard, Y., & Jeansoulin, R. (2002, March). Spatial data quality: From metadata to quality indicators and contextual end-user manual. *Proceedings of the OEEPE/ ISPRS Joint Workshop on Spatial Data Quality Management,* Istanbul, Turkey.

Downes, S. (2003). Design and reusability of learning objects in an academic context: A new economy of education? *USDLA Journal, 17*(1).

Downes, S. (2004, June). *Quality standards: It's all about teaching and learning? Proceedings of NUTN,* Kennebunkport, ME.

Dron, J., Boyne, C., & Mitchell, R. (2002). Evaluating assessment using n-dimensional filtering. *Proceedings of the AACE E-Learn Conference.*

Duval, E. (2006). LearnRank: Towards a real quality measure for learning. In U. Ehlers & J.M. Pawlowski (Eds.), *European handbook for quality and standardization in e-learning.* Berlin: Springer-Verlag, 457-463.

Duval, E., & Hodgins, W. (2004). Making metadata go away: Hiding everything but the benefits. *Proceedings of the International Conference on Dublin Core and Metadata Applications* (DC2004), Shanghai, China.

Duval, E., Hodgins, W., Sutton, S., & Weibel, S.L. (2002). Metadata principles and practicalities. *D-Lib Magazine, 8.* Retrieved August 26, 2006, from http://www.dlib.org/dlib/april02/ weibel/04weibel.html

EQO (European Quality Observatory). (2004). *The EQO model, v.1.2a.* Retrieved August 26, 2006, from *http://www.eqo.info/files/EQO-Model-1.2a.pdf*

ETB. (2002). Recommended data model format to be used as a standard by national systems

to include national/local resources in the EU Treasury Browser. *European Treasury Browser (ETB), D4.2.*

Eysenbach, G., Köhler, C., Yihune, G., Lampe, K., Cross, P., & Brickley, D. (2001). A metadata vocabulary for self- and third-party labeling of health Web sites: Health Information Disclosure, Description and Evaluation Language (HIDDEL). *Proceedings of AIMA 2001.* Retrieved 8 August, 2007 from http://www.medcertain. org/pdf/AMIA2001-final-edited-hiddel.pdf

GESTALT (Getting Educational Systems Talking Across Leading-Edge Technologies). (1999). *D0401 courseware metadata design.* Retrieved August 26, 2006, from http://www.fdgroup. co.uk/gestalt/

Guy, G., Powell, A., & Day, M. (2004). Improving the quality of metadata in e-print archives. *Ariadne, 38.*

Hanani, U., Shapira, B., & Shoval, P. (2001). Information filtering: Overview of issues, research and systems. *User Modeling and User-Adapted Interaction, 11,* 203-259.

Hillman, D., Dusshay, N., & Phipps, J. (2004). Improving metadata quality: Augmentation and recombination. *Proceedings of the International Conference on Dublin Core and Metadata Applications* (DC-2004), Shanghai, China.

IEEE LOM. (2002). *Standard for learning object metadata.* IEEE 1484.12.1-2002, IEEE Learning Technology Standards Committee.

Insight. (2005). *Insight dossier quality criteria.* European Schoolnet. Retrieved August 26, 2006, from http://insight.eun.org/ww/en/pub/insight/ thematic_dossiers/qualitycriteria.htm

INSPIRE (Infrastructure for Spatial Information in Europe). (2005). *Requirements for the definition of the INSPIRE implementing rules for metadata.* Author.

ISO 15836. (2003). *Information and documentation—the Dublin Core metadata element set.* International Organization for Standardization.

IVOA (International Virtual Observatory Alliance). (2004). *Resource metadata for the virtual observatory, version 1.01.* Retrieved August 26, 2006, from http://www.ivoa.net/

Kumar, V., Nesbit, J., & Han, K. (2005). Rating learning object quality with distributed Bayesian belief networks: The why and the how. *Proceedings of the 5th IEEE International Conference on Advanced Learning Technologies* (ICALT'05).

Lemire, D., Boley, H., McGrath, S., & Ball, M. (2005). Collaborative filtering and inference rules for context-aware learning object recommendation. *International Journal of Interactive Technology & Smart Education, 2*(3).

Manouselis, N., & Costopoulou, C. (2006). Quality in metadata: A schema for e-commerce. *Online Information Review (OIR), Special Issue on Advances in Digital Information Services and Metadata Research, 30*(3), 217-237.

MedCIRCLE. (2002, September). Towards a collaborative, open, semantic Web of trust for health information on the Web: Interoperability of health information gateways. *Proceedings of the Med-CIRCLE Workshop: Collaboration for Internet Rating, Certification, Labeling and Evaluation of Health Information,* Belgium.

Miller, B.N., Konstan, J.A., & Riedl, J. (2004). PocketLens: Toward a personal recommender system. *ACM Transactions on Information Systems, 22*(3), 437-476.

Moen, W.E., Stewart, E.L., & McClure, C.R. (1998). Assessing metadata quality: Findings and methodological considerations from an evaluation of the U.S. Government Information Locator Service (GILS). *Proceedings of the 5th International Forum on Research and Technology Advances in Digital Libraries* (ADL '98). IEEE Computer Press.

Muirhead, B., & Haughey, B. (2003). *An assessment of the learning objects, models and frameworks developed by the Learning Federation Schools Online Curriculum Content Initiative Australia.* Prepared for the Le@rning Federation, Australia.

Nesbit, J., Belfer, K., & Vargo, J. (2002). A convergent participation model for evaluation of learning objects. *Canadian Journal of Learning and Technology,* 105-120.

Nesbit, J.C., & Li, J. (2004). Web-based tools for learning object evaluation. *Proceedings of the International Conference on Education and Information Systems: Technologies and Applications* (vol. 2, pp. 334-339).

Najjar, J., Wolpers, M., & Duval, E. (2006). Towards effective usage-based learning applications: Track and learn from user experience(s). *Proceedings of the IEEE International Conference on Advanced Learning Technologies* (ICALT 2006), The Netherlands.

NDN. (2004, November). *Quality metadata.* Position Paper, National Data Network (NDN) Metadata Workshop, Australia. Retrieved August 26, 2006, from http://www.nationaldatanetwork.org

NISO (National Information Standards Organization). (2004). *Understanding metadata.* NISO Press.

Ochoa, X., & Duval, E. (2006). Quality metrics for learning object metadata. *Proceedings of the World Conference on Educational Multimedia, Hypermedia and Telecommunications* (EDMEDIA 2006).

Oram, A. (Ed.). (2001). *Peer-to-peer: Harnessing the power of disruptive technologies.* O'Reilly.

Pawlowski, J. (2006). *ISO/IEC 19796-1: How to use the new quality framework for learning, education, and training.* Retrieved August 26, 2006, from http://www.qualityfoundation.org/ww/en/oub/efquel/qualityservices/publications.htm

Rafaeli, S., Dan-Gur, Y., & Barak, M. (2005). Social recommender systems: Recommendations in support of e-learning. *Journal of Distance Education Technologies, 3*(2), 29-45.

Recker, M.M., & Wiley, D.A. (2001). A non-authoritative educational metadata ontology for filtering and recommending learning objects. *Journal of Interactive Learning Environments, 9*(3), 255-271.

Recker, M.M., & Wiley, D.A. (2000, June). An interface for collaborative filtering of educational resources. *Proceedings of the 2000 International Conference on Artificial Intelligence,* Las Vegas, NV.

Recker, M., & Walker, A. (2003). Supporting 'word-of-mouth' social networks via collaborative information filtering. *Journal of Interactive Learning Research, 14*(1), 79-98.

Recker, M., Walker, A., & Lawless, K. (2003). What do you recommend? Implementation and analyses of collaborative filtering of Web resources for education. *Instructional Science, 31*(4/5), 229-316.

Robertson, J.R. (2005). Metadata quality: Implications for library and information science professionals. *Library Review, 54*(5), 295-300.

Shon, J., & Musen, M.A. (1999). The low availability of metadata elements for evaluating the quality of medical information on the World Wide Web. *Proceedings of the 1999 American Medical Informatics Association Symposium*(AMIA'99).

Shreeves, S.L., Riley, J., & Milewicz, E. (2006). Moving towards sharable metadata. *First Monday, 11*(8).

Steinacker, A., Ghavam, A., & Steinmetz, R. (2001). Metadata standards for Web-based resources. *IEEE Multimedia,* (January-March), 70-76.

Supekar, K. (2005). A peer-review approach for ontology evaluation. *Proceedings of the 8th International Protégé Conference,* Madrid, Spain.

Supekar, K., Patel, C., & Lee, Y. (2004). Characterizing quality of knowledge on semantic Web. In V. Barr & Z. Markov (Eds.), *Proceedings of the 17th International Florida Artificial Intelligence Research Society Conference* (FLAIRS'04). AAAI Press.

Sutton, S.A. (1999). Conceptual design and deployment of a metadata framework for educational resources on the Internet. *Journal of the American Society for Information Science, 50*(13), 1182-1192.

Ternier, S., Olmedilla, D., & Duval, E. (2005). *Peer-to-peer versus federated search: Towards more interoperable learning object repositories. In P.* Kommers & G. Richards (Eds.), (pp. 1421-1428).

Tzikopoulos, A., Manouselis, N., & Vuorikari, R. (2007). An overview of learning object repositories. In P. Northrup (Ed.), *Learning objects for instruction: Design and evaluation.* Hershey, PA: Idea Group.

Van Assche, F., & Vuorikari, R. (2006). A framework for quality of learning resources. In U. Ehlers & J.M. Pawlowski (Eds.), *European handbook for quality and standardization in e-learning.* Berlin: Springer-Verlag, 443-456.

Walker, A., Recker, M., Lawless, K., & Wiley, D. (2004). Collaborative information filtering: A review and an educational application. *International Journal of Artificial Intelligence and Education, 14,* 1-26.

Wayne, L. (2004, January). Quality metadata. *Proceedings of the 2004 ESRI Federal User Conference,* Washington, DC.

Wiley, D. (Ed.). (2002). *The instructional use of learning objects.* Bloomington. IN: AECT. Retrieved August 10, 2005, from *http://reusability. org/read/*

World Wide Web Consortium. (n.d.). *PICS-specification.* Retrieved August 10, 2005, from *http://www.w3c.org/PICS*

Yamada, T. (2004, May). Role of metadata in quality assurance of multi-country statistical data in the case of UNIDO industrial statistics. *Proceedings of the Conference on Data Quality for International Organizations,* Germany.

Section III
Using Social Networks for Information Retrieval

Chapter VI
Social Network Models for Enhancing Reference–Based Search Engine Rankings

Nikolaos Korfiatis
Copenhagen Business School, Denmark

Miguel-Ángel Sicilia
University of Alcala, Spain

Claudia Hess
University of Bamberg, Germany

Klaus Stein
University of Bamberg, Germany

Christoph Schlieder
University of Bamberg, Germany

ABSTRACT

In this chapter we discuss the integration of information retrieval information from two sources—a social network and a document reference network—for enhancing reference-based search engine rankings. In particular, current models of information retrieval are blind to the social context that surrounds information resources, thus they do not consider the trustworthiness of their authors when they present the query results to the users. Following this point we elaborate on the basic intuitions that highlight the contribution of the social context—as can be mined from social network positions for instance—into the improvement of the rankings provided in reference-based search engines. A review on ranking models in Web search engine retrieval along with social network metrics of importance such as prestige and centrality are provided as background. Then a presentation of recent research models that utilize both contexts is provided, along with a case study in the Internet-based encyclopedia Wikipedia, based on the social network metrics.

INTRODUCTION

Since the introduction of information technology, information retrieval (IR) has been an important branch of computer and information science, mainly due to the ability to reduce the time required by a user to gather contextualized information and knowledge (Baeza-Yates & Ribeiro-Neto, 1999). With the introduction of hypertext (Conklin, 1987), information retrieval methods and technologies have been able to increase their accuracy because of the high amount of meta-information available for the IR system to exploit. That is not only information about the documents per se, but information about their context and popularity. However the development of the World Wide Web has introduced another dimension to the IR domain by exposing the social aspect of information (Brown & Duguid, 2002) produced and consumed by humans in this information space.

Current ranking methods in information retrieval—which are used in Web search engines as well—exploit the references between information resources such as the hypertextual (hyperlinked) context of Web pages in order to determine the rank of a search result (Dhyani, Keong, & Bhowmick, 2002; Faloutsos, 1985). The well-known PageRank algorithm (Page, Brin, Motwani, & Winograd, 1998; Brin & Page, 1998) has proved to be a very effective paradigm for ranking the results of Web search algorithms. In the original PageRank algorithm, a single PageRank vector is computed, using the link structure of the Web, to capture the relative "importance" of Web pages, independent of any particular search query. Nonetheless, the assumptions of the original PageRank are biased towards measuring external characteristics. In fact, Page et al. (1998) conclude their article with the sentence: *"The intuition behind PageRank is that it uses information which is external to the Web pages themselves—their backlinks, which provide a kind of peer review."*

That is to say that backlinks[1] (i.e., incoming links) are considered as a positive evaluation of the respective Web site. The PageRank therefore does not distinguish whether the user setting the link agrees with the content of the other Web page or whether she or he disagrees. This fact underlines that current reference-based ranking algorithms often do not take into consideration that an information resource is a result of cognitive and social processes. In addition to its surrounding hyperlinks, a social context (Brown & Duguid, 2002) underlies the referencing of those resources.

This suggests that a critical point in improving link-based metrics would be that of augmenting or weighting the pure backlink or reference model with social information, provided that linking is in many cases influenced by social ties, and trustworthiness critically depends on the social relevance or consideration of the authors of the pages. Recently, several independent researchers have provided different models for this kind of social network analysis as applied to ranking or assessing the quality of Web pages (Sicilia & Garcia, 2005; Hess, Stein, & Schlieder, 2006; Stein & Hess, 2006) or activity spaces such as Usenet and wikis (Korfiatis & Naeve, 2005). Other approaches such as those presented by Borner, Maru, and Goldstone (2004) have also dealt with integrating different networks by analyzing the simultaneous growth of coauthor and citation networks in time.

The main objective of this chapter is to provide a survey for recently proposed measures on a document reference network that integrate information from a second source: a social network. Therefore, we provide a bridge to the areas of social network analysis (SNA) and ranking methods applied in information retrieval.

To this end this chapter is organized as follows: The next section describes the basic intuition behind the concepts and the definitions provided by this chapter. We then provide an insight to the classic models of citation and link-based ranking methods such as PageRank and HITS. Next we offer insight to sociometric models, which can be used to evaluate users, as well as a reference to the FOAF vocabulary, which is used to define social connections on the Web. An overview of two hybrid ranking models that integrate in an equal way both the social and hypertextual context follows, and we then provide a case study of modeling authoritativeness on data obtained from the English-language version of Wikipedia by using some of the metrics discussed earlier in the chapter. Finally, we present our conclusions and provide an outlook of future research directions that can be exploited towards the combined consideration of hypertextual and social context in a Web IR system such as a Web search engine.

BACKGROUND AND MOTIVATION

The original intuition behind the design of the World Wide Web and the Hypertext Markup (HTML) language is that authors can publish Web documents that can provide pointers to other documents available online. This simplified aspect of a hypertext model adapted by Tim Berners-Lee in the original design of the World Wide Web (Berners-Lee & Fischetti, 1999) has given to the Web the morphology of an open publication system which can evolve simultaneously by providing references and pointers to existing documents available. However, as in the original publication contexts where an author gains credibility due to the popularity of her or his productions/affiliations, the credibility/appropriateness of a page on the Web is to some extent correlated with its popularity. What the first search engines on the Web failed to capture was exactly this kind of popularity which attributes the appropriateness to the query results of the search engine.

Although advances in query processing have made the retrieval of the query results computationally efficient (Wolf, Squillante, Yu, Sethuraman, & Ozsen, 2002), the precision and the recall

of the Web document retrieval systems such as search engines is under the negative effects of issues such as the ambiguity inherent to natural language processing. Further, backlink models are blind to the authors of the pages, which entails that every link is equally important for the final ranking. This overlooks the fact that some links can be more relevant than others, depending on their authors or other parameters such as affiliation with organizations, and even in some cases, the links may have been created with a malicious purpose, such as spamming or the popular case of "Google bombing" (Mathes, 2005).

Probably the best example where the above phenomena are manifested is the field of scientometrics and in particular the scholar evaluation problem. Earlier from the introduction of the impact factor by Garfield (1972), several researchers considered the development of metrics that can assist the evaluation of a scholar based on the reputation of his scientific works usually denoted as references to his or her work (Leydesdorff, 2001).

In particular the scholar evaluation problem can be formalized as follows:

Considering a scholar S with a collection of scientific output represented by a set of scholarly productions/publications as $A = \{a_1, a_2, ..., a_n\}$, then his/her research impact B is the aggregation if the impact of the individual scholarly works as: $B = \Omega \{P(a_1), P(a_2), ..., P(a_n)\}$ where, Ω is an aggregation operation (e.g., averaging) over the popularity $P(a_i)$ of his or her research production a_i. To the above formalization a set of open issues exist:

- Regarding the variability of his/her research work, *how can we aggregate the impact of his production to a representative and generally accepted number?*
- How do we measure the popularity of the production? For example, *do we count the same the reference provided to a research*

work by a technical report and by a generally accepted "prestigious" journal?

Scientometrics provides insight to open issues in the evaluation of the importance of documents that represent the scientific production, whereas in our case we look into the evaluation of the importance of Web pages. We follow the assumption that those Web pages/documents are productions of social entities which transpose a degree of credibility from their social context.

Based on this assumption we develop, in the section that follows, a basic framework that underlines the core of the credibility models presented throughout the rest of this chapter both for the social and hypertextual context. As can be seen in Figure 1, our framework considers a kind of affiliation network (see definition bellow) where hypertext documents (Web pages) are connected to their authors.

This gives a two-layer network: the document reference layer with documents (e.g., Web pages) linking to other documents, and the social layer with actors (authors or reviewers of the documents) with social ties (e.g., trust between the actors, coauthorship, etc.).

Formal Representations

Before continuing with the models representing credibility in both social and hypertextual contexts, we should first have a look at the formalizations used in order to be able to comprehend the metrics and the models using them.

A social/hypertextual network is formalized as a graph $G := (V, E)$ which is an ordered pair of two sets. A set of vertices $V = (V_1, V_2, V_3, ..., V_n)$ which represents the social entities/pages, and a set of edges $E = (E_{11}, E_{12}, E_{21}, ..., E_{ij})$ where E_{ij} represents the adjacent connection between the nodes i and j. In abstract form the network structure can be represented as a symmetric matrix (adjacency matrix) in which the nodes are listed in both axes and a Boolean value is assigned to E_j, which depicts the existence of a relational tie between the entities, represented in E_j.

Depending on the type of network, the adjacent connection may be:

- **Edge:** Indicates a connection between two nodes. In that case the graph is in the general form: $G := (V, E)$. When the connection is

Figure 1. Layers of context in the mixed mode network of authors or readers (human icons) and Web resources (squares)

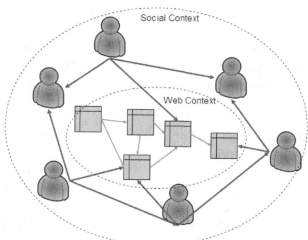

directed, the graph has the general form $G := (V, E, E_a)$ denoting that the connection is directional.

- **Signed edge:** Indicates a connection between two nodes which is assigned with a value. In that case, the graph is in the general form $G := (V, E, E_d)$ where the set E_d is the value set for the mapping $E \to E_d$. When the connection is directional, the graph has the general form $G := (V, E, E_a, E_d)$ where E_a and E_d is the directed connection and value set respectively.

An edge is often referenced to in the literature as *arc*. In a social network context, an edge and an arc differ based on the fact that an edge denotes a reciprocal connection whereas an arc is a directed one. However, when the network is a directed graph (digraph), those two terms become synonymous.

Furthermore, depending on the group size, a relation can be dichotomous, *trichotomous,* or connecting subgroups.

- A *dichotomous* relation is a bivalence type of relational tie where the valued set E_d is mapped to [0; 1]. Dichotomous relationships form units called dyads that are used to study indirect properties between two individual entities. On the Web, for example, the referring link from one page to another represents a dichotomous relation.

- A *trichotomous* or *triad* is a container of at most six dyads that can be either signed or unsigned. Usually in a triad, a dyadic relation is referenced by a third entity which provides a point of common affiliation. For instance, two pages are referenced by a directory page which can be studied in a triad.

- A *subgroup* relation is a more complex relation that acts as a container of triads where the members are interacting using a common flow or path.

Network Modes and Data

In principle, network data consists of two types of variables: *structural* and *compositional*. *Compositional* variables represent the attributes of the entities that form apart the network. This kind of data can be, for instance, the theme of the Web page. *Structural* variables define the ties between the network entities and the mode under which the network is formed. Depending on the domain considered, different terminologies can be used.

Depending on the measurement of structural variables, a network can have a mode. The term mode refers to the number of entities that the structural variables address in the network.

In particular, we can have the two following types of networks:

- **One-mode network:** This is the basic type of network where structural variables address the relational ties between entities belonging on the same set. The Web is in an abstract form a one-mode network linking Web documents.

- **Two-mode network or affiliation network:** This type of network contains two sets of entities, that is, authors and articles. An affiliation network is a special kind of two-mode network where at least one member of the set has a relational tie with the member of the other set. For example, an author has written an article. The networks studied through the rest of this chapter are affiliation networks, where authors produce documents with which they are affiliated.

Table 1. Example structural and compositional variables for different applications/domains

Structural Variables	Compositional Variables
links	Web pages/documents
References/citations	Papers/articles

In social network theory several other kinds of network exist such as ego-centered networks or networks based on special dyadic relations. As already mentioned, we intend to study only affiliation networks such as the author-article network or the reviewer-article network.

REFERENCE-BASED RANKINGS IN WEB CONTEXT

As noted earlier, using the hyperlink structure of the Web (or any linked document repository) to compute document rankings is a very successful approach (visible in the success of Google). The basic idea of link structure-based ranking methods is that the prominence of a document p_d can be determined by looking at the documents citing p_d (and the documents cited by p_d).[2] A paper cited by many other papers must be somehow important, otherwise it would not be cited so much. And a Web page linked by many other pages gains prominence (visibility).

Another view is the random surfer model. If a user starts on an arbitrary Web page, follows some link to another page, follows a link from this page to a third one, and so on, the likelihood for getting a certain page will depend on two aspects: from how many other pages it is linked and how visible the linking pages are.

PageRank

In 1976, Pinski and Narin computed the importance (rank) vis_d of a scientific journal p_d by using the weighted sum of the ranks vis_k of the journals p_k with papers citing p_d.[3] A slightly modified version of this algorithm (the PageRank algorithm) is used by the search engine Google[4] to calculate the visibility vis_d of a Web page p_d:

$$vis_d = (1-\alpha) + \alpha \sum_{p_k \in R_d} \frac{vis_k}{|C_k|} ,$$

where R_d is the set of pages citing p_d, and C_k is the set of pages cited by P_k.

This resembles the idea of a random surfer. Starting at some Web page p_a with probability α, she follows one of (C_a) links, while with $(1-\alpha)$ she stops following links and jumps randomly to some other page. Therefore, $(1-\alpha)$ can be considered as a kind of basic visibility for every page. From the ranked document's perspective, a page p_d can be reached by a direct (random) jump with probability $(1-\alpha)$ or by coming from one of the pages $p_k \in R_d$, where the probability to be on p_k is vis_k.

The equation shown above gives a recursive definition of the visibility of a Web page because vis_a depends on the visibility of all pages p_i citing p_a, and vis_i depends on the visibilities of the pages citing p_i and so on. For n pages this is a system of n linear equations that has a solution. In praxis, solving this system of equations for some million pages would be much too expensive (it takes too much time), therefore an iterative approach is used (for details, see Page et al., 1998).

Even the iterative approach is rather time consuming; the rank (visibility) of all pages is not computed at query time (when users are waiting for their search results), but all documents are sorted by visibility offline, and this sorted list is used to fulfill search requests by selecting the first k documents matching the search term.[5]

HITS

The hypertext induced topic selection (HITS) is an alternative approach using the network structure for document ranking introduced by Kleinberg (1999). Kleinberg identifies two roles a page can fulfill: hub and authority. Hubs are pages referring to many authorities (e.g., linklists), authorities are pages that are linked by many hubs. Now for each page p_d, its hub-value h_d and its authority value a_d can be computed:

$$h_d = \delta \sum_{p_k \in C_d} a_k \,, \quad a_d = \lambda \sum_{p_l \in R_d} h_l$$

Here a page p_d has a high h_d if it links many authorities (i.e., pages p_i with high a_i). In other words, it is a good hub if it knows the important pages. The other way around, p_d has a high a_d if it is linked by many good hubs, that is, it is listed in the important link lists. While the authority a_d gives the visibility of the document ($vis_d = a_d$), h_d is only an auxiliary value.

But HITS not only differs from PageRank by the equations used to calculate the visibility. While the linear equation system is solved iteratively in both algorithms, they differ in the set of pages used. As PageRank does the calculation off-line on all pages $p_i \in P$ and at query time selects the first k matching pages from this presorted list, HITS in a first step selects all pages matching the search term at query time (this gives a subset $M \subset P$) and then adds all pages linked by pages from M ($M^C = \bigcup_{p_i \in M} C_i$) and all pages linking pages from M ($M^R = \bigcup_{p_i \in M} R_i$). Then h_d and a_d are computed for all pages $p_d \in M' = (M^C \cup M \cup M^R)$. Only including pages somehow relevant to the search query (matching pages and neighbors) may improve the quality of the ranking, but produces high costs at query time, for a_d and h_d are not computed off-line because M' is dependent on the search term. This is a problem in praxis because a single search term can have up to some million matching Web pages, even if there are strategies for pre-calculation.[6]

Other Approaches

There are other link structure-based ranking algorithms, for example, the hilltop algorithm,[7] which in a first step identifies so-called expert pages (pages linking to a number of unaffiliated pages[8]) and then each page is ranked by the rank of the expert pages it is linked by, or the

TrustRank algorithm (Gyongyi, Garcia-Molina, & Pedersen, 2004), where link spam is semi-automatically identified by using a small seed of user-rated pages.

All these algorithms are best suited for networks with cyclic link structures. Repositories with mainly acyclic reference structure like citation networks of scientific papers (where each paper cites older ones) or online discussion groups where each thread consists of one initial posting and sequences of replies/follow-ups, need other visibility measures, such as those provided by Malsch et al. (2006), where creation time of a document is much more important (as scientific papers or postings are not changed after publishing in contrast to Web pages).

Linking and Evaluating Users

Ranking is not only a phenomenon that takes places in the Web, but derives from the archetype stratification of a society into degrees of power and dominance. In principle, in social contexts two types of ranking exist: explicit (formal) and implicit (informal). In explicit ranking it is declared who is the one who has the authority to command due to insignia, symbols, or status that he or she is being attributed from the beginning. On the other side, in implicit ranking it is the opinion and the behaviors of the surrounding entities that facilitate who has the authority to command and decide.

Both implicit and explicit forms of ranking may exist depending on the purpose of the social group and the kind of interactions between the members. However, our study is focused only on implicit forms of ranking where status is a social attribute that emerges rather than being set. In sociology there are several kinds of studies that tend to explain how status emerges, therefore several research models exist. Those models are analyzed further in the following sections.

Sociometric Status and Prominence

In a social group one recognizes several strata that characterize the members with a kind of implicit rank that is known in social science literature as "status" (Katz, 1953). Usually in a sociological interpretation, status denotes power expressed in different contexts such as political or economical. The most basic theoretical implication of status is the availability of choices the entity receives in the network which gives the entity the advantage of negotiation over the others. Depending on the topology of the network, status can be attributed to several nodes of the sociogram (see Figure 2).

In SNA studies, status is depicted upon the generalization of the location of the actor in the network. In particular, status is addressed by how strategic the position of that entity in a network is (e.g., how it affects the position of the others). Theoretical aspects of status were defined by Moreno and Jennings (1945) as the instances of the sociometric "star" and "isolate."

Quantifications of status employ techniques of graph theory such as the centrality index (Sabidussi, 1966; Freeman, 1979; Friedkin, 1991) which have been adjusted to the various representations of ties in a network. In our case we summarize the two most noteworthy measures of an actor in a directed network; the measures are "prestige" and "centrality."

Prestige

A prestige measure is a direct representation of status which often employs the non-reciprocal connections/choices provided to that entity along with the influence that this entity might provide to the neighboring entities. In principle, prestige is a non-reciprocal characteristic of an entity. That means that if the entity is considered prestigious by another entity, it does not mean that this entity will consider the referring entity prestigious as well.

Inner Degree

The simplest measure of prestige is the inner degree index or the popularity of an entity, which is defined as follows. Considering a graph $G := (V, E_A)$ and E_A, the set of the directed connections $E = (e_{1,1}, e_{1,2}, \ldots\ldots, e_{i,j})$ between the members of the set V then the inner degree K_i^{in} of a vertex V_i is the sum of the incoming connections to that vertex.

Figure 2. Types of connection degree in the network. It is obvious that the sociometric "star" (first diagram) is considered the one with the highest inner degree, thus is more popular. When there is reciprocity, the degree of influence can be used to provide an indication of prestige in the network.

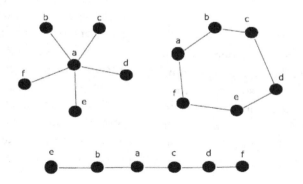

$$K_i^{in} = \sum_{j=1} e_{j,i}$$

Degree of Influence and Proximity Prestige

However, the inner degree index of a vertex makes sense only in cases where a directional relationship is available (the connection is non-reciprocal), and this cannot be applied in the study of non-directed networks. In that case the prestige is computed by the influence domain of the vertex. For a non-directed graph $G := (V, E, \overline{E})$, the influence domain of a vertex V_i is the number or proportion of all other vertices that are connected by a path to that particular vertex.

$$\overline{d_i} = \frac{1}{N-1} \sum_{j=1} \overline{e}_{j,i}$$

On the above measure E represents the set of paths between the vertices V_i and V_j, and $N-1$ is the number of all available nodes in the graph G (the total number of nodes $N = |V|$ minus the node that is subject to the metric).

Having the degree of influence, we can compute the "proximity prestige" (PP_i) by normalizing the degree of the vertex by the degree of influence such as:

$$PP_i = \frac{k_i^{in}}{\overline{d_i}}$$

Centrality

Unlike prestige measures that rely mainly on directional relations of the entities, the centrality index of a graph can be calculated in various ways, taking also into account the non-directional connections of the vertex that is examined. The most noteworthy measures of centrality are classified by the degree of analysis they employ in the graph.

Actor Degree Centrality

Actor degree centrality is the normalized index of the degree of an actor divided by the maximum number of vertices that exist in a network. Considering a graph $G = (V, E)$ with n vertices, then the actor degree centrality $C_d(n_i)$ will be:

$$C_d(n_i) = \frac{d(n_i)}{n-1}$$

where $n-1$ is the number of the remaining nodes in the graph G. Actor degree centrality is often interpreted in the literature as the "ego density" (Burt, 1982) of an actor since it evaluates the importance of the actor based on the ties that connect him or her to the other members of the network. The higher the actor degree centrality is, the most prominent this person is in a network, since an actor with a high degree can potentially directly influence the others.

Closeness or Distance Centrality

Another measure of centrality, the closeness centrality, considers the "geodesic distance" of a node in a network. For two vertices a geodesic is defined as the length of the shortest path between them. For a graph $G = (V, E)$, the closeness centrality $C_c(V_i)$ of a vertex V_i is the sum of geodesic distances between that vertex and all the other vertices in the network.

$$C_c(V_i) = \frac{n-1}{\sum_{i=1} d(u_i, u_n)}$$

where the function $d(u_i, u_n)$ calculates the length of the shortest path between the vertices i and j, and n-1 is the number of all other vertices in the network. The closeness centrality can be interpreted as a measurement of the influence of a vertex in a graph: the higher its value, the easier it is for that vertex to spread information into that network. Distance centrality can be valuable in networks where the actor possesses transitive properties that through transposition can be spread through direct connections such as the case of reputation.

Betweenness Centrality

Betweenness is the most celebrated measure of centrality since it not only measures the prominence of a node based on the position or the activity, but also the influence of the node in information or activity passed to other nodes Considering a graph $G = (V, E)$ with n vertices, the betweenness $C_B(u)$ for vertex $n \in V$ is:

$$C_B(u) = \frac{\sum_{s \neq u \neq t \in V} \sigma_{st}(u)}{(n-1)(n-2)}$$

where $C_B(u) = 1$ if and only if the shortest path from s to t passes through v and 0 otherwise. Betweenness can be the basis to interpret roles such as the "gatekeeper" or the "broker," which are extensive studies in communication networks. A vertex is considered as a "gatekeeper" if its betweenness and inner degree is relatively high. The "broker" is a vertex that has relatively high outer degree and betweenness.

The FOAF Vocabulary

Although sociometric models can provide several pathways on evaluating the importance of users, there is a crucial need for an accurate way of mining the relations between them in order to be able to apply those models. This can be done by using expressive vocabularies such as FOAF.

The Friend-of-a-Friend vocabulary (Brickley & Miller, 2005) is an expressive vocabulary set whose syntax is based on RDF syntax (Klyne & Carroll, 2004) and which is gaining popularity nowadays as it is used to express the connections between social entities in the Web along with their hypertextual properties such as their homepages or e-mails. In a best-case scenario, the author of a Web page (information resource) will attach his FOAF profile in the resource in order to make it identifiable as an own production by the visitors of that page. This can be observed clearly in cases such as blogs where the information resource represents the person that expresses his or her views through the blog. Furthermore connection between blogs also represents a kind of a directional dichotomous tie between the authors of those blogs.

In FOAF, standard RDF syntax is used to describe the relations between various acquaintances (relations) of the person described by the FOAF profile. This relation is depicted in the

Table 2. Some representative elements of the FOAF vocabulary and the representation of the relational tie

Vocabulary Element	Description	Type of Relational Tie
foaf:knows	links foaf:persons	Direct
foaf:member	Provides affiliation/membership (relates an entity with a social group)	indirect
foaf:maker	Indicates authorship (relates an information resource with its creator)	indirect
foaf:based_near	Indicates a spatial affiliation of a social entity	indirect
foaf:currentproject	Indicates a temporal affiliation of a social entity with a project or an activity	indirect

<foaf:knows> predicate which denotes that the person who has a description of <foaf:knows> in his profile for another person, has a social connection with that person as well. For example a FOAF profile for one of the authors of this chapter and the connection he has with his coauthors can be described by the fragment of RDF code seen in Box 1.

Research on descriptions of social relations in the semantic Web[9] is an undergoing effort which has been initiated lately to address the various concerns and sociological implications

for the expressiveness of social connections on the Web. One particular issue is that although the FOAF vocabulary (see Table 2) has a set of properties for the description of several kinds of relationships, the <foaf:knows> property is the most common relation that is expressed in a publicly available FOAF profile. According to the general discussion in the FOAF project, the reason for this is that many users prefer not to express their strength of social connections publicly than to do it in a general way which the <foaf:knows> property implies.

Box 1.

```xml
<?xml version="1.0" encoding="UTF-8" ?>
<rdf:RDF
    xmlns:xml="http://www.w3.org/XML/1998/namespace"
    xmlns:rdf="http://www.w3.org/1999/02/22-rdf-syntax-ns#"
    xmlns:rdfs="http://www.w3.org/2000/01/rdf-schema#">
<foaf:Person rdf:nodeID="friend1">
    <foaf:name>Nikolaos Korfiatis</foaf:name>
    <foaf:mbox rdf:resource="mailto:nk.inf@cbs.dk"/>
    </foaf:Person>
<foaf:Person rdf:nodeID="friend2">
 <foaf:name>Claudia Hess</foaf:name>
 <foaf:mbox rdf:resource="mailto:claudia.hess@wiai.uni-bamberg.de"/>
    </foaf:Person>
<foaf:Person rdf:nodeID="friend3">
    <foaf:name>Klaus Stein</foaf:name>
    <foaf:mbox rdf:resource="mailto:klaus.stein@wiai.uni-bamberg.de"/>
    </foaf:Person>
<foaf:Person rdf:nodeID="me">
    <foaf:title>Dr. </foaf:title>
    <foaf:givenName>Miguel-Angel</foaf:givenName>
    <foaf:family_name>Sicilia</foaf:family_name>
    <foaf:mbox rdf:resource="mailto:msicilia@uah.es"/>
    <foaf:knows rdf:nodeID="friend1"/>
    <rel:collaboratesWith rdf:nodeID="friend2"/>
    <rel:collaboratesWith rdf:nodeID="friend3"/>
    </foaf:Person>
</rdf:RDF>
```

Within well-defined application domains, however, more expressive constructs are required for describing the relationships between persons. Using the social relationships for recommending sensitive information such as Avesani, Massa, and Tiella (2005) in Moleskiing, a platform for exchanging information on ski tours (e.g., snow conditions, risk of avalanches), it is highly critical to get this information only from persons that you consider as trustworthy, and not from everyone you know (or who is known by some of your friends). Golbeck, Parcia, and Hendler (2003) therefore provided an extension to the FOAF vocabulary so that users can explicitly specify their degree of trust in another person. Specifying the degree of trust in someone with respect to her or his recommendations of scientific papers gives, according to the trust ontology[10] by Golbeck et al. (2003), as shown in Box 2.

EVALUATING WEB PAGE IMPORTANCE THROUGH THE ANALYSIS OF SOCIAL TIES

This section presents two research models to integrate social network data into document reference network-based measures: the PeopleRank approach and the trust-enhanced document rankings approach. The algorithms presented improve the measures on the document reference network by using propagated information from the social network.

Integrating Imprecise Expressions of the Social Context in PageRank

Sicilia and Garcia (2005) have introduced an approach for integrating the social context of an information resource into the core of ranking algorithms such as PageRank. Although a flavor of PageRank (PageRank with priors) can be used to normalize existing rankings, the core of the method relies on the expression of the relational ties of the social context (e.g., connections in a social network) using imprecise expressions.

The idea is that of using imprecise assessments of social relationships as a weighting factor for algorithms like PageRank, whereas imprecise expressions map better to social relation due to the difficulty of making an accurate estimation of the strength of the relational ties and their influence to the rest of the structure members.

The model considers two cases of social relations: (a) those that are formal/declared and can be mined from direct social connections, and (b) those that are informal/assumed and can be inferred by common properties such as affiliation.

The model begins by computing a metric called PeopleRank (PPR). PPR is based on the declared

Box 2.

```
<foaf:Person rdf:ID="Claudia">
    <trust:trustsRegarding>
        <trust:TopicalTrust>
            <trust:trustSubject
rdf:resource="#RecommendationsForPapers"/>
            <trust:trustedPerson rdf:resource="#Klaus"/>
            <trust:trustValue>9</trust:trustValue>
        </trust:TopicalTrust>
    </trust:trustsRegarding>
</foaf:Person>
```

Table 3. Intuitions behind the development of the PeopleRank algorithm (Adapted from Sicilia & Garcia, 2005)

PageRank	PeopleRank
Intuitively, pages that are well cited from many places around the Web are worth looking at.	Intuitively, the trust on the quality of pages is related to the degree of confidence we have on their authors.
Also, pages that have perhaps only one citation from something like the Yahoo! homepage are also generally worth looking at.	Pages authored or owned by people with a larger positive prestige should somewhat be considered more relevant.

relationships <foaf:knows> connecting pairs of <foaf:Person> specifications. As mentioned earlier, the FOAF vocabulary has deliberately avoided more specific forms of relation like friendship or endorsement, since social attitudes and conventions on this topic vary greatly between countries and cultures.

In consequence, the strength is provided explicitly as part of the link. In the case of absence of such value, an "indefinite" middle value is used. With the above, the PeopleRank can be defined by simply adapting the original PageRank definition:

We assume a social entity/person A that has persons $T_1 \ldots T_n$ which declare they know him/her (i.e., provide FOAF social pointers to it). The parameter d is a damping factor which can be set between 0 and 1…Also C(A) is defined as the number of (interpreted) declarations of backlinks going out of A's FOAF profile.

In the above definition we consider as an interpreted declaration of backlink the non-direct connection between two persons that can be inferred by other FOAF elements such as the FOAF affiliation.

Following the above definition the PeopleRank of a person $A(PpR(A))$ can be defined as follows:

$$PpR(A) = (1-d) + d\sum_{i=1}^{n} \frac{PpR(T_i)}{C(T_i)}$$

Even though the idea of ranking by peer's declarations seems intuitive and is coherent with the concepts explained in this chapter, the original intuitive justification provided for PageRank requires a reformulation. Table 3 provides the original and the socially oriented justifications.

An important parameter of the PpR computation is that declarations of social awareness should be interpreted. Here the management of vagueness plays a role, since there is no single model or framework that provides a metric for social distance.

The relevance r of a social tie in that model is provided by the following general expression, which provides a value for each edge (e_1, e_2) in the directed graph formed by the explicitly declared social relationships.

For a set of peers p_1, p_2, we define social relevance as $r(p_1, p_2) = S(p_1, p_2) \cdot e(p_1, p_2)$, asserting that $p_1 \neq p_2$.

The relevance r of an edge is determined from a degree of strength S (in a scale of fuzzy numbers [~0; ~ 10]) weighted by a degree of evidence e about the relationship. These strengths could be provided by extending the current FOAF schema with an additional attribute. Since we consider the variable S as a fuzzy variable, we can define membership in a fuzzy set such as S ε {close friend, acquaintance, distant friend,…} and a membership function that expresses the quantifications of the variable S from its linguistic form.

The quantification can be done by the expression of the linguistic variable in the FOAF schema.

The second fuzzy variable in the relevance function is the evidence of the relation. As already mentioned, we infer evidence from non-directional connections (e.g., affiliations). The more common affiliations exist between two actors in the network, the more relevant the connection is, since the evidence is used as a normalization factor.

Degrees of evidence support a notion of "external" evidence on the relation that completes the subjectively stated strength. The following expression provides a formalization for this evidence that is based both on the perceptions of "third parties" and/or affiliations.

$$e((p_1, p_2)) = \max(\Phi_{i \in U} S^{P_i}(p_1, p_2), P(p_1, p_2))$$

asserting again that $p_i \neq p_1 \neq p_2$ and having $i \in U$. According to this expression, the strengths of a social tie in a group of users U are aggregated through simple fuzzy averaging (Φ) and the evidence provided by third parties p_i; for example, work in common projects in which two persons $P(p_1, p_2)$ (p1; p2) collaborate $P(p_1, p_2)$ is obtained from FOAF declarations.

Concretely if we follow the affiliation by the FOAF descriptor, for example foaf:Project, people coworking in a project (as declared by <foaf:pastProject>) are credited an amount of 1, while people that were coworkers (as declared by <foaf:pastProject>) are credited an amount of 0.1 per common past project.

Figure 3 provides an abstract description of the process. The ComputeSocialRelevance procedure crawls the social network of the actors/people in order to extract the social relevance factor *r* based on the social connections. Then the PageRank for each document is calculated taking for each edge as input the r factor of the social relevance between the authors. In case the documents are written by the same author, the social relevance is set to zero.

Of course the above model can be modified and extended with more parameters such as expressions of negative and positive evaluations in the relational ties (e.g., in the case of a citation or a review). However it provides an initial straightforward model for the integration of imprecise expressions of social ties in the PageRank from which further empirical analysis could be carried out. Furthermore the procedure presented by this model, unlike several information retrieval algorithms, considers a social relation as an imprecise assessment to which a quantification provided by the actors in the form of Boolean values (e.g., knows or not) fails to capture other important elements such as strength and consider it as an evaluation factor.

Figure 3. The steps of the PpR algorithm

```
COMPUTEPAGERANKSOCIAL(S, D)
    ▷ D is the document graph
    ▷ S is the people graph

1   S ← COMPUTESOCIALRELEVANCE(S)
2   for each v ∈ VERTEX(D)
            do
3               v.source.relevance ←
                    NODES(S)[v.source].relevance

4   D ← WEIGHTEDPAGERANK(D)
```

Integrating Trust Networks and Document Reference Networks

An alternative approach for integrating different types of networks has been presented by Hess et al. (2006) and Stein and Hess (2006). They propose to integrate information from a trust network between persons and a document reference network. A trust network has been chosen as a social network because trust relationships represent a strong basis for recommendations. In contrast to social networks based only on a 'knows' or 'coworkers' relationship, trust relationships are more expressive, although more difficult to obtain. Trust networks cannot automatically be extracted from data on the Web, but users must indicate their trust relationships, as they are doing it already in an increasing number of trust-based social networks. Examples for such trust networks are the epinions Web of trust in which users rate other users with respect to the quality of their product reviews, or social networking services such as Orkut and Linked-in, in which you can rate your friends with respect to their trustworthiness (among other criteria such as 'coolness'). In trust networks, trust values can be inferred for indirectly connected persons by using trust metrics such as those presented in Goldbeck, Parsia, and Hendler (2003) or Ziegler and Lausen (2004). This reflects the fact that we trust in the real world the friends of our friends to a certain degree. Trust is therefore not transitive in the strict mathematical sense, but decreases with each additional step in the trust chain. In contrast to the measures presented in this chapter, most trust metrics calculate highly personalized trust values for the users in the network: a trust value for a user is always computed from the perspective of a specific user. The evaluations of one and the same user can therefore greatly vary between users depending on their personal trust relationships.

We can distinguish two roles that actors play in the trust networks: they can either be the authors or the reviewers of documents. The term 'reviewer' encompasses all persons having an opinion about the document, such as persons who read the document or editors who accepted the document for publication. Both cases are addressed in the following separately, leading to two different trust-enhanced visibility functions.

Case 1: Reviewers and Documents

In this first type of a two-layer-architecture, a trust network between reviewers is connected with a document reference network. In the document reference network, documents are linked via citations or hyperlinks. In the second layer, reviewers make statements about the degree of trust they have in other reviewers in making 'good' reviews, that is, above all that they apply similar criteria to the evaluation as themselves. Depending on the trust metric that is used for inferring trust values between indirectly connected persons, trust statements are in [0, 1] with 0 for no trust and 1 for full trust, or even [–1, 1] ranging from distrust[11] to full trust. Both layers are connected via reviews—that is, reviewers express their opinions on documents.

We have now two types of information, firstly the reviews of documents made by persons in which the requesting user has a certain degree of trust—that is, *trust-weighted reviews*—and secondly the *visibility* of the documents calculated on the basis of the document network. We now integrate the trust-weighted reviews in the visibility function and hence personalize it. This new trust-review-weighted-visibility function (in the following called twr-visibility) has the property that reviews influence the rank of a document to the degree of trust in the reviewer—that is, a review by someone deemed as highly trustworthy influences the rank to a considerable part, whereas reviews of less trustworthy persons have few influence. Having only untrustworthy reviewers, the user likely prefers a recommendation merely based on the visibility of the documents.

This architecture permits us to deal with two interpolation problems. Firstly, propagating trust values in the trust network makes it possible to consider reviews of users who are directly linked via a trust statement as well as indirectly via some "friends," that is, via chains of trust. Secondly, reviews influence not only the visibility of the reviewed papers but also indirectly the visibility of other papers, namely of those papers cited by the reviewed documents. Figure 4 illustrates these interpolations. Person 1 asks for a recommendation about document 4 that has not directly been reviewed, but which visibility is influenced by the twr-visibility of document 2 that has been reviewed by a person deemed as trustworthy by person 1.

The following function gives the twr-visibility for a document p_d in which r_d is the review of document p_d and t_{r_d} is the trust in the reviewer. The trust in the reviewer is directly taken as the trust in the review.

$$vf^{TWR}(p_d) = t_{r_d} r_d + (1 - t_{r_d}) vf(p_d)$$

The trust in the reviewers of a document therefore determines to which degree the trust-weighted reviews influence the twr-visibility. In the case that the trust in the reviewer is not absolute (trust = 1.0), the twr-visibility of the documents citing this document determines its twr-visiblity. Reviews by trustworthy persons therefore influence indirectly the twr-visibility of not directly evaluated documents. The vf^{TWR} function permits use of any visibility function such as the PageRank formula for the propagation of the trust-enhanced visibilities. The indirect connections in the trust network are computed before calculating the twr-visibility. Any trust metric can be used for the propagation of the trust statements. The above presented function therefore represents a general framework for integrating trust and document reference networks. A detailed description of

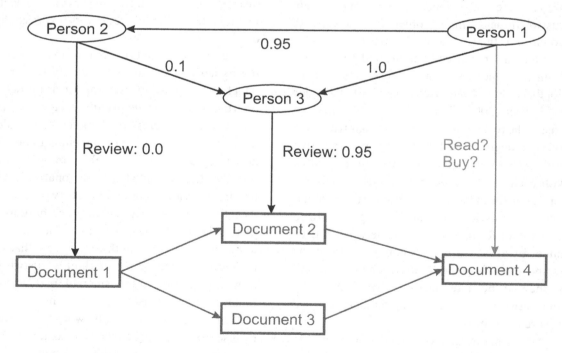

Figure 4. Interpolation in a document and reviewer network (From Hess et al., 2006)

this approach and a simulation demonstrating the personalization provided by this function is in Hess et al. (2006).

Case 2: Authors & Documents

In the second case, the trust network is built up between authors of documents. The trust statements refer to the trust in the quality and accurateness of the evaluated author's documents. As in the case of the reviewer network, the range of the trust values depends on the trust metric chosen. Authors are connected via an 'is-author' relationship with the documents they have written. Documents can be written by several persons. 'Is-author'-edges are not weighted. The structure of the document network is identical as in the first case: references connect the documents.

This two-layered architecture permits calculation of a trust-weighted visibility for each document in the document reference network. The idea is that the semantics of links will differ based on whether there is a trust or a distrust relationship between the citing and the cited author. This reflects the fact that a link can be set in different contexts. On the one hand, a link can affirm the authority, the importance, or the high quality of a document, for example the citing author confirms the results of the original work by his or her own experiments and therefore validates it. On the other, disagreement can be expressed in a link ranging from different opinions to suspicions that information is incorrect or even faked.

Several steps are required to compute the trust-weighted visibility:

1. Trust relationships between the authors of a citing and the cited paper are attributed to the reference between the documents in the document network. In the case of coauthorship, more than one trust value is available. Assuming that the opinions of coauthors do not vary extremely, the average of the trust values is attributed to the reference.

2. The trust values that are attributed to the references have to be transformed into edge weights, so an edge between two documents p_a and p_b has a weight $w_{a \to b}$, reflecting the relationship (trust) between the authors of the corresponding papers. This step is necessary as attributed trust values might be negative due to distrust between the authors. In a visibility function however, we need edge weights > 0. A mapping function defines how trust values are transferred into edge weights. Depending on the definition of the mapping function, different trust semantics can be realized. The mapping function can for instance be defined in a way that only such references are heavy weighted which express high trust whereas another definition could give a high weight to distrust values in order to get an overview on papers which are not appreciated in a certain community.

3. The trust-enhanced visibility of the documents can now be calculated by a visibility function that considers the edge weights. We illustrate this general framework by using a concrete visibility function for calculating the trust-weighted visibility, namely the PageRank. The original PageRank formula is modified such that each page p_i contributes not any longer with $\frac{vis_i}{|C_i|}$ (with C_i being the set of pages cited by p_i) to the visibility vis_d of another page p_d but distributes its visibility according to the edge weight, so we get:

$$vis_d = (1 - \alpha) \sum_{p_i \in R_d} \frac{w_{i \to d}}{\sum_{p_j \in C_k} w_{i \to j}} vis_i$$

This function can further be personalized so that it calculates individual recommendations for each user. It can also be adapted such that documents are highly ranked which are controversially discussed. This approach again is a general framework. Other visibility functions can be applied instead of the PageRank.

A Social Information Retrieval Case Study on Wikipedia

Having presented metrics of social and hyper-textual evaluation, we choose as a case study to model the authoritativeness of a system rich with social interactions such as Wikipedia. Wikipedia is based on wiki software (Leuf & Cunningham, 2001) and is considered one of the most successful collaborative editing projects on the Web since it currently contains over one million articles[13] and has an extensive community of contributors contributing content and improving the quality of the articles.

Traditional encyclopedias such us Britannica are often characterized with a high level of credibility by domain experts, taking into account the background process that has resulted (domain authorities contribute to the final outcome).

On the other hand, since it uses the WikiWiki system, Wikipedia allows the editing and creation of encyclopedic articles by anyone who wishes to contribute. Its primary target is to provide free editing access and gather knowledge representing the consensus of the term presented and thus not to evaluate the contributing authorities.

However, as the content increases along with the contributing sources (see Figure 1.2), a critical issue arises regarding the credibility of Wikipedia as an authoritative reference source (Lih, 2004; Lipczynska 2005). The question is extended not only to the outcome (article) but also to the process of shaping the article, in which a contributor would allow another authority to submit, change, or delete a contribution accepted or not accepted by him or her. Wikipedia has internal mechanisms of managing those cases such as a permission ranking system, where a contributor is accredited by the level of participation in the shaping of the article, as well as a discussion tab on most of the articles or notifications and warnings regarding the content.

Therefore Wikipedia is an ideal case for social information retrieval since its hyperlink context is attributing an ever-growing popularity with a set of disputes regarding the trustworthiness of its content and the expertise of the contributors in most of the articles.

Furthermore since it facilitates a large amount of social connections over a common affiliation, we consider it an interesting example to discuss authoritativeness over evolving documents.

In our case we consider the following social interactions:

- When a contributor edits content that has been submitted by someone else, then it establishes a tie with him or her. This is depicted by an acceptance factor which represents the percentage of the content of the previous contributor that is visible after.
- Every contributor that has a single or more contribution to the article establishes a relational tie with the other content contributors of the article. Evidence of participation in common projects strengthens this tie.

As can be seen in Figure 5, we define two different networks—the articles network and the contributors network—from where we can extract both the social and the hypertextual context for our case study.

Before continuing to the development of metrics, we need to further define the information sets from which we will extract the networks that will be provided as input to our metrics.

In the context of an encyclopedia, we define the following information sets:

- **Domain:** A collection of articles which tackle a common subject (e.g., philosophy).
- **Category:** A collection of domains which have a common categorical and etymological root. For example, the domains philosophy and economics have a kind of connection in the category of social sciences.

Within the above sets, the following network layers are defined:

- **The articles network:** Every article in Wikipedia contains references to other articles as well as external references. A set of links used for classification purposes is also available in most of the active articles of the encyclopedia. Every article represents a vertex in the article network and the internal connections between the articles the edges of the network.

- **The contributors network:** Wikipedia is a collaborative writing effort, which means that an article has multiple contributors. We assume that a contributor establishes a relationship with another contributor if they work on the same article. In the resulted weighted network, each contributor is represented by a vertex and their social ties (positive or negative) are represented by an edge, denoting the sequence of their social interaction. The contributors network relies on a set of directed and inferred relationships. In particular there is the direct tie (contributor X edits the content of the contributor Y) but also an inferred tie (contributor X and contributor Y work on the same article). This makes the importance of the contributors network higher since the content on the articles network relies much on the interaction by the member of the contributors network.

In this case study our focus is to examine a set of metrics for both social- and document-based relevance. However, both metrics must be able to be combined in order to extract an overall indicator of authoritativeness/trustworthiness. The development of those metrics is based on the following assumptions:

- The more decentralized the editing of an article, then the better this article represents a consensus about it.
- The contributors whose content has been most accepted (seen from the result of the diff operation in the wiki) are attributed a level of authority regarding the article.
- This level of authority remains only in the domain of the article. However, domains which belong in the same topic can retain the level of authority for a contributor.

The graph that we model is a signed directed network, with arcs signed as a factor depicting

Figure 5. Network layers in the Wiki publication model. Contributors are linked together by working on common projects (articles) in the same topic.

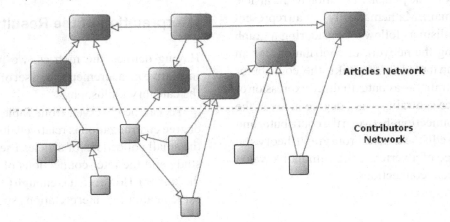

the level of acceptance of the content submitted by contributor *A* and accepted by contributor *B*. In order to model the authoritativeness of contributors, we selected the degree centrality. In our case study, we use the degree centrality index, which is the simplest definition of centrality and as mentioned is based on the incoming and outgoing adjacent connections to other contributors in an article graph. To measure the centrality at an individual level, we define the contributor degree centrality; and to an article level, the article degree centralization which represents the variability of contributor degree centrality over the specific article.

Contributor Degree Centrality

As already discussed, the inner degree (in a graph theoretic interpretation, the amount of edges coming into a node) represents the choices the actor has over a set of other actors. However, in our wiki network model, the amount of incoming edges represents edits to the text; therefore the metric of inner degree is the opposite, meaning that the person with the higher inner degree has the largest amount of objection/rejection in the contributor community and thus receives a kind of negative evaluation from his or her fellow contributors. On the other hand, the outer degree of the vertex represents edits/participation in several parts of the article and thus gives a clue to the activity of the person in relation to the article and the domain. Mathematically we can represent such formalism as follows. Considering a graph representing the network of contributors for an article contributed in the wiki, the contributor degree centrality—a contextualized expression of actor degree centrality—is a degree index of the adjacent connections between the contributor and others who edit the article. From graph theory, the outer degree of a vertex is the cumulative value of its adjacent connections:

$$C_D(n_i) = d(n_i) = \sum_j x_{ij}$$

The adjacent x_{ij} represents the relational tie between the contributors and their contribution over the domain of the article. This also is characterized by the visibility of the contribution in the final article and can be either 1 or 0. To provide the centrality, we divide the degree with the highest obtained degree from the graph, which in graph theory is proved to be the number of remaining vertices (g) minus the ego ($g - 1$). Therefore the contributor degree centrality can be calculated as an instance of the actor centrality index:

$$C'_D(n_i) = \frac{d(n_i)}{g - 1}$$

Article Degree Centralization

We define an article's degree centralization C_{DM} as the variability of the individual contributor centrality indices. The $C_D(n^*)$ represents the largest observed contributor degree centrality:

$$C_{DM} = \frac{\sum_i^g [C_D(n^*) - C_D(n_i)]}{(g - 1)(g - 2)}$$

Again we divide the variability with the highest variability observed in the graph in order to get a normalized calculation.

Interpretation of the Results

Having defined the metrics, we provide some indicative measurements for a set of articles from the category philosophy.

As can be observed from Table 5, the article degree centralization is relatively low because of the small collections of articles used in the case study and the inter-connections of the actors in the domain. However, it is enough to let us discuss some qualitative interpretations such as:

Table 4. Contributor degree centrality for the Wikipedia article "Immanuel Kant"

Cluster (Outerdegree)	Freq	Freq%	CumFreq	CumFreq%	Representative
1	1	0.4329	1	0.4329	65.6.92.153
2	199	86.1472	200	86.5801	82.3.32.71
4	14	6.0606	214	92.6407	80.202.248.28
6	6	2.5974	220	95.2381	Snowspinner
8	3	1.2987	223	96.5368	Tim Ivorson
10	1	0.4329	224	96.9697	StirlingNewberry
12	2	0.8658	226	97.8355	24.162.198.123
16	2	0.8658	228	98.7013	JimWae
18	1	0.4329	229	99.1342	Jjshapiro
20	1	0.4329	230	99.5671	SlimVirgin
31	1	0.4329 s	231	100	Amerindianart

Table 5. Articles used in the case study along with the number of contributors and their degree centralization

Article Name	Number of Contributors	Article Degree Centralization (max 1)
Adam Smith	276	0.039114
Aristotle	274	0.0232
Immanuel Kant	231	0.20484
Johann Wolfgang von Goethe	242	0.016682
John Locke	292	0.008581
Karl Marx	232	0.006601
Ludwig Wittgenstein	220	0.006328
Philosophy	280	0.00254
Plato	284	0.001207
Socrates	289	0.000405

- The dispersion of the actor indices denotes how dependent this article is on individual contributors. For instance, if an article has a very low degree of centralization, then it means that the social process to shape it was highly distributed, thus resulting in an article which has been submitted by multiple authorities. In our case, the articles represent a low degree of centralization, which means that contributions have been done by individuals with interests in other domains as well.

- The range of the group degree centralization reflects the heterogeneity of the authoring sources of the article. In our case, the article "Immanuel Kant" has a significantly higher degree of centralization, which means that it has been contributed by authorities most concentrated in the domain of the article who thus have contributed to other articles.

Contributors with higher inter-relation over the same domain represent higher authorities based on the assumptions that their interest spans the domain to which the article belongs, and therefore they have conducted background research regarding the material they have contributed. On the other hand contributors with lesser authority tend to have their content erased/objected by contributors with higher authority.

It should be noted that the measures developed and presented in this case study do not actually measure the "subjective" quality of an article since such a task is a cognitive process characterized by a high level of complexity.

Those measures can contribute in the direction of providing an indicator of "consensus" related to an article and thus assert that it does not provide controversial views or expressions of a small group of persons (especially in articles with political content). Thus a level of neutrality expressed in the writing of this article is asserted.

In the context of social-based information retrieval, those metrics can correlate with a degree of acceptance of the Wikipedia article by the domain experts and therefore provide a more valuable trustworthiness factor than traditional metrics that can measure only popularity and not trustworthiness.

CONCLUSION AND OUTLOOK

In this chapter we have provided background on backlink models, social network concepts, and their potential application to a combined model of Web retrieval that considers the links but also the relations between the creators of the documents and the links.

However, to incorporate the metrics discussed in this chapter, there must be a process that can provide a roadmap to that direction. The following steps highlight an abstract procedure on how to integrate information from a social network in the computation of document rankings:

1. Define the compositional and structural variables on both levels (actors, documents, and their connections),
2. Compute measures on the nodes (actors) of the social network and propagate them down to the nodes (documents) in the document network,
3. Propagate edge weights from the social network down to the corresponding edges of the document network to get weighted edges on the document network, or
4. Apply some ranking algorithm on the document network modified by 2 or 3 to compute social network enhanced rankings.

Current information retrieval models that use links to compute rankings as measures of the popularity of the Web pages fail to consider the social context that is tacit in the authorship of the pages and their links. Social network analysis provides sound models for dealing with these kind of models and can be combined with existing backlink models to come up with richer models.

Applying these steps gives improved ranking algorithms to build better search engines, which inherently integrate information about authors or reviewers of documents to provide better results. The algorithms described in this section therefore allow use of information about the authors of Web pages or about reviews from other users to build better information retrieval mechanisms. This also allows the identification of untrustworthy information, as information from unreliable sources and link spam.

However, research issues are open to the direction of applying such models in real context since information about the social context is something that is very difficult to extract and model. The Semantic Web can contribute to this direction by advancing the development and use of vocabularies that can express social relations in various ways and associate them with content. Nevertheless, privacy issues should be also considered since the expression of social relations in a publicly accessible information space is something that exhibits vulnerabilities in cases such as "phishing" attacks and social engineering (Levy, 2004).

REFERENCES

Avesani, P., Massa, P., & Tiella, R. (2005). A trust-enhanced recommender system application: Moleskiing. *Proceedings of the 20th ACM Symposium on Applied Computing,* Santa Fe, NM.

Baeza-Yates, R., & Ribeiro-Neto, B. (1999). *Modern information retrieval.* Harlow, UK: Addison-Wesley.

Berners-Lee, T., & Fischetti, M. (1999). *Weaving the Web: The original design and ultimate destiny of the World Wide Web by its inventor.* San Francisco: Harper.

Borner, K., Maru, J.T., & Goldstone, R.L. (2004). The simultaneous evolution of author and paper networks. *Proceedings of the National Academy of Sciences* (vol. 101, pp. 5266-5273).

Brickley, D., & Miller, L. (2005). *FOAF vocabulary specification.*

Brin, S., & Page, L. (1998). The anatomy of a large-scale hypertextual Web search engine. *Proceedings of the 7th International Conference on the World Wide Web,* Brisbane, Australia.

Brown, J.S., & Duguid, P. (2002). *The social life of information.* Boston: Harvard Business School Press.

Burt, R.S. (1980). Models of network structure. *Annual Review of Sociology, 6,* 79-141.

Conklin, J. (1987). Hypertext: An introduction and survey. *IEEE Computer, 20*(9), 17-41.

Dhyani, D., Keong, N.W., & Bhowmick, S.S. (2002). A survey of Web metrics. *ACM Computing Surveys, 34*(4), 469-503.

Faloutsos, C. (1985). Access methods for text. *ACM Computing Surveys, 17*(1), 49-74.

Freeman, L.C. (1979). Centrality in social networks: Conceptual clarification. *Social Networks, 1*(3), 215-239.

Friedkin, N.E. (1991). Theoretical foundations for centrality measures. *American Journal of Sociology, 96*(6), 1478-1504.

Friedkin, N.E. (1998). *A structural theory of social influence (structural analysis in the social sciences).* Cambridge: Cambridge University Press.

Garfield, E. (1972). Citation analysis as a tool in journal evaluation. *Science, 178*(4060), 471-479.

Golbeck, J., Parsia, B., & Hendler, J. (2003). Trust networks on the semantic Web. *Proceedings of Cooperative Intelligent Agents,* Helsinki, Finland.

Gyongyi, Z., Garcia-Molina, H., & Pedersen, J. (2004). Combating Web spam with TrustRank. *Proceedings of VLDB* (vol. 4).

Hess, C., Stein, K., & Schlieder, C. (2006). Trust-enhanced visibility for personalized document recommendations. *Proceedings of the 21st ACM Symposium on Applied Computing,* Dijon, France.

Hubbell, C.H. (1965). An input-output approach to clique identification. *Sociometry, 28*(4), 377-399.

Katz, L. (1953). A new status index derived from sociometric analysis. *Psychometrika, 18,* 39-43.

Kleinberg, J.M. (1999). Authoritative sources in a hyperlinked environment. *Journal of the ACM, 46*(5), 604-632.

Klyne, G., & Carroll, J.J. (2004). *Resource description framework (RDF): Concepts and abstract syntax.* W3C recommendation, World Wide Web Consortium.

Korfiatis, N., & Naeve, A. (2005). Evaluating wiki contributions using social networks: A case study on Wikipedia. *Proceedings of the 1st Online Conference on Metadata and Semantics Research* (MTSR'05). Rinton Press.

Leuf, B., & Cunningham, W. (2001). *The wiki way: Collaboration and sharing on the Internet.* San Francisco: Addison-Wesley Professional.

Levy, E. (2004). Criminals become tech savvy. *Security & Privacy Magazine, 2*(2), 65-68.

Leydesdorff, L. (2001). *The challenge of scientometrics: The development, measurement, and self-organization of scientific communications.* Universal.

Lih, A. (2004). Wikipedia as participatory journalism: Reliable sources? Metrics for evaluating collaborative media as a news resource. *Proceedings of the International Symposium on Online Journalism.*

Lipczynska S. (2005). Power to the people: The case for Wikipedia. *Reference Reviews, 19*(2).

Malsch, T., Schlieder, C., Kiefer, P., Lubcke, M., Perschke, R., Schmitt, M., & Stein, K. (2006). Communication between process and structure: Modeling and simulating message-reference-networks with COM/TE. *Journal of Artificial Societies and Social Simulation.*

Mathes, A. (2005). *Filler Friday: Google bombing.* Retrieved May 27, 2006, from *http://uber.nu/2001/04/06/*

Page, L., Brin, S., Motwani, R., & Winograd, T. (1998). *The PageRank citation ranking: Bringing order to the Web.* Technical Report, Stanford Digital Library Technologies Project, USA.

Pinski, G., & Narin, F. (1976). Citation influence for journal aggregates of scientific publications: Theory, with application to the literature of physics. *Information Processing and Management, 12*(5), 297-312.

Sabidussi, G. (1966). The centrality index of a graph. *Psychometrika, 31,* 581-603.

Scott, J. (2000). *Social network analysis: A handbook* (2nd Ed.). London/Thousands Oaks, CA: Sage.

Sicilia, M.A., & Garcia, E. (2005). Filtering information with imprecise social criteria: A FOAF-based backlink model. *Proceedings of the 4th Conference of the European Society for Fuzzy Logic and Technology* (EUSLAT), Barcelona, Spain.

Stein, K., & Hess, C. (2006). Information retrieval in trust-enhanced document networks. In Behrendt et al. (Eds.), *Semantics, Web and mining.* Berlin: Springer-Verlag.

Wolf, J.L., Squillante, M.S., Yu, P.S., Sethuraman, J., & Ozsen, L. (2002). Optimal crawling strategies for Web search engines. *Proceedings of the 11th International Conference on the World Wide Web* (pp. 136-147), Honolulu, HI.

Ziegler, C.N., & Lausen, G. (2004). Spreading activation models for trust propagation. *Proceedings of the IEEE International Conference on E-Technology, E-Commerce and E-Service* (EEE04), Taipei, Taiwan.

ENDNOTES

[1] With the term backlink, we refer to the backwards reference given to an object by another referring object. The most well-known type of a backlink is the citation provided to scientific articles and scholarly work.

[2] Technically a document reference network is a graph with documents as nodes and references (links) as directed edges. The visibility of a node is determined by analyzing the link structure.

3   The basic idea of this algorithm goes back to Seelay (1949), who used it in sociometrics (first published in Katz, 1953), but without normalization by the number of outgoing edges and without damping term (which was introduced by Hubbell, 1965).

4   We do not really know how Google does its ranking. They claim that their ranking algorithm is based on PageRank with modifications.

5   For the technical details, see Brin and Page (1998).

6   There is no obvious reason not to use the hub and authority approach for off-line calculation on the whole Net. There are search engines claiming to use a HITS-based algorithm, but without giving detailed information.

7   Also patented by Google.

8   Unaffiliated means that they do not belong to the same organization. This is determined by comparing URLs, IP addresses, and network topology.

9   See the Proceedings of the 1st FOAF Workshop, Galway.

10 The trust ontology is available at *http://trust. mindswap.org/ont/trust.owl* (last access date: May 30).

11 Although distrust statements are difficult to handle in propagation: Should I trust someone who is distrusted by someone I distrust? Or should I distrust this person even more?

12 Statistics and data for the English Language Wikipedia. For further information about the current size of Wikipedia, the reader can visit: *http://en.wikipedia.org/wiki/Wikipedia:Statistics* (last access date: May 30, 2006).

Chapter VII
From PageRank to Social Rank:
Authority-Based Retrieval in Social Information Spaces

Sebastian Marius Kirsch
University of Bonn, Germany

Melanie Gnasa
University of Bonn, Germany

Markus Won
University of Bonn, Germany

Armin B. Cremers
University of Bonn, Germany

ABSTRACT

Social information spaces are characterized by the presence of a social network between participants. In this chapter we present methods for utilizing social networks for information retrieval by applying graph authority measures to the social network. We show how to integrate authority measures in an information retrieval algorithm. In order to determine the suitability of the described algorithms, we examine the structure and statistical properties of social networks, and present examples of social networks as well as evaluation results.

INTRODUCTION

While the core concepts of information retrieval have been traced back as far as 4,000 years by some authors (Manber, 1992), the field itself is comparatively recent. The development of automated information retrieval systems has always been closely tied to available computing power. As increasing amounts of data and processing power become available, new methods are being developed which utilize these resources for information retrieval—often drawing on ideas or concepts that are much older. For example, the field of Web retrieval, one of the largest applications of information retrieval at the moment, did not exist until the Web itself (Berners-Lee, Cailliau, Luotonen, Nielsen, & Secret, 1994) was invented. At the same time, the most prominent methods for Web retrieval (Page, Brin, Motwani, & Winograd, 1999) draw upon ideas developed in related fields decades earlier (Pinski & Narin, 1976).

On the other hand, the idea of finding information using social relations and social networks is an ancient one. Indeed, before the advent and ubiquitous availability of modern communication media, it was the only method of finding information: If one wanted to know something, one had to ask someone—an acquaintance, a friend, or the reference desk librarian. Being well connected in the social network of one's peers was of paramount importance to ensure that one stayed well informed about current events. Scores of letters exchanged between scientists in the last centuries are testimony of the importance of communication and social relations for scientific work.

Closely connected is the idea of social rank and of authority. It is not only important how many people one knows, but also to know the right people—in order to be able to ask the right questions to the right people, and in order to get the right answers. Well-connected people are also crucial for disseminating information and spreading new ideas.

When communication networks—precursors of the Internet such as the ARPANET or Usenet—were invented, one of their first purposes was communication not between machines, but between users: electronic mail, newsgroups, and real-time communication. The cost of interacting with many people sank dramatically, and this made e-mail one of the "killer applications" for the budding computer networks.

Social Networks, Social Information Spaces, and Social Information Retrieval

Social networks become increasingly interesting with the shift of computer systems away from devices for computation towards communication media. Although social networks exist without any computer support, in recent years many different networks were formed, using the Internet as their main platform.

Besides a shared interest, the formation of social networks in real life is often determined by external factors—age, sex, geography, or a crucial experience (e.g., relocation or war.) Since virtual networks or communities are unconstrained by such external factors, the shared interest becomes a predominant determinant. The participants' identification with the group and the group's self-made norms also play an important role (see Dholakia, Bagozzi, & Klein Pearo, 2004).

The earliest applications of computer networks were electronic mail, mailing lists, and discussion boards. Especially in recent years, the World Wide Web shifted from content provision towards an interactive information space. Content (information) is not only provided by the providers of Web sites. Technologies like Wikis (Fuchs-Kittowski & Köhler, 2005), blogs (e.g., BlogSpot), or community support systems provide mechanisms that allow every user to add or change the content of this information space, with respect to access rights and correct authorization. We collectively refer to those interaction-enabling technologies as "Web 2.0" or the "social Web."

Technology serves as a new basis for a much older concept: social networks. People who share the same interests form a group. They know people within the group and share information with each other.

The glue that keeps them together is trustworthiness. Information given by a known person is trusted more than the one given by unknown people. In particular, those feelings of trust can be enhanced in a transitive way: if somebody knows someone who gives important information, both relationships between these three people hold for a certain reliability of information that is passed along this path.

The simplest kind of community is one where all members know each other. As a community grows—since normally every person knows somebody who is unknown to some others—we find that there are some members who can be seen as the "inner circle" (with many contacts within the community) or as relation-spreading hubs (Granovetter, 1973), and others who are not as well integrated. The members and the connections between them define the structure of a community. (Knowledge communities are a special kind of social network with the main idea that information is passed between their members.)

The exchange between experts (scientists, business people, etc.) has changed in many ways since the World Wide Web has become part of daily life. Now communities become virtual, which means that the community is built on the Web as a platform, and members of the community may be geographically dispersed all over the world (Wenger & Snyder, 2000; Lueg, Davenport, Robertson, & Pipek, 2001). The main ideas (as described above) stay the same, but new problems due to the geographically distributed structure of the community arise. Missing trust between the members of a community is the result. New concepts as awareness (Won & Pipek, 2004) must be developed and integrated in community systems. The intention here is to inform members about the activities within the community. (Activities within a virtual community normally are communication activities.) Knowledge about other members' activities seems to be the first precondition to provide confidence in the community.

As one can see the ties between members within a community differ in intensity. This degree of relationship between two members can be measured by different aspects, for example the intensity of communication between them,

the similarity of interests, and the similarity of the circle of friends.

In a community support system, high-intensity links can be used to assess the importance of information for a member. The more members strongly linked to a certain person are interested in a piece of information, the more—so we assume—this piece of information might be important for this person. In this way, if somebody searches for a special piece information, the search result may be ranked according to whether this piece of information was relevant for his or her colleagues or not. Here, we used some significant characteristics (ties between members) for assessing information. We call this *social network analysis* on a micro level.

Furthermore, the existence of communities and ties between people who work within the information space can be used for similar analyses which work on the macro level. As Granovetter (1973) stated, *weak ties* are particularly important for information dissemination and diffusion. Whereas *strong ties* are governed by external factors such as family relationships, weak ties depend on shared interests and social compatibility. They are therefore a stronger indication of an individual's personality and characteristics, which in turn makes them more useful for information retrieval purposes. Since an individual can have disproportionately more weak ties than strong ties, weak ties also facilitate the information flow between communities.

Information retrieval can be enriched by analyzing those social ties, especially the weak ties. We can liken social network analysis to adding a new dimension to information retrieval: conventional information retrieval algorithms mostly work representations of the retrievable content (the documents) and of the user's information needs (the queries.) This is a rather narrow view in that ignores important aspects of the creation and usage of information: information is produced and consumed by individuals, and an individual's information usage does not occur in a social vacuum. Most individuals are connected to other like-minded people in a social network. Analyzing these relations allows for a deeper understanding of the environment in which information is produced. For example, we can connect documents to their authors. By analyzing the social network of the author, we can connect him to other authors, who are in turn connected to their documents. In this example, social network analysis provides locality and context for a document. Other approaches may ignore other authors' documents and concentrate on the social network in order to extract information helping to rank a document. (One such approach is described in this chapter.)

A depiction of the entities and relations partaking in social information retrieval is found in Figure 1. The lower tier represents the domain of conventional information retrieval—documents, queries, and the relations between them. The upper tier represents social network analysis, which concerns itself with individuals and their relations with each other. By combining the two levels, new relations become apparent: relations between individuals and pieces of information. Of course, this model only lists a subset of all possible relations between individuals, documents, and queries, and any given social retrieval system will only use a subset of relations.

Social information retrieval adds these relations to the domain models and uses them to improve retrieval effectiveness. In the following sections, we describe how those analyses can be integrated into information retrieval and so form the idea of social information retrieval.

Examples of Social Media

We already mentioned examples of social media in the preceding sections; in this section, we explore their characteristics and suitability for social information retrieval in more depth. Since social retrieval depends on certain characteristics of the corpus—in particular on the presence of a social network—it is important to know the corpus.

Figure 1. A domain model for social information retrieval, listing entities, and possible relations between them

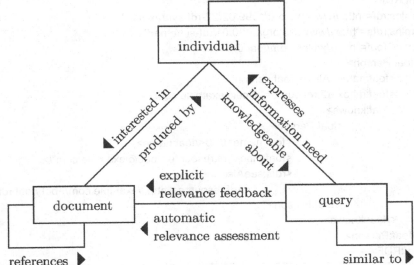

Electronic *mailing lists* and *newsgroups* were among the earliest applications for computer networks. They are still among the most prominent communication media, though their importance is waning with the rise of *Web-based discussion forums* and *chat rooms*. Their characteristics are sufficiently similar to subsume them all under the term "electronic messaging systems." Mailing lists and newsgroups are a fertile ground for social retrieval techniques, because of the sheer amount of information exchanged via those media. The importance of retrieval systems for these media is further exacerbated by the fact that the information published via them is very often not re-published in a more suitable or accessible form on the Web. Archives of mailing lists and newsgroups are easily available via several repositories on the Internet; authorship information and social relations between authors (as formed via public communication) can be extracted from header lines in a straightforward way.

The World Wide Web in its current association is not a social medium in the sense that it fulfills the requirements for social information retrieval: there is currently no method for extracting authorship information or social networks between the authors of Web pages from the Web at large. Nevertheless, we can identify several subsets of the Web which contain the necessary information and are suitable for social information retrieval.

The goal of the *Semantic Web* (Berners-Lee, Hendler, & Lassila, 2001) is to provide a standard way for publishing information on the Web with precise, machine-readable semantics. This goal is accomplished using a standardized information interchange format, XML (eXtensible Markup Language), as well as knowledge representation languages defined using this interchange format, such as RDF (Resource Description Framework) and OWL (Web Ontology Language). Vocabularies and ontologies defined using these knowledge representation languages are then used to define objects and classes with precisely defined seman-

Figure 2. An XML fragment using the Friend-Of-A-Friend schema. This XML fragment establishes the existence of a person called "Alice" with an e-mail address of "alice@example.com," and expresses the fact that Alice knows a person called "Bob" with e-mail address "bob@example.com." Further information about Bob is published under the address "http://example.com/~bob/foaf.rdf."

```
<rdf:RDF
  xmlns:rdf="http://www.w3.org/1999/02/22-rdf-syntax-ns#"
  xmlns:rdfs="http://www.w3.org/2000/01/rdf-schema#"
  xmlns:foaf="http://xmlns.com/foaf/0.1/">
  <foaf:Person>
    <foaf:name>Alice</foaf:person>
    <foaf:mbox rdf:resource="alice@example.com"/>
    <foaf:knows>
      <foaf:Person>
        <foaf:name>Bob</foaf:name>
        <foaf:mbox rdf:resource="bob@example.com"/>
        <rdfs:seeAlso
          rdf:resource="http://example.com/~bob/foaf.rdf"/>
      </foaf:Person>
    </foaf:knows>
  </foaf:Person>
</rdf:RDF>
```

Figure 3. An XML fragment linking a document to its author, using the Dublin Core metadata vocabulary and the Friend-of-a-Friend schema

```
<rdf:RDF
  xmlns:rdf="http://www.w3.org/1999/02/22-rdf-syntax-ns#"
  xmlns:rdfs="http://www.w3.org/2000/01/rdf-schema#"
  xmlns:dc="http://purl.org/dc/elements/1.1/"
  xmlns:foaf="http://xmlns.com/foaf/0.1/">
  <rdf:Description rdf:about="http://www.example.com/~alice/">
      <dc:title>Alice's Homepage</dc:title>
      <dc:creator>
            <foaf:Person>
                    <foaf:name>Alice</foaf:name>
                    <foaf:mbox rdf:resource="alice@example.com" />
                    <rdfs:seeAlso rdf:resource="http://www.example.com/~alice/foaf.rdf" />
            </foaf:Person>
      </dc:creator>
  </rdf:Description>
</rdf:RDF>
```

tics and relations. One such vocabulary is the FOAF standard (Brickley & Libby, 2005), which contains an ontology for describing individuals and relations between them. An example of a FOAF description is found in Figure 2. Similarly, the Dublin Core standard (Dublin Core Metadata Initiative, 2005) contains a vocabulary for attaching metadata to documents, and in particular for expressing authorship of a document (see Figure 3 for an example). Combined, these two standards allow us to describe relations between documents and individuals, as well as between individuals, in a machine-readable manner on the Web.

Web logs or *blogs* are Web sites that continually publish new articles and as such are a kind of online diary—written either by a single individual or by a group of people. Blogs usually allow interaction between users either by comments or by so-called "trackback links," which are links from one person's blog to an article on another blog. Authorship information must usually be extracted from the documents using information extraction techniques, and social relationships must be inferred from comments and trackbacks. Some blog services, for example LiveJournal (Six Apart Ltd., 2005), already provide this information in machine-readable form.

A *wiki* is a collaborative authoring system distinguished by the fact that it welcomes contributions from users by allowing every user of the system to create, edit, and delete content at will. The first wiki, called WikiWikiWeb from the Hawaiian word for "quick," was created in 1995 by Ward Cunningham as a supplement to the Portland Pattern Repository, a Web site about software design patterns. Most wiki implementations keep a log of a document's history, recording the author and the changes made to a document. Social relations can be inferred by coauthorship or by communication via special "talk" pages.

STATISTICAL PROPERTIES OF SOCIAL NETWORKS

The preceding section introduced social networks and motivated their application for information retrieval. In this section, we introduce basic notation for modeling social networks as graphs. We also define measures that allow us to character-

Figure 4. An example of a social network comprising five individuals

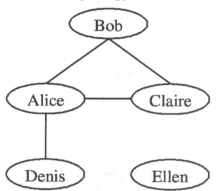

ize the structure of graphs in a concise manner. Social networks differ from other naturally occurring and artificial networks in a number of key characteristics, some of which are described at the end of the chapter.

These models and characteristics are key to developing retrieval algorithms which utilize social networks, as they allow us to draw parallels between social networks and related areas of information retrieval.

Notation and Terminology

Social networks are usually modeled as graphs. A *graph G* consists of a set of *vertices V* (also called *nodes*) representing individuals, and a set of edges *E* connecting the nodes. In the example in Figure 4, we see a set of nodes consisting of five individuals: Alice, Bob, Claire, Denis, and Ellen. The edges connecting these individuals represent social relationships: Alice has a social tie (e.g., a friendship or an acquaintanceship) with Bob and Claire, Denis has a social tie with Alice, and so on.

When modeling social networks, one often assumes that edges are *undirected,* meaning that if Alice has a social tie with Bob, then Bob also has a social tie with Alice. While this is a valid assumption, it is not always appropriate; for example, people with a different social rank may have differing views on what constitutes a social

tie. A student may consider himself acquainted with his professor, while the professor may not consider this passing acquaintance a social tie. In a *directed* graph, edges have a direction: If Alice considers Bob a friend, this does not imply that Bob considers Alice a friend.

One may also attach a *weight* to edges in a graph; weights are usually positive numbers. When modeling social networks, weights are used to model the strength of a relationship: a passing acquaintance has a lower weight than an intimate friendship. However, it is often difficult to measure the strength of a relationship and convert it to a numerical value that allows for comparisons. For example, one may still feel a very strong bond to a person one meets only once a year.

The example in Figure 4 is unweighted and undirected. Directed and weighted graphs have a greater expressive power. Undirected graphs can be converted to directed graphs by substituting every undirected edge by two directed edges. Unweighted graphs can be converted to weighted graphs by attaching a unit weight to each edge.

The *degree δ* of a node is the number of edges incident to it. For directed graphs, one often distinguishes between the *in-degree δ^-* (the number of edges terminating at the node) and the *out-degree δ^+* (the number of edges starting at the node.)

A *path* is a sequence of edges so that the endpoint of each edge of the path is the starting point of the next edge. The *length* of a path is the number of edges on the path. The *shortest path* between two nodes is a path with the minimum number of edges, or the minimal sum of edge weights for weighted graphs.

A *connected component* of an undirected graph is a subgraph so that there exists a path between each pair of nodes in the subgraph. A *weak component* of a directed graph is a subgraph so that the corresponding subgraph in the underlying undirected graph is connected.

The *adjacency matrix* of a graph with nodes $v_1,...,v_n$ is an $n{\times}n$ matrix with a value of 1 in row i and column j if there exists an edge from v_i to v_j (or the weight of the edge for weighted graphs), and a value of 0 otherwise.

Measures for Graphs

Looking beyond the level of individual nodes and edges, there are a number of measures which describe a graph's macroscopic properties.

When talking about paths in a graph, one is usually interested in the shortest paths between two nodes. The *average shortest path length* is the average length of all shortest paths between any two nodes in a graph; in network terms, it measures the average number of "hops" needed to get from one node in the network to another. The *diameter* of a graph is the maximum length of a shortest path and is therefore the maximum number of "hops" needed to connect two nodes. Since the distance between two nodes that cannot be reached from each other is customarily defined as infinity, it usually only makes sense to measure the diameter of one component of the graph.

For graphs that consist of more than one component, one may be interested in the size of the largest component. Random graph theory predicts that graphs with more than log n edges per node for a graph with n nodes will have a single *giant connected component,* with the other components being on a lower order of magnitude compared to the giant component.

Typical Properties of Social Networks

The statistical properties of social networks deviate from purely random networks in a number of ways, some of which are shared with other naturally occurring networks. Since these statistical properties influence the design of algorithms for social retrieval, we review some of them in this section.

The fact that social networks tend to have a very short average shortest path length is by now well known beyond the circle of sociologists and network analysts, having been the subject of numerous scientific and popular articles as well as a play. On average, if two individuals in a social network can be connected by a chain of acquaintances, these chains tend to be rather short—less than 10—even in networks with millions of participants. Milgram (1967) coined the term "small world" for this property. The largest chains of acquaintances—the *diameter* of the social network—tend to be comparatively short too. This property places a limit on the usefulness of algorithms that explore a social network by traversing social ties: after a few steps, most of the network will be explored.

On the other hand, the low average shortest path length makes social networks ideal for information dissemination, as information will reach most of the network in just a few steps. In fact, this property is shared by communication networks such as the Internet, or neural networks.

Social networks also tend to be highly clustered. If Alice has two friends, Bob and Claire, there is a high likelihood that Bob and Claire also know each other. This situation is psychologically desirable, since it allows Alice to spend time with Bob and Claire at the same time, thus strengthening two social ties at the same time, instead of dividing her time between her two friends. This high degree of clustering also accounts for a sense of community and a sense of locality in the social network for the individual.

Figure 5. The degree distribution of a social network with 1,277 individuals, derived from a mailing list corpus, plotted on a linear scale on the left (a) and on a doubly logarithmic scale on the right (b). The dashed line is a power-law distribution $Pr(\delta(v)=k) \sim k^{-\gamma}$ with $\gamma \approx 1.09$.

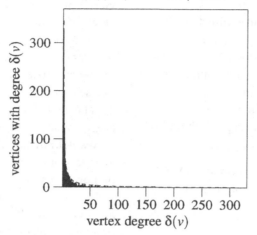

The degree distribution of a graph is the probability for a node to have a given degree. Random networks have a degree distribution which follows the Poisson distribution. In difference, the degree distributions of social networks tend to follow a power law: the probability of a node having degree k is proportional to $k^{-\gamma}$. This implies that the vast majority of nodes will have a very low degree, while a few nodes will have a very high degree. An example of such a degree distribution is shown in Figure 5.

This degree distribution has been found to be typical for a number of naturally occurring networks; several models currently exist that explain this distribution, one of the first being the "preferential attachment model" by Barabási and Albert (1999). In a social networks, the high-degree nodes serve as multipliers for information dissemination.

The increasing availability of data about large networks has led to a boom in social network analysis since the mid-1990s. Whereas previously, processing power and data availability limited social network analysis to several hundred or thousand nodes, the largest currently researched networks contain millions of participants. Co-

authorship networks compiled from databases of scientific publications contain more than two million participants (Newman, 2001). Data about movie actors is available for download from the Internet Movie DataBase (http://www.imdb/com) and contains about one million actors.

A number of other large networks have statistical properties similar to those of social networks. Examples of such networks are communication networks such as the Internet, the power grid, or neural networks. Of particular interest for information retrieval is the *Web graph*—the network of Web pages linking to each other. Current Web search engines index in excess of eight billion Web pages; experiments concerning the graph structure of the Web were performed on subsets of more than two hundred million Web pages—several orders of magnitude larger than currently available social networks.

GRAPH AUTHORITY MEASURES ON SOCIAL NETWORKS

While the graph model is an elegant and natural model for social networks, it is limited in its applications for information retrieval. In a graph, a single node is characterized not only by its intrinsic properties, but also by its relation to other nodes—and transitively by the relations of its neighboring nodes to other nodes. Ultimately, the whole network must be taken into account in order to characterize a single node.

The field of *associative retrieval* concerns itself with information retrieval on graphs. A number of information retrieval systems working directly on a graph structure have been proposed and implemented (e.g., Salton, 1963). The *spreading activation search* algorithm is a prominent technique in this field (Preece, 1981; see also Crestani, 1997, for an overview of spreading activation in information retrieval). However, none of these systems has seen widespread adoption to date.

Because graphs are rather unwieldy in this respect, it is desirable to characterize a node in relation to the whole graph by a single attribute, which can be attached to the node itself. *Graph authority measures* represent a class of techniques for this purpose. Authority measures assign a numeric measure of importance to each node according to its position in the graph.

We can broadly distinguish between local authority measures and global measures. Local measures take only the node and its immediate neighbors into account, while global measures use the complete graph for determining the authority measure.

Local Authority Measures

An example of a local authority measure is the number of neighbors of a node (its *degree*); for directed graphs, one may distinguish between the number of edges starting from a node (its *out-degree*) and the edges terminating in a node (its *in-degree*). For weighted graphs, one may sum over the weights of the starting or terminating edges and use this sum as an authority measure.

As described above, the importance of a graph depends not only on its neighbors, but also transitively on more distant nodes. Therefore, local measures are limited in their expressivity.

Global Authority Measures

Global authority measures alleviate this problem of expressivity by taking more than the immediate neighbors of a node into account. Global authority measures can be subdivided into graph-based methods and spectral methods. Whereas graph-based measures use properties of the graph such as path lengths, spectral measures use properties of the adjacency matrix or derived matrices.

An example of a graph-based measure is the *centrality* of a node. Centrality is the average length of shortest paths from a node to all other nodes. In other words, centrality answers the question: Given a node, how many steps does it take on average to reach any of the other nodes in the graph by the shortest possible path? This measure has been widely used to determine the center of a social network (see, e.g., Smeaton, Keogh, Gurrin, McDonald, & Sodring, 2002) or the "Oracle of Bacon at Virginia," a Web site analyzing the collaboration network of movie actors..

The *betweenness centrality* (Freeman, 1979) is a related definition of centrality. Betweenness is the sum of the probabilities for all pairs of nodes that a shortest path between them passes through the given node: For any two nodes, there may be a number of shortest paths connecting them, all having the same length. A given node may lie on some of these shortest paths, but not on others. The betweenness of a node can be seen as the sum of the probabilities that a given node would participate in an exchange or communication between two other nodes (presuming that the messages would indeed be routed through the graph by the shortest path).

Because both centrality measures are based on the notion of shortest paths between nodes, they fall short in environments where a shortest path between two nodes may not exist. In real-world social networks, which tend to be composed of several components, one usually has to restrict them to the largest connected component. Likewise, one usually applies them to the underlying undirected graph for directed social networks.

While these measures of authority are widely used in social network analysis, the related fields of bibliometrics and, by extension, Web retrieval have developed more sophisticated authority measures. These measures do not work on the graph itself, but on its adjacency matrix, or matrices derived from the adjacency matrix. Since they use linear algebra methods, in particular eigenvector decomposition, on these matrices, we call them *spectral methods*.

In bibliometrics, authority rankings are used as a "measure of standing" for an individual publication, for the importance of a journal, or even the scientific community of a country. When measuring the importance of a publication based on how often it is cited by other publications, it quickly becomes apparent that this simple count is not sufficient: some citations, for example citations from seminal works, are more important than others.

This leads to the following self-referential definition of authority: A publication is authoritative if it is cited by many authoritative publications. While this definition may seem strange at first, it forms the basis of one of the most prominent authority measures in information retrieval, the *PageRank algorithm* (Page et al., 1999) for Web retrieval. We will examine this algorithm in detail in the following section.

The PageRank Web Authority Measure

Web authority measures like PageRank are a way of solving the *abundance problem* (Kleinberg, 1999) of Web retrieval: among billions of Web pages, millions of which match the search keywords, how to find high-quality pages that answer the user's question? Web authority measures try to solve this problem by treating links from one page to another as a vote of confidence (or authority) for the page that is linked to. If many other pages link to a specific page, it is likely to be of a high quality—if not, why would the authors of the linking pages care to include a link?

The simplest Web authority measure is the number of pages linking to a page: the in-degree mentioned previously. PageRank takes an approach based on the idea of different pages having different amounts of authority proposed in the last section.

PageRank assumes that there is only a fixed amount of authority that is distributed among all pages. At the start of the algorithm, all pages have the same amount of authority. In each iteration, every page distributes its own authority equally among all pages it links to and receives authority from all pages that link to it. If the authority can percolate freely from any page to any other page (i.e., the underlying graph is ergodic), the amount of authority of each page will stabilize after a few iterations.

This principle can be generalized to other kinds of graphs. Given is a graph G with a set of nodes $V=\{v_1,...,v_n\}$, edges $E\subseteq V\times V$, edge weights c_{ij} for the edge between node v_i and v_j and a PageRank vector $r=(r_1,...,r_n)$. Before the first iteration, the PageRank vector is initialized with $r^0=(\frac{1}{n},...,\frac{1}{n})$. In each iteration, its components are updated according to:

$$r_i^{t+1} = \sum_{(v_j,v_i)\in E} \frac{c_{ij}r_j^t}{\sum_{(v_j,v_k)\in E} c_{jk}}$$

until the vector converges. If not every node in the graph can be reached from every other node, this computation is not guaranteed to converge. In order to ameliorate this problem, one usually adds a fixed amount of authority to each node in every iteration, while proportionally decreasing the amount received via incoming edges:

$$r_i^{t+1} = \frac{\epsilon}{n} + (1-\epsilon) \sum_{(v_j,v_i)\in E} \frac{c_{ij}r_j^t}{\sum_{(v_j,v_k)\in E} c_{jk}}$$

ϵ is usually set to a value between 0.1 and 0.3, depending on how far the graph deviates from the assumption that every node is reachable from every other node.

We call PageRank a spectral method because the PageRank vector is the maximal eigenvector of a matrix derived from the adjacency matrix of the graph: Let M be a row-normalized version of the adjacency matrix A:

$$(M)_{ij} \frac{(A)_{ij}}{\sum_k (A)_{ik}}$$

Then the PageRank vector $\mathbf{r}$ is the maximal eigenvector of:

$$\left(\frac{\epsilon}{n} \mathbf{1} + (1-\epsilon)M \right)^T$$

The PageRank algorithm given above is an application of the *power method* for computing the maximal eigenvector of a matrix. When computed with this algorithm, the sum of the components of the PageRank vector is 1.

Figure 6 shows a PageRank computation for an example of a social network. As expected, Alice has the highest PageRank value, followed by Bob and Claire with identical values, since they have the same place in the topology of the graph. The disconnected member of the network, Ellen, has the lowest PageRank value. The PageRank vector has been scaled so that the average of its values is 1. We can confirm that the PageRank vector is indeed an eigenvector of the matrix by multiplying it with the matrix.

A more realistic example of social networks are scientific coauthorship networks. In such a network, individuals are linked with each other if they have jointly published a scientific article. When applying the PageRank algorithm to the coauthorship network of the proceedings of the first 25 years of the ACM SIGIR conference, the following authors attain the highest PageRank values:

Figure 6. A step-by-step PageRank computation for an example of a social network

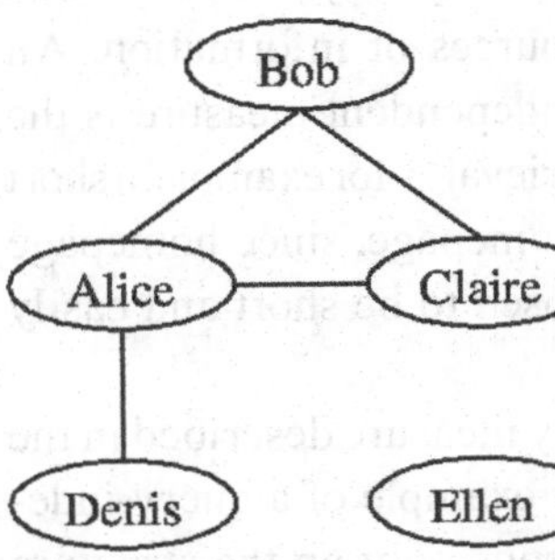

$$
\begin{pmatrix}
0 & 1 & 1 & 1 & 0 \\
1 & 0 & 1 & 0 & 0 \\
1 & 1 & 0 & 0 & 0 \\
1 & 0 & 0 & 0 & 0 \\
0 & 0 & 0 & 0 & 0
\end{pmatrix}
\Rightarrow
\begin{pmatrix}
0 & \frac{1}{3} & \frac{1}{3} & \frac{1}{3} & 0 \\
\frac{1}{2} & 0 & \frac{1}{2} & 0 & 0 \\
\frac{1}{2} & \frac{1}{2} & 0 & 0 & 0 \\
1 & 0 & 0 & 0 & 0 \\
\frac{1}{5} & \frac{1}{5} & \frac{1}{5} & \frac{1}{5} & \frac{1}{5}
\end{pmatrix}
\Rightarrow
$$

adjacency matrix · row-normalized

$$
\begin{pmatrix}
\frac{1}{15} & \frac{13}{45} & \frac{13}{45} & \frac{13}{45} & \frac{1}{15} \\
\frac{2}{5} & \frac{1}{15} & \frac{2}{5} & \frac{1}{15} & \frac{1}{15} \\
\frac{2}{5} & \frac{2}{5} & \frac{1}{15} & \frac{1}{15} & \frac{1}{15} \\
\frac{11}{15} & \frac{1}{15} & \frac{1}{15} & \frac{1}{15} & \frac{1}{15} \\
\frac{1}{5} & \frac{1}{5} & \frac{1}{5} & \frac{1}{5} & \frac{1}{5}
\end{pmatrix}
\Rightarrow
\begin{pmatrix}
\frac{1}{15} & \frac{2}{5} & \frac{2}{5} & \frac{11}{15} & \frac{1}{5} \\
\frac{13}{45} & \frac{1}{15} & \frac{2}{5} & \frac{1}{15} & \frac{1}{5} \\
\frac{13}{45} & \frac{2}{5} & \frac{1}{15} & \frac{1}{15} & \frac{1}{5} \\
\frac{13}{45} & \frac{1}{15} & \frac{1}{15} & \frac{1}{15} & \frac{1}{5} \\
\frac{1}{15} & \frac{1}{15} & \frac{1}{15} & \frac{1}{15} & \frac{1}{5}
\end{pmatrix}
\Rightarrow
\begin{pmatrix}
1.63 \\
1.12 \\
1.12 \\
0.75 \\
0.38
\end{pmatrix}
$$

with teleport ($\varepsilon = \frac{1}{3}$) · transposed · dom. eigenvector

Rank	Name	PageRank Score
1.	Bruce W. Croft	7.929
2.	Clement T. Yu	4.716
3.	James P. Callan	4.092
4.	Norbert Fuhr	3.731
5.	Susan T. Dumais	3.731
6.	Mark Sanderson	3.601
7.	Nicholas J. Belkin	3.518
8.	Vijay V. Raghavan	3.303
9.	James Allan	3.200
10.	Jan O. Pederson	3.135

PageRank scores were computed for $\epsilon=0.3$ and were normalized. We see that the PageRank algorithm indeed manages to identify 10 of the most authoritative authors in the field of information retrieval during the last 25 years.

SOCIAL INFORMATION RETRIEVAL WITH GRAPH AUTHORITY MEASURES

A graph authority measure on a social network as described in the previous section assigns an authority score to each individual. It is not immediately obvious to what end this can be used for information retrieval, since in information retrieval we are usually not interested in finding a particular individual; instead, we want to find documents. Conventional information retrieval algorithms assign authority or relevance scores to documents rather than individuals.

We can use the idea that an author's authority is indicative of the quality of his documents, by assigning authority scores to documents based on authorship. How to do this depends on the corpus we use. When each document has exactly one author, we can simply assign this author's authority score to the document; this is the case

for messages on mailing lists, for example. When a document has multiple authors, for example a scientific publication, there are several possibilities: We can use the maximum authority score of the authors, the minimum authority score, or an average of the scores. In environments where we can determine how much a single author contributed to a document, we can also use a weighted average. This is the case in collaborative authoring environments such as wikis, where one may count the number of edits made on a document by each author or the number of changed lines.

When retrieving relevant documents as regards a query, information retrieval systems can combine different kinds of information about a document. Pure text retrieval systems use only the content to find relevant documents. In a hyperlinked environment such as the Web, a search engine uses link-related information, for example the anchor text used in the linking pages—indeed, this anchor text is often a better indicator of a document's topic than the content of the document itself.

While the last two sources of evidence depend on the content of the query, there also exist *query-independent* sources of information. An example of a query-independent measure is the URL length in Web retrieval—for example, a short URL can indicate a homepage, since homepage URLs are usually chosen to be short and easily memorizable.

The social authority measure described in the last section is another example of a query-independent score: it depends only on the structure of the social network and the document's author, but not on the query.

In order to produce a ranked list of relevant documents as regards a query, this query-independent score must be combined with a score that expresses a document's relevance as regards a query; this is also called *data fusion*.

Craswell, Robertson, Zaragoza, and Taylor (2005) distinguish between three different methods for combining query-independent evidence with query-dependent evidence: combination of scores, combination of ranked lists, and use of query-independent evidence as priors for language modeling.

When combining scores, one combines the score of a conventional text retrieval algorithm, for example the vector space model or BM25, with the query-independent score, either by way of simple multiplication or using a linear combination. The advantage of multiplication is that this method has no tunable parameters and is invariant to normalization of the authority score.

The vector space model and the BM25 probabilistic model are linear combinations of scores; as detailed by Craswell et al. (2005), a query-independent term can be added to a BM25 score while preserving ranking. When using a linear combination between scores, care must be taken into account for differing distributions of the relevance score and the authority score. PageRank scores follow a power-law distribution (Pandurangan, Raghavan, & Upfal, 2002; Donato, Laura, Leonardi, & Millozzi, 2004; Craswell et al., 2005). See also Figures 7 and 8, similar to the distribution of term frequencies in a corpus.

(The distribution that governs term frequencies is also known as Zipf's Law).

Craswell et al. (2005) suggest transforming PageRank by:

$$w\frac{r}{k+r} \text{ or } w\frac{r^a}{k^a+r^a}$$

where r is the PageRank score and w, k, and a are constants which have to be determined by experiment. These formulas are similar to the term weighting formula:

$$\frac{tf}{k+tf}$$

in the BM25 weighting scheme. Other possible transformations are $w \log r$ or $w(1+e^{b-\log r})^{-1}$ (Zaragoza, Craswell, Taylor, Saria, & Robertson, 2004).

When combining evidence based on ranks, one produces two ranked lists—one sorted by the query-independent score and one sorted by the relevance score—and combines these lists based on ranks. The immediate advantage of

Figure 7. A cumulative distribution of PageRank for a social network with 1,277 individuals, derived from a mailing list corpus; PageRank computed using ϵ=0.3. The dashed line is a plot of a Pareto distribution $Pr(R \leq r) = 1 - \left(\frac{r}{r_m}\right)^\gamma$, using a maximum likelihood estimate of r_m=0.69 and γ=3.78.

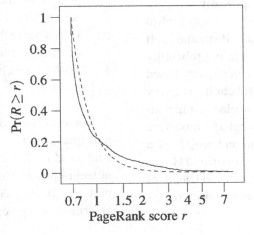

Figure 8. A plot of the probability density for the same Pareto distribution, with individual data points plotted as a scatterplot

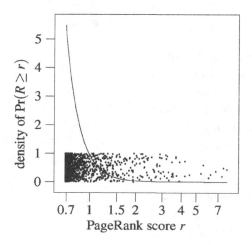

rank-based combination is that this method does not depend on the distribution of the underlying scores used to produce the rankings; this fact makes rank-based combination very attractive for meta-search engines which often know only the ranked lists of the underlying search engines, but not the actual scores. Dwork, Kumar, Naor, and Sivakumar (2001) describe several methods for rank aggregation in Web retrieval, for example by minimizing the distance between the final rank list and the individual ranked lists. Upstill, Craswell, and Hawking (2003) use a relevance score to find highly relevant documents, and re-rank the top n documents by the query-independent score; the parameter n is determined empirically.

Language modeling is a fairly new approach to information retrieval, proposed by Ponte and Croft (1998). In language modeling, a prior probability for a document is combined with a query-based probability. Since the prior probability is query independent, it presents an ideal place for including an authority measure. Language modeling systems usually use the document length as a prior probability; Westerveld, Kraaij, and Hiemstra (2001) and Kraaij, Westerveld, and Hiemstra (2002) present a system that uses authority scores as prior probabilities.

The techniques described so far form a repertoire for formulating social retrieval algorithms. We have described all necessary elements; by combining them, we arrive at the following algorithm for retrieval with social authority measures:

1. Extract authors and the social network from the corpus
2. Compute PageRank scores for the authors in the social network
3. Assign PageRank scores to documents by authorship
4. For a query, determine the set of relevant documents using a conventional text retrieval method, and compute relevance scores for each document
5. Combine the PageRank scores of the relevant documents with the relevance scores
6. Sort the result set by the combined scores and return it

For each step of the algorithm, there exist multiple possible techniques. An exhaustive study and evaluation of different combinations of techniques on different corpora has not been performed to date. An evaluation of one particular algorithm, using vector space retrieval and multiplicative combination of scores, will be given in the next section.

EVALUATION

For system evaluation, we need either a real or a simulated setting which involves all social information retrieval processes. In general, the effectiveness of the system depends on all user search sessions. We assume an explicit user cooperation without any system manipulations; however, the specific requirements of an optimal evaluation setting are more complex. For future work on this prototype, we are exploring the requirements of an optimal system evaluation. We also demonstrate the effectiveness of social information retrieval in a mailing list archive.

Optimal Evaluation Setting

The basic evaluation environment of an optimal setting is composed of a user-based and a group-based environment. At first, the user-based evaluation environment is influenced by three issues: the user's behavior, the user's collection, and the user's interaction. For an evaluation, all three issues must be available for a user to participate in the evaluation setting. All users and their individual environments build the overall group-based environment that is necessary to evaluate the impact of social information retrieval.

An optimal evaluation environment covers all three issues of a user and a group of users and is the most general requirement of an optimal evaluation setting. We derived from this requirement two additional elements concerning the input and the output of the setting:

- **Evaluation corpus:** A test collection is an essential part of the evaluation setting because it must support the components of the system. Thus, we require a corpus includ-

ing content information, a social network, and user actions. In general, standardized test collections are based only on content information and relevance assessments for specific evaluation tasks. For each task, a perfect system must retrieve all relevant documents that have been specified by human assessors and pooling. Instead, social information retrieval relies on a social network and authority information. An evaluation corpus for an optimal setting can fulfill these prerequisites either with simulated data or user tests.

- **Evaluation metric:** An evaluation metric provides a measure of performance. The choice of an optimal setting also determines the appropriate evaluation metric. For an optimal setting, we need user-centered evaluation metrics. Such metrics allow users to measure the system performance for each individual. Dhyani, Ng, and Bhowmick (2002) provide a detailed survey of Web metrics, but none of these measures consider user-centered aspects. For social information retrieval, we need a measure of the individual user satisfaction. Such a measure is difficult to quantify because several aspects can influence the metric. In a naïve way, each user's information need is satisfied when he or she receives relevant information in an adequate search time. This informal definition includes two objective user assessments: the relevance of information and the amount of time spent searching. Both factors depend on the user and the type of information needed. On one hand, for highly specific information needs (e.g., a search for contact information of a company), the number of Web sites that satisfy this information need is limited. Also the amount of time that a user is willing to spend for this type of information need is very low. On the other hand, the more unspecific information needs are, the more time is needed for the search. We conclude that user-centered metrics are essential for an optimal evaluation setting for social information retrieval. Further research is necessary to define such a measure which is beyond the scope of this work.

All requirements show that an optimal setting is mainly user driven. The specific environment cannot be simulated with a set of predefined retrieval tasks. An optimal setting considers individual information needs, which cannot be automatically assigned to specific users. In order to notice the increase of a social rank over time, a representative number of users is required. Thus, the application of the optimal setting to a real evaluation setting assumes that first, a group of users collect their queries over a certain time period. The evaluation corpus must be complex enough to extract the required environment. All decisions for a real evaluation strategy attempt to decompose the complexity of an optimal setting. Such a decomposition is an approximation of the optimal setting. First evaluation results will be given in the next section.

EVALUATION RESULTS

While an optimal evaluation scenario as detailed in the last section is of course desirable, it is not easily attained. The user-driven nature of the optimal scenario presents difficulties in the collection of data and the execution of the evaluation.

A more conventional evaluation of authority-based social retrieval techniques is presented in Sebastian Marius Kirsch (2005). The described experiments evaluate social retrieval in a batch-retrieval setting, using a known-item retrieval scenario, and measure performance using average rank and inverse average inverse rank against vector-space retrieval as a baseline method.

In an experiment using a mailing list corpus with 44,108 messages from 1,834 different e-mail addresses, social retrieval techniques led to an improvement of inverse average inverse rank of up to 25% in regard to the baseline technique. The average rank of the retrieved documents increased at the same time: average rank is dominated by documents which are retrieved late in the result list, whereas inverse average inverse rank is dominated by documents retrieved early. As noted by Page et al. (1999), authority-based

Figure 9. Degree distribution of the coauthorship network of 25 years of SIGIR proceedings (a) and PageRank distribution of the same network (b). The degree distribution does not follow a power-law distribution; it seems to follow an exponential distribution $Pr(\delta(v)=k) \sim \exp\left(\dfrac{-k}{k_c}\right)$ with $k_c \approx 2.9$. Due to the highly fractured social network, the PageRank algorithm fails to produce consistent scores.

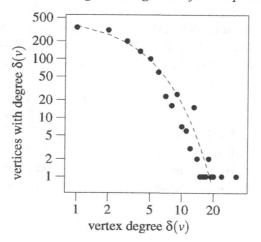

retrieval techniques work best for underspecified queries, which generate many documents, only some of which are actually relevant.

A second experiment was conducted using a corpus of 1,041 scientific publications by 1,397 authors from 25 years of proceedings of the SIGIR conference. This experiment is significant in that it challenges several assumptions about social retrieval implicit in this chapter. The social network of this corpus is highly fractured, with the largest component comprising just 22.3% of the social network (as compared to 70-90% for other social networks). As can be seen from Figure 9, neither the degree distribution nor the PageRank distribution follows a power law: the degree distribution is closer to an exponential distribution, whereas the PageRank scores fail to satisfy a simple distribution. These facts limit the applicability of PageRank-based retrieval techniques.

Experiments on the SIGIR corpus further revealed that while social retrieval is quite well suited to finding overviews and reviews, it is rather unsuited for finding ground-breaking publications. As noted by Granovetter (1973), innovators tend to be at the margins of the social network, because they do not conform to the norms of the community—which may well be the reason that allows them to innovate. They "think outside of the box" without being bound to the mode of thinking of the community.

Authority-based retrieval, by assigning high scores to well-connected individuals, biases the results away from innovators and towards multipliers. Multipliers are hubs in the social network and serve as disseminators of information. They are often early adopters of successful ideas and ensure that ideas flow from the innovator to the rest of the network.

This fact makes retrieving documents by multipliers a valuable function for social retrieval systems, since the path from the multiplier to the innovator is typically very short. In the experiments described in Sebastian Marius Kirsch (2005), the multiplier usually references the innovator directly, enabling quick access to the innovative document by following a single reference.

CONCLUSION

Social networks are the fabric underlying all social information spaces. In this chapter we examined their importance for information dissemination and for the formation of communities. We described some of their statistical properties, as they influence the choice of algorithms for retrieval using social networks.

We identified graph authority measures as a tool for retrieval in social information spaces and described a number of authority measures, focusing on PageRank as an algorithm of choice for social retrieval. An example of PageRank on a scientific coauthorship network supports its suitability for determining the authority of an individual in a social network.

We described how to integrate PageRank on a social network into an information retrieval system as a query-independent measure. We gave three different methods for this task, leading to the formulation of an algorithm for retrieval in social information spaces using authority measures.

An optimal evaluation scenario for social retrieval was described, stressing the fact that evaluation of such techniques needs to be user centered. Results of an evaluation using conventional methods gave insights into the performance of authority-based retrieval and into its limitations.

The application of social retrieval with authority measures is limited by three different aspects:

1. The presence of a social network is a prerequisite for social retrieval; unless individuals and their relations with each other can be identified, social retrieval is not applicable.

2. For small corpora or highly fractured social networks, the described algorithms may give unexpected results.
3. Authority-based retrieval in general is biased towards multipliers instead of innovators, limiting the ability to find innovative individuals.

The current interest in social information spaces and "social software" motivates retrieval methods that are tailor-made for these kinds of applications. Authority-based retrieval is one such method that allows users to derive tangible benefits from the participation in a social information space, namely improved retrieval performance. The described methods are applicable for a wide range of social information spaces, which provide a fertile ground for their evaluation.

REFERENCES

Barabási, A.-L., & Albert, R. (1999). Emergence of scaling in random networks. *Science, 286,* 509-512.

Berners-Lee, T., Cailliau, R., Luotonen, A., Nielsen, H.F., & Secret, A. (1994). The World Wide Web. *Communications of the ACM, 37*(8), 76-82.

Berners-Lee, T., Hendler, J., & Lassila, O. (2001). The semantic Web. *Scientific American, 284*(5), 34-43.

Craswell, N., Robertson, S., Zaragoza, H., & Taylor, M. (2005). Relevance weighting for query independent evidence. In G. Marchionini, A. Moffat, J. Tait, R. Baeza-Yates, & N. Ziviani (Eds.), *Proceedings of the 28th Annual International ACM SIGIR Conference on Research and Development in Information Retrieval* (pp. 416-423), Salvador, Brazil.

Crestani, F. (1997). Application of spreading activation techniques in information retrieval. *Artificial Intelligence Review, 11*(6), 453-482.

Dholakia, U.M., Bagozzi, R.P., & Klein Pearo, L. (2004). A social influence model of consumer participation in network- and small-group-based virtual communities. *Journal of Research in Marketing, 21*(3), 241-263.

Dhyani, D., Ng, W.K., & Bhowmick, S.S. (2002). A survey of Web metrics. *ACM Computing Surveys, 34*(4), 469-503.

Donato, D., Laura, L., Leonardi, S., & Millozzi, S. (2004). Large scale properties of the Webgraph. *European Physical Journal B, 38,* 239-243.

Dublin Core Metadata Initiative. *DCMI metadata terms.* Retrieved August 30, 2005, from *http://dublincore.org/documents/dcmi-terms/*

Dwork, C., Kumar, R., Naor, M., & Sivakumar, D. (2001). Rank aggregation methods for the Web. In V.Y. Shen, N. Saito, M.R. Lyu, & M.E. Zurko (Eds.), *Proceedings of the 10th International Conference on the World Wide Web* (pp. 613-622), Hong Kong.

Freeman, L.C. (1979). Centrality in social networks. Conceptual clarification. *Social Networks, 1,* 215-239.

Fuchs-Kittowski, F. & Köhler, A. (2005). Wiki-communities in the context of work processes. In D. Riehle (Ed.), *Proceedings of the 2005 International Symposium on Wikis* (WikiSym 2005) (pp. 33-39), San Diego, CA.

Granovetter, M.S. (1973). The strength of weak ties. *American Journal of Sociology, 78*(6), 1360-1380.

Kirsch, S.M. (2005). *Social information retrieval.* Diploma Thesis, Rheinische Friedrich-Wilhelms-Universität Bonn, Germany.

Kleinberg, J.M. (1999). Authoritative sources in a hyperlinked environment. *Journal of the ACM, 46*(5), 604-632.

Kraaij, W., Westerveld, T., & Hiemstra, D. (2002). The importance of prior probabilities for entry page search. In M. Beaulieu, R. Baeza-Yates, S.H. Myaeng, & K. Jarvelin (Eds.), *Proceedings of the 25th Annual International ACM SIGIR Conference on Research and Development in Information Retrieval* (pp. 27-24), Tampere, Finland.

Lueg, C., Davenport, E., Robertson, T., & Pipek, V. (2001). Actions and identities in virtual communities of practice. *Proceedings of the 7th European Conference on Computer Supported Cooperative Work* (ECSCW 2001), Bonn, Germany.

Manber, U. (1992). Foreword. In W.B. Frakes & R. Baeza-Yates (Eds.), *Information retrieval. Data structures & algorithms* (pp. v-vi). Indianapolis, IN: Prentice-Hall.

Milgram, S. (1967). The small-world problem. *Psychology Today, 2,* 60-67.

Newman, M.E.J. (2001). The structure of scientific collaboration networks. *Proceedings of the National Academy of Sciences of the United States of America, 98*(2), 404-409.

O'Reilly, T. (2006). *What Is Web 2.0—design patterns and business models for the next generation of software.* Retrieved January 3, 2007, from *http://www.oreillynet.com/pub/a/oreilly/tim/ news/2005/09/30/what-is-web-20.html?page=1*

Page, L., Brin, S., Motwani, R., & Winograd, T. (1999). *The PageRank citation ranking: Bringing order to the Web.* Technical Report No. 1999-66, Stanford University, USA.

Pandurangan, G., Raghavan, P., & Upfal, E. (2002). Using PageRank to characterize Web structure. In O. Ibarra & L. Zhang (Eds.), *Proceedings of the 8th Annual International Conference on Computing and Combinatorics* (pp. 330-339). Singapore: Springer.

Pinski, G., & Narin, F. (1976). Citation influence for journal aggregates of scientific publications: Theory, with application to the literature of physics. *Information Processing and Management, 12*(5), 297-312.

Ponte, J.M., & Croft, W.B. (1998) A language modeling approach to information retrieval. *Proceedings of the 21st Annual International ACM SIGIR Conference on Research and Development in Information Retrieval* (pp. 275-281), Melbourne, Australia.

Preece, S.E. (1981). *A spreading activation network model for information retrieval.* PhD Thesis, University of Illinois at Urbana-Champaign, USA.

Salton, G. (1963). Associative document retrieval techniques using bibliographic information. *Journal of the ACM, 10*(4), 440-457.

Six Apart Ltd. (n.d.). *Live journal bot policy.* Retrieved January 3, 2007, from *http://www. livejournal.com/bots/*

Smeaton, A., Keogh, G., Gurrin, C., McDonald, K., & Sodring, T. (2002). Analysis of papers from twenty-five years of SIGIR conferences: What have we been doing for the last quarter of a century? *SIGIR Forum, 36*(2), 39-43.

Upstill, T., Craswell, N., & Hawking, D. (2003). Query-independent evidence in home page finding. *ACM Transactions on Information Systems, 21*(3), 286-313.

Wenger, E., & Snyder, W.M. (2000). Communities of practice: The organizational frontier. *Harvard Business Review,* (January-February), 139-145.

Westerveld, T., Kraaij, W., & Hiemstra, D. (2001) Retrieving Web pages using content, links, URLs and anchors. In E.M. Vorhees & D.K. Harman (Eds.), *Proceedings of the 10th Text Retrieval Conference* (TREC-10) (pp. 663-672). Gaithersburg, MD: National Institute of Standards and Technology.

Won, M. & Pipek, V. (2004). Sharing knowledge on knowledge—the eXact Peripheral Expertise Awareness System. *Journal of Universal Computer Science, 9*(12), 1388-1397.

Zaragoza, H., Craswell, N., Taylor, M., Saria, S., & Robertson, S. (2004). Microsoft Cambridge and TREC-13: Web and HARD tracks. In E.M. Vorhees & L.P. Buckland (Eds.), *Proceedings of the 13th Text Retrieval Conference* (TREC-13). Gaithersburg, MD: National Institute of Standards and Technology.

Chapter VIII
Adaptive Peer–to–Peer Social Networks for Distributed Content–Based Web Search

Le-Shin Wu
Indiana University, USA

Ruj Akavipat
Indiana University, USA

Ana Gabriela Maguitman
Universidad Nacional del Sur, Argentina

Filippo Menczer
Indiana University, USA

ABSTRACT

In this chapter we propose a collaborative peer network application called 6Search (6S) to address the scalability limitations of centralized search engines. Each peer crawls the Web in a focused way, guided by its user's information context. Through this approach, better (distributed) coverage can be achieved. Each peer also acts as a search "servent" (server + client) by submitting and responding to queries to/from its neighbors. This search process has no centralized bottleneck. Peers depend on a local adaptive routing algorithm to dynamically change the topology of the peer network and search for the best neighbors to answer their queries. We present and evaluate learning techniques to improve local query routing. We validate prototypes of the 6S network via simulations with 70–500 model users based on actual Web crawls. We find that the network topology rapidly converges from a random network to a small-world network, with clusters emerging from user communities with shared interests. We finally compare the quality of the results with those obtained by centralized search engines such as Google.

BACKGROUND AND MOTIVATION

Centralized search engines have difficulties in achieving good coverage of the Web (Lawrence & Giles, 1999) because the Web is large, fast growing, and fast changing (Brewington & Cybenko, 2000; Fetterly, Manasse, Najork, & Wiener, 2003; Ntoulas, Cho, & Olston,, 2004). Further, various biases introduced to address the needs of the "average" user imply diminished effectiveness in satisfying many atypical search needs. Examples of bias include interfaces (advanced search features are often buried and poorly documented), ranking (in favor of precision and popularity, to please the majority of users who do not look beyond the first few hits), and coverage (well-connected pages are easy for a crawler to find and thus more likely to be indexed (Najork & Wiener, 2001)).

We identify the above limitations as problems of scale in spite of enormous progress in crawling (Cho & Garcia-Molina, 2002), indexing (Dean & Ghemawat, 2004), and retrieval and ranking (Brin & Page, 1998); the "one-engine-fits-all" model does not—cannot—scale well with the size, dynamics, and heterogeneity of the Web and its users.

Topical or vertical search engines are one approach to address this problem. Effective topical crawling algorithms have been designed to support specialized portals (Chakrabarti, Berg, & Do, 1999; Menczer & Belew, 2000; Menczer, Pant, & Srinivasan, 2004). However, these efforts are generally aimed to very limited information spaces—digital libraries, Web sites, databases—and are not designed to scale with searching the Web at large.

It is evident that distributed systems are part of the answer to the scale problem. Peer social networks are increasingly seen as a candidate framework for distributed Web search applications. A social network is a social structure between participants who are connected through various social relationships. In the real world,

we discover that people can successfully find relevant information for questions by just asking the "right" people through their social network, although the network is extremely dynamic (for example, people may not be available all time, people may change their interests anytime, or people can decide not to respond to requests, etc.). Thus, a peer-to-peer (P2P) social network searching system is a network that uses the social network as the basis to route queries for information retrieval. Each peer in the network acts just as a person in the social network:

- Peers are independent
- A peer can enter and leave the network at any time
- Peers learn and store profiles of other peers with a view to their potential for answering prospective queries
- Peers discover new peers through their current neighbors

By simulating the information finding mechanism in a social network of people, the peer network collectively tries to route the queries to the "right" peers according to some peer selection algorithms which predict the degree of match between queries and peers.

A P2P computer social network relies on the computing power and bandwidth of the participants in the network rather than concentrating it in a relatively few servers (Wikipedia, 2005). The most popular use of a P2P network is for file sharing. Applications such as Gnutella (*http://www.gnutella.com*), BitTorrent (*http://www.bittorrent.com*), and KaZaa (*http://www.kazaa.com*) allow peers to share content files, mostly media related, among peers without having to set up dedicated servers and acquiring large bandwidth to support the whole community. The P2P file sharing application is by no means replacing the dedicated servers in content distribution. It simply provides an alternative for content distribution by trading the speed and reliability of dedicated servers for the ease of sharing, lower cost, fault tolerance, and lower bandwidth requirement for a file sharer. In a similar way as P2P file sharing applications are used to facilitate content distribution, P2P applications can be developed to facilitate Web search.

There is extensive work on peer network searching applications in the AI and IR literature. (There are too many examples to list here; the reader is referred to the review in Lua, Crowcroft, J., Pias, 2005, and Risson & Moors, 2004, as starting points.) One model proposed by the YouSearch project is to maintain a centralized search registry for query routing (similar to Napster), and moreover enrich the peers with the capability to crawl and index local portions of the Web (Bawa, Jr, Rajagoplan, & Shekita, 2003). Unfortunately, the central control in this approach makes it difficult to adapt the search process to the heterogeneous and dynamic contexts of the peer users.

A completely decentralized approach is the Gnutella model, in which queries are sent and forwarded blindly by each peer. The problems of this approach are that peers flooded by requests cannot manage the ensuing traffic, and that the topology is uncorrelated with the interests of the peer users. As a result, the basic Gnutella model does not scale well with the number of users and queries. Adaptive, content-based routing has been proposed to overcome this difficulty in the file sharing setting. NeuroGrid (Joseph, 2002) employs a learning mechanism to adjust metadata describing the contents of nodes. A similar idea has been proposed to distribute and personalize Web search using a query-based model and collaborative filtering (Pujol, Sanguesa, & Bermudez, 2003). Search, however, is disjoint from crawling, making it necessary to rely on centralized search engines for content.

An intermediate approach between the flood network and the centralized registry is to store index lists in distributed, shared hash tables (Suel et al., 2003). In pSearch (Tang, Xu, & Dwarkadas, 2003), latent semantic analysis (Deerwester, Du-mais, Landauer, & Harshman, 1990) is performed over such distributed hash tables to provide peers with keyword search capability. This is a promising approach, however Li et al. (2003) argue that full-text Web search is infeasible in both the flood model and the distributed hash table model.

Another alternative is a hybrid peer network, where multiple special directory nodes (hubs) provide construct and use content models of neighboring nodes to determine how to route query messages through the network (Lu & Callan, 2003). In a hybrid peer network, leaf nodes provide information and use content-based retrieval to decide which documents to retrieve for queries.

In this chapter we propose an alternative model for peer-based Web search which uses the same idea of content-based models of neighboring nodes, but without assuming the presence of special directory hubs. Each peer is both a (limited) directory hub and a content provider; it has its own topical crawler (based on local context), which supports a local search engine—typically but not necessarily a small one. Queries are first matched against the local engine and then routed to neighbor peers to obtain more results. Initially the network has a random topology (like Gnutella), and queries are routed randomly as in the flood model. However, the protocol includes a learning algorithm by which each peer uses the results of its interactions with its neighbors (matches between queries and responses) to refine a model of the other peers. This model is used to dynamically route queries according to the predicted match with other peers' knowledge. The network topology is thus modified on the fly based on learned contexts and current information needs. Similar ideas are receiving increasing attention in the P2P search literature (Crespo & Garcia-Molina, 2002; Kalogeraki, Gunopulos, & Zeinalipour-Yazti, 2002; Yang & Garcia-Molina, 2002).

The key idea of the proposed peer search network is that the flooding problem can be alleviated by intelligent collaboration between the peers. This should lead to an emergent clustered topology in which neighbor communities tend to form according to clusters of peers with shared interests and domains. In fact we predict that the ideal topology for such a network would be a "small world" (Watts & Strogatz, 1998). This topology allows for any two peers to reach each other via a short path (small diameter) while maximizing the efficiency of communication within clustered peer communities. Following Milgram's famous experiments on "six degrees of separation" (Watts & Strogatz, 1998), we named our model 6Search (6S).

Outline and Contributions

After a brief introduction, we start by presenting the 6S protocol and algorithms including the message primitives, neighbor management, neighbor modeling, and adaptive query routing. Then we describe the architecture of the 6S system which integrates the protocol and algorithm. In the remainder of the chapter, we explain how we conduct an experiment to test our 6S system based on real Web data, and we discuss our results. We also propose an alternative evaluation approach for a peer network system. Finally, we conclude by summarizing our results and discussing future work. The following findings are our main contributions:

- The 6S nodes rapidly discover the content locality among their peers, displaying a topology that converges to a small-world network after each peer has routed as few as five to six queries, and this change in topology leads to an increase in the quality of the results.
- The collective search performance of the system improves as more sophisticated learning algorithms are employed by the peers to route queries, and as more network resources become available; conversely performance degrades softly as bandwidth and CPU cycles become more scarce.

- The 6S peers achieve a search quality that is comparable to that of Google, and significantly outperforms that obtained by a centralized search engine with the same resources (size of crawl set) as the 6S peer collective.
- The 6S algorithms scale very well up to 500 peers, the maximum number of users we were able to simulate in a closely controlled testing environment, giving us confidence for the public release of an open prototype.

6S PROTOCOL AND ALGORITHM

As shown in Figure 1, the 6S application (personal search engine) layer sits between the user and the peer network layer. The 6S peer network protocol acts as an application layer between the search engine and the network (TCP/IP) layer. The application also interfaces with the network using the HTTP protocol for crawling the Web.

The 6S peer network layer provides the means to find results (hits) by querying the indexes built by peer search engines. When the user submits

Figure 1. 6S protocol stack

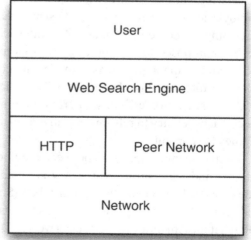

a query to his or her personal search engine, the latter can retrieve hits from its local index database and augment the results by searching the peer network for additional hits.

The design of our protocol is based on the following considerations:

1. Peers are independent
2. A peer can enter and leave the network at any time
3. A peer should not be overwhelmed by other peers
4. A query should not be propagated indefinitely
5. A peer may choose not to respond or forward some queries
6. The architecture should make it difficult to create denial of service (DoS) attacks using the service

Below we discuss the message primitives that the protocol uses for communication. The following section discusses the algorithm and parameters of each message type.

Message Primitives

We do not wish to design an overly complex protocol, which could hinder the development of improved protocols in the future. In the following, we present the most fundamental primitives that we feel one cannot do without. Here we use a simple XML syntax to illustrate peer network messages. Our prototype protocol is based on these primitives. There are a few additional primitives that we are considering for future implementations as they would enable richer peer interactions and more sophisticated search and learning algorithms. Those are omitted for brevity. It should also be noted that from the network layer (TCP/IP), peers can identify each other during communication (from their IP addresses, say), so this information is omitted in the peer network primitives.

Query Message

```
<Query>
   <ID></ID>
   <TTL></TTL>
   <timestamp></timestamp>
   <body>
      <word> kwd1 </word><weight> wt1 </weight>
      :
      <word> kwd2 </word><weight> wt2 </weight>
   </body>
   <ownerid></ownerid>
</Query>
```

The query message is used by a peer to pass its queries to other peers on the network. A query owner identification may optionally be attached to the query. We allow this option into the primitive since a peer may need to identify itself to other peers.

A peer sends a query consisting of its query keywords and the corresponding weight of each keyword (weights can be 1 by default). Attached with each query are ID, TTL (time to live), and timestamp. An owner identification can be attached as a sign that one wants to discover new neighbors. The ID and timestamp are added to help differentiate each query. Given two peers, the ID has to be locally unique.

The purpose of TTL is to limit the forwarding of a query (see below) such that a query will not survive in the network too long and move too far from the originating peer. This is a standard technique to limit congestion and loops in any network protocol. The TTL is decreased for every forward, and a query will not be forwarded when TTL reaches 0. In 6S we may allow for the amount by which the TTL is decreased by a peer to depend on local variations of the protocol.

Query Response

```
<QueryResponse>
   <timestamp></timestamp>
   <body>
      <hit>
      <score></score>
      <url></url>
      <summary></summary>
      <info></info>
      </hit>
      :
   </body>
   <ownerid></ownerid>
</QueryResponse>
```

The query response is used by a peer to respond to other peers' search queries. As in the query message primitive, an optional owner ID is provided so that the responder may identify itself. Once a peer receives a query, it will decide whether it should respond or not. If it decides to respond, it will match the query against its local index database and return N_h results (hits) in the response message.

Moreover, depending on the similarity between the query and its neighbor profiles, the peer may also select some of its neighbors and forward the query to them, as will be illustrated in detail later. Then the peer will forward its neighbors' responses, if any, back to the peer who originated the query.

We impose a restriction on the way that a peer replies to a forwarded query. The response must be sent to the neighbor that forwarded the query, and not directly to the peer who originated the query. This is because we want to prevent potential DoS attacks created by exploiting the response system. If a peer responds to a forwarded query by sending a reply directly to the source, someone can inject a query with a large TTL into the network together with a spoofed return address. Then all the responses will be directed to that address, overwhelming the target machine.

Profile Request

```
<ProfileRequest></ProfileRequest>
```

The profile request is needed to let a peer request profiles from others. The profile describes what a peer has indexed and is ready for sharing. We use the pull mechanism because it spares a peer from the load of having to propagate updates for its own profile. The cost of a peer having to request profile information should be lower than that of having to keep track of all peers that store one's profile.

Profile Response

```
<ProfileResponse>
   <body>
      <word></word>
      :
      <word></word>
   </body>
</ProfileResponse>
```

This primitive allows a peer to respond to a request for its own profile. Such a profile initially consists of a simple list of terms. Later, as peers learn about their neighbors' expertise from query responses, profiles are updated with more information. More complex profiles and updating algorithms will be described in more detail later.

Neighbor Management

Since our goal is to allow peers to form communities without centralized control, a peer needs to find new peers and evaluate their quality and match. In our design, we choose not to have peers aggressively flooding the network looking for other peers unless it is necessary to do so, such as when the peer enters the network for the first time or when all known peers are not available. Otherwise, a peer would discover new peers

Figure 2. 6S neighbor discovery

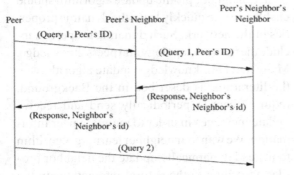

through its current neighbors. The process that we use in our prototype is to let a peer attach its contact ID with the query in the ownerid field. If the peer that receives a query wants to become a neighbor of the requesting peer, it will respond with its own contact ID in the ownerid field of the response message. The new neighbor peers can later contact each other directly. For example, illustrated in Figure 2, a peer sent out Query 1 with its contact ID attached. One of its Neighbor's Neighbors replied to Query 1 and also attached the contact ID with response message. Since this peer had the contact information about its Neighbor's Neighbor now, for the next query—Query 2, it can send this query to its Neighbor's Neighbor directly without passing through other peers.

In addition to the mechanism for discovering new neighbors, we also need to consider the issue of how often or when a peer will want to find more neighbors. A simple approach is to give each peer a fixed number of slots for neighbors N_n. This number can vary among peers depending on their bandwidth and computational power to process neighbor data. We assume that N_n is fixed for each peer. A peer will search for new peers when its neighbor slots are not full or when it wants to find better neighbors than the currently known peers.

Each peer may of course know about more than N_n peers. Let us call $N_k(t)$ the number of peers known at time t. This number can grow arbitrarily, but probably will be capped at some parameter determined by the peer application's

available memory or storage. A peer must prune neighbor information as needed.

Many neighbor management algorithms in the P2P literature require peers to send update messages in order to maintain valid network information when peers leave the network. In contrast, a 6S peer does not need to send any message when it wants to leave the network because our query routing algorithm, which will be discussed later in detail, animatedly updates the neighbor profiles based on queries and responses in the system.

Neighbor Modeling and Adaptive Query Routing

6S relies on adaptive query routing to shape its dynamic network topology. To support adaptive query routing, each peer learns and stores profiles of other peers with a view to their potential for answering prospective queries. A neighbor profile is the information a particular peer maintains to describe its knowledge about what that neighbor stores in its search engine index and is ready for sharing. By checking profile information, peers try to increase the probability of choosing the appropriate neighbors to route their queries.

Akavipat, Wu, and Menczer (2004) implemented a simple method to initialize and maintain peer profiles: first ask a neighbor for its description, defined as a list of n most frequent keywords in the neighbor's index; then perform a crude update to this list by adding query terms for which the neighbor returns good responses. The score of a keyword in such a neighbor profile is the highest similarity score of the responses a neighbor returns for that keyword. This method, albeit crude and fragile (due to its dependency on information supplied by neighbors), was shown to give rise to an efficient network topology and promising initial results.

Let us now improve on the reliability and robustness of the simple learning algorithms above by introducing a better profile representation and a novel soft updating scheme. Interactions with peers reveal information of varying reliability. For example, a direct response to a query is telling about a peer's knowledge with respect to that query, but may also reveal (less reliable) information about the peer's knowledge relative to other queries. We want to capture all available information in profiles, but must discriminate information on the bases of its reliability. To this end, let each peer maintain two profile matrices W^f and W^e for focused and expanded information, respectively. Each profile matrix has the same structure: rows correspond to terms and columns to peers. Thus an element w_{ip} of W is the contribution of term i to the profile of known peer $p(p = 1, ..., N_k)$.

Each peer starts with both neighbor profiles empty. After participating in query forwarding and responding, different updates will be made to each type of profile.

- **Focused profile:** Weights w_{ip}^f are updated initially based on p's response to a neighbor profile request message, and successively through query-response interaction–namely for terms i in queries submitted or forwarded to p. When a peer receives responses to a query Q, it compares the incoming hits with its local hits. Based on this comparison, the peer makes an assessment about p's knowledge with respects to terms $i \in Q$.

- **Expanded profile:** Weights w_{jp}^e are updated through query-response interaction analogously to the focused profile, but for terms $j \notin Q$ that co-occur with terms $i \in Q$ in a hit page d returned by p and have a higher term frequency: $TF(j, d) > \max_i TF(i, d)$. If a certain set of documents is a good response for a certain query, then it may as well be a good response for queries that are well represented in the set. Thus the expanded profile implements a form of query expansion, which we expect to speed up learning since queries are typically short, and thus W^f is typically rather sparse.

The neighbor profile update algorithm should enable peers to quickly learn the dynamic properties of the network. Such dynamic properties include the network topology and peers' knowledge. Many neighbor knowledge update algorithms in the literature, as described in the Background, require peers to periodically send and receive update messages in order to maintain peer information. We want our neighbor learning algorithm to instead dynamically update the neighbor profiles according to the natural interactions in the system, namely queries and responses.

In Akavipat et al.'s (2004) implementation, a peer updated its neighbor profiles only when a score of any neighbor hit was better than at least one of the top N_h local scores. In such cases the query keywords were added into the neighbor profile with the best score of the neighbor hit as the new weight. Let us now modify the algorithm so that the peer will always update its neighbor profile no matter whether the score of the neighbor hit is better or worse than the local score. Furthermore, instead of using the best score as the new value for term weights, we propose the following learning rule to update the weights of the query terms in the neighbor profile matrices:

$$w_{ip}(t+1) = (1-\gamma) \cdot w_{ip}(t) + \gamma \cdot \frac{S_p + 1}{S_l + 1} \quad (1)$$

where t is a time step, S_p and S_l are the average scores of p's hits and the local hits respectively in response to the query Q, and γ is a learning rate parameter $(0 < \gamma < 1)$. The terms i subject to this learning rule depend on Q and the profile matrix (focused or expanded) as described above.

The actual set of N_n neighbors, that is, those to whom queries are sent, is selected dynamically for each query at time t among the $N_k(t)$ known peers. Sophisticated algorithms have been proposed for determining the quality of peers (Kamvar, Schlosser, & Garcia-Molina, 2003). Here instead we propose a very simple adaptive routing algorithm to manage neighbor information and to use such information for dynamically selecting neighbors to query:

1. When a peer is first discovered, a profile is requested. A description for the peer is then initialized with the list of keywords contained in the peer's profile.

2. Responses from neighbors (and neighbors' neighbors, and so on) to query Q are evaluated and used to update the description of each known peer:

   (a) The hit average scores (S_p) of hits received from neighbors and the local hit average scores (S_l) are computed.

   (b) Update W^f using Equation 1 for terms in Q.

   (c) If $S_p > S_l$, update W^e using Equation 1 for terms not in Q that occur in the hits received from neighbors more frequently than the query terms.

   (d) The discovery signal ownerid is sent with the next query to that neighbor.

   (e) New peers that respond to discovery signals are added to the list of known peers, with their profile.

3. For the next query Q', known peers are ranked by similarity σ between the query and the peer profiles computed as follows:

$$\sigma(p, Q') = \sum_{i \in Q'} [\alpha \cdot w_{ip}^f + (1 - \alpha) \cdot w_{ip}^e] \quad (2)$$

where α is a reliability parameter regulating the contributions of focused and expanded profiles. Typically $0.5 < \alpha < 1$ to reflect higher confidence in focused profile weights as they come from direct responses to queries.

4. The top N_n ranked among known peers are selected as neighbors and sent Q'.

5. Go to step 2.

6S ARCHITECTURE

Using the protocol described earlier, we create the architecture of a peer as shown in Figure 3. Each peer has a local search engine with its own index database. The peer not only processes its own local queries, but also the queries that are passed to it by other peers. The peer contains five basic modules, allowing us to easily test and modify each component separately. The system is implemented in Java to take advantage of a number of code libraries available from other sources.

The *user interface module* is where the peer search system accepts queries from the user and displays the results back to the user. When the user enters a query, this module distributes it to three other modules (combinator, local search, and neighbor information) where the query is further processed.

The *local search module* handles the search task on a local index created from shared personal files, bookmarked pages, and pages crawled by the local Web crawler. We use the open-source search engine Nutch (*http://lucene.apache.org/nutch/*) as the local indexing and database code.

For the topical crawler, we use a *best-N-first* search algorithm developed by Menczer et al. (2004; Pant, Bradshaw, & Menczer, 2003; Pant, Srinivasan, & Menczer, 2003), which has been proven very effective against a number of crawling algorithms. A detailed description of this crawling algorithm is outside the scope of this chapter and can be found in the above references. Briefly, the crawler is given a set of seed URLs to start from and a set of topic keywords. The URLs to be visited are prioritized by the similarity between the topic and the page in which a URL is encountered. Some additional mechanisms guarantee that the crawler is sufficiently exploratory. This crawler is also publicly available from *http://informatics.indiana.edu/fil/IS/JavaCrawlers*.

The peer crawler can be seeded with pages bookmarked by the user, or hits returned by a

Figure 3. 6S peer architecture

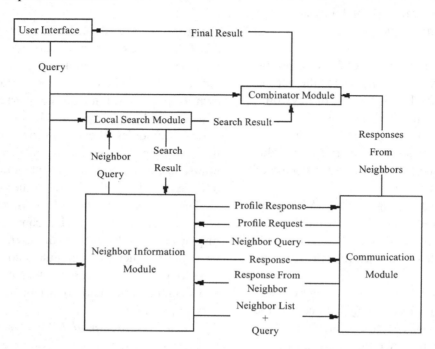

search engine based on a user profile, or pages visited recently by the user. The topic keywords, if not given explicitly by the user, can be extracted from the user profile or from the queries submitted by the user to search engines during the day.

The results of a search are sent to different modules based on the origin of the query. If the query comes from the user, the results are sent first to the combinator module to be merged with hits obtained from other peers, and they are also sent to the neighbor information module to assist in evaluating neighbors' responses to that query. If the query comes from another peer, the results will be sent back to that peer by the neighbor information and communication modules.

The *neighbor information module* handles how a peer responds to the others, which includes evaluating qualities of each neighbor and determining which known peers are best neighbors for sending or forwarding a particular query. The module contains a database that stores known

peer information, which is continually updated according to the algorithm, which is described earlier, each time that a response is received. The module also handles how much information is provided in response to neighbor requests for a peer profile.

As mentioned earlier, the evaluation of a new peer begins with a description received from that peer. Since Nutch provides an interface for retrieving the highest frequency terms from a search index, we use this as a simple way for a peer to create its own profile, to be sent to other peers upon request. This is done by extracting the most frequent terms from the local index database.

When the neighbor information module receives a query, whether from a user or from other peers, it dynamically selects a set of neighbors from its database of known peers, based on the query. The N_n parameter can be set by the user to limit the maximum number of neighbors to whom the module can forward queries.

Table 1. The seven ODP topics used to model communities of users with shared interests in our first simulation

No.	Topic Keywords
1	Science/Environment/Products and Services
2	Science/Astronomy/Software
3	Science/Social Sciences/Archaeology
4	Shopping/Home and Garden/Cleaning
5	Sports/Tennis/Players
6	Recreation/Boating/Boatbuilding
7	Computers/Software/Freeware

Figure 4. Simulator pseudo code

```
Initialize all peers
Initialize simulated network at random
While not terminated
  For each peer
    If user submits a query
      Process query on local search engine
      Send query to appropriate neighbors
    EndIf
    If a response to a previous query is received
      If response is for local user
        Evaluate neighbor
        Combine hits with other hits
        Output to user
      Else
        Forward response to query sender
      EndIf
    EndIf
    If a query is received
      Process query on local search engine
      Send response back
      If TTL > 0
        Decrease TTL
        Forward query to appropriate neighbors
      EndIf
    EndIf
    If a request for profile is received
      Generate profile
      Send profile to requester
    EndIf
  EndFor
EndWhile
```

The *combinator module* combines and re-ranks the hits obtained from the local search module with those contained in responses received from peer neighbors.

The *communication module* acts as the interface between the peer application and the peer network layer. It is responsible for all communication with other peers. The tasks of this module include passing queries, results, and other messages between the other modules of the local peer and the external peers.

EXPERIMENTAL SETUP

To analyze the behavior of 6S peer network interactions, we created a simulator to do two different types of simulations that allow us to model synthetic users and run their queries over real indexes obtained from actual distributed Web crawls. The goal of the simulator in our experiments outlined below is to study the statistics of 6S's emergent peer network topology and the feasibility of the 6S framework using large peers and using a large number of peers.

Our simulator takes a snapshot of the network for every time step. In a time step of the simulator, all of the peers process all of their buffered incoming messages and send all of their buffered outgoing messages. This may include the generation of a local query as well as responding to the queries received by other peers and forwarding them. The pseudo code for the simulator is shown in Figure 4.

There are $N = 70$ peers in our first simulation experiment and $N = 500$ peers in our second simulation. In order to study whether the adaptive routing algorithm of the 6S network can generate network topologies that capture the interests shared by user communities, thus reducing query flooding problems, we modeled synthetic users belonging to 7 (for the first simulation) and 50 (for the second simulation) different groups of 10 users each. Each group is associated with a general topic. Each peer has its own search engine database, but for the peers in a given group, the search engines are built by topical crawlers focusing on the same topic. For example if a group's topic is "sports," then all the peer search engines in this group focus on different aspects of sports. Two points are to be emphasized here. First, while the simulated peers in this experiment are associated with relatively narrow topics, this is not a 6S general requirement; peer topics can have arbitrary generality matching single users or communities of users. Second, while we simulate these communities to see if the peer network can discover them, any individual peer has no more knowledge about other peers in its group than about all other peers.

Group topics are chosen from the Open Directory (ODP, *http://dmoz.org*) to simulate the group structure according to a simple methodology developed to evaluate topical crawlers (Srinivasan, Pant, & Menczer, 2005). The topics corresponding to the groups in our first simulation (with 70 peers) are shown in Table 1. For each group, we extract a set of 100-200 URLs from the ODP subtree rooted at the category node corresponding to the group's topic. Random subsets are assigned to the peer crawlers as seeds. So the search engines within each group differ from each other according to the different sets of crawled pages (starting from different sets of seeds). We use the same strategy to setup our second simulation, but instead of 7 topics we choose 50 different topics.

Given a set of topic keywords and a set of seed URLs, the best-N-first crawler was run off-line for each peer to harvest the pages that would be indexed to build the peer's search engine. For our first simulation, we crawled about 10,000 Web pages for each peer (for a total of 700,000 pages). And for our second simulation, we crawled about 1,000 Web pages for each peer (for a total of 500,000 pages). The Nutch package was then used to index these pages and build each peer's search engine.

Each peer is allowed to know about all of the other peers (N_k = 69 for first simulation and N_k = 499 for second simulation) and to have N_n = 5 neighbors. At the beginning of each experiment, the peer network is initialized as a random Erdos-Renyi graph, that is, each peer is assigned five random neighbors drawn from a uniform distribution, irrespective of groups.

Each peer in our experiments has 10 queries as its own local queries. The queries are related with the peer's group topic. The queries used in our experiments are 3-5 word strings such as "environmental products services" and "manufacturing selling system parts." The queries for each peer in our first simulation were generated by randomly picking keywords from the ODP descriptions of the Web sites whose URLs were used as seeds for the peer's crawler. The queries for each peer in our second simulation were generated by extracting the title words of a Web site. If a title had more than five words, then we randomly picked five words from the title as a query. The peer that has a local query from a certain Web site and the peer that used the URL of this Web site as a seed for the peer's crawler must belong to the same group. Since we have 10 peers in one group and 10 queries per peer, we have 100 queries per group and a total of 700 and 5,000 queries in the first and second simulations respectively.

Finally we set the profile learning rate to γ = 0.3 (Equation 1), the profile reliability parameter to α = 0.8 (Equation 2), and the TTL to 3. We ran the simulator for about 10,000 time steps for the first simulation (corresponding to 1,000 queries issued per peer) and 1,200 time steps for the second simulation (corresponding to 120 queries issued per peer). Since there are only 10 distinct queries per peer, each query is submitted several times in the course of a simulation. In these simulations the peers have static content, as only one crawl takes place per peer. Therefore it is not necessary to request a peer's profile more than once.

Our first experiment was performed on IU's AVIDD-B Linux cluster with 208 2.4~GHz Prestonia processors using a General Parallel File System and a gigabit Ethernet connection to Abilene Internet2 and Internet. Each 10,000-page crawl took less than one hour. The 70 crawls could be run in parallel. A complete simulation run took approximately six hours. Our second experiment was distributed over five dual 2.8~GHz Linux machines, each running 100 peers. A complete simulation run took approximately 24 hours.

ANALYSIS FOR FEW LARGE PEERS

Let us analyze the results obtained from the first simulation, in which we model a relatively small network with relatively large peers (i.e., indexing relatively large crawl sets). Here we consider only the simple learning algorithm for query routing, while later in this chapter we consider the richer profile representation with query expansion and the soft update rule.

Emerging Network Topology

With the purpose of showing the variation of the network topology at different simulation time steps, we need to introduce two network statistics, the *cluster coefficient* and the *diameter*. The cluster coefficient for a node is the fraction of a node's neighbors that are also neighbors of each other. This was computed in the directed graph based on each peer's N_n neighbors. Thus, in our simulation, with $N_n = 5$, the total number of possible directed links between neighbors is $N_n(N_n - 1) = 20$. The overall cluster coefficient C is computed by averaging across all peer nodes. The diameter D is defined as the average shortest path length ℓ across all pairs of nodes. Since the network is not always strongly connected, some pairs do not have a directed path ($\ell = \infty$). To address this problem, we use the harmonic mean of shortest paths:

$$D = (\frac{N}{N-1}\sum_{ij}\ell_{ij}^{-1})^{-1} \qquad (3)$$

where N is the number of nodes. The diameter D thus defined can be computed from all pairs of nodes irrespective of whether the network is connected. C and D are measured at each time

Figure 5. Small-world statistics of the 6S peer network

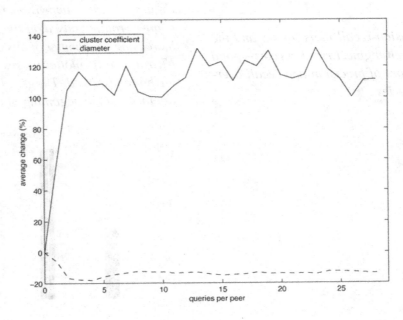

Figure 6. Peer network connectivity for all groups (left two) and for one of the groups (right two). Left: Initial neighbor links. Right: Final neighbor links.

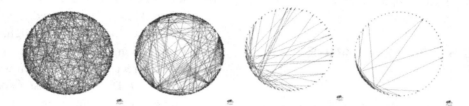

step in a simulation run diameter, while the cluster coefficient increases very rapidly and significantly, stabilizing around a value twice as large as that of the initial random graph after only five queries per peer. Figure 5 shows that the 6S diameter remains roughly equal to the initial random graph.

These conditions define the emergence of a small-world topology in our peer network (Watts & Strogatz, 1998). This is a very interesting finding, indicating that the peer interactions cause the peers to route queries in such a way that communities of users with similar interests cluster together to find quality results quickly, while it is still possible to reach any peer in a small number of steps.

To illustrate the small-world phenomenon, Figure 6 shows the dynamics of the peer network topology. We see the change both for the whole network and for the neighborhood of a single group (corresponding to Topic 7 in Table 1). The 10 nodes corresponding to peers in this group are placed around the 8 o'clock position. On the left we see the initial random connections; on the right we see the connections in the final network. One can observe that there are more local (within group) links and fewer long (cross-group) links on the right-hand side, revealing the emergence of local clusters in the network topology as the semantic locality is discovered among peers.

Figure 7. Precision-recall plots for 6S and the centralized search engine. Error bars correspond to standard errors of precision and recall averaged across queries.

Figure 8. Relative improvement in F-measure due to query routing based on simple learning and to increasing the number of hits per query response Nh from 5 to 10, plotted versus the total number of top hits considered. The gray bars measurements are taken at the beginning of the simulation

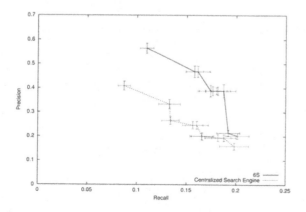

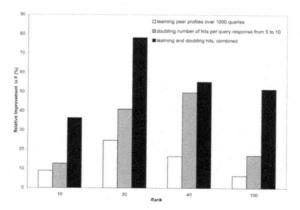

Quality of Results

In order to compare the performance of the 6S network approach with the traditional centralized search engine approach, we need to evaluate the quality of results obtained through 6S and compare them to the results obtained from centralized search engines based on the same queries. We build a centralized search engine using the same amount of network resources as a 6S run; we crawled and indexed 700,000 pages from the same seeds but using a traditional (breadth-first) crawler rather than a topical crawler. We issue the same queries used for 6S and collect 100 top hits for each query.

We want to use precision-recall plots as a tool to compare the performance between different types of search engines. To calculate precision and recall values, it is necessary to obtain a relevant set of pages for each query. As a context for relevance, we must consider that queries are submitted in our simulation by model users. To capture the users' relevance contexts, we extend each of the 700 peer queries with a single most

Figure 9. Average fraction of neighbors that are connected to peers in the same group as themselves, and diameter of peer network versus time. Time is measured in number of simulation steps, and one query is issued by each peer every 8 steps. So 200 steps are equivalent to 25 queries per peer.

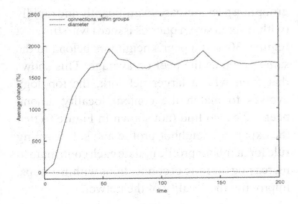

frequent term from the profile of the peer submitting the query. Each extended query is submitted off-line to a separate centralized search engine, built just for evaluation purposes, that combines the 70 peers' search engine databases; the top 100 hits returned are used as the relevant set of each query. For example, to get the relevant set of peer 4's query "environmental products services," we extend the above query with the most frequent term "health" in peer 4's local search engine database. So the query used to obtain the relevant set is "environmental products services health." Note that we are not granting 6S an unfair advantage because these profile terms used to obtain relevant sets are not used by 6S peers when processing queries.

Figure 7 shows the precision-recall plots comparing quality of results by 6S and the centralized search engine. 6S significantly outperforms the centralized search engine. This occurs because of the collaboration among peers—queries are successfully routed to those peers who can return highly relevant hits owing to their stronger focus relative to user interests.

Figure 8 shows that performance improves as peers learn to route queries to the appropriate neighbors and as the number of hits N_h that peers return in response to queries increases. Performance is measured by the F-measure, which combines precision and recall through their harmonic mean. The relatively small improvement due to the simple learning algorithm motivated our design of more sophisticated adaptive query routing schemes, and suggests that most of the advantage enjoyed by this version of 6S (cf. Figure 7) is due to focused coverage rather than to the rudimentary learning algorithm. The effect of N_h is larger; more communication can only improve performance—in the limit of complete communication, the network would combine all the focused crawls in a centralized fashion. However, there is a cost associated with communication: network traffic grows linearly with N_h. Yet, as N_h goes from 5 to 10 and traffic doubles, performance improves

Table 2. Average precision at 10 of Google and 6S

	$\langle P_{10} \rangle$	$S_{\langle P_{10} \rangle}$	95% Confidence Interval
Google	0.079678	0.00095	(0.0778, 0.0816)
6S	0.078380	0.00062	(0.07714, 0.07962)

Figure 10. Precision-recall plots for three learning schemes, taken at the start of the simulation (top), after 504 time steps or 63 queries per peer (middle), and after 1,000 time steps or 125 queries per peer (bottom)

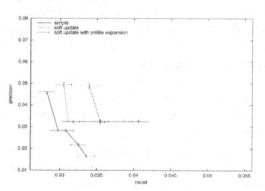

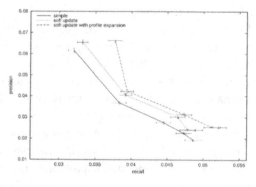

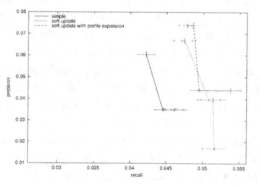

by less than a factor of 2. More experiments are needed to study the trade-off between network traffic and search effectiveness.

ANALYSIS FOR MANY SMALL PEERS

Let us analyze the results obtained from the second simulation, in which we model a larger network (one order of magnitude more peers) with relatively lightweight peers (one order of magnitude smaller crawls). Here we focus on the evaluation of the different learning algorithms supporting query routing. We also want to see if peers with similar interests can still find each other even though the network is much larger and the ratio of related peers is smaller compared to the first simulation (1/50 rather than 1/7). Finally we will compare the performance of 6S with that of a real-world centralized search engine, namely Google.

Emerging Network Topology

Even with larger network size, our experiment shows that with adaptive query routing, a peer can still quickly find another peer with a similar focus. Due to the smaller ratio between the size of peer groups and the size of the network, the clustering coefficient does not grow appreciably from its random network value in this simulation. Yet we observe in Figure 9 that the average fraction of neighbors that are in the same interest group as a peer increases significantly and rapidly (within six to seven queries issued) with time. At regime, 30% of a peer's neighbors belong to the same group as the peer on average. This shows that even with a larger network, the topology evolves to match the content locality among peers. We also find (not shown in Figure 9) that the expanded neighbor profile and soft learning rule for neighbor profile update each contribute to increasing the ratio of connections within groups, improving the locality of the network.

Quality of Results

To evaluate the query routing algorithm, here we use two baseline query routing algorithms that do not employ the expanded profile W^e: (1) *simple* updates W^f by replacing w_{ip}^f with the best hit score from p; (2) *soft update* uses W^f with the update rule in Equation 1. The relevant sets in the second simulation are simply the sets of URLs classified by the ODP under the same topic as the page whose title is used as query.

We show precision-recall snapshots in Figure 10. The snapshots are made at time steps 8, 504, and 1,000. Already at the start we observe a difference in performance between the learning algorithms. One might be surprised by such a difference after the first query since all peers in each simulation begin with empty profiles. However, during the four time steps the first query took to propagate (it can only travel as far as half the round trip), adaptive peers in the query path had already learned about their neighbors, hence they could better forward the query.

Besides showing that all query routing schemes take advantage of the learning and improve their performance over time, Figure 10 also confirms that the more sophisticated learning algorithms outperform the simpler ones, with the best performance achieved by combining expanded profiles and the soft profile update rule.

As a last analysis we wanted to compare the quality of the average results obtained by 6S peers with those returned by a real-world search engine. To this end we queried the Google Web API. As a summary performance measure, we employed the commonly used average precision at 10, $\langle P_{10} \rangle$. As shown in Table 2, the difference in performance between the two systems is not statistically significant, suggesting that 6S can be competitive with much larger search engines—the number of pages indexed by Google is about 104 times larger than those of the entire 6S network in our simulation.

The comparison with Google must be inter-preted carefully. The pages used as relevant sets in this experiment (ODP pages) are well known to Google, and using their titles as queries allowed Google to retrieve and rank very highly the pages with those titles. However, 6S peers can exploit their context and share their knowledge via collaboration during the search process, while Google has a single, universal ranking function and cannot exploit such context. Thus Google did not rank as highly pages that our model users considered relevant because they were highly related to the page used to compose the query. Another factor to be considered is that Google may have returned other relevant pages that were not in our relevant sets; our automatic assessment methodology would not allow us to give credit for those. Despite this caveat, we find the comparative result very encouraging.

ALTERNATIVE EVALUATION

In the evaluation discussed earlier, we plot precision vs. recall, a standard technique in information retrieval, in order to evaluate the quality of results obtained through either different search engines or different query routing algorithms. But the precision-recall plots for search evaluation on real Web data have a drawback, which is the construction of the relevant sets for queries. The most intuitive way for generating the relevant set of a query is using human assessment. People can make their decisions about whether a Web page is relevant to a query or not after viewing the content of the page. But it is impossible for people to access all the Web pages on the Internet. To overcome this recall problem, we used two different approaches to construct the relevant set of queries in simulations of a 6S P2P network with few large peers and a 6S P2P network with many small peers. In our first simulation, we appended a user's context term to the original query, and then submitted this modified query into a centralized search engine which combined all of the network peers' knowledge. We picked the top 100 hits returned by the centralized search engine as the relevant set for this query. In our second simulation, the relevant set of a query was the set of URLs classified by the ODP under the same topic as the page whose title was used as that particular query. These two approaches were designed for a fair evaluation that would in one case take context into account, in the other use an independent source of relevance assessments (the ODP). However, it is difficult to eliminate all bias (either in favor of a centralized search engine or in favor of 6S) when comparing two completely different search paradigms. For example, the number of Web pages indexed by Google is much larger than those in the 6S system. So when doing the precision and recall computation, some query results returned by the centralized search engine might be classified as irrelevant simply because they are not in the predefined relevant set of our experiment, even if they were actually relevant.

Leake, Maguitman, and Reichherzer (2005) introduces two novel criterion functions for evaluating retrieval performance: *global coherence* and *coverage*. These two functions generalize the well-known IR measures of precision and recall. However, in contrast to precision and recall, the measures of global coherence and coverage do not require that all relevant resources be precisely identified. Instead, these measures are applicable as long as an approximate description of the potentially relevant material is available.

Let us review the definitions of *global coherence* and *coverage*. Assume $R = \{r_1,...,r_m\}$ is a set containing approximate descriptions of potentially relevant material, where each r_i is a collection of keywords. Let $A = \{a_1,...,a_n\}$ be the set of retrieved resources, with a_i also represented as a collection of keywords. A measure of *similarity* between a retrieved resource a_i and a relevant resource r_j can be computed using, for example, the *Jaccard coefficient*, defined as:

$$Similarity(a_i, r_j) = \frac{|a_i \cap r_j|}{|a_i \cup r_j|} \quad (4)$$

Then, the *accuracy* of resource a_i in R is defined as follows:

$$Accuracy(a_i, R) = \max_{r_j \in R} Similarity(a_i, r_j) \quad (5)$$

The accuracy of a retrieved resource a_i provides an estimate of the precision with which the keywords in a_i replicate those of relevant resources.

Once the *Accuracy* of each retrieved result has been computed, it can be used to obtain a measure of *Global_Coherence* as follows:

$$Global\_Coherence(A, R) = \frac{\sum_{a_i \in A} Accuracy(a_i, R)}{|A|} \quad (6)$$

The *Global_Coherence* function measures the degree to which a retrieval mechanism succeeded in keeping its focus within the theme defined by a set of relevant resources. This is similar to the IR notion of precision, except that we use a less restrictive notion of relevance: by using a measure

Table 3. Average and standard deviation of global coherence and coverage of On-Topic, 6S, and Random across 50 topics

Global Coherence	μ	σ	95% Confidence Interval
Random	0.036	0.016	(0.032.0.041)
6S	0.052	0.020	(0.047,0.058)
On-Topic	0.063	0.020	(0.057,0.068)
Coverage	μ	σ	95% Confidence Interval
Random	0.015	0.006	(0.013,0.016)
6S	0.024	0.012	(0.020,0.027)
On-Topic	0.033	0.013	(0.030,0.037)

of accuracy instead of considering exact matches, we overcome the drawback of binary classification of relevancy.

It is important to note that a high global coherence value does not guarantee acceptable retrieval performance. For example, if the system retrieves only a single resource that is similar to some relevant resource, the global coherence value will be high. Because search mechanisms should also maximize the number of relevant resources retrieved, we introduce a coverage factor to favor those strategies that retrieve many resources similar to a target set of relevant resources. We define a criterion function able to measure *coverage* as a generalization of the standard IR notion of recall, seen in below as equation (7).

A performance evaluation based on our criterion functions requires access to a set of terms taken to characterize potentially relevant resources (a target set R) for a given query. For our task we used the ODP directory to construct relevant sets as follows.

Let $t_1...t_m$ be third-level topics in the ODP directory and let $q_{1...}q_m$ be m queries associated with these topics. With the aim of constructing a relevant set R_i for each query q_i, we extract the descriptions of URLs from the ODP subtrees rooted at the topic t_i. Each $r \in R_i$ is then defined as a set of keywords extracted from these descriptions, and it represents a potentially relevant result for query q_i.

To verify whether the global coherence and coverage measures can be used as performance evaluation tools, we conducted a preliminary experiment. The goal of this experiment was to compare the global coherence and coverage measures applied to a set of *On-Topic* results (i.e., results focused on the topic under con-

sideration) against the performance measures applied to a *Random* set of results. We expected our performance evaluation measures to return significantly higher values for the *On-Topic* set than for the *Random* one. In this experiment, we used the same $m = 50$. ODP topics from our second simulation and applied the procedure described above to construct the relevant set R. For a given topic, the *On-Topic* retrieved set ($A_{On-Topic}$) was created using 10 URLs within that topic subtree in the ODP directory. To construct the *Random* retrieved set (A_{Random}), we used a method similar to the one used to construct the *On-Topic* set but, instead of extracting URLs from the subtree under the relevant topic, we randomly selected 10 URLs from the whole ODP directory. Finally, our performance evaluation framework was validated by comparing the global coherence and coverage of the *On-Topic* and *Random* retrieved sets. The results, which are included in Table 3 (together with an evaluation for 6Search performance to be described next), show that the *On-Topic* retrieved set truly has significantly better performance than the *Random* retrieved set both in terms of global coherence and coverage. This outcome also indicates that the global coherence and coverage for the *On-Topic* and *Random* sets are feasible upper and lower bounds for measuring the performance of a search system.

Let us now apply this evaluation approach for assessing the performance of the 6S system. To this end, we selected one query from each group in our second simulation (for a total of $m = 50$ queries) and considered the top $N = 10$ hits retrieved by the 6Search system. Table 3 shows that the quality of the results returned by the 6S system is significantly better than the Random baseline both in terms of global coherence and coverage.

$$Coverage(A, R) = \frac{\sum_{r_i \in R} Accuracy(r_i, A)}{|R|} = \frac{\sum_{r_i \in R} \max_{a_j \in A} Similarity(a_j, r_i)}{|R|} \qquad (7)$$

DISCUSSION

In this chapter we introduced a collaborative peer network application called 6Search, with which we intend to study the idea that the scalability limitations of centralized search engines can be overcome via distributed Web crawling and searching. We also described adaptive routing algorithms to dynamically change the topology of the peer network based on commonality of interests among users, so as to avoid the problem of flooding queries which has plagued other attempts to search over peer networks. The results presented here seem to support the idea that adaptive routing can work with real data and that critical network structure can emerge spontaneously from the local interactions between peers, capturing the locality of content interests among them. Our experiments also suggest that 6Search can outperform centralized search engines, which cannot take advantage of user context in their crawling and searching processes.

One can observe a sharp drop in precision as recall increases (Figures 7 and 10), which corresponds to the drop in F-measure as each peer considers more hits (Figure 8). The reason is that each neighbor contributes a small number N_h of hits, so in order to increase recall, a peer must consider a larger pool of neighbors, some of which may belong to different topical communities.

One of the challenges in effectiveness comparison is how to evaluate different systems such as 6S and centralized search engines in an unbiased way. By our preliminary experiment results, we have shown that the *global coherence* and *coverage* are promising approaches to compare the performance of different systems. These measures confirm that 6S can provide users with relevant results.

Let us briefly discuss redundancy of coverage. We believe that minimizing overlap between pages indexed by peers is neither desirable nor practical. Clearly one would not want all peers to be identical, but this is a very unlikely scenario;

peers will be driven by user profiles built from their daily queries, their stored documents, their bookmarks, and so forth. Such profiles will generate heterogeneous profiles and lead to broad coverage of the Web. Redundancy will likely occur for popular pages likely to be of interest to a large number of people. This kind of redundant coverage is good for both performance (local data yield faster results) and robustness (duplication ensures availability).

FUTURE WORK

We are currently extending the evaluation with global coherence and coverage to 5,000 queries to better quantify the performance of our 6S system. We will also repeat the same computation for the results returned by Google to compare the distributed and centralized approach.

As a project in its infancy stage, 6S has many directions for further development. One technique proposed in a semantic Web setting—where peers query for RDF data (Tempich, Staab, & Wranik, 2004) that we intend to test for Web searching—is query relaxation, whereby a peer assumes that a neighbor may have knowledge about a topic/query if it has knowledge about a more specific version of the topic/query. While our application is arguably more difficult due to the unstructured nature

Figure 11. A screen shot of the 6S application

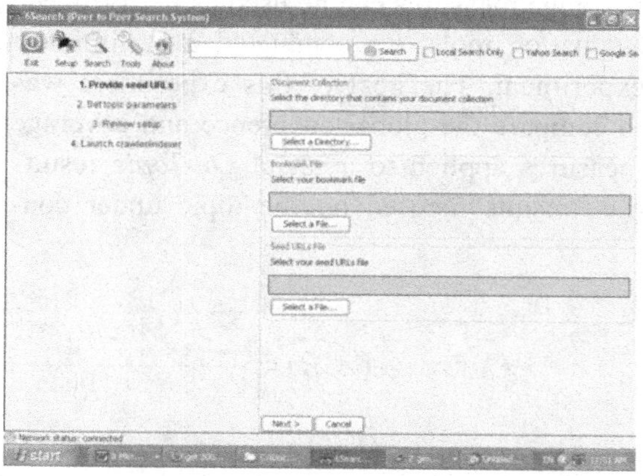

of generic Web pages, we hope that the promising scalability results obtained for semantic Web data will generalize to Web IR.

A number of improvements and extensions of the 6S network architecture and protocols are under consideration. Additional IR techniques such as various lexical similarity functions and term weighting schemes can be applied, as well as richer representation for profiles, for example, LSI (Deerwester et al., 1990).

A robust algorithm is to be developed for combining hits from peers in the combinator module, thus allowing for heterogeneous scoring by peer search engines. Strategies based on semi-supervised learning have proven effective for merging results in hierarchical peer networks, where peers can aggregate query-based document samples from neighbors into centralized (hub) databases (Lu & Callan, 2004). In a framework like 6S, this may be possible to a limited extent as we do not require special hubs. We are designing an appropriate randomized ranking function to allow for probabilistic updates of peer profiles.

Additional learning algorithms will be analyzed for adaptive query routing. For example, one could mine the streams of queries and responses that are forwarded though a peer. In the Gnutella v0.6 file sharing network, peers tend to issue queries that are very similar to their own content (Asvanund et al., 2003). This suggests that a profile should be updated based on queries in addition to query responses. Another possibility is to extend the 6S protocol by including requests for profiles of a neighbor's neighbors. Several promising heuristics for adaptive query routing proposed in the literature (Crespo & Garcia-Molina, 2002; Kalogeraki et al., 2002; Yang & Garcia-Molina, 2002) will be explored. Referral should also be investigated as an alternative mechanism for adapting the network topology based on local reinforcement interactions (Singh, Yu, & Venkatraman, 2000). Finally, we plan to study the use of reinforcement learning algorithms for identifying good neighbors from

not only their individual performance but also that of their neighborhoods.

In parallel with the above algorithmic extensions, implementation of a working 6S servent (server + client) application is underway. Figure 11 offers a view of the current prototype's user interface. We are developing a prototype based on the JXTA framework (Waterhouse, 2001) which will integrate the 6S protocol, topical crawler, document index system, search engine system, and network communication system; we plan to release the prototype to the open-source community. Testing the peer communication protocols in real environments over TCP/IP will allow us to study the robustness of the system from a security standpoint, for example, with respect to DoS attacks. Can malicious users gain unfair advantage or disrupt the network? Most importantly, the prototype is necessary in order to move from simulated to real users in the evaluation of the proposed approach. For example, it would not be sufficient to simply test the system on real queries that are publicly available because these are not labeled or associated with particular users, and therefore do not capture the relationships that exist between different users. Peer collaborative Web search is based on real users driving the interaction between peers so that the network can discover, form, and leverage communities of users with common interests. Testing the prototype in a realistic setting will also allow us to tune our protocols and algorithms. For example, while a peer may decide not to share its knowledge with other peers, we will consider whether the information available to a peer should be dependent on the information it is willing to share. Finally, JXTA provides for mechanisms to bootstrap a peer into the network. Simple mechanisms employed by many file sharing peer networks rely on a registry for first joining the network. An advantage of our approach is that adaptive query routing should rapidly adjust the connections of the new peer and prevent overload on the registry.

REFERENCES

Akavipat, R., Wu, L.-S., & Menczer, F. (2004). Small world peer networks in distributed Web search. *Proceedings of the Alternate Track Papers and Posters of the 13th International World Wide Web Conference,* New York.

Asvanund, A., Bagala, S., Kapadia, M., Krishnan, R., Smith, M., & Telang, R. (2003). Intelligent club management in P2P networks. *Proceedings of the Workshop on Economics of Peer to Peer Systems,* Berkeley, CA.

Bawa, M., Jr, R.B., Rajagoplan, S., & Shekita, E. (2003). Make it fresh, make it quick—searching a network of personal Webservers. *Proceedings of the 12th International World Wide Web Conference,* Budapest, Hungary.

Brewington, B.E., & Cybenko, G. (2000). How dynamic is the Web? *Proceedings of the 9th International World Wide Web Conference,* Amsterdam, The Netherlands.

Brin, S., & Page, L. (1998). The anatomy of a large-scale hypertextual Web search engine. *Computer Networks, 30*(1-7), 107-117.

Chakrabarti, S., Berg, M., & Dom, B. (1999). Focused crawling: A new approach to topic-specific Web resource discovery. *Computer Networks, 31*(11-16), 1623-1640.

Cho, J., & Garcia-Molina, H. (2002). Parallel crawlers. *Proceedings of the 11th International World Wide Web Conference,* Honolulu, HI.

Crespo, A., & Garcia-Molina, H. (2002). Routing indices for peer-to-peer systems. *Proceedings of the 22nd International Conference on Distributed Computing Systems* (ICDCS'02), Vienna, Austria.

Dean, J., & Ghemawat, S. (2004). MapReduce: Simplified data processing on large clusters. *Proceedings of the 6th Symposium on Operating System Design and Implementation* (OSDI04), San Francisco, CA.

Deerwester, S., Dumais, S., GW, F., Landauer, T., & Harshman, R. (1990). Indexing by latent semantic analysis. *Journal of the American Society for Information Science, 41,* 391-407.

Fetterly, D., Manasse, M., Najork, M., & Wiener, J. (2003). A large-scale study of the evolution of Web pages. *Proceedings of the 12th International World Wide Web Conference,* Budapest, Hungary.

Joseph, S. (2002). NeuroGrid: Semantically routing queries in peer-to-peer networks. *Proceedings of the International. Workshop on Peer-to-Peer Computing,* Pisa, Italy.

Kalogeraki, V., Gunopulos, D., & Zeinalipour-Yazti, D. (2002). A local search mechanism for peer-to-peer networks. *Proceedings of the 11th International Conference on Information and Knowledge Management* (CIKM'02), McLean, VA.

Kamvar, S., Schlosser, M., & Garcia-Molina, H. (2003). The EigenTrust algorithm for reputation management in P2P networks. *Proceedings of the 12th International World Wide Web Conference,* Budapest, Hungary.

Lawrence, S., & Giles, C. (1999). Accessibility of information on the Web. *Nature, 400,* 107-109.

Leake, D., Maguitman, A., & Reichherzer, T. (2005, July). Exploiting rich context: An incremental approach to context-based Web search. *Proceedings of the International and Interdisciplinary Conference on Modeling and Using Context* (CONTEXT'05), Paris, France.

Li, J., Loo, B., Hellerstein, J., Kaashoek, F., Karger, D., & Morris, R. (2003). On the feasibility of peer-to-peer Web indexing and search. *Proceedings of the 2nd International Workshop on Peer-to-Peer Systems,* Berkeley, CA.

Lu, J., & Callan, J. (2003). Content-based retrieval in hybrid peer-to-peer networks. *Proceedings of* the 12th International Conference on Information and Knowledge Management (CIKM'03), New Orleans, LA.

Lu, J., & Callan, J. (2004). Merging retrieval results in hierarchical peer-to-peer networks. *Proceedings of the 27th Annual International ACM SIGIR Conference on Research and Development in Information Retrieval*, Sheffield, UK.

Lua, E.K., Crowcroft, J., & Pias, M. (2005). A survey and comparison of peer-to-peer overlay network schemes. *IEEE Communications Surveys and Tutorials, 7*(2).

Menczer, F., & Belew, R. (2000). Adaptive retrieval agents: Internalizing local context and scaling up to the Web. *Machine Learning, 39*(2-3), 203-242.

Menczer, F., Pant, G., & Srinivasan, P. (2004). Topical Web crawlers: Evaluating adaptive algorithms. *ACM Transactions on Internet Technology, 4*(4), 378-419.

Najork, M., & Wiener, J.L. (2001). Breadth-first search crawling yields high-quality pages. *Proceedings of the 10th International World Wide Web Conference*, Hong Kong.

Ntoulas, A., Cho, J., & Olston, C. (2004). What's new on the Web?: The evolution of the Web from a search engine perspective. *Proceedings of the 13th International World Wide Web Conference*, New York.

Pant, G., Bradshaw, S., & Menczer, F. (2003). Search engine—crawler symbiosis. *Proceedings of the 7th European Conference on Research and Advanced Technology for Digital Libraries* (ECDL), Berlin.

Pant, G., Srinivasan, P., & Menczer, F. (2003). Crawling the Web. *Web Dynamics*.

Pujol, J., Sanguesa, R., & Bermudez, J. (2003). Porqpine: A distributed and collaborative search engine. *Proceedings of the 12th International*

World Wide Web Conference, Budapest, Hungary.

Risson, J., & Moors, T. (2004). *Survey of research towards robust peer-to-peer networks: Search methods*. Sydney, Australia: University of New South Wales.

Singh, M., Yu, B., & Venkatraman, M. (2000). Community-based service location. *Communications of the ACM, 44*(4), 49-54.

Srinivasan, P., Pant, G., & Menczer, F. (2005). A general evaluation framework for topical crawlers. *Information Retrieval, 8*(3), 417-447.

Suel, C., Mathur, T., Wu, J.-W., Zhang, J., Delis, A., Kharrazi, M. et al. (2003). ODISSEA: A peer-to-peer architecture for scalable Web search and information retrieval. *Proceedings of the International Workshop on the Web and Databases* (WebDB), San Diego, CA.

Tang, C., Xu, Z., & Dwarkadas, S. (2003). Peer-to-peer information retrieval using self-organizing semantic overlay networks. *Proceedings of ACM SIGCOMM'03*, Karlsruhe, Germany.

Tempich, C., Staab, S., & Wranik, A. (2004). REMINDIN': Semantic query routing in peer-to-peer networks based on social metaphors. *Proceedings of the 13th International World Wide Web Conference*, New York.

Waterhouse, S. (2001). *JXTA search: Distributed search for distributed networks*. Santa Clara, CA: Sun Microsystems.

Watts, D., & Strogatz, S. (1998). Collective dynamics of "small-world" networks. *Nature, 393*, 440-442.

Yang, B., & Garcia-Molina, H. (2002). Improving search in peer-to-peer networks. *Proceedings of the 22nd International Conference on Distributed Computing Systems* (ICDCS'02), Vienna, Austria.

Section IV
Social Issues

Chapter IX
The Ethics of Social Information Retrieval

Brendan Luyt
Nanyang Technological University, Singapore

Chu Keong Lee
Nanyang Technological University, Singapore

ABSTRACT

In this chapter we discuss some of the social and ethical issues associated with social information retrieval. Using the work of Habermas, we argue that social networking is likely to exacerbate already disturbing trends towards the fragmentation of society and a corresponding decline reduction in social diversity. Such a situation is not conducive to developing a healthy, democratic society. Following the tradition of critical theorists of technology, we conclude with a call for responsible and aware technological design with more attention paid to the values embedded in new technological systems.

INTRODUCTION

The development of social information retrieval systems has begun to generate interest among information scientists eager to apply such techniques to the development of ever more advanced searching tools. The goal is a laudable one. Current information retrieval systems are mediocre at best in terms of either user friendliness or, alternatively, in their ability to sort through the enormous number of documents generated on an ever-growing basis by our networked societ-

ies. Yet in the haste to apply social information retrieval techniques, are we running the risk of creating new problems? In this chapter we wish to sound a note of caution to those involved in this burgeoning field. To do so we introduce the work of the political theorist Jurgen Habermas, and in particular his concepts of the public sphere and communicative action. These concepts provide the necessary context for our discussion of the social and ethical implications of social information retrieval. We then draw on the well-established sociological concept of homophily to argue that social networking is likely to exacerbate already disturbing trends towards the fragmentation of society that Habermas identifies. Specifically, we suggest that the effects of homophily engendered by these new technologies are likely to erode further the public sphere and the ability to engage in communicative action with deleterious effects on the skills needed to create communities at precisely a time in our history when they are most needed. We conclude with a call for responsible and aware technological design. In the tradition of critical theorists of technology such as Langdon Winner, we suggest that more attention needs to be paid to consciously embedding values in technological systems.

THE RISE AND FALL OF THE PUBLIC SPHERE

The notion of the public sphere, that is, a place where rational debate is both possible and widely engaged in, is most closely associated with the German political theorist Jurgen Habermas and his book, *The Structural Transformation of the Public Sphere.* For Habermas, the idea of the public sphere was intimately associated with a new kind of space. Prior to the 18th century, space had tended to be separated into private and public areas. The private realm was associated with the family, but public space was tied to the state, and in particular, the monarch. The court was the center of this arena in the middle ages and the early modern period of European history. During the course of the 18th century, in England at least, a third space opened up, one that was public, but which was not centered on the royal court. This was the space of coffee shops, aristocratic salons, and printing presses. Here, rising members of the capitalist class could come together as independent individuals to debate issues relating to the conduct of state affairs that previously had been the preserve of secular or ecclesiastical authority. The development of this third space, neither court nor

family, eventually led to the creation of a public sphere as it allowed two enabling characteristics to be met. First, coffee shops and salons rapidly became places where the outcome of debate were determined by rational argument, rather than tradition or authority. Second, status differences were increasingly bracketed or, in other words, "left at the door." Instead of a person's rank or level of social prestige determining who could say what, debate in the nascent public sphere required only the ability to engage in rational discourse. Out of such discourse, it was thought by participants, an enlightened public opinion could be wrought, one in opposition to the feudal state and one which had in mind the good of the entire society rather than any particular group.

Once in place, however, the bourgeois public sphere rapidly declined in the nineteenth and twentieth centuries. Habermas identifies the cause of this decay in the re-feudalization of society, a return in many ways to the society of spectacle that characterized the public space of the middle ages with its elaborate ceremonies and protocols connecting kings and bishops with their people. A number of factors are held responsible for this decline. The first was the tendency of the public sphere to fuse with the state and private realm. The bracketing of inequalities was increasingly made impossible as more and more people acquired the education, time, and resources to participate in the public sphere. Instead of being "left at the door," inequalities became the topic of debate and, later, amelioration. At the same time as the private realm, with its host of inequalities, was under increasing scrutiny, the state was intruding in the public sphere, picking up on the discussions increasingly taking place there around issues of inequality in order to develop the welfare state. The result was that the public sphere found itself increasingly sidelined through the creation of large organizations (trade unions, business associations, lobby groups) whose missions were to mediate between the state and individuals. These organizations pursued particular interests, so that negotiated compromises rather than the ascertaining of the general interest became the aim of discussion. Furthermore, as they became more powerful, they increasingly viewed the individual as needing management through public relations techniques rather than capable of being engaged in dialogue and rational debate. The technology of mass media was also a contributory factor to the re-feudalization of the public sphere—an important point that we will return to later. As radio and television became commonplace, they tended to replace the culture of print which preceded them. But, Habermas argues, they were not equal to the task of creating a community of readers engaged in rational debate. Their immediacy and intimacy meant that emotional appeals increasingly trumped reasoned deliberations. And the segmentation of audiences that they encouraged meant that there could be no single public capable of being addressed through discourse. In all these ways, citizens gradually "lost the sense of the pleasures and virtues of argument" (Calhoun, 1992), becoming passive consumers of culture instead.

Of course, the historical reality of the public sphere was less than ideal. Gender, race, and class inevitably excluded large numbers of individuals. However, it is as an ideal that the concept is of significance to us today. The public sphere, imperfect though it might have been, was still a space in which was created far more than in other places an "ideal speech situation." It allowed more people than ever before equal opportunities to discourse. This ability led to the possibility of not just strategic action on the part of speakers (that is, action designed to manipulate an individual into supporting an aim of the speaker), but what Habermas calls communicative action (language used to generate a shared understanding). By engaging in communicative action, actors could, in a dialectic process, arrive at a mutual understanding of their world beyond that associated with goal-driven instrumentality and which included assessments of normative and subjective claims.

In so doing these actors could reproduce and transmit the cultural knowledge that underpins meaningful human existence. The decay of the public sphere continues a long running trend of the destruction of places or institutions where communicative action takes place. To understand why this is the case, we need to explore Habermas' twin concepts of lifeworld and system. By lifeworld, Habermas refers to the "enormous fund of non-explicit, taken-for-granted notions" used "to seek shared understanding about something in the objective, social, or subjective world" (Brand, 1990). This is the common knowledge that communicative action draws on for help in its work of mutual understanding, but also which it preserves and passes on to others. In the earliest human societies—egalitarian hunter-gatherers, for example—the lifeworld and communicative action would have been sufficient to sustain both the material and symbolic reproduction of society. But as these societies became more complex, the task of coordinating their survival became progressively delegated to subsystems that did not rely on communicative action, but instead on mechanisms designed to ensure compliance without understanding (money, political office, and most especially legal systems). The system, in search of legitimacy from the public, increasingly ate into, or to use Habermas' term, colonized the lifeworld in areas previously the exclusive preserve of cultural reproduction (mass media, for example), social integration (family affairs), and socialization (education). Of course, the expansion of the system has brought benefits (laws against child abuse and labor, for example), but as Habermas notes it has also brought about growing dependence on the state, and a general sense of alienation and feelings of helplessness among individuals when faced with the often inscrutable actions of large bureaucratic entities in both the private and public sectors. In the face of this colonialization, the public sphere, where communicative action was the norm, acts as an example of how another method of coordinating society is possible. Thus it is vitally important that it be revitalized or at least not allowed to shrink any further. How can this be achieved?

According to Habermas, hope is to be found in the new social movements. These movements, products of the socio-cultural upheavals of the 1960s, place at the center of public attention issues that do not directly revolve around the world of money or narrow political advantage, but rather issues of lifestyle and human choice. Environmentalism, feminism, and the anti-nuclear movement are a few examples of the vast range of issues that new social movements address. Habermas argues that these groups are a response to the colonization of the lifeworld. They reject the routine operations of the system in favor of developing new methods of coordination and, most importantly, places for public discussion. In the places opened up by the activities of new social movements, people can come together to discuss and debate, thereby planting the seeds for a new public sphere based on the ideals of communicative action. New communication technologies (e-mail, Web, mobile telecommunications, and so on) have all been seen as conducive to the aims of new social movements. They enabled the protests, and more importantly from a long-term perspective, much of the debate against the World Trade Organization (WTO) and the lobbying of the Jubilee movement against African debt. The Zapatistas would never have survived the onslaught of the Mexican army without their ability to use the Internet to mobilize global public opinion. And the Bush administration faced a larger-than-expected domestic battle in its race to invade Iraq again thanks to the debate carried on over the networks of new communication technology.

Social information retrieval would appear on the surface to be another enabling tool in the arsenal of new social movements fighting the battle to re-establish communicative action as a basis for decision making in our complex societies. Technologies such as social bookmarking, blogs, and social tagging are powerful tools that allow in-dividuals to form communities based on common interests, and which create spaces for interaction and, at least potentially, debate. However, there is a problem with this rosy scenario and it goes by the sociological name of 'homophily.'

THE PROBLEM OF HOMOPHILY

McPherson, Smith-Lovin, and Cook (1991) define homophily as "the principle that a contact between similar people occurs at a higher rate than among dissimilar people." Homophily is a concept with a long history. In the social sciences, references to homophily go back to the 1920s and 1930s with studies showing that children made friends faster if the individuals had demographic traits in common. Since that time further research has demonstrated the same pattern with respect to numerous kinds of relationships: gender, race, ethnicity, age, religion, education, occupation, social class, prestige, behaviors, and values. From an examination of these studies, McPherson et al. (1991) conclude that: "In general the patterns of homophily are remarkably robust over these widely varying types of relations" (p. 418). For our purposes the important point to note from the findings of these studies is that information that flows through networks tends to be localized, that is, the social characteristics of a particular human node of the network in many ways determines network distance.

Homophily is a problem for the public sphere as a place for communicative action. This is because communicative action is based on rational debate between individuals, and this requires social diversity (one cannot sustain debate without a set of actors speaking from different perspectives). It emerges from differences in one's ethnic, cultural, or educational backgrounds; one's differences in personality, preferred cognitive style, and blend of intelligences; and one's race, creed, ancestry, language, nationality, gender, sexual orientation, political affiliation, or socio-economic status.

Habermas is not alone in valuing diversity for its effects on human communities. Using a human-maze large enough that problem solvers had no global sense of the problem, and one that had many optimal and non-optimal solutions, Johnson (1999) has shown that diversity is critical to the ability of communities to find better and more robust solutions to problems. When the problem solvers learn about the maze, they create a diversity of experience, inching with each try to the optimal solution. The problem solvers are handicapped because they have no global perspective (remember that to simulate a complex problem, the maze is large). Here is where diversity helps. The individual problem solvers can combine their individually diverse experiences into a powerful collective experience, so that larger collectives of individuals manage to find the minimum path much more easily than if they had been a smaller group or lone participant. It is important to note that this enhanced performance is due to diversity, that is, the unique contributions from each individual and not the superior contribution of any single problem solver in the collective.

The widely acclaimed management scholar Moss Kanter (1988) has put forward another compelling reason for ensuring diversity and, although she does not specifically use the term, the public sphere. She stresses that for all five types of innovation, namely product, process, technological, administrative, and evolutionary, to be supported, diversity must be guaranteed. This is because innovation typically crosses boundaries, with many of the best ideas being interdisciplinary and interfunctional in origin. The development of such "new combinations" benefits from the broader perspective and information brought from the "outside" through diversity. To her, cross-fertilization can be achieved by the "kaleidoscopic thinking" possessed by people with "cosmopolitan" rather than "local" orientations. Stressing the importance of contact with people outside the field, Kanter warns of the dangers of "occupational psychosis" or "trained incapacity"

that await "those who concentrate on only one area and interact only with those who are similar in outlook to become less able over time to learn new things." Kanter is, in fact, warning of the dangers of homophily.

Under conditions of pure homophily, it is unlikely that anything resembling a public sphere could come into existence. What made its development possible was the creation of institutions that exerted enough force to counter the effects of homophily, generating instead an oasis of diversity. Oldenburg (1997) talks about "The Great Good Place" that existed in profusion in the United States in the not-so-distant past in his book of the same title. The subtitle of his book "Cafes, Coffee Shops, Community Centers, Beauty Parlors, General Stores, Bars, Hangouts and How They Get You Through the Day" brings to mind some of these often overlooked institutions that helped bridge the gap between age, gender, and other demographic variables (Oldenburg, 1997). Institutions such as these, which Oldenburg calls the 'Third Place', make possible the debates underpinning genuine communication. What are Third Places? He asserts that to understand this concept, one has to first understand the First and Second Places. According to Oldenburg, the First Place is the home. The home is the most important place of all, as it is the first regular and predictable environment of the growing child and the one that will have the greatest impact upon his or her development. It will harbor individuals long before the workplace is interested in them and well after the world of work casts them aside. The Second Place is the work setting; it reduces the individual to a single, productive role. It performs the dual role of fostering competition and motivating people to rise above their fellow colleagues, and also provides the means to a living, improves the material quality of life, and structures endless hours of time for a majority who could not structure it on their own. The Third Place is a generic designation for a great variety of public places that host the regular, voluntary, informal, and happily anticipated gatherings of the individual beyond the realms of home (The First Place) and work (The Second Place).

Oldenburg describes the Third Place variously as "informal public gathering places," "happy gathering places," "congenial meeting places," "a home away from home," and "a place where unrelated people can relate." Decrying the segregation, isolation, and compartmentalization that characterizes modern society, Oldenburg stresses that a Third Place has distinct community-building function, as it allows for ease of association by providing a convivial atmosphere based on the camaraderie of people who see themselves as equals. Its egalitarian ethos ensures that it remains a place where people will always be welcome and that serves everyone. It acts as a "home away from home" where unrelated people can relate, and therefore it encourages people to mix and encourages generation gaps to be bridged, as participants from different generations can enjoy each others' company. A Third Place also allows participants to learn to be at ease with other people, and so it performs a socialization function. Oldenburg provides several examples of the Third Place in different countries: the British pubs, the American-German beer garden, and the Italian piazzas and taverns.

The Third Place makes for an excellent public sphere because it is a neutral ground for discussions, debates, and banter. It is an intellectual and political forum in which participants place value on good conversation and on enjoying other people, primarily for the company they offer instead of focusing on the instrumentalities of the interaction. The Third Place is where unplanned meetings can be anticipated. Although the examples furnished above give the impression that the Third Place is a place where food is consumed (and Oldenburg himself suggested that the food and drinks served in Third Places should be cheap), this is not strictly a requirement. Drug stores, post offices, libraries, the gym, and staircase landings are indeed excellent Third

Places. What is important is that the sustaining activity in a Third Place has to be conversation. Given the role that Third Places play in promoting diversity, interaction, and discussion, a question one has to ask is: Which social information retrieval system today incorporates all the features of the Third Space?

HOMOPHILY, THE PUBLIC SPHERE, AND SOCIAL INFORMATION RETRIEVAL

To phrase the question differently: How likely is social information retrieval to support rather than suppress the creation of such enabling institutions? There is evidence that the latter is more likely the outcome. Barry Wellman, in his examination of the sociological effects of existing "personalized networking," writes that "this is a time for individuals...not groups. The all-embracing collectivity has become a fragmented, personalized network" (Wellman, 2001). Other scholars reach similar conclusions. Robert Axelrod, exploring the emergent properties of agent-based models of cultural dissemination, concludes that electronic communication is likely to produce a polarization of communicative interaction, not based on geographical location as currently is the norm, but through the choice of individuals. Furthermore he argues that the level of polarization may be even stronger with electronic communication than with geographically dependent systems (Axelrod, 1997). Robyn Brothers (2000) is perhaps the most pessimistic regarding the ability of computer-mediated communications to foster the necessary conditions for a renewed public sphere, arguing that "electronic communication in general has increasingly isolated citizens who once would have interacted in some public forum (e.g., a town hall, a public square, the local café, etc.), calling into question the arena so central to the functioning of democracy." The instrument of this dysfunctional development lies in "the dynamics of collective identity formation through shared interests," which, Brothers believes, is an integral by-product of the development of the new communications technologies (Brothers, 2000). Similarly, Van Alstyne and Brynjolfsson (2005) are critical of "the claim that a global village is the inexorable result of increased connectivity," arguing that current communication technology could equally result in the balkanization of the Internet into groups of like-minded individuals pursuing their own interests. The result of such balkanization, they add, although sometimes economically efficient, also raises issues of inequality for those excluded from the networks, a lowering of social cohesiveness, and a reduction of the creativity associated with "intellectual cross-pollination" (Van Alstyne & Brynjolfsson, 2005). McGehee (2001) described a mental attitude adopted by Matsushita founder, Konosuke Matsushita, called *sunao mind*. This attitude of openness to new and radical ideas allows one to listen with genuine interest and concern and without judgment. Precisely such a mindset is required for intellectual cross-pollination, but with the ascendancy of personalized networks, such a mindset will be difficult to cultivate.

To give a few concrete examples of the problem we are documenting here, consider that over two-thirds of the searches on the World Wide Web are conducted on either Google or Yahoo! (Sullivan, 2005), meaning that people looking for documents on, say, "knowledge management" are likely to encounter only Google- and Yahoo-centric ones. One has to remember that any single search engine indexes a fraction of the Web and that the search results of any search engine are generated using a single, proprietary algorithm. Therefore two-thirds of the people searching the Web are uncovering documents located in a fraction of the Web and searched using a single algorithm. Diversity is reduced accordingly. Similarly, customers of Amazon and Barnes & Noble are being told what books other readers of a particular title are reading, tempting

them to purchase those other books and in the process again reducing diversity by creating small clusters of readers who have essentially read the same books. Social networking Web sites have a similar effect. Consider the following examples. Classmates.com links old boys and old girls from a school together. Friendster, MySpace, and Buzz-Oven link like-minded friends, Generation @-ers, and teens. The foundations for the social links within all these sites are the similar interests, profiles, tastes in music, and so on of their users. Diversity is defeated in such sites. This situation is all the more serious when we consider the fact that MySpace alone claims to have attracted more than 40 million members.

Online communities of practice (CoPs) are another example of phenomena that have the potential to stifle heterogeneity and encourage homophily. CoPs are collections of like-minded people who share common professional objectives and whose collaborative relationships support the goals of a particular organization. Two prominent examples are Nikonians (a CoP for users of Nikon photographic equipment) and Techforums (developed by Buckland Labs for its clients). Among the reasons why so many people are enamored of and are starting communities of practice in both profit and non-profit settings are the benefits to be achieved in being able to better capture knowledge, share best practices, solve problems quickly, drive innovation, enable professional development, reduce business costs, and socialize and support organizational learning. But in as far as CoPs are also vehicles for homophily, they extinguish diversity.

HANDLING HOMOPHILY FOR THE PUBLIC SPHERE IN SOCIAL INFORMATION RETRIEVAL SYSTEMS

Of course, we do not wish to dismiss social information retrieval, nor suggest that it does not have benefits. What we are saying here is that this is the time to embed the values we see as important in the technology we produce. Here it is useful to examine the work of Langdon Winner (1989), who looks at technology from the perspective of a political theorist. Winner argues that technology has political effects of two kinds. The first of these occurs when a technological development "becomes a way of settling an issue in the affairs of a particular community" (Winner, 1989). Winner gives us as an example the introduction of the mechanical tomato harvester in California during the 1960s. This invention appeared in a social context where large and small tomato farmers co-existed in the same area, each employing a great deal of temporary labor to bring in the tomato harvest. In this case the machine decided two issues: the size of the optimal land holding for tomato farmers and the size of the necessary labor force. Large farms became the only economical way to produce tomatoes, so that small farmers were increasingly bought out by their bigger neighbors. And the labor force shrunk dramatically in size as the mechanical harvesters made human labor in the fields superfluous.

The second kind of political effect technology is capable of producing, according to Winner, is built into the technology from the beginning. These are "inherently political" technologies, "man-made systems that appear to require or to be strongly compatible with particular kinds of political relationships" (Winner, 1989). A prime example of such a technology is nuclear power, which tends to require centralized management, highly specialized expertise, and authoritarian control, if disaster is to be prevented. It is a technology not readily compatible with democratic traditions. Both the effects of the tomato harvester and nuclear power are most definitely political, as they affect the ways of life of both employees and communities, but it is important to note here, as Winner does, that this does not mean that they represent some sort of "conspiracy" against the world. Each technology was developed by reason-

ably caring and concerned people who wanted to make a positive difference to their world. What is the problem then? Simply that, as Winner points out, our societies have been "technologically somnambulist"—we have been sleeping while our technologies play out their political roles undisturbed. Instead of thinking about what values we want our society to embody and acting to make sure that our technologies reflect and enable those values, we have been content to let the mantra of efficiency and productivity remain our sole guides to technological development. Winner would have us look at the development of each new technology as akin to a piece of parliamentary legislation.

Legislation (in properly functioning political systems) is intently scrutinized by members of the political party, in power as well as the opposition parties and other groups outside the governing apparatus, the aim being to identify the flaws and weak points before the bill is passed, as well as to make sure that it reflects the values of the society it will help structure. Winner argues that we need to similarly subject technology to the same kind of intense scrutiny before it becomes a part of our society: "Many crucial choices about the form and limits of our regimes of instrumentality must be enforced at the founding, at the genesis of each new technology. It is here that our best purposes must be heard" (Winner, 1989, p. 58). So, where does this leave us in relation to social information retrieval? We would like to suggest two directions for developers of social information retrieval systems to explore.

Firstly, developers should attempt to bridge the barriers between different groups. What are these barriers and how can one come to grips with them? Ashkenas, Ulrich, Jick, and Kerr (2002) have developed a framework to understand the invisible boundaries that impose real and imaginary barriers between people. Their framework can be productively used to understand and address the effects of homophily when designing social information retrieval systems. They propose three types of boundaries that need to be eliminated and suggest that they can be understood by using the metaphor of a multi-story building. Firstly, vertical boundaries are represented by the floors and ceilings of the building. These boundaries separate people by hierarchical levels, titles, status, and rank. Eliminating vertical boundaries may require the system to provide features such as anonymization. Secondly, horizontal boundaries are represented by the walls between the rooms on each floor. These are boundaries between separate, but equal communities (photographers and stamp collectors, for example). Eliminating horizontal boundaries requires the social information retrieval system to provide a bridge to enable communication between the different groups. This can be achieved by alerting members of different communities to the fact that there are other communities within the retrieval system. Pelz and Andrews (1966) give us some clue as to the frequency that these alerts should be issued. His research indicates that two years is all it takes for people of different backgrounds to get "homogenized" in their thoughts so that designers of retrieval systems should think of heterogenizing the membership within this timeframe. Thirdly, the external boundary is represented by the fence between the users of one system with those of another. Dissolving external boundaries will require different social information retrieval systems to be interoperable. For example, the owners of different systems (e.g., Classmates.com and Friendster) could provide bridges between the two services to facilitate mutual exploration and discovery of their members' interests. This assumes that the two companies find it commercially beneficial to do so and raises a host of other questions which cannot detain us now; suffice to say that it is likely that the private benefits of niche marketing would outweigh the social good of encouraging heterogeneity.

Our final point begins with the commonplace observation that the aim of much information retrieval research is to make finding information easier or, in other words, more efficient. Thus it shares the same general perspective that animates the majority of technological development today. But perhaps we should take a step back for a moment, hold our breath, and ask a seemingly unthinkable question: Should our efforts be directed towards making information easier to find? If we assume that efficiency is the only value worthy of being embedded in technology, then the question seems ridiculous, but could there be other values that are not advanced or even actually harmed by such an approach? We would argue in the affirmative. Given the deterioration of the public sphere and the doubt surrounding the ability of electronic communications as they now stand to sustain, let alone enhance the capabilities for communicative action, it may be time for information retrieval experts to think about embedding values other than efficiency into the systems they create. Social information retrieval seems especially appropriate in this regard as it is a relatively new development and therefore susceptible to deliberate interventions that aim to influence the effects of the technology. In particular, and from the perspective of this chapter, what are needed are mechanisms that address the effects of homophily and plan for the creation of spaces where debate between opposing positions can occur. But this cannot be done unless the basic assumption that social information retrieval is a "good thing" because it is somehow more efficient is questioned, debated, and clarified. This chapter hopes to start such a debate.

REFERENCES

Alstyne, M., & Brynjolfsson, E. (2005). Global village or cyber-Balkans? Modeling and measuring and integration of electronic communities. *Management Science, 51*(6), 851-868.

Ashkenas, R., Ulrich, D., Jick, T., & Kerr, S. (2002). *The boundaryless organization: Breaking the chains of organizational structure* (2nd ed.). San Francisco: Jossey-Bass.

Axelrod, R. (1997). The dissemination of culture: A model with local convergence and global polarization. *Journal of Conflict Resolution, 41*(2), 203-226.

Brand, A. (1990). *The force of reason: An introduction to Habermas' Theory of Communicative Action.* Sydney, Australia: Allen & Unwin.

Brothers, R. (2000). The computer-mediated public sphere and the cosmopolitan ideal. *Ethics and Information Technology, 2*(2), 91-98.

Calhoun, C. (1992). *Habermas and the public sphere.* Cambridge, MA: MIT Press.

Habermas, J. (1991). *The structural transformation of the public sphere.* Cambridge, MA: MIT Press.

Johnson, N.L. (1999). *The science of social diversity.* Retrieved January 17, 2007, from http://ishi.lanl.gov/Documents_1/DiveristyScience.pdf

Kanter, R.M. (1988). When a thousand flowers bloom: Structural, collective, and social conditions for innovation in organization. *Research in Organizational Behavior, 10,* 169-211.

McGehee, T. Jr. (2001). *Whoosh: Business in the fast lane.* New York: Perseus.

McPherson, M., Smith-Lovin, L., & Cook, J. (2001). Birds of a feather: Homophily in social networks. *Annual Review of Sociology, 27,* 415-444.

Oldenburg, R. (1997). *The great good place: Cafes, coffee shops, community centers, beauty parlors, general stores, bars, hangouts and how they get you through the day.* New York: Marlowe & Company.

Pelz, D., & Andrews, F. (1966). *Scientists in organizations.* New York: John Wiley & Sons.

Sullivan, D. (2005). *comScore MediaMatrix search engine ratings.* Retrieved January 17, 2007, from http://searchenginewatch.com/reports/article.php/2156431

Wellman, B. (2001). Physical place and cyberplace: The rise of personalized networking. *International Journal of Urban and Regional Research, 25*(2), 227-252.

Winner, L. (1989). *The whale and the reactor: A search for limits in an age of high technology.* Chicago: University of Chicago Press.

Chapter X
The Social Context
of Knowledge

Daniel Memmi
Université du Québec à Montréal, Canada

ABSTRACT

Information and knowledge have become a crucial resource in our knowledge-based, computer-mediated economy. But knowledge is primarily a social phenomenon, on which computer processing has had only a limited impact so far, in spite of impressive advances. In this context have recently appeared various collaborative systems that promise to give access to socially situated information. We argue that a prior analysis of the social context is necessary for a better understanding of the whole domain of collaborative software. We will examine the variety and functions of information in modern society, where collaborative information management is now the dominant type of occupation. In fact, real information is much more complex than its usual technical sense: one should distinguish between information and knowledge, as well as between explicit and tacit knowledge. Because of the notable importance of tacit knowledge, social networks are indispensable in practice for locating relevant information. We then propose a typology of collaborative software, distinguishing between explicit communities supported by groupware systems, task-oriented communities organized around a common data structure, and implicit links exploited by collaborative filtering and social information retrieval. The latter approach is usually implemented by virtually grouping similar users, but there exist many possible variants. Yet much remains to be done by extracting, formalizing, and exploiting implicit social links.

INTRODUCTION

The development of computers and electronic networks has considerably advanced our society's capacity for information processing, and the very

scale of this global phenomenon raises quite a few questions. Yet electronic data processing is by now so pervasive in advanced societies that it is easy to forget how recent it all is: computer science started about the time of World War II, but personal computers, the Internet, and the Web only go back a couple of decades in spite of their explosive progress.

As a matter of fact, information processing (i.e., the collection, creation, elaboration, and transmission of useful knowledge) has been around for as long as human history, and has become more and more important with the advent of modern bureaucratic industrial states two centuries ago. Recent technological developments take place within this social framework, which determines their shape, usage, and direction. The interaction between pre-existing social practices and new technologies is then an obvious issue to consider.

So how do human beings and organizations process information in today's technological, computer-mediated environment? How do they interact with each other through electronic networks? How can they put recent technical advances to the best possible use? And what future directions can be foreseen? To try and answer such questions, it would be useful to first analyze human information processing in more detail.

The classical approach, prevalent notably in cognitive psychology, has been to focus on individual information processing capabilities (Neisser, 1967; Mandler, 1985). A body of studies on perception, learning, recall, association and inference, and so forth has been performed on individual subjects in laboratory conditions. Much has been learned in this way on human information processing: for example our limited short-term memory, perceptual schemas, associative recall, probabilistic learning, and inference mechanisms are by now fairly well-established findings.

These studies have however been increasingly criticized for dealing mostly with isolated subjects performing artificial tasks in unrealistic ("non-ecological") environments. One has seen in the past 20 years a gradual shift to the study of situated and collective cognition. There has been more emphasis so far on physically situated rather than socially situated behavior, but the general trend is clear (Clark, 1998; Harnad & Dror, 2006).

Researchers in this growing movement try to understand how human beings perform tasks and solve problems in real physical and social situations. What they may lose in precision and experimental control, they hope to gain in scope and realism. Such an approach seems more relevant to the complex socio-technical environment in which human information processing must take place today.

The recent emergence of virtual communities which has been made possible by the Internet and other electronic networks is also a phenomenon worth investigating. These communities constitute a novel, computer-mediated form of social grouping, combining in variable proportion traditional social relations with more functional, goal-oriented features. Virtual communities should be studied as a collective entity rather than a mere collection of individual participants (Kollock & Smith, 1999; Rheingold, 2000; Memmi, 2006).

Understanding the social and technical context of individual information processing is important for several reasons. Beside the inherent interest of this subject, studying the way human beings use their social skills and social networks to acquire relevant information would help develop better information retrieval systems. As a matter of fact, there has recently appeared a variety of collaborative software systems inspired by human task-oriented social interactions.

Even if socially situated knowledge management cannot be totally reproduced with computers, software systems can be designed to borrow from the most pertinent aspects of human collective processing. Such distributed systems will also fit better the manner in which human beings naturally operate and solve tasks within society, and should thus prove easier to use. More generally, we will see how studying the role and use of knowledge in our society may prove useful to software designers and developers.

Our main thesis will be that information retrieval and information management in general should profit greatly from the study of socially situated information processing by human beings. This text intends to survey fundamental issues more than recent technical solutions. Understanding the nature and functions of knowledge in society appears necessary for long-term advances. We thus hope to bring some order to a fairly diverse range of proposals and to point to new research directions.

In this chapter we will therefore describe in turn: (1) the social and economic context of human information processing, (2) the nature and varieties of knowledge as well as its social pathways, and (3) various technical methods that have been devised to make use of the social aspects of human information processing.

We will resort in rather eclectic fashion to several disciplines, notably cognitive psychology, structural sociology, economics, management theory, and of course computer science and software design. But our main goal throughout will be to replace present work in collaborative software systems within the context of socially situated human cognition.

SOCIAL CONTEXT

We will start by showing more precisely how information processing can be seen as socially situated. This point of view will also have concrete technical consequences for the design of software systems.

The Social Import of Information

Far from being a purely individual phenomenon, information is intimately interwoven with the social and economic fabric of human groups. Social life is not possible without a constant exchange of information within groups and organizations.

Because the social functions of information are still largely underestimated, they deserve much more emphasis.

In this respect, one might want to make a distinction between raw information and knowledge acquired by human beings. Whereas information could be formulated objectively, knowledge is inherently a cognitive phenomenon and knowledge acquisition is a complex process. This distinction will prove useful later on, but following common usage, we will use the two terms more or less interchangeably for the time being.

Information can be defined in various ways, notably in probabilistic terms, but its practical function is to reduce uncertainty and to answer questions, allowing us to avoid dangers, fulfill goals, solve problems, and plan for the future. Information obviously has a biological survival function: all life forms, from insects to mammals, need information about their environment in order to find food and mates, avoid predators, and seek appropriate living conditions.

Information comes from the environment, be it physical, biological, or social. But most of our human environment is in fact a social one. Like most primates and many mammals, mankind is a highly social species and social situations are an integral art of our daily life. In modern urban society, moreover, we live in a mostly artificial, man-made environment replete with social functions and meanings.

As I look out of my window while writing this, I can see mostly buildings, whether residential or commercial, cars and traffic, and people walking by, many of them probably to or from work. This physical urban environment is actually a social environment. In my home, radio, television, telephone, fax machine, the Internet, papers, and magazines keep me informed about the larger world. The workplace is also a place of high informational density, where information is constantly exchanged and elaborated upon so as to perform complex social tasks.

As an ordinary member of modern society, I am extremely well connected with my environment, which turns out to be a highly social one. We could indeed be defined as social beings by the rich pattern of informational interactions we regularly maintain with our surroundings. Sociologists and anthropologists have often remarked that social cohesion is both ensured and demonstrated by regular exchanges of goods and services (Mauss, 1923), and information most probably plays a similar role, from office gossip to the Internet.

More concretely, a constant flow of information is obviously necessary for the coordination of social activities. This is true at all levels of social organization, from small business firms to the highest levels of government. The more complex the social and economic organization, the more important coordination activities become (Mintzberg, 1979). At the same time, communication is often highly ritualized and the practical functions of information blend insensibly with its cohesive role. For instance, office memos carry useful information while reaffirming organizational structure.

Another factor to consider is the economic value of information. It is a fact that is not yet sufficiently recognized, that information (or more accurately, human knowledge) has been the dominant source of growth and wealth in advanced societies for more than half a century. Investment in education, research and development, management, and other intangible factors has now overtaken investment in physical assets both in value and contribution to economic productivity and growth (Kendrick, 1994).

It is knowledge, and not physical investment in plants and machines, that is now the driving force in our post-industrial society. Knowledge-based domains such as electronics, computers and data processing, aeronautics, aerospace, biotechnology, and pharmaceutical companies clearly are the most dynamic, productive, wealthiest, and fastest-growing sector of the economy.

And this is not a temporary phenomenon, but a solid long-term trend.

In short, most of our information originates from social situations, fulfills social and economic functions, and knowledge has become crucially important in a modern economy. Information must therefore be considered within its social context in order to really understand its functions and uses, and information processing techniques should also be seen in this context.

Toward the Information Society

Information processing is then not only an individual activity, it is the blood flow that keeps our societies running and prospering. Knowledge-intensive occupations and organizations have accordingly become more and more important: research and education, engineering, high-tech companies, consulting activities, law firms, financial services, health care, and so forth. A whole class of "knowledge workers" has emerged whose jobs consist mostly of handling and elaborating information on a daily basis (Drucker, 1992).

Knowledge workers not only handle information, but also create, transform, acquire and store, transmit and exchange, apply, and teach all forms of knowledge. They usually do so in a highly collaborative manner. For various reasons, the management of knowledge in many modern organizations tends to be a collective, distributed activity.

Information being an intangible asset, it is easily duplicated (especially with electronic techniques) and lends itself to cumulative development, a fact that encourages its dissemination and collective production and use. Network effects reinforce this tendency: it is often all the more advantageous to use an informational product (such as software) when it has many more users. Knowledge workers value collaborative work accordingly.

So information and knowledge are used mainly in social situations, even when processed by individuals. Information processing in real life is socially situated, and individual uses are secondary and derived from social goals. Not only most of the information we handle fulfills social functions, it is also managed collectively. As a consequence, useful or necessary information is to be found as much (if not more) in social circles as in libraries or databases.

The growing importance of information in a knowledge-oriented society has also been considerably accelerated by the recent developments in electronic information processing. Social and professional changes have gone hand in hand with technological advances—progress in one area taking place in synergy with evolutions in another. What is striking is not only the enormous increase in computing power available on the job in many professions, but its distributed character and the connectivity between individual computers.

Centralized mainframes have been replaced by cohorts of ubiquitous personal computers, and everybody is now connected to everybody and everything else by the Internet. More than the arrival of computers, the prominent fact of our time is the advent and rapid spread of electronic networks. They have made possible an amazing acceleration in the speed and quantity of information exchanged in our society.

At the same time, and this is of course no coincidence, sociologists have noticed an evolution toward a "network society" of loose, temporary, flexible relationships (Castells, 1996; Wellman, 1999). Instead of staying within closed groups, many social actors tend to shift from one connection to another as required by a different tasks or objectives. Traditional organizations give way to more flexible arrangements, and the Internet has proven to be the obvious tool to switch between diverse social links, regardless of time and distance.

The powerful conjunction between social changes and technological advances makes the information flow ever more important and significant. A network society can only function by constantly exchanging information, and a network structure is the appropriate organization for an information society (Shapiro & Varian, 1999). Computers, electronic networks, urban life, as well as rapid transit systems provide the technical infrastructure for this kind of social life.

The recent movement known as "Web 2.0" is characteristic of this socio-technical evolution (O'Reilly, 2005). This encompasses a loose collection of software tools and applications fostering social relations and collaborative work on the Internet. In this approach, the Web is seen as a platform for various social communication applications. Such tools accelerate even more the present trend toward a network society.

One may speculate about the causes and effects in this global evolution, and whether social changes or technical advances have been the dominant factor. But is clear that changes in different areas have reinforced one another, forming a coherent system that is reshaping our whole society. *Collective, distributed knowledge processing is now the prototypical occupation in today's information society.*

Technical Consequences

Because of these various social, cultural, and technical changes, human information processing is thus becoming more and more a collective, collaborative activity. Information can still be accessed individually in books, libraries, databases, or on the Web, but the sheer volume of accessible information makes social guidance or filtering practically inevitable. And more often than not, pertinent information resides partly in people's heads or expertise, and not in explicit documents, whether physical or electronic.

The constantly increasing complexity of tasks and problems makes it necessary to first locate the right person in order to perform a given task or solve a problem, and this requires a particular kind of social expertise. The diversity and dispersion of information, the fact that various sources of information must be put together and reformulated to become relevant, usually require some human collaboration. And one cannot stay within a small familiar circle of close colleagues or acquaintances to find all the required answers.

The information needed is often to be found somewhere within or by way of a larger social network of professionally related people. These networks may be formal (employees of a firm, professional organizations) or informal (personal address book, casual professional contacts), but they must be searched to locate information or knowledge that could not be found otherwise. Information retrieval thus becomes a social problem.

This means that *the whole domain of information retrieval should be fundamentally rethought in the light of the social nature of human knowledge.* Information has too often been thought of as some kind of objective material, detached from its social environment and use. This simplistic approach has probably made possible the first developments of information retrieval techniques, but one will not advance beyond those techniques without considering the ways in which human beings process knowledge in society.

Classical information retrieval has dealt fairly successfully with how to represent texts, how to evaluate semantic proximity, and how to index and retrieve documents efficiently (Salton & McGill, 1983; Baeza-Yates, 1999; Manning & Schütze, 1999). But new questions should now be considered: Who is the most likely person able to answer a request? How can we find this person quickly and efficiently? How can one represent people and social links? How can one use social expertise and distributed knowledge to recommend or filter documents?

This is the general setting in which must be seen the recent developments of collaborative software, social filtering, recommendation systems, and similar work. The present interest in such systems is no accident, but rather a sign of our times. We will describe below concrete technical approaches, but we must discuss beforehand the variety of knowledge forms involved in social processes.

NATURE OF KNOWLEDGE

We will now analyze in more detail how human beings manage information in real social situations and how they handle different varieties of knowledge.

A Simple Example

To illustrate this discussion, let us start with a concrete example. Let us suppose your organization has asked you to write or prepare a report on free and open source software, a subject you might not know too well. So how would you go about it? The first step might be to visit a library, looking up the computer science section directly, or consulting the catalog. But there just are not many books on the subject, they are still unlikely to be found in a public library, and relevant articles are scattered among so many journals.

Nowadays, your first reflex would probably be to use a search engine instead, to find references on the Web. But you will then be flooded with a profusion of references, of various relevance and quality. Which ones should you read and use? Can you trust these references to reflect a consensus in the domain? Or are they unorthodox divagations? Should you start with this long official report by a reputable organization or does this unassuming Web page offer a decent summary?

At this point, you will probably try to locate a knowledgeable colleague or acquaintance, somebody who could give you a leg up by recommending a few basic references or by inspecting your first list of references. He or she might also explain how to best exploit those sources, and tell you things about the domain that are not easily found in written documents. And if he happens to be a practitioner of open software, the discussion could become quite lively and really interesting....

He might assert, for instance, that popular discussions on the subject tend toward wishful thinking and unsubstantiated ideological claims. He could, however, recommend two or three studies in which one can find the real professional status and economic support of free software developers. This would probably help you write a better, more informed report on the matter.

But how can you be sure your colleague really knows what he is talking about? Well, you can never be totally sure (until you become an expert yourself). But if he has been recommended by close colleagues of yours, if he has been involved in this subject for years, if he belongs to an association dealing with free software, you might be reasonably confident. If he does not belong to your organization, you will probably try to evaluate somehow the competence of his organization and his own standing, before you trust his advice.

And how does one locate the right person? In most cases, this is done simply by asking personal acquaintances deemed to be closer than you to the information required. For instance, if you do not know anybody working on free software, you might ask a software engineer or your system manager to recommend somebody else to consult. By following two or three such links, you will quickly find a knowledgeable expert.

Such a simple strategy has been shown to be fairly efficient. In a well-known experiment, people in the United States were asked to forward a letter through personal acquaintances only, in order to reach a target person whose occupation was mentioned, but not the exact address (Travers & Milgram, 1969). People were instructed to hand over the letter to somebody they thought closer to the target, geographically or professionally, and the process would be repeated from one person to the next. Not all letters reached the final target, but those that arrived at their destinations took no more than five steps on average. This is a good example of the "small-world" phenomenon (Watts, 1999).

We often use a similar strategy when looking for preliminary information on a subject we do not know much about yet. In other words, *we first perform a kind of social look-up in order to access relevant information or knowledge.*

This fairly straightforward example illustrates some of the points we will now elaborate upon: the difficulty for an individual to manage socially distributed information on his own, the need for social guidance, the problem of trust, how help can be found by exploiting social links, the importance of tacit knowledge and personal expertise, the role and structure of social groups, and so forth. The issue will then be how to formalize and exploit these social phenomena.

The well-known Internet bookseller Amazon.com offers prospective buyers a simplified version of such social guidance. When a book on a given subject is found through Amazon's search engine, the system displays a list of ratings and comments on this book by former buyers and users. This is still very crude (the trustworthiness of the ratings is questionable), but this is an effort to help individual online buyers with social advice.

Varieties of Knowledge

Yet to fully understand human information processing, it must be realized that we are actually dealing with different forms of information or knowledge which are managed in different ways. To begin with, one should distinguish between *information* and *knowledge,* a distinction we have glossed over so far. Although usage varies somewhat, information is basically the raw material of information processing, whereas knowledge has been acquired by human beings through a learning process.

Information can be found in physical form, for instance in written documents, databases, images, and recordings. Information may be defined objectively in probabilistic terms according to information theory: the quantity of information contained in a message is inversely proportional to (the logarithm of) its probability of occurrence. This mathematical approach has proven its worth in signal processing and telecommunications, but its application to human cognition is debatable, as it proves hard to separate information from its practical context of use.

Knowledge, for its part, is inherently personal or social: knowledge is information acquired by human beings. Knowledge must be learned in context, individually or collectively, before being put to use to accomplish human goals and functions. The very notion of knowledge is inseparable from cognitive and social processes, while information could be defined more narrowly as a property of the physical world.

The point is that even if information can be objectively quantified for engineering purposes, *only knowledge is of real social and economic importance.* But knowledge is also difficult to acquire. Information may be copied or reproduced mechanically, but knowledge must be assimilated by humans before it can be used. And specialized knowledge can only be acquired by well-prepared specialists, restricting its effective social range of application.

The increasing division of labor, the complexity of technical knowledge, and the pace of innovation make it more and more difficult to ensure the transmission of knowledge within organizations and firms. Training or tutoring mechanisms may be devised, but bringing together the appropriate people remains a problem for learning to succeed. One must find both adequate experts and well-prepared apprentices. This is very much a social problem, which must first be solved for knowledge transmission to take place.

Another important distinction is between *explicit* and *tacit* knowledge, or perhaps more accurately between explicit information and tacit knowledge (usage is unfortunately not coherent here). Explicit knowledge or information is public

and formalized, in linguistic or mathematical form notably. Books, journals, textual documents of all kinds, Web sites, databases, and so forth—all contain explicit knowledge, as long as one knows the linguistic or formal conventions necessary to interpret their content.

Information retrieval and computer science deal mostly with explicit information, so that it is too easy to forget that this is only one kind of knowledge. Real social life, however, makes frequent use of other forms of knowledge as well, which can be grouped together under the general label of tacit or implicit knowledge (Polanyi, 1966; Baumard, 1999). There is in fact a variety of forms of tacit knowledge (such as body language, common sense, work expertise, procedural knowledge, etc.), and one might distinguish further between unformulated and unconscious knowledge, but we will not attempt a more detailed analysis here.

Tacit knowledge is knowledge that has been acquired from practical experience: medical expertise, technical know-how, teaching experience, and management skills are forms of tacit knowledge. This cannot be learned from books alone, as learning by doing is a necessary component. Organized tutoring may help, but transmission will then be from person to person, which proves to be a slow and cumbersome process. *Tacit knowledge remains a serious bottleneck in the information society.*

One should also notice that tacit knowledge is often collective. Many organizations perform (more or less adequately) thanks to collective routines and procedures that are distributed among many actors and are often left unformalized. The knowledge inherent in organizational functions is not expressed publicly, and no single actor knows the whole picture. This lack of clarity may lead to serious inefficiencies.

Tacit or implicit knowledge is thus hard to learn and to pass on, and the computer revolution has so far not helped very much in this respect. As tacit knowledge is unfortunately an essential part of social life and economic performance, this is an area that begs for more consideration from knowledge management in general and information retrieval in particular. We feel that serious advances could be expected in this domain.

Last but not least, *social knowledge* is the (largely implicit) knowledge necessary to make use of social relationships so as to perform tasks and solve problems. It is an important component of most professions, but one that is usually learned by long practice and experience. The social skills and expertise necessary to find information needed for a given task, ensure social cooperation, and negotiate common rules are crucial to task performance in most lines of work.

Social knowledge has not yet been given sufficient recognition, however, and is rarely discussed, described, or formalized. Sociologists have been interested in the social structure of groups and how this constrains individual choices and strategies (e.g., Lazega, 2001). But there has been much less emphasis on individual knowledge of these constraints, on how they might be represented and processed cognitively. This calls for more research in social psychology.

To be able to access or use social knowledge would be quite useful for information retrieval systems. Finding the appropriate expert most likely to answer a technical question, for example, is often a better idea than searching the Web by oneself. Though the issue is usually not presented directly in this way, we will see below that collaborative software systems have started to incorporate elements of social expertise.

Social Networks

It should be obvious by now that an important part of human knowledge management takes place by way of social links and requires appropriate social expertise. Social networks have fortunately been studied and formalized by structural sociology, and there is a sizable body of methods and techniques to draw upon (Wassermann & Faust, 1994).

Social networks are a simplified model of social relationships, schematic enough to be represented and handled mathematically on a computer. The basic data structure is a graph, where nodes stand for social actors (individuals or groups) and links represent social relations. Links are usually not labeled, but may have an associated numerical value (standing for the strength or frequency of the relation). This graph is in turn implemented as a matrix on which various operations can be performed.

If the matrix represents direct links, indirect relations (requiring several steps through the network) can be found by computing successive powers of the basic matrix. For instance the square of the matrix will show two-step relations, the cube of the matrix three-step relations, and so on. Many other operations are also possible, and there are various algorithms for extracting from the social graph densely linked subgroups of nodes.

This approach is obviously a drastic simplification of the complexity of real human relationships, but the formal structure of such models can already be very revealing. In particular, the structural subgroups that can be extracted automatically from the graph correspond to social groupings of actors, working on similar tasks and exchanging information about common concerns. Structural subgroups are usually functional groups as well.

For example, after mapping the network of collaboration relationships between 71 lawyers in an American law firm, it is possible to find 11 dense subgroups corresponding to specific locations or specialties (see Lazega, 2001). As these subgroups also interact with one another, they can be seen as forming a higher-level network with fewer nodes, a kind of summary of the basic network. The whole process requires some human interpretation, but reveals social facts that are simply not obvious to the naked eye.

The position of an actor within the social network is usually significant: it shows the centrality or prominence of the actor, and the resources and information he has immediate access to. The network also shows the nodes and paths an actor would have to follow in order to access more remote information. Sociologists tend to interpret structural positions in terms of power relationships: central positions are strategic while actors located at the margins have to go through others to access various resources (Burt, 1992).

From our point of view, however, the main issue to consider is that *structural networks determine social access to information.* Central actors have quick and easy access to socially embedded knowledge, while marginal actors might have to contend with longer access routes. The social expertise necessary to retrieve socially situated information comprises social skills (such as diplomacy or bargaining tactics), but also the basic ability to perceive and exploit the social structure as such.

Social expertise may remain more or less unconscious, but the deliberate "networking" behavior of the ambitious professional is also quite common. Many professionals know the importance of "weak ties": useful information and opportunities are often obtained through casual relations which thus deserve to be strenuously cultivated (Granovetter, 1973). At the same time, developing and using a network of close contacts in the workplace is often a prerequisite to successful work performance.

Social information retrieval and problem solving by human beings is thus achieved through social networks, which govern information circulation and information flow. Formalizing this structure should be very helpful in order to model human knowledge management skills and capabilities, and possibly to design better collaborative software systems.

Now the development of electronic transmission networks has made it possible to extract automatically many social relations, as they leave electronic traces. For instance one may note the pattern of e-mail messages exchanged within an organization and formalize it as a graph. Of course, not all social interactions are reflected in electronic messaging, but e-mail traffic is obviously significant in many modern organizations. Web browsing is also a more indirect source of social affinities, which can be exploited to retrieve social information.

As a matter of fact, collaborative software systems make use of social links and social information, directly or indirectly. They might have been consciously designed in this way, but this may also be the result of practical attempts to solve an informational problem.

TECHNICAL APPROACHES

After this review of human information processing in social context, it is now time to consider how the insights gained during this study can be used to design social information systems. This should also help us put in perspective recent work in collaborative software.

Typology of Collaborative Software

There is already a variety of collaborative systems, but one can try to regroup various proposals into a few classes. We would like to propose a general typology of these systems, using a few relevant features to differentiate between them.

What collaborative systems have in common is the modeling of a social environment and use of social expertise to access relevant information. They differ, however, in the manner, explicit or implicit, in which they model the social community that serves as context for information purposes. Some systems provide users with an explicit representation of a social group, which may be consciously accessed as such. Other systems use social links implicitly, and the end users do not have to be aware of the underlying social structure (we prefer calling such links *implicit* rather than tacit because they might be totally unconscious).

Another pertinent distinction is whether the focus of operations is on the group itself or on the informational task being performed. Virtual communities tend to be task oriented and more impersonal than real communities, and some collaborative systems will emphasize the task more than the social group. In such a case, representing the task at hand is the central issue, and the explicit or implicit representation of the group structure becomes of secondary importance.

One should also remember that a collaborative information system does not have to reproduce faithfully every aspect of human information processing. There are fruitful lessons to learn from studying socially situated human cognition, but a software system can do things differently (and more efficiently in some ways) than the human mind. For example, social expertise about how to retrieve relevant knowledge may be implicitly built into a computer system, whereas a human being would have to search his social network consciously.

In fact some software systems stick closely to the structure and functioning of real human groups, and exhibit the same limitations in terms of group size or cognitive load. We would contend that virtual communities may well function differently, and that collaborative software should be designed accordingly. On the other hand, present software is still far from the complexity and capabilities of human social processing, so that there remains much to be learned from real human cognition.

Still, collaborative systems may also be classified in different ways, notably by using more technical criteria. The manner in which individual participants, relationships, and communities are represented and the clustering algorithms are used to regroup similar actors, the data structures and implementation techniques could also be used to differentiate between systems. But the emphasis being here on social issues, a classification based on community type seems more appropriate to this discussion.

To sum up, we think that work on collaborative systems up to now can be roughly classified into three main types: building explicit communities, building task-oriented communities, and using implicit social links.

Building Explicit Communities

This is the most obvious direction, and this research field is often known as *groupware* (Favela & Decouchant, 2003). Such systems try to make as explicit as possible the structure of the group, the biography and interests of participants, their role and status, and the history of interactions. The goals, tasks, common tools, past actions, and current problems can be posted publicly. The rationale is that group awareness and explicit interactions are conducive to better problem solving.

In a hospital setting for instance, there is an intense exchange of information between various medical staff (physicians, nurses, laboratory technicians, etc.), and timely access to correct information is clearly vital. But medical staff is highly mobile, and information is heterogeneous (verbal exchanges, textual records, images, etc.) and rapidly changing. The collective task to be performed (taking care of patients) is therefore highly distributed and in constant evolution.

And the problem is not just information distribution, but rather one of coordination between different actors and collective decision making. Although they often communicate through common objects (such as whiteboards and clipboards), medical personnel must be aware of each other, because the source and time of information may be crucial. A multi-agent architecture can then be used to locate or notify the right person at the right time with the appropriate information (Munoz, Gonzalez, Rodriguez, & Favela, 2003). In this way interactions are made explicit but also kept under tight control.

Yet groupware systems, properly speaking, can only function for small groups of participants. When the number of active members reaches more than 30 or 40 people, personal information and individual interactions may prove overwhelming. On the other hand, high awareness about individual group members may lead to personal relations and allow focusing a search for information on the person most likely to know the answer to a problem.

In this way, groupware systems try to reproduce the functioning of small social groups as we traditionally know them: family and friends, office life, workgroups, neighborhood associations, and so forth. Such systems are often used in a close professional context (e.g., a hospital or a firm) where people already know each other or are likely to meet face to face sooner or later. In this case, groupware will reinforce or assist real or potential social relationships, but will not create unexpected links.

Groupware design presents interesting technical challenges for computer scientists: managing synchronous and asynchronous communication between participants in various and changeable locations, transmission of heterogeneous data (including text files, messages, images, and sound), maintaining the coherence of common data structures, and so on. Sophisticated systems have been developed, notably for healthcare environments and computer-supported collaborative learning. But these systems are not widely used, probably because they are still too cumbersome and not appropriate for many social groups.

Groupware can be useful in professional domains requiring intensive social links with focused interactions dealing with very specific tasks. The density and quality of interactions require fairly elaborate software to update and transmit information in a graceful and readable way, with heterogeneous data and more and more mobile users. But groupware is inadequate and unwieldy for larger groups and casual interactions.

Another possibility is to use the social network that can be inferred from Web pages, social interactions, and common interests to locate experts on a given subject (Kautz, Selman, & Shah, 1987). This might be the only way to find tacit information, which is not publicly available. This approach may also be developed to improve information retrieval by taking advantage of the social links of document authors for instance—well-connected authors are probably more reliable (Kirsch, Gnasa, & Cremers, 2006). But we will see below how to exploit implicit links.

Still another research direction that has not yet been developed much in computer science would be to post an explicit structure for the social network in a given domain. So this would also be an explicit representation, but a more schematic and lighter one.

We have seen that structural sociology has elaborated formal models of social groups considered as networks of relations (Wassermann & Faust, 1994). The complexity of real social interactions is deliberately simplified so as to represent a group by a graph, in which nodes are actors and links are relations. Social interactions are reduced to simple relations, such as collaboration, advice, or influence.

Without going into more detail, the point is that structural sociology is well formalized and sufficiently advanced to offer relevant representation tools for larger communities. Representing groups with hundreds of members is not a problem, and the nature of links (edges in a graph) is simpler and more abstract. For larger communities, these formal methods might be a better source of inspiration than current groupware techniques.

From a practical point of view, structural methods could be used to map the current state of a community and to show participants their position in the network, the coherence of the structure, what the sub-groups are, the dynamic evolution of the network, and so forth. This would be another way to raise group awareness, not in personal terms but from a structural, more abstract perspective.

In a large firm, for example, it might be useful to be able to identify structural subgroups in order to find appropriate contacts on a functional rather than a personal basis. Although this is technically possible and software systems are now available for this purpose, they are not really used in practice, perhaps because they are felt to be too revealing and intrusive.

Still, when participation is only occasional or unique, and when interactions are mostly impersonal, the notion of structural network loses significance. If all interactions take place through a common workspace, the most one could probably hope for is to make it easy for users to enter the system and to deal with common objects. A good data structure and convenient access and modification procedures are then necessary.

Building Task-Oriented Communities

Virtual communities are frequently task oriented. Computer-mediated communities are often quite different from traditional social groups, a fact that is too rarely acknowledged in the literature. By comparison with traditional groups, participation in virtual communities is more impersonal, often temporary or anonymous, with a lower level of emotional involvement. These communities are mostly goal oriented: participants contribute to a common goal or task, but are less interested in personal relationships.

In such a case, group activities revolve around a common data structure (forum, discussion thread, Web site, wiki, database, etc.) that shows the current state of the task in progress and is regularly updated. This is a *blackboard* model, where all interactions go through a central data structure rather than by means of particular links.

Such an architecture was originally proposed for the Hearsay-II speech understanding system as an efficient method to coordinate the operation of various modules: all communication between

modules takes place through the blackboard (Lesser & Erman, 1977). In our domain, this can be seen as a form of situated cognition, determined by a common public environment which is represented here by a central blackboard.

Since most of the information necessary for group activities is posted on this blackboard, *information retrieval can be done by accessing the common workspace.* Information management is collective, in the sense that the blackboard somehow summarizes the whole history of group interactions and contains all the information deemed relevant by the group. This is another form of collaborative retrieval, but of an indirect and impersonal kind.

One reason that may explain the prevalence of this type of communication is simply that it minimizes the complexity of interactions. The number of potential point-to-point links between n actors is n(n-1)/2, which grows like the square of the number of actors. But the number of interactions with a common data structure only increases linearly with the number of participants, a much more manageable proposition for larger groups.

There is in fact no sharp boundary between explicit communities and blackboard-mediated groups, and the distinction is not always clear. For example, in hospital wards, the "blackboard" (actually a whiteboard) is only one source of information among others. Yet there is a strong tendency in modern life, notably in virtual communities, toward more impersonal, functional, flexible social groups organized around a common task or goal. Such groups have their own informational requirements, which must be served by access to a simple, robust, easily maintained blackboard structure.

The recent *wiki* technique is a good example of user-friendly blackboard management system. A wiki is basically an interactive Web site with simple and easy editing procedures. Registered participants may post text messages on the site, and they can also augment, comment on, or modify previous messages. So everybody can contribute to the site, but interventions must be signed and the history of modifications is kept automatically. In practice, a moderator is useful to check interventions before they are posted.

The well-known online encyclopedia Wikipedia has been (and still is) developed in this way with very good results overall (*www.wikipedia.org*). The quality of entries is not always consistent, and there have been a few problems with inaccuracies or vandalism (hence the importance of competent moderators). But on the whole Wikipedia has proven to be a successful collective, collaborative enterprise and a model of what could be accomplished online.

Although it is in fact a more complex phenomenon, the development of free or open source software may also be seen as a task-oriented activity (Feller, Fitzgerald, Hissam, & Lakhnani, 2005). A software project under development serves as a common object which is repeatedly corrected and improved by a wide community of programmers and testers, many of whom do not interact on a personal basis. This community is strongly structured, however, with a small inner core of project leaders surrounded by concentric circles of contributors and critics, so that this would really be a hybrid example between personal and impersonal relations.

Using Implicit Social Links

Other software systems do not post group structure or common data. This is usually the case with collaborative information retrieval, collaborative filtering, and recommender systems. There exist many variants, but the basic idea consists of exploiting the implicit structure of a group of users in order to find relevant documents, filter search results, or recommend information or products. The grouping may be made public in some systems, but is usually not handled by the users themselves, who might remain totally unaware of this virtual structure.

These collaborative systems work by computing similarities between human users and by taking advantage of the resemblance to share information between similar users (Resnick, Iacovou, Suchak, Bergstrom, & Riedl, 1994; Shardanand & Maes, 1995; Adomavicius & Tuzhilin, 2005). For example one may recommend movies, books, music, or other products to a given user by finding "similar" users and quoting their best choices. Or one may retrieve or filter documents by noting which documents have been retrieved or used by groups of similar users.

To throw some light on the variety of such systems, one may want to make several distinctions between them. Although real systems often blur these distinctions, the following categories of collaborative systems may be useful:

- **Collaborative filtering (recommender systems):** These systems recommend (or rank) products, services, or documents for the benefit of an individual user by collecting the preferences of similar users.
- **Collaborative retrieval systems:** These retrieve (or filter) relevant documents by using the profiles of similar users. Poor initial queries can thus be augmented with more expert information.
- **Active (explicit) rating:** Users explicitly take the time to rate or recommend products. People are amazingly willing to do so (probably as a form of self-expression, in order to promote a product they like, out of sheer sociability, etc.), but their active intervention is required.
- **Passive (implicit) rating:** Information on user preferences is collected by noting significant user actions (buying products, Web browsing, bookmarking, downloading files, etc.). This can be done automatically, but user tastes are inferred, not directly measured.

This general approach requires establishing an interest profile for each end user, and choosing a similarity measure so as to be able to compare users in a coherent way. By analogy with classical information retrieval methods, each user is usually characterized by a vector of relevant features, and users are compared by computing their proximity in vector space. The group profile used as a basis for recommendations can then simply be the average of member profiles.

There have been quite a few variations, such as employing statistical correlation, angle or distance between vectors, or various clustering algorithms to estimate user resemblance, but the determination of a user profile is of course crucial to the operation of the system. One may want to compare different methods, but results depend on the task and the nature of the data (Breese, Heckerman, & Kadie, 1998).

Instead of comparing users to find subgroups of users with similar interests, it is also possible to compare and cluster items with regard to user preferences (this is what Amazon.com does). If you like a particular item, the system can then recommend similar items. But the latter method is in fact a dual representation of the former: one may equivalently represent users in item space or items in user space, but a choice can be made for reasons of implementation.

Collaborative systems unfortunately suffer from a "cold-start" problem: a critical mass of users and user preferences is needed for the system to prove valuable. There is then little incentive for initial users to join the club, and some way must be found to attract them in order to build this critical mass. Symbolic rewards might help in this regard (the pleasure of participating in an innovative experiment for example).

One should also be aware that rankings depend on the particular rating method chosen to evaluate the relevance of documents or products. We have seen that the rating of a particular item could be determined by explicit user evaluations, by semantic proximity to user profiles, or by recording user actions concerning this item. Evaluations may depend both on user profiles and user actions in variable combinations.

In short, *implicit collaborative systems work by setting up groupings of similar users* and then exploiting these virtual groups to retrieve or recommend socially supported items. Collecting individual ratings (whether explicit or not) about items is a prerequisite to calculating their overall social value in the group of reference.

Another example of the implicit use of social structure is offered by PageRank, Google's ranking algorithm for Web pages (Brin & Page, 1998). This famous search engine retrieves pages in classical fashion (by computing their textual similarity to a user query) but then orders them by exploiting the structure of Web links. The page ranking is meant to solve the frequent problem of information overflow with too many answers to a query.

More precisely, Web pages are ranked by the sum of hyperlinks pointing to them from other Web sites, each link being weighted with the value of the pointing site, determined recursively in the same way by considering its own incoming links. The ranking of a site thus increases with the number and value of sites pointing to it. A careful matrix implementation of the graph of hyperlinks speeds up the recursive value computation.

The hyperlink structure used by the PageRank algorithm is in fact the public trace of an implicit social consensus. Web sites with numerous incoming links are better known (and tend to attract even more new links) as they have been judged more relevant by other Web site publishers. This is a measurable form of hyperspace reputation on the Web, which is presumably a good indicator of the interest and trustworthiness of a Web page. The success of Google is largely due to the clever use of this social indicator.

Peer-to-peer file sharing systems such as Napster, Gnutella, or KaZaA have also been very successful, to the horror of major music companies. They work by distributing requests through a network of participants so as to find users with similar tastes. Music files or other documents can then be exchanged among like-minded participants. Napster employed a central server to store and compare user profiles, but in more recent systems both data and processing are totally distributed throughout the network (Memmi & Nérot, 2003; Wang, Pouwelse, Lagendijk, & Reinders, 2006).

Peer-to-peer architectures can be used for file sharing, information retrieval, and collaborative filtering. But the implicit links between users do not have to be made public for the system to work, thus allowing a minimum of privacy.

In spite of their differences, these various collaborative systems all make use of distributed, implicit, socially situated knowledge by building or revealing virtual communities. Relevant information is accessed through social links, and retrieval algorithms embody social expertise about information handling. But individual systems users are not made directly aware of the underlying group structure.

TRENDS AND PERSPECTIVES

Even though our survey has not been exhaustive, the diversity of approaches and collaborative systems is striking. So the question arises whether one can discern general tendencies among recent research work. It is by no means clear at this time that one approach will predominate over the others, but we would like to venture a few general observations and suggest likely developments.

Following the typology proposed above, explicit communities and task-oriented groups are the most obvious phenomena and have probably attracted more initial attention as a basis for computer-aided communication. But it seems to us that *there remains more to discover about implicit social links,* so that interesting novel techniques may be expected to appear in this direction. Because more and more information is becoming available in electronic form about human relationships, new ways will be found to exploit such information.

For example, commercial transactions and work connections often leave electronic traces which can used for informational purposes. Profiling people by their commercial or browsing behavior can also be used to put together virtual groups with similar interests and needs. On the other hand, such techniques could also prove very intrusive, posing difficult ethical and social problems about individual privacy.

We believe that more detailed analyses of human social information processing would be a fruitful source of new techniques. We have tried here to show the wealth and complexity of social information processes, but we still do not know enough about such common social mechanisms. Studying and modeling collective information management should bring about new insights and suggest new approaches.

Unfortunately, interest in this area has traditionally been dispersed among very different disciplines, which do not communicate very well with each other. Sociology, economics, and management studies notably have contributed valuable observations about human knowledge management, but this is too rarely a central concern and approaches vary widely. Fundamental research in this domain is then more likely to be a source of inspiration to computer science than to provide a store of directly applicable models.

Accessing and making use of tacit knowledge has hardly started, and usually only indirectly. In spite of the social and economic importance of this type of knowledge, it only becomes accessible online as a by-product of explicit communication links on the Internet. No systematic effort has been made so far to address this question by computer, although the problem is largely recognized in real life (tutoring relationships and training schemes are basically meant to ensure the transmission of implicit or tacit knowledge).

Profiling individuals by their electronic behavior is the most likely route in order to gain access to the tacit knowledge they might possess, but for privacy reasons this is probably feasible only within work situations and inside organizations. And as to collective tacit knowledge (the kind of knowledge that makes a company more or less efficient), one simply knows very little about how to describe or formalize such distributed information.

We would also like to suggest that a generic platform or general toolbox for collaborative software design would be a good idea for experimenting with various methods. It would help build prototypes and new software systems. Such a platform should contain the main representation and processing techniques we have seen so far, with capacities for exchanging information between different approaches. Common data representations would make it possible to share information among various tools.

A recent example of this kind of open toolbox can be found in the Sakai project (*www.sakaiproject.org*). This is a free collaborative environment which contains many of the communication techniques currently available for virtual communities. The emphasis is on education and e-learning, but the software can easily be extended to other areas.

In our view, such a toolbox should include in particular the following methods:

- Current communication tools (e-mail, chat, forums);
- Blackboard facilities (a wiki structure, for example);
- Social network simulation software;
- Social network analysis software; and
- Common profiling and clustering algorithms.

Most of these software tools are already available, but in different domains, and they are rarely employed together. For example, elaborate methods have been developed for social network analysis, and software packages are easily obtainable (e.g., Ucinet or Structure), but they have mostly been used by sociologists. Electronic mail is widely used, but communication patterns are rarely collected and studied. Putting together different methods would make data available for analysis, and help investigate a complex and multidisciplinary field of enquiry.

To sum up, socially situated human information management is an intricate, multi-faceted domain, which we still do not understand well enough to reproduce in all its wealth and power. More fundamental studies are needed, as well as more friendly generic research tools. It is time for a global approach and for comprehensive software tools in order to improve our capacity for useful and efficient collaborative software design.

CONCLUSION

We have tried to show here how human information processing takes place in a social context and to what extent human beings use this context to retrieve information and solve problems. Shifting the emphasis from individual to social processes greatly improves our ability to understand and reproduce real human abilities. Studying and modeling socially situated information processing is therefore an important source of inspiration for the design of better collaborative information systems.

Of course, technology does not have to imitate life. It has often been the case in the history of computer science that efficient solutions to practical problems were derived mostly from technical considerations. Computers do not work by duplicating human thought processes faithfully, but by exploiting the speed and accuracy of electronic devices. Technical constraints and possibilities may have their own logic.

For high-level abilities, however, and especially when dealing with new areas to model, analyzing human cognitive processes is often both a prerequisite and a good start for system design. In the domain of information retrieval and knowledge management, studying closely the way human society performs its knowledge tasks by using distributed, collaborative processes has proven to be a fruitful approach. We are convinced that useful design ideas are still to be gained in this manner.

REFERENCES

Adomavicius, G., & Tuzhilin, A. (2005). Toward the next generation of recommender systems: A survey of the state-of-the-art and possible extensions. *IEEE Transactions on Knowledge and Data Engineering, 17*(6).

Baeza-Yates, R. (1999). *Modern information retrieval.* Boston, MA: Addison Wesley.

Baumard, P. (1999). *Tacit knowledge in organizations.* London: Sage.

Breese, J.S., Heckerman, D., & Kadie, C. (1998). Empirical analysis of predictive algorithms for collaborative filtering. *Proceedings of the 14th Conference on Uncertainty in Artificial Intelligence.*

Brin, S., & Page, L. (1998). *The anatomy of a large-scale hypertextual Web search engine.* Computer Science Department, Stanford University, USA.

Burt, R.S. (1992). *Structural holes: The social structure of competition.* Cambridge, MA: Harvard University Press.

Castells, M. (1996). *The rise of the network society.* Oxford: Blackwell.

Clark, A. (1998). *Being there: Putting brain, body, and world together again.* Cambridge, MA: MIT Press.

Drucker, P.F. (1992). *The age of discontinuity.* New York: Harper & Row.

Favela, J., & Decouchant, D. (Eds.). (2003). *Groupware: Design, implementation and use.* Berlin: Springer-Verlag.

Feller, J., Fitzgerald, B., Hissam, S.A., & Lakhnani, K.R. (2005). *Perspectives on free and open source software.* Cambridge, MA: MIT Press.

Granovetter, M.S. (1973). The strength of weak ties. *American Journal of Sociology, 78,* 1360-1380.

Harnad, S., & Dror, I.E. (Eds.). (2006). Distributed cognition—special issue. *Pragmatics and Cognition, 14*(2).

Kautz, H., Selman, B., & Shah, M. (1997). Referral Web: Combining social networks and collaborative filtering. *Communications of the ACM, 40*(3).

Kendrick, J.W. (1994). Total capital and economic growth. *Atlantic Economic Journal, 22*(1).

Kirsch, S., Gnasa, M., & Cremers, A. (2006). Beyond the Web: Retrieval in social information spaces. *Proceedings of the 28th European Conference on Information Retrieval.*

Kollock, P., & Smith, M. (Eds.). (1999). *Communities in cyberspace.* London: Routledge.

Lazega, E. (2001). *The collegial phenomenon.* Oxford: Oxford University Press.

Lesser, V., & Erman, L. (1977). A retrospective view of the Hearsay-II architecture. *Proceedings of the 5th IJCAI* (pp. 790-800).

Mandler, G. (1985). *Cognitive psychology.* Hillsdale, NJ: Lawrence Erlbaum.

Manning, C.D., & Schütze, H. (1999). *Foundations of statistical natural language processing.* Cambridge, MA: MIT Press.

Mauss, M. (1924). Essai sur le don. *Année Sociologique 1923-1924.*

Memmi, D., & Nérot, O (2003). Building virtual communities for information retrieval. In J. Favela & D. Decouchant (Eds.), *Groupware: Design, implementation and use.* Berlin: Springer-Verlag.

Memmi, D. (2006). The nature of virtual communities. *AI and Society, 20*(3).

Mintzberg, H. (1979). *The structuring of organizations.* Englewood Cliffs, NJ: Prentice Hall.

Munoz, M.A, Gonzalez, V.M., Rodriguez, M., & Favela, J. (2003). Supporting context-aware collaboration in a hospital: An ethnographic informed design. In J. Favela & D. Decouchant (Eds.), *Groupware: Design, implementation and use.* Berlin: Springer-Verlag.

Neisser, U. (1967). *Cognitive psychology.* New York: Appleton-Century-Crofts.

O'Reilly, T. (2005) *What is Web 2.0.* Retrieved from *http://www.oreillynet.com/pub/a/oreilly/tim/news/2005/09/30/what-is-web-20.html*

Polanyi, M. (1966). *The tacit dimension.* London: Routledge & Kegan Paul.

Rheingold, H. (2000). *The virtual community.* Cambridge, MA: MIT Press.

Resnick, P., Iacovou, N., Suchak, M., Bergstrom, P., & Riedl, J. (1994). GroupLens: An open architecture for collaborative filtering of Netnews. *Proceedings of the 1994 Conference on Computer-Supported Cooperative Work.*

Salton, G., & McGill, M. (1983). *Introduction to modern information retrieval.* New York: McGraw-Hill.

Shapiro, C., & Varian, H.R. (1999). *Information rules: A strategic guide to the network economy.* Cambridge, MA: Harvard Business School Press.

Shardanand, U., & Maes, P. (1995). Social information filtering: Algorithms for automating "word of mouth." *Proceedings of the 1995 Conference on Human Factors in Computing Systems.*

Travers, J., & Milgram, S. (1969). An experimental study of the small world problem. *Sociometry, 32,* 425-443.

Wang, J., Pouwelse, J., Lagendijk, R., & Reinders, M. (2006). Distributed collaborative filtering for peer-to-peer file sharing systems. *Proceedings of the 21st Annual ACM Symposium on Applied Computing.*

Wasserman, S., & Faust, K. (1994). *Social network analysis: Methods and applications.* Cambridge: Cambridge University Press.

Watts, D.J. (1999). *Small worlds.* Princeton, NJ: Princeton University Press.

Wellman, B. (Ed.). (1999). *Networks in the global village.* Boulder, CO: Westview Press.

Section V
Social Information Seeking Models

Chapter XI
Social Information Seeking in Digital Libraries

George Buchanan
University of Wales, Swansea, UK

Annika Hinze
University of Waikato, New Zealand

ABSTRACT

Information seeking is a complex task, and many models of the basic, individual seeking process have been proposed. Similarly, many tools now exist to support "sit-forward" information seeking by single users, where the solitary seeker interacts intensively with a search engine or classification scheme. However, in many situations, there is a clear interaction between social contexts beyond the immediate interaction between the user and the retrieval system. In this chapter we demonstrate a number of contrasting uses of the social aspects of information seeking, and through those propose, demonstrate, and realize social models of information seeking that complement existing information seeking models and technologies. These include: information sharing among humanities researchers; creation of profiles for continuous, ongoing searching of medical material; and the capture of models of user behaviors in an interactive, mobile tourist information system. From the human perspective we illustrate differing social techniques and issues including: explicit and implicit sharing; seeking facilitated by subject (medical, academic) experts and search experts (librarians); and anonymized and attributed social environments. Whereas many papers focus on particular social retrieval technologies, in this chapter we abstract a number of different approaches to present underlying principles, architectures, and models that can be adopted for a wider range of applications. We focus on digital library (DL) technology, as DLs have well-accepted architectures that support a wide variety of information seeking tools. We also address the key related issue of models of information seeking—models that have strongly influenced the design of DL technologies.

BACKGROUND

Social information seeking studies the many ways in which communication and interaction between people influence their information seeking. To take one simple example, humans often share "pearls of wisdom" through informal, off-line discussions. This form of interchange has been observed in many different domains including engineering, academe, and the clinical world. Though such off-line communications are inaccessible to computer systems, they form a critical foundation for much of the actual information seeking of the users of digital libraries and online encyclopedias. Failing to understand the consequences of this hidden activity on interactive information seeking will result in a shortfall in the quality and effectiveness of online information retrieval tools.

The pervasive nature of social interaction within information seeking already leaves its fingerprints on public Web sites. For example, many news and technical Web sites support simple "e-mail this article" tools that facilitate information sharing between collaborators at a basic level. Similarly, Amazon.com has placed a considerable investment in providing collaborative filtering to support recommendations for its customers. Finally, Google's PageRank algorithm (Brin & Page, 1998) and the related work of Chakrabarti, Joshi, Punera, and Pennock (2002) on online communities of interest are, in fact, prime examples of the successful harnessing of social information—the human creation of Web links between sites—to improve the effectiveness of automated document retrieval systems. However, persuasive as these "real-world" examples may be, they represent a fragmented veneer beneath which is, at present, a lack of systematic science and, often, a considerable degree of conjecture as to which elements should be evaluated to create a "social" information retrieval infrastructure.

Technical Background

The projects reported and synthesized in this chapter all originate in the domain of digital library research. There are many competing definitions of digital libraries, from those emphasizing the significance of the institution that operates the library, to highly techno-centric definitions that focus upon the combination of particular functions. Our definition, and the one upon which this chapter is built, is that a digital library is an indexed and organized collection of digital documents, where inclusion in the library is determined by the institution or individual who operates the library. Implicit in this definition is an assumption that selection of a document for inclusion in the library is based upon its intellectual quality and its relevance to the purpose of the collection. Similarly, the indexation and organization of the library is assumed to include features analogous to a traditional library of printed documents—for example, subject classification hierarchies, and author and title indexes. These indexes are expected to be supplemented by those that can only realistically be created by a computerized index—for example, of the full text of the documents.

One key concept that we have borrowed from hypertext research is also critical to understanding the role of digital library systems in our research. Halasz (1988), in a seminal work, introduced the distinction between computation *within* a hypertext and computation *over* a hypertext. The first concept applies to internal processing that occurs in the creation and operation of the system itself; the second to the ability to access the content of a hypertext whilst it is in operation, and perform some external processing over the content. One practical example may clarify the distinction: a Web server may operate an online store, such as Amazon, while an external computer (e.g., Google) creates a searchable index over the content of many Web servers, including the store, and indexes it. In this context, the store's Web server is performing computation 'within' the store, while the search computer is computing 'over' the store. Some of our examples will use computation within the library, adjusting and extending its services internally, while others operate over one or more libraries.

In this chapter we reflect on several different projects that have been undertaken at Middlesex University, the University of Waikato, University College London, and the University of Wales over a six-year time span. These varying individual studies coalesce to form a deeper insight into the underlying design space for social information seeking, and identify both areas where research is maturing and fields where many new insights remain to be achieved.

The chapter will proceed in five parts: First, we will briefly introduce a number of popular information seeking models, and discuss their relevance to social information seeking. Second, we describe the different social settings in which our research has been performed before, thirdly, presenting the tools and environments that we have created to support the interpersonal aspects of human information seeking. We then discuss the varied social and technical systems we have shown, identifying underlying principles related to information seeking models and technologies. Fifth and finally, we conclude the chapter with a review of the accomplishments of social information retrieval to date, and an outlook to future research.

MODELING INFORMATION SEEKING

This part of the chapter will outline key information seeking models introduced by Marchionini, Belkin, Ellis, Kuhlthau, and Ingwersen (1982). Each of these models has been influential in the development of information seeking tools, though each emphasizes different aspects of the search process. Taking the models in turn, we will identify

the degree of social information seeking captured within the model already, and also discuss the means by which social information seeking can be included.

Marchionini's Information Seeking Model

Marchionini et al.'s (1995) eight-stage model may be compared with the classic 'Waterfall' model of software development. It is a linear, sequential model in which each step progresses logically from the previous one (see Figure 1). Unlike the models that follow, Marchionini's represents interactive search only; other strategies for discovering information, such as discussion with peers, browsing classification topics online, or browsing library shelves, are not represented.

In principle, any of the stages of Marchionini's model could be social—however, most of the direct interaction with the search engine (stages 4 to 6) is unlikely to have an immediate social context unless searching is being done collaboratively. For the sake of brevity, we will not discuss that possibility in this chapter.

However, other phases—such as the selection of sources (3), extraction of information (7), and reflection (8)—will often occur in a social sphere. For example, a student may discuss material with a peer or a supervising academic.

Belkin's ASK Model

A second key model in interactive search is Belkin's Anomalous State of Knowledge (ASK) model (Belkin et al., 1982). This model focuses on the searcher's uncertainty about information, and in contrast to Marchionini's model, it was primarily created to explain the gap between information retrieval systems and the user's mental model of their information need. The proposition of the underlying ASK hypothesis is that users often do not know what they are searching for, and they need guidance and cues on how to fol-

Figure 1. Marchionini et al.'s (1995) model of the information seeking process

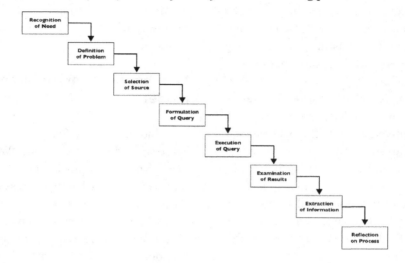

low an effective process. Consequently, the ASK model emphasizes the choice of low-level searching tactics to resolve doubt about a topic and the user's state of knowledge at each point. However, the tactics exist much at the level described by Marchionini et al. (1995), and the model of the user is primarily cognitive. The cognitive part does not include any form of "social cognition." Consequently, Belkin's model remains fixed upon the individual and his or her direct interaction with the retrieval system.

Ellis' Information Seeking Model

The behavioral model of information seeking introduced by Ellis (1989) is a strong contrast against the models of both Belkin and Marchionini. Like Marchionini, Ellis emphasizes a number of 'behaviors' or actions that can be performed in the course of information seeking. Unlike Marchionini, he does not present a linear model—a seeker may switch from one behavior to another, and then return. Just as little is his model limited to interactive querying—each behavior could be achieved by a number of means such as interactive searching, consultation with colleagues, or browsing library shelves. Ellis' behaviors are:

- **Starting:** Identifying and using initial sources.
- **Chaining:** Following existing leads, or finding documents that use known items.
- **Browsing:** Scanning lists (tables of contents, chapter titles) within found texts.
- **Differentiating:** Distinguishing the quality and relevance of each document.
- **Monitoring:** Keeping up to date in areas that are already known.
- **Extracting:** Studying retrieved material in detail for conclusive details.
- **Verifying:** Checking the reliability of extracted facts.
- **Ending:** Resolving final uncertainties, reaching conclusions.

However, though the model is not linear, there is a certain assumption of progress from the 'starting' activity of identifying some initial sources to the 'ending' activity of summarizing what has been found (Wilson, 1999). The six other stages certainly will interleave. For example, a researcher may find a new citation in the process of 'extracting' detailed information from a found document and move onto 'chaining' that new lead to discover further material.

Ellis' model, like that of Kuhlthau which follows, has been influential in moving research on information seeking from a focus on interactive search seen in Marchionini's model onto a wider view that includes interactive search, but also encompasses the discovery of leads and ongoing monitoring on topics where the initial, intensive searching has been done. In terms of social information seeking, however, Ellis' model is no more precise or explicit that Marchionini's. The task of 'chaining'—following up on new leads—is as disconnected from the source of the lead (which may be social) as it is from the method of chaining (e.g., visiting a Web site or library).

Kuhlthau's Model

Marchionini's and Ellis' models present two contrasting views of the seeking process, and both are highly influential. Kuhlthau's (2002) model brings together a number of the properties of these other two models. Though contemporary with both Marchionini and Ellis, Kuhlthau echoes the process emphasis of the former, and the cyclical, repetitive, and unpredictable flow of the latter. Like Belkin, she focuses on doubt and uncertainty, and associates changes in these feelings with progress through the information seeking process, resolving eventually in success and relief or failure and disappointment. Her six stages of the information seeking process are: Initiation, Selection, Exploration, Formulation, Collection, and Presentation. The critical point in the process is the Formulation stage when the user's information need becomes better defined and focus increases. The following collection process gathers together the best information, and as it progresses, the user's anxiety falls and confidence grows.

Though this emotional focus may lead one to expect some recognition of the social aspects of the process, the definition of the different activities in Kuhlthau's model is devoid of any social note. As with Ellis' model, though there is a clear

opportunity for social factors both to influence each activity and to be used to fulfill parts of the process, this is not realized.

Ingwersen's Model

The recent information seeking model of Ingwersen and Järvelin (2005) presents different 'actors' in the information seeking process. Both components of the computer system and the human searcher are seen as 'actors'. However, in this model, the idea of a *social context* is added as another 'actor'. This is a welcome addition to the conception of the information seeking process. However, when one turns to the model in detail, the description of the effect of the social context, there is a lack of detail.

There are only a few examples of the effect of social interaction, and the most developed description explains how a pair of question-and-answer interactions with a colleague would be represented in the model. The model also is focused upon a single user interacting with a search system. This fails to fully capture situations where a number of people may collaboratively search for information—for example, at the beginning of a group project or where a number of researchers use a collaborative information seeking tool.

This new model therefore makes a key step forward in reflecting the social aspect of information seeking. However, it is not focused on social information seeking, and it fails to provide a model of social information seeking.

Summary

In this section, we have reviewed five key information seeking models. The focus of our interest was the degree to which social aspects of information seeking are explicitly represented. In each case, we found that the models provided scope for including social information seeking, but lacked structured, formal representation of it. Linear, process-centered models that focus on interactive search, such as Marchionini's or Belkin's, may be seen as unlikely candidates for representing the wider influences and inputs of community. On the other hand, one may expect that behavioral models such as Ellis' and Kuhlthau's would have a clearer representation of social aspects of information seeking, given their generally broader view. However, it is only in the novel model of Ingwersen and Järvelin that we start to see social elements of information seeking represented.

Strong models of an activity support the development of effective tools to support that work. The deeper and more structured understanding of the information seeking process provided by the models above have led to improved information retrieval and digital library technologies. If we are to build a strong foundation for building social information seeking tools, then our information seeking models must be extended to reflect the social attributes, activities, and decision making of the information seeking process. Indeed, special models of social information seeking may well be required to better capture the processes and information use that occur when searching has a strongly collaborative- or community-centered context.

Social information seeking has existed long before the introduction of digital technologies. Thus, we can build our models of social information seeking from both recent research around digital systems, and more established research regarding physical information environments such as libraries.

INFORMATION SEEKING IN SOCIETY

In the previous section, we noted that social aspects of information seeking are poorly represented in established, accepted models. However, there is abundant evidence from studies of information seeking that social considerations, goals, techniques, and inputs play critical roles in the pursuit of useful information. In this section, we will provide an insight into the social information seeking issues for a set of sample domains. In the following section, we will demonstrate the inclusion of these social aspects in implemented systems. Supporting and contrasting research from other sources will be introduced to clarify and expand the discussion of each domain.

Schools and the Classroom: Sharing Among Peers

We studied the activity of children creating independent works, but working collaboratively to find and store inspiring pieces, and reviewing each other's work (Theng et al., 2001). Much of their seeking occurred within a social context—either searching the pieces written by their friends, or with their classmates exploring the Web for material that could give the inspiration for a story.

In this case, there was a strong need to represent the social context in the digital library system. The class was involved in the design of the DL system through a participative design process. This led to the creation of a number of different shared spaces within the digital library through which students could collaborate electronically. However, this electronic domain supplemented rather than replaced the pupil's face-to-face interaction in class. Much of the student's use of the system occurred in regular, scheduled class time in the school's computer room.

The electronic provision of shared document space supported the continued discussion of ideas at home or outside school hours. Pupils usually placed material into these spaces at the end of or after class time. During class, students would typically work together at the one machine. However, shared document spaces only allowed the interchange of documents within the library, and the writing and sharing of comments on the documents. Students also discovered material outside of the time when they were primarily using the DL. In these situations, e-mail was frequently used to share ideas or send URLs of interesting material. Often these messages referred to documents not yet in the library, or to ideas or concepts rather than any document at all. The structured interaction of the library fit poorly with the fluid and opportunistic flow of this supplementary social exchange.

Students had also been arranged into formal groups of up to five as part of the class activity. Feedback was supposed to be given by each member of the group on the essays being written by the others. However, though this system did work, the pupils strongly preferred having feedback from friends. For different essays, different friends would be preferred. The KidsDL system was therefore extended to support document exchange and comments between the members of both fixed formal groups and ad-hoc informal groups.

The needs we found in this situation varied from collaboration within the information seeking environment to communication outside it, and a wide range of formality of structure. The challenge was providing a consistent system that could encompass this diversity without causing confusion through inconsistency.

Academic Research: Collaboration and Competition

Together with other researchers, we have studied the pursuit of academics. Our own focus is on humanities academics. In the humanities, there is an oft-quoted division between 'truffle hunters' who seek out obscure pieces that illuminate a known problem, and 'parachutists' who synthesize material from a variety of sources to identify large-scale themes. These contrasting approaches often lead to different social interactions. For parachutists, a high value is often placed on exchanging useful information, whereas truffle hunters tend to jealously guard their rare sources until they are ready to publish.

Our research has revealed that in information seeking, experienced researchers often rely on their academic community to locate information. In part, this social context supplies precise information (e.g., suggested papers with title and author information), and in part, it provides guidance regarding the special terminology of unfamiliar fields. Another social aspect that is important is the use of personal homepages on the Web to track the current activity of key people whose interests mirror or complement those of the researchers themselves.

However, though there is a significant social element to the information seeking of academics, this is not reflected in the digital tools available to them. Furthermore, some readily available electronic media, such as mailing lists, are little used either to communicate informally or to discuss research. There are three key reasons for this: first, the digital technology is unfamiliar and the rewards uncertain, which results in a low take-up; second, the digital domain does not provide forums which have prestige in the community itself; and third, public digital forums do not allow for the selectivity of whom one is talking to, which can be controlled both face to face and via personal e-mail. Thus, the social context in which the humanities researcher operates provides an unappealing alternative to face-to-face contact using established skills at conferences with academic esteem. These dynamics work at the community level: so just as significant communication towards finding important literature occurs within the community, so the community's established patterns reduce the scope for widening digital take-up.

In the humanities, therefore, collaboration can be tinged with a need to restrict awareness of special material. Furthermore, there is a poor fit between the digital tools and the key social interactions within the research community. The barriers within digital communication need to be lowered while ensuring that a researcher's 'pearls' are not given away without their explicit action.

The Medical World: Information Intermediaries, Patients, and Clinicians

In clinical environments, there is a need to manage uncertainty in a safety-critical environment. Social issues are highly complex—as there are conflicting demands between the strong separation of clinical disciplines, a need to work effectively in teams, and often highly hierarchical power structures. The success or failure of individual information systems is often determined not by technical issues, but rather the social determiners of acceptability.

Effective information seeking support has embraced these tensions and practices by placing expert information intermediaries (librarians) in existing medical teams, adding another strongly defined role to the group. Our recent work has extended from this starting point, looking at the additional complications that emerge when supporting patients with chronic illnesses. In this context, patients often need to obtain information relevant to their condition on an ongoing basis, as the disease changes. Describing their need requires both clinical and information expertise, yet the search engine must identify documents that are comprehendible to the patient themselves. This adds further complexity to an already challenging situation.

One view of the information seeking challenge for the patient can be to place him or her on an informal team constituted of the medical experts involved in the patient's care and the patient him or herself. This team is a heterogeneous collection of skills and abilities, but the collective knowledge of every member may be needed to identify the patient's precise information needs. Information seeking is already an identified challenge within clinical teams, and recent research has demonstrated the advantages that can be gained by adding a specialist information intermediary (e.g., a specialist medical librarian) who provides information finding support to the other team members. This is a promising avenue to explore when viewing the patient as a further member of a clinical team.

Social contexts also work within the community of patients: increasingly, those who suffer chronic diseases often share practical advice on coping with their conditions through online discussion boards. Private discussions often emerge from these boards, communicated by personal e-mails and Internet messaging systems.

Information seeking is therefore a collaborative process, with the patient at the center. Either the patient is part of a team, perhaps assisted by a clinical librarian. Relevance judgments about material are often made in concert with their fellow patients, and sometimes their medical practitioner.

Tourism: Collaborative Filtering, Sparse Data, and Dynamic Environments

Finally, we have been studying the delivery of information in mobile environments, and our recent work has pursued the use of tourist information as the target context. In this environment, there are two levels of social issues. First, a tourist may be traveling with other people (e.g., family or friends) who have different interests. This means successful information seeking needs to work within multiple constraints. Second, there will be other tourists who are visiting or have visited the same location. This second level of social interaction means that the tourist can gain information, both explicit and implicit, about the environment from other tourists. The social context is, therefore, both a constraint and a provider of information.

In the case of tourism, seekers have low attention and often do not want to perform intensive information seeking. The focus of research is in using minimal and low-attention information tools over many individuals to build models of a user that provide a broad understanding of the individual's interests. The objective of the model is not to pinpoint a user's exact needs, but rather to exclude items of little or no interest.

Summary

These varied social contexts provide a wide span of information use, information seeking behavior, and social models. This broad coverage of the social aspects of the human search for information has provided a deep insight into the underlying patterns of behavior and the technical solutions that provide effective information systems in each context. Social considerations can limit the adoption of digital tools, but can also provide a source of data that can be leveraged to increase the precision achieved by search engines and browsing interfaces. Social exchanges take many forms: from complex informal and dynamic networks of peers found in the incidental exchanges between tourists through formal peer groups in the classroom to structured teams with specialized roles in clinical practice. Clearly, differing specific models will be needed to encompass the challenges, requirements, and practices of each situation. In this chapter, however, we will focus on presenting a generalized model that can be populated with the particulars of an actual situation of use.

In the digital domain, there is a ready opportunity to use the data acquired in one part of the user's information work to support his or her activity in another. For example, as we saw in KidsDL, a student's essay writing and the comments supplied to friends and classmates provide a potential insight into the student's information preferences and needs. However, electronic communication can also provide a spur to active information seeking, as demonstrated in the cases of e-mail exchanges between academics, yet little has been done to streamline or integrate this electronic exchange into a digital information seeking workflow. Bulletin boards provide a rich and valued interactive environment that is similarly disconnected, or at best loosely connected

with structured information repositories—that is, digital libraries, which the same user community will regularly consult for critical information. Therefore, our current digital environments have considerable scope for improved support of information seeking.

We will now turn to studying our implemented systems, before continuing onto an identification of common human behaviors and technical solutions.

IMPLEMENTED SYSTEMS

In this section we will briefly introduce both systems created by ourselves and other researchers, highlighting the response to the challenges noted above. Reference will be made to existing publications, but key architectural diagrams will be reproduced in expanded form.

KidsDL

The KidsDL project (Theng et al., 2001) has already been described. There, we briefly introduced selected parts of the system. Here, we will discuss these elements in detail.

The digital library was implemented using the well-established open-source digital library system 'Greenstone.' Greenstone has a highly developed and well-defined architecture that reflects the construction of other key digital library systems, and indeed large-scale, structured information repositories generally (Bainbridge et al., 2001; Adams & Blandford, 2004, 2005).

At a simple level, Greenstone has a receptionist component that presents the system to the user in a readily usable interface. It hides the underlying complexity of the server that holds the library collections and performs retrieval and storage functionality from the user. Typically, the receptionist is accessed through a standard Web browser. Beyond this, the server level is divided into different 'filters' or services, and the receptionist into separate 'actions'. For example, interactive search is provided by one service, hierarchical browsing by topic through another. Each separate service is often—though not always—reflected directly in an action in the receptionist interface. The exceptions include a user authentication service, which can be used to identify individual users and restrict their interaction library to those items that best suit their needs or those features to which they have authorized access. Clearly, this service could be used by any number of user-focused actions in the receptionist.

An overall view of this architecture is illustrated in Figure 2.

In the KidsDL project, we extended the Greenstone architecture model in a number of ways. Most of the modifications were achieved by adding additional actions to the receptionist and services to the server. Generally, therefore, the principles of the DL architecture remained unchanged. However, a brief reference to the diagram of the KidsDL system in Figure 3 will immediately reveal that the extensions to the basic architecture were extensive.

First, a review system was added to the library. Similar social extensions to digital libraries have been suggested before (Goh & Leggett, 2000). However, in this case the review system could be used by both the class teacher and by fellow students. As we noted above, the students who could review a paper were either in formal groups set by the teacher, or informally selected friends and classmates.

Second, the library had to develop a broad range of information spaces. Greenstone supports the creation of a number of discrete 'collections' that are separate, discrete sets of documents. Each collection usually contains items that have a common topic, author, or genre, as deemed appropriate by the library administration. In the KidsDL, this conception was adjusted to provide individual collections where works-in-progress were stored, group collections for essays were available for peer review, along with established collections for finished works, materials that were selected by the teacher to provide inspiration or examples, and so forth.

A number of the features of the extended DL system were co-opted by the pupils in the course of social information seeking. For example, reviews could provide suggestions and references to other documents. The target documents of these queries may be in the KidsDL itself, other DLs, the school library, online, or at unknown locations (e.g., a specific book without reference to where it might be found).

However, interaction still occurred beyond the library. Figure 3 therefore represents only part of the broader information seeking environment. In Figure 4, we see an extended view that now simplifies the model of the DL, but extends the

Figure 2. A simplified view of Greenstone's architecture

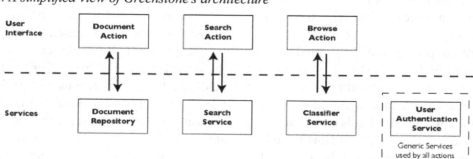

Figure 3. The KidsDL architecture

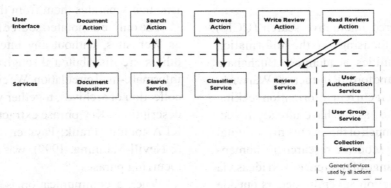

Figure 4. The digital library in the wider communication environment

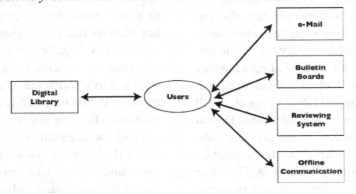

social representation of the environment. Unusually, the DL systems' features support information exchange between users. This provides only one conduit of many for communication between the pupils. These exchanges may be face to face or remote, synchronous or asynchronous, precise (e.g., book title and author) or imprecise ('find out more about what others have said about Caesar's character'). Searching may also be collaborative (e.g., tasks given to a specific group of pupils) in both formal or informal groups as well as individual.

While the KidsDL was very successful and clearly demonstrated the benefits of the collaborative design process, it revealed some new challenges in creating social information seeking tools. First, it was hard to foresee all the social communication that would occur. As students

and teachers were operating in a familiar environment, regular, formal communication was readily identified early in the design process. However, informal exchanges and feedback, unplanned collaboration, and exchange were in practice essential to the successful operation of the classroom. The highly structured approach of the digital library delivered good support for the formal communication required, and the review system facilitated a great deal of unplanned (or at least, unanticipated) information sharing.

However, the KidsDL was circumvented when the students were engaged in more fluid tasks. Familiar, unstructured tools were used more when informal and unplanned interaction occurred—as it frequently did. Integration between the more fluid environments (such as e-mail) and the DL was weak.

UCIS Project (Humanities)

In the user-centered interactive search (UCIS) project, we are focusing on the information seeking of humanities academics (Buchanan, Cunningham, Blandford, Rimmer, & Warwick, 2005). Much of their current information seeking uses social sources, as we have already noted. However, though much of this occurs in the digital domain, including scouring researcher's homepages and the exchange of references and ideas via e-mail, this interaction generally occurs outside the information seeking environment itself.

We are currently investigating how the gap between the existing uses of digital technologies and, for example, the digital library can be bridged. To achieve this goal, we are exploiting a number of information mining tools created in the course of the New Zealand Digital Library project—well known for its creation of the Greenstone Digital Library system introduced in the previous subsection. Examples of such tools are bibliographic, proper name, and citation mining tools. These use compression and data mining techniques to extract data from full text. Classically, these techniques are used to extract metadata from documents, and subsequently to index the documents.

In the UCIS project, however, we adjust this strategy to extract metadata from interpersonal communication (e.g., e-mails) and subsequently use it in either retrieving documents from information sources or identifying specific information sources. Here, we will focus upon the latter strategy.

Within the humanities, one common community activity is the creation of annotated lists of information sources, for example, lists of archival repositories, complete with descriptions of their holdings. Often, for any single researcher, the information that will eventually form the sources for one article will have been gleaned from many different sources. Indeed, senior researchers who we have interviewed have reported that the determination to find more difficult-to-find items and

investigating neglected archives is one characteristic that separates them from their juniors.

The online annotated source lists are operated as Web sites, without any internal indexation; others are distributed through mailing lists or informal e-mail circulation. We created an indexed collection of archives, together with their source descriptions. Key phrase extraction, through the KEA toolkit (Frank, Paynter, Witten, Gutwin, & Nevill-Manning, 1999), was used to identify recurring phrases.

When a communication is received by the system, it extracts what bibliographic, citation, or proper name text it can, together with any key phrases that match those discovered in the sources lists. Together, these are used to identify matching repositories. Each of those can also be searched to identify matching works within the repository. The practical challenge at this point is to be sufficiently selective with the final result set, and not repeatedly alert the user to the same archival repository. To achieve this, a trace is maintained on previous recommendations to the user. A heuristic is used whereby the weight used to rank repositories is halved for a given repository for a given user after five recommendations (a recommendation is only counted if it falls within the top five repositories in a list—lower

Figure 5. UCIS e-mail ingest architecture

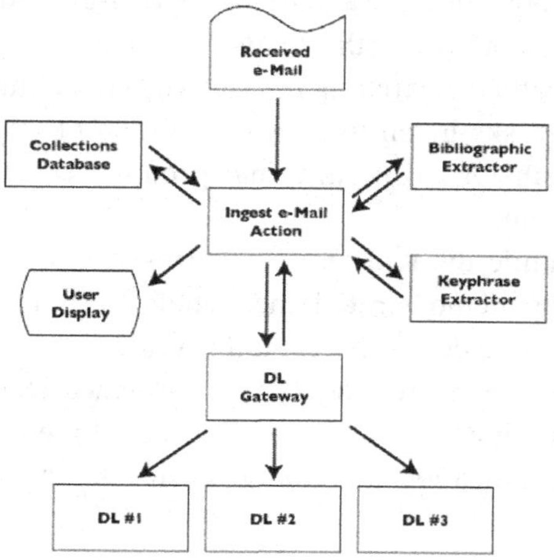

ranks are discarded for the purposes of the recommendation count). A heuristic lower-bound cut on match scoring is also used to limit the size of the recommended set, and to avoid spurious and unreliable matches.

The architecture for this solution is seen in Figure 5. The technical details for the components such as the extraction tools for bibliographies and key phrases can be found in earlier papers (Frank et al., 1999; Yeates, Witten, & Bainbridge, 2001). The strategy is promising, but much can be done to improve the precision of matching, using community scores and building 'community-of-interest' indexes as suggested by Chakrabati et al. (2002). However, it demonstrates how informal information seeking can be bridged to connect with formal, organized information collections.

Med-GS

Turning to information seeking in the medical domain, and onto more dynamic information seeking environments, we have studied the collaborative, shared information tasks that occur between medical professionals and patients. In this case, the focus has been on the complex information work that occurs in consequence of press coverage of medical conditions. This often triggers patient enquiries into how new information affects their treatment or condition. From the clinical perspective, however, patients use very different terms and language, and have different needs and goals compared to what other medical professionals would seek. Therefore, there is a social and linguistic barrier to communication.

A common solution to such semantic difficulties would be to deploy ontological support. However, we used a simpler, proven, technique using a thesaurus (Jaana Kristensen, 1993) and a generic alerting system for digital libraries (Buchanan & Hinze, 2005).

With the Med-GS system that we have developed (see Figure 6), incoming source documents (e.g., press alerts) from established media-alerting services are matched against profiles of information needs that represent the interests of patients. To overcome the differences in language used by the media on one hand and medical professionals on the other, the source documents have key "everyday language" medical terms (e.g., chicken pox) extracted, and where necessary these are then translated using a thesaurus into the proper clinical terminology (e.g., varicella). Terminology that is consistent across clinical and common usage are passed forward without translation. The extracted medical terms are then passed onto a filtering system that uses standard alerting (event-based) technology.

The filtering system contains profiles—akin to stored queries—that represent a clinician's information needs and clinical interest. Immediate task information (e.g., patient conditions) are also stored in contextual profiles that provide further profile content for more precise matching.

When the extracted and translated material from an incoming press alert matches an infor-

Figure 6. The MedGS architecture

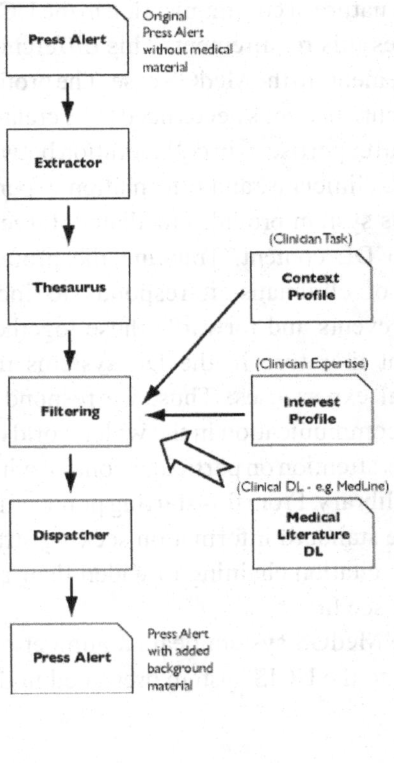

221

mation profile, then the filtering system recalls supplementary documents from one or more digital libraries, using standard DL access protocols (e.g., Z39.50). The press release is then delivered to the clinician (e.g., via e-mail), together with the selected matching DL literature, for example, reports from specialist medical information services such as MedLine.

The architecture used for this scenario can, however, also be used with alternative thesauri or reconfigured architecture to support patient requirements in similar circumstances.

Some of the elements we met regarding humanities communication can be compared with the MedGS architecture. In both cases a communication—a press release or e-mail—is used to garner material from a set of digital libraries. There are, however, differences. Researchers in an academic discipline share a technolect—a specialized language within their domain. However, in the MedGS system, medical experts are divided from their patients by differences in language. Likewise, in the MedGS case the releases need to be filtered, whereas the person-to-person nature of communication in the UCIS case removes this requirement. This difference adds requirements to the MedGS case. The profiles that represent a patient's needs need to be created with care and expertise—in collaboration between the patient, clinicians, and information experts.

This system provides mediated, targeted access to DL content. Tracking the professional needs of clinicians, it responds to incoming media events and forwards those together with relevant literature in the DL systems that the medical expert uses. Thus, we respond to the social communication in the wider world context to focus attention on particular content within the digital library. From this starting point, clinicians can use standard information seeking strategies such as citation chaining to widen their reading as they see fit.

The MedGS system bears a number of similarities to the UCIS system presented in the previous subsection; social communication is used to identify and retrieve material in a number of DL systems. However, in this case there was a significant language problem and also there is an absence of explicit recommendation that may occur in the case of UCIS. In the next subsection we find another use of a system across a number of DLs that explores the use of social factors in a different way—building recommendations without there being explicit social communication.

TIP

Mobile information systems of all forms operate within a number of constraints: limitations of processing power, network speed, storage capacity, and display size. Given these design constraints, and the human-computer interaction issues that consequently emerge (e.g., due to restricted screen estate), the overall information system needs to ensure that as much data of value is provided with as little overhead as possible.

The Tourist Information Provider (TIP) system represents one of the few mobile information systems that has matured over several significant redesigns as limitations are progressively circumvented or even exploited to create a comprehensive and sophisticated information tool (Hinze & Jumanee, 2005). Here, we will focus upon the current generation of TIP (TIP 2.5), which can exploit a number of techniques that use social information to improve the fit of delivered or displayed information to the user's needs. The primary forms of exploiting the social information are TIP's travel recommender, which attempts to bring to the user's attention sights or activities that particularly match his or her interests, and TIP's review component. The underlying techniques are broadly similar to the social filtering technologies used in Amazon and other online retailers. However, the mobile context, transient activity, and information delivery focus mean that specific design criteria emerge in TIP that are absent in large-scale, long-term recommendation systems.

TIP offers several recommendation services: some capture explicit social groups, some use implicit social groups that are formed by the user's travels, and the review component allows for browsing in other users' textual feedback (reviews) regarding travels and sights visited.

Explicit social groups can be defined by the traveler to the system as a list of friends which will then be taken into account for recommendations. Only those sights are recommended that received positive (numeric) feedback from friends. Our system also allows for the extension of the social circle to friends of friends, with degrading trust values the further the person is located within the social network from the traveler. Using social information increases the traveler's trust in the given recommendations.

Implicit social groups are typically formed based on similarity of user feedback. Travelers receive a recommended list of those sights that have been rated positively by people with similar interests or location. One prevalent problem for these kinds of recommendations using implicit social groups is the sparcity of data: new users may not have visited any sights yet, or they are too dissimilar to other users (so-called grey sheep)—both may lead an inability or low quality in determining the social group and thus a failure to produce effective recommendations. Our remedies are twofold.

First, social groups are determined based on a number of characteristics such as similarity of (explicit) user profiles, proximity of the travelers' current locations, or similarity of travel histories (Hinze & Jumanee, 2005). This information is either used directly or via estimation of user feedback to determine social groups. In this way, we are using socially relevant information to improve the retrieval and precision of recommendations.

Our second approach supports explicit user interaction. Typical recommendations are given to the traveler automatically after he or she visits a sight. Our review component captures travelers' textual feedback about single sights or longer travels. Interested travelers can then search and browse these reviews. They can also comment and rate other people's reviews. Using recommendations, reviews, and ratings, travelers can form a social online community.

Summary

These systems have been developed on standard digital library components. However, they vary considerably in the form of the capture of the social context, and its use to leverage the performance of information seeking itself. Nonetheless, there are some underlying principles that recur: using social factors to weight or score documents, providing a social or collaborative interface to common library features, supporting an explicit social space in the library, and/or supporting searches of social targets (e.g., people).

As we have successively demonstrated with architectures for digital libraries, information alerting services, and mobile information systems, robust and flexible systems can be created to provide tailorable features where final deployment needs vary widely provided that the underlying components remain consistent, if reconfigured in different ways. Two approaches have also been illustrated: extending a library internally through a componentized architecture as seen with the KidsDL and UCIS systems, while in the case of MedGS and TIP systems we used the DL itself as a component in a widened system.

In the next section, we will focus on the general patterns that can be drawn from the systems discussed here, in terms of both information seeking models and DL architectures.

ARCHITECTURES AND MODELS

Having studied our solution systems in the previous section, we conclude by abstracting architectural forms that satisfy the demands of a variety of social information systems. Similarly, we will identify extensions to the existing information seeking models that explicitly address social factors.

In terms of requirements, social information seeking can include four different forms of finding information: interactive search, interactive browsing, information alerts, and tailored recommendations. Each of these facilities can be offered without social support, but each can benefit from the additional information a social context can provide. Separate from this, social influences to the information seeking process can also be divided into four: individual seeking activated by social inputs (e.g., a citation), seeking improved by weighting a model of the social context, seeking with a social goal (e.g., finding a person's Web page), or seeking undertaken as a shared social task. Just as seeking often, in fact, moves between its four forms and combines them, so social seeking can move between or combine its four influences. Starting from a standard componentized digital library architecture, we will demonstrate an extended architecture that adds social modeling to that architecture.

This section will first discuss extensions to the five information seeking models introduced early in this chapter. It will then propose an extended form of the well-accepted DL architectures of Suleman and Fox (2002) and Bainbridge et al. (2001).

Extending Information Seeking Models

In the previous two sections, we have met four systems that support information seeking in a social context. Here, we return to view the information seeking models introduced earlier, and contrast them with the social information seeking activity already presented and supported in implemented systems noted above.

Gary Marchionini's iterative model of the interactive search process has a clear focus that does not fit with some of the information seeking tasks that we have presented here. For example, it does not fit at all with the Med-GS system, where the activity is one of responding to incoming changes in the information environment (alerts). Such misfits are outside the scope of the model and can be discarded. However, the model fits well with the information seeking performed by the pupils using the KidsDL system, and some of the active information seeking performed by humanities users and tourists. Much of this seeking is iterative, and the social context can readily be incorporated by viewing social influences and inputs as aspects of each stage in the process—in other words, retaining the sequence and activities within the process, but adding a social aspect to each. An alternative approach would be to deploy Ingwersen's modeling of social issues as a discrete factor that is separated from the interaction itself, yet indirectly influences it.

This latter, segregated approach may seem attractive. However, it fails to capture the active role of social interaction in some information seeking—for example, where a group of pupils sits together to find information, or a team of researchers collectively seek papers relevant to a project. Therefore, explicit inclusion within the model better represents social information seeking than the abstracted view favored by Ingwersen.

Kuhlthau's emphasis of process and sequence suggests a similar approach to that we found in Marchionini's model—retaining sequence and incorporating an explicit representation of social factors within each process.

However, in contrast, Ellis' broadly similar model emphasizes strategies and behaviors over sequence. Thus, we are again faced by the question of whether social information seeking should be placed within specific strategies, or as an explicit, separate role. To decide on that issue, we need to return to the information seeking activity reported here, and re-evaluate it within Ellis' model. The answers are not straightforward. A group of researchers collectively seeking papers may well use a number of Ellis' strategies, whether sitting together at one machine or distributed over a network. For example, chaining of references can be used in either case. In this example, the social attribute may provide a context for the goals and for the evaluation of relevance, but has no effect on the structure of the strategy itself.

The choice of sources and tools is more involved. Users may choose tools with social features or because of social influences (e.g., colleague familiarity or recommendation). Though the pursuit of an individual's homepage is similar to chaining, it is also part of constructing a model of the researchers (i.e., authors) within the information domain. This construction of a mental picture of the information domain is in and of itself an information seeking task. Similarly, identifying a fellow tourist whose recommendations you trust is separate to choosing specific sights. This 'meta-task' is perhaps more fitted to explicit representation as an activity in its own right within Ellis' model. Ellis himself has made similar judgments in extending his original model (Ellis, Cox, & Hall, 1993).

Thus, we add the activity of 'Identifying Authorities' to the information seeking task. As already discussed, this is often a social activ-ity. Similarly, a user's understanding of what is relevant will often depend on his or her social content—be it peers, classmates, or professors. Though seekers have clear information goals, they will adjust their strategies to match the expectations of their peers. We suggest that the task of 'Identifying Relevance Criteria' could usefully be explicitly modeled within Ellis' model.

Turning finally to Ingwersen and Järvelin's model, this already includes social attributes within the model. We have already noted the lack of explicit capture of how the social factors interact with the model, and the fact that the model identifies the social environment as a contextual issue within which direct interaction occurs. However, this model fails to properly represent collaborative information seeking. Given the model's proposition as a cognitive model, extending it to represent collaborative seeking would require an encapsulation of social cognition, which is in itself a major undertaking. This significant challenge cannot yet be properly met, as much fundamental research needs to be undertaken to support any proposed model. Thus, a social information seeking analogue of Ingwersen's model remains a significant challenge for future research.

Figure 7. An example of representing social factors within Marchionini's model

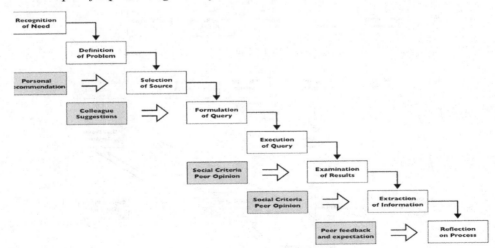

Architectures for Social Information Seeking

Having viewed our models of information seeking, we can make two immediate observations: first, that within process-oriented models such as Marchionini and, to a lesser extent, Kuhlthau, social information seeking adds further factors to each stage in the process; and second, when new behaviors are included within behavioral models such as Ellis', we see new, discrete items in our model. Differing software architectures and levels of abstraction will correspond to one or other of these forms of change. Thus, when we turn to architectures for information seeking tools, we can expect to repeat the same pattern.

For example, in an interactive search tool, the fundamental retrieval behavior will not change.

However, ranking may be affected by the popularity of items, or special recommendations may be added. Conversely, when we add a support for collaborative filtering (e.g., recommendations in the TIP system), we do not simply adjust an existing feature. Rather, we add an entirely new concept to the system architecture.

In Figure 2 above, we presented a typical digital library architecture. Different retrieval services are provided as separate components in a modular service-based architecture. The DL interface mediates user interaction with the underlying services. In contrast, in Figure 8 we present the same model extended with a composite set of extensions from the different systems introduced above. Within the existing framework for a DL architecture, we find a new service that supports recommendations.

Figure 8. Generic DL architecture, with additional recommendation, alerting, and communication services to provide a social context

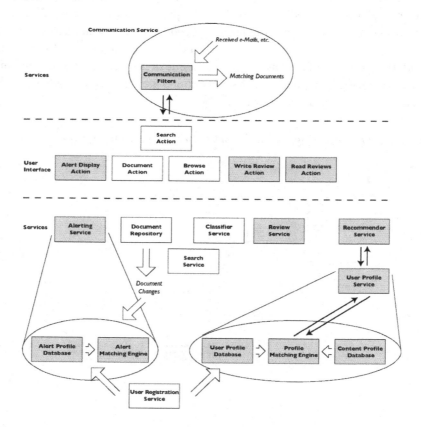

A key element of social information seeking is identifying the community or communities within which a user is placed. As noted above, users may even wish to have informal and casually created communities. In Figure 8 we abstract a social context service that can be used to model the user's current community. The community in question may be a composite of named communities; an informal, transient group; or a formal, ongoing context (e.g., research group). This social context service is used to provide underlying social data for any use of social factors in the running of the library—be it extending established services (search, browsing) or novel ones (reviews, recommendations).

Beyond the social context provided by reviews and recommendations based on other users, alerts can be supported. In contrast to a recommendation service, which can be used to filter all material in the library, the alerting service focuses only on new or changed material in the library. As noted above, this is often achieved in concert between 'ordinary' readers—patients in the earlier case—and information experts such as librarians. Alerts can be created by such experts not only for a specific user, but also for entire classes of users. To achieve this, both systems use identity information from the underlying user registration (authentication) service seen in earlier DL architectures above (e.g., Figure 2).

However, Figure 8 represents the provision of social support *within* a digital library. Conversely, if we return to the support of humanities academics, we see support for seeking *across* different DL systems. A further configuration of library and society can also be found in the support of humanities academics—where a DL collection is built from the homepages of known researchers. This provides a complementary tool that may assist the selection of appropriate libraries for a user's search.

A third architectural aspect emerges from a critical social activity—communication. As we saw across our four applications, messages between users, or received by users, can provide critical information to support their broader information seeking task. This is not seen in full in Figure 8, for clarity, but could be achieved as already described above.

Summary

In addressing either digital library architectures or information seeking models, we retain the existing basic frameworks. Changes essentially take one of two forms: new items in the higher abstraction, or alterations to existing elements. In the case of DL architectures, however, the separation of user interface layers and underlying services more often allow for the encapsulation of social aspects in discrete components. Conversely, in models of information seeking, social aspects are harder to clearly separate. An example is readily identified in the judgment of a document as relevant: whatever the underlying technology, this is ultimately a decision made in the mind of the information seeker. To what degree the decision is personal or social is probably impossible to determine. However, in creating technical support for social information seeking, we do not have to capture the human mind; rather, we support it with transparent tools.

Social information seeking can be found in all sorts of forms, but ultimately the issue of communication between people is key. Whether collaboratively seeking, reviewing each others' work, responding to media releases, or exploring on holiday, communication underpins the process. Therefore, in both models and architecture, support for effective social information seeking pivots on closing the gap between human communication and the digital library.

CONCLUSION

Social information seeking extends the existing simple models of information seeking to better capture the full range of social factors that so determine how humans actually enact and direct seeking tasks. There are many areas where traditional models already provide sterling support for the development of effective seeking tools. However, for some tasks, the additional social factors add considerably to the range of provided user tools, and improve existing ones.

We have extended information seeking models and digital library architectures to encompass these new dimensions. However, a considerable degree of work needs to be done. No doubt new systems will extend and challenge the appropriate divisions of social factors in both models and architectures. Indeed, we anticipate that such changes will be faced in the near future. Our existing model does not directly address social and cultural issues such as hierarchies and power, which, as Adams and Blandford (2004) demonstrated, can have a huge influence on the appropriate behaviors. Similarly, we do not directly address common social forums such as blogs, chat rooms, and bulletin boards. Finally, our approach does not yet do justice to the rich opportunities for including library patrons into the life of the library, as proposed by Goh and Leggett (2000). Each of these factors can be addressed in the design and implementation of components within our architecture, but a more systematic taxonomy could yield significant advantages.

The provision of social information seeking in a library context is only in its infancy. We have much further to go than we have yet traveled.

REFERENCES

Adams, A., & Blandford, A. (2004). The unseen and unacceptable face of digital libraries. *International Journal on Digital Libraries, 4*(2), 71-81.

Adams, A., & Blandford, A. (2005). Digital libraries' support for the user's 'information journey'. *Proceedings of ACM/IEEE JCDL* (pp. 160-169).

Bainbridge, D., Buchanan, G., McPherson, J.R., Jones, S., Mahoui, A., & Witten, I.H. (2001). Greenstone: A platform for distributed digital library applications. *Proceedings of ECDL* (pp. 137-148).

Belkin, N.J, Oddy, R.N., & Brooks, H.M. (1982). Ask for information retrieval: Part I. Background and theory. *Journal of Documentation, 38*(2), 61-71.

Brin, S., & Page, L. (1998). The anatomy of a large-scale hypertextual (Web) search engine. *Proceedings of the 7th World Wide Web Conference* (vol. 30, pp. 1-7, 107-117).

Buchanan, G., & Hinze, A. (2005). A generic alerting service for digital libraries. *Proceedings of the Joint Conference on Digital Libraries* (pp. 131-140).

Buchanan, G., Cunningham, S.J., Blandford, A., Rimmer, J., & Warwick, C. (2005). Information seeking by humanities scholars. *Proceedings of the European Conference on Digital Libraries* (pp. 218-229).

Chakrabarti, S., Joshi, M., Punera, K., & Pennock, D.M. (2002). The structure of broad topics on the Web. *Proceedings of WWW 2002* (pp. 251-262).

Ellis, D. (1989). A behavioral model for information retrieval system design. *Journal of Information Science, 5*(4/5), 237-247.

Ellis, D., Cox, D., & Hall, K. (1993). A comparison of the information seeking patterns of researchers in the physical and social sciences. *Journal of Documentation, 49*(4), 356-369.

Frank, E., Paynter, G., Witten, I., Gutwin, C., & Nevill-Manning, C. (1999), Domain-specific key phrase extraction. *Proceedings of the 16th International Joint Conference on Artificial Intelligence* (pp. 668-673). San Francisco: Morgan Kaufmann.

Goh, D., & Leggett, J. (2000). Patron-augmented digital libraries. *Proceedings of the ACM Conference on Digital Libraries* (pp. 53-163). New York: ACM Press.

Halasz, F.G. (1988). Reflections on NoteCards: Seven issues for the next generation of hypermedia systems. *Communications of the ACM, 31*(7), 836-852.

Hinze, A., & Junmanee, S. (2005). Providing recommendations in a mobile tourist information system. *Proceedings of ISTA* (pp. 86-100).

Ingwersen, P., & Järvelin, A. (2005). *The turn.* Elsevier.

Jaana Kristensen, J. (1993). Expanding end-users' query statements for free text searching with a search-aid thesaurus. *Information Processing and Management, 29*(6), 733-744.

Kuhlthau, C.C. (2002). *Seeking meaning: A process approach to library and information sciences* (2nd ed.). Libraries Unlimited.

Marchionini, G. (1995). *Information seeking in electronic environments.* Cambridge: Cambridge University Press.

Suleman, H., & Fox, E.A. (2002). Designing protocols in support of digital library componentization. *Proceedings of the European Conference on Digital Libraries* (ECDL) (pp. 568-582). Berlin: Springer-Verlag (LNCS 2458).

Theng, Y.L., Mohd-Nasir, N., Buchanan, G., Fields, B., Thimbleby, H.W., & Cassidy, N. (2001). Dynamic digital libraries for children. *Proceedings of the Joint Conference on Digital Libraries* (JCDL) (pp. 406-415).

Wilson, T.D. (1999). Models in information behavior research. *Journal of Documentation, 55*(3), 249-270.

Witten, I.H., Boddie, S.J., Bainbridge, D., & McNab, R.J. (2000). Greenstone: A comprehensive open-source digital library software system. *Proceedings of the ACM Conference on Digital Libraries* (pp. 113-121).

Yeates, S., Witten, I.H., & Bainbridge, D. (2001). Tag insertion complexity. *Proceedings of the Data Compression Conference* (pp. 243-252).

Chapter XII
Relevant Intra–Actions in Networked Environments

Theresa Dirndorfer Anderson
University of Technology, Sydney (UTS), Australia

ABSTRACT

In this chapter the author uses a study of human assessments of relevance to demonstrate how individual relevance judgments and retrieval practices embody collaborative elements that contribute to the overall progress of that person's individual work. After discussing key themes of the conceptual framework, the author will discuss two case studies that serve as powerful illustrations of these themes for researchers and practitioners alike. These case studies—outcomes of a two-year ethnographic exploration of research practices—illustrate the theoretical position presented in part one of the chapter, providing lessons for the ways that people work with information systems to generate knowledge and the conditions that will support these practices. The author shows that collaboration does not have to be explicit to influence searcher behavior. It seeks to present both a theoretical framework and case studies that can be applied to the design, development, and evaluation of collaborative information retrieval systems.

INTRODUCTION

Relevance is a central concept for information retrieval used as a measurement for evaluating information systems. However, it is a concept that significantly extends far beyond this traditional domain, since it is also at the heart of the human communication of meaning. It is an essentially human construct that is embedded in the everyday practices of communication, information seeking,

and knowledge generation. In this chapter we look at the social and contextual dimensions of human relevance judgments, particularly within the complexity of computer-mediated information activities. When examined from the searcher's—as opposed to the system's—perspective, the social and collaborative aspects are seen to be far more embedded in these practices than is accounted for in many depictions of collaborative information retrieval. The inherently interactive character of human relevance judgments means that social and private aspects are interwoven in the seeking and gathering of information. Human relevance judgments are radically different from those of information retrieval systems, and thus our understanding of collaborative systems must take into account the 'real-life' experiences of searchers and searcher communities.

The aim of this chapter is to demonstrate the emergent, socially situated character of human assessments of relevance and to discuss the implications for the design and development of collaborative information systems. After discussing key themes of the conceptual framework, we discuss two case studies that serve as powerful illustrations of these themes for researchers and practitioners alike. These case studies—outcomes of a two-year ethnographic exploration of research practices—illustrate the theoretical position presented in part one of the chapter. The extracts from the detailed accounts of the two informants demonstrate how they draw on interactions with colleagues (e.g., face-to-face, e-mail, casual as well as formal encounters) and with ideas communicated in their own works as well as those of other researchers. Thus, in this chapter we provide both a theoretical framework and case studies that can be applied to the design, development, and evaluation of collaborative information retrieval systems.

A CONCEPTUAL FRAMEWORK FOR RELEVANCE AS A SOCIALLY SITUATED PHENOMENON

This first part of the chapter provides a conceptualization of relevance assessment that acknowledges the interplay between the individual (personal) and social (collaborative) elements of these human judgments. It is based on the framework developed for a longitudinal study of relevance assessments made in the context of scholarly research.

Relevance: A Fundamental Human Activity

In today's highly networked information environments, determining *relevance* is fundamental for finding the appropriate information to resolve problems and fill gaps from the overwhelming volume of what is available. It is the process by which encounters with "new" information are related to what is already familiar to us. Alfred Schutz positions *relevance* as a feature of our consciousness embodying enormous complexity. To illustrate his point, he uses the process of writing one of his influential essays on relevance, observing:

...although I spend but an hour at my desk, I traverse within this measurable period of our time an ongoing span of my inner life which condenses experiences, skills, and knowledge acquired in the greater part of my lifetime into the writing down of a single page. (Schutz, 1970, p. 10)

Schutz goes on to explain that, while the task might be experienced as a single activity, there are in fact "a set of heterogeneous activities" taking place (1970, p. 10). This observation can be compared to the "situated information retrieval" described nearly 30 years later by Hert (1997), who depicts searchers working simultaneously in different levels of time-space. Such research demonstrates the complexity and dynamism of the human judgments associated with locating and using information. It also alerts us to the fact that there are no straightforward explanations for the way judgments of relevance are made.

If we are to understand the human processes used for judging relevance in situations driven by the searcher, relevance has to be examined in the context of everyday practice. The notion of an "everyday context" of relevance is raised in a number of papers examining information seeking behaviors (e.g., Chatman, 1996; Given, 2002; Savolainen, 1995). Harter (1992) and Saracevic (1996b) also speak of intuitive meanings of *relevance* in an everyday context, pointing out that we apply it effortlessly when using information, without having to define what relevance is. Schamber (1994) goes so far as to suggest that addressing the "everyday, intuitive meaning" (p. 36) of relevance is possible only in a holistic, situational perspective to information behavior.

The dynamic, multi-dimensional view of relevance described by information science researchers like Saracevic, Harter, and Greisdorf draws on the discussions of relevance in philosophical and communication domains. This interdisciplinary perspective is increasingly recognized as a necessity for addressing the complexity of *relevance*: "...a concept that engenders more than a simple dichotomy of choice" (Greisdorf, 2000, p. 70).

Harter (1992) describes relevance assessment as a "mental act," implying the exploration of judgments of relevance made in a search situation should be related to research in areas of human communication such as discourse, meaning, and cognition. Supporting earlier statements by Harter, Saracevic (1996b) draws on major theories about relevance from philosophy and communication for his discussion of relevance. According to Saracevic, any theory of human judgments of relevance has to incorporate its intuitive understanding. The concept of relevance is embedded in human cognition. This intuitive understanding confers certain attributes on *relevance*:

...it is based on cognition; it involves interaction, frequently communication; it is dynamic; it deals with appropriateness or effectiveness; and it is expressed in a context, the matter at hand. (Saracevic, 1996b, p. 203)

He describes the everyday practice of *relevance* and argues that the general, intuitive quality of relevance must be included in information science's portrayal of the concept.

Saracevic, Harter, and Greisdorf cite the work of Schutz (1970) as well as Sperber and Wilson (1986) and their use of *relevance* to explain the complexities of human interactions, interpreting relevance as an interacting system of multiple relevances. For Schutz (1970), relevance is to be studied in the sphere of perception. His system of relevances contains three basic interdependent and dynamically interacting relevances: topical, interpretative, and motivational. He also clearly states that:

...there are no such things as isolated relevances. Whatever their type, they are always interconnected and grouped together in systems. (Schutz, 1970, p. 43)

This framework links the problem situation to interpretation and intention at the point a judgment is made.

For Sperber and Wilson (1986), relevance drives human communication. Arguing that communication relies on a mutual "knowing," they view relevance as a way of knowing. Inferences, interpretation, and the context of communication are central to their view of relevance. Cognition, they suggest, is organized to maximize relevance. People can intuitively distinguish relevant from irrelevant information (and degrees of relevance), but cannot readily express these distinctions. Achieving the best cognitive effect with the least amount of effort—our goal, according to Sperber and Wilson (1986)—requires an individual to focus on what seems to them to be the most relevant information available (see for example discussion, Sperber & Wilson, 1986, pp. 118-120).

As the research described here suggests, we have come to realize that searcher satisfaction with information retrieval systems centers on locating relevant information. However, this research has also shown us that there judging relevance is not straightforward. Greisdorf, Harter, and Saracevic all suggest the significance of Sperber and Wilson's principles for the study of relevance in information retrieval research is that they can help explain the differences and similarities between system results and searcher judgments of what is "relevant" for them (e.g., Greisdorf, 2000, p. 69; Saracevic, 1996b, p. 206).

While relevance may always be intuitive, it does not always appear logical to an outside observer, human or machine. As Dewey explains, relevance is neither always explicit, nor always syntactical (Ekbia & Maguitman, 2001). Similarly, the theoretical work of Capurro (1992, 2000), Hjørland (1997, 2000), and Leydesdorff (2000) discussing the role of pre-existing knowledge—or "pre-understanding"—in mediating interactions with information systems suggests that relevance is part of a much wider process of human cognition. As Green (2001) observes, the intuitive understandings of humans are not shared by computational devices like retrieval systems.

In summary, drawing on these philosophical explorations of relevance, we begin to get a picture of relevance as a complex and dynamic means of communicating judgments. We do not fully understand how intuitive judgments about the relevance of a topic or content of a document take shape, nor do we fully understand how such judgments are communicated. However, we can see, as Green (2001) suggests, that understanding the ways that relationships are communicated and judged is an important step in the development of more responsive information systems. Furthermore, this communication approach makes clear that judgments of relevance made by an individual cannot exist in isolation from either the larger task at hand or the social world of the individual. As will be discussed in the next section, this context constitutes interaction with both people and information systems.

Information Seeking and Retrieval Processes: Social Context and Interaction

The understandings of relevance presented in the previous section led us to see relevance as a relation that arises through the expression of that relation in a particular context. Park's (1992, 1994) framework connects relevance evaluation with stages of search process and the context of the information problem. Contextual variables of the search process can differ from user to user (Park, 1992). The interplay of these elements of the search process helps explains the variability of relevance assessment reported in empirical research (e.g., Schamber, 1994). This section briefly discusses the broader context of such judgments—the information seeking, retrieval, and use processes.

Studying information behavior in social contexts is seen as essential for understanding the way those contexts shape action and interpretation. Seeking and retrieving information are firmly situated in "everyday life" experiences by information science researchers like Given (2002), Huotari and Chatman (2001), Talja (2002), and Savolainen (1995). Conceptualizing information seeking as a natural component of everyday practice relates to Bourdieu's *habitus* (e.g., 1990, pp. 52-65). Savolainen (1995), for instance, provides an illustration of the application of Bourdieu's framework. Similarly, Leydesdorff (2000) relates Habermas' portrayal of events in the "lifeworld" to the study of communicating and searching for information in social contexts. Hert (1997), Marchionini (1995), and Vakkari (1999) all illustrate how *information retrieval* can be seen as a component of this information seeking process. More specifically, retrieval is a communication process in which judgments of relevance are made.

The act of retrieving something from an information retrieval system is not a single interaction, but a complex process of interaction of representations communicated between a searcher and a system. People interact with many different layers of representation during information retrieval (Hjørland, 2002; Saracevic, 1996a, 1996b). Ingwersen's "poly-representation" model of information retrieval portrays searchers as interactively processing representations of the current topical information need, underlying problem space and actual work task (Ingwersen, 1996). This model of information retrieval is in line with a rhizomatic depiction of information contexts because, according to Burnett and McKinley (1998), it tries to deal with the multiplicity involved in information seeking and retrieval interactions.

Interactivity can be seen as both a human and system trait. The foundational work of Winograd and Flores (1987) emphasizes computers as tools for communication rather than computation. They are particularly concerned with the question of language and how it mediates human action in the computing environment (Capurro, 1992; Flores, 1998; Winograd & Flores, 1987). Similarly, Suchman (1987)—in another seminal work—demonstrates the significance of the interactional and social as well as the technical elements for interface design. In such work we can see the recognition that the searchers' experiences play a growing role in design and evaluation of systems. Furthermore, there is also an appreciation that not all aspects of that experience are explicitly structured.

Acknowledging information retrieval as an interactive process means information retrieval research must examine the interaction of all components of the information retrieval setting. Systems use has been shown to be related to information seeking stages by Kuhlthau (1991), Hert (1997), and Robins (2000). A searcher's interpretations of system responses impact upon their future choices, actions, and cognitive activities (Hert, 1992, 1997). For example, researchers have found that the early phases of this information seeking process are fraught with uncertainty and disorientation that led searchers to apply multiple types of information seeking strategies within a single episode (e.g., Hert, 1997; Robins, 1998; Spink, Greisdorf, & Bateman, 1999; Vakkari & Hakala, 2000; Xie, 2000).

The implications of seeing retrieval as an interactive process over time rather than a single interaction increases the focus on what Burnett

and McKinley (1998) call "interaction space." The interactive approach to this searcher context is also of value for explorations of practices like relevance assessment. Drawing on the work of Deleuze and Guattari, Burnett and McKinley present a *rhizomorphic model of information contexts*: "…a networked, hypertextual information seeking environment" (1998, p. 293). They recognize the "cognitive authority" conferred upon items contained in a particular database and the subsequent impact of this context upon a searcher's decisions with regard to an item (p. 287). They also discuss the notion of self and identity, and how information seeking is a negotiation process in which a searcher as an active "meaning maker" gains access to different selves and different communities through interaction with an information system. The rhizomorphic model replaces earlier notions of structured and predictable searcher-system interaction. It provides an image of interconnectivity, complexity, multiplicity, and fragmentation. This metaphor seems particularly appropriate for the depiction of relevance assessment and retrieval processes as dynamic and interactive social activities.

Relevance Assessment as a Socio-Cognitive Phenomenon

As was discussed in previous sections of this chapter, we have come to realize that, particularly from the human perspective, judging relevance is far from straightforward and that understanding system use means understanding human communicative practices. If we accept the principles of interactive information retrieval, human judgments of relevance—at the heart of information retrieval—involve judging the appropriateness of communication (be it verbal or written, sound or image) to the "matter at hand" (Schutz, 1970; Sperber & Wilson, 1986).

The role of the searcher's problem situation and dynamism of relevance judgments are examined by a number of researchers who draw attention to the situated character of relevance judgments. Relevance assessment, it has been shown, is the result of personal perception and contextual factors, like time, stages of the search process, and the context of the information problem (Mizzaro, 1998; Park, 1992; Tang & Solomon, 1998). Byström and Järvelin (1995), Wang and Soergel (1998), and Vakkari and Hakala (2000), for example, relate relevance judgments to problem stages. As a focus forms, clearer criteria for relevance also appear to emerge (Hjørland & Christensen, 2002; Vakkari, 2003). By mapping evaluations of relevance made by searchers in terms of time and the search process, the judgment of relevance is linked to stages of the search process, successive searches, and decision processes associated with work goals. The impact of that process also means that the order in which results are presented to a request impact on the judgment of relevance (e.g., Boyce, 1982; Eisenberg & Barry, 1988). Cool (1997) and Hert (1997) describe these factors and goals associated with retrieval practices as part of the searcher's *situation*.

As part of their argument for including a socio-cognitive relevance type in their framework, Cosijn and Ingwersen (2000) point out that it is "highly context dependent and associated with organizational strategies or scientific community interaction within" (p. 549). Hjørland (2002) argues for a more socio-cognitive perspective in information science, and the exploration of the ways that people interpret texts and the impact of organization and search contexts. The socio-cultural context of information seeking, he argues, implicitly establishes criteria for judging the relevance of information encountered during searching and retrieval practices (Hjørland, 2002).

As our understanding of various types of relevance has grown, the inadequacy of the binary judgment of relevant/not relevant has also been raised. Exploring relevance assessment as a socio-cognitive phenomenon thereby encompasses notions of *partial relevance* (e.g., Janes, 1994; Saracevic, Kantor, Chamis, & Trivison, 1988;

Spink et al., 1998), *relative relevance* (Borlund & Ingwersen, 1998), and *irrelevance* (e.g., Hjørland, 2000; Swanson, 1988; Wang & Soergel, 1998). Swanson (1988), for example, observes that there is an inherent flaw in uncritical acceptance of relevance as being "additive":

The possibility, for example, that two irrelevant documents might become relevant if put together has never been adequately considered as far as I know. (p. 93)

Zerubavel (1993) points out that, like relevance, the notion of *irrelevance* has a critical social dimension that ties our judgments to our socialization—culturally, professionally, personally—and to "rules of exclusion" (p. 399). Hjørland (2000; Hjørland & Christensen, 2002) takes a similar position in his observations about possible causes for the "nonrelevance" of search output. This work draws attention to the need for further research into the social as well as the individual factors contributing to such judgments during information seeking and use.

From such findings, we can conclude that a searcher's judgment of relevance is based upon criteria extending beyond topic matching between a document and a query. Kekäläinen and Järvelin (2002) refer to relevance that is not solely based on topicality as *higher-order relevance* and argue strongly that it plays a clear role in information retrieval interaction, which in turn means *higher-order relevance* must be incorporated into information retrieval system evaluation. Doing so, however, requires a fuller understanding of searcher judgments and the qualities of *higher-order relevance*. Taking a social interactionist perspective allows us to further conclude that even at an individual level, such judgments will involve engagement with the judgments and perceptions of the collective, which in turn brings with it recognition of collaborative elements. Accepting that this judgment process has both social and individual contexts to consider—this ties in well with the rhizomorphic model (Burnett & McKinley, 1998) described in the previous section.

Both individual and social elements of information need and relevance are worthy of consideration However, as Sundin and Johannisson point out (2005a, 2005b), it is not about privileging one element over the other, but rather applying a conceptual framework that moves in a more sociocultural direction. The work of Sundin and Johannisson demonstrates that information behavior research cannot focus on the rational individual, but instead needs to recognize the collective influence on individual experience. As they point out, although the presence of both socially and individually oriented aspects of information needs and relevance assessment were recognized as long ago as the 1980s, the social aspects of these concepts have not been explored to any great extent—certainly not in terms of the relationship between individual and collective aspects. For Sundin and Johannisson, the "communication approach" offers an alternative to a largely socially oriented or largely individually oriented approach:

The communication approach proposes a dialogic view of identity, knowledge formation and other social practices that unites an interest in the social aspects of information seeking practices with an interest in how individuals act upon the social by using linguistic and physical tools. (2005a, p. 113)

In particular, they make the case that information seeking and related activities like relevance assessment are social practices: institutionalized activities where rules become formalized and negotiated. Significantly, this approach accepts that there is a contingent character to these social elements that allows for a single individual or groups of individuals to influence the shaping of the social.

This approach serves as a reminder of the collective elements implied in Kelly's personal construct theory insofar as it has been applied to the information seeking framework of researchers like Kuhlthau (2004) and in turn has so significantly informed human information behavior research in recent times. Constructs, as patterns one formulates to make sense of the world, provide guidelines or frames of reference which in turn help determine the choices to be made in a given situation. Recognizing that there is both an individual and social element worthy of consideration draws attention to the fact that the 'constructs' discussed by Kelly are individual interpretations of rules of the community/communities of which the individual is a member.

Such theoretical positions compel us to recognize that relevance is a highly contextual sociocognitive phenomenon that emerges through engagement with people, ideas, and texts. Hert (1992) describes retrieval as a transformative process, where the searcher shapes search results. Neither the system nor the user can judge relevance in advance. Furthermore, the judgment of relevance or usefulness is not a single event simply based on text content. In scholarly research, for example, social networks and social sharing inform these decisions (Talja, 2002). Both information retrieval and relevance assessment need to be examined as "situated activities" intertwining social and individual elements. As will be discussed in the following section, examining that context in a way that does not diminish its complexity becomes critical.

Information Retrieval as Social-Material Intra-Action

Increasingly relevance has come to be recognized as a mediator of human activity: a "tool" used in relation to a goal—be that the retrieval of information from a system or the selection of texts when preparing a research paper (e.g., Hjørland & Christensen, 2002). To this end, the work of Lev Vygotsky and the activity theory perspective on cognition is helpful because of its perceived capacity to examine human activity within its social and cultural contexts. Vygotsky's approach, as typified by Hjørland (1997), Jacob (1992), and Lave (1988), portrays people actively constructing cognitive practices in a socio-cultural context. Hjørland (2002) makes the observation that socio-cognitive views study individual cognition from the social context rather than from the isolated mind or brain: "They are not working from the inside-out, but outside-in" (pp. 258-259).

Activity theory shifts the research focus from isolated individual to individuals acting in a specific setting. In Nardi's (1996) view:

...consciousness is located in everyday practice: you are what you do. And what you do is firmly and inextricably embedded in the social matrix of which every person is an organic part. (p. 7)

This perspective of people-in-activity provides a valuable framework for information retrieval researchers exploring relevance judgments and retrieval decisions situated in the research and retrieval processes of individuals. Traces of this activity perspective can be found in the work of Lave (1988) and Barad (1998), who are particularly valuable for the contribution they can make for theorizing the less explicit interactions and collaborations present in dynamic information retrieval situations.

Lave's research on cognition and learning offers further support for a framework that encompasses the interplay of the social system and individual experience (Lave, 1988). Lave sought to move beyond a dichotomous separation of social behavior from cognitive behavior, where "...one has system without individual experience, the other experience without system" (p. 150). Instead, "...'cognition' is constituted in dialectical relations among people acting, the contexts of their activity, and the activity itself" (p. 148). It is "...a nexus of relations between the mind at work and the world in which it works" (p. 1). Lave uses a framework based upon the emergent, contingent nature of

action. For her, addressing context involved not only an examination of physical aspects, but also the ways these features were defined by the participants. Her theoretical framework portrays context as consisting of two components: *arena* and *setting*. *Arena* refers to contextual aspects not directly negotiable by the individual: a "physically, economically, politically, and socially organized space-in-time" (Lave, 1988, p. 150). *Setting* refers to the context created by the individual during interaction with the *arena*—including interaction with other individuals. The focus is on neither the individual nor the environment, but the relation between the two. Context is not a single entity, but interplay between the *arena* and the *setting*. The focus is on neither the individual nor the environment, but the relation between the two, thereby providing a socio-cognitive framework for individual experience.

As Suchman and Trigg (1993) point out, Lave's framework addresses both "...the social and the material structuring of specifically situated activity systems" (p. 144). An appreciation of the socio-material relations present in a system provides a rich theoretical framework for the study of information retrieval systems. There are no simple dichotomies between the structure of an IR system and its content. Nor can the searcher's experience of the system and its content be completely separated from its structure (Hjørland, 1997). Applying Lave's framework, the IR system structure, beyond the control of the individual, becomes part of the *arena* in which searcher behavior is observed. The searcher's interpretation of that structure is represented in the notion of *setting*.

Barad (1998) takes this idea of socio-material interaction further with her description of *intra-action,* explaining that:

Apparatuses are not preexisting or fixed entities; they are themselves constituted through particular practices that are perpetually open to rearrangements, rearticulations, and other reworkings. (p. 7)

For Barad:

...what gets defined as a 'subject' (or 'object') and what gets defined as an 'apparatus' is intra-actively constituted through specific practices. (1998, p. 19, note 32)

Applying this position to relevance research, both searchers and their search tools/artifacts are to be viewed as "actors" in the practices of retrieval and relevance under observation. In particular, by framing such study in terms of *intra-action* offers a depiction of searcher-systems relations that draws together the fixed and the fluid, the collective and the individual, the personal and the collaborative in a more emergent construction of retrieval and assessment practices.

Suchman and Trigg (1993) draw on Lave's analysis in their discussion of "representational devices" as central actors in the structuring of practice. In later work, they observe:

Making technologies is, in consequence, a practice of configuring new alignments between the social and the material that are both localised and able to travel, stable and reconfigurable, intelligibly familiar and recognizably new. (Suchman, Trigg, & Blomberg, 2002, p. 164)

Like Barad (1998), they argue for a view of technologies "as the alignments of material and discursive practice" (Suchman et al., 2002, p. 164). These observations merit particular consideration for research of retrieval systems, as they were focusing particularly on technologies "that incorporate practices of coding and classification" (p. 164). Viewing the information retrieval system in socio-material terms means seeing it as a complex and interdependent system of dynamic and interrelated elements involving people (e.g., content providers, searchers, database managers), tools (hardware, software, machines), and information structures (content, rules, controls)—which Covi and Kling (1996) describe as a socio-technical system.

Barad's (1998) discussion of *intra-action* seems particularly appropriate for dealing with these practices. For a researcher, the texts and citations that are represented within a bibliographic database, for instance, embody the ideas of other researchers. The decision to select/not select, to pursue/not pursue relates to the searcher's interests, goals, ambitions, concerns, and view of self. When interacting with networked information systems, a searcher's understanding of the content represented on the screen evolves over time. An initial search request prompts a response produced by the system's interpretation of that request. Modified or discontinued search requests emerge, as the contents of a database are made accessible to the searcher. Viewing this iterative search process as *intra-action* accentuates this emergent quality. Barad's *intra-action* does more than offer us a socio-material perspective—it reminds us that these elements can be inextricably linked. Her approach encourages us to avoid unnatural dichotomies in searcher-system relations and to consider them instead as emergent constructions. Furthermore, it can also draw attention to the human-human communication that takes place when a judgment of relevance is made in this context.

A Framework for Relevance as a Socially Situated Activity

Issues of representation and relevance are critical components in human behavior and in the use of information systems. Using networked information resources to discover, locate, and retrieve information is a communicative process between and among creators, organizers, distributors, mediators, evaluators, and users of texts and their representations that is mediated by machines. Throughout these processes, determining relevance is fundamental for finding the appropriate information to resolve problems, make connections, and fill gaps from the overwhelming volume of what is available. It is the process by which encounters with "new" information are related to what is already familiar to us. Karamuftuoglu (1998, p. 1071) describes the knowledge function of retrieval systems as a "creative/inventive labor" that leads to the inventing and prescribing of relevance criteria on an ongoing basis.

A searcher's interaction with representations of texts centers on communication, language, and meaning. The conceptual discussion presented in the previous sections provide us with an integrative, non-dualistic position on the relationship between the individual and the social elements that can be discerned in practices like the seeking, retrieving, and judging of information. It builds upon portrayals of the emergent and socially situated character of relevance judgments (Karamuftuoglu, 1998; Sundin & Johannisson, 2005a, 2005b). Suchman (1987) makes the point that human-machine "interaction" blurs the lines between the physical and the social, between a tool that one uses and a person with whom one communicates. Information systems further challenge the idea of an interface as something separating human from machine because they act as tools with a primary function of linking people to the embodiment of ideas expressed by others. This socio-material framework suggests a view of collaboration that is far more embedded in individual system use than is traditionally portrayed in models of collaborative information retrieval.

CASES FROM ETHNOGRAPHIC RESEARCH

The conceptual framework described in the previous section was applied to an ethnographic study of the way academics engaged in research projects make judgments about the relevance of information when working with networked information systems. This second part of the chapter illustrates the capacity of this framework to make the blended, evolving qualities of human information behavior in such a context more explicit by presenting extended extracts from this study. Crafting such rich portrayals of the complex interplay between the social and individual elements present in locating and using information invites a broadening of the scope of collaborative information retrieval.

Study Background: The Methodology

In this chapter we draw on two years of ethnographic observation of two scholars engaged in the discovery, evaluation, use, and generation of information and knowledge as part of their own ongoing research practices. Both informants were experienced academics at, or near, the beginning of research projects involving the use of networked information systems (e.g., bibliographic databases, digital libraries, Web-based resources). They were also experienced users of these systems. The inquiry sought to understand the evolving character of human judgments of relevance, examining various expressions of the informants' topic and how each made sense of what they found as they engaged in the information seeking activities associated with their own research projects.

Fieldwork used process-oriented and user-oriented methods of discovery that allowed informants to shape the exploration of the practices surrounding the evolving understandings of their research topics. Engaging with these interpretive processes from within the informants' worlds meant allowing them to drive the circumstances and the manner in which their practices were examined, observing what they did and listening to their explanations of their actions. Audio and video tools recorded informants' 'talk-aloud' sessions as they searched and evaluated both networked and print information resources (e.g., citations, abstracts, and texts). They were also observed preparing documents as part of their research work, discussing their project with colleagues and delivering presentations about their work.

A diverse range of material was analyzed inductively, including search histories, audio and video recordings of search and evaluation sessions, meetings and discussions between informants and their colleagues, e-mail correspondence, and documents generated by the academics during their research. This ethnographic approach resulted in two narratives (a blend of anecdotes, vignettes, and analysis) portraying the research experiences of each informant and their evolving judgments of relevance over a two-year period.

John: Setting the Scene

John is a senior lecturer involved in a research project emerging from a workshop conducted a few months before our first meeting. His participation in the author's ethnographic study began shortly before he started collecting information for his own project exploring the relationship between evolution and design. John is clearly a very comfortable and capable user of networked resources, but does not like being called an "expert."[1]

During the observation period, John's research grew from a faculty project expected to last a couple of years to become an international venture expected to take at least five years. The project's scale changed as a result of John's engagement with the literature and his interactions with researchers about his ideas. In later months, he began working with a research assistant, who performed some of the database searches and document retrieval. John's interactions with both these filters of information (databases and human intermediary) were observed.

John is, in his own words, an "avid explorer of ideas." His wide reading of literature in his own and related fields was evident in his talk-aloud discussions when he voiced connections between the information under review and his understanding of the conceptual debates they contain. He describes himself as "someone with a natural curiosity about the world around me." This curiosity in his view makes him a very thorough

searcher. During one of our search discussions, John admitted to being "a bit of a bowerbird."

The exploratory nature of John's project meant that he was collecting research material from diverse domains. In the first year of his inquiry, he reduced a total of 7,945 citations from 24 databases to a collection of 902 articles marked for retrieval. He appeared to thoroughly enjoy the opportunity to explore this literature.

John: Conferences, Concept Maps, and "Foundation Papers"

We arrange a meeting just after John has returned from overseas, where an international team of research collaborators emerged as a result of his participation in a conference. He is excited about the new prospects of examining a broad collection of literature emerging in the social, economic, design, and ethics areas from the multicultural perspective he feels the project demands. For now he must attend to managerial issues related to the project—solidifying the international collaborations, organizing research assistants, establishing a database management system. But within a month or two, he plans to return his attention to exploring the social evolution literature and generating the momentum that he hopes will allow the project to eventually take on a life of its own.

Now that he has a research assistant (Martin), John hopes he will be able to keep some momentum going on this project. Martin has picked up where John left off with the searches of the social evolution literature. In total, the two of them have searched 22 databases under the topic "social evolution." John shows me the spreadsheet they have prepared to record the number of items identified in each database not only for "social evolution," but also for the other dimensions of the broader project. These are the headings that he first mentioned to me in April—the process features of evolution that provided the framework for his examination of the book literature discussed in his research proposal. The social evolution column alone includes nearly 8,000 citations, not counting for duplication across databases. Scanning these listings—and abstracts when available—has resulted in a collection of about 800 items that Martin is now in the process of locating.

A few months later I observe John and Martin as they sort their collection of over 300 articles into categories according to the relevance for their project, spending most of the morning reading these articles to determine where each document belongs. There is some discussion about different interpretations and judgments of significance, but generally they reach agreement. After two-and-a-half hours, they classify 145 documents as having "high relevance," 81 as "intermediate," and 67 as "low relevance." A further 30 documents end up in the "other" category—referring to other dimensions of the project like technology, economics, and law, which will be examined by other collaborators or at later stages in the project.

With this step completed, they can then focus on the content of the most relevant articles—the ones considered key works for the project at this point. Sorted into author categories, these "highly relevant" articles are arranged across several tables. John and Martin begin creating a keyword list that identifies terms representing their collection of articles and highlighting what is in their view most important. They draw these keywords out after revisiting the articles—glancing once again at titles, abstracts, and headings. By mid-afternoon, they have scanned all the "highly relevant" articles and filled one whiteboard with keywords and a frequency count for each term. Martin points to the board and explains:

These are the sort of words I suppose you're looking for when deciding whether they're relevant or not....

Once they have this list—the "taxonomy," as John calls it—they begin drawing a concept map incorporating these terms into a visual representation of "social evolution," the topic of their project.

The exercise is John's way of identifying what he had already collected and managing a way forward. Discussing the ideas emerging from today's activities is both exciting and satisfying for each of them—the "way in" to the literature that John has often talked about is slowly crystallizing on the boards before them.

He describes the map they have just created as a model that is static and dynamic at the same time. The diagram they have created will also help them work out how to analyze the content they have collected. Observing the construction of this map and his discussion of the process with Martin and me offers some insight into John's understanding of what, in his view, "social evolution" is all about. His world view and his expectations become clearer, as does the influence of particular writers and works on his project.

The map is not meant to be a permanent framework for the analysis. It is simply "an attempt in a fairly short period of time to make some kind of understanding of what we've been doing." When we next meet a week later, there is already a modified version in use. He points to the copy now spread out on the table and explains how it will guide their work:

Here we have a very crude interpretation of this literature that we've been going through. Now, with the benefit of that, let's start to read this and see whether this holds up or whether we need to continue to develop it. And I'm quite relaxed about the idea that this might come out totally different from what we've got here. But at least it's a starting point, it's something to challenge with our reading.

Continued evaluation of his own interpretations of terms on the keyword list or in the concept map—and discussions with Martin—will continue to help them makes sense of their reading. As observation of John's concept mapping showed, the texts he is reading and reviewing represented the voices of various researchers and positions he accepts as relevant to his project. The concept map is a "sounding board" that can be referred to when working with his "highly relevant" articles.

John uses his concept map as a guide to help him understand how—if at all—the documents he reviews fit into his research. Thus, he examines each document, looking for clues to its content—reading only as much as is required for his decision-making purpose. If he can make such a decision quickly by looking only at the article's title, author, abstract, keywords, or some combination of these elements, or if some other "trigger" about that article is known to him (such as his expectations of a particular author, the mention made by a colleague, or a review article), then so much the better. If this is not possible, however, he scans the article looking for enough information to make his decision. Ironically, it sometimes means spending more time on articles that end up in a "marginal," "low," or "other" pile than those ending up in his "highly relevant" collection.

Using relevance rankings helps ensure that the materials John and Martin identify as "highly relevant" are given priority. Finding a place for ideas and for information collected during the course of his exploration of the literature was important for John. Creating the categories for his collection of documents helped him work out how items fit together. This clustering does not stop John from using the documents for different projects. Some articles appear more relevant than others when it comes to accomplishing his immediate goals. Shortly after one such sorting session, for example, John removed two articles from his highly relevant collection temporarily because he wanted to use them to write a conference paper that he was preparing with Martin. John is very conscious of the place that these two items rightfully occupy in this major project, but is able to make a clear distinction between his short-term and long-term research needs.

John's research for this long-term project has led not only to the paper topic he is working on with Martin, but also to an invitation to participate in a plenary discussion at the same conference—for which he is currently preparing another paper. He is now preparing a total of three papers on varying aspects of this topic: the two mentioned already and the paper he is coauthoring with one of his faculty colleagues about this project for another international conference.

The big challenge he faces is dealing with what John refers to as the "islands of information" about his topic which, in his words, "need to be made into continents" within his writing timeframe. This creative process involves working through as many of the dozen or more texts he feels are key works before the submission deadlines. It also involves regular dialogues with international researchers, not as coauthors but rather as respected colleagues. His participation in Web-based communication associated with the plenary session, for instance, has raised a number of questions about the ideologies associated with social evolutionary perspectives, which in turn has prompted him to examine "the literature *around* social evolution." Through these engagements, the boundaries of what he considers relevant to his topic are widening.

Catherine: Setting the Scene

Catherine is a senior lecturer who, at the start of this investigation, had spent the last three years working part time on a doctoral thesis on journalism education. Our first meeting took place when she was about to start working on a new thesis chapter addressing key issues for journalism education. Like John, she does not consider herself an experienced searcher. However, she has used networked information resources extensively in industry and academic settings, and appeared very comfortable using the university's networked information resources.

A few months after beginning work on her new chapter, and with the start of the next semester less than a month away at that time, she ended up putting her thesis aside to prepare some reading lists for one of her courses. In the process, she decided to use her lecture preparation as a way to begin work on a later thesis chapter addressing journalism professional practice.

Teaching commitments and family issues seriously impacted upon the time she was able to devote to her research. Catherine is the type of person who finds it hard to say "no" to requests for assistance or student consultation. As a result, her work routine can become very fractured. Interruptions to the time she sets aside for searching because of phone calls, e-mail, messages, or people stopping by her office unexpectedly are constant. In my conversations with Catherine, I found that she fantasized frequently about the way she would pursue her thesis topic if she had the time. She also spoke about feeling isolated from the postgraduate community because she is working on her thesis part time.

Finding time to conduct searches and explore the literature was an important issue for Catherine. She was very enthusiastic about exploring her area of interest, but was constantly frustrated about the discontinuity associated with the "snippets" of time she had available.

Catherine: Finding the Right Words and a Place in her Field

Catherine is ready to conduct further searches on her topic. Until now she has repeatedly mentioned that she is dissatisfied with the results. More to the point, she often expresses frustration with herself for being unable to find the right way to get what she wants during the search sessions. This particular morning, however, something has changed. In sharp contrast to the frustration she exhibited when we met last week, she appears very enthusiastic and upbeat about the search she is about to conduct. She explains that she attended a conference yesterday at which papers were presented on topics related to her own. There is enthusiasm in her voice as she describes her experience.

The event also seems to have provided her with a new set of search terms. One session that was particularly valuable, she explains, made clear to her that there has been a shift in the terminology used in her field. Catherine describes this as a huge shift. Significantly, she now realizes that "training" is the word that she should be using in her searching:

Last time it was difficult to get what I wanted…and difficult to articulate what I wanted. I want to construct a new view of media from a different perspective—a perspective that I now realize is not there!

She decides that it might make sense to "go back a step and rethink what the possibility of finding information is.

She has yet to do any further work on the articles that she collected as a result of the search three weeks ago. However, she quickly reviews a particular article she was very pleased to find during the last search session, noting it still "looks useful." Discussion at yesterday's conference, she remarks, in fact further strengthens the argument that is reflected in that article.

Attending the conference has prompted her to "take a systematic approach" to today's search session and to generate a list of words and word combinations for her search requests. She pulls out a list of words and word combinations that she did not use in her first session. She thinks this strategy will unlock information from the databases that she is about to search.

At the end of this search session, Catherine discusses the day's experience as she gathers her papers alongside the computer. She feels "much better" than she did after the search she did three weeks ago:

I'm getting largely what I already know about…But I'm also rethinking what kind of information I can access…there's no point looking for what's not there, it's too depressing!

She describes her search strategy on this day as "more systematic" and her results as "much more useful" than last time. The encounters at the conference she has just attended have not only given her new search terms, but also provided her with a clearer appreciation of the scope of current debates in her field. Armed with a greater awareness of what is—and is not—being discussed by her peers, she speculates about possible explanations for the limited material she is locating, and she is able to see a way to move forward in her project.

Later in the year, Catherine is telling me about another paper she will be presenting at a professional conference on a topic motivated by her interest in "wanting to try and continue to participate in that [professional] association." She only really became involved the previous year, when she presented a paper based upon her pilot study. It generated a lot of discussion during the conference. The subsequent publication of the paper did not provoke much response, in her view, which disappointed her because she had hoped that some of the discussion of issues raised at the conference would continue.

So, the current topic that she has worked out for this second conference:

...is centrally related to what I am doing [in the thesis], but it's also something that I think will enable that process to continue of engaging with the other people in the field. I guess, part of what I see as being a purpose of the doctoral research is to be able to create a place for yourself in the field. So this seems like—it's not a direct continuation of what I did last time [at the conference] but it's certainly strongly related.

Motivation for work on this aspect of her thesis clearly extends beyond the thesis itself.

Catherine is cognizant of the place she wishes to create for herself in the field. Our discussion illustrates that she is very conscious of her potential role in this particular community's discussion of the issues she seeks to address. The context provided by the community in which she wishes to participate influences her research objectives and thereby her thesis. She explains that she has very deliberately selected the topic for the paper. In this instance, judgments she makes about what is appropriate for her own research are affected by her desire to engage in more fulsome discussion with her peers about her work. Mindful of the place she wishes to create for herself in her field, we see Catherine refashioning her research.

Discussion: Scholarly Research as an Illustration of the Interplay Between Personal and Social

Collaboration and socialization are more embedded and seemingly invisible than is often accounted for in models of collaborative information retrieval. Whether using networked information systems for searching or for managing material collected during the course of a project, the relevance judgments people make are mediated by computer interfaces but also shaped by interpersonal relations and face-to-face settings. The extracts from John's and Catherine's projects illustrate the way social and individual elements of their scholarly practices merge in relation to relevance assessment and the creative connection-building function of information seeking. In both cases, their individual research projects were shaped by encounters with other people—in mediated and personal encounters—in ways that were shown to inform their judgments about information.

The biggest challenge of academic work is not finding information, but being able to effectively manage our discovery and use of the ideas we encounter. Collaboration is embedded in scholarly research both implicitly and explicitly—a fact that must be considered in any exploration of how academics select and use relevant resources located during the searching of networked information systems such as bibliographic databases and digital libraries available through the Internet. Whether scholars work alone or as part of a team, the communication of ideas and investigations within their intellectual communities is a critical element of knowledge production in this context. The ethnographic research described here enriches previous research positing scholarly research as a form of social interaction (e.g., Fry, 2006; Meadows, 1990; Selden, 2001; Talja, 2002).

Exploring the social practices associated with academic work that might otherwise be considered an individual endeavor offers rich illustrations of ways academic information seeking can be viewed as a communal activity: interaction and collaboration can be embedded in seemingly individual tasks. This position on collaboration and interaction also reflects Barad's (1998) notion of intra-action, to emphasize the emergent quality of working with information and understandings about what constitutes a relevant piece of information in the course of dealing with information systems (human as well as mechanical), people, and texts of all kinds. Following Barad's position, the searcher and the information they are producing are co-constituted through these processes of meaning-making.

Observing and analyzing the interactions and collaborations that take place within scholarly research practices leads to potent illustrations of the knowledge production function of retrieval systems, which Karamuftuoglu (1998) contends foregrounds the social context in which any information system operates. It also contributes a detailed look at individual interpretations of community rules and norms. The collaborative or social aspects of human relevance judgments have often been discussed by researchers as distinct from personal judgments of relevance. Karamuftuoglu (1998, p. 1074), for example, discusses the "social view of relevance" in terms of a relation between a document and a discourse community, and "personal relevance" in terms of the individual's information needs. Zhang (2002) separates the collaborative judgments of peers

from that of an individual searcher, describing the subjectivity of the individual's judgments in a manner that ignores the social, interactive nature of an individual's information seeking and retrieval. In contrast to these approaches, the case studies presented in this chapter demonstrate that, from the searcher's perspective, distinguishing between personal and social aspects is not necessarily possible. For instance, conference attendance had a visible impact on the information behaviors in both the cases reported here. For John it set him on a path of research collaboration that informed both his individual and collaborative pursuits. For Catherine, it exposed her to the language of her research community at a critical point in her information seeking, helping her to revise her search criteria. In this last example, an interpersonal encounter was drawn into an information retrieval task despite being separated from it both in terms of time and space.

Individual and social qualities are not distinct from one another, but rather are interwoven in a searcher's experience with networked information systems. Talja's (2002) examination of the context of academic information seeking is of particular value to this discussion because of her focus "on sharing information about relevant documents and practices of finding relevant documents" (p. 145). She discusses the "scholar's communication network" and associated information sharing practices. She concludes that scholarly networks not only inform information seeking strategies, but the interpretation, use, and generation of information by a scholar (Talja, 2002, p. 155). The extracts from Catherine's and John's experiences demonstrate how their personal connections with scholarly networks influence their individual judgments of information and shape their research projects.

In conversations with John, he described how e-mail communication and personal meetings with international collaborators were shaping the categories created, the themes to be covered, and the extent of that coverage in his research.

A chance encounter with an informal eight-page document about thesis preparation that a colleague shared with Catherine helped her establish clearer limits for her research, making it easier for her to articulate what she wanted to cover in her research. In this frame of mind, she revisited some of the earlier material she had collected in the course of her research and located a document that provided the framework enabling her to move even further forward and utilize her other material in what she felt was an efficient way.

These case studies of scholarly research practices illustrate how the conceptual framework presented in the first part of this chapter can be applied to develop a fuller understanding of human relevance judgments. With their emphasis on the interplay between the social setting and an individual's construction of his or her "horizon," both Zerubavel's "sociomental" perspective (1993) and Hjørland's (2002) "socio-cognitive" approach to relevance support this idea of relevance as a socially situated activity.

When discussing their individual relevance judgments, John and Catherine demonstrate an awareness of their place within their respective research communities. In this way, they demonstrate the behaviors Sundin and Johannisson (2005a) discuss and the bi-directional influences made manifest in such judgments. Both informants articulate their desire to influence the research directions of their peers—along the lines of the social shaping described by Sundin and Johannisson. Equally, even in these extracts from more than two years of observation, the social or collective view of their respective communities is seen shaping the way they both move forward in their research. Collaboration and interaction do not have to be explicit to be influential.

The cases presented here draw attention to the socializing aspects of relevance assessment practices of people working with networked information, highlighting how collaboration with other people (both face to face and mediated by systems and texts) informs and is informed by an individual's engagement with networked information systems. Theorizing relevance assessment as intra-action leads to a portrayal of these judgments as emergent constructions, resulting from the interplay between social and personal, technical and human elements. The cases reported in this chapter suggest that, in scholarly research settings, even in a seemingly individual project, we can find evidence of decisions impacted by a scholar's awareness of and response to a wider, social context.

Implications and Conclusion

The social and collaborative aspects of relevance judgments are a critical part of any depiction of collaborative information retrieval. The framework and cases presented here offer an alternative to more traditional portrayals of collaborative information retrieval. As was demonstrated in the cases presented in this chapter, the embedded and inter-related character of these personal and social elements requires us to consider collaborative information retrieval in a way that does not create a separation between them. There are social dimensions of information retrieval at both explicitly collaborative and inter-psychological levels.

In our engagement with information systems, human and mechanical, there is continual interplay between individual and collective elements. Some of these collaborative aspects are embedded in the wider research practices prompting information system use and are not visible in the same way as other practices more conventionally considered collaborative. Nevertheless these aspects are a critical part of any depiction of collaborative information retrieval, suggesting that we need to devise frameworks that do not examine them in isolation from one another. Taking a holistic approach to relevance assessment demonstrates that relevance judgments are drivers of the search and research processes informants moved through during information seeking. Understanding the breadth of these human relevance judgments is critical for the design of information systems that wish to take into account the interplay between the personal and social features of these practices.

Collaboration is far more pervasive than simply engaging with others in online or direct encounters; it is embedded in research activities both implicitly and explicitly. Examining the expressions of relevance draws attention to the impact of the human practices of indexing and representation on informants' judgments. Practices such as the labeling of content and generation of representations contained within networked information systems are often invisible in depictions of the searcher-system relationship. Making them made more visible within these ethnographic stories sheds light on the ways that these representations are interpreted during the course of a research project. Analysis of the cases reported in this chapter suggests that searchers benefit from opportunities to review and re-word search requests so as to take into account the dynamics of their own search goals and the evolving discourse of their research communities. Such connections might also be well supported through collaborative metadata schemes, enabling the communication of alternative representations of content.

Examining the situatedness of information retrieval interactions is important for the design of context-sensitive information retrieval systems. The framework presented in the first part of this chapter contributes to this area by describing how relevance—as a communicative practice—is generated when searchers are engaged with information systems. The cases described in the second part provide lessons for the ways that people work with information systems to generate knowledge and the conditions that will support these practices. They demonstrate how individual relevance judgments and retrieval practices embody collaborative elements that contribute to the overall progress of that person's individual work. Collaboration does not have to be explicit to influence searcher behavior. Portraying these experiences as intra-action can help us explain and understand the range of encounters that inform and influence that behavior.

REFERENCES

Barad, K. (1998). Getting real: Technoscientific practices and the materialization of reality. *Differences: A Journal of Feminist Cultural Studies, 10*(2), 87 (84).

Borlund, P., & Ingwersen, P. (1998). Measures of relative relevance and ranked half-life: Performance indicators for interactive IR. In W.B. Croft, A. Moffat, C.J. van Rijsbergen, R. Wilkinson, & J. Zobel (Eds.), *Proceedings of the 21st ACM SIGIR Conference on Research and Development of Information Retrieval* (pp. 324-331), Melbourne. New York: ACM.

Bourdieu, P. (1990). *The logic of practice* (R. Nice, trans.). Cambridge, UK: Polity Press in association with Basil Blackwell.

Boyce, B. (1982). Beyond topicality. A two-stage view of relevance and the retrieval process. *Information Processing and Management, 18,* 105-189.

Burnett, K., & McKinley, E.G. (1998). Modeling information seeking. *Interacting with Computers, 10*(3), 285-302.

Byström, K., & Järvelin, K. (1995). Task complexity affects information seeking and use. *Information Processing & Management, 31*(2), 191-213.

Capurro, R. (1992). Informatics and hermeneutics. In C. Floyd, H. Züllighoven, R. Budde, & R. Keil-Slawik (Eds.), *Software development and reality construction* (pp. 363-375). Berlin/Heidelberg/New York: Springer.

Capurro, R. (2000). Hermeneutics and the phenomenon of information. In C. Mitcham (Ed.), *Metaphysics, epistemology, and technology.*

Research in philosophy and technology (vol. 19, pp. 79-85). JAI/Elsevier.

Chatman, E.A. (1996). The impoverished life-world of outsiders. *Journal of the American Society for Information Science, 47*(3), 193-206.

Cool, C. (1997, November 1-6). The nature of situation assessment in new information retrieval environments. In C. Schwartz & M. Rorvig (Eds.), *ASIS '97: Digital Collections: Implications for Users, Funders, Developers and Maintainers. Proceedings of the 60th ASIS Annual Meeting* (vol. 34, pp. 135-146), Washington, DC. Medford, NJ: Information Today for ASIS.

Cosijn, E., & Ingwersen, P. (2000). Dimensions of relevance. *Information Processing & Management, 36,* 533-550.

Covi, L., & Kling, R. (1996). Organizational dimensions of effective digital library use: Closed rational and open natural systems models. *Journal of the American Society for Information Science, 47*(9), 672-690.

Eisenberg, M.B., & Barry, C.L. (1988). Order effects: A study of the possible influence of presentation order on user judgments of document relevance. *Journal of the American Society for Information Science, 39*(5), 293-300.

Ekbia, H.R., & Maguitman, A.G. (2001, July 27-30). Context and relevance: A pragmatic approach. *Proceedings of the 3rd International and Interdisciplinary Conference on Modeling and Using Context* (vol. 2116, pp. 156-169), Dundee, UK. Heidelberg: Springer.

Flores, F. (1998). Information technology and the institution of identity: Reflections since understanding computers and cognition. *Information Technology and People, 11*(4), 351-372.

Fry, J. (2006). Scholarly research and information practices: A domain analytic approach. *Information Processing & Management, 42*(1), 299-316.

Given, L.M. (2002). The academic and the everyday: Investigating the overlap in mature undergraduates' information-seeking behaviors. *Library and Information Science Research, 24,* 17-29.

Green, R. (2001). Relationships in the organization of knowledge: An overview. In C.A. Bean & R. Green (Eds.), *Relationships in the organization of knowledge* (pp. 3-18). Dordrecht, The Netherlands: Kluwer Academic.

Greisdorf, H. (2000). Relevance: An interdisciplinary and information science perspective. *Informing Science, 3*(2), 67-71.

Harter, S.P. (1992). Psychological relevance and information science. *Journal of the American Society for Information Science, 43*(9), 602-615.

Hert, C.A. (1992). Exploring a new model for understanding information retrieval interactions. *Proceedings of ASIS' 92* (pp. 72-75).

Hert, C.A. (1997). *Understanding information retrieval interactions: Theoretical and practical implications.* Greenwich, CN: Ablex.

Hjørland, B. (1997). *Information seeking and subject representation: An activity theoretical approach to information science.* Westport, CN: Greenwood Press.

Hjørland, B. (2000). Relevance research: The missing perspective(s): "Non-relevance" and "epistemological relevance." *Journal of the American Society for Information Science, 51*(2), 209-211.

Hjørland, B. (2002). Epistemology and the socio-cognitive perspective in information science. *Journal of the American Society for Information Science and Technology, 53*(4), 257-270.

Hjørland, B., & Christensen, F.S. (2002). Work tasks and socio-cognitive relevance: A specific example. Brief communication. *Journal of the American Society for Information Science, 53*(11), 960-965.

Huotari, M.-L., & Chatman, E.A. (2001). Using everyday life information seeking to explain organizational behavior. *Library and Information Science Research, 23,* 351-366.

Ingwersen, P. (1996). Cognitive perspective of information retrieval interaction: Elements of a cognitive IR theory. *Journal of Documentation, 52*(1), 3-50.

Jacob, E. (1992). Culture, context and cognition. In M.D. LeCompte, W.L. Millroy, & J. Preissle (Eds.), *The handbook of qualitative research in education* (pp. 293-335). San Diego, CA: Academic Press.

Janes, J.W. (1994). Other people's judgments: A comparison of users' and others' judgments of document relevance, topicality and utility. *Journal of the American Society for Information Science, 45*(3), 160-171.

Karamuftuoglu, M. (1998). Collaborative information retrieval: Toward a social informatics view of IR interaction. *Journal of the American Society for Information Science, 49*(12), 1070-1080.

Kekäläinen, J., & Järvelin, K. (2002, July 21-25). Evaluating information retrieval systems under the challenges of interaction and multidimensional dynamic relevance. In H. Bruce, R. Fidel, P. Ingwersen, & P. Vakkari (Eds.), *Proceedings of the 4th International Conference on Conceptions of Library and Information Science* (CoLIS4) (pp. 253-270), Seattle, WA. Greenwood Village, CO: Libraries Unlimited.

Kuhlthau, C.C. (1991). Inside the search process: Information seeking from the user's perspective. *Journal of the American Society for Information Science, 42*(5), 361-371.

Kuhlthau, C.C. (2004). *Seeking meaning: A process approach to library and information services* (2nd ed.). Westport, CN: Libraries Unlimited.

Lave, J. (1988). *Cognition in practice: Mind, mathematics and culture in everyday life.* Cambridge, UK: Cambridge University Press.

Leydesdorff, L. (2000). Luhmann, Habermas and the theory of communication. *Systems Research and Behavioral Science, 17*(3), 273-288.

Marchionini, G. (1995). *Information seeking in electronic environments.* Cambridge/New York: Cambridge University Press.

Meadows, J. (1990, July 18-21). General overview, keynote address. In M. Feeney & K. Merry (Eds.), *Proceedings of the Conference on Information Technology and the Research Process* (pp. 1-13), Cranfield, UK. London: Bowker-Saur.

Mizzaro, S. (1998). How many relevances in information retrieval? *Interacting with Computers, 10*(3), 303-320.

Nardi, B.A. (1996). Activity theory and human-computer interaction. In B.A. Nardi (Ed.), *Context and consciousness: Activity theory and human-computer interaction* (pp. 7-16). Cambridge, MA: MIT Press.

Park, T.K. (1992). *The nature of relevance in information retrieval: An empirical study.* Unpublished PhD Thesis (UMI No. 9231644), Indiana University, USA.

Park, T.K. (1994). Toward a theory of user-based relevance: A call for a new paradigm of inquiry. *Journal of the American Society for Information Science, 45*(3), 135-141.

Robins, D. (1998, October 24-29). Dynamics and dimensions of user information problems as foci of interaction in information retrieval. In C.M. Preston (Ed.), *Proceedings of the 61st ASIS Annual Meeting on Information Access in the Global Information Economy* (vol. 35, pp. 327-341), Pittsburgh, PA. Medford, NJ: Information Today (for ASIS).

Robins, D. (2000). Interactive information retrieval: Context and basic notions. *Informing Science, 3*(2), 57-61.

Saracevic, T. (1996a). Interactive models of information retrieval (IR): A review and proposal. *Proceedings of the 59th Annual Meeting of the American Society for Information Science* (vol. 33, pp. 3-9).

Saracevic, T. (1996b). Relevance reconsidered '96. In P. Ingwersen & N.O. Pors (Eds.), *Proceedings of the 2nd International Conference on Conceptions of Library and Information Science: Integration in Perspective* (CoLIS 2) (pp. 201-218). Copenhagen: Royal School of Librarianship.

Saracevic, T., Kantor, P.B., Chamis, A.Y., & Trivison, D. (1988). A study of information seeking and retrieving. I: Background and methodology. *Journal of the American Society for Information Science, 39*(3), 161-176.

Savolainen, R. (1995). Everyday life information seeking: Approaching information seeking in the context of "way of life." *Library and Information Science Research, 17,* 259-294.

Schamber, L. (1994). Relevance and information behavior. *Annual Review of Information Science and Technology, 29,* 3-48.

Schutz, A. (1970). *Reflections on the problem of relevance. Edited, annotated, and with an introduction by Richard M. Zaner.* New Haven, CT/London: Yale University Press.

Selden, L. (2001). Academic information seeking—careers and capital types. *New Review of Information Behavior Research, 1*(2), 195-215.

Sperber, D., & Wilson, D. (1986). *Relevance: Communication and cognition.* Oxford: Basil Blackwell.

Spink, A., Greisdorf, H., & Bateman, J. (1998). From highly relevant to not relevant: Examining different regions of relevance. *Information Processing and Management, 34*(5), 599-621.

Spink, A., Greisdorf, H., & Bateman, J. (1999). A study of mediated successive searching during information seeking. *Journal of Information Science, 25*(6), 477-487.

Suchman, L. (1987). *Plans and situated actions: The problem of human-machine communication.* Cambridge, UK: Cambridge University Press.

Suchman, L., Trigg, R., & Blomberg, J.L. (2002). Working artefacts: Ethnomethods of the prototype. *British Journal of Sociology, 53*(2), 163-179.

Suchman, L.A., & Trigg, R.H. (1993). Artificial intelligence as craftwork. In S. Chaiklin & J. Lave (Eds.), *Understanding practice: Perspectives on activity and context* (pp. 144-178). Cambridge, UK: Cambridge University Press.

Sundin, O., & Johannisson, J. (2005a). The instrumentality of information needs and relevance. In F. Crestani & I. Ruthven (Eds.), *Proceedings of the Conference on Conceptions of Library and Information Science* (CoLIS 2005) (pp. 107-118). Berlin/Heidelberg: Springer-Verlag.

Sundin, O., & Johannisson, J. (2005b). Pragmatism, neo-pragmatism and sociocultural theory: Communicative participation as a perspective in LIS. *Journal of Documentation, 61*(1), 23-43.

Swanson, D.R. (1988). Historical note: Information retrieval and the future of an illusion. *Journal of the American Society for Information Science, 39*(2), 92-98.

Talja, S. (2002). Information sharing in academic communities: Types and levels of collaboration in information seeking and use. *New Review of Information Behavior Research, 3,* 143-159.

Tang, R., & Solomon, P. (1998). Toward an understanding of the dynamics of relevance judgment: An analysis of one person's search behavior. *Information Processing and Management, 34*(2/3), 237-256.

Vakkari, P. (1999). Task complexity, problem structure and information actions: Integrating studies on information seeking and retrieval. *Information Processing & Management, 35*(6), 819-837.

Vakkari, P. (2000, July 24-28). Relevance and contributing information types of searched documents in task performance. In N.J. Belkin, P. Ingwersen, & M.-K. Leong (Eds.), *Proceedings of the 23rd Annual International ACM SIGIR Conference on Research and Development in Information Retrieval* (vol. 34, pp. 2-9), Athens, Greece. New York: ACM Press.

Vakkari, P. (2003). Task-based information seeking. In B. Cronin (Ed.), *Annual review of information science and technology* (vol. 37, pp. 413-464). Medford, NJ: Information Today.

Vakkari, P., & Hakala, N. (2000). Changes in relevance criteria and problem stages in task performance. *Journal of Documentation, 56*(5), 540-562.

Wang, P., & Soergel, D. (1998). A cognitive model of document use during a research project. Study 1. Document selection. *Journal of the American Society for Information Science, 49*(2), 115-133.

Winograd, T., & Flores, F. (1987). *Understanding computers and cognition: A new foundation for design.* Reading, MA: Addison-Wesley.

Xie, H. (2000). Shifts of interactive intentions and information seeking strategies in interactive information retrieval. *Journal of the American Society for Information Science, 51*(9), 841-857.

Zerubavel, E. (1993). Horizons: On the sociomental foundations of relevance. *Social Research, 60*(2), 397-413.

Zhang, X. (2002). Collaborative relevance judgment: A group consensus method for evaluating user search performance. *Journal of the American Society for Information Science and Technology, 53*(3), 220-231.

ENDNOTE

[1]   All quotes within the extracts presented here are those of the two informants (John and Catherine) and are taken from transcripts of the author's engagements with them during the ethnographic study.

Chapter XIII
Publication and Citation Analysis as a Tool for Information Retrieval

Ronald Rousseau
KHBO (Association K.U. Leuven), Belgium

ABSTRACT

In this chapter an overview of citation analysis is presented, emphasizing its formal aspects as applied social network theory. As such citation linking can be considered a tool for information retrieval based on social interaction. It is indeed well known that following citation links is an efficient method of information retrieval. Relations with Web linking are highlighted. Yet, also social aspects related to the act of citing, such as the occurrence of invisible colleges, are discussed. I present some recent developments and my opinion on some future developments. In this way I hope the reader will realize how the fields of citation analysis and Webometrics can be helpful in building social information retrieval systems.

INTRODUCTION: DEFINITION OF CITATION ANALYSIS

We define citation analysis as that subfield of bibliometrics where patterns and frequencies of citations, given as well as received, are analyzed. Such an analysis is performed on the level of authors, journals, scientific disciplines, and any other useful unit or level. Citation analysis further studies relations between cited and citing units (documents, authors, countries, etc.). From an ap-

plication point of view, citation analysis may be considered as a collaborative peer effort to analyze and promote the quality of scholarly publication and research. For a review of citation analysis as a subfield of informetrics, we refer to Wilson (1999) and Borgman and Furner (2002).

Science is a social and accumulative endeavor, even if occasionally whole areas are overturned by new evidence. No scientific discovery or activity is conducted in splendid isolation, and new work is always based in some way on the work of predecessors. Citations reflect this social and accumulative aspect by linking the past with the present, and possibly the future. They represent an intrinsic part of the progress and development of science.

Contributions to scientific knowledge are often crystallized in the form of a scientific article. Such contributions may take the form of new facts, new hypotheses, new theories or theorems, new explanations, or a new synthesis of existing facts (Russell & Rousseau, 2002). In each case a transition has taken place from an existing, say 'old', situation to a 'new' one. The transition itself takes place in the head of the investigators with the help of scientific equipment and is usually invisible for outsiders, but scientific tradition requires that an author refers to earlier articles that relate to the theme of his or her paper. The author must clarify his or her starting point. 'The old' is revealed by identifying those predecessors whose concepts, methods, and discoveries have inspired or were used in developing 'the new'. Stated otherwise, the author acknowledges a group of inspirational articles written by earlier researchers by referring to them. The term 'referring' means here: mentioning in the proper context and giving an explicit bibliographical statement in the reference list. The older articles are then cited by—receive a citation from—the new one.

A similar process takes place when a new Web site is created and links are attached to existing Web sites. Yet, while the act of citing is accompanied with a time stamp, a time stamp on the Web (if it exists at all) usually gets lost very soon. Of course there is another important difference between the two types of linking. When article A cites article B, then because of this time factor, B will usually not cite A. Note though that recently Rousseau and Small (2005) published a strange case where a giant Escher staircase (Rousseau & Thelwall, 2004) was discovered between 13 articles. Between Web sites or Web pages, reciprocal linking is quite feasible. This

is, however, also true for citation links between journals or authors.

Articles connected to other articles through citation linking, journals connected to other journals and to itself, also by citation linking, scientists connected to colleagues through co-authorship—all these relations can be considered as special cases of networks or expressed in mathematical terminology as graphs. Consequently, graph theory and network analysis will constitute an important thread in this contribution. Information retrieval using citation analysis techniques takes advantages of the existence of these links. Garner (1967) was among the first to show the relation between citation indexing and general graph theory. For a deeper insight in all aspects of citation analysis, the reader is referred to *Citation Analysis in Research Evaluation* by Henk F. Moed (2005).

Although this contribution focuses on citation analysis and Web linking, we cannot ignore the enormous influence of the 'free online availability' movement. Preprint servers, open access (gold road), self-archiving (green road), institutional repositories, and other new modes of publication are changing the landscape of scholarly publishing (Bosc & Harnad, 2005; Brody, Kampa, Harnad, Carr, & Hitchock, 2003). It has been shown that open access increases later citation counts and that earlier Web usage can be used as a predictor for later citation counts (Brody, Harnad, & Carr, 2006). Web access has given rise to download counts as a new indicator.

What is the Relation Between Publication and Citation Analysis on the One Hand and Information Retrieval on the Other?

Citing is not a purely logical or objective act. It can be compared to decision making under partially unknown circumstances. As all other decisions it involves a socially determined choice. Using publication and citation data for evaluation purposes is certainly socially determined. It is, for one thing, influenced by the ease in which this information can be retrieved. It is also determined by which publication outlets are considered to be important by scientific peers (a particular type of social group) and which are considered to be less important: journals with a long tradition, the most recent specialization journals, conference proceedings of some international conferences, particular Web preprint servers. Under such circumstances it is a good idea to harness other users' experiences. This can be done by applying the results of publication and citation analysis. These results are, indeed, the final product of a very large number of 'votes'. It should also be recalled that Eugene Garfield created the Science Citation Index in the first place as a retrieval tool (Egghe & Rousseau, 1990).

CO-CITATIONS AND BIBLIOGRAPHIC COUPLING

In the previous section we talked about relations of the form Cites(A;B), or in words: A cites B. Now we move up one level of complexity and study relations of the form Cites(A; B,C), in words: A cites B and C; and Cites(A,B;C), in words: A and B cite C. In the first case we say that articles B and C are co-cited; in the second case we say that A and B are bibliographically coupled.

The technique of using bibliographic coupling for retrieval purposes and the term itself have been introduced by Kessler (1962, 1963). The bibliographic coupling strength of two articles is the number of times they are bibliographically coupled—that is, the number of articles their reference lists have in common. The notion of bibliographic coupling may be applied to articles, but also to books and other documents. Using the language of set theory, the bibliographic coupling strength of two documents may be defined as the number of elements in the intersection of their reference lists. The relative bibliographic

coupling strength is then the number of elements in the intersection of their reference lists, divided by the number of documents in the union of their reference lists (Sen & Gan, 1983). This is essentially the Jaccard index. We note that the 'related records' feature in ISI's databases uses the bibliographic coupling technique (Garfield, 1988; Atkins, 1999).

In 1973 the notion of co-citation (if not the term) was independently proposed by Marshakova (1973) and Small (1973). In the Russian literature bibliographic coupling is said to be 'retrospective' while co-citation is called 'prospective coupling'. The co-citation strength (or frequency) of two documents is the number of times they have been co-cited. As is the case for the notion of *bibliographic coupling,* also *co-citation* may be applied to other documents than articles, such as books. If C_A denotes the set of documents citing A, and C_B denotes the set of documents citing B, then the co-citation strength of A and B may be defined as the number of elements in the intersection of C_A and C_B. The relative co-citation frequency is then the number of elements in the intersection of C_A and C_B, divided by the number of documents in the union of C_A and C_B. This is again a Jaccard index.

The co-citation strength of two documents never decreases in time and so does the number of articles with which a fixed article has been co-cited. Co-citation histories—that is, how the co-citation strength and the relative co-citation strength change in time—have been studied by Rousseau (Egghe & Rousseau, 1990, III.4.3.2).

Being bibliographically coupled or being co-cited are symmetric relations: if A is co-cited with B, then B is co-cited with A. This relation, however, is in general not transitive: if A is co-cited with B, and B is co-cited with C, then A is not necessarily co-cited with C. If this relation were transitive, we would have natural groups (equivalence classes). As the co-citation relation is non-transitive, there are no equivalence classes and hence classification becomes a subjective problem. Classification may be done by considering connected components in the citation graph (but these can be overly large) or by a clustering algorithm (but here the groups, i.e., the clusters, depend on the used method and often a threshold value). Appropriately, and preferably automatically, naming the resulting clusters might be a challenging task. A recent approach by Schneider (2005) looks very promising in this respect. Sen and Gan (1983) also introduced the notions of indirect bibliographic coupling and indirect co-citation. We refer the reader to their article and Egghe and Rousseau (2002) for further information related to these notions.

Co-citation analysis may be performed on different types of actors: authors, journals, countries (as represented by authors), and so forth (Boyack, Klavans, & Borner, 2005; Ding, Chowdhury, & Foo, 2000). The most-used type of co-citation analysis is *author co-citation analysis* (ACA), introduced by White and Griffith (1981). ACA has mostly been used to analyze the intellectual structure of a given scientific field (McCain, 1990, 1991, 1995; White & McCain, 1998; Marion & McCain, 2001). In 1990 McCain published a technical overview of ACA, which has worldwide been adopted as a standard. In this overview McCain states that there are four main steps in an author co-citation analysis. First the raw data matrix (author co-citations) is compiled; next a conversion of this matrix to a proximity, association, or similarity matrix is performed. When this new data matrix has been generated, the third step is to perform a multivariate analysis of the relations between the authors represented in the matrix. In this step, cluster analysis, multidimensional scaling (MDS), factor analysis, and correspondence analysis have been used. Finally the interpretation and validation of the resulting influence network ends the work. ACA has been applied in many fields as illustrated by the contributions of the following colleagues: Braam, Moed, and van Raan (1991a, 1991b); Bayer, Smart, and McLaughlin (1990); Lin and Kaid (2000); Kreuzman (2001); Persson

(2001); and Reader (2001). Traditional ACA has been enhanced and extended by Chen (1999a, 1999b) and Chen and Paul (2001). They introduced Pathfinder network scaling as a replacement for MDS, leading to attractive three-dimensional visualizations of (among other examples) ACA networks. This approach, moreover, does not need a conversion from raw citation data when the Minkowski distance parameter r is set equal to ∞ (White, 2000, 2003). We finally note that author co-citations have been classified by Rousseau and Zuccala (2004).

Besides co-citation analysis, also other co-occurrences have been studied. It seems that the first such study was performed by Karl-Erik Rosengren in 1966. In 1968 Rosengren published a book called *The Literary System,* in which he introduced the co-mention approach to graphically display the frame of reference of fiction book reviewers (Rosengren 1966, 1968). In literary reviews of fiction books, he identified the most frequently mentioned authors and their co-occurrences. From these data he was able to draw a map with authors as nodes, while the distances between them were estimated using their co-occurrences (Persson, 2000).

In this chapter we will not discuss these other co-occurrence instances, except for co-linking. It should be mentioned though that formally (referring to the underlying mathematical structure), they have a lot in common with co-citations and bibliographic coupling.

MEASURING ASPECTS OF SOCIAL BEHAVIOR IN SCIENCE

Social ties are neither necessary for citation, as one may cite authors without knowing them personally, nor sufficient, as knowing someone is not reason enough to cite him or her (White, 2001). White, Wellman, and Nazer (2004) try to find an answer to the questions: "What drives citation? Is it primarily who citers know or what they know?" It is a question about social structure vs. intellectual structure. Using social network analysis techniques they studied the growth of intercitation over time of a group called "Globenet," a pseudonym for an international group of 16 researchers from seven disciplines. They found that co-citation is a powerful predictor of intercitation in journal articles, while being an editor or coauthor turned out to be an important predictor in the book to which all "Globenet" members contributed. The term 'intercitation' is used here as a general term referring to a member (or members) of a closed group citing one or more other members of this group. It was found that intellectual ties (shared content) were a better predictor than friendship. Yet, interciters communicated more than did non-interciters.

The above mentioned study is one of many that recently discussed the normative theory of citation vs. the theory that citations are a social construction (Moed & Garfield, 2004). The normative theory of citation claims that scientists give credit where credit is due, and this for purely scientific reasons. Proponents of the normative theory usually refer to the work of Robert K. Merton. Within the normative framework, citations can be used to trace intellectual and cognitive influence. This is an important hypothesis when applying citation analysis for information retrieval purposes or in research evaluation exercises. The constructive view takes the position that scientists cite to advance their own interest, convince others, and gain a dominant position in the scientific community (Moed & Garfield, 2004). Main proponents of this view are Gilbert (1977) and Cozzens (1989), who introduced the idea that referencing is mainly a rhetoric device to convince others of the value or truth of the claims put forward in an article. Baldi (1998) found that authors are likely to cite articles that are most relevant to their work in terms of intellectual content. In this respect they seem to be little concerned with the social characteristics of authors. In another study Moed

and Garfield (2004) found that in basic science, such as physics, astronomy, and molecular biology, the percentage of authoritative references decreased as bibliographies became shorter. The term "authoritative references" is defined here as references to papers that are already frequently cited. As scientists drop authoritative references more readily than other types, this implies that persuasion is not the major motivation to cite. Yet, this study also found that, certainly when reference lists become longer, they are diluted by citations to authoritative articles. It seems, however, that there is a circular reasoning in this argument, as authoritative articles are defined as frequently cited articles. We further note that the problem studied by Moed and Garfield has been recast in a model-theoretic framework (a power law) by Egghe, Rao, and Sahoo (2006).

The importance of social interaction among scientists was among the main topics covered by Cronin (2005) in his keynote address of the 10th International Conference of the International Society for Scientometrics and Informetrics (ISSI), at the Karolinska Institute, Sweden. How important are physical proximity and place in the construction of knowledge (and knowledge claims)? Is "to be where the action is" the reason why elite universities are 'elite' universities, and is the Web eroding this function (Kim, Morse, & Zingales, 2006)? Is the same true for scientific conferences? The topic of interaction between scientists leads us to the famous notion of an 'invisible college'.

Price (1963) adopted the old term 'invisible college' and gave it a new meaning as a group of elite scientists, mutually interacting to the advance of science. He used the term 'invisible college' to emphasize the informal pattern of interpersonal contact among such scientists. In a well-written and highly insightful article, Zuccala (2006a) addresses the invisible college concept, leading to a precision of Price's work. She proposes the following definition:

An invisible college is a set of interacting scholars or scientists who share similar research interests concerning a subject specialty, who often produce publications relevant to this subject and who communicate both formally and informally with one another to work towards important goals in the subject, even though they may belong to geographically distant research affiliates.

She links the study of invisible colleges to author co-citation analysis as developed by White and Griffith (1981). Maps resulting from an author co-citation analysis may then function as a roadmap for the scientist studying an invisible college. As members of an invisible college share common interests and often collaborate formally and informally, they can also be characterized by the saying 'birds of feather flock together' (Kretschmer, 1997; McPherson, Smith-Lovin, & Cook, 2001).

Although not a new feature (Garner, 1967), we see nonetheless that nowadays graph theory and network analysis techniques have become rather popular among scientists studying relations between journals (citing–cited) or research collaboration. Linking may occur between similar or between different concepts as in articles to articles (citing), scientists to scientists (collaboration), but also words to texts (a text is a collection of words), and persons to country (nationality: a country is a group of people with the same nationality). Recall that in traditional librarianship a library catalog links a book to the place number of a book, and hence to its shelf place in the library.

Examples of recent articles using techniques of social network analysis include: Giannakis and Croom (2001); Kretschmer (2004); Kretschmer, Kretschmer, and Kretschmer (2005); Liu and Wang (2005); White (2000); and Yin, Kretschmer, Hanneman, and Liu (2006). In relation to research evaluation, we remind the reader that outputs of technological and innovation research are in many cases not written up as such but appear as designs, applications, models, or know-how

(Jansz, 2000; Russell & Rousseau, 2002). We suggest that network analysis covering more than the traditional journal articles, for example, trade literature, may lead to a better understanding of the visibility and practical importance of such technological outputs.

Network analysis, as applied to citation studies, can be considered a structural approach. Structural approaches vs. frequency approaches is one axis along which Bollen, Van de Sompel, Smith, and Luce (2005) classify impact measures, the other axis being the difference between an author or a reader point of view.

Recently, Flom, Friedman, Strauss, and Neaigus (2004) introduced a new sociometric network measure, denoted as Q, for individual actors as well as for whole networks. This measure tries to capture the idea of bridges between two groups in a connected undirected network. The higher its value, the more this actor acts as a bridge between the two groups. This measure has been used to study collaboration links between England and Germany in the field of mechanics (Chen & Rousseau, in press).

One of the key authors in the application of network theory and multivariate statistics to citation analysis, scientific collaboration, and the Web is Loet Leydesdorff. In a series of articles (Leydesdorff, 2003, 2004a, 2004b, 2004c, 2006; Leydesdorff & Hellsten, 2005, 2006; Leydesdorff & Jin, 2005; Wagner & Leydesdorff, 2005), he investigated citation relations among journals using the Science Citation Index, the Social Science Citation Index, and a local Chinese database. Among many other aspects he studies the role of biconnected components in larger networks. We recall that a biconnected component of an undirected graph is a maximal set of edges such that for every triple of distinct vertices a, b, c, there exists a path from a to b, not containing c. The importance of biconnected components lies in the fact that they provide a robust definition of a cluster.

WEBOMETRICS

Generalities

The introduction of the World Wide Web led to an anticipation of major paradigmatic shifts in scientific communication. As a result the new subfield of Webometrics emerged. Webometrics is the name given to the innovative metric study of electronic communication by Almind and Ingwersen (1997). More precisely, Björneborn (2004; see also Björneborn & Ingwersen, 2001; Ingwersen & Björneborn, 2004) defines Webometrics as:

The study of the quantitative aspects of the construction and use of information resources, structures and technologies on the Web drawing on bibliometric and informetric approaches.

There are still numerous discussions on the validity of adapting traditional methods for the construction of production and citation data using electronic formats. One particular concern is the definition of what constitutes a valid publication on the Internet. The co-occurrence of the terms 'citation analysis' and 'Web' brings immediately Ingwersen's (1998) 'Web impact factor' to mind. What is the correct (or at least an acceptable) way of calculating Web impact factors and what is their validity in terms of measuring the impact of a particular Web space? One (loosely stated) definition of a Web impact factor is: the number of external inlinks divided by the number of pages found at the entity of which a Web impact factor is counted (typically this is a country or a university). It should be noted that impact factors for Web sites have also been proposed by Rodríguez i Gairín (1997).

The inlink degree of a node in a network is the number of inlinks, while the outlink degree is the number of outlinks. Authorities are Web nodes with a high inlink degree, while hubs are Web nodes with a high outlink degree. According to

Kleinberg (1999), hubs and authorities exhibit a mutually reinforcing relationship: a good hub will point to many authorities, and a good authority will be pointed at by many hubs. The 'hubs and authorities' approach is related to the Pinski-Narin influence weight citation measure (Pinski & Narin, 1976) and mimics the idea of 'highly cited documents' (authorities) and reviews (hubs). Trying to avoid the long scrolling list syndrome, link structure plays an important role in rankings obtained in Web information retrieval (see also Lempel & Moran, 2001). Clearly, from a graph-theoretic point of view, citation networks (author, article, journal) and Web networks are just special cases of the all-embracing mathematical term 'graph'.

Relations Between Citation Analysis and Web Links

How can we study references and relations from the Web to paper-based sources? Vaughan and Shaw (2003, 2005) were the first ones to make a full-scale investigation of this type of relation. They define Web citations as mentions of an article published in a paper-based source in a source on the Web. The term Web-to-print citation for this type of citation has been proposed by Van Impe and Rousseau (2006). Vaughan and Shaw propose an interesting classification of Web references in three categories, according to academic level:

- Research impact, similar to a classical reference;
- Other intellectual impact (reference in a syllabus, a popular science Web site, academic questions and answers, etc.); or
- Non-intellectual impact (reference in a table of contents, an online bibliography, an author's homepage, etc.).

Investigating journal articles in four scientific domains (biology, genetics, medicine, and multi-disciplinary sciences), Vaughan and Shaw found that about 30% of Web citations belonged to the first category. Clearly, the other categories are not negligible. Indeed, a citation in a syllabus or in course notes is important because it proves that the teacher thought the cited article to be of such value that it should be brought to the attention of future academics. Vaughan and Shaw (2005) discovered that, at least in the four domains studied by them, there exists a significant correlation between Web citation counts and classical citation counts. These four domains (biology, genetics, medicine, and multidisciplinary sciences) belong to the exact and medical sciences. If their findings could be confirmed in general (for other scientific domains, including the social sciences and the humanities), then the Vaughan-Shaw approach would, in particular, be very useful for citation studies in the humanities, where collecting classical (paper-based) citations is tedious. Web citation counts would then offer a relatively simple way to study the visibility of authors, articles, and journals in all, or at least many, humanities fields. A small-scale study by Van Impe and Rousseau (2006) in the fields of general history, history of the book and archaeology, and for articles written mainly in other languages than English (Dutch, French) was only moderately successful. Classical as well as Web-to-print citation scores were found to be too low to draw significant conclusions. The relation between citation analysis and Web link or Web popularity has also been investigated by Thelwall and Harries (2004).

Although Larson (1996), in one of the first Web-related studies, conducted an exploratory analysis of a co-linked set of Web sites related to geographic information systems, earth sciences, and satellite remote sensing, Web co-link analysis is nevertheless a relatively new technique. It is conceptually similar to co-citation analysis and bibliographic coupling studies. An improved HITS algorithm (Kleinberg, 1999) using the Web link structure has been proposed by Dean and Henzinger (1999). These algorithms make extensive use of the hubs and authorities concept.

Thelwall and Wilkinson (2004) found that using couplings and co-links led to improved recall, but not improved precision. Zuccala (2006b) compared a Web co-link analysis of mathematics institutes with an author co-citation analysis in the mathematical field of *singularity theory and its applications to wave propagation theory and dynamical systems*. She finds six motivations for linking between mathematical institutes:

- Social co-links occurring because some mathematics institutes have cooperative research programs;
- Navigational co-links, existing because several directories are listing the same groupings of mathematics institute homepages;
- Personal co-links: mathematicians have visited these institutes and present links on their homepage (in their institute) to show the places they have visited;
- Geographical co-links that have arisen because developers of Web pages are aware of the geographical closeness of some of the institutes;
- Historical co-links because some institutes have been operational for a lot longer than the other ones, thus are more recognized on the Web; and
- Prestige.

She concludes that the Web environment is much more complex than the publication environment, resulting in maps that are more difficult to interpret.

Björneborn (2004, 2005) studied what types of Web links, Web pages, and Web sites function as cross-topic connectors in small-world link structures across an academic Web space. In his investigations he found that the structure of the Web can better be compared to a corona, rather than a bow-tie, as suggested by Broder et al. (2000). Within the academic Web space, computer departments play a special role as connectors between other departments. In terms of social network indicators, this is expressed by the fact that they have a high betweenness centrality in the academic Web. In Kleinberg's (1999) terminology, this means that they often act as hubs and authorities.

After many years of experience, Thelwall (2006) notes that the enormous variety of genres on the Web makes applications of qualitative methodologies and pure logic problematic in large-scale Web studies. According to him, the Web is incapable of giving definitive answers to large-scale link analysis questions concerning social factors, such as those underlying link creations. He claims that a general theory of link analysis is not possible.

Notwithstanding the cautionary note mentioned above, Webometrics and cybermetrics are nowadays hot topics in the field of information science. For further information we refer the reader to Newman's (2003) review, offering a general framework for all types of networks; Ingwersen and Björneborn's (2005) article on Webometric methods; Thelwall, Vaughan, and Björneborn (2005) for a general review of the field; and Thelwall's (2004) book for a thorough introduction to Web link analysis.

FUTURE DEVELOPMENTS

In this section we briefly discuss some applications and features that might come to existence in the near future, or which we think are highly desirable, even though somewhat futuristic.

It is obvious that nowadays the monopoly position of Thomson Scientific is under attack by Google Scholar and Scopus (the Scopus Citation tracker), and other initiatives may follow soon. Moreover, more and more countries and regions are trying to start a local citation index (Jin & Wang, 1999; Wu et al., 2004).

Major changes to bibliographic and bibliometric methodologies are emerging with the increased presence of academic journals and other scholarly works on the Web. The enormous capability of the Web for storing and integrating information makes available unified (and hopefully, uniform) data sources for bibliometric analysis, accessible from any computer anywhere in the world. This could lead to the integration of local and regional citation indexes into a virtual world citation atlas (Russell & Rousseau, 2002).

A classical citation index informs the user when an article has been used, in which context, and by whom. The same information can be found on the Web by a technique called forward linking, the reverse of reference linking. Forward linking means that a published article is linked to the articles in which it is cited. Just as for classical citation indexes, it allows researchers to easily track the progression of a concept or discovery since its original publication (Steiner & Stanier, 2006). Forward linking can also be combined with citation recommender systems. These are systems that recommend which articles would be suitable for using, and hence referencing, in a research paper (McNee et al., 2002). The presence of every scholarly work ever written linked to every work it cites or is cited by in a universal Web-based bibliographic and citation database would solve many of the problems plaguing the construction of output and citation measures in a non-electronic environment.

The problem of the under-representation in international scientific databases of studies from developing and other countries written in non-English languages could eventually become a thing of the (non-electronic) past. Yet, it should be observed that also search engines and Web archives are biased in some ways (Thelwall & Vaughan; 20004; Vaughan & Thelwall, 2004). The prospect of on-the-spot translation of non-English articles on the Web (Stix, 2006) would lead to an increase in the visibility and citation levels of non-English-speaking scientists. Although this seems to be a far away dream, its realization would benefit many scientists in non-western countries. Online publishing ventures such as the establishment of global repositories for research would also increase the presence of studies from developing and other peripheral countries.

The fact that the Internet accentuates the value of individual pieces of information puts increasing emphasis on the individual article and rather less on the journal, a trend that could diminish the value given to journal impact factors in the short term and likely to cause their demise in the long term. Clustering articles on the Web by subject would allow these to be ranked according to their importance for different fields, a process that could also be used to identify inappropriate citations. Furthermore, with escalating networking in science, scientists will become increasingly aware of what their peers are doing. This could bring about a possible increase in the speed with which results are incorporated into the work of others thus reducing citation lags (Russell & Rousseau, 2002).

We also look forward to the opportunity for better accuracy in bibliometric data with the automatic softbot checking of bibliographic elements such as titles and authors directly from their original Web sources (Maes, 1994). We can also hope for greater access to the results of research from the social sciences and the humanities due to increased international presence through Web publishing (Van Impe & Rousseau, 2006).

Interesting for the active researcher would be a feature such as Liu and Maes' (2004) "What Would They Think" Web interface. In the application we have in mind, opinions of colleagues we hold in high esteem are modeled, so that we can access them when the real people are not available. In that way we could receive feedback on questions such as "What would X think if I approach the problem in this particular way?" We could even get an opinion from a group of people: "What would Y's research group think about this approach to research evaluation?"

Such opinions can be mined from introductory or discussion sections of articles, but also from talks made available on the Web, or even from scientific discussion lists.

Finally, we would like to mention that Q-measures have not yet been applied to citation studies, although they hold—in our opinion—a lot of promise.

FINAL REMARKS

In this article we focused on citation analysis as a tool for information retrieval and discussed some social implications of citation analysis. Relations with Web linking were highlighted. Scientists know that there are always new discoveries to be made, new questions to be asked, and thereby new areas for inquiry to be opened. This also holds for the field of informetrics and citation analysis as a subfield. As such we mentioned recent developments and tried to predict future developments.

Research evaluation may or may not use citation analysis techniques. For this reason not much emphasis is placed on it in our review. We refer the readers to the *Handbook of Quantitative Science and Technology Research* (Moed, Glänzel, & Schmoch, 2004). This handbook also deals with another aspect not covered in our article, namely the use of patent citations (e.g., Narin, Breitzman, & Thomas, 2004; Tijssen, Buter, & van Leeuwen, 2000).

Hundreds of articles have been published related to citation analysis. This contribution is not meant to give a complete picture, but just reflects our own view on the field. In particular, we did not cover any case studies. Surely many colleagues will feel that their work is unjustly overlooked. Our only excuse is that the reference list already contains more than 100 items.

ACKNOWLEDGMENT

The author thanks Jin Bihui and the editors of this book for helpful comments on a first draft of this article.

REFERENCES

Almind, T.C., & Ingwersen, P. (1997). Informetric analysis on the World Wide Web: Methodological approaches to Webometrics. *Journal of Documentation, 53,* 404-426.

Atkins, H. (1999). The ISI Web of science—links and electronic journals. *D-Lib Magazine, 5*(9). Retrieved January 23, 2007, from *http://www.dlib. org/dlib/september99/atkins/09atkins.html*

Baldi, S. (1998). Normative versus social constructivist processes in the allocation of citations: A network-analytic model. *American Sociological Review, 63,* 829-846.

Bayer, A.E., Smart, J.C., & McLaughlin, G.W. (1990). Mapping intellectual structure of a scientific subfield through author cocitations. *Journal of the American Society for Information Science, 41,* 444-452.

Björneborn, L. (2004). *Small-world link structures across an academic Web space: A library and information science approach.* Unpublished Doctoral Dissertation, Royal School of Library and Information Science, Denmark.

Björneborn, L. (2005). Identifying small-world connectors across an academic Web space—a Webometric study. In P. Ingwersen & B. Larsen (Eds.), *Proceedings of ISSI 2005* (pp. 55-66). Stockholm: Karolinska University Press.

Björneborn, L., & Ingwersen, P. (2001). Perspectives of Webometrics. *Scientometrics, 50,* 65-82.

Bollen, J., Van de Sompel, H., Smith, J.A., & Luce, R. (2005). Toward alternative metrics of journal impact: A comparison of download and citation data. *Information Processing & Management, 41,* 1419-1440.

Borgman, C.L., & Furner, J. (2002). Scholarly communication and bibliometrics. In B. Cronin (Ed.), *Annual review of information science and technology (vol. 36,* pp. 3-72). Medford, NJ: Information Today.

Bosc, H., & Harnad, S. (2005). In a paperless world a new role for academic libraries: Providing open access. *Learned Publishing, 18,* 95-99.

Boyack, K.W., Klavans, R., & Borner, K. (2005). Mapping the backbone of science. *Scientometrics, 64,* 351-374.

Braam, R.R., Moed, H.F., & van Raan, A.F.J. (1991a). Mapping of science by combined cocitation and word analysis. I: Structural aspects. *Journal of the American Society for Information Science, 42,* 233-251.

Braam, R.R., Moed, H.F., & van Raan, A.F.J. (1991b). Mapping of science by combined cocitation and word analysis. II: Dynamical aspects. *Journal of the American Society for Information Science, 42,* 252-266.

Broder, A., Kumar, R., Maghoul, F., Raghavan, P., Rajagopalan, S., Stata, R., Tomkins, A., & Wiener, J. (2000). Graph structure in the Web. *Computer Networks, 33,* 309-320.

Brody, T., Harnad, S., & Carr, L. (2006). Earlier Web usage statistics as predictors of later citation impact. *Journal of the American Society for Information Science and Technology, 57,* 1060-1072.

Brody, T., Kampa, S., Harnad, S., Carr, L., & Hitchock, S. (2003). Digitometric services for open archives environments. In T. Troch & I.T. Sølvberg (Eds.), *Research and advanced technology for digital libraries* (pp. 207-220). Berlin: Springer-Verlag (LNCS 2769).

Chen, C. (1999a). *Information visualisation and virtual environments.* London: Springer.

Chen, C. (1999b). Visualising semantic spaces and author co-citation networks in digital libraries. *Information Processing and Management, 35,* 401-420.

Chen, C., & Paul, R.J. (2001). Visualizing a knowledge domain's intellectual structure. *Computer, 34*(3), 65-71.

Chen, L., & Rousseau, R. (in press). Q-measures for binary divided networks: Bridges between German and English institutes in publications of the *Journal of Fluid Mechanics. Scientometrics.*

Cozzens, S. (1989). What do citations count? The rhetoric-first model. *Scientometrics, 15,* 437-447.

Cronin, B. (2005). Warm bodies, cold facts: The embodiment and emplacement of knowledge claims. In P. Ingwersen & B. Larsen (Eds.), *Proceedings of ISSI 2005* (pp. 1-12). Stockholm: Karolinska University Press.

Dean, J., & Henzinger, M.R. (1999). Finding related pages in the World Wide Web. *Computer Networks, 31,* 1467-1479.

Ding, Y., Chowdhury, G., & Foo, S. (2000). Journal as markers of intellectual space: Journal co-citation analysis of information retrieval area, 1987-1997. *Scientometrics, 47,* 55-73.

Egghe, L., Rao, Ravichandra I.K., & Sahoo, B.B. (2006). Proof of a conjecture of Moed and Garfield on authoritative references and extension to non-authoritative references. *Scientometrics, 66,* 537-549.

Egghe, L., & Rousseau, R. (1990). *Introduction to informetrics. Quantitative methods in library, documentation and information science.* Amsterdam: Elsevier.

Egghe, L., & Rousseau, R. (2002). Co-citation, bibliographic coupling and a characterization of lattice citation networks. *Scientometrics, 55,* 349-361.

Flom, P.L., Friedman, S.R., Strauss, S., & Neaigus, A. (2004). A new measure of linkage between two sub-networks. *Connections, 26*(1), 62-70.

Frandsen, T.F., & Rousseau, R. (2005). Article impact calculated over arbitrary periods. *Journal of the American Society for Information Science and Technology, 56,* 58-62.

Garfield, E. (1988). Announcing the SCI compact disc edition: CD-ROM gigabyte storage technology, novel software, and bibliographic coupling make desktop research and discovery a reality. *Current Contents, 22*(May 30).

Garner, R. (1967). A computer oriented graph theoretic analysis of citation index structures. In B. Flood (ed.), *Three Drexel information science studies* (pp. 1-46). Philadelphia, Drexel Institute of Technology.

Giannakis, M., & Croom, S. (2001). The intellectual structure of supply chain management: An application of the social network analysis and citation analysis to SCM related journals. *Proceedings of the 10th International Annual IPSERA Conference,* Jönköping, Sweden.

Gilbert, G.N. (1977). Referencing as persuasion. *Social Studies of Science, 7,* 113-122.

Ingwersen, P. (1998). The calculation of Web impact factors. *Journal of Documentation, 54,* 236-243.

Ingwersen, P., & Björneborn, L. (2005). Methodological issues of Webometric studies. In

H.F. Moed, W. Glänzel, & U. Schmoch (Eds.), *Handbook of quantitative science and technology research* (pp. 339-369). Dordrecht: Kluwer.

Jansz, C.N.M. (2000). Some thoughts on the interaction between scientometrics and science and technology policy. *Scientometrics, 47,* 253-264.

Jin, B.H., & Wang, B. (1999). Chinese Science Citation Database: Its construction and application. *Scientometrics, 45,* 325-332.

Kessler, M.M. (1962). *An experimental study of bibliographic coupling between technical papers.* Report, Lincoln Laboratory, Massachusetts Institute of Technology, USA.

Kessler, M.M. (1963). Bibliographic coupling between scientific papers. *American Documentation, 14,* 10-25.

Kim, E.H., Morse, A., & Zingales, L. (2006). *Are elite universities losing their competitive edge?* NBER Working Paper Series 12245.

Kleinberg, J.M. (1999). Authoritative sources in a hyperlinked environment. *Journal of the ACM, 46*(5), 604-632.

Kretschmer, H. (1997). Patterns of behaviour in co-authorship networks of invisible colleges. *Scientometrics, 40,* 579-591.

Kretschmer, H. (2004). Author productivity and geodesic distance in co-authorship networks, and visibility on the Web. *Scientometrics, 60,* 409-420.

Kretschmer, H., Kretschmer, U., & Kretschmer, T. (2005). Visibility of collaboration between immunology institutions on the Web including aspects of gender studies. In P. Ingwersen & B. Larsen (Eds.), *Proceedings of ISSI 2005* (pp. 750-760). Stockholm: Karolinska University Press.

Kreuzman, H. (2001). A co-citation analysis of representative authors in philosophy: Examin-

ing the relationship between epistemologists and philosophers of science. *Scientometrics, 51,* 525-539.

Larson, R.R. (1996). Bibliometrics of the World Wide Web: An exploratory analysis of the intellectual structure of cyberspace. In S. Hardin (Ed.), *Global complexity: Information, chaos and control. Proceedings of the 59th Annual Meeting of the ASIS.* Retrieved January 23, 2007, from *http://sherlock.berkeley.edu/asis96/asis96.html*

Lempel, R., & Moran, S. (2001). SALSA: The stochastic approach for link-structure analysis. *ACM Transactions on Information Systems, 19,* 131-160.

Leydesdorff, L. (2003). Can networks of journal-journal citations be used as indicators of change in the social sciences? *Journal of Documentation, 59,* 84-104.

Leydesdorff, L. (2004a). Clusters and maps of science journals on bi-connected graphs in the Journal Citation Reports. *Journal of Documentation, 60,* 371-427.

Leydesdorff, L. (2004b). Top-down decomposition of the *Journal Citation Report* of the *Social Science Citation Index*: Graph- and factor-analytical approaches. *Scientometrics, 60,* 159-180.

Leydesdorff, L. (2004c). The university-industry knowledge relationship: Analyzing patents and the science base of technologies. *Journal of the American Society for Information Science and Technology, 55,* 991-1001.

Leydesdorff, L. (2006). Can scientific journals be classified in terms of aggregated journal-journal citation relations using the *Journal Citation Reports? Journal of the American Society for Information Science and Technology, 57,* 601-613.

Leydesdorff, L., & Hellsten, I. (2005). Metaphors and diaphors in science communication: Mapping the case of stem-cell research. *Science Communication, 27,* 64-99.

Leydesdorff, L., & Hellsten, I. (2006). Measuring the meaning of words in contexts: An automated analysis of controversies about 'Monarch butterflies', 'Frankenfoods', and 'stem cells'. *Scientometrics, 67,* 231-258.

Leydesdorff, L., & Jin, B.H. (2005). Mapping the Chinese Science Citation Database in terms of aggregated journal-journal citation relations. *Journal of the American Society for Information Science and Technology, 56,* 1469-1479.

Lin, Y., & Kaid, L.L. (2000). Fragmentation of the intellectual structure of political communication study: Some empirical evidence. *Scientometrics, 47,* 143-164.

Liu, H., & Maes, P. (2004). What would they think? A computational model of attitudes. *Proceedings of the 9th International Conference on Intelligent User Interface* (IUI), Funchal, Portugal.

Liu, Z., & Wang, C.Z. (2005). Mapping interdisciplinarity in demography: A journal network analysis. *Journal of the American Society for Information Science and Technology, 31,* 308-316.

Maes, P. (1994). Agents that reduce work and information overload. Communications of the ACM, 37(7), 30-40.

Marion, L.S., & McCain, K.W. (2001). Contrasting views of software engineering journals: Author cocitation choices and indexer vocabulary assignments. *Journal of the American Society for Information Science and Technology, 52,* 297-308.

Marshakova, I.V.(1973). System of document connections based on references (in Russian). *Nauchno-Tekhnicheskaya Informatsiya, 2*(6), 3-8.

McCain, K.W. (1990). Mapping authors in intellectual space: A technical overview. *Journal of*

the American Society for Information Science, *41,* 433-443.

McCain, K.W. (1991). Mapping economics through the journal literature: An experiment in journal cocitation analysis. *Journal of the American Society for Information Science, 42,* 290-296.

McCain, K.W. (1995). The structure of biotechnology R&D. *Scientometrics, 32,* 153-175.

McNee, S.M., Albert, I., Cosley, D., Gopalkrishnan, P., Lam, S.K., Rashid, Konstan, J.A, & Riedl, J. (2002). On the recommending of citations for research papers. *Proceedings of CSCW'02* (pp. 116-125), New Orleans, LA.

McPherson, M., Smith-Lovin, L., & Cook, J.M. (2001). Birds of a feather: Homophily in social networks. *Annual Review of Sociology, 27,* 415-444.

Moed, H.F. (2005). *Citation analysis in research evaluation.* Dordrecht: Springer.

Moed, H.F., & Garfield, E. (2004). In basic science the percentage of 'authoritative' references decreases as bibliographies become shorter. *Scientometrics, 60,* 295-303.

Moed, H.F., Glänzel, W., & Schmoch, U. (Eds.). (2004). *Handbook of quantitative science and technology research. The use of publication and patent statistics in studies of S&T studies.* Dordrecht: Kluwer.

Narin, F., Breitzman, A., & Thomas, P. (2004). Using patent citation indicators to manage a stock portfolio. In H.F. Moed, W. Glänzel, & U. Schmoch (Eds.), *Handbook of quantitative science and technology research* (pp. 553-568). Dordrecht: Kluwer.

Newman, M.E.J. (2003). The structure and function of complex networks. *SIAM Review, 45,* 167-256.

Persson. O. (2000). The literature climate of Umeå—mapping public library loans. *Bibliometric Notes, 4*(5). Retrieved January 23, 2007, from *http://www.umu.se/inforsk/Bibliometric-Notes/BN5-2000/BN5-2000.htm*

Persson, O. (2001). All author citations versus first author citations. *Scientometrics, 50,* 339-344.

Pinski, G., & Narin, F. (1976).Citation influences for journal aggregates of scientific publications: Theory, with applications to the literature of physics. *Information Processing and Management, 12,* 297-312.

Price, D.J. de Solla (1963). *Little science, big science.* New York: Columbia University Press.

Reader, D.M. (2001). The intellectual structure of entrepreneurship: An author co-citation analysis. In M. Davis & C.S. Wilson (Eds.), *Proceedings of the 8th International Conference on Scientometrics & Informetrics* (pp. 587-596). Sydney: BIRG.

Rodríguez i Gairín, J.M. (1997). Valorando el impacto de la información en Internet: AltaVista, el 'Citation Index' de la Red. *Revista Espanola de Documentacion Scientifica, 20,* 175-181.

Rosengren, K.E. (1966). *The literary system.* Unpublished Licentiate Thesis in Sociology, University of Lund, Sweden.

Rosengren, K.E. (1968). *Sociological aspects of the literary system.* Stockholm: Natur och Kultur.

Rousseau, R., & Small, H. (2005). Escher staircases dwarfed. *ISSI Newsletter, 1*(4), 8-10.

Rousseau, R., & Thelwall, M. (2004). Escher staircases on the World Wide Web. *FirstMonday, 9*(6). Retrieved January 23, 2007, from *http://www. firstmonday.org/issues/issue9_6/rousseau/index. html*

Rousseau, R., & Zuccala, A. (2004). A classification of author co-citations: Definitions and search strategies. *Journal of the American Society of Information Science and Technology, 55,* 513-529.

Russell, J.M., & Rousseau, R. (2002). Bibliometrics and institutional evaluation. In R. Arvantis (Ed.), *Encyclopedia of life support systems (EOLSS). Part 19.3: Science and technology policy.* Oxford, UK: EOLSS.

Schneider, J.W. (2005). Naming clusters in visualization studies: Parsing and filtering of noun phrases from citation contexts. In P. Ingwersen & B. Larsen (Eds.), *Proceedings of ISSI 2005* (pp. 406-416). Stockholm: Karolinska University Press.

Sen, S.K., & Gan, S.K. (1983). A mathematical extension of the idea of bibliographic coupling and its applications. *Annals of Library Science and Documentation, 30,* 78-82.

Small, H. (1973). Co-citation in the scientific literature: A new measure of the relationship between two documents. *Journal of the American Society for Information Science, 24,* 265-269.

Steiner, U., & Stanier, C. (2006). Soft matter: The essential ingredient for success. *Soft Matter, 2,* 9-11.

Stix, G. (2006). The elusive goal of machine translation. *Scientific American, 294*(3), 70-73.

Thelwall. M. (2004). *Link analysis: An information science approach.* Amsterdam: Elsevier.

Thelwall, M. (2006). Interpreting social science link analysis research: A theoretical framework. *Journal of the American Society for Information Science and Technology, 57,* 60-68.

Thelwall, M., & Harries, G. (2004). Do the Web sites of higher rated scholars have significantly more online impact? *Journal of the American Society for Information Science and Technology, 55,* 149-159.

Thelwall, M., & Vaughan, M. (2004). A fair history of the Web? Examining country balance in the Internet Archive. *Library & Information Science Research, 26,* 162-176.

Thelwall, M., Vaughan, L., & Björneborn, L. (2005). Webometrics. *Annual Review of Information Science and Technology, 39,* 81-135.

Thelwall, M., & Wilkinson, D. (2004). Finding similar academic Web sites with links, bibliometric coupling and colinks. *Information Processing and Management, 40,* 515-526.

Tijssen, R., Buter, R.K., & van Leeuwen, Th.N. (2000). Technological relevance of science: An assessment of citation linkages between patents and research papers. *Scientometrics, 47,* 389-412.

Van Impe, S., & Rousseau, R. (2006). Web-to-print citations and the humanities. *Information - Wissenschaft und Praxis, 57,* 422- 426.

Vaughan, L., & Shaw, D. (2003). Bibliographic and Web citations: What is the difference? *Journal of the American Society for Information Science and Technology, 54,* 1313-1322.

Vaughan, L., & Shaw, D. (2005). Web citation data for impact assessment: A comparison of four science disciplines. *Journal of the American Society for Information Science and Technology, 56,* 1075-1087.

Vaughan, L., & Thelwall, M. (2004). Search engine coverage bias: Evidence and possible causes. *Information Processing and Management, 40,* 693-707.

Wagner, C.S., & Leydesdorff, L. (2005). Network structure, self-organization, and the growth of international collaboration in science. *Research Policy, 34,* 1608-1618.

White, H.D. (2000). Toward ego-centered citation analysis. In B. Cronin & H.B. Atkins (Eds.), *The Web of knowledge; a festschrift in honor of Eugene Garfield* (pp. 475-496). Medford, NJ: Information Today.

White, H.D. (2001). Authors as citers over time. *Journal of the American Society for Information Science and Technology, 52,* 87-108.

White, H.D. (2003). Pathfinder networks and author cocitation analysis: A remapping of paradigmatic information scientists. *Journal of the American Society for Information Science and Technology, 54,* 423-434.

White, H.D., & Griffith, B. (1981). Author cocitation: A literature measure of intellectual structure. *Journal of the American Society for Information Science, 32,* 163-171.

White, H.D., & McCain, K. (1998). Visualizing a discipline: An author cocitation analysis of information science, 1972-1995. *Journal of the American Society for Information Science, 49,* 327-355.

White, H.D., Wellman, B., & Nazer, N. (2004). Does citation reflect social structure? Longitudinal evidence from the "Globenet" interdisciplinary research group. *Journal of the American Society for Information Science and Technology, 55,* 111-126.

Wilson, C.S. (1999). Informetrics. *Annual Review of Information Science and Technology, 34,* 107-247.

Wu, Y., Pan, Y., Zhang, Y., Ma, Z., Pang, J., Guo, H., Xu, B., & Yang, Z. (2004). China Scientific and Technical Papers and Citations (CSTPC): History, impact and outlook. *Scientometrics, 60,* 385-394.

Yin, L.C., Kretschmer, H., Hanneman, R.A., & Liu, Z.Y. (2006). Connection and stratification in research collaboration: An analysis of the COLLNET network. *Information Processing & Management, 42,* 1599-1613.

Zuccala, A. (2006a). Modeling the invisible college. *Journal of the American Society for Information Science and Technology, 57,* 152-168.

Zuccala, A. (2006b). Author cocitation analysis is to intellectual structure as Web cocitation analysis is to...? *Journal of the American Society for Information Science and Technology, 57,* 1486-1501.

Section VI
Applications and Case Studies in Social Information Retrieval

Chapter XIV
Personalized Information Retrieval in a Semantic-based Learning Environment

Antonella Carbonaro
University of Bologna, Italy

Rodolfo Ferrini
University of Bologna, Italy

ABSTRACT

Active learning is the ability of learners to carry out learning activities in such a way that they will be able to effectively and efficiently construct knowledge from information sources. Personalized and customizable access on digital materials collected from the Web according to one's own personal requirements and interests is an example of active learning. Moreover, it is also necessary to provide techniques to locate suitable materials. In this chapter, we introduce a personalized learning environment providing intelligent support to achieve the expectations of active learning. The system exploits collaborative and semantic approaches to extract concepts from documents, and maintaining user and resources profiles based on domain ontologies. In such a way, the retrieval phase takes advantage of the common knowledge base used to extract useful knowledge and produces personalized views of the learning system.

INTRODUCTION

Most of the modern applications of computing technology and information systems are concerned with information-rich environments, the modern, open, large-scale environments with autonomous heterogeneous information resources (Huhns & Singh, 1998; Cooley, Mobasher, & Srivastava, 1997). The effective and efficient management of the large amounts and varieties of information they include is the key to the above applications.

The Web inherits most of the typical characteristic of an information-rich environment: information resources can be added or removed in a loosely structured manner, and it lacks global control of the content accuracy of those resources. Furthermore, it includes heterogeneous components with mutual complex interdependencies; it includes not just text and relational data, but varieties of multimedia, forms, and executable code. As a result, old methods for manipulating information sources are no longer efficient or even appropriate. Mechanisms are needed in order to allow efficient querying and retrieving on a great variety of information sources which support structured as well as unstructured information.

In order to foster the development of Web-based information access and management, it is relevant to be able to obtain a user-based view of available information. The exponential increase of the size and the formats of remotely accessible data allows us to find suitable solutions to the problem. Often, information access tools are not able to provide the right answers for a user query, but rather, they provide large supersets thereof (e.g., in Web search engines). The search for documents uses queries containing words or describing concepts that are desired in the returned documents. Most content retrieval methodologies use some type of similarity score to match a query describing the content, and then they present the user with a ranked list of suggestions (Belkin & Croft, 1992). Designing applications for supporting the user in accessing and retrieving Web information sources is one of the current challenges for the artificial intelligence community.

In a distributed learning environment, there is likely to be large number of educational resources (Web pages, lectures, journal papers, learning objects, etc.) stored in many distributed and differing repositories on the Internet. Without any guidance, students will probably have great difficulty finding the reading material that is relevant for a particular learning task. The metadata descriptions concerning a learning object (LO) representation provide information about properties of the learning objects. However, the sole metadata does not provide qualitative information about different objects nor provide information for customized views. This problem is becoming particularly important in Web-based education where the variety of learners taking the same course is much greater. In contrast, the courses produced using adaptive hypermedia or intelligent tutoring system technologies are able to dynamically select the most relevant learning material from their knowledge bases for each individual student. Nevertheless, generally these systems cannot directly benefit from existing repositories of learning material (Brusilovsky & Nijhavan, 2002).

In educational settings learning objects can be of different kinds, from being files having static content (like HTML, PDF, or PowerPoint presentation format) or in sophisticated interactive format (like HTML pages loaded with JavaScript or Java applet, etc.). Audio files, video clips, or Flash animations could also constitute learning objects. An LO comprises a chunk of content material, which can be re-used or shared in different learning situations. Such a re-use of content from one system to another makes LO standardized so that it can be adopted across different computer platforms and learning systems. The IEEE Standard for Learning Object Metadata (LOM)[1] is the first accredited standard for learning object technology.[2]

Presently there are countless LOs available for commercial and academic use. Because of time and capability constraints, however, it is almost impossible both for a learner and a teacher to go through all available LOs to find the most suitable one. In particular, learning object metadata tags may facilitate rapid updating, searching, and management of content by filtering and selecting only the relevant content for a given purpose (Carbonaro, 2004). Searchers can use a standard set of retrieval techniques to maximize their chances of finding the resources via a search engine (Recker,

Walker, & Lawless, 2003). Nevertheless, the value searching and browsing results depend on the information and organizational structure of the repository. Moreover, searching for LOs within heterogeneous repositories may become a more complicated problem. What we are arguing in this chapter is that one can alleviate such difficulties by using suitable representations of both available information sources and a user's interests in order to match as appropriately as possible user information needs, as expressed in his or her query and in any available information. The representation we propose is based on ontologies representing the learning domain by means of its concepts, the possible relations between them and other properties, the conditions, or regulations of the domain. In the digital library community, a flat list of attribute/value pairs is often assumed to be available. In the Semantic Web community, annotations are often assumed to be an instance of an ontology. Through the ontologies the system will express hierarchical links among entities and will guarantee interoperability of educational resources. Recent researches on ontologies have shown the important role they can play in the e-learning domain (Dzbor, Motta, & Stutt, 2005).

In this context, standard keyword search is of very limited effectiveness. For example, it does not allow users and the system to search, handle, or read concepts of interest, and it does not consider synonymy and hyponymy that could reveal hidden similarities potentially leading to better retrieval. The advantages of a concept-based document and user representations can be summarized as follows: (i) ambiguous terms inside a resource are disambiguated, allowing their correct interpretation and, consequently, a better precision in the user model construction (e.g., if a user is interested in computer science resources, a document containing the word 'bank' as it is meant in the financial context could not be relevant); (ii) synonymous words belonging to the same meaning can contribute to the resource model definition (for example, both 'mouse' and

'display' bring evidence for computer science documents, improving the coverage of the document retrieval); (iii) synonymous words belonging to the same meaning can contribute to the user model matching, which is required in recommendation process (for example, if two users have the same interests, but these are expressed using different terms, they will considered overlapping); and (iv) classification, recommendation, and sharing phases take advantage of the word senses in order to classify, retrieve, and suggest documents with high semantic relevance with respect to the user and resource models.

For example, the system could support computer science last-year students during their activities in courseware like bio computing, internet programming, or machine learning. In fact, for these kinds of courses, it is necessary to have the active involvement of the student in the acquisition of the didactical material that should integrate the lecture notes specified and released by the teacher. Basically, the level of integration depends both on the student's prior knowledge in that particular subject and on the comprehension level he wants to acquire. Furthermore, for the mentioned courses, it is necessary to continuously update the acquired knowledge by integrating recent information available from any remote digital library.

The rest of the chapter is organized as follows. The next section describes background and literature review proposing significant examples of semantic-based e-learning systems. We then illustrate our personalized learning retrieval framework detailing proposed system requirements and architecture. We propose a concept-based semantic approach to model resource and user profiles providing word sense disambiguation process and resource representation, and provide some notes about test implementation and experimental sessions. Some final considerations and comments about future developments conclude the chapter.

BACKGROUND AND LITERATURE REVIEW

The research on e-learning and Web-based educational systems traditionally combines research interests and efforts from various fields, in order to tailor the growing amount of information to the needs, goals, and tasks of the specific individual users. Semantic Web technologies may achieve improved adaptation and flexibility for users, and new methods and types of courseware which will be compliant with the semantic Web vision. In the following sections we will describe some examples of existing projects thanks to which we will be able to outline what the current research on these fields offers. They are based on ontologies and standards that have an important role in the representation of LOs. Heflin (2004) defined an ontology as a structure in which defined terms are used to describe and represent an area of knowledge. Moreover, ontologies include computer-usable definitions of basic concepts in the domain and the relationships among them. Ontologies could be used to share domain information in order to make that knowledge reusable. The W3C standard language for ontology creation is OWL. More detailed review on ontology-based applications in education can be found in Kanellopoulos, Kotsiantis, and Pintelas (2006).

Edutella

Edutella (*http://edutella.jxta.org/*) is defined as a multi-staged effort to scope, specify, architect, and implement an RDF-based[3] metadata infrastructure for P2P-networks for exchanging information about learning objects. Edutella P2P architecture is essentially based on JXTA and RDF. JXTA (*http://www.jxta.org/*) is an open source technology that provides a set of XML-based protocols supporting different kinds of P2P applications.

According to Mendes and Sacks (2004), three types of services that a peer can offer are defined in an Edutella network:

- **Edutella query service:** This is the basic service in the framework. It presents a common, RDF-based query interface (the Query Exchange Language–RDF-QEL) for metadata providing and consuming through the Edutella network.
- **Edutella replication:** This provides replication of data within additional peers to ensure data persistence
- **Edutella mapping, mediation, clustering:** This kind of service manages metadata allowing semantic functionality of the global infrastructure.

An important point to underline is that Edutella does not share resource content but only metadata.

Smart Space for Learning

Smart Space for Learning is the result of the Elena project work (*http://www.elena-project. org*). According to Stojanovic, Stojanovic, and Volz (2002), a Smart Space for Learning can be defined as a set of service mediators which support the personalized consumption of heterogeneous educational services provided by different management systems. Learning services are entities designed to satisfy a specific purpose (e.g., the delivery of a course). They may use resources as learning objects (e.g., exercises and exams) and Web services to interface the formers with learners. WSDL and WSDL-S are languages to syntactically and semantically describe a Web service.

The system architecture of a Smart Space for Learning is essentially composed of two building blocks: an Edutella network and a set of ontologies. In a Smart Space for Learning, providers of learning services are connected to a learning management system that is based on Edutella. Ontology has to describe the learning domains using concepts and relations that may be referred to in the annotations of the learning services.

HyCo

HyCo (García, Berlanga, Moreno, García, & Carabias, 2004) stands for Hypermedia Composer; it is a multiplatform tool that supports the creation of learning materials. HyCo is the result of the development of an authoring tool created in order to define ALDs.

According to Berlanga and García (2005), ALDs are learning units that contain personalized behavior in order to provide each student with a learning flow which is to be adequate to his or her characteristics. ALDs are semantically structured in order to allow reusability.

The last version of HyCo also manages a kind of resource named SLO. An SLO is a learning object compliant with IMS metadata (*http://www.imsglobal.org/metadata/index. cfm*). Every resource created with HyCo is turned into an SLO. Whenever the conversion process is finished, an XML file is generated for the new SLO and stored in a repository.

Magpie

Magpie (*http://kmi.open.ac.uk/projects/magpie/*) provides automatic access to complementary Web sources of knowledge by associating a semantic layer to a Web page. This layer depends on one of a number of ontologies, which the user can select. When an ontology is selected, the user can also decide which classes are to be highlighted on the Web page. Clicking on an instance of a class from the selected ontology gives access to a number of semantic services. Magpie is proposed in a learning context to help students of a course in climate science understand the subject. The provided semantic services are integrated into the browsing navigation both in active and passive user involvement.

Ontology Mapping

The *ontology space* holds all the ontologies used by the system. The distributed nature of ontology development has led to a large number of different ontologies covering the same or overlapping domains. In this scenario it is possible that a particular sub-domain can be modeled by using different ontologies and, in general, if the ontology space contains n elements, the same sub-domain can be modeled n times, one for each ontology maintained by the system. This could be very useful in ontology mapping. *Ontology mapping* is the process whereby two ontologies are semantically related at the conceptual level, and the source ontology instances are transformed into the target ontology entities according to those semantic relations. Ontology mapping though is not an easy task; it has been widely treated in literature, and some crucial problems are listed below:

1. **The lack of a universally recognized standard for ontology:** On the Web a number of ontologies are available, but they are developed using different languages.
2. **The difficulty of commonly modeling the knowledge domain:** Different developers could have different visions of the domain, and they could give most weight to some aspect rather than other one.
3. **The granularity of the domain to be represented may be different in different communities:** Different communities may have overlapping sub-domains, but concepts and relations could have been developed with a different granularity.

While the first point represents a technical problem, the last two are related to the physical ontology design and development. In particular, the second case represents a fixed domain in which different developers produce different ontologies, while the third case refers to different communities having the same domain but with a different perspective of the involved semantics.

In the literature, one can distinguish three different approaches for ontology mapping. For each of them we propose an example application:

Automatic Mapping

- **MAFRA** (Maedche, Motik, Silva, & Volz, 2002) aims to automatically detect similarities between entities belonging to source and target ontologies. The overall process is composed of five steps. First, data are normalized; second, similarity between entities are calculated according to a previously proposed algorithm, then the mapping is obtained through the semantic bridging phase, and finally transformation of instances and checking of the achieved results are executed.
- **IF-Map** (Kalfoglou, 2003) is a semi-automatic method for ontology mapping. The authors make the assumption that if two communities want to share their knowledge, they must refer their local ontologies to a reference ontology. The overall process is obtained by composing the following four major steps: ontology harvesting, in which ontologies are acquired; translation, as the IF-Map method is specified in Horn logic, the data are translated in prolog clauses; IF-Map, the main mapping mechanism; and, finally, the display result step.

Manual Mapping

- **SKOS** (SKOS Core Vocabulary specification, *http://www.w3.org/TR/swbp-skos-core-spec/ 2005*; SKOS Mapping Vocabulary specification, *http://www.w3.org/2004/02/skos/ mapping/spec/ 2005*) is a group of RDF-based vocabularies developed to support the interoperability between different types of knowledge organization

systems. In particular, SKOS consists of three RDF vocabularies:

- *SKOS Core:* Provides a model for expressing contents and structures of different kind of concept schemas.
- *SKOS Mapping:* Provides vocabularies for describing mappings between concept schemas.
- *SKOS Extension:* Contains extensions to the SKOS Core useful for specialized applications.

For example one could use SKOS Core to translate knowledge structures like taxonomies or thesauri into a common format, and subsequently he can create a mapping between them by using SKOS Mapping.

Semi-Automatic Mapping

As an example of semi-automatic tool for ontology mapping, we would like to illustrate the one proposed in Ehrig and Sure (2004). The implemented approach is based on manually encoded mapping rules. The rules are then combined to achieve better mapping results compared to one obtained using only one at a time. In order to learn how to combine the methods, both manual and automatic approaches are introduced.

PERSONALIZED LEARNING RETRIEVAL FRAMEWORK

System Requirements

Traditional approaches to personalization include both content-based and user-based techniques (Dai & Mobasher, 2004). If, on one hand, a content-based approach allows the definition and maintenance of an accurate user profile (for example, the user may provide the system with a list of keywords reflecting his or her initial interests, and the profiles could be stored in form of weighted keyword vectors and updated on the basis of explicit relevance feedback), which is particularly valuable whenever a user encounters new content, on the other hand it has the limitation of concerning only the significant features describing the content of an item. Differently, in a user-based approach, resources are processed according to the rating of other users of the system with similar interests. Since there is no analysis of the item content, these information management techniques can deal with any kind of item, being not just limited to textual content. In such a way, users can receive items with content that are different from those received in the past. On the other hand, since a user-based technique works well if several users evaluate each item, new items cannot be handled until some users have taken the time to evaluate them, and new users cannot receive references until the system has acquired some information about the new user in order to make personalized predictions. These limitations are often referred to as sparsity and start-up problems (Melville et al., 2002). By adopting a hybrid approach, a personalization system is able to effectively filter relevant resources from a wide heterogeneous environment like the Web, taking advantage of common interests of the users and also maintaining the benefits provided by content analysis.

A hybrid approach maintains another drawback: the difficulty of capturing semantic knowledge of the application domain—that is, concepts, relationships among different concepts, inherent properties associated with the concepts, axioms or other rules, and so forth.

A semantic-based approach to retrieving relevant LOs can be useful to address issues like trying to determine the type or the quality of the information suggested from a personalized learning environment. In this context, standard keyword search has a very limited effectiveness. For example, it cannot filter for the type of information (tutorial, applet or demo, review questions, etc.), the level of information (aimed to secondary school students, graduate students, etc.), the prerequisites

for understanding information, or the quality of information. Some examples of semantic-based e-learning systems can be found in Mendes and Sacks (2004), in Lytras and Naeve (2005), and in the last paragraph of this chapter.

The aim of this chapter is to present our personalized learning retrieval framework based on both collaborative and semantic approaches. The collaborative approach is exploited both in retrieving tasks (to cover recommendation and resource sharing tasks) and in semantic coverage of the involved domain. The semantic approach is exploited introducing an ontology space covering domain knowledge and resource models based on word sense representation. The ontologies are updated as time goes on to reflect changes in the research domain and user interests. Also the ontology level exploits system collaborative aspect.

In Carbonaro (2005), we introduced the InLinx (Intelligent Links) system, a Web application that provides an online bookmarking service. InLinx is the result of three filtering components integration, corresponding to the following functionalities:

1. **Bookmark Classification (content-based filtering):** The system suggests the more suitable category that the user can save the bookmark in, based on the document content; the user can accept the suggestion or change the classification by selecting another category he considers the best for such a given item.

2. **Bookmark Sharing (collaborative filtering):** The system checks for newly classified bookmarks and recommends them to other users with similar interests. Recipient users can either accept or reject the recommendation once they receive the notification.

3. **Paper Recommendation (content-based recommendation):** The system periodically checks if a new issue of some online journal has been released; then, it recommends the plausible appealing documents, according to the user profiles.

Over the years we have designed and implemented several extensions of the original architecture such as personalized category organization and mobile services (Andronico, Carbonaro, Colazzo, & Molinari, 2004). Most recently, we have introduced concepts for classification, recommendation, and document sharing in order to provide a better personalized semantic-based resource management. Generally, recommender systems use keywords to represent both the users and the resources. Another way to handle such data is by using hierarchical concept categories. This issue will enable users and the system to search, handle, or read only concepts of interest in a more general manner, providing a semantic possibility. For example, synonymy and hyponymy can reveal hidden similarities, potentially leading to better classification and recommendation. We called the extended architecture EasyInfo.

In this chapter we present the introduction of an ontology layer in our e-learning domain to describe the content and the relations between the various resources. It will formulate an exhaustive representation of the domain by specifying all of its concepts and the existing relations. Through the ontologies the system will express hierarchical links between entities and will guarantee interoperability of educational resources. We decide to maintain the several existing ontologies that each user knows. This approach allows us to easily compare the knowledge of a user with his or her personal ontologies without having a single consensual ontology that will accommodate all his or her needs. In this section we describe our approach to support personalization retrieval of relevant learning resources in a given Web-based learning system. This framework distinguishes between the generic user and the system administrator points of view.

Marco: A User Seeking Resources

Web technologies will continue to mature, and learning through the World Wide Web will become increasingly popular, particularly in distance education systems. Teachers can distribute lecture notes and other required materials via the Web, so Marco gets the opportunity to freely and autonomously use learning materials by collecting other related materials on the Web as well.

Active learning is the ability of learners to carry out learning activities in such a way that they will be able to effectively and efficiently construct knowledge from information sources. That is, Marco should be able to acquire, apply, and create knowledge and skills in the context of personal requirements and interests (Lee, 1999). Marco expects more than being able to filter, retrieve, and refer to learning materials. He prefers to have personalized access to library materials that he can customize according to his personal requirements and interests.

Therefore, new tools should allow the learners to integrate their selections from digital information sources and create their own reference sources. Moreover, in order to give intelligent support to achieve the expectations of active learning, it is also necessary to provide techniques to locate suitable materials. These mechanisms should extend beyond the traditional facilities of browsing and searching, by supporting active learning and by integrating the user's personal library and remote digital libraries. The user will be able to carry out learning activities when browsing both the personal and the remote digital libraries, therefore he can build personalized views on those materials while turning them into an accessible reference collection.

Because of the complexity of the system as well as the heterogeneity and amount of data, the use of semantics is crucial in this setting. For example, semantic description of resources and student profiles can be used to cluster students or resources with similar content or interests.

From a functional point of view, Marco needs a procedure to submit new material integrating the existing personal and remote libraries which consist of the following two phases:

Figure 1. System architecture

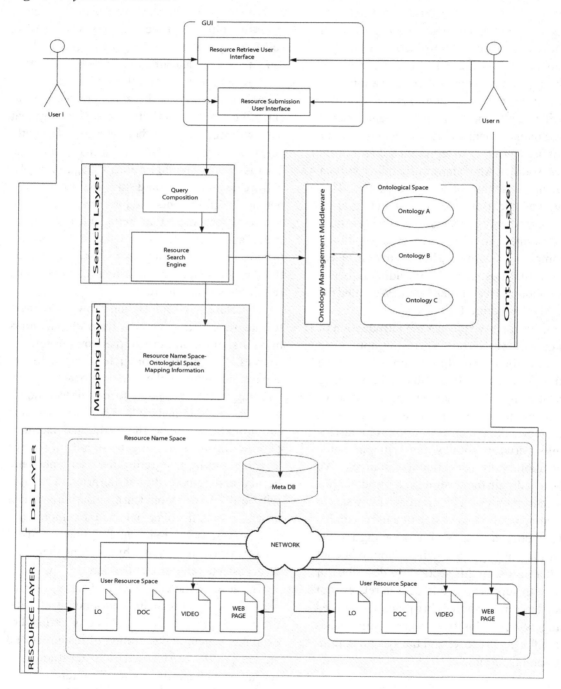

1. An interface to submit new resources to the system, and
2. An interface to propose the mapping between the submitted resource and the ontology concepts.

Francesco: Learning System Administrator

Francesco wants to offer a personalized e-learning system that is able to respond to the effective user needs and modifiable user behavior and interests. The keyword profiling approach suffers because of a polysemy problem (the presence of multiple meanings for one term) and a synonymy problem (the presence of multiple words having the same meaning). If user and resource profiles do not share the same exact keywords, relevant information can be missed or wrong documents could be considered as relevant. Francesco wants an alternative method that is able to learn semantic profiles capturing key concepts, and which represents user and resource contents. The concepts should be defined in some ontologies. Moreover, Francesco wants to offer a procedure to map resources with respect to an ontology by creating an open and flexible ontology space describing the learning domain, in order to avoid specialized retrieving.

From a functional point of view, Francesco needs a procedure to organize the ontology space consisting of the following three phases:

1. An interface to add, remove, and modify ontologies belonging to the ontology space;
2. An interface to execute ontology mapping; and
3. An interface to propose the mapping between resources submitted by users and the ontology concepts.

System Architecture

As shown in Figure 1, the proposed architecture is divided into five different layers:

- **Search layer:** In this layer the user can specify his or her query and subscribe new resources to the system.
- **Ontology space layer:** In this the layer the system logically maintains the system ontologies.
- **Mapping layer:** This layer organizes the structure in which the mapping between resources and ontology concepts.
- **DB layer:** In this layer are stored all the

Figure 2. Query composition GUI

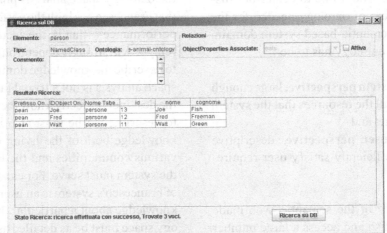

meta-information about the resources—that is, information like title, author, physical location, and so on.

- **Resource layer:** This layer stores the different learning resources.

The following sections describe in more detail each layer.

Search Layer

This is the layer where the user can query the system for resources and propose new ones. Through the GUI the user composes his or her query by using the *Query Composition* module (see Figure 2). A simple query specifying only keyword is not enough for a semantic search. The query composer interacts with the ontology management middleware in order to navigate the ontology and allows the user to choose not only the concept, but also a property associated with it.

Once the query has been composed, the Query Composition module passes the query to the Resource Search Engine. This module interacts with the ontology space and queries the mapping layer retrieving a list, eventually empty, of resources to be proposed to the user.

Ontology Space Layer

In this section we would like to center our discussion on the kind of ontology needed for the description of a semantic-based system domain. In particular, the ontology has to be:

- **From the system perspective:** large enough to describe all the resources that the system must manage; and
- **From the user perspective:** descriptive enough to efficiently satisfy user requirements.

The emergence of the semantic Web made it possible to publish and access a large number of ontologies; their widespread use by different communities represents the backbone for semantically rich information sharing. The sharing of ontology, though, is not a solved problem. With the proposed domain requirements in mind, we need to maintain the view of each system user on the personal ontology without altering its original schema, while assuming that the different communities desire to share knowledge to infer the relationships among their concepts and to amplify the effectiveness of the system response. For example, let us consider an example taken from Kalfoglou and Schorlemmer (2003) that shows the issues one has to take into account when attempting to align specified English and French concepts. We argue that promoting services to support group collaboration among users involved in the learning process could be a useful approach to solve such problems.

According to Stutt and Motta(2004), there are a lot of 'knowledge neighborhoods' built around some topic by handling different learning resources, ontologies, and users. It is necessary to create an ontology space comprising more than one global ontology, even partially overlapping, belonging to different knowledge neighborhoods. So doing, it is possible to propose to a huge user-maintained repository, and also create links and automatic search to another community.

At this point we need to outline a crucial aspect: the ontology space analysis phase. We can think that Francesco has built the perfect system, but the performance—that is, the accuracy in the query reply—will strongly depend on the ontology used to describe the knowledge domain. The ontology space analysis is not a trivial task; not only must the designer perfectly know the domain he wants to describe, but he must also have an excellent knowledge both of the living ontologies in the various communities and the kind of users that the system must serve. For example, if the target of Francesco's system is an user with an in-depth knowledge about a particular domain, the ontology space must be as detailed as possible. On the contrary, if the expected user is at a more scholastic level, the domain will be more general and with less detailed information. These choices are related to the design phase of the system, but they cannot be a binding obstacle for future improvements. Communities and their domains evolve in time, and as a consequence, the representation of the overall system domain must evolve.

Ontology mapping is not a trivial task. If, at first glance, the biggest problem seems to be related to highly time-consuming aspects of the subsequent process, it is easy to verify that matching of concepts belonging to different ontologies can be considered the hardest part of the work. Initially, the purpose of manually mapping different ontologies can seem a titanic effort, so the first idea is the development of an automatic tool able to solve the task. Unfortunately, this approach has problems with accuracy of matching. An automatic tool such as MAFRA could solve the mapping process in little time and certainly the results are not prone to classical human errors. But other errors may occur and we think that they can be even more dangerous. An automatic tool, for example, will find it difficult to detect semantic differences between concepts belonging to different and complex ontologies. Moreover, the accuracy of algorithms and rules used for automatic semantic relationship deduction between different schemas could not be satisfactory.

In particular, a human error could be related to the absent-mindedness of the mapper and can be categorized as syntactical mistakes. These kinds of errors, or a big percentage of them, can be detected through the help of a parser. On the contrary, an accuracy problem is a semantical error and is much more difficult to identify. This kind of error could reduce the expected performance improvement deriving from ontology use.

A manual process is necessary because the semantic relationships that can occur between ontologies are too complex to be directly learned by machines. For this reason, in order to avoid semantic errors, one can adopt a manual map-

ping approach; however, it could be unacceptably expensive.

At the time of writing, the mapping process is an open problem in our architecture. For our test cases we used a manual mapping, but a semi-automatic ontology mapping tool is in development.

Mapping Layer

Another crucial aspect of the proposed system is the resource mapping phase. The resource representation may be accomplished using two different strategies:

1. **By using a list containing ontology concepts**: this solution represents a good resource representation and it is easily practicable;
2. **By using a subgraph of the ontology space**: this solution could represent in more detail the learning resources, but it is more difficult to implement.

The main difference between the two mentioned strategies is related to concept properties. Without the properties the subgraph can be conformed to the concept list; nevertheless, the properties allow differentiation between similar resources.

Generally, the choice depends on the domain one has to manage. If the resource space is composed of resources made up of generic domain topics, then the first solution may be the best one. On the contrary, if the resources are extremely detailed, the graph model may be the best choice. We have chosen the first proposed model; our choice is limited by the interaction with the resource representation produced by the disambiguation module of EasyInfo, which is similar to a concept list expressed in an XML-based language. In future works we intend to go through this limitation also supporting the graph model.

In the last part of this section, we describe the resource ontology mapping task. As shown in

Figure 1, all the information about resources are maintained within the DB; through the DB layer it provides a Resource Name Space to other system modules. More precisely, the Resource Name Space is the set of logical names of the resources managed by the system. For this reason, the list of ontology concepts is mapped with a record of the database.

Most of the efforts in the field of mapping between ontologies and databases have been spent in the directions of heterogeneous database integration. The purpose of such an approach is to map a database record to a list of ontology concepts in order to give a semantical representation of the data they represent.

In our architecture the database maintains all the meta information about the learning resources such as title, author, physical location,

Figure 3. XML-based language to express the resource mapping process

```
<?xml version="1.0" encoding="UTF-8" ?>
<!DOCTYPE Map (View Source for full doctype...)>
- <Map>
  - <DBConnection>
      <NameDB>testDB</NameDB>
      <Login>root</Login>
      <Password />
    </DBConnection>
  - <Ontologies>
    + <Ontology>
    + <Ontology>
    + <Ontology>
    + <Ontology>
    </Ontologies>
  - <ClassesMap>
    + <ClassMap type="Inferred">
    + <ClassMap type="Asserted">
    - <ClassMap type="Inferred">
        <TableName>animali</TableName>
      + <IDRow>
        <PrefixOntology>pean</PrefixOntology>
        <IDObject>animal</IDObject>
      </ClassMap>
    - <ClassMap type="Asserted">
        <TableName>animali</TableName>
      - <IDRow>
          <KeyValue>2</KeyValue>
        </IDRow>
        <PrefixOntology>pean</PrefixOntology>
        <IDObject>duck</IDObject>
      </ClassMap>
    </ClassesMap>
  </Map>
```

Figure 4. A screenshot of the GUI for the mapping phase

and so on. Through the DB, the system provides a Resource Name Space in which each element represents a single resource. Both system and users can refer to resources by using their logical name and all the other information handled within the Database Layer. In order to give an ontological–logical–resource representation, we have to create an ontological–physical–database mapping. In the rest of this section, we refer to some existing techniques of mapping between databases and ontologies.

- *Kaon reverse* (Stojanovic et al., 2002) is a KAON plug-in for semi-automatically mapping relational database to ontologies. In the first step of this approach, the relational database model is transformed into an ontology structure expressed in F-Logic (Kifer, 1995). In the second step, the database content is migrated into the created ontology. If needed, the F-Logic structure can be translated in RDF.

- *D2R* (Bizer, 2003) is defined as a declarative XML-based language used to describe mappings between relational database schemas and OWL[4] ontologies without changing the database schema. The D2R mapping process comprises the following steps:
  - selection of a record set from the database,
  - grouping of the record set by the d2r: group By attribute,
  - creation of class instances, and
  - mapping of the grouped record set data to instance properties.

- *Deep annotation* (Handschuh, Staab, & Volz, 2003) is defined as a manual annotation process that uses information properties, information structures, and information context in order to derive mapping between database schema and ontologies. This approach proposes the annotation of Web pages maintaining DB content by using information about the database schema. In this way, a client can map the public mark up of the Web page to its own ontology.

Our first approach was inspired by the ones proposed in Kaon Reverse. We studied a two-step process for the semi-automatic mapping between database schemas and ontologies. We had taken into consideration the approach proposed in D2R, and we have developed an XML-based language to express the resulting mapping (see Figure 3). In order to improve the accuracy of the mapping process, we have adopted the idea of manual mapping proposed in Deep Annotation. Although the resource manual mapping can be considered time consuming, we have preferred the accuracy of the resource representation rather than the quickness of the overall process.

DB Layer

In the DB layer we maintain all the meta-information about the resources, information like title, author, physical location, and so on. As previously described, this layer provides the Resource Name Space, which is the set of resource logical names managed by the system.

Resource Layer

This is the layer of resources. A resource can be maintained both on the same machine in which the system is running and in a remote accessible machine. All the information about resources are stored in the DB layer.

CONCEPT-BASED SEMANTIC APPROACH TO MODEL RESOURCE AND USER PROFILES

Word Sense Disambiguation Process

In order to substitute keywords with univocal concepts into user and resource profiles, we must build a process called Word Sense Disambiguation (WSD). Given a sentence, a WSD process identifies the syntactical categories of words and interacts with an ontology both to retrieve the exact concept definition and to adopt some techniques for semantic similarity evaluation among words. We use GATE (Cunningham, Maynard, Bontcheva, & Tablan, 2002) to identify the syntactic class of the words and WordNet (Fellbaum, 1998), which is one of the most used reference lexicons in the Word Sense Disambiguation task.

The use of the described Word Sense Disambiguation step reduces classification errors due to ambiguous words, thus allowing better precision in the succeeding recommendation and sharing phases. For example, if the terms "procedure," "subprogram," and "routine" appear in the same resource, we consider three occurrences of the same sysnset "{06494814}: routine, subroutine, subprogram, procedure, function (a set sequence of steps, part of larger computer program)" and not one occurrence for each word.

Moreover, the implemented WSD procedure allows more accurate document representation. For example, let us process two sentences containing the "mouse" polysemous word. The disambiguation process applied to the first sentence "The white cat is hunting the mouse" produces the following WordNet definition:

{2244530}: mouse (any of numerous small rodents typically resembling diminutive rats having pointed snouts and small ears on elongated bodies with slender usually hairless tails), while

the same process applied to the second sentence "The mouse is near the pc" produces the following result:

{3651364}: mouse, computer mouse (a hand-operated electronic device that controls the coordinates of a cursor on your computer screen as you move it around on a pad; on the bottom of the mouse is a ball that rolls on the surface of the pad; "a mouse takes much more room than a trackball").

To the best of our knowledge, no systems use a concept-based semantic approach to model resource and user profiles in a learning environment.

Resource Representation

Many systems build document and user representations by taking into account some word properties in the document, such as their frequency and their co-occurrence. Nevertheless, we described how a purely word-based model is often not adequate when the interest is strictly related to the resource semantic content. We now describe how the novice user and resource semantic profiles differ from the old ones in taking into account word senses representing user and resource contents.

In the early version of our system, we adopted a representation based on the Vector Space Model (VSM), the most frequently used model in information retrieval (IR) and text learning. Since the resources of the system are Web pages, it was necessary to apply a sequence of contextual processing to the source code of the pages in order to obtain a vector representation. To filter information resources according to user interests, we must have a common representation both for the users and the resources. This knowledge representation model must be expressive enough to synthetically and significantly describe the information content. The use of the VSM allows updates of the user profile in accordance with consulted information resources (Salton, 1989).

To guarantee a customizable architecture, the system needs to construct and maintain user profiles. For a particular user, it is reasonable to think that processing a set of correctly classified relevant and inappropriate documents from a certain domain of interest may lead to identifying the set of relevant keywords for such a domain at a certain time. Thus, the user domain-specific sets of relevant features, called prototypes, may be used to learn how to classify documents. In particular, in order to consider the peculiarity of positive and negative examples, we define positive prototype for a class c_j, a user u_i at time t, as a finite set of unique indexing terms, chosen to be relevant for c_j, up to time t. Then we define a negative prototype as a subset of the corresponding positive one, whereas each element can be found at least once in the set of documents classified as negative examples for class c_j. Positive examples for a specific user u_i and for a class c_j are represented by the explicitly registered documents or accepted by u_i in c_j, while negative examples are either deleted bookmarks, misclassified bookmarks, or rejected bookmarks that happen to be classified into c_j.

After the WSD, our resources are represented by using a list of WordNet concepts obtained by the described architecture from the words in the documents and their related occurrence. Our hypothesis is that concept-based document and user representations produce retrieved documents with high semantic relevance with respect to the user and resource models.

EXPERIMENTAL DOMAIN

The following paragraphs describe how we consider the resource content to propose a fitted technique in a personalized information retrieval framework. The automatic retrieval of relevant learning objects is obtained by considering students and learning material profiles, and by adopting filtering criteria based on the value of selected metadata fields. Our experiments are based on SCORM[5]-compliant LOs. For example, we use the student's knowledge of domain concept to avoid recommendation of highly technical papers to a beginner student or popular magazine articles to a senior graduate student. For each student, the system evaluates and updates his or her skill and technical expertise levels.

We use artificial learners to get a flavor of how the system works. We created SCORM-compliant learning material using the abstract of several papers in .html version from scientific journals published on the Web. We linked an imsmanifest SCORM file to each paper. Then, we simulated 10 users with different initial profiles (based on the field of interest and on the skill level) and saved, in four turns, 10 learning resources for each user, obtaining 400 LOs. The main advantage of the described approach is the semantic accuracy growth. To give a quantitative estimation of the improvement induced by a concept-based approach, we are executing a comparative experiment between word-based user and resource models on one side and concept-based user and resource models on the other one. In particular, in order to evaluate the collaborative approach, we have considered different initial student profiles. The several components influencing the choice of recommendation receivers are:

- **User interest in the category of recommended resource:** The system maintains a user vs. category matrix that, for a specific user, stores the number of times he or she shows interest for a certain class, saving a bookmark in that class.
- **Confidence level between users:** We use a matrix maintaining the user's confidence factor, ranging from 0.1 to 1, to represent how many documents recommended by a specific user are accepted or rejected by another one. The confidence factor is not bi-directional.

- **Relation between the class prototype of recommended resource and the class prototype of other categories:** To obtain a fitting recommendation, we apply the Pearson-r correlation measure to a weighted user-category matrix in which classes related to the class of the recommended bookmark are enhanced.

To verify the effectiveness of the EasyInfo module on the recommendation process, we considered a certain snapshot of the user/category matrix and of the confidence factor matrix. Then, we observed the behavior of the system while performing the same recommendation task both using and without using the EasyInfo extension.

For simplicity, we have considered three users, user1, user2 and user3, and three resources, r1, r2, and r3. In the first case, whenever user1 saves (or accepts) r1, the system will recommend it to user2 who has a high interest in that topic (independent of similarity among user profiles). The same resource will not be recommended to user3 because the system is not able to discover similarity between two students by simply using word-based user and resource models. In the second case, the same resource could also be recommended to user3 who is conceptually similar to user1, even if the similarity is not evident in a simple word matching system. Moreover, the system is able to discover word sense similarities between r1 and r3 and to propose r3 both to user2 and user3, thus allowing better personalization.

CONSIDERATIONS

This chapter addresses key limitations with existing courseware on the Internet. Humans want immediate access to relevant and accurate information. There has been some progress in combining learning with information retrieval, however, these advances are rarely implemented in e-learning courseware. With this objective in mind, we described how to propose a personalized information retrieval framework, considering student and learning material profiles, adopting filtering criteria based on the value of selected metadata fields, and capturing not only structural but also semantics information. We showed how the semantic technologies can enhance the traditional keyword approach by adding semantic information in the resource and user profiles.

Summarizing, the key elements of the described system could be highlighted as follows. The system provides immediate portability and visibility from different user locations, enabling access to a personal bookmark repository just by using a Web browser. The system assists students in finding relevant reading material providing personalized learning object recommendations. The system directly benefits from existing repositories of learning material by providing access to large amounts of digital information. The system reflects continuous ongoing changes of the practices of its members, as required by a cooperative framework. The system proposes resource and student models based on word senses rather than simply on words exploiting a word sense-based document representation.

REFERENCES

Andronico, A., Carbonaro, A., Colazzo, L., & Molinari, A. (2004). Personalisation services for learning management systems in mobile settings. *International Journal of Continuing Engineering Education and Lifelong Learning*.

Belkin, N.J., & Croft, W.B. (1992). Information filtering and information retrieval: Two sides of the same coin. *Communications of the ACM, 35*(12), 29-38.

Berlanga, A.J., & García, F.J. (2005). IMS LD reusable elements for adaptive learning designs. *Journal of Interactive Media in Education, 11*(Special Issue).

Bizer, C. (2003). D2R MAP—a database to RDF mapping language. *Proceedings of the 12th International World Wide Web Conference*.

Brusilovsky, P., & Nijhavan, H. (2002). A framework for adaptive e-learning based on distributed re-usable learning activities. *Proceedings of the World Conference on E-Learning* (E-Learn 2002), Montreal, Canada.

Budanitsky, A., & Hirst, G. (2001). Semantic distance in WordNet: An experimental, application-oriented evaluation of five measures. *Proceedings of Workshop on WordNet and Other Lexical Resources of the 2nd Meeting of the North American Chapter of the Association for Computational Linguistics*, Pittsburgh, PA.

Carbonaro A. (2004). Learning objects recommendation in a collaborative information management system. *IEEE Learning Technology Newsletter, 6*(4).

Carbonaro, A. (2005). Defining personalized learning views of relevant learning objects in a collaborative bookmark management system. In *Web-based intelligent e-learning systems: Technologies and applications*. Hershey, PA: Idea Group.

Cooley R., Mobasher, B., & Srivastava, J. (1997). Web mining: Information and pattern discovery on the World Wide Web. Proceedings of the 9th International Conference on Tools with Artificial Intelligence (ICTAI '97).

Cunningham, H., Maynard, D., Bontcheva, K., & Tablan, V. (2002). GATE: A framework and graphical development environment for robust NLP tools and applications. *Proceedings of the 40th Anniversary Meeting of the Association for Computational Linguistics*, Budapest.

Dai, H., & Mobasher, B. (2004). Integrating semantic knowledge with Web usage mining for personalization. In A. Scime (Ed.), *Web mining: Applications and techniques* (pp. 276-306). Hershey, PA: Idea Group.

Dzbor, M., Motta, E., & Stutt, A. (2005). Achieving higher-level learning through adaptable semantic Web applications. *International Journal of Knowledge and Learning, 1*(1/2).

Ehrig, M., & Sure, Y. (2004, May). Ontology mapping—an integrated approach. In C. Bussler, J. Davis, D. Fensel, & R. Studer (Eds.), *Proceedings of the 1st European Semantic Web Symposium* (pp. 76-91), Heraklion, Greece. Berlin: Springer-Verlag (LNCS 3053).

Fellbaum, C. (Ed.). (1998). *WordNet: An electronic lexical database.* Cambridge, MA: MIT Press.

García, F.J., Berlanga, A.J., Moreno, M.N., García, J., & Carabias, J. (2004). *HyCo—an authoring tool to create semantic learning objects for Web-based e-learning systems* (pp. 344-348). Berlin: Springer-Verlag (LNCS 3140).

Handschuh, S., Staab, S., & Volz, R. (2003). On deep annotation. *Proceedings of the 12th International World Wide Web Conference.*

Heflin, J. (2004, February). OWL Web Ontology Language use cases and requirements. Retrieved from http://www.w3.org/TR/Webont-req/

Huhns, M.N., & Singh, M.P. (1998). *Multiagent systems in information-rich environments. Cooperative information agents II* (pp. 79-93). (LNAI 1435).

Kalfoglou, Y., & Schorlemmer, M. (2003). IF-Map: An ontology mapping method based on information-flow theory. In S. Spaccapietra et al. (Eds.), *Journal on data semantics.* (LNCS 2800).

Kanellopoulos, D., Kotsiantis, S., & Pintelas, P. (2006, February). Ontology-based learning applications: A development methodology. *Proceedings of the 24th Iasted International Multi-Conference Software Engineering,* Austria.

Kifer, M., Lausen, G., & Wu, J. (1995). Logical foundations of object-oriented and frame-based languages. *Journal of the ACM, 42*(4), 741-843.

Koivunen, M., & Miller, E. (2002). W3C semantic Web activity. In E. Hyvonen (Ed.), *Semantic Web kick-off in Finland* (pp. 27-44). Helsinki: HIIT.

Leacock, C., & Chodorow, M. (1998). Combining local context and WordNet similarity for word sense identification. In C. Fellbaum (Ed.), *WordNet: An electronic lexical database* (pp. 265-283). Cambridge, MA: MIT Press.

Lee, J. (1999). Interactive learning with a Web-based digital library system. *Proceedings of the 9th DELOS Workshop on Digital Libraries for Distance Learning.* Retrieved from *http://courses. cs.vt.edu/~cs3604/DELOS.html*

Lytras, M.D., & Naeve, A. (Eds.). (2005). *Intelligent learning infrastructure for knowledge intensive organizations.* London: Information Science.

Maedche, A., Motik, B., Silva, N., & Volz, R. (2002). MAFRA—a mapping framework for distributed ontologies. *Proceedings of EKAW (Knowledge Engineering and Knowledge Management) 2002.* Berlin: Springer-Verlag (LNCS 2473).

Mendes, M.E.S., & Sacks, L. (2004). Dynamic knowledge representation for e-learning applications. In M. Nikravesh, L.A. Zadeh, B. Azvin, & R. Yager (Eds.), *Enhancing the power of the Internet—studies in fuzziness and soft computing* (vol. 139, pp. 255-278). Berlin/London: Springer-Verlag.

Nagarajan, R. (2002). Content-boosted collaborative filtering for improved recommendations. *Proceedings of the 18th National Conference on Artificial Intelligence,* Canada.

Recker, M., Walker, A., & Lawless, K. (2003). What do you recommend? Implementation and analyses of collaborative filtering of Web resources for education. *Instructional Science, 31,* 229-316.

Resnik, P. (1995). *Disambiguating noun groupings with respect to WordNet senses.* Chelmsford, MA: Sun Microsystems Laboratories.

Salton, G. (1989). *Automatic text processing: The transformation, analysis and retrieval of information by computer.* Reading, MA: Addison-Wesley.

Stojanovic, L., Stojanovic, N., & Volz, R. (2002). Migrating data-intensive Web sites into the semantic Web. *Proceedings of the 17th ACM Symposium on Applied Computing* (pp. 1100-1107).

Stutt, A., & Motta, E. (2004). Semantic learning Webs. *Journal of Interactive Media in Education, (10).*

Tang, T., & McCalla, G. (2005). Smart recommendation for an evolving e-learning system: Architecture and experiment. *International Journal on E-Learning, 4(1), 105-129.*

ENDNOTES

[1]   *http://grouper.ieee.org/p1484/wg12/files/ LOM_1484_12_1_v1_Final_Draft.pdf*

[2]   *http://ltsc.ieee.org*

[3]   RDF is the W3C recommendation for the creation of metadata about resources. With RDF, one can make statements about a resource in the form of a subject–predicate–object expression. The described resource is the subject of the statement, the predicate is a specified relation that links the subject, and the object is the value assigned to the subject through the predicate.

[4]   OWL is the W3C recommendation for the creation of new ontology optimized for the Web. The Web Ontology Language OWL is a semantic markup language for publishing and sharing ontologies on the World Wide Web. OWL is developed as a vocabulary extension of RDF, and it is derived from the DAML+OIL Web Ontology Language. For these reasons it provides a greater machine interpretability of Web content than the one supported by its predecessors. Essentially, with OWL one can describe a specific domain in terms of class, properties, and individuals. It has three increasingly expressive sublanguages: OWL Lite, OWL DL, and OWL Full.

[5]   SCORM (Sharable Courseware Object Reference Model) is a suite of technical standards that enable Web-based learning systems to find, import, share, reuse, and export learning content in a standardized way. It is a specification of the Advanced Distributed Learning Initiative (*http://www. adlnet.org/*).

Chapter XV
Multi–Agent Tourism System (MATS)

Soe Yu Maw
University of Computer Studies, Yangdon, Myanmar

Myo-Myo Naing
University of Computer Studies, Yangdon, Myanmar

ABSTRACT

In this chapter we propose the architecture of the multi-agent tourism system (MATS). Tourism information on the World Wide Web is dynamic and constantly changing. It is not easy to obtain relevant and updated information for individual user needs. A multi-agent system is defined as a collection of agents that work in conjunction with each other. The objective of MATS is to provide the most relevant and updated information according to the user's interests. It consists of multiple agents with three main tiers such as the Interface Module, Information Management Module, and Domain-Related Module. We propose the Rule-based Personalization with Collaborative Filtering technique for effective personalization in MATS which can address the limitations of pure collaborative filtering such as scalability, sparsity, and cold-start problems.

INTRODUCTION

The World Wide Web has become an important way to get information and the ideal environment for publishing information on the Internet. The information on the World Wide Web is distributed, dynamic, and heterogeneous. Users are frustrated with the information obtained by using search engines because of the problem of information overload. It is time consuming to search for relevant information that they need. When surfing Web sites, users are demanding more powerful tools that are capable of integrating and interpreting the vast amount of heterogeneous information available on the Web (Breese & Kadie, 1998). One possible approach is to personalize the Web site by creating a system that responds to user queries by aggregating information from several sources depending upon who the user is. Personalization means knowing who the user is, what the user wants, and recognizing a specific user based on a user profile.

Personalization is dynamic, proactive, and personable (Connor, 2001). The interest in personalization has increased as a way to filter information and reduce information overload. We consider personalization to retrieve and share user information in a social network. The social community is the network of interest (personal information of users) and the relationship of users. Kirsch, Gnasa, and Cremers (2006) describes that social information retrieval system as the ability to acquire information that meets the users' needs through a combination of information retrieval systems and social networks. In social networks, users are described by a relationship, and these relations are used to communicate and share information.

According to Avery and Zeckhauser (1997) and Shearin and Lieberman (2001), Web sites have access to incredible amounts of data about users, their preferences, and their behavior. They also have the ability to dynamically generate all aspects of their Web sites. As a result, there is a great deal of interest in personalization software that can customize the experience of individual users to a Web site or accommodate the message being communicated to the users in order to optimize the effectiveness of the Web site.

Agent-based technology can potentially solve complex, dynamic online decision support tasks and offer a new opportunity in utilizing Web resources. An agent-based system can interact much more personally with the users. Agents are sophisticated computer programs that act autonomously on behalf of the users in a distributed environment. Intelligent agents can search the relevant information and make recommendations to the individual user. Because of the flexible and dynamic characters of intelligent agents, they are

being used widely as an interface system between the user and the World Wide Web for different applications.

During the last few years, a wide range of different Web-based tourism-related agents has been established. The acceptance and consequently the competitiveness of a tourism system are mainly determined by the quantity and quality of the data it provides. Therefore, most existing tourism systems try to fulfill the tourist's request (interest) from an extensive data collection (Rumetshofer & Wob, 2005). In the tourism domain, there is a vast amount of information available about accommodation, transportation, restaurants, and sightseeing places, and it is troublesome to get the right information to the right person at the right time.

The objective of our research is to provide an efficient multi-agent based tourism information system that is able to overcome the information overload problem, and to improve the scalability, sparsity, accuracy, and quality of recommendations.

With this view, we propose a multi-agent tourism system (MATS) to assist users in retrieving and integrating tourism information on the World Wide Web effectively and efficiently. MATS consists of multiple agents with three main tiers: the Interface Module, Information Management Module, and Domain Related Module. In this system, the core technique for the Personalization Agent is the Rule-based Personalization with Collaborative Filtering technique. It identifies the user by retrieving the user's profile and filters the information to provide only those that match the user's interest. The information relevant to the user can be obtained by two options. One option is to ask the user to fill in the form, and another option is to use cookies that can be used to track where the user travels over the site. Several agents in each tier perform their relevant tasks to provide the required pieces of information from each domain to satisfy the user's request.

Motivation and Contributions

The information on the Web is chaotic and ever increasing. The user cannot retrieve information that is relevant to his or her request easily. Agents have widely been proposed as a solution to the information overload (Wooldridge, 2002, p. 248). Krupansky (2005) defined an agent as "a computer program capable of flexible and autonomous action in a dynamic environment, usually an environment containing other agents." Agents on the Internet mostly perform information retrieval, filtering, and gathering in context. In order to perform this, agents interoperate and coordinate with each other. An agent is able to collate and manipulate information obtained from the information sources in order to answer queries posed by users and other information agents. The information sources include traditional databases, flat files, knowledge bases, programs, as well as other information agents. We use an agent-based architecture for our system because the various information sources and personalization components are inherently distributed and autonomous. In a multi-agent system architecture, each agent is autonomous, cooperative, coordinated, intelligent, and able to communicate with other agents to fulfill the user's needs. Krupansky (2005) states that agents have social ability—that is, they communicate with the user, the system, and other agents as required.

The World Wide Web, which contains distributed and semi-structured information resources, obviously presents enormous potential; but it also presents a number of difficulties (Wooldridge, 2002, pp. 248-249). The most obvious difficulty from the user's viewpoint of the World Wide Web is colloquially known as the "information overload" problem. The sheer volume of information available to users makes it hard to filter out irrelevancies. Search engines such as Google (*www.google.com*) and Yahoo (*www.yahoo.com*) attempt to alleviate this problem by indexing largely unstructured and unmanaged informa-

tion on the Web. Search engines are one of the commonly used tools for information gathering. Though these tools are valuable and useful, they have several limitations. For example, search engines only provide the user with the location or the address of the information rather than the information that the users need. Search engines order the user's results based on the small amount of information available in the user's queries and by Web site popularity, rather than individual user interests. So all users see the same results for the same query, even if they have wildly different interests and backgrounds. To meet these requirements, personalization is suggested.

Willy (2001) states that Web personalization is the process of customizing the content and structure of a Web site to the specific and individual needs of each user. He also described personalization as a process of gathering and storing information about users, analyzing the information, and based on the analysis, delivering the information to each user at the right time (Willy, 2001). Hyldegaard and Seiden (2004) concluded that Web personalization has observed two types of approaches from the technical point of view: profile-based personalization and behavior-based personalization. Profile-based personalization is based on the matching of a user profile and content profile. Profile-based personalization can be divided into customization and rule-based personalization. Behavior-based personalization is also known as collaborative information filtering. According to Mobasher, Cooley, and Srivastava (2000), Web personalization can generally be categorized into three major types: decision rule-based filtering, content-based filtering, and collaborative filtering. Our system is mainly related to rule-based filtering and collaborative filtering. We briefly discuss the main features of each approach and then look into more specific relevant approaches in the MATS architecture section.

Decision rule-based filtering systems, such as Broadvision (*www.broadvision.com*), allow

Web site administrators to specify rules based on factual data such as user demographics or static profiles (collected through a registration process), other kinds of collected data, or session history. The rules are used to affect the content served to a particular user. The limitation of this approach is that it generates many rules so that it is very slow to train.

Content-based filtering approaches, such as those used by WebWatcher (Shardanand & Maes, 1995), rely on content similarity of Web documents to personal profiles obtained explicitly or implicitly from users. Content-based filtering is most suitable when the objects are easily analyzed by computer and the user's decision about object suitability is not subjective. This approach has difficulty capturing different types of content (e.g., images, video clips, etc.) and has a problem of overspecialization.

Collaborative filtering systems, such as Firefly (Joachims, Freitag, & Mitchell, 1997) and Net Perception (*www.netperception.com*), typically take explicit information in the form of user ratings or preferences, and through a correlation engine, return information that is predicted to closely match the user's preference. Pure collaborative filtering can solve most problems of a pure content-based approach—the content is not limited to the text document. However, there are still some limitations in pure collaborative filtering such as sparsity and scalability, which we discuss in the collaborative filtering section.

The following are the contributions that we present in this chapter.

- As a main contribution, we propose an agent-based architecture of a tourism system that assists users in retrieving and integrating information from the World Wide Web.
- We also propose a Rule-based Personalization with Collaborative Filtering (RPCF) technique, which can give the user information effectively and efficiently according to the user's interests and behaviors.

- We elaborate the proposed RPCF algorithm that produces better recommendations and more accurate results than the traditional collaborative filtering algorithm, and we demonstrate how our proposed method can provide accurate information for the tourism domain.

Organization

The chapter is organized as follows. In the next section, we discuss some related work of existing multi-agent tourism systems, and their weaknesses. In the third section we present the architecture of our proposed Multi-Agent Tourism System (MATS) in detail along with the proposed method and algorithms. The experimental results of our proposed method are described in the fourth section to illustrate the efficiency and effectiveness of our proposed method. The last section concludes the chapter with some future trends.

RELATED WORK

Before we present our proposed architecture, we discuss the definitions and background of the system and review some related work.

Tourism, as an enterprise, deals with many activities. Some of these activities include tour guides, accommodation, transportation, food, marketing, banking and cash transfer, insurance, communications, medicine, advertisement, trip planning, hospitability, entertainment, and so on. In order to give better services to users, it is necessary to use more powerful methods for retrieving information.

Agent-Based Tourism Systems

Buhalis and Licata (2002) discuss the future of e-tourism intermediaries, while Rayman-Bacchus and Monlina (2001) predict the business issues and trends of Internet-based tourism. However, they did not focus on a tourist's requirements or a software development perspective. Stabb et al. (2002) point out the possible use of semantics for intelligent systems for tourism as well as the importance of catching user needs and decision styles, but without details of how to achieve it.

Information gathering on the Internet about tourist destinations is less effective than it is supposed to be. The reason is that there is no organized URL directory for users to know how and where to access such information. Users might have to browse several sites before reaching the desired information. If the user does not know the addresses of the relevant Web sites, it is quite hard or even impossible to get the information from those Web sites.

Niknafs, Shiri, and Javidi (2003) used a case-based reasoning (CBR) technique in e-tourism, which is one of the applied categories of e-government. It is used for finding the suggestions of travel schedules for tourists. However, case-based reasoning has some limitations. Since the case base is large, the retrieval speed is slow. CBR depends on pre-indexing, which is a time-consuming process. It is impossible to retrieve a case in which case data is missing or unknown.

Yeung, Tung, and Yen (1998) presented a multi-agent-based tourism kiosk that aims at enhancing the effectiveness and efficiency of information retrieval on tourism information. However the system was implemented only to support a specific geographic area (i.e., Hong Kong). It cannot support manual interaction in the decision process. It is inadequate for an integrated solution.

For the implementation of the intelligent multimedia travel agent system (IMTAS), Lenz (1996) used case-based reasoning techniques. IMTAS improves traditional tourism information systems with a decision support system (DSS), guiding the customer during information search, as well as with multimedia facilities providing up-to-date information about specific destinations. Lenz has suggested different scenarios of how tourists could interact with three different types of agents:

the CBR agent, the World Wide Web agent, and the interface agent. A CBR system like IMTAS has several shortcomings. It cannot perform in domains where there is no content associated with items, or where the content is difficult to analyze. Another major limitation of all the CBRs that identify a product (for example, in the hotel case scenario, the hotel product has the attributes of cost and location, such as the cost=100$ and the location=London, so the user can query only these attributes contained in this product) with a case is that users can query the case base only referring to attribute of the product. It is not a flexible approach for the coordination and integration of information and services.

Recently, Chiu, Cheung, and Leung (2005) proposed a multi-agent information system (MAIS) framework for mobile workforce management (MWM) with an in-depth study on how to integrate these technologies for a scalable MWM MAIS but without considering the application of semantics.

Social Information Retrieval Methods

An information retrieval system can be defined as leading the users to those documents that will best enable them to satisfy their need for information. Traditional information retrieval methods fail to address the fact that information production and consumption are social activities. Kirsch et al. (2006) tackled this problem by extending the domain model of information retrieval to include social networks for information retrieval. They presented an attempt to leverage a social network for information retrieval. They proposed a model for social information retrieval which integrates the domains of social network analysis and information retrieval. Their aim is to improve the retrieval performance by providing retrieval techniques.

Resnick, Iacovou, Suchak, Bergstrom, and Riedl (1994) and Konstan et al. (1997) introduced an automated collaborative filtering system using a neighborhood-based algorithm. GroupLens provided social information filtering to the personalized predictions for Usenet new articles. It used both Pearson correlation coefficients to weigh user similarity and all available correlated neighbors to compute a final prediction. Sarwar et al. (1998) designed and implemented a model for integrating content-based ratings into a collaborative filtering system. The filterbot model allows collaborative filtering systems to address sparsity and early rater problems by tapping the strength of content filtering techniques.

The Recommender system proposed by Hill, Stead, Rosenstein, and Furnas (1995) and Shardanand and Maes (1995) expanded upon the original GroupLens algorithm. They generate recommendations on music and movies respectively, suggesting collaborative filtering to be applicable to many different types of media. Ringo (Hill et al., 1995) is a social information filtering system which makes personalized music recommendations. It computed a weighted average of ratings from all users in the neighborhood. Bellcore (Shardanand & Maes, 1995) used Pearson correlation to weigh the average of ratings from all users in the neighborhood. Bellcore used Pearson correlation to weigh a random sample of neighbors, selected the best neighbors, and performed a full multiple regression on them to create prediction.

Goldberg, Nichols, Oki, and Terry (1992) built a system for filtering e-mail called Tapestry which allowed users to annotate messages. Tapestry is one of the first computer-based collaborative filtering systems, designed to support a small, close-knit community of users. The collaborative filtering provided by Tapestry was not automated and required users to construct complex queries in a special query language designed for the task. Many systems use statistical techniques to provide personal recommendations of documents by finding a group of other users (neighbors) that have a history of agreeing with the target user.

The applications of rating-based collaborative filtering now exist in a variety of domains including books, music, movies, and information. While collaborative filtering has been a significant success, there are several problems that researchers and commercial applications have distinguished. It suffers from two fundamental problems: sparsity and scalability. In our system, we therefore first apply the rule-based personalization technique to address the sparsity problem which can reduce the consideration set of items. We use the combination of Rule-based Personalization with Collaborative Filtering technique to improve the accuracy, sparsity, and scalability of collaborative filtering algorithm.

MATS ARCHITECTURE

Today, the Internet has blossomed as a distributed open system where heterogeneous software agents come and go. However, there are no well-established protocols or languages on the 'agent level' (higher than TCP/IP), and the structure of the network itself keeps changing (Vlassis, 2003). In such an environment, multi-agent system technology can be used to develop agents that act on behalf of a user and are able to negotiate with other agents in order to achieve their goals.

Wooldridge (2002) described a multi-agent system as a collection of software agents that works in conjunction with each other. In a multi-agent system architecture, each agent is autonomous, cooperative, coordinated, intelligent, rational, and able to communicate with other agents to fulfill the user's needs. Each agent type has different application-specific capabilities and agency properties. In order to have autonomy, an agent must possess a certain degree of intelligence, allowing it to survive in a dynamic and heterogeneous environment.

In this section, we present the architecture of our proposed Multi-Agent Tourism System (MATS). Figure1 shows MATS's architecture that consists of:

- Interface Module
- Information Management Module
- Domain-Related Module
- Knowledge Repository

MATS operates through the following steps.

For User Request/Query Operations

1. The Interface Module accepts requests to find the user information in the user profile. If it exists, it sends the request to the Information Management Module to find the relevant information with the user's interest. Otherwise, it creates the user profile and sends the request to the Information Management Module.
2. The Interface Module sends the request for query information to the Information Management Module.
3. The Information Management Module processes the request and sends it to the Domain-Related Module for specifying relevant agent.
4. The Domain-Related Module retrieves information from the corresponding database in the Knowledge Repository and returns the response to the Information Management Module.
5. The Information Management Module returns the response to the Interface Module.
6. The Interface Module presents the response information to the user.

For Update/Maintenance Operations

1. When information changes (such as additions/removals) occur in the target Web sites, the Information Agent from the Information Management Module sends this information to Domain-Related Module.

2. In the Domain-Related Module, the Domain Agent specifies the relevant agent and sends this information to the corresponding agent.
3. These corresponding agents update the relevant databases.

INTERFACE MODULE

The Interface Module consists of the Interface Agent and Personalization Agent. The Interface Agent is capable of communicating with other agents within the system and the users. It manages the presentation of information and elicits input from the user, maintains user profiles, and in general it represents the end user's interests in the system.

User Profile Creation

The Personalization Agent retrieves the user profile based on the user's choices and behaviors. Personalization is concerned adapting to the in-

Figure 1. Architecture of multi-agent tourism system (MATS)

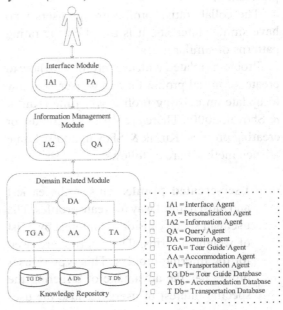

dividual needs, interests, and preferences of each user. According to the profile of a specific user, the Personalization Agent can recognize who the user is. In order to provide the information relevant to the user's interest, we need to create a user profile. Kuflik and Shoval (2000) described that the quality of the user profile has a major impact on the performance of the information filtering. In general, there are three types of user profiles:

- Content-based profile,
- Rule-based profile, and
- Collaborative profile.

The content-based profile represents instances using a vector of terms. The vector of terms, which may be weighted, represents the document content. It consists of attributes such as descriptive, structural, and administrative metadata, varying with the type of content.

In the rule-based profile, rules are created from the answers provided by users on questions about information usage and filtering behaviors. It may include contextual attributes, such as geographic location, and the user's interests and preferences.

The collaborative profile groups users who have similar interests. It is based on the rating patterns of similar users.

Problems related with user profiles are how to create an initial profile for a new user and how to update an existing profile over time (Kuflik & Shoval, 2000). There are various methods for creating profiles (Kuflik & Shoval, 2000). Some of such methods are as follows:

- **User-created profile:** This is the easiest and most natural way to create profiles. The user can specify his or her interest by a list of weighted terms. These terms are used for the filtering process. This type of user profile has the advantage of targeting the specific interest of users because the user

can specify his or her interest profile directly. However, some users are not willing to give their data.

- **System-created profile by automatic Indexing:** A set of data items are analyzed by software in order to identify the most frequent and meaningful terms in the text. Those terms consist of the user profile. These terms are weighted according to the frequency of their appearance. This type of profile is less accurate than a user-created profile.

- **System plus user-created profile:** This is the combination of the above two approaches. First, the initial profile is created automatically (by automatic indexing). Next, the user reviews the proposed profile and updates it by adding or deleting. The user can adjust the profile created by the system. This method can provide better flexibility and is more accurate than the other method.

- **System-created profile based on learning by artificial neural network (ANN):** In this method, an ANN is trained based on a sample set of data items that have already been judged relevant by the user.

- **User profile inherited from a user stereotype:** A user-stereotype is represented as a content-based profile, which is a set of demographic and social attributes as well as the features of classes of users.

For the purpose of our MATS system, we adopt the System plus User-Created Profile approach. There are two ways to acquire user information: explicit personalization and implicit personalization in MATS.

Explicit Personalization

In explicit personalization, users are explicitly asked to fill in the forms in order to obtain the user profile information. Therefore, more responsibility is transferred to the user application as specialized functionality, that is, a user interface is provided that allows users to insert, modify, and apply personal information to the services. If the user elects to create a user profile, he or she will be asked to furnish a user name or an e-mail address that will save as a user name, and a password to use each time he or she logs in. The user will also be asked to provide contact information, including address and telephone numbers, as well as to identify his or her interests. When the user has completed the form, the collected information is created as the user content profile.

For example, when a user requests a tour schedule, the system requests the user to complete the Tour Enquiry Form explicitly. In this form, the user needs to fill the user name, contact, telephone number, e-mail address, contact address, town or city, country, the date of the user visit, how long the user spends on his or her tour, total number of people traveling, and user interest places. When the user has completed this form, the Personalization Agent creates the user profile using the submitted form information.

Implicit Personalization

An implicit personalization process includes a component that monitors users' behavior and makes changes to their profiles according to their behavior. Here, the problem is how to create an initial profile for a new user if the information is not available. When the user does not choose to create the user profile, this is done by gathering information from user behavior by using cookies. User behavior includes mouse activities, scrollbar activities, keyboard activities, and so on (Claypool, Le, Wased, & Brown, 2001). Mouse activities include the number of mouse clicks and the time spent moving the mouse in milliseconds. Scrollbar activities include the number of mouse clicks on the horizontal and vertical scroll bars and time spent scrolling. Keyboard activities include Page Up, Page Down, Up Arrow, and Down Arrow (Claypool et al., 2001).

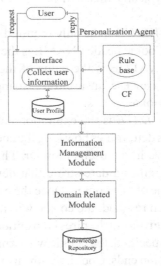

Figure 2. Architecture of Personalization Agent

Cookies

Mayer-Schönberger (2005) defines cookies as pieces of information generated by a Web server and stored in the user's computer, ready for future access. They can be used by a server to recognize authenticated users and to personalize the Web pages of a site depending on the preferences of a user. The main purpose of cookies is to identify users and possibly prepare customized Web pages for them. Cookies are used for storing a user's ID and password for specific Web sites. Each time the user logs on to the Web site, the browser will check to see if the user has any pre-defined preferences (via cookies). If the user has preference cookies, the browser will send the cookies to the server along with the user's request for a Web page. When a new user arrives, the site creates a new ID in the database and sends the ID as a cookie. Each cookie has six parameters described as follows:

    Set-Cookie:
    NAME = VALUE;
    Expire = DATE;
    Path = PATH;
    Domain = DOMAIN_NAME;
    Secure

Set-Cookie is a header as part of an HTTP response; typically this will be generated by a CGI Script.

NAME=VALUE is the only required attribute on the Set-Cookie header. NAME is the name of the cookie. VALUE is the value of the cookie. The server can use an arbitrary string as the value of a cookie.

Expire = DATE is the expiration date of the cookie. This determines how long the cookie will remain active in the user's browser. The Expire attribute specifies a date string that defines the valid lifetime of that cookie. Once the expiration date has been reached, the cookie will no longer be stored or given out. Expires is an optional attribute. If not specified, the cookie will expire when the user session ends. Cookies with an expiration date are called persistent cookies.

The date string is formatted as: Wdy, DD-Mon-YYYY HH:MM:SS GMT

Path=PATH, the path attribute, is used to specify the subset of URLs in a domain for which the cookie is valid. If the path is not specified, it is assumed to be the same path as the document being described by the header which contains the cookie.

Domain=DOMAIN_NAME, the domain attribute, takes the path parameter one step further. This makes the cookie accessible to pages on any of the servers when a site uses multiple serves in a domain.

If a cookie is marked *Secure*, it will only be transmitted if the communications channel with the host is a secure one. Currently this means that secure cookies will only be sent to HTTPS (HTTP over SSL) servers. This can only be used under a secure server condition. If secure is not specified, a cookie is considered safe to be sent in the clear over unsecured channels.

An example cookie to be used in creating a user profile is as follows:

Set-Cookie:
HOTEL = SEDONA_0001;

Expires = Thu, 27 July 2006 20:00:00 GMT;
Path=/;
Domain = http://www.sedonahotels.com.sg/index.asp ;
Secure;

THE PROPOSED METHOD

In this section, we describe our proposed method for the Personalization Agent in MATS. The Personalization Agent performs filtering of information in order to satisfy specific user requirements. Mobasher et al. (2000) and Sung (2002) state that most of the existing Web personalization systems can be generally classified into three types: rule-based systems, content-based filtering systems, and collaborative filtering systems. Rule-based systems allow Web site administrators to specify rules used to determine the contents served to individual users. Content-based filtering systems associate every user with a profile to filter content. Collaborative filtering systems utilize the similarity among profiles of users to recommend interesting materials.

The goal of the Personalization Agent in MATS is to sort through large volumes of dynamically generated information and present to the user those that are likely to satisfy his or her information requirement. In order to identify information that satisfies a user's interest, we propose a Rule-based Personalization with Collaborative Filtering method to acquire the filtered information that evaluates the user's interest. Our proposed method is able to make good matches between user interest and those users seeking the information.

Before describing our proposed method, we briefly discuss rule-based personalization, collaborative filtering, and their weaknesses. We then discuss how we modify information to achieve the best recommendations in our Personalization Agent.

Rule-Based Personalization

Rule-based personalization refers to the personalization resulting from a match of user profile with content profile based on rules (Instone, 2004). This form of personalization implements rules based on a user's profile. The rule-based approach uses the collected data and then defines a set of rules to tailor the content based on the facts specified in the user profile. It is an important way to expose the relevant content to the user. This approach is a simple and straightforward way of personalization to get the relevant information. It determines the quality of personalization experience accordingly. The major drawback to Rule-based Personalization is its limited applicability. The key to this scheme is that we must know ahead of time what the promotion or personalization should be. This is rather strict, and must constantly be evaluated and adjusted depending on the business's needs. The scale of this scheme can also be very large if more detailed personalization is required (Payne, 2000). In addition, just using a rule-based approach generates many rules and involves complex rule maintenance. And the rules must be changed to account for every use situation, or risk failing to meet user expectations and decreasing the site's usefulness. In the characteristics of rule-based personalization, the input data is the user and the content profile, and the output data is the exposed context-dependent content and services.

We therefore combine rule-based personalization with some filtering techniques, either before or after the filtering process, to develop the best recommendation. Initially, our rule-based personalization contains much of the problem-solving knowledge.

For example, if the user queries the names of hotels with a cost between $50 and $60 and the location is in Yangon, the rule is as follows:

Rule: **if** (cost $\geq$ $50 && cost $\leq$ $60) **&&** (location = Yangon)
   then (show hotel name)

rule-based personalization is an important function to expose relevant content to the user, such as matching the user's interest or role, in our proposed method.

Collaborative Filtering

According to Resnick et al. (1994), collaborative filtering is often referred to as social filtering. It focuses on the behavior of users on the items that are to be recommended. The social approach resembles the real-life recommendation. The social filtering system plays a significant role in reducing information overload and providing users with information relevant to their specific interest. The task of collaborative filtering is to predict the interest of an active user to a target item based on user profile. The collaborative filtering system works by collecting user feedback in the form of ratings for item in a given domain, and exploiting similarities and differences among profiles of several users in determining how to recommend an item (Melville, Mooney, & Nagarajan, 2002). The collaborative filtering system can perform in domains where there is not much content associated with items or where the content is difficult to analyze.

Collaborative filtering draws recommendations from a variety of other users with similar interests and involves gathering data on user preferences and behavior, and then uses that data to algorithmically produce recommendations for new users. Collaborative filtering solves the problem of personalization of content for an essentially unknown user.

The effectiveness of a collaborative filtering system depends on the size of the sample, capture of data, speed, and algorithm. A collaborative filtering algorithm should be able to give personalized suggestions by using evaluation from the users that have the same preferences. There are two general classes of collaborative filtering algorithm: memory-based methods and model-based methods (Zeng, Xing, & Zhou, 2003).

The memory-based methods are the most popular prediction techniques in collaborative filtering applications. They utilize the entire user-item database to generate predictions. The user-based collaborative filtering algorithm is a memory-based algorithm (Yu, Wen, Xu, & Ester, 2001; Yu, Xu, Tao, Ester, & Kriegel, 2002).

The model-based collaborative filtering methods use the user's preferences to learn a model, which is then used for predictions. Model-based methods are not suitable for environments in which user preference models must be updated rapidly or frequently (Zeng et al., 2003).

Various algorithms have been used with collaborative filtering, both recommendation systems and similarity measures. The technologies that have been applied to the recommendation system are Bayesian networks, Pearson Correlation Coefficient, Clustering, Cosine Correlation and Horting, and so forth (Kangas, 2002). Among these methods, the Bayesian networks are only feasible for environments in which the knowledge of user preferences is changing slowly with respect to the time needed to build the model, but these models are not suitable for environments in which user preference models must be updated rapidly or frequently (Breese & Kadie, 1998). The clustering technique usually produces fewer personal recommendations than other methods. In some cases, the clusters have worse accuracy than the nearest neighbor algorithm (Kangas, 2002). We therefore adopt the Pearson Correlation Coefficient for similarity measure between users and describe the experimental result of the RPCF algorithm.

Although pure collaborative filtering is very useful for prediction systems, it has some weaknesses: sparsity and cold-start problems (Papagelis, Plexousakis, & Kutsuras, 2005).

Sparsity is the major limitation of collaborative filtering. It occurs when the number of items far exceeds what an individual can rate, and only a few total numbers of items available in the database are rated by the users. Most users do not rate most items and hence the user-item matrix is typically very sparse. In the tourism domain, it is possible to get the very sparse user-item matrix because most of the users are not willing to rate the item from various sites.

Cold-Start refers to the situation in which an item cannot be recommended. This problem applies to new and obscure items, and is particularly detrimental to users with eclectic tastes. It is hard to get many ratings from new users, so such users cannot get the accurate recommendation. The reason is that there is difficulty finding the neighborhood.

Therefore, pure collaborative filtering has difficulty in making recommendations for new items since it requires a body of data before it can make recommendations.

To overcome the abovementioned problems of pure rule-based personalization and pure collaborative filtering systems, we propose a Rule-based Personalization with Collaborative Filtering algorithm to produce the best recommendations.

Figure 3 shows the Recommendation process by RPCF algorithm for hotel enquiry. In this system, when a user requests information about hotels, the rule-based personalization retrieves the user profile and evaluates the rule to select the contents that meet the condition of the rules. According to the rules executed by rule-based personalization, it searches for the hotel informa-

Figure 3. Recommendation process by RPCF for hotel enquiry

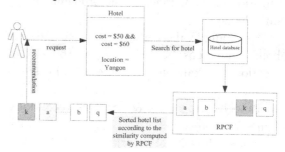

tion in the hotel database. In this, RPCF evaluates the prediction of hotel according to the similarity and weight. The accuracy of prediction is done by means of Mean Absolute Error (MAE), which evaluates the performance of the RPCF algorithm. After processing these steps, the user is responded to with the recommendation most relevant to the user's request.

PROPOSED RPCF ALGORITHM

Our proposed rule-based personalization with collaborative filtering algorithm is as follows:

1. Generate rules by using rule-based personalization from user query input.
2. Compute the similarity measure between users by means of the Person Correlation Coefficient.
3. Weight the similarity by the number of item ratings and select the neighboring user that has the highest similarity rating with the active user.
4. Compute a prediction from the ratings of neighbor.
5. Use Mean Absolute Error for evaluating the accuracy of a prediction.

This RPCF algorithm aims to identify users that have relevant interests by calculating similarity between user profiles.

In step 1, the rule-based personalization is performed as the example, as shown in rule-based personalization. This step generates the content rules based on the user query input. The content rules are in the form IF condition THEN action.

Collaborative filtering works by collecting user feedback in the form of ratings for items in a given domain, and exploiting similarities and differences among profiles of several users in determining how to recommend an item or how to

give the prediction for the active user's interest. A subset of users is chosen based on their similarity to the active user, and a weighted combination of their ratings is used to produce predictions for the active user. Similarity is a powerful way to retrieve interesting information from a large repository. The threshold of correlation coefficient ranges from -1.00 to +1.00. The value of -1.00 represents a perfect negative correlation while a value of +1.00 represents a perfect positive correlation. A value of 0.00 represents a lack of correlation.

In step 2, the following Pearson Correlation Coefficient function is used to compute the similarity measure between the user's preference functions (Cann, 2004).

$$S(a,b) = \frac{\sum_{i=1}^{N}(x_{a,i} - \overline{x_a})(x_{b,i} - \overline{x_b})}{\sqrt{\sum_{i=1}^{N}(x_{a,i} - \overline{x_a})^2 * \sum_{i=1}^{N}(x_{b,i} - \overline{x_b})^2}} \quad (1)$$

where S (a, b) is the similarity of user a and b, N is the number of items, and $x_{a,i}$ and $x_{b,i}$ are the ratings given to the item i by user a and b. $\overline{x_a}$ and $\overline{x_b}$ are the average ratings (mean) of user a and b.

A higher collection value indicates more accurate recommendations. Pearson's Correlation Coefficient only measures the overlapping items between users. In step 3, the Significance-Weighting method as shown in Equation 2 (Cann, 2004) is used to devalue the correlation based on few co-rated items:

$$W(a,b) = S(a,b) * \frac{n}{50} \quad (2)$$

If two users have less than 50 commonly rated items, we apply a significance weight of n/50, where n is the number of co-rated items.

If there are more than 50 co-rated items, then a significance weight of 1 is applied which means we leave the correlation unchanged.

In step 4, predictions are computed from the weighted combination of the neighbor, which is defined in Papagelis et al. (2005) as:

$$P_{a,i} = \bar{x}_a + \frac{\sum_{b=1}^{M}(x_{b,i} - \bar{x}_b)}{\sum_{b=1}^{M}W(a,b)} * W(a,b) \qquad (3)$$

where, M is the number of users in the neighborhood and $P_{a,i}$ is the prediction of the active user a on the target item i.

Step 5 evaluates the accuracy of a predictor by comparing predicted values with user-provided values. To evaluate the accuracy of prediction, we use MAE (Papagelis et al., 2005) as the evaluation metric as follows:

$$MAE = \frac{1}{n} * \sum_{i=1}^{n}\left|x_{a,i} - p_{a,i}\right| \qquad (4)$$

where, $p_{a,i}$ is the predicted value of user a on item i, $x_{a,i}$ is the rating given to item i by user a, and n is the number of actual ratings in an item set. MAE is the mean absolute error between the predicted value and the actual value of users within the test data. The lower the MAE, the more accurate the prediction is.

INFORMATION MANAGEMENT MODULE

There are two main purposes of the Information Management Module. One is to store the data in corresponding databases, and the other is to attain the requested query and decide which pieces of information to retrieve from the database. It consists of Information Agent and Query Agent.

Information Agent

The Information Agent manages the data to be stored in corresponding databases whenever the changes or updates of information occur. The Information Agent sends the collected information to the Domain-Related Module in order to store them locally in the Knowledge Repository. The Information Agent can serve the information needs of users in specific domains. It also collects and manipulates the tourism information from many distributed information sources which are constructed independently. It is the main entity of MATS that grabs the information from any site that is interested in offering services, such as tourism information. There are two main issues to be solved in collecting information. The first one manually performs which site to choose that is related to the user's interest, and the second is to extract the detailed information automatically from that relevant site by using an existing wrapper (Zhao, Meng, Wu, Raghavan, & Yu, 2005). It also passes the queries that come from the Information Agent and retrieves the resulted queries information from the Query Agent.

Query Agent

An important capability of the Information Management Module is the ability to retrieve the information flexibly and efficiently. The Query Agent retrieves the pieces of information from the Knowledge Repository through the Domain-Related Module and returns the results to the Personalization Agent. It uses KQML to retrieve queries during interaction from other agents.

KQML

KQML is an agent communication language that enables similar software agents to communicate with each other via predefined performatives (Finin, Fritzson, McKay, & McEntire, 1994). It is the first de facto standard agent communication language, and many agent platforms support KQML. A performative specifies the format of any given message and dictates how an agent should respond to the message. In our system, we use KQML as an agent communication language—as a language and protocol for exchanging information and knowledge. It is both a message format and a message handling protocol to support run-time knowledge sharing among agents.

A KQML message consists of a 'performative', its associated arguments which include the real content of the message, and a set of optional arguments 'transport', which describe that content in a manner that is independent of the syntax of the content language and perhaps the sender and receiver.

The syntax of KQML is based on balanced parentheses. The initial element of the list is the performative; the remaining elements are the performative's arguments as keyword/value pairs. Because the language is relatively simple, the actual syntax is not significant and can be changed if necessary in the future. The set of performatives forms the core of the language.

In MATS, KQML can be seen as a layered language that consists of three layers (Finin et al., 1994): content layer, message layer, and communication layer. The content layer depicts the actual content of the message, in the program's own representation language. The message layer determines the kind of interaction. The primary functions of the message layer are to identify the protocol to be used to deliver the message and to supply a performative which the sender attaches to the content. The communication layer encodes a set of features to the message that describe the lower-level communication parameters, such as the identity of the sender and recipient, and a unique identifier associated with the communication.

For example, a message representing a query about the detail information of a hotel might be encoded as:

```
(evaluate :sender Query Agent
      :receiver Domain Agent
      :language KQML
      :content (ask_detail:
          :type hotel
          :price hotel
          :room Family
          :name Sedona Hotel
      )
)
```

In this message, the KQML *performative* is 'evaluate', the *sender* of the message is 'Query Agent' from the Information Management Module, the *receiver* of the message is 'Domain Agent', and the *content* is (ask_detail:type hotel, price hotel, room family, name Sedona Hotel). The Domain Agent searches which agent has the information of the Sedona Hotel and sends a KQML message to the Hotel Agent for information as follows:

```
(evaluate :sender Query Agent
      :receiver Hotel Agent
      :language KQML
      :content (ask_detail:
      :from Query Agent
      :type hotel
      :price hotel
      :room Family
      :name Sedona Hotel
      )
)
```

If the hotel exists, the Hotel Agent sends the result from the Hotel Database to the Domain Agent.

```
(evaluate :sender Hotel Agent
      :receiver Domain Agent
      :language KQML
      :content (tell_detail:
          :from Query Agent
          :type hotel
```

```
:price hotel
:room Family
:name Sedona Hotel
:result ([address: No. 1 Kaba Aye
Pagoda Road, Yankin Towship,
Yangon]
    [Telephone: 951-666900]
    [price of Family room: $150
    per day]
    )
  )
)
```

The Domain Agent sends the retrieved result back to the Query Agent, and it displays the request to the use through the Interface Module.

DOMAIN-RELATED MODULE

The Domain-Related Module consists of the Domain Agent and many other agents corresponding to the tourism domain such as Tour Guide Agent, Accommodation Agent, and Transportation Agent.

Domain Agent

The Domain Agent is capable of accomplishing specialized tasks such as database queries and delivering specific domain solutions. The Domain Agent is responsible for choosing the type of query for retrieving hotels, restaurants, tourism information, and so forth. It is the system's gateway to specific sources of travel services to other agents. It receives queries from the Information Agent and passes them to each domain-related agent. These retrieve the required data from the corresponding database and return the desired information to the Information Management Module. When information changes, such as add or remove occurs in the interested Web sites, each domain-related agent updates the corresponding database.

KNOWLEDGE REPOSITORY

The Knowledge Repository consists of tourism information for each domain in a standard structure like a relational table, and its operations include SELECT, INSERT, UPDATE, and DELETE. It is a repository for a collection of computerized data files. The purpose of the Knowledge Repository is to maintain information and make that information available on demand. It stores information about tourism, accommodation, transportation, and so forth.

Tour Guide Database

The tour guide database consists of tourism information such as tour packages like full-package tours, private tours, group tours, guided tours, customized guided tours, and places of interest, and they can be classified according to different criteria, for example the type of places, historical monuments, beaches, mountains, religious places, museums, and so forth.

Accommodation Database

The accommodation database contains information about hotels and restaurants. For each hotel, we maintain the detailed information such as the standard of hotel, its category, price, the services available (types of rooms, availability of bar or restaurant, swimming pool, gym, garage or parking, beauty parlor, and so on), and information about its location (in the down-town area, close to places of interests, close to markets, close to industrial sites, etc.).

Transportation Database

The transportation database contains information about car rental services such as full-day downtown area, half-day downtown area, from airport to hotel, hotel to famous sightseeing places, and so on. International airline schedules and fares, domestic airline schedules and fares, train schedules and fares, bus service, taxi service, and others—all of this information is stored in corresponding databases in the Knowledge Repository. Each item in the database is maintained and updated by corresponding agents whenever the information is changed in various information sources.

EXPERIMENTAL RESULTS OF THE RPCF ALGORITHM

This section describes the experimental results of the RPCF algorithm. We use the hotel ratings datasets from Travelocity (*www.travelocity.com*) to evaluate the algorithm. The dataset contains (2,721) ratings from (40,995) user reviews for (740) hotels. Each user can rate a hotel to express his or her willingness to stay at this hotel. A rating is a number ranging from 1 to 5; a higher score indicates a higher preference. We evaluate some of the datasets taken from Travelocity. We now consider 30 users of ratings on 20 hotels for the prediction rating of user1 on hotel5.

Table 1 shows the comparison of the RPCF algorithm and the pure collaborative filtering algorithm of similarity, weight, prediction, and MAE. The similarity and prediction of these two algorithms have some differences in values, but

Table 1. Comparison of similarity, weight, prediction, and MAE of two algorithms

Users	RPCF Algorithm				Pure CF Algorithm			
	Sim	Weight	Pred	MAE	Sim	Weight	Pred	MAE
u1,u2	-0.3	-0.1	4.2	0.01	0	-0.1	4.5	-0.1
u1,u3	0.1	0	4	0	0.1	0	4	0
u1,u4	0.2	0.1	4	0	0.2	0	4.1	0
u1,u5	0	0	4.1	0.01	0	0	4.1	0
u1,u6	-0.1	0	4.1	0	0	0	3.8	0.1
u1,u7	-0.5	-0.2	3.8	0	0	-0.1	3.5	0.1
u1,u8	0	0	3.5	0	0	0	3.6	0
u1,u9	0.1	0	3.4	0	0.1	0	3	0.2
u1,u10	0.6	0.2	3.4	0	0.6	0.1	3.1	0
u1,u11	0.3	0.1	3.1	0	0.3	0.1	3.1	0
u1,u12	0.3	0.1	2.8	0.02	0.3	0.1	2.8	0.1
u1,u13	-0.2	-0.1	2.9	0	0	0	2.3	0.2
u1,u14	-0.2	-0.1	2.1	0.01	0	0	3.6	-0.5
u1,u15	0.2	0.1	3.9	0.02	0.2	0	4	0.1
u1,u16	-0.3	-0.1	4	0	0	-0.1	3.7	0.1
u1,u17	0	0	3.7	0	0.2	0	3.6	0.1
u1,u18	-0.2	-0.1	3.6	0	0	0	3.5	0.1
u1,u19	-0.3	-0.1	3.3	0	0	-0.1	3.2	0.1
u1,u20	0.1	0	3.2	0	0.1	0	3	0.1
u1,u21	-0.1	0	3	0	0	0	2.8	0.1
u1,u22	0.3	0.1	2.8	0.01	0.3	0.1	2.9	0
u1,u23	0	0	2.9	0.02	0	0	4.5	-0.5
u1,u24	-0.1	0	4.4	0	0	0	4.4	0
u1,u25	-0.2	-0.1	4.5	0	0	0	4.2	0.1
u1,u26	-0.3	-0.1	4.3	0.01	0	-0.1	4.1	0.1
u1,u27	0	0	4.2	0	0	0	4	0.1
u1,u28	0.1	0	4	0	0.1	0	4	0
u1,u29	-0.1	0	4	0	0	0	4	0
u1,u30	0.1	0	3.9	0	0.1	0	4	0

Sim=Similarity
Pred=Prediction

the weight value is roughly the same. However, RPCF obviously improves the MAE.

Figure 4 shows the comparison results of similarity for the RPCF algorithm and the pure collaborative filtering algorithm. The similarity values are computed by Pearson's Correlation Coefficient. The similarity values range from -1 to +1. The higher the similarity value, the smaller the neighborhood size. While the pure collaborative filtering shows the similarity value is 'zero', which means the two users have no correlation, RPCF shows how dissimilar the ratings of these two users are by a negative correlation value. The more exact the similar value, the more accurate the prediction value is.

Figure 5 shows the comparison of the weight for the two algorithms. The weight can be scaled by using the similarity of user pairs. We obtain the highest weight by multiplying the highest similarity pairs with the number of co-rated items over commonly rated items.

Figure 6 shows the comparison of prediction for the two algorithms. The prediction value of rating is for user1 on hotel 5. We compute the prediction based on the highest similarity and weight. So we get few errors which improve the accuracy of prediction. In this figure, some prediction values of pure collaborative filtering are higher than RPCF because it depends on the rating values given by the user—for example, (user 1 and user 2) pair and (user1 and user 23) pair and so on.

As shown in Figure 7, while the fluctuation of MAE of pure collaborative filtering is high, the MAE of RPCF is quite stable. This figure shows that RPCF outperforms pure collaborative filtering

Figure 4. Comparison of similarity between two algorithms

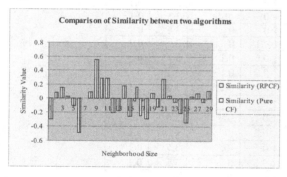

Figure 6. Comparison of prediction between two algorithms

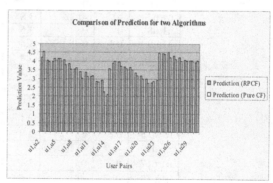

Figure 5. Comparison of weight between two algorithms

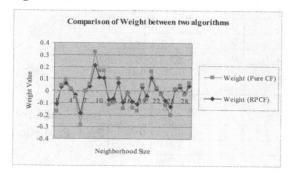

Figure 7. Comparison of MAE between two algorithms

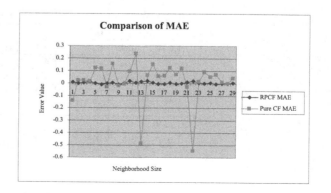

in MAE, meaning that RPCF made predictions with fewer (even without) errors.

CONCLUSION

Information on the World Wide Web is distributed, dynamic, and heterogeneous. So, it is not easy to get the relevant and updated information needed by each individual user. In this chapter we have introduced the Personalization Agent for Multi-Agent Tourism System and proposed a Rule-based Personalization with Collaborative Filtering technique. MATS can provide users efficiently and effectively with information that is relevant to the user's request. Users are able to interact with an autonomous agent environment in an interactive and user-friendly way. We use KQML as an agent communication language. In our system, the user has two options: filling out a form and saving user information in the user profile, or applying the cookies which provide an easier way to gather information about the user. In order to provide relevant information for the user's interest, the system maintains the various types of tourism information and provides the updated information according to the user's profile. Experimental results show that our proposed method also improves scalability, accuracy, and quality of recommendation.

All agents in MATS are written in Java and access the relational databases via the Java Database Connectivity (JDBC) or Microsoft's Open Database Connectivity (ODBC) interfaces. Since MATS is still in the ongoing stage of implementation, the following areas of future work need to be carried out to provide a complete working system on the Web:

- The current implementation of MATS has not fully provided the update/maintain information operation whenever the information is changed in various information sources.

We must focus on how to automatically update the contents of the Knowledge Repository in order to provide users with the most recent tourism information on the Web.

- We must also focus on building the automatic wrapper around an existing Knowledge Repository by using hierarchical clustering techniques to extract the pieces of relevant information from the Web page without human intervention.

- We must extend the current work to mobile devices. We will focus on applications that collect and deliver information by using small-screen mobile devices such as PDAs and smart phones.

REFERENCES

Abrahams, B., & Dai, W. (2005). Architecture for automated annotation and ontology based querying of semantic Web resources. Proceedings of the 2005 IEEE/WIC/ACM International Conference on Web Intelligence (WI'05), (pp. 413-417).

Andrew, S. (n.d). Cookies. Retrieved April 29, 2006, from http://www.quirksmode.org/js/cookies.html

Avery, C., & Zeckhauser, R. (1997). Recommender systems for evaluating computer messages. Communication of the ACM, 40(3), 88-89.

Breese, J., & Kadie, C. (1998). Empirical analysis of predictive algorithms for collaborative filtering. Proceedings of the 14th Annual Conference on Uncertainty in Artificial Intelligence (UAI-98) (pp. 43-52).

Burger, F., Kroiss, P., Pröll, B., Richtsfeld, R., Sighart, H., & Starck, H. (1997). TIS@ WEB—database supported tourist information on the Web. Proceedings of the 4th International Information and Communication Technologies in Tourism 1997 (ENTER'97), Edinburgh, Scotland.

Cann, J.A. (2004). Maths from scratch for biologists: Correlation (pp.91-144). Retrieved March 14, 2006, from http://www-micro.msb.le.ac.uk/1010/DH3.html

Chiu, D.K.W., Cheung, S.C., & Leung, H.F. (2005). A multi-agent infrastructure for mobile workforce management in a service oriented enterprise. Proceedings of the 38th Annual Hawaii International Conference on System Sciences (HICSS'05) (Track 3, p. 85c).

Claypool, M., Le, P., Wased, M., & Brown, D. (2001, January 14-17). Implicit interest indicators. Proceedings of the 6th International Conference on Intelligent User Interfaces (IUI '01) (pp. 33-40), Santa Fe, NM.

Connor, O. (2001). Personalization comes full circle, part 2. Retrieved April 27, 2006, from http://www.clickz.com/experts/crm/crm-strat/article.php/14341

Finin, T., Fritzson, R., McKay, D., & McEntire, R. (1994, November 29-December 2). KQML as an agent communication language. Proceedings of the 3rd International Conference on Information and Knowledge Management (CIKM '94) (pp. 456-463), Gaithersburg, MD.

Goldberg, D., Nichols, D., Oki, B.M., & Terry, D. (1992). Using collaborative filtering to weave an information tapestry. 35(12), 61-70.

Hill, W., Stead, L., Rosenstein, M., & Furnas, G. (1995, May 7-11). Recommending and evaluating choices in a virtual community of use. Proceedings of the SIGCHI Conference on Human Factors in Computing Systems (pp. 194-201), Denver, CO.

Hyldegaard, J., & Seiden, P. (2004). My e-journal: Exploring the usefulness of personalized access to scholarly articles and services. Information Research, 9(3).

Instone, K. (2004). Information architecture perspective on personalization. Retrieved February 23, 2006, from http://instone.org/files/Instone-IAPrzChapter.pdf

Joachims, T., Freitag, D., & Mitchell, T. (1997). WebWatcher: A tour guide for the World Wide Web. Proceedings of the 15th International Joint Conference on Artificial Intelligence (IJCAI97) (pp. 770-775), Nagoya, Japan.

Kangas, S. (2002). Collaborative filtering and recommendation systems. Research Report TTE-2001-35, LOUHT-Project, VTT Tietotekniikka. Retrieved March 26, 2006, from http://www.vtt.fi/inf/julkaisut/muut/2002/collaborativefiltering.pdf

Kirsch, S.M., Gnasa, M., & Cremers, A.B. (2006, April 10-12). Beyond the Web: Retrieval in social information spaces. Advances in Information Retrieval, Proceedings of the 28th European Conference on ECIR (vol. 3936/2006, pp. 84-95), London.

KMI. (n.d.). KQML performatives. Retrieved January 28, 2006, from http://kmi.open.ac.uk/people/emaunela/JATLiteBean/KQMLperf.html

Konstan, J.A., Miller, B.N., Maltz, D., Herlocker, J.L., Gordon, L.R., & Riedl, J. (1997). GroupLens: Applying collaborative filtering to Usenet news. 40(3), 77-87.

Krupansky, J.(2005). Definition: Agent, activity, advancing the science of software agent technology. Retrieved February 5, 2006, from http://www.agtivity.com/def/agent.htm

Kuflik, T., & Shoval, P. (2000, July 24-28). Generation of user profiles for information filtering: Research agenda (poster session). Proceedings of the 23rd Annual International ACM SIGIR Conference on Research and Development in Information Retrieval (SIGIR'00) (pp. 313-315), Athens, Greece.

Lenz, M. (1996). IMATS: Intelligent multimedia travel agent system. Proceedings of the ENTER'96 Conference, Innsbruck.

Maw, S.Y., & Naing, M.-M. (2006, February). Personalization agent for multi-agent tourism system. Proceedings of the 4th International Conference on Computer Application (ICCA'06) (pp. 117-124), Yangon, Myanmar.

Maw, S.Y., Naing, M.-M., & Thein. N.L. (2006, November 6-8). RPCF algorithm for multi-agent tourism system (poster session). Proceedings of the 2006 IEEE International Symposium on Micro-NanoMechatronics and Human Science (MHS 2006), Nagoya, Japan.

Mayer-Schönberger, V. (2005). The cookie concept. Retrieved March 3, 2006, from http://www.cookiecentral.com/c_concept.htm

Melville, P., Mooney, J., & Nagarajan, R. (2002). Content-boosted collaborative filtering for improved recommendations. *Proceedings of the 18th National Conference on Artificial Intelligence* (AAAI-2002) (pp. 187-192), Edmonton, Canada.

Middleton, S.E., Shadbolt, N.R., & De Roure, D.C. (2004). Ontological user profiling in recommender systems. *ACM Transactions on Information Systems, 22*(1), 54-88.

Mobasher, B., Cooley, R., & Srivastava, J. (2000). Automatic personalization based on Web usage mining. *43*(8), 142-151.

Niknafs, A.A., Shiri, M.E., & Javidi, M.M. (2003). A case-based reasoning approach in e-tourism: Tour itinerary planning. *Proceedings of the 14th International Workshop on Database and Expert Systems Applications* (DEXA'03) (p. 818), Iran.

Papagelis, M., & Plexousakis, D. (2004, September 27-29). Qualitative analysis of user-based and item-based prediction algorithms for recommendation agents. *Proceedings of the 8th International CIA Workshop* (pp.152-166), Erfurt, Germany.

Papagelis, M., Plexousakis, D., & Kutsuras, T. (2005). Alleviating the sparsity problem of collaborative filtering using trust inferences. *Trust Management, 3477*, 224-239.

Payne, C. (2000). Personalization technique. Retrieved January 4, 2006, from http://www.wdvl.com/Authoring/ASP/Personalization/techniques.html

Resnick, P., Iacovou, N., Suchak, M., Bergstrom, P., & Riedl, J. (1994, October 22-26). GroupLens: An open architecture for collaborative filtering of Netnews. Proceedings of the 1994 ACM Conference on Computer Supported Cooperative Work (CSCW '94) (pp. 175-186), Chapel Hill, NC.

Rumetshofer, H., & Wob, W. (2005). Semantic maps and meta-data enhancing e-accessibility in tourism information systems. Proceedings of the 16th International Workshop on Database and Expert Systems Applications (DEXA'05) (pp. 881-885), Austria.

Sarwar, B.M., Konstan, J.A., Borchers, A., Herlocker, J., Miller, B., & Riedl, J. (1998, November 14-18). Using filtering agents to improve prediction quality in the GroupLens research collaborative filtering system. Proceedings of the 1998 ACM Conference on Computer Supported Cooperative Work (CSCW'98) (pp. 345-354), Seattle, WA.

Shardanand, U., & Maes, P. (1995, May 7-11). Social information filtering: Algorithms for automating "word of mouth." Proceedings of the SIGCHI Conference on Human Factors in Computing Systems (pp. 210-217), Denver, CO.

Shearin, S., & Lieberman, H. (2001, January 14-17). Intelligent profiling by example. Proceedings of the 6th International Conference on Intelligent User Interfaces (IUI '01), Santa Fe, NM.

Statsoft. (n.d.). Basic statistics. Retrieved February 10, 2006, from http://www.statsoft.com/textbook/stbasic.html#index

Sung, H.H. (2002, November). Helping online customers decide through Web personalization. Proceedings of the Conference on IEEE Intelligent Systems (vol. 17, no. 6, pp. 34-43), Kyungpook National University, Korea.

UMBC. (n.d.). What is KQML? Retrieved January 28, 2006, from http://www.cs.umbc.edu/kqml/whats-kqml.html

Vlassis, N. (2003). A concise introduction to multiagent systems and distributed AI. Retrieved January 14, 2006, from http://staff.science.uva.nl/~vlassis/cimasdai/

Webdesign. (n.d.). Cookies: HTTP cookies—Web cookies. Retrieved January 25, 2006, from http://Webdesign.about.com/od/cookies

Webdesign. (2005). How to write Web cookies. Retrieved March 20, 2006, from http://Webdesign.about.com/b/a/136789.htm

Webopedia. (n.d.). Do cookies compromise security? Retrieved January 1, 2006, from http://www.Webopedia.com/DidYouKnow/Internet/2002/Cookies.asp

Wikipedia. (n.d.). Collaborative filtering. Retrieved March 3, 2006, from http://en.wikipedia.org/wiki/Collaborative_filtering

Willy, C. (2001, April 17). Web site personalization. Retrieved May 31, 2005, from http://www-128.ibm.com/developerworks/Websphere/library/techarticles/hipods/personalize.html

Wooldridge, M. (2002). An introduction to multiagent system. Chichester, UK: John Wiley & Sons.

Yeung, C., Tung, P.F., & Yen, J. (1998). A multiagent based tourism kiosk on Internet. *Proceedings of the 31st Annual Hawaii International Conference on System Sciences* (vol. 4, p. 452).

Yu, K., Wen, Z., Xu, X., & Ester, M. (2001). Feature weighting and instance selection for collaborative filtering. *Proceedings of the 2nd International Workshop on Management of Information on the Web—Web Data and Text Mining* (MIW'01) (pp. 285-290).

Yu, K., Xu, X., Tao, J., Ester, M., & Kriegel, H.P. (2002). Instance selection techniques for memory-based collaborative filtering. *Proceedings of the 2nd SIAM International Conference on Data Mining* (SDM'02). Retrieved February 21, 2006, from *http://citeseer.ist.psu.edu/yu02instance.html*

Zeng, C., Xing, C.X., & Zhou, L.Z. (2003). Similarity measure and instance selection for collaborative filtering. *Proceedings of the 12th International Conference on the World Wide Web* (WWW'03) (pp. 652-658), Budapest, Hungary.

Zhao, H., Meng, W., Wu, Z., Raghavan, V., & Yu, C. (2005, May 10-14). Fully automatic wrapper generation for search engines. *Proceedings of the 14th International World Wide Web Conference Committee* (IW3C2) (pp. 66-75), Chiba, Japan.

Chapter XVI
Hybrid Recommendation Systems:
A Case Study on the Movies Domain

Konstantinos Markellos
University of Patras, Greece

Ionna Mousourouli
University of Patras, Greece

Penelope Markellou
University of Patras, Greece

Angeliki Panayiotaki
University of Patras, Greece

Aristotelis Mertis
University of Patras, Greece

Athanasios Tsakalidis
University of Patras, Greece

ABSTRACT

Recommendation systems have been used in e-commerce sites to make product recommendations and to provide customers with information that helps them decide which products to buy. They are based on different methods and techniques for suggesting products with the most well known being collaborative and content-based filtering. Recently, several recommendation systems adopted hybrid approaches by combining collaborative and content-based features as well as other techniques in order to avoid their limitations. In this chapter we investigate hybrid recommendations systems and especially the way they support movie e-shops in their attempt to suggest movies to customers. Specifically, we introduce an approach where the knowledge about customers and movies is extracted from usage mining and onto-logical data in conjunction with customer movie ratings and matching techniques between customers. This integration provides additional knowledge about customers' preferences and allows the production of successful recommendations. Even in the case of the cold-start problem where no initial behavioral information is available, the approach can provide logical and relevant recommendations to the customers. The provided recommendations are expected to have higher accuracy in matching customers' preferences and thus higher acceptance by them. Finally, we describe future trends and challenges, and discuss the open issues in the field.

INTRODUCTION

With the evolution of the Web, the overall business environment has undergone significant changes. The ability of companies to transact business with partners and customers anywhere in the world has become not only a reality but also a necessity. In this context, it is becoming evident that the next evolution in business is a global Web economy. However, this networked economy is notably characterized by the impersonal nature of the online environment and the extensive use of information technology (IT), as opposed to face-to-face contact for transactions.

Since Internet technologies and infrastructures to support electronic commerce (e-commerce) are now in place, attention is paid to psychological factors that affect its acceptance by online consumers and their perceptions of online transactions. One such factor is *individuality* of e-customers, seen to be an important key to the proliferation of e-commerce. The question is how easily Internet users become e-customers and which are the internal "mechanisms" and external factors that participate in an e-purchase. The primary problem arises from the fact that shoppers with varying needs, preferences, and backgrounds navigate through extensive and complex Web structures and are overwhelmed by too many options and too much information that they have to deal with, the majority of which is often irrelevant to their needs and interests. Generally, search engines are used for filtering pages according to explicit users' queries. However, their results are often poor since the produced lists are long, unmanageable, and contain irrelevant pages (Middleton, De Roure, & Shadbolt, 2004).

Many e-shops consider analyzing customers' behavior, developing marketing strategies to create new consuming markets, and discovering hidden loyal customers as the key factors of success. Therefore, new techniques to promote electronic business become essential, and Web personalization is one of the most popular techniques. According to Eirinaki and Vazirgiannis (2003):

Personalization is defined as any action that adapts the information or services provided by a Web site to the knowledge gained from the users' navigational behavior and individual interests, in combination with the content and the structure of the site.

In this direction, the recent Web technological advances help online companies to acquire an individual customer's information in real-time and at low cost. Based on this information, they construct detailed profiles and provide personalized e-services. Thus, e-shops have now the opportunity to improve their performance by addressing the individual's needs and preferences, increasing satisfaction, promoting loyalty, and establishing one-to-one relationships. Personalization is expected to be one of the means for driving e-commerce and e-business forward.

Recommendation or recommender systems (RSs) (Adomavicius & Tuzhilin, 2005) that comprise popular forms of personalization are becoming significant business tools. They emerged in the middle of 1990s and from novelties used by a few Web sites have changed to important tools incorporated into many e-commerce applications (e.g., Amazon.com, eBay.com, CDNow.com, etc.) in order to help customers find products to purchase. Specifically, these systems take advantage of users' and/or communities' opinions in order to support individuals to identify the information or products most likely to be interesting to them or relevant to their needs and preferences. For example, an RS can remember the articles that a user has read. The next time he visits the site, the system can recommend new articles to him based on the ones he has read before.

The recommendations may be implemented in many forms (Brusilovsky, 2001):

- Personalized offers, prices, products, and services;
- Inserting or removing thematic units, sections, paragraphs;
- Sorting, hiding, unhiding, adding, removing, highlighting links; and/or
- Optional explanations or detailed information, and so forth.

According to Schafer, Konstan, and Reidl (2001), RSs can enhance the sales of e-commerce sites in various ways:

- **Converting visitors to buyers:** The visitors often navigate an e-commerce site without purchasing anything. RSs can help them find products they wish to purchase.
- **Increasing cross-sell:** RSs improve cross-sell by suggesting additional products for the customer to purchase. If the recommendations are good, the average order size should increase. For instance, a site might recommend additional products in the checkout process, based on those products already in the shopping cart.
- **Building e-loyalty:** In a world where a site's competitors are only a click or two away, gaining consumers' loyalty is an essential business strategy. RSs improve e-loyalty by creating a value-added relationship between the site and the customer. Sites invest in learning about their customers, use RSs to operationally learn, and present custom interfaces that match consumer needs. Consumers repay these sites by returning to the ones that best match their needs. The more a customer uses the RS—teaching it what he wants—the more loyal he is to the site.

The dilemma of how to choose the most suitable products and services is a challenging research problem. Various approaches have been used to produce recommendations, for instance *collaborative filtering* typically based on product ratings explicitly defined by the users. The system recommends which products have been evaluated positively by similar user(s) whose ratings are in the strongest correlation with the current user. Another approach is *content-based filtering,* which uses product features and recommends products to users that have similar features with those they rated highly during the past. Besides these two techniques, *demographic filtering* employs demographic data (e.g., age, gender, profession) to infer recommendation rules, and *statistics-based techniques* like best-seller characteristics are used, usually when no personalization technique is applicable. Each of these techniques individually has major advantages and drawbacks.

In this context, we present the way *hybrid recommendations systems* that combine various approaches can be used by e-commerce applications, and specifically we focus on movie e-shops. The following section presents definitions and background information on existing recommendation approaches, refers to the most important research and commercial efforts in the movie e-shops domain that support intelligent recommendations, and compares and discusses them. Moreover, we justify why hybrid technologies provide intelligent and more comprehensive experiences to customers. A new approach for a movie e-shop is introduced, where the knowledge about customers and movies is extracted from usage mining and ontological data in conjunction with customer-movie ratings and matching techniques between customers. This integration provides additional knowledge about customers' preferences and allows the production of successful recommendations. Even in the case of the *cold-start problem* where no initial behavioral information is available, the approach can provide logical and relevant recommendations to the customers. The provided recommendations are expected to have higher accuracy in matching customers' preferences and thus higher acceptance by them. The final sections describe future trends and challenges, and discuss issues that still remain unclear and should be addressed.

BACKGROUND

Collaborative filtering (Goldberg, Nichols, Oki, & Terry, 1992; Resnick, Iacovou, Suchak, Bergstrom, & Riedl, 1994; Shardanand & Maes, 1995; Sarwar, Karypis, Konstan, & Riedl, 2001; Basilico & Hofmann, 2004) tries to model the way people take recommendations from friends, which would be the ideal situation. Its advantages include the capability of application in cross-domain recommenders and the simplicity compared to other recommendation techniques, as it does not need feature extraction or item representation but only ratings. Its drawbacks include the so-called *new-item problem,* where a new item is not recommended unless a notable number of users rate it; the more common *new-user problem,* where a new user is registered and has not rated enough items so that the recommender can make accurate recommendations; and the *sparsity problem,* where the number of available ratings are much larger than the ratings to be predicted by the recommender. Collaborative filtering is also vulnerable to attacks from vicious users. The attacks can either be promotions of an item or nuking.

Content-based filtering (Balabanovic & Shoham, 1997; Pazzani, 1999; Mooney & Roy, 2000), on the other hand, presents similar limitations as collaborative filtering. As it is based on item-to-item filtering, sometimes the recommendation results lack diversity. The feature extraction process when it comes to, for example, multimedia content can be rather difficult and a proper representation for the objects is not easy. The new user problem still exists here. However, content-based filtering can work more easily with implicit feedback methods like keeping record of the purchase or search history, compared with collaborative filtering which most of the times needs explicit rating of items.

Demographic filtering (Pazzani, 1999) can be used for inferring recommendations based on stereotypes. However, issues like how the user information will be obtained and what the privacy policy of the company is towards the customers need further consideration. Especially, privacy is a significant objective in demographic filtering and collaborative filtering methods. Lastly, *statistics-based methods* (Schafer et al., 2001) provide no personalization, but users can appreciate their results as they are easy to implement. Many systems incorporate them into the recommendation strategy as a stable technique.

Due to the shortcomings of each recommendation method, *hybrid models* (Burke, 2002) have been proposed in order to combine the robustness and eliminate the drawbacks of the individual techniques. *Hybrid recommender systems* combine more than one recommendation technique in order to provide users with more accurate recommendations. As a result, hybrids act on more than one data source (collaborative data, content data, or demographic data) and provide seven ways to combine individual recommendation techniques into a hybrid one. The most straightforward is the *weighted combination,* which uses each technique to generate a recommendation score for each item, and then it calculates the mean or the weighted mean of the scores to provide the final recommendation score for each item. The *mixed combination* runs all recommendation algorithms simultaneously and produces the final recommendation list by merging the lists generated by the individual algorithms. The *switching combination* evaluates a criterion that determines what technique will be used for a certain recommendation request. The *feature combination* hybrid treats collaborative data as additional content data and employs content-based techniques on the augmented feature vector set. The *cascade hybrid* runs all techniques sequentially; each technique receives the recommendation list of the previous technique as input and refines the items by re-ranking them in the input set. The *feature augmentation hybrid* also runs all techniques sequentially, but here, each recommendation technique receives a rating or a classification produced by the previous algorithms as input. Finally, in the *meta-level hybrid,* each technique receives the model generated by the previous technique, and not just instances produced by it, as input.

In the remainder of this section, we survey the latest hybrid RSs, sorted by application domain.

Movies Domain

The MovieMagician system (Grant & McCalla, 2001) combines collaborative and content-based filtering by creating relativistic cliques (cliques of users having similar interest about movies of a certain kind). Movies' features are organized in a granularity hierarchy, having broader terms at the top, like "Genre," and narrower terms at the bottom levels, like "Action." This way, each movie can be realized as an instantiation of this hierarchy and the similarity of two movies can be determined by how much their hierarchies overlap. Each time a movie is instantiated, a similarity list is created—that is, a list of all similar movies to that movie. User preference is acquired through an overall rating on a seven-point scale about the movie or through individual feature rating (i.e., actors, plot, etc.). In order to predict a rating for an unseen movie, the system calculates cliques of users having similar interest with the active user about the specific movie and its similarity list, and then ranks users with regard to how similar they are with the active user. The recommended rating will be the rating of the most similar user in the clique. A very important feature that MovieMagician incorporates is the explanation of movie recommendations by means of personalized reviews.

Melville, Mooney, and Nagarajan's (2002) approach, called content-boosted collaborative filtering (CBCF), uses a content-based predictor to create a full pseudo user ratings matrix based on the sparse user ratings matrix provided by the EachMovie dataset. Then, collaborative filtering is used by applying the Pearson correlation formula on the full pseudo user-ratings matrix. The content-based predictor uses a naïve Bayesian text classifier on the movie content having a vector of bag-of-words like title or cast as input and producing the predicted rating to the unseen movies as output. The collaborative filtering algorithm used is a neighborhood-based algorithm that firstly computes with the Pearson correlation the similarity of all users with the active user; it then selects the N top highest similarities and computes the prediction with the weighting combination of the top-N most similar users.

Recommendz (Garden, 2004) is a cross-domain system that uses both collaborative and content-based filtering to generate recommendations, and the final recommendation is created with a weighted combination. It provides users with the ability, just like MovieMagician, to rate individual features of a movie. Moreover, the system encourages the provision of different types of feedback: overall rating of movie, selection of a relevant movie's feature, and specification of quantity of that feature in the item and of the degree to which the presence of this feature is positive or negative. Also, users can add their own features that they think best characterize a movie, although such ability can import many redundant features. The hybrid filtering algorithm incorporates three similarity metrics to measure the similarity between two users: the Pearson correlation of the overall ratings of the items, the Pearson correlation of particular features, and the Pearson correlation of the common features rated. These three similarities are combined into a weighted average to produce the recommended rating of the active user towards a movie.

CinemaScreen (Salter & Antonopoulos, 2006; CinemaScreen, 2006) is also a system that provides movie recommendations. Firstly, it uses collaborative filtering to produce an initial recommendation list and then it passes that list as input to a content-based algorithm. This way the system bypasses the new item problem, as the final recommendation list may include movies that it has not rated, but that has features similar to movies that other people have rated. The system uses a Web robot to collect information about movies and show times from multiple sources on the Internet. The collaborative filtering algorithm is a typical neighborhood-based one—that is, it calculates the users having similar rating history with the active user using the Pearson correlation. However, the system uses a threshold to distinguish significantly similar users—that is, users showing high similarity with the active user. The rating of the active user is acquired by the weighted mean of the neighborhood users' ratings. Afterwards the collaborative filtering recommendation list is fed to the content-based filtering algorithm. Here, each movie's rating is added to the score of each of the movie's features (actors, directors, genre, etc.) and then the mean is calculated for each feature. The three scores calculated express the degree of user preference towards each feature. Then, for each actor, the system searches the movies in which they have appeared and adds up the actor's score to each movie's score. The same procedure is followed for the directors and genres. Finally, the average of the scores is calculated for each movie, and so the final predicted ratings for the movies are acquired.

Schafer et al. (2004) propose a slightly different kind of recommendation model, a meta-recommender system. A meta-recommender system accesses many different information sources and/or recommender systems and returns results related to a user query that reflects an ephemeral need. An instance of this model for the movie domain, MetaLens, has an initial preference screen where the active user can select the features that the recommended movies like to have and the weight of each feature. The system forms the user demands as a query and forwards it to the sources of information, specifically Yahoo Movies, Rotten Tomatoes, and Movielens. Yahoo Movies provides movies information, Rotten Tomatoes provides movie reviews, and Movielens provides person-alized recommendations based on collaborative filtering. The results returned from all sources are united and ranked according to the extended Boolean model and then are displayed to the active user. The strengths of such a recommender system are the capability for both ephemeral and persistent recommendations and the combination of multiple recommendation techniques. A recent optimization on MetaLens' interface had resulted in DynamicLens (Schafer, 2005), which uses the MetaLens inner engine as is and additionally unites the preference and recommendation screens into one. The user can select the features he or she likes and see dynamically the recommendations they induce, making it easier for the user to select the correct features and weights.

TV Domain

In the TV domain, PTV (Smyth & Cotter, 2000) encounters the TV programs and channels overload due to digital TV advent. PTV is a Web-based recommender that combines case-based reasoning and collaborative filtering. The system maintains a database storing users' registration information and their ratings about programs. Information in the profile includes general user preferences like preferred channels and viewing times, as well as programs the user prefers or hates. PTV also maintains a case-based database, which stores information about all programs. Each case is a feature vector and the similarity between two cases is the weighted sum between corresponding features. In order to be able to calculate similarity of user preferences and a given case, the profile is converted to a profile schema, a feature-based representation of the profile. The system thus calculates item-to-item similarity to find programs similar to those they have previously liked. User-based collaboration filtering is also used; it calculates k more similar profiles and retrieves r programs that exist in those, and is absent for the active user's profile.

Research Papers and Books Domain

The TechLens[+] (Torres, McNee, Abel, Konstan, & Riedl, 2004) recommender system addresses the research paper overload problem by recommending papers that researchers are likely to be interested in. It combines a k-nearest neighbor collaborative filtering algorithm together with a TF-IDF (Van Rijsbergen, 1979) content-based filtering algorithm in order to generate recommendations. Among different combination implementations, the mixed approach had the best performance. In this approach, the two recommender algorithms run in parallel and merge their results into the final recommendation research paper list. The list is ranked according to a score resulting from the addition of the score ranks in the two algorithms. TechLens[+] maintains a one-paper history profile that expresses a researcher's current interests. This paper is acquired explicitly from user feedback.

In Huang, Chung, and Chen (2004), a graph-based hybrid approach (GBHA) is used in the domain of books integrating collaborative and content-based filtering. In this approach, the books, customers, and purchase transactions are modeled in a two-layer graph composed of a layer of book nodes, a layer of customer nodes, and links from the customer nodes to the book nodes, representing purchases. Each customer and each book is represented by feature vectors containing demographic data, such as sex and title respectively. The edges connecting nodes in the same layer represent the similarity of the connecting nodes, computed by a similarity function. The recommendation algorithm is referenced now as a graph search algorithm. To produce a book rating for the active customer, we calculate the shortest path from active customer's node in the customer layer to the specific book's node in the book layer. If the path contains only book-to-book similarity weights, the recommendation is purely content-based, while if it contains only customer-to-customer and purchase history links, it uses purely collaborative filtering. So, a path containing both types of edges uses a hybrid approach.

Quickstep (Middleton, 2003), also applied in the paper domain, uses a topic classifier to classify the Web page research browses in a topic ontology. A training set is used initially to bootstrap the classifier. However, later on, it is enriched by the classified papers the whole community of system's users browse. So, they are used as a sharing pool of information and add the sense of collaboration in the system. Quickstep uses unobtrusive feedback in order to acquire the browsed papers and only uses explicit feedback when it displays the recommendation list. For every user, it maintains a profile that is a topic list including the classified papers, and it applies a time decay function in order to keep record of researchers' current interests. The final recommendations result from correlating the users' current topics of interest and papers classified to those topics. Finally, the results are ranked according to a value called recommendation confidence, which is based on how confident the system is about the correctness of the classification. FoxTrot, an enhanced version of Quickstep, has several additions, such as capability for searching the paper database, visualization of the user profile so that feedback can be elicited easier, and computation of a recommendation list through both collaborative and content-based filtering. The usage of topic ontology in both systems gives the opportunity for inferring user preferences without explicit user browsing.

Other Domains

Windowls (Kazienko & Kolodziejski, 2005) is a hybrid RS used in an e-commerce windsurfing site. It supports content-based filtering by means of an association rules algorithm in order to track items that are frequently bought together. For logged users, it provides persistent personalization using collaborative and demographic filtering. Users are asked to provide personal data, which are being associated with their likes, dislikes, or behavior. Also, collaborative filtering takes advantage of a user's frequently rated items to recommend products that others, who have similar taste, have bought. An interesting property of Windowls is that of adaptivity. Each recommendation method has a weight that, according to the degree that each user selects the products recommended by it, is adapted to reflect how useful the customer finds the method.

Stef (Guo, Zhang, Chew, & Burdon, 2005) is another RS implemented to support businesses to choose exhibitions abroad to assist their exports. It combines item collaborative and content-based filtering based on products' semantic features. Stef utilizes SPR (Semantic Product Relevance), a model that consists of semantic similarity and product taxonomy. Semantic similarity, expressed by a five-scale rating, is assigned by domain experts to show the relevance of a product class with another class, subclass, or superclass. Product taxonomy, represented by a tree structure, groups the similar products into subclasses of products. The recommendation process initially utilizes the correlation-based similarity measure to calculate similarity between two items, then it performs semantic similarity calculation of target product and product category using the vector cosine similarity measure and adds up the two similarity values in order to acquire the final similarity score. The k highest scores are chosen as the most similar items and are recommended to the user.

Viscors (Kim, Lee, Cho, & Kim, 2004) is an RS implemented for the mobile Web to assist customers to choose the wallpapers they like. For new customers, it utilizes collaborative filtering based on the customer profile, which is the ratings matrix. The collaborative filtering module calculates the k nearest neighbor based on the Pearson correlation and then it generates a recommendation list based on a score called Purchase Likeness Score, which comprises unseen images. Thereafter, the customer can either buy a wallpaper or use it as a query to find wallpapers similar to it. This capability combines Content-Based Information Retrieval (CBIR) and feedback: the query wallpaper is compared based on its visual low-level features with the wallpaper database, and the best matches are returned. The user can mark the recommender wallpapers as preferred or non-preferred, a process that continuously refines the initial query until the current interests of the customer are learned.

FDRAS (Jung, Na, & Lee, 2003) is a system used for textile recommendation. A number of sensibility adjectives describing textiles have been collected, and 512 users give their five-scale estimation of how much an adjective matches a textile. The means of the ratings are calculated, and the adjectives with the top five means are selected for each textile. When the user logs in, he or she is asked to rate a number of textiles and thereafter he or she can be offered recommendations with a two-way method. Traditional collaborative filtering with the Pearson correlation is used together with representative attribute neighborhood in order to cluster the neighbors based on age, gender, and zip code. Also, content-based filtering is used through color histograms and textile design coefficients. The predictions of both methods are calculated for a given textile, and then the two scores are added to give the final score.

In the following tables, a comparison of the above RSs is provided.

The profile representation used by most systems is the classic user-item ratings matrix. Feature vectors are used by the paper recommenders TechLens and the graph-based model (GBHA). In addition, Quickstep uses an ontology to express the user profile as a structured tree of high-level concepts. The recommenders usually start with an empty profile and wait for user interaction in order to obtain user preference information. FDRAS, the fashion recommender, stands as an exception here, as it requires the rating of a number of texture samples in order to obtain a training set and bootstrap the recommender. Also, Quickstep has the desirable property, where users can manually add, anytime, preference information through the visualized representation of the profile.

Referring to the learning models used by the recommenders, CBCF uses the naïve classifier to fill up the user-item matrix according to the existing values. Quickstep uses a k-nearest neighbor classifier to classify the various papers into concepts. The two multimedia recommenders, Viscors and FDRAS, use content-based im-

Table 1. Comparison of various RSs

	User-item matrix	Feature vectors	History of purchases	Demographic features	Stereotyping	Training set	Manual	IR techniques, i.e., TF-IDF	Clustering	Classifiers	Explicit feedback	Implicit feedback	Semantic feedback	Domain knowledge	Weighted	Mixed	Meta-level	Cascade	Feature augmented	Switching	Feature combination
MovieMagician	X							X			X		X	X					X		
CBCF	X							X		X	X								X		
Recommendz	X										X		X		X						
CinemaScreen	X										X								X		
MetaLens																					
PTV	X	X							X	X	X					X					
Quickstep	X					X	X		X	X	X			X					X		
GBHA		X	X								X									X	
TechLens	X	X						X			X					X					
Viscors	X		X				X		X		X							X			
Stef	X	X									X			X	X						
FDRAS	X					X			X		X			X							
Windowls	X				X							X	X		X						

Table 2. Specific features for RSs comparison

Column	Description
User-item ratings	Matrix storing the historical user ratings.
Feature vectors	Vectors of features that represent an item. The vectors usually store an integer or Boolean value that indicates the amount of a feature in an item.
History of purchases	Historical data usually in forms of listings.
Demographic	Demographic data about users, e.g., age, sex, occupation, etc.
Stereotyping	Use of demographic features to build stereotypes in order to classify users in certain categories.
Training set	A set of examples to initialize the profile of a user or to train a classifier.
Manual	User sets his own parameters.
IR techniques	Information retrieval techniques, for example, TF-IDF algorithm.
Clustering	Grouping.
Classifiers	Neural nets, decision trees, association rules, etc.
Explicit feedback	User explicitly provides information.
Implicit feedback	User behavior is observed, and information about the user is inferred.
Semantic feedback	User provides information about particular features of the items he or she prefers.
Domain knowledge	Uses domain knowledge.
Weighted	Uses weighted combination hybrid.
Mixed	Uses mixed combination hybrid.
Meta-level	Uses meta-level combination hybrid.
Cascade	Uses cascade combination hybrid.
Feature augmented	Uses feature-augmented combination hybrid.
Switching	Uses switching combination hybrid.
Feature combination	Uses feature combination hybrid.

age retrieval techniques like color histogram in order to find similar pictures. FDRAS uses also clustering based on demographic data like sex and age. The other systems are based primarily on profile-item similarity matching techniques and use no learning model.

The type of relevance feedback that is mostly used is explicit feedback, which can explicitly provide positive and negative user preference. However, some systems use implicit feedback, like Quickstep and TechLens. These systems observe users browsing unobtrusively and infer user preference based on that. Although implicit feedback has some major drawbacks against explicit feedback, in some application domains, users are more reluctant to provide detailed preference information. In these cases, the hybrid method, the usage of both explicit and implicit feedback, is the best solution. There is also a special kind of explicit feedback, semantic feedback, where users rate specific item features. Semantic feedback can provide a more detailed evaluation of an item and a better representation for user preference. Only MovieMagician and Recommendz use this kind of feedback for the movie domain.

Lastly, the recommenders have been classified into the combination classes presented in Burke (2002). The weighted combination is used by the Stef and Windowls systems. This combination is the most straightforward and simple, while it offers flexibility to update the weight of each individual technique. However, theoretically, it does not solve the new item problem, being unjust against the less rated items, as collaborative filtering will contribute little or not at all in the final score of new items. In the mixed hybrid, used by PTV and TechLens, the new item problem is overcome as the content-based module generates a special list with the k more similar items. The feature augmentation hybrid is the most frequently used. The MovieMagician system uses a collaboration-via-content combination, calculating in the beginning a list of similar movies for each movie and then applying collaborative filtering on all movies.

CBCF uses the same combination by means of the naïve classifier to predict the ratings for the movies the user has not rated. A switching hybrid has been used by the graph-based recommender (GBHA). The system switches the two techniques according to which layer the best path from active customer to target book traverses. In Viscors, a kind of cascade combination is used. Collaborative filtering is used first and then content-based filtering for the wallpapers the user selects.

GENERAL PROCESS OF RECOMMENDATION SYSTEMS

Even though RSs are complex applications that combine several models, algorithms, and heuristics, most of them perform the basic steps of the Knowledge Discovery in Databases (KDD) process. This process includes the following steps: Data Selection, Data Pre-Processing and Transformation, Data Analysis, Interpretation and Evaluation, and Presentation (Geyer-Schulz & Hahsler, 2002), as depicted in Figure 1.

Data Selection

This step refers to the selection of the data set that will be used to produce recommendations and can stem from various sources. Collecting accurate and sufficient data comprises a crucial task of every RS. Specifically, it can include data about the *user* (demographics, user knowledge, skills, capabilities, interests, preferences, goals, etc.), the *usage* (selective actions, ratings, usage frequency, action correlations or sequences, etc.), and the *usage environment*—hardware, software, and physical (browser version, available plug-ins, bandwidth, display/input devices). Data can be collected either *explicitly* (the user is asked to provide them using questionnaires, fill-in preference forms, etc.) or *implicitly* (the data are derived without initiating any interaction with the users using acquisition rules, plan

Figure 1. General process of RSs

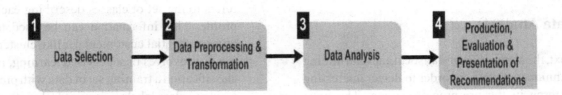

recognition, and stereotype reasoning). However, in both approaches, we must deal with different but equally serious problems. In the case of explicit profiling, users are often negative about filling in questionnaires and revealing personal information online; they comply only when required and even then the submitted data may be poor or false. On the other hand, in implicit profiling, even though the source of information is not biased by the user's negative attitude, the problems encountered derive once again from the invaded privacy concern and the loss of anonymity. Personalization is striving to identify users, records their online behavior in as much detail as possible, and extract needs and preferences in a way they do not notice, understand, or control (Kramer, Noronha, & Vergo, 2000; Mesquita, Barbosa, & Lucena, 2002). The most important data sources that an RS can use are: registration, login/password, history file, navigation, search keywords, support, product/service evaluation, and so forth.

Data Pre-Processing and Transformation

The next step in the recommendation process after data collection (a task that is in continuous execution) is data preparation, which involves data cleaning and data transformation into internal representation models that will allow for further processing and updating. Data cleaning removes all irrelevant entries from the Web server logs in order to facilitate their manipulation. For instance, entries that do not reveal actual usage information

are removed, and missing data are completed. Moreover, data compression algorithms can be used in this stage in order to reduce the size and dimension of the data and achieve efficient mining of the patterns. The problems that we often face during this phase include: *user identification, session identification, path completion,* and *transaction identification.*

- **User identification:** Registration and login/password procedures, as well as the combination of other heuristics, can be used for assuring the identification of unique users.
- **Session identification:** Session is a set of user clicks across one or more Web servers, and session identification aims to group the page accesses of each individual user into sessions. Time windows can be used to identify the different sessions of a user.
- **Path completion:** This problem is caused by local caching and proxy server activities creating gaps in user access paths. A referrer log for identifying the page that the request came from and also the site topology can be used to fully cover this issue.
- **Transaction identification:** This problem (grouping the references of each user) can be solved by using time windows that partition a user session based on time intervals (specified thresholds).

The map of the data into required structures can then be performed. These models can be either *individual* or *aggregate* (when working with groups of users) profiles.

Data Analysis

Next, the application of statistical and data mining techniques follows, in order to detect interesting patterns in the pre-processed data. The most well-known techniques used for data analysis include *clustering, classification* and *association rule mining, sequential pattern discovery,* and *prediction*. In this chapter we focus on clustering, and classification and association rule mining. A more detailed description of these techniques follows.

- **Clustering:** Clustering algorithms are used mainly for segmentation purposes. Their aim is to detect "natural" groups in data collections (e.g., customer profiles, product databases, transaction databases, etc.). They compute a measure of similarity in the collection in order to group together items that have similar characteristics. The items may be either users that demonstrate similar online behavior or pages that are utilized by users in a similar way. The produced groups (database segmentation into clusters of similar people, e.g., customers, prospects, most valuable or profitable customers, most active customers, lapsed customers, etc.) can be based on many different customer attributes (e.g., navigation behavior, buying behavior, or demographics). There are several clustering algorithms available: Hierarchical Agglomerative Clustering (HAC) (Rasmussen, 1992; Willett, 1988), k-means clustering (MacQueen, 1967), Self-Organizing Maps (SOMs), or Kohonen clustering (Kohonen, 1997).
- **Classification:** The main objective of classification algorithms is to assign items to a set of predefined classes. These classes usually represent different user profiles, and classification is performed using selected features with high discriminative ability as refers to the set of classes describing each profile. This information can be used to attract potential customers. Unlike clustering that involves unsupervised learning, in classification a training set of data with pre-assigned class labels is required (classification is categorized as a supervised machine learning technique). Then the classifier (by observing the class assignment in the training set) learns to assign new data items in one of the classes. It is often the case that clustering is applied before classification to determine the set of classes. Some widely used classification algorithms are: K-nearest neighbor (KNN), decision trees, naïve Bayes, and neural networks (Chakrabarti, 2003).

- **Association rule mining:** Association rules connect one or more events. Their aim is to discover associations and correlations between different types of information without obvious semantic dependence. In the Web personalization domain, this method may indicate correlations between pages not directly connected and reveal previously unknown associations between groups of users with specific interests (Agrawal, Imielinski, & Swami, 1993; Chen, Park, & Yu, 1996, 1998). Such information may prove valuable for e-commerce and e-business Web sites since it can be used to improve customer relationship management (CRM). The most well-known algorithm for discovering association rules is Apriori (Agrawal & Srikant, 1994).

Production, Evaluation, and Presentation of Recommendations

After data analysis, the extracted knowledge has to be converted into intelligent information, interaction, or interface for each customer. In this step the revealed patterns should be interpreted in order to be understandable from the users. Indeed, every pattern comprises a separate e-marketing opportunity, and its validity, novelty, and usefulness should be evaluated and managed differently. Finally, the RS presents the produced recommendations in a suitable form. Their purpose is to provide access to specific items through promotional links, such as those supplied by cross-selling or up-selling options. For example:

- **Cross-selling:** This suggests products related to the one(s) the user is currently viewing. In many cases, these are complementary products—for example, proposing a music CD with a book, or batteries with toys.
- **Up-selling:** This suggests products perhaps more expensive or advanced to the one(s) the user has chosen. The customer will be informed about products available in the next (upper) price level, which he may not have known about. The degree of applicability of this tactic depends on the type of products, and this applies to cross-selling as well.
- **Opinions of other customers:** These suggest additional products that the customer may also like to purchase, based on what other customers (considered as like-minded) have bought.
- **History data:** Analyzing the history of past purchases (stored in a transaction database), the e-shop is able to offer customers a targeted range of choices that are most likely to fit their profile.

Shortcomings

Most RSs do not take into consideration semantic characteristics, resulting in poor prediction accuracy. Without deeper semantic knowledge about the underlying domain, the RS cannot handle heterogeneous and complex objects based on their properties and relationships. In the next section, we introduce a hybrid RS approach that

tries to overcome shortcomings of most RSs and produce full personalization. In this way, we can offer every user different recommendations that change during his or her navigation.

INTEGRATION OF ONTOLOGICAL AND USAGE MINING DATA

The pilot e-shop rents movies to the customers and produces recommendations based on Web usage mining techniques, semantic metadata, customer-product ratings, and matching techniques between customers. The operation of the e-shop is simple and straightforward. In the case of a new customer, the e-shop motivates him or her to become a member by filling in the registration form. In this way the e-shop collects the necessary initial information about the customer in order to support him or through his or her navigation. In the case of an known customer, the e-shop identifies him or her via a login/password procedure and provides a personalized greeting. Then the customer navigates the e-shop, selects movies from the online catalog or uses the search facility, is informed about their features (e.g., story, cast, etc.), adds them to his or her basket, and pays for the renting total. Moreover, the customer can rate a specific movie using a range from 1 to 10, where 1 stands for a very bad movie and 10 stands for a very good one. The approach incorporates classification and association rule mining. The following sections describe the way recommendations are produced. The proposed recommendation approach is depicted in Figure 2.

E-Shop Ontological Schema

Many online shops adopt a basic classification schema for the provided items. This schema can be depicted as a tree, where the root represents the most general class, the internal nodes represent all intermediate classes, and the leaves stand for the specific items. Its role is important especially in the knowledge discovery process, since it represents the e-shop's dependent knowledge and may affect the results. In this framework, the proposed recommendation approach is based on an ontological schema, which has been incorporated in a pilot e-shop that rents movies to customers. The Web site consists of a collection of pages containing information about movies' attributes such as title, category, studio, actor, director, producer, awards, year, duration, audience, story, and so forth. The initial data have been retrieved from the Internet Movie Database (*http://www.imbd.com*), organized in the ontological schema, and enhanced in order to comprise a rich superset covering all needed concepts and relations.

The ontology underneath formulates a representation of the e-shop domain by specifying all of its concepts, the relations between them, and other properties, conditions, and "regulations." It allows semantic annotation and has the ability to perform semantic querying and ontology-based browsing. The ontology "building" was a complex and time-consuming task and was based on our intuition in order to depict all e-shop notions, organize their taxonomic hierarchies, and represent their relationships. The development was akin to the definition of a set of data and their structure. In this way, the ontology can be considered as a

knowledge base that is used further for extracting useful knowledge. Specifically, its role is to be used as an input for the mining phase in order to extract, combine, and transform the existing implicit and explicit knowledge (user class, history profile, e-shop content, and structure) into new forms. For the implementation of the ontology, we use the Protégé Editor (Stanford, 2006). Protégé framework can implement a robust OWL (Web ontology language) environment. The output of this task is a list of possible recommendations.

A subset of the e-shop ontology is depicted in Figure 3. In particular, the ontology creates connections between movies according to different attributes that characterize them. By using the specific customer's history file, the system figures out his or her preferences. For example, it can be found if the customer likes or dislikes watching movies:

- From a certain category (e.g., "action," "drama," "comedy," "westerns," "musicals," etc.);
- By a certain director (e.g., "Steven Spielberg," "Francis Ford Copolla," "Sydney Pollack," etc.);
- With a certain actor (e.g., "Sean Penn," "Nicole Kidman," "Brad Pitt," "Julia Roberts," etc.); or

Figure 2. Proposed recommendation approach

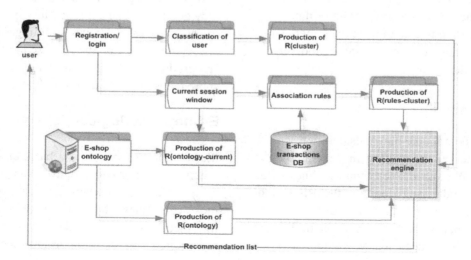

- With other attribute combinations.

When one or more matching criteria are met, then other movies can be discovered according to the ontological schema, movies that have similar attributes with those that the customer has already rented. In the case of a new customer (history file=∅), the information from his or her registration form is analyzed, and the recommendations are based on the ontology.

Customer Classification

The main purpose of the classification step is to assign customers to a set of predefined classes. These classes represent different user profiles, and classification is performed by using selected features with high discriminative ability as refers to the set of classes describing each profile. The features that determine a specific class can be tuned and typically include userID, age, sex, nationality, occupation, as well as education, preferences, and so forth. For example, from the class "rent comedies," customers that like to rent comedies and customers that do not can be extracted. The profile of an active buyer can be as the one depicted in Table 3. Consider the attributes and the values presented in Table 4, and suppose we want to decide if the next unknown user X rents comedies or not:

$$X=\{userID=101, age=22, sex=w, occupation=student, education=medium\}$$

In classification, a training set of data with pre-assigned class labels is required (classification is categorized as a supervised machine learning technique). Then the classifier (by observing the class assignment in the training set) learns to assign new data items in one of the classes. It is often the case that clustering is applied before classification to determine the set of classes.

We have based our categorization model on a naïve Bayes classifier (Hand, Mannila, & Smyth, 2002), where each snapshot X consists of a set of attributes $x_1, x_2, \ldots x_n$. We have defined m classes $C_1, C_2, \ldots C_m$. Given an unknown snapshot X for which we do not know its class, the classifier predicts that X belongs to the class with the higher probability. The classifier assigns X in class C_i if $P(C_i|X) > P(C_j|X)$ for $1 \leq j \leq m$, $j \neq i$. According to Bayes theorem, $P(C_i|X)=P(X|C_i)*P(C_i)/P(X)$. $P(X)$ is constant for all snapshots, so we need to maximize the expression $P(X|C_i)*P(C_i)$. For categorizing X, we compute the probability $P(X|C_i)*P(C_i)$ for each class C_i. X will be assigned in class C_i if $P(X|C_i)*P(C_i) > P(X|C_j)*P(C_j)$ for $1 \leq j \leq m$, $j \neq i$. This means that X is assigned in the class with the maximum probability.

This classification model may be revised

Figure 3. Part of the e-shop ontology (extended version of Mobasher, Jin, & Zhou, 2004)

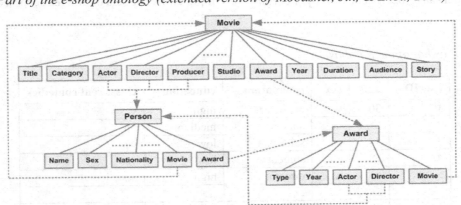

Table 3. Part of a user profile

userID	"67"
age	"30"
sex	"male"
occupation	"seller"
education	"higher"

as time passes and updated based on collected transactions data. Additionally, user assignment to classes might be used for provoking interactions among users and also enhancing collaboration and communication. Moreover, it provides to e-shop the ability to perceive a useful insight of the "virtual communities." For each class, a set of recommendations is attached. These recommendations are lists with, for example, the best and worst movies that other users, "close" to the current, have contributed.

Association Rule Mining on Click-Streams

The model tracks all user actions as successive page requests recorded in server logs. Log files are then cleaned from all redundant information (such as secondary, automatically generated requests for page images, etc.). Combining the remaining requests with information about the way Web site content is structured, the system distils user accesses to movies pages. The set of movies, which have been accessed by a certain

user during all past visits to the e-shop, are stored in the user profile, and this is where the generator seeks for discovering association rules.

An association rule example follows:

$$\{movie_i, movie_j\} \rightarrow \{movie_x\} \text{ with support=0.02 and confidence=0.68.}$$

The above rule conveys the relationship that users who accessed $movie_i$ and $movie_j$ also tend (with a confidence of 68%) to be interested in $movie_x$. Support represents the fact that the set $\{movie_i, movie_j, movie_x\}$ is observed in 2% of the sets of movies accessed.

Other examples of association rules include:

- 60% of the users that rent the movie "Lord of the Rings—The Fellowship" in sequence select "Lord of the Rings—The Two Towers" and "Lord of the Rings—The Return of the King."
- 75% of the users who visited the "Shrek" movie belong to the 15-20 age group.
- 25% of the users who rent the movie "Harry Potter" were in the 20-30 age group and lived in Athens.
- 45% of the users who accessed the e-shop started from page "Top movies of the week."

The discovered association rules may use as input either the sets of movies accessed by all us-

Table 4. A snapshot of the database

userID	age	sex	occupation	education	class: rent comedies
1	30	w	engineer	high	yes
2	25	m	student	medium	no
3	34	m	salesman	low	yes
4	18	m	student	low	yes
5	45	w	director	high	no
...	...	...	...	...	...
100	28	w	artist	high	yes

ers or just the ones accessed by users that belong to the same class as the current one. Another option is to use both approaches and suggest the union of discovered topics. This scenario is very useful when association rules inside classes fail to produce reliable recommendations due to lack of adequate input.

Production of Recommendations

This section describes in detail the algorithm that the e-shop uses for the production of movie recommendations. These recommendations are suggested to the customer in the form of "customers who liked/rented this movie also rented…." The filtering procedure is based on a different kind of data. More precisely, it depends on the cluster, in which the user was classified, his or her click-streams, his or her transaction history and ratings, and the Web site ontology metadata. The main idea is to generate an initial set of recommendations combining all the aforementioned data and then prune (using a pre-defined threshold-α) this set and sort the remaining items in an ascending order (first the movie with the higher predicted rate).

We separate two cases according to the existence of a user's history data:

- **Case 1: When the user is a known one and system has kept track of his history.** We define as $M_{History}$ the set of movies that the user has watched and rated. In this case, the system, according to $M_{History}$, finds the users "close" to him with similar history and ratings. We define this set of users as U_L. Every user U_i that belongs to U_L is associated with a number s_i that depicts the similarity of U_i with the current user. Also, we define as U_M the set of users that belong to U_L and have seen movie M. Moreover, according to $M_{History}$ the model uses the ontology to discover the associations between the items that the user has rated. Therefore, we define

as $R_{ontology}$ the list of recommendations that derive from the ontology based on the user's history file.

- **Case 2: When the user is a new one.** In this case, the system uses information from the user's registration and consequently the initial class in which she has been assigned to. We define as U_K the set of users in the class that have similar attributes with the current one. These attributes are the information that the user gave to the system after filling in the registration form, for example age, sex, occupation, education, preferences, and so forth. Every user U_i that belongs to U_K is associated with a number s_i that depicts the similarity of U_i with the current user according to the aforementioned attributes. We define as U_M the set of users that belong to U_K and have watched movie M. Every class is attached to a set of movies. We define as $R_{cluster}$ the recommended movies according to the user's class.

Continuing, we define as $W_{current}$ the current session window, which contains the movies that the user has accessed in the current transaction. We can produce a recommendation in accordance to a user's current click-stream by using association rules and the site ontology. So for $R_{rules-current}$ we mean the recommendations that derive from the current session window and association rules mining, and for $R_{ontology-current}$ we consider the recommendations that derive from the current session window and the ontology.

We use two methods for processing the information of current session as we achieve better predictions by their combination. Each method uses different ways to predict the user's preferences—that is, association rules encapsulate the navigational behavior of users, while the ontology reflects the connections between items' attributes and discovers patterns that explain a user's preferences.

In sequence, we name $R_{initial}$ the initial recommendation set that will be filtered by the algorithm and ordered in ascending form. It is computed by the union of $R_{ontology-current}$, $R_{rules-current}$, and in the first case (when the user has historical data) we use $R_{ontology}$, while in the second case (when the user is a new one) we use $R_{cluster}$.

Consequently, we compute $R_{initial}$ for each case as follows:

- *Case 1:* $R_{initial} = R_{ontology-current} \cup R_{rules-current} \cup R_{ontology}$
- *Case 2:* $R_{initial} = R_{ontology-current} \cup R_{rules-current} \cup R_{cluster}$

The algorithm used for producing recommendations to the customers of the e-shop is presented in Table 5. As far as similarity among users is concerned, we consider that every user has a vector with the movies he or she has rated (i.e., a history vector). For example, we assume X and Y are two users. We define as X_R and Y_R their history vectors and R_X and R_Y the sets with their rated movies respectively. Then C is the set with the rated movies that they have in common, so $C = R_X \cap R_Y$. If the users do not have any movie in common, then $C = \varnothing$. Additionally, we define X_C and Y_C, the vectors with the movies that both users have rated (movies that belong to C).

A limitation that arises in this step concerns the percentage of common rated movies in relation to all rated movies. For example, if the user X has rated 60 movies, $R_X = 60$, and the user Y has rated 40 movies, $R_Y = 40$, and their common movies are only 5, $C = 5$, then these users are not considered as similar. In order to consider two users as similar, they should have more than 50% of the one with the fewer rated movies in common.

Then the similarity between users X and Y is the distance between vectors X_C and Y_C and can be computed from the following formula:

$$sim(X_C, Y_C) = \sqrt{\sum_{i=1}^{N} (R(X_C, M_i) - R(Y_C, M_i))^2}$$

When the user is a new one, we compute the similarity among users in the same class. In this case, we use the attributes that derived from the registration form. These attributes have a certain position in the vector which describes the user's profile. For example, if the attributes are age, sex, occupation, and education, then an instance of this vector for user X could be {22, 0, 3, 2}. This means:

{age=22, sex=male, occupation=student, education=medium}

In other words, every attribute takes values that correspond to certain information, for example, occupation=3 denotes a student.

The computation of similarity among users is a very time-consuming task. It is easy to infer

Table 5. The algorithm used for producing recommendations

Input
U: all users U_i: user with ID i M: all movies M_j: movie j $M_{History}$: movies that the customer has rated $R_{initial}$: initial recommendations
Algorithm

For each M_i in $R_{initial}$
    If $M_{History} = \varnothing$ then
        Find U_m in U_K
    Else Find U_m in U_L
    For each U_j in U_m
        $r_{Mi} = R_{Mi,Uj} * s_j$
        if $r_{Mi} > \alpha$ then
            $R = R \cup \{M_i\}$
    end
end

Output
A list R of movie recommendations in ascending order (first the movie with the biggest r) that user U_i has not seen and probably would like to see

that in the case of a large e-shop with many users and a rich variety of movies, the complexion of similarity's computation can be very difficult.

To summarize, we have used the explicit data that the user provides during his or her registration in order to categorize him or her into a class of predefined groups. These groups (classes) are static and generated according to system's characteristics. A user can belong to many different classes. This classification cannot be altered in accordance with the user's navigational activity. It is static and can only be modified if the user changes his or her preferences—that is, his or her registration data. On the other hand, we have used the association rules and the ontology of the site. This information derives dynamically from the user's navigational activity. Rules' extraction is performed during the off-line process, while the discovery of the proper ones (according to current session window) is performed during the online process. Association rules are created with Apriori algorithm (Agrawal et al., 1993), and the algorithm is implemented in C++. Screenshots of the movie RS are depicted in Figure 4.

For the evaluation of our approach, we use two data sets. The first set includes 100 snapshots of the ontological scheme of the pilot movie e-shop. A spider is used to mine the information from HTML pages and store them in the database. The second set includes data for the navigation users' behaviors that were collected from the log files. This set now includes 25 users and 218 separate visits. Then, we follow the next steps:

- We collect samples of users' ratings for the movies that they have watched.
- For each user u we calculate r_{um} rating that the model predicts the user will give to movie m (user has not watched movie m).
- We present to the user the Web page that includes all information about movie m that has the bigger r_{um}.
- We ask the user to rate movie m without

Figure 4. The pilot movie e-shop

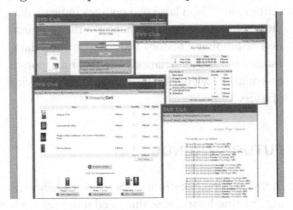

watching the movie based on the Web page data.

- We ask the user to watch the movie and re-rate it.

We define as estimated-rating er_{um} the rating that user u gives without watching movie m and as actual-rating ar_{um} the rating after the user has watched the movie. We use the mean absolute error (MAE) to calculate the mean deviation between the prediction and the actual ratings of a user. Specifically, we calculate:

$$\left| E_{er} \right| = \frac{\sum_{u \in U'} \sum_{m \in M'} \left| er_{um} - r_{um} \right|}{\# \, predictions}$$

$$\left| E_{ar} \right| = \frac{\sum_{u \in U'} \sum_{m \in M'} \left| ar_{um} - r_{um} \right|}{\# \, predictions}$$

$$\left| E_{ear} \right| = \frac{\sum_{u \in U'} \sum_{m \in M'} \left| er_{um} - ar_{um} \right|}{\# \, predictions}$$

for measuring the accuracy of recommendations where U' is the set of users for which the RS made predictions and M' is the set of movies that they have not seen yet. The experiments showed firstly that estimated ratings from the actual ratings of users differ by as much as 8.99%. The RS predicted ratings r_{um} deviate from the estimated ratings by as much as 9.68%, while from the actual ratings, 10.38%. These percentages indicate that the whole process is strengthened by the combination of ontology, history files, registration data, usage data, and association rules that incorporate essential knowledge for the navigational behavior of users.

FUTURE TRENDS

In this section, we discuss some issues concerning existing hybrid RSs that need more research and the trends of future hybrid recommendation technology.

First of all, not all possible combinations of recommendation techniques have been fully explored. Our survey did not include any meta-level recommenders, any feature combination hybrid, nor a cascade implementation as defined in the Introduction section. Moreover, only collaborative and content-based filtering were studied. Further, Burke (2002) studies knowledge-based techniques and demographic filtering combinations. Finally, more research is needed on how to select the most effective combination for each scenario. Although a rough insight has been provided in Burke (2002) and in our survey, a more detailed trade-off analysis would be appropriate.

Hybrid recommendation is based both on content data and on collaborative data. So, the reliability of both data sources should be checked in order to defend the system against plotted attacks to influence system behavior. A content-based attack on a Web recommender, for instance, would include false metadata information in Web pages, so that the system would not categorize them properly. Recently, shilling or profile injection attacks have gained much interest. In this case, the attacker, either human or agent, creates multiple profiles and provides appropriate ratings for particular products in order to influence the recommendations. The desired influence can be pushing or nuking a product that is increasing or

decreasing the recommendation frequency of the product, or merely sabotaging the recommender's integrity by decreasing recommendation accuracy. So, the content-based module, when possible, should be able to analyze the content information integrity of the items, while the collaborative filtering module should provide defense against several attack models. Another solution is the usage of multiple data sources, both content and collaborative, an approach followed by meta-recommenders.

A permanent issue in RSs is privacy. Hybrid recommenders are most likely to integrate collaborative filtering and/or demographic filtering techniques, and thus users are required to disclose personal information. Surveys have shown that customers hesitate to do that in fear of how the e-commerce companies will employ it. The usage of multiple data sources of demographic and collaborative data perplexes things more. The user should understand the company's privacy policy and have the option to choose whether he or she allows the usage of his or her data for recommendation purposes in other sites or not. Kobsa and Teltzro (2005) present an effective way of communicating privacy statements with the customer. The privacy policy is broken into pieces and is distributed to the context that each piece refers to. Each time a customer is asked to provide a bit of personal data, comprehensive information is given on how the data will be used and why they are needed. The communication of privacy policy is one step towards acquiring the trust of customers.

Hybrid recommendation is an important step towards personalization; however, it should be complemented with new technologies to build an even more robust recommendation infrastructure. Our survey showed that only a few of the systems made use of domain knowledge and ontologies. Semantic Web technology, meaning literally machine understandability, can offer more potential current recommendation technology. User preference could be represented in terms of high-level concepts and relationships, and new sophisticated algorithms could understand them and correlate them to a well-built common knowledge representation (Pazzani, 2005). This next step shall give an accuracy leap in recommendations.

The emergence of the semantic Web and the wide usage of other decentralized infrastructures like the grid or peer-to-peer systems will also influence the future development of RSs. Most implementations so far are based on simple client-server architecture and are therefore centralized—that is, a server performs all the computations and stores all the data. The adoption of a decentralized model (Ziegler, 2005) has multiple benefits. Firstly, decentralized infrastructures can give a solution to the problem of privacy, as both data storage and calculation can be done locally on each network node. Also, a central service provider is not necessary as network nodes function independently. Through their own sites or homepages, organized in a machine understandable form, information can be acquired about user preferences and trust circle by means of links to other sites. Lastly, speed and scalability problems, which exist in current projects, will dissolve.

CONCLUSION

Recommendation systems are special personalization tools that help users find interesting information and services in complex online shops. Even though today's e-commerce environments have greatly evolved and now incorporate techniques from other domains and application areas, such as Web mining, semantics, artificial intelligence, user modeling, and profiling, setting up a successful recommendation system is not a trivial or straightforward task. In this chapter we argue that by monitoring, analyzing, and understanding the behavior of customers, their demographics, opinions, preferences, and history, as well as taking into consideration the specific e-shop ontology and by applying Web mining techniques,

the effectiveness of produced recommendations may be significantly improved. In this way, the e-shop may eventually upgrade user interaction, increase its usability, convert visitors to buyers, retain current customers, and establish long-term and loyal one-to-one relationships.

Specifically, after a survey of the RS field, we introduce a recommendation approach for e-shops that extends Web usage-based techniques by incorporating semantic annotations in order to better meet the customers' preferences. The preliminary evaluation experiments show that the whole process has been enhanced by the combination of a site's ontology, user history files, user registration data, and association rules—a combination that encompasses all necessary knowledge about users' navigational attitudes. Currently, we are working on collecting further data in order to extensively evaluate the approach using more metrics such as coverage that measure the ability of the system to produce all pages that users are likely to visit.

An important point of future consideration relates to the close dependence of the algorithm from the e-shop ontological schema, which can be overbalanced by the association rule mining. Rules catch all users' navigational activity and their relative behavior on products. Another interesting area of work concerns the improvement of algorithm performance by decreasing its complexity, which is augmented analogically with the number of products, users, and their history files. Finally, it will be interesting to investigate different approaches to combine various information channels in order to generate more accurate recommendations.

REFERENCES

Adomavicius, G., & Tuzhilin, A. (2005). Toward the next generation of recommender systems: A survey of the state-of-the-art and possible extensions. *IEEE Transactions on Knowledge and Data Engineering, 17*(6), 734-749.

Agrawal, R., & Srikant, R. (1994). Fast algorithms for mining association rules. In C. Santago, J. Bocca, M. Jarke, & C. Zaniolo (Eds.), *Proceedings of the 20th VLDB Conference* (pp. 487-499). San Francisco: Morgan Kaufmann.

Agrawal, R., Imielinski, T., & Swami, A. (1993). Mining association rules between sets of items in large databases. *Proceedings of the ACM SIGMOD International Conference on Management of Data* (pp. 207-216).

Balabanovic, M., & Shoham, Y. (1997). Fab: Content-based, collaborative recommendation. *Communications of the ACM, 40*(3), 66-72.

Basilico, J., & Hofmann, T. (2004). Unifying collaborative and content-based filtering. *Proceedings of the 21ˢᵗ International Conference on Machine Learning* (vol. 69, p. 9). New York: ACM Press.

Brusilovsky, P. (2001). adaptive hypermedia. User Modeling and User Adapted Interaction, 11(1/2), 87-110.

Burke, R. (2002). Hybrid recommender systems: Survey and experiments. User Modeling and User-Adapted Interaction, 12(4), 331-370.

Burke, R., Mobasher, B., & Bhaumik, R. (2005, January 9). Identifying attack models for secure recommendation, Beyond Personalization: A Workshop on the Next Stage of Recommender Systems Research, in conjunction with the 2005 International Conference on Intelligent User Interfaces (IUI'05) (pp. 19-25), San Diego, CA.

Chakrabarti, S. (2003). Mining the Web: Discovering knowledge from hypertext data. San Francisco: Morgan Kaufmann.

Chen, M., Park, J., & Yu, P. (1996). Data mining for path traversal patterns in a Web environment. Proceedings of the 16th International Conference on Distributed Computing Systems (pp. 385-392).

Chen, M., Park, J., & Yu, P. (1998). Efficient data mining for path traversal patterns. IEEE Transactions Knowledge and Data Engineering, 10(2), 209-221.

CinemaScreen. (2006). Retrieved January 5, 2006, from http://www.cinemacreen.co.uk

Ding, Y., Fensel, D., Klein, M., Omelayenko, B., & Schulten, E. (2004). The role of ontologies in e-commerce. In S. Staab & R. Studer (Eds.), *International handbooks on information systems: Handbook on ontologies* (pp. 593-615). Berlin/Heidelberg: Springer-Verlag.

Eirinaki, M., & Vazirgiannis, M. (2003). Web mining for web personalization. *ACM Transactions on Internet Technology, 3*(1), 1-27.

Garden, M. (2004). *On the use of semantic feedback in recommender systems.* Master's Thesis, McGill University, Canada.

Geyer-Schulz, A., & Hahsler, M. (2002). Evaluation of recommender algorithms for an Internet information broker based on simple association rules and on the repeat-buying theory. In B. Masand, M. Spiliopoulou, J. Srivastava, & O. Zaiane (Eds.), *Proceedings of WEBKDD* (pp. 100-114), Edmonton, Canada.

Goldberg, D., Nichols, D., Oki, B.M., & Terry, D. (1992). Using collaborative filtering to weave an information tapestry. *Communications of the ACM, 35*(12), 61-70.

Grant, S., & McCalla, G. (2001). A hybrid approach to making recommendations and its application to the movie domain. *Proceedings of the 14th Biennial Conference of the Canadian Society on Computational Studies of Intelligence: Advances in Artificial Intelligence* (pp 257-266). London: Springer-Verlag (LNCS 2056).

Guo, X., Zhang, G., Chew, E., & Burdon, S. (2005, December 5-9). A hybrid recommendation approach for one-and-only items. In S. Zhang & R. Jarvis (Eds.), *Proceedings of 18th Australian*

Joint Conference on Artificial Intelligence (pp. 457-466), Sydney, Australia. Berlin/Heidelberg: Springer-Verlag (LNCS).

Hand, D., Mannila, H., & Smyth, P. (2001). *Principles of data mining* (pp. 353-356). Boston: MIT Press.

Huang, Z., Chung, W., & Chen, H. (2004). A graph model for e-commerce recommender systems. *Journal of the American Society for Information Science & Technology, 55*(3), 259-274.

Jung, K., Na, Y., & Lee, J. (2003). *Creating user-adapted design recommender system through collaborative filtering and content based filtering* (pp. 204-208). Berlin: Springer-Verlag (LNCS 2902).

Kazienko, P., & Kolodziejski, P. (2005). *WindOwls—adaptive system for the integration of recommendation methods in e-commerce* (pp. 218-224). Berlin/Heidelberg: Springer-Verlag (LNAI).

Kim, C., Lee, J., Cho, Y., & Kim, D. (2004). VISCORS: A visual-content recommender for the mobile Web. *IEEE Intelligent Systems, 19*(6), 32-39.

Kobsa, A., & Teltzrow, M. (2005, January 9). Impacts of contextualized communication of privacy practices and personalization benefits on purchase behavior and perceived quality of recommendation, *Beyond Personalization: A Workshop on the Next Stage of Recommender Systems Research, in conjunction with the 2005 International Conference on Intelligent User Interfaces* (IUI'05) (pp. 48-53), San Diego, CA.

Kohonen, T. (1997). *Self-organizing maps*. New York: Springer-Verlag.

Kramer, J., Noronha, S., & Vergo, J. (2000). A user-centered design approach to personalization. *Communications of the ACM, 8,* 45-48.

Lam, S.K., & Riedl., J. (2004). Shilling recommender systems for fun and profit. *Proceedings of the 13th International Conference on the World Wide Web* (pp. 393-402). New York: ACM Press.

Li, Y., Meiyun, Z., & Yang, B. (2005, August 15-17). Analysis and design of e-supermarket shopping recommender system. *Proceedings of the 7th International Conference on Electronic Commerce* (ICEC'05) (pp. 777-779), Xian, China.

MacQueen, J. (1967). Some methods for classification and analysis of multivariate observations. In L.M. Le Cam & J. Neyman (Eds.), *Proceedings of the 5th Berkeley Symposium on Mathematical Statistics and Probability* (pp. 281-297). University of California Press.

Melville, P., Mooney, R., & Nagarajan, R. (2002). Content-boosted collaborative filtering for improved recommendations. *Proceedings of the 18th National Conference on Artificial Intelligence* (AAAI-02) (pp. 187-192).

Mesquita, C., Barbosa, S.D., & Lucena, C.J. (2002). Towards the identification of concerns in personalization mechanisms via scenarios. Proceedings of 1st International Conference on Aspect-Oriented Software Development, Enschede, The Netherlands. Retrieved January 5, 2006, from http://trese.cs.utwente.nl/AOSD-EarlyAspectsWS/Papers/Mesquita.pdf

Middleton, S.E. (2003). *Capturing knowledge of user preference with recommender systems*. PhD Thesis.

Middleton, S.E., De Roure, D.C., & Shadbolt, N.R. (2004). Ontology-based recommender systems. In S. Staab & R. Studer (Eds.), *International handbooks on information systems: Handbook on ontologies* (pp. 477-498). Berlin/Heidelberg: Springer-Verlag.

Mobasher, B., Jin, X., & Zhou, Y. (2004). Semantically enhanced collaborative filtering on the Web. In Berendt et al. (Eds.), *Proceedings of the European Web Mining Forum*. Berlin: Springer-Verlag (LNAI).

Mooney, R., & Roy, L. (2000, June 2-7). Content-based book recommending using learning for text categorization. *Proceedings of the 5th ACM Conference on Digital Libraries* (pp. 195-204), San Antonio, TX.

O'Donovan, J., & Smyth, B. (2006, January 29-31). Is trust robust? An analysis of trust-based recommendation. *Proceedings of the 11th International Conference on Intelligent User Interfaces*. New York: ACM Press.

Pazzani, M. (1999). A framework for collaborative, content-based and demographic filtering. *Artificial Intelligence Review, 13*(5-6), 393-408.

Pazzani, M.J. (2005, January 9). Beyond idiot savants: Recommendations and common sense. *Beyond Personalization: A Workshop on the Next Stage of Recommender Systems Research, in conjunction with the 2005 International Conference on Intelligent User Interfaces* (IUI'05) (pp. 99-100), San Diego, CA.

Rasmussen, E. (1999). Clustering algorithms. In W.B. Frakes & R. Baeza-Yates (Eds.), *Information retrieval: Data structure and algorithms*. Englewood Cliffs, NJ: Prentice Hall.

Resnick, P., Iacovou, N., Suchak, M., Bergstrom, P., & Riedl, J. (1994). GroupLens: An open architecture for collaborative filtering of Netnews. *Proceedings of the ACM Conference on Computer Supported Cooperative Work* (pp. 175-186).

Salter, J., & Antonopoulos, N. (2006). CinemaScreen recommender agent: Combining collaborative and content-based filtering. *IEEE Intelligent Systems, 21*(1), 35-41.

Sarwar, B., Karypis, G., Konstan, J., & Riedl, J. (2001). Item-based collaborative filtering recommendation algorithms. *Proceeding of the 10th World Wide Web Conference* (pp. 285-295).

Schafer, J.B. (2005, January 9). DynamicLens: A dynamic user-interface for a meta-recommendation system. *Beyond Personalization: A Workshop on the Next Stage of Recommender Systems Research, in conjunction with the 2005 International Conference on Intelligent User Interfaces* (IUI'05) (pp. 72-76), San Diego, CA.

Schafer, J.B., Konstan, J.A., & Reidl, J. (2004). The view through MetaLens: Usage patterns for a meta-recommendation system. *IEE Proceedings Software, 151*(6), 267-279.

Schafer, J.B., Konstan, J.A., & Riedl, J. (2001). E-commerce recommendation applications. *Data Mining and Knowledge Discovery, 5*(1/2), 115-153.

Shardanand, U., & Maes, P. (1995). Social information filtering: Algorithms for automating "word of mouth." *Human Factors in Computing Systems ACM CHI* (pp. 210-217).

Smyth, B., & Cotter, P. (2000). A personalized television listings service. *Communications of the ACM, 43*(8), 107-111.

Stanford. (2006). Protégé editor. Retrieved August 2006 from http://protege.stanford.edu

Torres, R., McNee, S.M., Abel, M., Konstan, J.A., & Riedl, J. (2004). Enhancing digital libraries with TechLens+. *Proceedings of the 4th ACM/IEEE Joint Conference on Digital Libraries* (JCDL 2004) (pp. 228-236).

Van Rijsbergen, C.J. (1979). *Information retrieval* (2nd ed.). Butterworths.

Willett, P. (1988). Recent trends in hierarchic document clustering: A critical review. *Information Processing and Management, 24*(5).

Ziegler, C.N. (2005). *Towards decentralized recommender systems*. PhD Thesis, Albert-Ludwigs-Universität Freiburg, Germany.

Compilation of References

Abowd, G.D., Dey, A.K., Abowd, G., Orr, R., & Brotherton, J. (1997). *Context-awareness in wearable and ubiquitous computing.* GVU Technical Report GIT-GVU-97-11. Retrieved September 2, 2006, from http://www-static. cc.gatech.edu/fce/pubs/iswc97/wear.html

Abrahams, B., & Dai, W. (2005). Architecture for automated annotation and ontology based querying of semantic Web resources. Proceedings of the 2005 IEEE/WIC/ACM International Conference on Web Intelligence (WI'05), (pp. 413-417).

Adams, A., & Blandford, A. (2002). Acceptability of medical digital libraries. *Health Informatics Journal, 8*(2), 58-66.

Adams, A., & Blandford, A. (2004). The unseen and unacceptable face of digital libraries. *International Journal on Digital Libraries, 4*(2), 71-81.

Adams, A., & Blandford, A. (2005). Digital libraries' support for the user's 'information journey'. *Proceedings of ACM/IEEE JCDL* (pp. 160-169).

Adomavicius, G., & Tuzhilin, A. (2005). Toward the next generation of recommender systems: A survey of the state-of-the-art and possible extensions. *IEEE Transactions on Knowledge and Data Engineering, 17*(6), 734-749.

Adomavicius, G., & Tuzhilin, A. (2005). Towards the next generation of recommender systems: A survey of the state-of-the-art and possible extensions. *IEEE Transactions on Knowledge and Data Engineering, 17*(6), 734-749.

Agarwal, N.K., & Poo, D.C.C. (2006). Meeting knowledge management challenges through effective search. *International Journal of Business Information Systems, 1*(3), 292-309.

Agrawal, R., & Srikant, R. (1994). Fast algorithms for mining association rules. In C. Santago, J. Bocca, M. Jarke, & C. Zaniolo (Eds.), *Proceedings of the 20th VLDB Conference* (pp. 487-499). San Francisco: Morgan Kaufmann.

Agrawal, R., Imielinski, T., & Swami, A. (1993). Mining association rules between sets of items in large databases. *Proceedings of the ACM SIGMOD International Conference on Management of Data* (pp. 207-216).

Akavipat, R., Wu, L.-S., & Menczer, F. (2004). Small world peer networks in distributed Web search. *Proceedings of the Alternate Track Papers and Posters of the 13th International World Wide Web Conference,* New York.

Alavi, M., & Leidner, D.E. (2001). Review: Knowledge management and knowledge management systems: Conceptual foundations and research issues. *MIS Quarterly, 25*(1), 107-136.

Almind, T.C., & Ingwersen, P. (1997). Informetric analysis on the World Wide Web: Methodological approaches to Webometrics. *Journal of Documentation, 53,* 404-426.

Alstyne, M., & Brynjolfsson, E. (2005). Global village or cyber-Balkans? Modeling and measuring and integration of electronic communities. *Management Science, 51*(6), 851-868.

Anderson, M., Ball, M., Boley, H., Greene, S., Howse, N., Lemire, D., & McGrath, S. (2003). RACOFI: A rule-applying collaborative filtering system. *Proceedings of IEEE/WIC COLA'03,* Halifax, Canada (NRC 46507).

Andrew, S. (n.d). Cookies. Retrieved April 29, 2006, from http://www.quirksmode.org/js/cookies.html

Andronico, A., Carbonaro, A., Colazzo, L., & Molinari, A. (2004). Personalisation services for learning management systems in mobile settings. *International Journal of Continuing Engineering Education and Lifelong Learning.*

Ashkenas, R., Ulrich, D., Jick, T., & Kerr, S. (2002). *The boundaryless organization: Breaking the chains of organizational structure* (2nd ed.). San Francisco: Jossey-Bass.

Asmus, J., Bonner, C., Esterhay, D., Lechner, A., & Rentfrow, C. (2005, December 6). *Instructional design technology trend analysis.* Denver: University of Colorado. Retrieved September 1, 2006, from http://elgg.net/collinb/files/1136/2967/TrendAnalysisWeb.pdf

Asvanund, A., Bagala, S., Kapadia, M., Krishnan, R., Smith, M., & Telang, R. (2003). Intelligent club management in P2P networks. *Proceedings of the Workshop on Economics of Peer to Peer Systems,* Berkeley, CA.

Atkins, H. (1999). The ISI Web of science—links and electronic journals. *D-Lib Magazine, 5*(9). Retrieved January 23, 2007, from *http://www.dlib.org/dlib/september99/atkins/09atkins.html*

Avery, C., & Zeckhauser, R. (1997). Recommender systems for evaluating computer messages. Communication of the ACM, 40(3), 88-89.

Avesani, P., Massa, P., & Tiella, R. (2005). A trust-enhanced recommender system application: Moleskiing. *Proceedings of the 20th ACM Symposium on Applied Computing,* Santa Fe, NM.

Axelrod, R. (1997). The dissemination of culture: A model with local convergence and global polarization. *Journal of Conflict Resolution, 41*(2), 203-226.

Baecker, R.M. (Ed.). (1992). *Readings in groupware and CSCW.* San Francisco: Morgan Kaufmann.

Baeza-Yates, R. (1999). *Modern information retrieval.* Boston, MA: Addison Wesley.

Baeza-Yates, R., & Ribeiro-Neto, B. (1999). *Modern information retrieval.* New York: ACM Press.

Bainbridge, D., Buchanan, G., McPherson, J.R., Jones, S., Mahoui, A., & Witten, I.H. (2001). Greenstone: A platform for distributed digital library applications. *Proceedings of ECDL* (pp. 137-148).

Balabanovic, M., & Shoham, Y. (1997). Fab: Content-based, collaborative recommendation. *Communications of the ACM, 40*(3), 66-72.

Baldi, S. (1998). Normative versus social constructivist processes in the allocation of citations: A network-analytic model. *American Sociological Review, 63,* 829-846.

Barabási, A.-L., & Albert, R. (1999). Emergence of scaling in random networks. *Science, 286,* 509-512.

Barad, K. (1998). Getting real: Technoscientific practices and the materialization of reality. *Differences: A Journal of Feminist Cultural Studies, 10*(2), 87 (84).

Bartlett, K. (2001, June 15). *Backlash vs. third-party annotations from MS smart tags.* Retrieved August 26, 2006, from http://lists.w3.org/Archives/Public/www-annotation/2001JanJun/0115.html

Basilico, J., & Hofmann, T. (2004). Unifying collaborative and content-based filtering. *Proceedings of the 21st International Conference on Machine Learning* (vol. 69, p. 9). New York: ACM Press.

Bates, M. (1989). The design of browsing and berrypicking techniques for the online search interface. *Online Review, 13*(5), 407-424.

Battelle, J. (2004). GlobalSpec: Domain specific search and the semantic Web. *John Battelle's Searchblog.* Retrieved May 24, 2006, from http://battellemedia.com/archives/000519.php

Baumard, P. (1999). *Tacit knowledge in organizations.* London: Sage.

Bawa, M., Jr, R.B., Rajagoplan, S., & Shekita, E. (2003). Make it fresh, make it quick—searching a network of personal Webservers. *Proceedings of the 12th International World Wide Web Conference,* Budapest, Hungary.

Bayer, A.E., Smart, J.C., & McLaughlin, G.W. (1990). Mapping intellectual structure of a scientific subfield through author cocitations. *Journal of the American Society for Information Science, 41,* 444-452.

Beard, K. (1996). A structure for organizing metadata collection. *Proceedings of the 3rd International Conference/Workshop on Integrating GIS and Environmental Modeling,* Santa Fe, NM.

Belkin, N.J, Oddy, R.N., & Brooks, H.M. (1982). Ask for information retrieval: Part I. Background and theory. *Journal of Documentation, 38*(2), 61-71.

Belkin, N.J. (1984). Cognitive models and information transfer. *Social Science Information Studies, 4*(2-3), 111-129.

Belkin, N.J. (2000). Helping people find what they don't know. *Communications of the ACM, 43*(8), 58-61.

Belkin, N.J., & Croft, B.W. (1992). Information filtering and information retrieval: Two sides of the same coin? *Communications of the ACM, 35*(12), 29-36.

Berlanga, A.J., & García, F.J. (2005). IMS LD reusable elements for adaptive learning designs. *Journal of Interactive Media in Education,* 11(Special Issue).

Berners-Lee, T., & Fischetti, M. (1999). *Weaving the Web: The original design and ultimate destiny of the World Wide Web by its inventor.* San Francisco: Harper.

Berners-Lee, T., Cailliau, R., Luotonen, A., Nielsen, H.F., & Secret, A. (1994). The World Wide Web. *Communications of the ACM, 37*(8), 76-82.

Berners-Lee, T., Hendler, J., & Lassila, O. (2001). The semantic Web. *Scientific American, 284*(5), 34-43.

Bharat, K., & Broder, A.Z. (1998). A technique for measuring the relative size and overlap of Web search engines. *Proceedings of the 7th International World Wide Web Conference (WWW7)* (pp. 379-388).

Billsus, D., & Pazzani, M. (1998). Learning collaborative information filters. *Proceedings of the 15th International Conference on Machine Learning* (pp. 46-54). San Francisco: Morgan Kaufmann. Retrieved May 28, 2006, from http://www.ics.uci.edu/~pazzani/Publications/MLC98.pdf

Bizer, C. (2003). D2R MAP—a database to RDF mapping language. *Proceedings of the 12th International World Wide Web Conference.*

Björneborn, L. (2004). *Small-world link structures across an academic Web space: A library and information science approach.* Unpublished Doctoral Dissertation, Royal School of Library and Information Science, Denmark.

Björneborn, L. (2005). Identifying small-world connectors across an academic Web space—a Webometric study. In P. Ingwersen & B. Larsen (Eds.), *Proceedings of ISSI 2005* (pp. 55-66). Stockholm: Karolinska University Press.

Björneborn, L., & Ingwersen, P. (2001). Perspectives of Webometrics. *Scientometrics, 50*, 65-82.

Blake, C., & Pratt, W. (2002, November 18-21). Collaborative information synthesis. *Proceedings of ASIST 2002* (pp. 44-56), Philadelphia.

Bollen, J., Van de Sompel, H., Smith, J.A., & Luce, R. (2005). Toward alternative metrics of journal impact: A comparison of download and citation data. *Information Processing & Management, 41*, 1419-1440.

Borgman, C.L. (1996). Why are online catalogs still hard to use? *Journal of the American Society for Information Science, 47*(7), 493-503.

Borgman, C.L., & Furner, J. (2002). Scholarly communication and bibliometrics. In B. Cronin (Ed.), *Annual review of information science and technology (vol. 36,* pp. 3-72). Medford, NJ: Information Today.

Borlund, P., & Ingwersen, P. (1998). Measures of relative relevance and ranked half-life: Performance indicators for interactive IR. In W.B. Croft, A. Moffat, C.J. van Rijsbergen, R. Wilkinson, & J. Zobel (Eds.), *Proceedings of the 21st ACM SIGIR Conference on Research and Development of Information Retrieval* (pp. 324-331), Melbourne. New York: ACM.

Borner, K., Maru, J.T., & Goldstone, R.L. (2004). The simultaneous evolution of author and paper networks. *Proceedings of the National Academy of Sciences* (vol. 101, pp. 5266-5273).

Bosc, H., & Harnad, S. (2005). In a paperless world a new role for academic libraries: Providing open access. *Learned Publishing, 18*, 95-99.

Bourdieu, P. (1990). *The logic of practice* (R. Nice, trans.). Cambridge, UK: Polity Press in association with Basil Blackwell.

Boyack, K.W., Klavans, R., & Borner, K. (2005). Mapping the backbone of science. *Scientometrics, 64*, 351-374.

Boyce, B. (1982). Beyond topicality. A two-stage view of relevance and the retrieval process. *Information Processing and Management, 18*, 105-189.

Braam, R.R., Moed, H.F., & van Raan, A.F.J. (1991). Mapping of science by combined cocitation and word analysis. I: Structural aspects. *Journal of the American Society for Information Science, 42*, 233-251.

Brand, A. (1990). *The force of reason: An introduction to Habermas' Theory of Communicative Action.* Sydney, Australia: Allen & Unwin.

Breese, J., & Kadie, C. (1998). Empirical analysis of predictive algorithms for collaborative filtering. *Proceedings of the 14th Annual Conference on Uncertainty in Artificial Intelligence (UAI-98)* (pp. 43-52).

Breese, J.S., Heckerman, D., & Kadie, C. (1998). Empirical analysis of predictive algorithms for collaborative filtering. *Proceedings of the 14th Conference on Uncertainty in Artificial Intelligence.*

Brewington, B.E., & Cybenko, G. (2000). How dynamic is the Web? *Proceedings of the 9th International World Wide Web Conference,* Amsterdam, The Netherlands.

Brickley, D., & Miller, L. (2005). *FOAF vocabulary specification.*

Brin, S., & Page, L. (1998). The anatomy of a large-scale hypertextual Web search engine. *Proceedings of the 7th International Conference on the World Wide Web,* Brisbane, Australia.

Brin, S., & Page, L. (1998). The anatomy of a large-scale hypertextual Web search engine. *Computer Networks, 30*(1-7), 107-117.

Broder, A., Kumar, R., Maghoul, F., Raghavan, P., Rajagopalan, S., Stata, R., Tomkins, A., & Wiener, J. (2000). Graph structure in the Web. *Computer Networks, 33,* 309-320.

Brody, T., Harnad, S., & Carr, L. (2006). Earlier Web usage statistics as predictors of later citation impact. *Journal of the American Society for Information Science and Technology, 57,* 1060-1072.

Brody, T., Kampa, S., Harnad, S., Carr, L., & Hitchock, S. (2003). Digitometric services for open archives environments. In T. Troch & I.T. Sølvberg (Eds.), *Research and advanced technology for digital libraries* (pp. 207-220). Berlin: Springer-Verlag (LNCS 2769).

Brothers, R. (2000). The computer-mediated public sphere and the cosmopolitan ideal. *Ethics and Information Technology, 2*(2), 91-98.

Brown, J.S., & Duguid, P. (2002). *The social life of information.* Boston: Harvard Business School Press.

Brusilovsky, P. (2001). adaptive hypermedia. *User Modeling and User Adapted Interaction, 11*(1/2), 87-110.

Brusilovsky, P., & Nijhavan, H. (2002). A framework for adaptive e-learning based on distributed re-usable learning activities. *Proceedings of the World Conference on E-Learning* (E-Learn 2002), Montreal, Canada.

Buchanan, G., & Hinze, A. (2005). A generic alerting service for digital libraries. *Proceedings of the Joint Conference on Digital Libraries* (pp. 131-140).

Buchanan, G., Cunningham, S.J., Blandford, A., Rimmer, J., & Warwick, C. (2005). Information seeking by humanities scholars. *Proceedings of the European Conference on Digital Libraries* (pp. 218-229).

Budanitsky, A., & Hirst, G. (2001). Semantic distance in WordNet: An experimental, application-oriented evaluation of five measures. *Proceedings of Workshop on WordNet and Other Lexical Resources of the 2nd Meeting of the North American Chapter of the Association for Computational Linguistics,* Pittsburgh, PA.

Burger, F., Kroiss, P., Pröll, B., Richtsfeld, R., Sighart, H., & Starck, H. (1997). TIS@WEB—database supported tourist information on the Web. Proceedings of the 4th International Information and Communication Technologies in Tourism 1997 (ENTER'97), Edinburgh, Scotland.

Burke, R. (2002). Hybrid recommender systems: Survey and experiments. *User Modeling and User-Adapted Interaction, 12,* 331-370.

Burke, R., Mobasher, B., & Bhaumik, R. (2005, January 9). Identifying attack models for secure recommendation, Beyond Personalization: A Workshop on the Next Stage of Recommender Systems Research, in conjunction with the 2005 International Conference on Intelligent User Interfaces (IUI'05) (pp. 19-25), San Diego, CA.

Burnett, K., & McKinley, E.G. (1998). Modeling information seeking. *Interacting with Computers, 10*(3), 285-302.

Burt, R.S. (1980). Models of network structure. *Annual Review of Sociology, 6,* 79-141.

Burt, R.S. (1992). *Structural holes: The social structure of competition.* Cambridge, MA: Harvard University Press.

Butler, B. (2001). KnowBit reference information: A knowledge base specification. *Proceedings of the NISO Standards Review Meeting.*

Butterworth, R. (2006). *The Accessing our Archival and Manuscript Heritage project and the development of the 'Helpers' Web site.* Middlesex University Interaction Design Centre Technical Report IDC-TR-2006-001. Retrieved June 8, 2006, from http://www.cs.mdx.ac.uk/research/idc/tech_reports.html

Butterworth, R. (2006). Designing digital library resources for users in sparse, unbounded social networks. In Gonzalo et al. (Eds.), *Proceedings of the 10th European Conference on Research and Advanced Technology for Digital Libraries* (pp. 184-195). Berlin: Springer-Verlag (LNCS 4172).

Butterworth, R. (2006). Information seeking and retrieval as a leisure activity." In Blandford & Gow (Eds.), *Proceedings of the 1st International Workshop on Digital Libraries in the Context of Users' Broader Activities.* Retrieved June 8, 2006, from http://www.uclic.ucl.ac.uk/events/dl-cuba2006/dl-cuba.pdf

Butterworth, R., & Davis Perkins, V. (2005). Assessing the roles that a small specialist library plays to guide the development of a hybrid digital library. In F. Crestani & I.

Ruthven (Eds.), *Information Context: Nature, Impact, and Role: Proceedings of the 5th International Conference on Conceptions of Library and Information Sciences* (pp. 200-211). Berlin: Springer-Verlag (LNCS 3507).

Byström, K., & Järvelin, K. (1995). Task complexity affects information seeking and use. *Information Processing & Management, 31*(2), 191-213.

Calhoun, C. (1992). *Habermas and the public sphere.* Cambridge, MA: MIT Press.

Cann, J.A. (2004). Maths from scratch for biologists: Correlation (pp.91-144). Retrieved March 14, 2006, from http://www-micro.msb.le.ac.uk/1010/DH3.html

Capurro, R. (1992). Informatics and hermeneutics. In C. Floyd, H. Züllighoven, R. Budde, & R. Keil-Slawik (Eds.), *Software development and reality construction* (pp. 363-375). Berlin/Heidelberg/New York: Springer.

Capurro, R. (2000). Hermeneutics and the phenomenon of information. In C. Mitcham (Ed.), *Metaphysics, epistemology, and technology. Research in philosophy and technology* (vol. 19, pp. 79-85). JAI/Elsevier.

Carbonaro A. (2004). Learning objects recommendation in a collaborative information management system. *IEEE Learning Technology Newsletter, 6*(4).

Carbonaro, A. (2005). Defining personalized learning views of relevant learning objects in a collaborative bookmark management system. In *Web-based intelligent e-learning systems: Technologies and applications.* Hershey, PA: Idea Group.

Case, D.O. (2002). *Looking for information: A survey of research on information seeking, needs, and behavior.* San Diego: Academic Press, Elsevier.

Castells, M. (1996). *The rise of the network society.* Oxford: Blackwell.

Chaffee, J., & Gauch, S. (2000). Personal ontologies for Web navigation. *Proceedings of the 9th International Conference on Information and Knowledge Management* (CIKM'00) (pp. 227-234).

Chakrabarti, S. (2003). Mining the Web: Discovering knowledge from hypertext data. San Francisco: Morgan Kaufmann.

Chakrabarti, S., Berg, M., & Dom, B. (1999). Focused crawling: A new approach to topic-specific Web resource discovery. *Computer Networks, 31*(11-16), 1623-1640.

Chakrabarti, S., Joshi, M., Punera, K., & Pennock, D.M. (2002). The structure of broad topics on the Web. *Proceedings of WWW 2002* (pp. 251-262).

Chatman, E.A. (1996). The impoverished life-world of outsiders. *Journal of the American Society for Information Science, 47*(3), 193-206.

Chen, C. (1999). *Information visualisation and virtual environments.* London: Springer.

Chen, C. (1999). Visualising semantic spaces and author co-citation networks in digital libraries. *Information Processing and Management, 35,* 401-420.

Chen, C., & Paul, R.J. (2001). Visualizing a knowledge domain's intellectual structure. *Computer, 34*(3), 65-71.

Chen, H., & Dumais, S.T. (2000). Bringing order to the Web: Automatically categorizing search results. *Proceedings of CHI'00, Human Factors in Computing Systems* (pp. 145-152).

Chen, L., & Rousseau, R. (in press). Q-measures for binary divided networks: Bridges between German and English institutes in publications of the *Journal of Fluid Mechanics. Scientometrics.*

Chen, M., Hearst, M., Hong, J., & Lin, J. (1999). Cha-Cha: A system for organizing intranet search results. *Proceedings of the 2nd USENIX Symposium on Internet Technologies and SYSTEMS* (USITS), pp. 47-58.

Chen, M., Park, J., & Yu, P. (1996). Data mining for path traversal patterns in a Web environment. Proceedings of the 16th International Conference on Distributed Computing Systems (pp. 385-392).

Chen, M., Park, J., & Yu, P. (1998). Efficient data mining for path traversal patterns. IEEE Transactions Knowledge and Data Engineering, 10(2), 209-221.

Chi, E.H., & Pirolli, P. (2006, February). Social information foraging and collaborative search. *Proceedings of the HCIC Workshop,* Fraser, CO.

Chiu, D.K.W., Cheung, S.C., & Leung, H.F. (2005). A multi-agent infrastructure for mobile workforce management in a service oriented enterprise. Proceedings of the 38th Annual Hawaii International Conference on System Sciences (HICSS'05) (Track 3, p. 85c).

Cho, J., & Garcia-Molina, H. (2002). Parallel crawlers. *Proceedings of the 11th International World Wide Web Conference,* Honolulu, HI.

Chuang, S.L., & Chien, L.F. (2002). Towards automatic generation of query taxonomy: A hierarchical query clustering approach. In V. Kumar, S. Tsumoto, P.S. Yu, & N. Zhong (Eds.), *Proceedings of IEEE 2002 International Conference on Data Mining* (pp. 75-82). Los Alamitos, CA: IEEE Computer Society.

CinemaScreen. (2006). Retrieved January 5, 2006, from http://www.cinemacreen.co.uk

Clark, A. (1998). *Being there: Putting brain, body, and world together again*. Cambridge, MA: MIT Press.

Claypool, M., Le, P., Wased, M., & Brown, D. (2001, January 14-17). Implicit interest indicators. Proceedings of the 6th International Conference on Intelligent User Interfaces (IUI '01) (pp. 33-40), Santa Fe, NM.

Cohen, W., & Fan, W. (2000). Web-collaborative filtering: Recommending music by crawling the Web. In I. Herman & A. Vezza (Eds.), *Proceedings of the 9th International World Wide Web Conference on Computer Networks: The International Journal of Computer and Telecommunications Networking* (pp. 685-698). Amsterdam, The Netherlands: North-Holland.

Coleman, A.S., Smith, T.R., Buchel, O.A., & Mayer, R.E. (2001). Learning spaces in digital libraries. In Constantopoulos & Sølvberg (Eds.), *Proceedings of the Conference on Research and Advanced Technology for Digital Libraries* (ECDL 2001) (pp. 251-262). Berlin: Springer-Verlag.

Conklin, J. (1987). Hypertext: An introduction and survey. *IEEE Computer, 20*(9), 17-41.

Connor, O. (2001). Personalization comes full circle, part 2. Retrieved April 27, 2006, from http://www.clickz.com/experts/crm/crm-strat/article.php/14341

Cool, C. (1997, November 1-6). The nature of situation assessment in new information retrieval environments. In C. Schwartz & M. Rorvig (Eds.), *ASIS '97: Digital Collections: Implications for Users, Funders, Developers and Maintainers. Proceedings of the 60th ASIS Annual Meeting* (vol. 34, pp. 135-146), Washington, DC. Medford, NJ: Information Today for ASIS.

Cooley R., Mobasher, B., & Srivastava, J. (1997). Web mining: Information and pattern discovery on the World Wide Web. Proceedings of the 9th International Conference on Tools with Artificial Intelligence (ICTAI '97).

Cosijn, E., & Ingwersen, P. (2000). Dimensions of relevance. *Information Processing & Management, 36*, 533-550.

Covi, L., & Kling, R. (1996). Organizational dimensions of effective digital library use: Closed rational and open natural systems models. *Journal of the American Society for Information Science, 47*(9), 672-690.

Cox, A. (2005). What are communities of practice? A comparative review of four seminal works. *Journal of Information Science, 31*(6), 527-540.

Cozzens, S. (1989). What do citations count? The rhetoric-first model. *Scientometrics, 15,* 437-447.

Craswell, N., Robertson, S., Zaragoza, H., & Taylor, M. (2005). Relevance weighting for query independent evidence. In G. Marchionini, A. Moffat, J. Tait, R. Baeza-Yates, & N. Ziviani (Eds.), *Proceedings of the 28th Annual International ACM SIGIR Conference on Research and Development in Information Retrieval* (pp. 416-423), Salvador, Brazil.

Crespo, A., & Garcia-Molina, H. (2002). Routing indices for peer-to-peer systems. *Proceedings of the 22nd International Conference on Distributed Computing Systems* (ICDCS'02), Vienna, Austria.

Crestani, F. (1997). Application of spreading activation techniques in information retrieval. *Artificial Intelligence Review, 11*(6), 453-482.

Cronbach, L.J. (1951). Coefficient alpha and the internal structure of tests. *Psychometrika, 16*(3), 297-334.

Cronin, B. (2005). Warm bodies, cold facts: The embodiment and emplacement of knowledge claims. In P. Ingwersen & B. Larsen (Eds.), *Proceedings of ISSI 2005* (pp. 1-12). Stockholm: Karolinska University Press.

Cross, R., Borgatti, S.P., & Parker, A. (2002). Making invisible work visible: Using social network analysis to support strategic collaboration. *California Management Review, 44*(2), 25-46.

Cui, H., Wen, J., Nie, J., & Ma, W. (2002). Probabilistic query expansion using query logs. In D. Lassner, D.D. Roure, & A. Iyengar (Eds.), *Proceedings of the 11th International Conference on World Wide Web* (pp. 325-332). New York: ACM Press.

Cunningham, H., Maynard, D., Bontcheva, K., & Tablan, V. (2002). GATE: A framework and graphical development environment for robust NLP tools and applications. *Proceedings of the 40th Anniversary Meeting of the Association for Computational Linguistics,* Budapest.

Currier, S., Barton, J., O'Beirne, R., & Ryan, B. (2004). Quality assurance for digital learning object repositories: Issues for the metadata creation process. *ALT-J Research in Learning Technology, 12*(1), 5-20.

DaeEun, K., & Sea Woo, K. (2001). Dynamics of expert groups to recommend Web documents. In Constantopoulos & Sølvberg (Eds.), *Proceedings of the Conference on Research and Advanced Technology for Digital Libraries* (ECDL 2001) (pp. 275-286). Berlin: Springer-Verlag.

Dahlen, B.J., Konstan, J.A., Herlocker, J.L., Good, N., Borchers, A., & Riedl, J. (1998). *Jump-starting movielens:*

User benefits of starting a collaborative filtering system with 'dead data'. University of Minnesota TR 98-017.

Dai, H., & Mobasher, B. (2004). Integrating semantic knowledge with Web usage mining for personalization. In A. Scime (Ed.), *Web mining: Applications and techniques* (pp. 276-306). Hershey, PA: Idea Group.

Dean, J., & Ghemawat, S. (2004). MapReduce: Simplified data processing on large clusters. *Proceedings of the 6th Symposium on Operating System Design and Implementation* (OSDI04), San Francisco, CA.

Dean, J., & Henzinger, M.R. (1999). Finding related pages in the World Wide Web. *Computer Networks, 31,* 1467-1479.

Deerwester, S., Dumais, S., GW, F., Landauer, T., & Harshman, R. (1990). Indexing by latent semantic analysis. *Journal of the American Society for Information Science, 41,* 391-407.

Devillers, R., Gervais, M., Bedard, Y., & Jeansoulin, R. (2002, March). Spatial data quality: From metadata to quality indicators and contextual end-user manual. *Proceedings of the OEEPE/ISPRS Joint Workshop on Spatial Data Quality Management,* Istanbul, Turkey.

Dhillon, I.S., Mallela, S., & Kumar, R. (2002). Enhanced word clustering for hierarchical text classification. *Proceedings of the 8th ACM SIGKDD International Conference on Knowledge Discovery and Data Mining* (pp. 191-200).

Dholakia, U.M., Bagozzi, R.P., & Klein Pearo, L. (2004). A social influence model of consumer participation in network- and small-group-based virtual communities. *Journal of Research in Marketing, 21*(3), 241-263.

Dhyani, D., Keong, N.W., & Bhowmick, S.S. (2002). A survey of Web metrics. *ACM Computing Surveys, 34*(4), 469-503.

Ding, Y., Chowdhury, G., & Foo, S. (2000). Journal as markers of intellectual space: Journal co-citation analysis of information retrieval area, 1987-1997. *Scientometrics, 47,* 55-73.

Ding, Y., Fensel, D., Klein, M., Omelayenko, B., & Schulten, E. (2004). The role of ontologies in e-commerce. In S. Staab & R. Studer (Eds.), *International handbooks on information systems: Handbook on ontologies* (pp. 593-615). Berlin/Heidelberg: Springer-Verlag.

Donato, D., Laura, L., Leonardi, S., & Millozzi, S. (2004). Large scale properties of the Webgraph. *European Physical Journal B, 38,* 239-243.

Downes, S. (2003). Design and reusability of learning objects in an academic context: A new economy of education? *USDLA Journal, 17*(1).

Downes, S. (2004, June). *Quality standards: It's all about teaching and learning? Proceedings of NUTN,* Kennebunkport, ME.

Dretske, F. (1981). *Knowledge and the flow of information.* Cambridge, MA: MIT Press

Dron, J., Boyne, C., & Mitchell, R. (2002). Evaluating assessment using n-dimensional filtering. *Proceedings of the AACE E-Learn Conference.*

Drucker, P.F. (1992). *The age of discontinuity.* New York: Harper & Row.

Dublin Core Metadata Initiative. *DCMI metadata terms.* Retrieved August 30, 2005, from *http://dublincore.org/documents/dcmi-terms/*

Dumais, S.T., & Chen, H. (2000). Hierarchical classification of Web content. *Proceedings of SIGIR-00, the 23rd ACM International Conference on Research and Development in Information Retrieval* (pp. 256-263).

Duval, E. (2006). LearnRank: Towards a real quality measure for learning. In U. Ehlers & J.M. Pawlowski (Eds.), *European handbook for quality and standardization in e-learning.* Berlin: Springer-Verlag, 457-463.

Duval, E., & Hodgins, W. (2004). Making metadata go away: Hiding everything but the benefits. *Proceedings of the International Conference on Dublin Core and Metadata Applications* (DC2004), Shanghai, China.

Duval, E., Hodgins, W., Sutton, S., & Weibel, S.L. (2002). Metadata principles and practicalities. *D-Lib Magazine, 8.* Retrieved August 26, 2006, from http://www.dlib.org/dlib/april02/weibel/04weibel.html

Dwork, C., Kumar, R., Naor, M., & Sivakumar, D. (2001). Rank aggregation methods for the Web. In V.Y. Shen, N. Saito, M.R. Lyu, & M.E. Zurko (Eds.), *Proceedings of the 10th International Conference on the World Wide Web* (pp. 613-622), Hong Kong.

Dzbor, M., Motta, E., & Stutt, A. (2005). Achieving higher-level learning through adaptable semantic Web applications. *International Journal of Knowledge and Learning, 1*(1/2).

Egghe, L., & Rousseau, R. (1990). *Introduction to informetrics. Quantitative methods in library, documentation and information science.* Amsterdam: Elsevier.

Egghe, L., & Rousseau, R. (2002). Co-citation, bibliographic coupling and a characterization of lattice citation networks. *Scientometrics, 55,* 349-361.

Egghe, L., Rao, Ravichandra I.K., & Sahoo, B.B. (2006). Proof of a conjecture of Moed and Garfield on authoritative references and extension to non-authoritative references. *Scientometrics, 66,* 537-549.

Ehrig, M., & Sure, Y. (2004, May). Ontology mapping—an integrated approach. In C. Bussler, J. Davis, D. Fensel, & R. Studer (Eds.), *Proceedings of the 1st European Semantic Web Symposium* (pp. 76-91), Heraklion, Greece. Berlin: Springer-Verlag (LNCS 3053).

Eirinaki, M., & Vazirgiannis, M. (2003). Web mining for web personalization. *ACM Transactions on Internet Technology, 3*(1), 1-27.

Eisenberg, M.B., & Barry, C.L. (1988). Order effects: A study of the possible influence of presentation order on user judgments of document relevance. *Journal of the American Society for Information Science, 39*(5), 293-300.

Ekbia, H.R., & Maguitman, A.G. (2001, July 27-30). Context and relevance: A pragmatic approach. *Proceedings of the 3rd International and Interdisciplinary Conference on Modeling and Using Context* (vol. 2116, pp. 156-169), Dundee, UK. Heidelberg: Springer.

Ellis, D. (1989). A behavioral model for information retrieval system design. *Journal of Information Science, 5*(4/5), 237-247.

Ellis, D. (1993). A comparison of the information seeking patterns of researchers in the physical and social sciences. *Journal of Documentation, 49*(4), 356-369.

Ellis, D., Allen, D., & Wilson, T.D. (1999). Information science and information systems: Conjunct subjects, disjunct disciplines. *Journal of the American Society for Information Science, 50*(12), 1095-1107.

Ellis, D., Cox, D., & Hall, K. (1993). A comparison of the information seeking patterns of researchers in the physical and social sciences. *Journal of Documentation, 49*(4), 356-369.

EQO (European Quality Observatory). (2004). *The EQO model, v.1.2a.* Retrieved August 26, 2006, from *http://www.eqo.info/files/EQO-Model-1.2a.pdf*

ETB. (2002). Recommended data model format to be used as a standard by national systems to include national/local resources in the EU Treasury Browser. *European Treasury Browser (ETB), D4.2.*

Eysenbach, G., Köhler, C., Yihune, G., Lampe, K., Cross, P., & Brickley, D. (2001). A metadata vocabulary for self- and third-party labeling of health Web sites: Health Information Disclosure, Description and Evaluation Language (HIDDEL). *Proceedings of AIMA 2001.* Retrieved 8 August, 2007 from http://www.medcertain.org/pdf/AMIA2001-final-edited-hiddel.pdf

Faloutsos, C. (1985). Access methods for text. *ACM Computing Surveys, 17*(1), 49-74.

Fang, X., Chen, P., & Chen, B. (2005). User search strategies and search engine interface design. In R.W. Proctor & K.-P.L. Vu (Eds.), *Handbook of human factors in Web design* (pp. 193-210). Mahwah, NJ: Lawrence Erlbaum.

Favela, J., & Decouchant, D. (Eds.). (2003). *Groupware: Design, implementation and use.* Berlin: Springer-Verlag.

Fayyad, U.M., Piatetsky-Shapiro, G., Smyth, P., & Uthurusamy, R. (Eds.). (1996). *Advances in knowledge discovery and data mining.* Menlo Park, CA: AAAI Press.

Fellbaum, C. (Ed.). (1998). *WordNet: An electronic lexical database.* Cambridge, MA: MIT Press.

Feller, J., Fitzgerald, B., Hissam, S.A., & Lakhnani, K.R. (2005). *Perspectives on free and open source software.* Cambridge, MA: MIT Press.

Fetterly, D., Manasse, M., Najork, M., & Wiener, J. (2003). A large-scale study of the evolution of Web pages. *Proceedings of the 12th International World Wide Web Conference,* Budapest, Hungary.

Fidel, R. (1994). User-centered indexing. *Journal of the American Society for Information Science, 45*(8), 572-576.

Finin, T., Fritzson, R., McKay, D., & McEntire, R. (1994, November 29-December 2). KQML as an agent communication language. Proceedings of the 3rd International Conference on Information and Knowledge Management (CIKM '94) (pp. 456-463), Gaithersburg, MD.

Flom, P.L., Friedman, S.R., Strauss, S., & Neaigus, A. (2004). A new measure of linkage between two sub-networks. *Connections, 26*(1), 62-70.

Flores, F. (1998). Information technology and the institution of identity: Reflections since understanding computers and cognition. *Information Technology and People, 11*(4), 351-372.

Fowell, S., & Levy, P. (1995). Developing a new professional practice: A model for networked learner support in higher education. *Journal of Documentation, 51*(3), 271-280.

Frandsen, T.F., & Rousseau, R. (2005). Article impact calculated over arbitrary periods. *Journal of the American Society for Information Science and Technology, 56*, 58-62.

Frank, E., Paynter, G., Witten, I., Gutwin, C., & Nevill-Manning, C. (1999), Domain-specific key phrase extraction. *Proceedings of the 16th International Joint Conference on Artificial Intelligence* (pp. 668-673). San Francisco: Morgan Kaufmann.

Freeman, L.C. (1979). Centrality in social networks. Conceptual clarification. *Social Networks, 1*, 215-239.

Freeman, L.C. (1979). Centrality in social networks: Conceptual clarification. *Social Networks, 1*(3), 215-239.

Freyne, J., Smyth, B., Coyle, M., Balfe, E., & Briggs, P. (2004). Further experiments on collaborative ranking in community-based Web search. *Artificial Intelligence Review, 21*(3-4), 229-252.

Friedkin, N.E. (1991). Theoretical foundations for centrality measures. *American Journal of Sociology, 96*(6), 1478-1504.

Friedkin, N.E. (1998). *A structural theory of social influence (structural analysis in the social sciences)*. Cambridge: Cambridge University Press.

Fry, J. (2006). Scholarly research and information practices: A domain analytic approach. *Information Processing & Management, 42*(1), 299-316.

Fu, L., Goh, D.H., Foo, S., & Na, J.C. (2003). Collaborative querying through a hybrid query clustering approach. In T.M.T. Sembok, H.B. Zaman, H. Chen, S.R. Urs, & S.H. Myaeng (Eds.), *Digital libraries: Technology and management of indigenous knowledge for global access* (pp. 111-122). Berlin: Springer-Verlag (LNCS 2911).

Fu, L., Goh, D.H.-L., Foo, S.S.-B., & Supangat, Y. (2004, September 12-17). Collaborative querying for enhanced information retrieval. *Proceedings of ECDL 2004* (pp; 378-388), Bath, UK.

Fuchs-Kittowski, F. & Köhler, A. (2005). Wiki-communities in the context of work processes. In D. Riehle (Ed.), *Proceedings of the 2005 International Symposium on Wikis* (WikiSym 2005) (pp. 33-39), San Diego, CA.

García, F.J., Berlanga, A.J., Moreno, M.N., García, J., & Carabias, J. (2004). *HyCo—an authoring tool to create semantic learning objects for Web-based e-learning systems* (pp. 344-348). Berlin: Springer-Verlag (LNCS 3140).

Garden, M. (2004). *On the use of semantic feedback in recommender systems.* Master's Thesis, McGill University, Canada.

Garfield, E. (1972). Citation analysis as a tool in journal evaluation. *Science, 178*(4060), 471-479.

Garfield, E. (1988). Announcing the SCI compact disc edition: CD-ROM gigabyte storage technology, novel software, and bibliographic coupling make desktop research and discovery a reality. *Current Contents, 22*(May 30).

Garner, R. (1967). A computer oriented graph theoretic analysis of citation index structures. In B. Flood (ed.), *Three Drexel information science studies* (pp. 1-46). Philadelphia, Drexel Institute of Technology.

GESTALT (Getting Educational Systems Talking Across Leading-Edge Technologies). (1999). *D0401 courseware metadata design.* Retrieved August 26, 2006, from http://www.fdgroup.co.uk/gestalt/

Geyer-Schulz, A., & Hahsler, M. (2002). Evaluation of recommender algorithms for an Internet information broker based on simple association rules and on the repeat-buying theory. In B. Masand, M. Spiliopoulou, J. Srivastava, & O. Zaiane (Eds.), *Proceedings of WEBKDD* (pp. 100-114), Edmonton, Canada.

Giannakis, M., & Croom, S. (2001). The intellectual structure of supply chain management: An application of the social network analysis and citation analysis to SCM related journals. *Proceedings of the 10th International Annual IPSERA Conference*, Jönköping, Sweden.

Gilbert, G.N. (1977). Referencing as persuasion. *Social Studies of Science, 7*, 113-122.

Given, L.M. (2002). The academic and the everyday: Investigating the overlap in mature undergraduates' information-seeking behaviors. *Library and Information Science Research, 24*, 17-29.

Glance, N. (2001). Community search assistant. In C. Cidner & J. Moore (Eds.), *Proceedings of the 6th International Conference on Intelligent User Interfaces* (pp. 91-96). New York: ACM Press.

Goh, D., & Leggett, J. (2000). Patron-augmented digital libraries. *Proceedings of the ACM Conference on Digital Libraries* (pp. 53-163). New York: ACM Press.

Goh, D.H., Fu, L., & Foo, S. (2005). Collaborative querying using the query graph visualizer. *Online Information Review, 29*(3), 266-282.

Goh, J.M., Poo, D.C.C., & Chang, K.T.T (2004, July 8-11). Incorporating contextual cues into electronic repositories. *Proceedings of the 8th Pacific-Asia Conference on Information Systems* (pp. 472-484), Shanghai, China.

Golbeck, J., Parsia, B., & Hendler, J. (2003). Trust networks on the semantic Web. *Proceedings of Cooperative Intelligent Agents,* Helsinki, Finland.

Goldberg, D., Nichols, D., Oki, B.M., & Terry, D. (1992). Using collaborative filtering to weave an information tapestry. *Communications of the ACM, 35*(12), 61-70.

Golder, S., & Huberman, B.A. (2005). *The structure of collaborative tagging systems.* Retrieved May 28, 2006, from http://www.hpl.hp.com/research/idl/papers/tags/tags.pdf

Google Technology. (2004). Our search: Google technology. *About Google.* Retrieved May 27, 2006, from *http://www.google.com/technology/*

Gordon, M., & Pathak, P. (1999). Finding information on the World Wide Web: The retrieval effectiveness of search engines. *Information Processing and Management, 35,* 141-180.

Granovetter, M.S. (1973). The strength of weak ties. *American Journal of Sociology, 78*(6), 1360-1380.

Grant, S., & McCalla, G. (2001). A hybrid approach to making recommendations and its application to the movie domain. *Proceedings of the 14th Biennial Conference of the Canadian Society on Computational Studies of Intelligence: Advances in Artificial Intelligence* (pp 257-266). London: Springer-Verlag (LNCS 2056).

Green, A. (1990). What do we mean by user needs? *British Journal of Academic Librarianship, 5,* 65-78.

Green, R. (2001). Relationships in the organization of knowledge: An overview. In C.A. Bean & R. Green (Eds.), *Relationships in the organization of knowledge* (pp. 3-18). Dordrecht, The Netherlands: Kluwer Academic.

Green, S.J. (1998). Automated link generation: Can we do better than term repetition? *Computer Networks and ISDN Systems, 30,* 75-84.

Greisdorf, H. (2000). Relevance: An interdisciplinary and information science perspective. *Informing Science, 3*(2), 67-71.

Gruber, T. (1993). *Toward principles for the design of ontologies used for knowledge sharing.* Technical Report KSL 93-04, Stanford University Knowledge Systems Laboratory, USA.

Gruber, T.R. (1993). *A translation approach to portable ontology specifications.* Tech Report Logic-92-1, Department of Computer Science, Stanford University, USA.

Guo, X., Zhang, G., Chew, E., & Burdon, S. (2005, December 5-9). A hybrid recommendation approach for one-and-only items. In S. Zhang & R. Jarvis (Eds.), *Proceedings of 18th Australian Joint Conference on Artificial Intelligence* (pp. 457-466), Sydney, Australia. Berlin/Heidelberg: Springer-Verlag (LNCS).

Guy, G., Powell, A., & Day, M. (2004). Improving the quality of metadata in e-print archives. *Ariadne, 38.*

Gyongyi, Z., Garcia-Molina, H., & Pedersen, J. (2004). Combating Web spam with TrustRank. *Proceedings of VLDB* (vol. 4).

Habermas, J. (1991). *The structural transformation of the public sphere.* Cambridge, MA: MIT Press.

Halasz, F.G. (1988). Reflections on NoteCards: Seven issues for the next generation of hypermedia systems. *Communications of the ACM, 31*(7), 836-852.

Hammond, T., Hanny, T., Lund, B., & Scott, J. (2005). Social bookmarking tools (I). *D-Lib Magazine, 11*(4). Retrieved May 28, 2006, from http://www.dlib.org/dlib/april05/hammond/04hammond.html

Hammouda, K.M., & Kamel, M.S. (2004). Efficient phrase-based document indexing for Web document. *IEEE Transactions on Knowledge and Data Engineering 16*(10), 1279- 1296. Washington, DC: IEEE Computer Society Press.

Hanani, U., Shapira, B., & Shoval, P. (2001). Information filtering: Overview of issues, research and systems. *User Modeling and User-Adapted Interaction, 11,* 203-259.

Hand, D., Mannila, H., & Smyth, P. (2001). *Principles of data mining* (pp. 353-356). Boston: MIT Press.

Handschuh, S., Staab, S., & Volz, R. (2003). On deep annotation. *Proceedings of the 12th International World Wide Web Conference.*

Harnad, S., & Dror, I.E. (Eds.). (2006). Distributed cognition—special issue. *Pragmatics and Cognition, 14*(2).

Harter, S.P. (1992). Psychological relevance and information science. *Journal of the American Society for Information Science, 43*(9), 602-615.

Hatcher, L. (1994). *A step-by-step approach to using the SAS(R) system for factor analysis and structural equation modeling.* Cary, NC: SAS Institute.

Hawking, D., Paris, C., Wilkinson, R., & Wu, M. (2005, August 9). Context in enterprise search and delivery. *Proceedings of the ACM SIGIR 2005 Workshop on Information Retrieval in Context* (IRiX) (pp. 14-16), Salvador, Brazil.

Heaney, M. (1999). *An Analytical Model of Collections and their Catalogs.* Retrieved June 8, 2006, from http://www.ukoln.ac.uk/metadata/rslp/model/amcc-v31.pdf

Heflin, J. (2004, February). OWL Web Ontology Language use cases and requirements. Retrieved from http://www.w3.org/TR/Webont-req/

Herlocker, J.L., Konstan, J.A., & Riedl, J. (2000, December 2-6). Explaining collaborative filtering recommendations. *Proceedings of the 2000 ACM Conference on Computer Supported Cooperative Work (CSCW'00)* (pp. 241-250). Philadelphia.

Herlocker, J.L., Konstan, J.A., Terveen, L.G., & Riedl, J.T. (2004). Evaluating collaborative filtering recommender systems. *ACM Transactions on Information Systems, 22*(1), 5-53.

Hert, C.A. (1992). Exploring a new model for understanding information retrieval interactions. *Proceedings of ASIS' 92* (pp. 72-75).

Hert, C.A. (1997). *Understanding information retrieval interactions: Theoretical and practical implications.* Greenwich, CN: Ablex.

Hess, C., Stein, K., & Schlieder, C. (2006). Trust-enhanced visibility for personalized document recommendations. *Proceedings of the 21st ACM Symposium on Applied Computing,* Dijon, France.

Hill, W., Stead, L., Rosenstein, M., & Furnas, G. (1995, May 7-11). Recommending and evaluating choices in a virtual community of use. Proceedings of the SIGCHI Conference on Human Factors in Computing Systems (pp. 194-201), Denver, CO.

Hill, W., Stead, L., Rosenstein, M., & Furnas, G. (1995). Recommending and evaluating choices in a virtual community of use. *Proceedings of the Human Factors in Computing Systems (CHI '95) Conference* (vol. 1, pp. 194-201). New York: ACM.

Hillman, D., Dusshay, N., & Phipps, J. (2004). Improving metadata quality: Augmentation and recombination. *Proceedings of the International Conference on Dublin Core and Metadata Applications* (DC-2004), Shanghai, China.

Hinze, A., & Junmanee, S. (2005). Providing recommendations in a mobile tourist information system. *Proceedings of ISTA* (pp. 86-100).

Hjørland, B. (1997). *Information seeking and subject representation: An activity theoretical approach to information science.* Westport, CN: Greenwood Press.

Hjørland, B. (2000). Relevance research: The missing perspective(s): "Non-relevance" and "epistemological relevance." *Journal of the American Society for Information Science, 51*(2), 209-211.

Hjørland, B. (2002). Epistemology and the socio-cognitive perspective in information science. *Journal of the American Society for Information Science and Technology, 53*(4), 257-270.

Hjørland, B., & Christensen, F.S. (2002). Work tasks and socio-cognitive relevance: A specific example. Brief communication. *Journal of the American Society for Information Science, 53*(11), 960-965.

Hofstede, M. (2000). A collection of special search engines. *Universiteitsbibliotheek.* Retrieved May 28, 2006, from http://www.leidenuniv.nl/ub/biv/specials.htm

Huang, Z., Chung, W., & Chen, H. (2004). A graph model for e-commerce recommender systems. *Journal of the American Society for Information Science & Technology, 55*(3), 259-274.

Hubbell, C.H. (1965). An input-output approach to clique identification. *Sociometry, 28*(4), 377-399.

Huhns, M.N., & Singh, M.P. (1998). *Multiagent systems in information-rich environments. Cooperative information agents II* (pp. 79-93). (LNAI 1435).

Huotari, M.-L., & Chatman, E.A. (2001). Using everyday life information seeking to explain organizational behavior. *Library and Information Science Research, 23,* 351-366.

Hydlegärd, J. (2006). Collaborative information behavior—exploring Kuhlthau's information search process model in a group-based educational setting. *Information Processing and Management, 42,* 276-298.

Hyldegaard, J., & Seiden, P. (2004). My e-journal: Exploring the usefulness of personalized access to scholarly articles and services. Information Research, 9(3).

IEEE LOM. (2002). *Standard for learning object metadata.* IEEE 1484.12.1-2002, IEEE Learning Technology Standards Committee.

Ingwersen, P. (1996). Cognitive perspective of information retrieval interaction: Elements of a cognitive IR theory. *Journal of Documentation, 52*(1), 3-50.

Ingwersen, P. (1998). The calculation of Web impact factors. *Journal of Documentation, 54,* 236-243.

Ingwersen, P., & Björneborn, L. (2005). Methodological issues of Webometric studies. In H.F. Moed, W. Glänzel, & U. Schmoch (Eds.), *Handbook of quantitative science and technology research* (pp. 339-369). Dordrecht: Kluwer.

Ingwersen, P., & Järvelin, A. (2005). *The turn.* Elsevier.

Ingwersen, P., & Jarvelin, K. (2004, July 29). Information retrieval in contexts. *Proceedings of the ACM SIGIR 2004 Workshop on Information Retrieval in Context* (pp. 6-9), Sheffield, UK.

Insight. (2005). *Insight dossier quality criteria.* European Schoolnet. Retrieved August 26, 2006, from http://insight.eun.org/ww/en/pub/insight/thematic_dossiers/quality-criteria.htm

INSPIRE (Infrastructure for Spatial Information in Europe). (2005). *Requirements for the definition of the INSPIRE implementing rules for metadata.* Author.

Instone, K. (2004). Information architecture perspective on personalization. Retrieved February 23, 2006, from http://instone.org/files/Instone-IAPrzChapter.pdf

International Council on Archives. (1999*). ISAD(G): General international standard archival description* (2nd ed.). Retrieved June 8, 2006, from *http://www.icacds.org.uk/eng/ISAD(G).pdf*

ISEdb (Internet Search Engine Database). (2005). *Specialty search engines.* Retrieved May 28, 2006, from http://www.isedb.com/html/Internet_Search_Engines/Specialty_Search_Engines/

ISO 15836. (2003). *Information and documentation—the Dublin Core metadata element set.* International Organization for Standardization.

IVOA (International Virtual Observatory Alliance). (2004). *Resource metadata for the virtual observatory, version 1.01.* Retrieved August 26, 2006, from http://www.ivoa.net/

Jaana Kristensen, J. (1993). Expanding end-users' query statements for free text searching with a search-aid thesaurus. *Information Processing and Management, 29*(6), 733-744.

Jacob, E. (1992). Culture, context and cognition. In M.D. LeCompte, W.L. Millroy, & J. Preissle (Eds.), *The handbook of qualitative research in education* (pp. 293-335). San Diego, CA: Academic Press.

Janes, J.W. (1994). Other people's judgments: A comparison of users' and others' judgments of document relevance, topicality and utility. *Journal of the American Society for Information Science, 45*(3), 160-171.

Jansz, C.N.M. (2000). Some thoughts on the interaction between scientometrics and science and technology policy. *Scientometrics, 47,* 253-264.

Järvelin, K., & Ingwersen, P. (2004). Information seeking research needs extension towards tasks and technology. *Information Research, 10*(1), paper 212. Retrieved from *http://InformationR.net/ir/10-1/paper212.html*

Jin, B.H., & Wang, B. (1999). Chinese Science Citation Database: Its construction and application. *Scientometrics, 45,* 325-332.

Joachims, T. (1997). Text categorization with support vector machines: Learning with many relevant features. *Proceedings of ECML-98, the 10th European Conference on Machine Learning* (pp. 137-142).

Joachims, T., Freitag, D., & Mitchell, T. (1997). WebWatcher: A tour guide for the World Wide Web. Proceedings of the 15th International Joint Conference on Artificial Intelligence (IJCAI97) (pp. 770-775), Nagoya, Japan.

Johnson, N.L. (1999). *The science of social diversity.* Retrieved January 17, 2007, from http://ishi.lanl.gov/Documents_1/DiveristyScience.pdf

Joseph, S. (2002). NeuroGrid: Semantically routing queries in peer-to-peer networks. *Proceedings of the International. Workshop on Peer-to-Peer Computing,* Pisa, Italy.

Jung, K., Na, Y., & Lee, J. (2003). *Creating user-adapted design recommender system through collaborative filtering and content based filtering* (pp. 204-208). Berlin: Springer-Verlag (LNCS 2902).

Kalfoglou, Y., & Schorlemmer, M. (2003). IF-Map: An ontology mapping method based on information-flow theory. In S. Spaccapietra et al. (Eds.), *Journal on data semantics.* (LNCS 2800).

Kalogeraki, V., Gunopulos, D., & Zeinalipour-Yazti, D. (2002). A local search mechanism for peer-to-peer networks. *Proceedings of the 11th International Conference on Information and Knowledge Management* (CIKM'02), McLean, VA.

Kamvar, S., Schlosser, M., & Garcia-Molina, H. (2003). The EigenTrust algorithm for reputation management in P2P networks. *Proceedings of the 12th International World Wide Web Conference,* Budapest, Hungary.

Kanellopoulos, D., Kotsiantis, S., & Pintelas, P. (2006, February). Ontology-based learning applications: A development methodology. *Proceedings of the 24th Iasted International Multi-Conference Software Engineering,* Austria.

Kangas, S. (2002). Collaborative filtering and recommendation systems. Research Report TTE-2001-35, LOUHT-Project, VTT Tietotekniikka. Retrieved March 26, 2006, from http://www.vtt.fi/inf/julkaisut/muut/2002/collaborativefiltering.pdf

Kanter, R.M. (1988). When a thousand flowers bloom: Structural, collective, and social conditions for innovation in organization. *Research in Organizational Behavior, 10,* 169-211.

Karamuftuoglu, M. (1998). Collaborative information retrieval: Toward a social informatics view of IR interaction. *Journal of the American Society for Information Science, 49*(12), 1070-1080.

Katz, L. (1953). A new status index derived from sociometric analysis. *Psychometrika, 18,* 39-43.

Kautz, H., Selman, B., & Shah, M. (1997). Referral Web: Combining social networks and collaborative filtering. *Communications of the ACM, 40*(3).

Kawin Interactive. (2003, January 1). *Kawin Vortalbuilding.com: Your gateway to the universe.* Retrieved May 24, 2006, from http://elibrary.line56.com/detail/RES/1098686731_907.html

Kazienko, P., & Kolodziejski, P. (2005). *WindOwls—adaptive system for the integration of recommendation methods in e-commerce* (pp. 218-224). Berlin/Heidelberg: Springer-Verlag (LNAI).

Kekäläinen, J., & Järvelin, K. (2002, July 21-25). Evaluating information retrieval systems under the challenges of interaction and multidimensional dynamic relevance. In H. Bruce, R. Fidel, P. Ingwersen, & P. Vakkari (Eds.), *Proceedings of the 4th International Conference on Conceptions of Library and Information Science* (CoLIS4) (pp. 253-270), Seattle, WA. Greenwood Village, CO: Libraries Unlimited.

Kendrick, J.W. (1994). Total capital and economic growth. *Atlantic Economic Journal, 22*(1).

Kessler, M.M. (1962). *An experimental study of bibliographic coupling between technical papers.* Report, Lincoln Laboratory, Massachusetts Institute of Technology, USA.

Kessler, M.M. (1963). Bibliographic coupling between scientific papers. *American Documentation, 14,* 10-25.

Khoussainov, R., & Kushmerick, N. (2003). Learning to compete in heterogeneous Web search environments. *Proceedings of the 18th International Joint Conference on Artificial Intelligence (IJCAI-03).*

Kifer, M., Lausen, G., & Wu, J. (1995). Logical foundations of object-oriented and frame-based languages. *Journal of the ACM, 42*(4), 741-843.

Kim, C., Lee, J., Cho, Y., & Kim, D. (2004). VISCORS: A visual-content recommender for the mobile Web. *IEEE Intelligent Systems, 19*(6), 32-39.

Kim, E.H., Morse, A., & Zingales, L. (2006). *Are elite universities losing their competitive edge?* NBER Working Paper Series 12245.

Kirsch, S., Gnasa, M., & Cremers, A. (2006). Beyond the Web: Retrieval in social information spaces. *Proceedings of the 28th European Conference on Information Retrieval.*

Kirsch, S.M. (2005). *Social information retrieval.* Diploma Thesis, Rheinische Friedrich-Wilhelms-Universität Bonn, Germany.

Kirsch, S.M., Gnasa, M., & Cremers, A.B. (2006, April 10-12). Beyond the Web: Retrieval in social information spaces. Advances in Information Retrieval, Proceedings of the 28th European Conference on ECIR (vol. 3936/2006, pp. 84-95), London.

Kleinberg, J.M. (1999). Authoritative sources in a hyperlinked environment. *Journal of the ACM, 46*(5), 604-632.

Klyne, G., & Carroll, J.J. (2004). *Resource description framework (RDF): Concepts and abstract syntax.* W3C recommendation, World Wide Web Consortium.

KMI. (n.d.). KQML performatives. Retrieved January 28, 2006, from http://kmi.open.ac.uk/people/emaunela/JATLiteBean/KQMLperf.html

Kobsa, A., & Teltzrow, M. (2005, January 9). Impacts of contextualized communication of privacy practices and personalization benefits on purchase behavior and perceived quality of recommendation, *Beyond Personalization: A Workshop on the Next Stage of Recommender Systems Research, in conjunction with the 2005 International Conference on Intelligent User Interfaces* (IUI'05) (pp. 48-53), San Diego, CA.

Kohonen, T. (1997). *Self-organizing maps.* New York: Springer-Verlag.

Koivunen, M., & Miller, E. (2002). W3C semantic Web activity. In E. Hyvonen (Ed.), *Semantic Web kick-off in Finland* (pp. 27-44). Helsinki: HIIT.

Kollock, P., & Smith, M. (Eds.). (1999). *Communities in cyberspace*. London: Routledge.

Komarjaya, J., Poo, D.C.C., & Kan, M.-Y. (2004, September 12-17). Corpus-based query expansion in online public access catalogs. *Proceedings of ECDL 2004* (pp. 221-231). Bath, UK.

Konstan, J. (2004). Introduction to recommender systems: Algorithms and evaluation. *ACM Transactions on Information Systems, 22*(1), 1-4.

Konstan, J.A., Miller, B.N., Maltz, D., Herlocker, J.L., Gordon, L.R., & Riedl, J. (1997). GroupLens: Applying collaborative filtering to Usenet news. *Communications of the ACM, 40*(3), 77-87.

Korfiatis, N., & Naeve, A. (2005). Evaluating wiki contributions using social networks: A case study on Wikipedia. *Proceedings of the 1st Online Conference on Metadata and Semantics Research* (MTSR'05). Rinton Press.

Kraaij, W., Westerveld, T., & Hiemstra, D. (2002). The importance of prior probabilities for entry page search. In M. Beaulieu, R. Baeza-Yates, S.H. Myaeng, & K. Jarvelin (Eds.), *Proceedings of the 25th Annual International ACM SIGIR Conference on Research and Development in Information Retrieval* (pp. 27-24), Tampere, Finland.

Kramer, J., Noronha, S., & Vergo, J. (2000). A user-centered design approach to personalization. *Communications of the ACM, 8*, 45-48.

Kretschmer, H. (1997). Patterns of behaviour in co-authorship networks of invisible colleges. *Scientometrics, 40*, 579-591.

Kretschmer, H. (2004). Author productivity and geodesic distance in co-authorship networks, and visibility on the Web. *Scientometrics, 60*, 409-420.

Kretschmer, H., Kretschmer, U., & Kretschmer, T. (2005). Visibility of collaboration between immunology institutions on the Web including aspects of gender studies. In P. Ingwersen & B. Larsen (Eds.), *Proceedings of ISSI 2005* (pp. 750-760). Stockholm: Karolinska University Press.

Kreuzman, H. (2001). A co-citation analysis of representative authors in philosophy: Examining the relationship between epistemologists and philosophers of science. *Scientometrics, 51*, 525-539.

Krupansky, J.(2005). Definition: Agent, activity, advancing the science of software agent technology. Retrieved February 5, 2006, from http://www.agtivity.com/def/agent.htm

Kuflik, T., & Shoval, P. (2000, July 24-28). Generation of user profiles for information filtering: Research agenda (poster session). Proceedings of the 23rd Annual International ACM SIGIR Conference on Research and Development in Information Retrieval (SIGIR'00) (pp. 313-315), Athens, Greece.

Kuhlthau, C.C. (1991). Inside the search process: Information seeking from the user's perspective. *Journal of the American Society for Information Science, 42*(5), 361-371.

Kuhlthau, C.C. (2002). *Seeking meaning: A process approach to library and information sciences* (2nd ed.). Libraries Unlimited.

Kuhlthau, C.C. (2004). *Seeking meaning: A process approach to library and information services* (2nd ed.). Westport, CN: Libraries Unlimited.

Kumar, V., Nesbit, J., & Han, K. (2005). Rating learning object quality with distributed Bayesian belief networks: The why and the how. *Proceedings of the 5th IEEE International Conference on Advanced Learning Technologies* (ICALT'05).

Lam, S.K., & Riedl., J. (2004). Shilling recommender systems for fun and profit. *Proceedings of the 13th International Conference on the World Wide Web* (pp. 393-402). New York: ACM Press.

Lancaster, F.W. (1968). *Information retrieval systems: Characteristics, testing and evaluation*. New York: John Wiley & Sons.

Lancaster, F.W. (2003). *Indexing and abstracting in theory and practice*. London: Facet.

Larson, R.R. (1996). Bibliometrics of the World Wide Web: An exploratory analysis of the intellectual structure of cyberspace. In S. Hardin (Ed.), *Global complexity: Information, chaos and control. Proceedings of the 59th Annual Meeting of the ASIS*. Retrieved January 23, 2007, from *http://sherlock.berkeley.edu/asis96/asis96.html*

Lave, J. (1988). *Cognition in practice: Mind, mathematics and culture in everyday life*. Cambridge, UK: Cambridge University Press.

Lawrence, S., & Giles, C. (1999). Accessibility of information on the Web. *Nature, 400,* 107-109.

Lawrence, S., & Giles, C.L. (2000). Accessibility of information on the Web. *Intelligence, 11*(1), 32-39.

Lazega, E. (2001). *The collegial phenomenon*. Oxford: Oxford University Press.

Leacock, C., & Chodorow, M. (1998). Combining local context and WordNet similarity for word sense identification. In C. Fellbaum (Ed.), *WordNet: An electronic lexical database* (pp. 265-283). Cambridge, MA: MIT Press.

Leake, D., Maguitman, A., & Reichherzer, T. (2005, July). Exploiting rich context: An incremental approach to context-based Web search. *Proceedings of the International and Interdisciplinary Conference on Modeling and Using Context* (CONTEXT'05), Paris, France.

Lederman, P. (2005). Implementing a taxonomy solution. *AIIM E-Doc, 19*(2), 25-26.

Lee, J. (1999). Interactive learning with a Web-based digital library system. *Proceedings of the 9th DELOS Workshop on Digital Libraries for Distance Learning.* Retrieved from *http:// courses.cs.vt.edu/~cs3604/DE-LOS.html*

Lemire, D., Boley, H., McGrath, S., & Ball, M. (2005). Collaborative filtering and inference rules for context-aware learning object recommendation. *International Journal of Interactive Technology & Smart Education, 2*(3).

Lempel, R., & Moran, S. (2001). SALSA: The stochastic approach for link-structure analysis. *ACM Transactions on Information Systems, 19,* 131-160.

Lenz, M. (1996). IMATS: Intelligent multimedia travel agent system. Proceedings of the ENTER'96 Conference, Innsbruck.

Lesser, V., & Erman, L. (1977). A retrospective view of the Hearsay-II architecture. *Proceedings of the 5th IJCAI* (pp. 790-800).

Leuf, B., & Cunningham, W. (2001). *The wiki way: Collaboration and sharing on the Internet.* San Francisco: Addison-Wesley Professional.

Levy, D.M., & Marshall, C.C. (1994). What color was George Washington's white horse? A look at assumptions underlying digital libraries. *Proceedings of Digital Libraries '94* (pp. 163-169). College Station, TX.

Levy, E. (2004). Criminals become tech savvy. *Security & Privacy Magazine, 2*(2), 65-68.

Lewis, D.D. (1998). Naive (Bayes) at forty: The independence assumption in information retrieval. *Proceedings of ECML-98, the 10th European Conference on Machine Learning* (pp. 4-15). Berlin: Springer-Verlag (LNCS 1398).

Leydesdorff, L. (2000). Luhmann, Habermas and the theory of communication. *Systems Research and Behavioral Science, 17*(3), 273-288.

Leydesdorff, L. (2001). *The challenge of scientometrics: The development, measurement, and self-organization of scientific communications.* Universal.

Leydesdorff, L. (2003). Can networks of journal-journal citations be used as indicators of change in the social sciences? *Journal of Documentation, 59,* 84-104.

Leydesdorff, L. (2004). Clusters and maps of science journals on bi-connected graphs in the Journal Citation Reports. *Journal of Documentation, 60,* 371-427.

Leydesdorff, L. (2004). Top-down decomposition of the *Journal Citation Report* of the *Social Science Citation Index*: Graph- and factor-analytical approaches. *Scientometrics, 60,* 159-180.

Leydesdorff, L. (2004). The university-industry knowledge relationship: Analyzing patents and the science base of technologies. *Journal of the American Society for Information Science and Technology, 55,* 991-1001.

Leydesdorff, L. (2006). Can scientific journals be classified in terms of aggregated journal-journal citation relations using the *Journal Citation Reports*? *Journal of the American Society for Information Science and Technology, 57,* 601-613.

Leydesdorff, L., & Hellsten, I. (2005). Metaphors and diaphors in science communication: Mapping the case of stem-cell research. *Science Communication, 27,* 64-99.

Leydesdorff, L., & Hellsten, I. (2006). Measuring the meaning of words in contexts: An automated analysis of controversies about 'Monarch butterflies', 'Frankenfoods', and 'stem cells'. *Scientometrics, 67,* 231-258.

Leydesdorff, L., & Jin, B.H. (2005). Mapping the Chinese Science Citation Database in terms of aggregated journal-journal citation relations. *Journal of the American Society for Information Science and Technology, 56,* 1469-1479.

Li, J., Loo, B., Hellerstein, J., Kaashoek, F., Karger, D., & Morris, R. (2003). On the feasibility of peer-to-peer Web indexing and search. *Proceedings of the 2nd International Workshop on Peer-to-Peer Systems,* Berkeley, CA.

Li, Y., Meiyun, Z., & Yang, B. (2005, August 15-17). Analysis and design of e-supermarket shopping recommender system. *Proceedings of the 7th International Conference on Electronic Commerce* (ICEC'05) (pp. 777-779), Xian, China.

Lieberman, H. (1995). Letizia: An agent that assists Web browsing. In C.S. Mellish (Ed.), *Proceedings of the 14th International Joint Conference on Artificial Intelligence* (pp. 924-929). Montréal, Canada: Morgan Kaufmann.

Lih, A. (2004). Wikipedia as participatory journalism: Reliable sources? Metrics for evaluating collaborative media as a news resource. *Proceedings of the International Symposium on Online Journalism.*

Lin, Y., & Kaid, L.L. (2000). Fragmentation of the intellectual structure of political communication study: Some empirical evidence. *Scientometrics, 47,* 143-164.

Lipczynska S. (2005). Power to the people: The case for Wikipedia. *Reference Reviews, 19*(2).

Liu, H., & Maes, P. (2004). What would they think? A computational model of attitudes. *Proceedings of the 9th International Conference on Intelligent User Interface* (IUI), Funchal, Portugal.

Liu, Z., & Wang, C.Z. (2005). Mapping interdisciplinarity in demography: A journal network analysis. *Journal of the American Society for Information Science and Technology, 31,* 308-316.

Loom Ontosaurus. (1998). *Loom Web browser.* Intelligent Systems Division, Information Sciences Institute, University of Southern California, USA.

Lu, J., & Callan, J. (2003). Content-based retrieval in hybrid peer-to-peer networks. *Proceedings of the 12th International Conference on Information and Knowledge Management* (CIKM'03), New Orleans, LA.

Lu, J., & Callan, J. (2004). Merging retrieval results in hierarchical peer-to-peer networks. *Proceedings of the 27th Annual International ACM SIGIR Conference on Research and Development in Information Retrieval,* Sheffield, UK.

Lua, E.K., Crowcroft, J., & Pias, M. (2005). A survey and comparison of peer-to-peer overlay network schemes. *IEEE Communications Surveys and Tutorials, 7*(2).

Lueg, C., Davenport, E., Robertson, T., & Pipek, V. (2001). Actions and identities in virtual communities of practice. *Proceedings of the 7th European Conference on Computer Supported Cooperative Work* (ECSCW 2001), Bonn, Germany.

Lytras, M.D., & Naeve, A. (Eds.). (2005). *Intelligent learning infrastructure for knowledge intensive organizations.* London: Information Science.

Machlup, F. (1980). *Knowledge: It's creation, distribution, and economic significance* (vol. 1). Princeton, NJ: Princeton University Press.

MacQueen, J. (1967). Some methods for classification and analysis of multivariate observations. In L.M. Le Cam & J. Neyman (Eds.), *Proceedings of the 5th Berkeley Symposium on Mathematical Statistics and Probability* (pp. 281-297). University of California Press.

Maedche, A., Motik, B., Silva, N., & Volz, R. (2002). MAFRA—a mapping framework for distributed ontologies. *Proceedings of EKAW (Knowledge Engineering and Knowledge Management) 2002.* Berlin: Springer-Verlag (LNCS 2473).

Maes, P. (1994). Agents that reduce work and information overload. Communications of the ACM, 37(7), 30-40.

Malsch, T., Schlieder, C., Kiefer, P., Lubcke, M., Perschke, R., Schmitt, M., & Stein, K. (2006). Communication between process and structure: Modeling and simulating message-reference-networks with COM/TE. *Journal of Artificial Societies and Social Simulation.*

Manber, U. (1992). Foreword. In W.B. Frakes & R. Baeza-Yates (Eds.), *Information retrieval. Data structures & algorithms* (pp. v-vi). Indianapolis, IN: Prentice-Hall.

Mandler, G. (1985). *Cognitive psychology.* Hillsdale, NJ: Lawrence Erlbaum.

Manning, C.D., & Schütze, H. (1999). *Foundations of statistical natural language processing.* Cambridge, MA: MIT Press.

Manouselis, N., & Costopoulou, C. (2006). Quality in metadata: A schema for e-commerce. *Online Information Review (OIR), Special Issue on Advances in Digital Information Services and Metadata Research, 30*(3), 217-237.

Marchionini, G. (1995). *Information seeking in electronic environments.* Cambridge: Cambridge University Press.

Marchionini, G. (1997). *Information seeking in electronic environments.* Cambridge, UK: Cambridge University Press (Cambridge Series on Human-Computer Interaction).

Marchiori, M. (1997). The quest for correct information on the Web: Hyper search engines. *Proceedings of WWW6, the 6th International World Wide Web Conference* (pp. 265-276).

Marion, L.S., & McCain, K.W. (2001). Contrasting views of software engineering journals: Author cocitation choices and indexer vocabulary assignments. *Journal of the American Society for Information Science and Technology, 52,* 297-308.

Marshakova, I.V. (1973). System of document connections based on references (in Russian). *Nauchno-Tekhnicheskaya Informatsiya, 2*(6), 3-8.

Mathes, A. (2004, December). Folksonomies: Cooperative classification and communication through shared metadata. *Proceedings of the Computer Mediated Communication Doctoral Seminar* (LIS590CMC), Urbana-Champaign, IL. Retrieved September 2, 2006, from http://www.adammathes.com/academic/computer-mediated-communication/folksonomies.html

Mathes, A. (2005). *Filler Friday: Google bombing.* Retrieved May 27, 2006, from *http://uber.nu/2001/04/06/*

Mauss, M. (1924). Essai sur le don. *Année Sociologique 1923-1924.*

Maw, S.Y., & Naing, M.-M. (2006, February). Personalization agent for multi-agent tourism system. Proceedings of the 4th International Conference on Computer Application (ICCA'06) (pp. 117-124), Yangon, Myanmar.

Maw, S.Y., Naing, M.-M., & Thein. N.L. (2006, November 6-8). RPCF algorithm for multi-agent tourism system (poster session). Proceedings of the 2006 IEEE International Symposium on Micro-NanoMechatronics and Human Science (MHS 2006), Nagoya, Japan.

Mayer-Schönberger, V. (2005). The cookie concept. Retrieved March 3, 2006, from http://www.cookiecentral.com/c_concept.htm

McCain, K.W. (1990). Mapping authors in intellectual space: A technical overview. *Journal of the American Society for Information Science, 41,* 433-443.

McCain, K.W. (1991). Mapping economics through the journal literature: An experiment in journal cocitation analysis. *Journal of the American Society for Information Science, 42,* 290-296.

McCain, K.W. (1995). The structure of biotechnology R&D. *Scientometrics, 32,* 153-175.

McGehee, T. Jr. (2001). *Whoosh: Business in the fast lane.* New York: Perseus.

McNee, S.M., Albert, I., Cosley, D., Gopalkrishnan, P., Lam, S.K., Rashid, Konstan, J.A, & Riedl, J. (2002). On the recommending of citations for research papers. *Proceedings of CSCW'02* (pp. 116-125), New Orleans, LA.

McPherson, M., Smith-Lovin, L., & Cook, J. (2001). Birds of a feather: Homophily in social networks. *Annual Review of Sociology, 27,* 415-444.

McPherson, M., Smith-Lovin, L., & Cook, J.M. (2001). Birds of a feather: Homophily in social networks. *Annual Review of Sociology, 27,* 415-444.

Meadows, J. (1990, July 18-21). General overview, keynote address. In M. Feeney & K. Merry (Eds.), *Proceedings of the Conference on Information Technology and the Research Process* (pp. 1-13), Cranfield, UK. London: Bowker-Saur.

MedCIRCLE. (2002, September). Towards a collaborative, open, semantic Web of trust for health information on the Web: Interoperability of health information gateways. *Proceedings of the MedCIRCLE Workshop: Collaboration for Internet Rating, Certification, Labeling and Evaluation of Health Information,* Belgium.

Melville, P., Mooney, J., & Nagarajan, R. (2002). Content-boosted collaborative filtering for improved recommendations. *Proceedings of the 18th National Conference on Artificial Intelligence* (AAAI-2002) (pp. 187-192), Edmonton, Canada.

Memmi, D. (2006). The nature of virtual communities. *AI and Society, 20*(3).

Memmi, D., & Nérot, O (2003). Building virtual communities for information retrieval. In J. Favela & D. Decouchant (Eds.), *Groupware: Design, implementation and use.* Berlin: Springer-Verlag.

Menczer, F., & Belew, R. (2000). Adaptive retrieval agents: Internalizing local context and scaling up to the Web. *Machine Learning, 39*(2-3), 203-242.

Menczer, F., Pant, G., & Srinivasan, P. (2004). Topical Web crawlers: Evaluating adaptive algorithms. *ACM Transactions on Internet Technology, 4*(4), 378-419.

Mendes, M.E.S., & Sacks, L. (2004). Dynamic knowledge representation for e-learning applications. In M. Nikravesh, L.A. Zadeh, B. Azvin, & R. Yager (Eds.), *Enhancing the power of the Internet—studies in fuzziness and soft computing* (vol. 139, pp. 255-278). Berlin/London: Springer-Verlag.

Mesquita, C., Barbosa, S.D., & Lucena, C.J. (2002). Towards the identification of concerns in personalization mechanisms via scenarios. Proceedings of 1st International Conference on Aspect-Oriented Software Development, Enschede, The Netherlands. Retrieved January 5, 2006, from http://trese.cs.utwente.nl/AOSD-EarlyAspectsWS/Papers/Mesquita.pdf

Meyer, H.A. (2006). *Topic search engines.* Retrieved May 28, 2006, from http://www.allsearchengines.com/

Middleton, S.E. (2003). *Capturing knowledge of user preference with recommender systems.* PhD Thesis.

Middleton, S.E., De Roure, D.C., & Shadbolt, N.R. (2004). Ontology-based recommender systems. In S.

Staab & R. Studer (Eds.), *International handbooks on information systems: Handbook on ontologies* (pp. 477-498). Berlin/Heidelberg: Springer-Verlag.

Middleton, S.E., Shadbolt, N.R., & De Roure, D.C. (2004). Ontological user profiling in recommender systems. *ACM Transactions on Information Systems, 22*(1), 54-88.

Mika, P. (2005, November 6-10) Ontologies are us: A unified model of social networks and semantics. *Proceedings of the 4th International Semantic Web Conference (ISWC 2005)*, Galway, Ireland. Retrieved September 2, 2006, from http://www.cs.vu.nl/~pmika/research/papers/ISWC-folksonomy.pdf

Milgram, S. (1967). The small-world problem. *Psychology Today, 2*, 60-67.

Miller, B.N., Konstan, J.A., & Riedl, J. (2004). PocketLens: Toward a personal recommender system. *ACM Transactions on Information Systems, 22*(3), 437-476.

Miller, G.A., Beckwith, R., Fellbaum, C., Gross, D., & Miller, K. (1990). Introduction to WordNet: An online lexical database. *International Journal of Lexicography, 3*(4), 235-244.

Mintzberg, H. (1979). *The structuring of organizations.* Englewood Cliffs, NJ: Prentice Hall.

Mitchell, J.C. (1969). The concept and use of social networks. In J.C. Mitchell (Ed.), *Social networks in urban situations* (pp. 1-50). Manchester, UK: University of Manchester Press.

Mizzaro, S. (1998). How many relevances in information retrieval? *Interacting with Computers, 10*(3), 303-320.

Mladenic, D. (1998). *Machine learning on non-homogeneous, distributed text data.* PhD Thesis, Faculty of Computer and Information Science, University of Ljubljana, Slovenia.

Mobasher, B., Cooley, R., & Srivastava, J. (2000). Automatic personalization based on Web usage mining. *43*(8), 142-151.

Mobasher, B., Jin, X., & Zhou, Y. (2004). Semantically enhanced collaborative filtering on the Web. In Berendt et al. (Eds.), *Proceedings of the European Web Mining Forum.* Berlin: Springer-Verlag (LNAI).

Moed, H.F. (2005). *Citation analysis in research evaluation.* Dordrecht: Springer.

Moed, H.F., & Garfield, E. (2004). In basic science the percentage of 'authoritative' references decreases as bibliographies become shorter. *Scientometrics, 60*, 295-303.

Moed, H.F., Glänzel, W., & Schmoch, U. (Eds.). (2004). *Handbook of quantitative science and technology research. The use of publication and patent statistics in studies of S&T studies.* Dordrecht: Kluwer.

Moen, W.E., Stewart, E.L., & McClure, C.R. (1998). Assessing metadata quality: Findings and methodological considerations from an evaluation of the U.S. Government Information Locator Service (GILS). *Proceedings of the 5th International Forum on Research and Technology Advances in Digital Libraries* (ADL '98). IEEE Computer Press.

Mooney, R., & Roy, L. (2000, June 2-7). Content-based book recommending using learning for text categorization. *Proceedings of the 5th ACM Conference on Digital Libraries* (pp. 195-204), San Antonio, TX.

Morahan-Martin, J., & Anderson, C.D. (2000). Information and misinformation online: Recommendations for facilitating accurate mental health information retrieval and evaluation. *CyberPsychology & Behavior, 3*(5), 731-746.

Mori, M., & Yamada, S. (2000, October 30-November 4). Adjusting to specialties of search engines using Meta Weaver. *Proceedings of the World Conference on the WWW and Internet (WebNet 2000)* (pp. 408-412). San Antonio, TX.

Morville, P. (2002, February 21). *Social network analysis.* Retrieved August 30, 2006, from http://semanticstudios.com/publications/semantics/000006.php

Muirhead, B., & Haughey, B. (2003). *An assessment of the learning objects, models and frameworks developed by the Learning Federation Schools Online Curriculum Content Initiative Australia.* Prepared for the Le@rning Federation, Australia.

Munoz, M.A, Gonzalez, V.M., Rodriguez, M., & Favela, J. (2003). Supporting context-aware collaboration in a hospital: An ethnographic informed design. In J. Favela & D. Decouchant (Eds.), *Groupware: Design, implementation and use.* Berlin: Springer-Verlag.

Muresan, G., & Harper, D.J. (2001). Document clustering and language models for system-mediated information access. *Proceedings of the 5th European Conference on Research and Advanced Technology for Digital Libraries* (pp. 438-449).

Nagarajan, R. (2002). Content-boosted collaborative filtering for improved recommendations. *Proceedings of the 18th National Conference on Artificial Intelligence*, Canada.

Najjar, J., Wolpers, M., & Duval, E. (2006). Towards effective usage-based learning applications: Track and learn from user experience(s). *Proceedings of the IEEE International Conference on Advanced Learning Technologies* (ICALT 2006), The Netherlands.

Najork, M., & Wiener, J.L. (2001). Breadth-first search crawling yields high-quality pages. *Proceedings of the 10th International World Wide Web Conference,* Hong Kong.

Nakata, K. (2001). A grounded and participatory approach to collaborative information exploration and management. *Proceedings of the 34th Annual Hawaii International Conference on System Sciences* (HICSS-34), Maui, HI.

Narayanan, S., Koppaka, L., Edala, N., Loritz, D., & Daley, R. (2004). Adaptive interface for personalizing information seeking. *CyberPsychology & Behavior, 7*(6), 683-688.

Nardi, B.A. (1996). Activity theory and human-computer interaction. In B.A. Nardi (Ed.), *Context and consciousness: Activity theory and human-computer interaction* (pp. 7-16). Cambridge, MA: MIT Press.

Nardi, B.A., & O'Day, V. (2000). *Information ecologies.* Boston: MIT Press.

Narin, F., Breitzman, A., & Thomas, P. (2004). Using patent citation indicators to manage a stock portfolio. In H.F. Moed, W. Glänzel, & U. Schmoch (Eds.), *Handbook of quantitative science and technology research* (pp. 553-568). Dordrecht: Kluwer.

NDN. (2004, November). *Quality metadata.* Position Paper, National Data Network (NDN) Metadata Workshop, Australia. Retrieved August 26, 2006, from http://www.nationaldatanetwork.org

Neisser, U. (1967). *Cognitive psychology.* New York: Appleton-Century-Crofts.

Nesbit, J., Belfer, K., & Vargo, J. (2002). A convergent participation model for evaluation of learning objects. *Canadian Journal of Learning and Technology,* 105-120.

Nesbit, J.C., & Li, J. (2004). Web-based tools for learning object evaluation. *Proceedings of the International Conference on Education and Information Systems: Technologies and Applications* (vol. 2, pp. 334-339).

Newman, M.E.J. (2001). The structure of scientific collaboration networks. *Proceedings of the National Academy of Sciences of the United States of America, 98*(2), 404-409.

Newman, M.E.J. (2003). The structure and function of complex networks. *SIAM Review, 45,* 167-256.

Nichols, D.M., Pemberton, D., Dalhoumi, S., Larouk, O., Belisle, C., & Twidale, M.B. (2000, September 18-20). DEBORA: Developing an interface to support collaboration in a digital library. *Proceedings of ECDL 2000* (pp. 239-248). Lisbon, Portugal.

Niknafs, A.A., Shiri, M.E., & Javidi, M.M. (2003). A case-based reasoning approach in e-tourism: Tour itinerary planning. *Proceedings of the 14th International Workshop on Database and Expert Systems Applications* (DEXA'03) (p. 818), Iran.

NISO (National Information Standards Organization). (2004). *Understanding metadata.* NISO Press.

North, E.J., North, J., & Benade, S. (2004). Information management and enterprise architecture planning—a juxtaposition, *Problems and Perspectives in Management, 4,* 166-179.

Ntoulas, A., Cho, J., & Olston, C. (2004). What's new on the Web?: The evolution of the Web from a search engine perspective. *Proceedings of the 13th International World Wide Web Conference,* New York.

Nunnaly, J. (1978). *Psychometric theory.* New York: McGraw-Hill.

O'Donovan, J., & Smyth, B. (2006, January 29-31). Is trust robust? An analysis of trust-based recommendation. *Proceedings of the 11th International Conference on Intelligent User Interfaces.* New York: ACM Press.

O'Reilly, T. (2005) *What is Web 2.0.* Retrieved from *http://www.oreillynet.com/pub/a/oreilly/tim/news/2005/09/30/what-is-web-20.html*

O'Reilly, T. (2006). *What Is Web 2.0—design patterns and business models for the next generation of software.* Retrieved January 3, 2007, from *http://www.oreillynet.com/pub/a/oreilly/tim/news/2005/09/30/what-is-web-20.html?page=1*

Ochoa, X., & Duval, E. (2006). Quality metrics for learning object metadata. *Proceedings of the World Conference on Educational Multimedia, Hypermedia and Telecommunications* (EDMEDIA 2006).

Ogure, T., Nakata, K., & Furuta, K. (2001). Ontology processing for technical information retrieval. *Proceedings of the 1st International Conference on Universal Access in Human-Computer Interaction* (pp. 1503-1507), New Orleans, LA.

Oldenburg, R. (1997). *The great good place: Cafes, coffee shops, community centers, beauty parlors, general stores, bars, hangouts and how they get you through the day.* New York: Marlowe & Company.

Oram, A. (Ed.). (2001). *Peer-to-peer: Harnessing the power of disruptive technologies.* O'Reilly.

Page, L., Brin, S., Motwani, R., & Winograd, T. (1998). *The PageRank citation ranking: Bringing order to the Web.* Technical Report, Stanford Digital Library Technologies Project, USA.

Page, L., Brin, S., Motwani, R., & Winograd, T. (1999). *The PageRank citation ranking: Bringing order to the Web.* Technical Report No. 1999-66, Stanford University, USA.

Pandurangan, G., Raghavan, P., & Upfal, E. (2002). Using PageRank to characterize Web structure. In O. Ibarra & L. Zhang (Eds.), *Proceedings of the 8th Annual International Conference on Computing and Combinatorics* (pp. 330-339). Singapore: Springer.

Pant, G., Bradshaw, S., & Menczer, F. (2003). Search engine—crawler symbiosis. *Proceedings of the 7th European Conference on Research and Advanced Technology for Digital Libraries* (ECDL), Berlin.

Pant, G., Srinivasan, P., & Menczer, F. (2003). Crawling the Web. *Web Dynamics.*

Papadopoullos, A. (2004). Answering the right questions about search. *EContent leadership series: Strategies for...search, taxonomy & classification* (supplement to July/August 2004 *EContent and Information Today*, pp. S6-S7). Retrieved May 29, 2006, from http://www.pro-com-strasser.com/docs/Convera_Right_Questions.pdf

Papagelis, M., & Plexousakis, D. (2004, September 27-29). Qualitative analysis of user-based and item-based prediction algorithms for recommendation agents. *Proceedings of the 8th International CIA Workshop* (pp.152-166), Erfurt, Germany.

Papagelis, M., Plexousakis, D., & Kutsuras, T. (2005). Alleviating the sparsity problem of collaborative filtering using trust inferences. *Trust Management, 3477,* 224-239.

Park, T.K. (1992). *The nature of relevance in information retrieval: An empirical study.* Unpublished PhD Thesis (UMI No. 9231644), Indiana University, USA.

Park, T.K. (1994). Toward a theory of user-based relevance: A call for a new paradigm of inquiry. *Journal of the American Society for Information Science, 45*(3), 135-141.

Pawlowski, J. (2006). *ISO/IEC 19796-1: How to use the new quality framework for learning, education, and training.* Retrieved August 26, 2006, from http://www.qualityfoundation.org/ww/en/oub/efquel/qualityservices/publications.htm

Payne, C. (2000). Personalization technique. Retrieved January 4, 2006, from http://www.wdvl.com/Authoring/ASP/Personalization/techniques.html

Pazzani, M. (1999). A framework for collaborative, content-based and demographic filtering. *Artificial Intelligence Review, 13*(5-6), 393-408.

Pazzani, M.J. (2005, January 9). Beyond idiot savants: Recommendations and common sense. *Beyond Personalization: A Workshop on the Next Stage of Recommender Systems Research, in conjunction with the 2005 International Conference on Intelligent User Interfaces* (IUI'05) (pp. 99-100), San Diego, CA.

Pelz, D., & Andrews, F. (1966). *Scientists in organizations.* New York: John Wiley & Sons.

Persson, O. (2001). All author citations versus first author citations. *Scientometrics, 50,* 339-344.

Persson. O. (2000). The literature climate of Umeå—mapping public library loans. *Bibliometric Notes, 4*(5). Retrieved January 23, 2007, from *http://www.umu.se/inforsk/BibliometricNotes/BN5-2000/BN5-2000.htm*

Pinski, G., & Narin, F. (1976). Citation influence for journal aggregates of scientific publications: Theory, with application to the literature of physics. *Information Processing and Management, 12*(5), 297-312.

Pinski, G., & Narin, F. (1976).Citation influences for journal aggregates of scientific publications: Theory, with applications to the literature of physics. *Information Processing and Management, 12,* 297-312.

Plassard, M.-F. (Ed). (1998). *Functional requirements for bibliographic records: Final report of the IFLA study group on functional requirements for bibliographic records.* UBCIM. Retrieved June 8, 2006, from http://www.ifla.org/VII/s13/frbr/frbr.pdf

Polanyi, M. (1966). *The tacit dimension.* London: Routledge & Kegan Paul.

Ponte, J.M., & Croft, W.B. (1998) A language modeling approach to information retrieval. *Proceedings of the 21st Annual International ACM SIGIR Conference on Research and Development in Information Retrieval* (pp. 275-281), Melbourne, Australia.

Porter, A.N. (1999). *The council for world mission and its archival legacy*. London: SOAS.

Powell, A., Heaney, M., & Dempsey, L. (2000). RSLP collection description. *D-Lib Magazine, 6*(9). Retrieved January 5, 2007, from http://www.dlib.org/dlib/september00/powell/09powell.html

Preece, S.E. (1981). *A spreading activation network model for information retrieval*. PhD Thesis, University of Illinois at Urbana-Champaign, USA.

Price, D.J. de Solla (1963). *Little science, big science*. New York: Columbia University Press.

Procter, R., Goldenberg, A., Davenport, E., & McKinlay, A. (1998). Genres in support of collaborative information retrieval in the virtual library. *Interacting with Computers, 10*(2), 157-175.

Pujol, J., Sanguesa, R., & Bermudez, J. (2003). Porqpine: A distributed and collaborative search engine. *Proceedings of the 12th International World Wide Web Conference*, Budapest, Hungary.

Pujol, J.M., Sanguesa, R., & Bermudez, J. (2003, May 20-24). Porqpine: A distributive and collaborative search engine. *Proceedings of the 12th International World Wide Web Conference* (WWW2003, p. S25), Budapest, Hungary. Retrieved May 27, 2006, from http://www2003. *org/cdrom/papers/poster/p341/p341-pujol.html.html*

Quillian, M.R. (1968). Semantic memory. In M. Minsky (Ed.), *Semantic information processing*. Boston: MIT Press.

Rafaeli, S., Dan-Gur, Y., & Barak, M. (2005). Social recommender systems: Recommendations in support of e-learning. *Journal of Distance Education Technologies, 3*(2), 29-45.

Raghavan, V., & Sever, H. (1995). On the reuse of past optimal queries. In E.A. Fox, P. Ingwersen, & R. Fidel (Eds.), *Proceedings of the 18th International ACM-SIGIR Conference on Research and Development of Information Retrieval* (pp. 344-350). New York: ACM Press.

Rasmussen, E. (1999). Clustering algorithms. In W.B. Frakes & R. Baeza-Yates (Eds.), *Information retrieval: Data structure and algorithms*. Englewood Cliffs, NJ: Prentice Hall.

Reader, D.M. (2001). The intellectual structure of entrepreneurship: An author co-citation analysis. In M. Davis & C.S. Wilson (Eds.), *Proceedings of the 8th International Conference on Scientometrics & Informetrics* (pp. 587-596). Sydney: BIRG.

Recker, M., & Walker, A. (2003). Supporting 'word-of-mouth' social networks via collaborative information filtering. *Journal of Interactive Learning Research, 14*(1), 79-98.

Recker, M., Walker, A., & Lawless, K. (2003). What do you recommend? Implementation and analyses of collaborative filtering of Web resources for education. *Instructional Science, 31*(4/5), 229-316.

Recker, M.M., & Wiley, D.A. (2000, June). An interface for collaborative filtering of educational resources. *Proceedings of the 2000 International Conference on Artificial Intelligence*, Las Vegas, NV.

Recker, M.M., & Wiley, D.A. (2001). A non-authoritative educational metadata ontology for filtering and recommending learning objects. *Journal of Interactive Learning Environments, 9*(3), 255-271.

Rennie, J.D.M., Shih, L., Teevan, J., & Karger, D.R. (2003). Tackling the poor assumptions of naive Bayes text classifiers. *Proceedings of the 20th International Conference on Machine Learning* (pp. 616-623).

Resnick, P., & Varian, H.R. (1997). Recommender systems. *Communications of the ACM, 40*(3), 56-58.

Resnick, P., Iacovou, N., Suchak, M., Bergstrom, P., & Riedl, J. (1994). GroupLens: An open architecture for collaborative filtering of Netnews. *Proceedings of the 1994 Conference on Computer Supported Collaborative Work (CSCW'94)* (pp. 175-186).

Resnik, P. (1995). *Disambiguating noun groupings with respect to WordNet senses*. Chelmsford, MA: Sun Microsystems Laboratories.

Rheingold, H. (2000). *The virtual community*. Cambridge, MA: MIT Press.

Risson, J., & Moors, T. (2004). *Survey of research towards robust peer-to-peer networks: Search methods*. Sydney, Australia: University of New South Wales.

Robertson, J.R. (2005). Metadata quality: Implications for library and information science professionals. *Library Review, 54*(5), 295-300.

Robertson, S.E. (1981). The methodology of information retrieval experiment. In K. Sparck Jones (Ed.), *Information retrieval experiment* (pp. 9-31). Butterworths.

Robins, D. (1998, October 24-29). Dynamics and dimensions of user information problems as foci of interaction in information retrieval. In C.M. Preston (Ed.), *Proceedings of the 61st ASIS Annual Meeting on Information*

Access in the Global Information Economy (vol. 35, pp. 327-341), Pittsburgh, PA. Medford, NJ: Information Today (for ASIS).

Robins, D. (2000). Interactive information retrieval: Context and basic notions. *Informing Science, 3*(2), 57-61.

Rodríguez i Gairín, J.M. (1997). Valorando el impacto de la información en Internet: AltaVista, el 'Citation Index' de la Red. *Revista Espanola de Documentacion Scientifica, 20,* 175-181.

Rosengren, K.E. (1966). *The literary system*. Unpublished Licentiate Thesis in Sociology, University of Lund, Sweden.

Rosengren, K.E. (1968). *Sociological aspects of the literary system*. Stockholm: Natur och Kultur.

Rousseau, R., & Small, H. (2005). Escher staircases dwarfed. *ISSI Newsletter, 1*(4), 8-10.

Rousseau, R., & Thelwall, M. (2004). Escher staircases on the World Wide Web. *FirstMonday, 9*(6). Retrieved January 23, 2007, from *http://www.firstmonday.org/issues/issue9_6/rousseau/index.html*

Rousseau, R., & Zuccala, A. (2004). A classification of author co-citations: Definitions and search strategies. *Journal of the American Society of Information Science and Technology, 55,* 513-529.

Rumetshofer, H., & Wob, W. (2005). Semantic maps and meta-data enhancing e-accessibility in tourism information systems. Proceedings of the 16th International Workshop on Database and Expert Systems Applications (DEXA'05) (pp. 881-885), Austria.

Russell, J.M., & Rousseau, R. (2002). Bibliometrics and institutional evaluation. In R. Arvantis (Ed.), *Encyclopedia of life support systems (EOLSS). Part 19.3: Science and technology policy*. Oxford, UK: EOLSS.

Sabidussi, G. (1966). The centrality index of a graph. *Psychometrika, 31,* 581-603.

Sahami, M., & Heilman, T.D. (2006). A Web-based kernel function for measuring the similarity of short text snippets. *Proceedings of the 15th international Conference on the World Wide Web* (pp. 377-386). New York: ACM Press.

Salter, J., & Antonopoulos, N. (2006). CinemaScreen recommender agent: Combining collaborative and content-based filtering. *IEEE Intelligent Systems, 21*(1), 35-41.

Salton, G. (1963). Associative document retrieval techniques using bibliographic information. *Journal of the ACM, 10*(4), 440-457.

Salton, G. (1989). *Automatic text processing: The transformation, analysis and retrieval of information by computer*. Reading, MA: Addison-Wesley.

Salton, G., & McGill, M. (1983). *Introduction to modern information retrieval*. New York: McGraw-Hill.

Saracevic, T. (1996). Interactive models of information retrieval (IR): A review and proposal. *Proceedings of the 59th Annual Meeting of the American Society for Information Science* (vol. 33, pp. 3-9).

Saracevic, T. (1996). Relevance reconsidered '96. In P. Ingwersen & N.O. Pors (Eds.), *Proceedings of the 2nd International Conference on Conceptions of Library and Information Science: Integration in Perspective* (CoLIS 2) (pp. 201-218). Copenhagen: Royal School of Librarianship.

Saracevic, T., Kantor, P.B., Chamis, A.Y., & Trivison, D. (1988). A study of information seeking and retrieving. I: Background and methodology. *Journal of the American Society for Information Science, 39*(3), 161-176.

Sarwar, B., Karypis, G., Konstan, J., & Riedl, J. (2001). Item-based collaborative filtering recommendation algorithms. *Proceeding of the 10th World Wide Web Conference* (pp. 285-295).

Sarwar, B.M., Konstan, J.A., Borchers, A., Herlocker, J., Miller, B., & Riedl, J. (1998, November 14-18). Using filtering agents to improve prediction quality in the GroupLens research collaborative filtering system. Proceedings of the 1998 ACM Conference on Computer Supported Cooperative Work (CSCW'98) (pp. 345-354), Seattle, WA.

Savolainen, R. (1995). Everyday life information seeking: Approaching information seeking in the context of "way of life." *Library and Information Science Research, 17,* 259-294.

Schafer, J.B. (2005, January 9). DynamicLens: A dynamic user-interface for a meta-recommendation system. *Beyond Personalization: A Workshop on the Next Stage of Recommender Systems Research, in conjunction with the 2005 International Conference on Intelligent User Interfaces* (IUI'05) (pp. 72-76), San Diego, CA.

Schafer, J.B., Konstan, J.A., & Reidl, J. (2004). The view through MetaLens: Usage patterns for a meta-recommendation system. *IEE Proceedings Software, 151*(6), 267-279.

Schafer, J.B., Konstan, J.A., & Riedl, J. (2001). E-commerce recommendation applications. *Data Mining and Knowledge Discovery, 5*(1/2), 115-153.

Schamber, L. (1994). Relevance and information behavior. *Annual Review of Information Science and Technology, 29,* 3-48.

Schmidt, K., & Simone, C. (2000). Mind the gap! Towards a unified view of CSCW. *Proceedings of the 4th International Conference on the Design of Cooperative Systems* (COOP2000), Sophia Antipolis, France.

Schneider, J.W. (2005). Naming clusters in visualization studies: Parsing and filtering of noun phrases from citation contexts. In P. Ingwersen & B. Larsen (Eds.), *Proceedings of ISSI 2005* (pp. 406-416). Stockholm: Karolinska University Press.

Schutz, A. (1970). *Reflections on the problem of relevance. Edited, annotated, and with an introduction by Richard M. Zaner.* New Haven, CT/London: Yale University Press.

Scott, J. (2000). *Social network analysis: A handbook* (2nd Ed.). London/Thousands Oaks, CA: Sage.

Selden, L. (2001). Academic information seeking—careers and capital types. *New Review of Information Behavior Research, 1*(2), 195-215.

Sen, S.K., & Gan, S.K. (1983). A mathematical extension of the idea of bibliographic coupling and its applications. *Annals of Library Science and Documentation, 30,* 78-82.

Setten, M.V., & Hadidy, F.M. (n.d.). *Collaborative search and retrieval: Finding information together.* Retrieved February 20, 2004, from *https://doc.telin.nl/dscgi/ds.py/ Get/File-8269/GigaCE-Collaborative_Search_and_ Retrieval Finding_Information_Together.pdf*

Shapiro, C., & Varian, H.R. (1999). *Information rules: A strategic guide to the network economy.* Cambridge, MA: Harvard Business School Press.

Shardanand, U., & Maes, P. (1995). Social information filtering: Algorithms for automating 'word of mouth'. *Proceedings of the Conference on Human Factors in Computing Systems (ACM CHI'95)* (pp. 210-217). Denver, CO.

Shearin, S., & Lieberman, H. (2001, January 14-17). Intelligent profiling by example. Proceedings of the 6th International Conference on Intelligent User Interfaces (IUI '01), Santa Fe, NM.

Sherman, C. (2006, January 19). *Survey: Google, Yahoo still favorites in North America.* Retrieved May 29, 2006, from http://searchenginewatch.com/searchday/article. php/3578491

Shih, L., Chang, Y., Rennie, J., & Karger, D. (2002). Not too hot, not too cold: The bundled-SVM is just right! *Proceedings of the ICML-2002 Workshop on Text Learning.*

Shon, J., & Musen, M.A. (1999). The low availability of metadata elements for evaluating the quality of medical information on the World Wide Web. *Proceedings of the 1999 American Medical Informatics Association Symposium*(AMIA'99).

Shreeves, S.L., Riley, J., & Milewicz, E. (2006). Moving towards sharable metadata. *First Monday, 11*(8).

Sicilia, M.A., & Garcia, E. (2005). Filtering information with imprecise social criteria: A FOAF-based backlink model. *Proceedings of the 4th Conference of the European Society for Fuzzy Logic and Technology* (EUSLAT), Barcelona, Spain.

Silverstein, C., Henzinger, M., Marais, H., & Moricz, M. (1998). Analysis of a very large AltaVista query log. *Technical Report 1998-014.* Palo Alto, CA: Digital Systems Research Center.

Singh, M., Yu, B., & Venkatraman, M. (2000). Community-based service location. *Communications of the ACM, 44*(4), 49-54.

Six Apart Ltd. (n.d.). *Live journal bot policy.* Retrieved January 3, 2007, from *http://www.livejournal.com/ bots/*

Small, H. (1973). Co-citation in the scientific literature: A new measure of the relationship between two documents. *Journal of the American Society for Information Science, 24,* 265-269.

Smeaton, A., Keogh, G., Gurrin, C., McDonald, K., & Sodring, T. (2002). Analysis of papers from twenty-five years of SIGIR conferences: What have we been doing for the last quarter of a century? *SIGIR Forum, 36*(2), 39-43.

Smyth, B., & Cotter, P. (2000). A personalized television listings service. *Communications of the ACM, 43*(8), 107-111.

Smyth, B., Balfe, E., Boydell, O., Bradley, K., Briggs, P., Coyle, M., & Freyne, J. (2005, July 31-August 5). A live-user evaluation of collaborative Web search. *Proceedings of the 19th International Joint Conference on Artificial Intelligence (IJCAI-05)* (pp. 1419-1424). Edinburgh, Scotland.

Smyth, B., Balfe, E., Briggs, P., Coyle, M., & Freyne, J. (2003). Collaborative Web search. *Proceedings of the 18th International Joint Conference on Artificial*

Intelligence (IJCAI-03) (pp. 1417-1419). San Francisco: Morgan Kaufmann.

Soboroff, I., Nicholas, C., & Pazzani, M. (Eds.). (1999). *Proceedings of the SIGIR-99 Workshop on Recommender Systems,* Berkley, CA.

Sperber, D., & Wilson, D. (1986). *Relevance: Communication and cognition.* Oxford: Basil Blackwell.

Spink, A., Greisdorf, H., & Bateman, J. (1998). From highly relevant to not relevant: Examining different regions of relevance. *Information Processing and Management, 34*(5), 599-621.

Spink, A., Greisdorf, H., & Bateman, J. (1999). A study of mediated successive searching during information seeking. *Journal of Information Science, 25*(6), 477-487.

Srinivasan, P., Pant, G., & Menczer, F. (2005). A general evaluation framework for topical crawlers. *Information Retrieval, 8*(3), 417-447.

Stanford. (2006). Protégé editor. Retrieved August 2006 from http://protege.stanford.edu

Starr, B., Ackerman, M.S., & Pazzani, M. (1996). Do-I-Care: A collaborative Web agent. *Proceedings of the Human Factors in Computing Systems Conference (CHI '96)* (pp. 273-274). New York: ACM.

Statsoft. (n.d.). Basic statistics. Retrieved February 10, 2006, from http://www.statsoft.com/textbook/stbasic.html#index

Stein, K., & Hess, C. (2006). Information retrieval in trust-enhanced document networks. In Behrendt et al. (Eds.), *Semantics, Web and mining.* Berlin: Springer-Verlag.

Steinacker, A., Ghavam, A., & Steinmetz, R. (2001). Metadata standards for Web-based resources. *IEEE Multimedia,* (January-March), 70-76.

Steiner, U., & Stanier, C. (2006). Soft matter: The essential ingredient for success. *Soft Matter, 2,* 9-11.

Stix, G. (2006). The elusive goal of machine translation. *Scientific American, 294*(3), 70-73.

Stojanovic, L., Stojanovic, N., & Volz, R. (2002). Migrating data-intensive Web sites into the semantic Web. *Proceedings of the 17th ACM Symposium on Applied Computing* (pp. 1100-1107).

Stutt, A., & Motta, E. (2004). Semantic learning Webs. *Journal of Interactive Media in Education,* (10).

Suchman, L. (1987). *Plans and situated actions: The problem of human-machine communication.* Cambridge, UK: Cambridge University Press.

Suchman, L., Trigg, R., & Blomberg, J.L. (2002). Working artefacts: Ethnomethods of the prototype. *British Journal of Sociology, 53*(2), 163-179.

Suchman, L.A., & Trigg, R.H. (1993). Artificial intelligence as craftwork. In S. Chaiklin & J. Lave (Eds.), *Understanding practice: Perspectives on activity and context* (pp. 144-178). Cambridge, UK: Cambridge University Press.

Suel, C., Mathur, T., Wu, J.-W., Zhang, J., Delis, A., Kharrazi, M. et al. (2003). ODISSEA: A peer-to-peer architecture for scalable Web search and information retrieval. *Proceedings of the International Workshop on the Web and Databases* (WebDB), San Diego, CA.

Suleman, H., & Fox, E.A. (2002). Designing protocols in support of digital library componentization. *Proceedings of the European Conference on Digital Libraries* (ECDL) (pp. 568-582). Berlin: Springer-Verlag (LNCS 2458).

Sullivan, D. (2000, April 4). The vortals are coming! The vortals are coming! Retrieved May 24, 2006, from http://searchenginewatch.com/sereport/article.php/2162541

Sullivan, D. (2002, February 20). *Specialty search engines.* Retrieved March 23 and May 28, 2006, from http://searchenginewatch.com/links/article.php/2156351

Sullivan, D. (2005). *comScore MediaMatrix search engine ratings.* Retrieved January 17, 2007, from http://searchenginewatch.com/reports/article.php/2156431

Sundin, O., & Johannisson, J. (2005). The instrumentality of information needs and relevance. In F. Crestani & I. Ruthven (Eds.), *Proceedings of the Conference on Conceptions of Library and Information Science* (CoLIS 2005) (pp. 107-118). Berlin/Heidelberg: Springer-Verlag.

Sundin, O., & Johannisson, J. (2005). Pragmatism, neo-pragmatism and sociocultural theory: Communicative participation as a perspective in LIS. *Journal of Documentation, 61*(1), 23-43.

Sung, H.H. (2002, November). Helping online customers decide through Web personalization. Proceedings of the Conference on IEEE Intelligent Systems (vol. 17, no. 6, pp. 34-43), Kyungpook National University, Korea.

Supekar, K. (2005). A peer-review approach for ontology evaluation. *Proceedings of the 8th International Protégé Conference,* Madrid, Spain.

Supekar, K., Patel, C., & Lee, Y. (2004). Characterizing quality of knowledge on semantic Web. In V. Barr & Z. Markov (Eds.), *Proceedings of the 17th International Florida Artificial Intelligence Research Society Conference* (FLAIRS'04). AAAI Press.

Sutton, S.A. (1999). Conceptual design and deployment of a metadata framework for educational resources on the Internet. *Journal of the American Society for Information Science, 50*(13), 1182-1192.

Swanson, D.R. (1988). Historical note: Information retrieval and the future of an illusion. *Journal of the American Society for Information Science, 39*(2), 92-98.

Swearingen, K., Lyman, P., Varian, H.R., Charles, P., Good, N., Jordan, L.L., & Pal, J. (2003). *How much information?* Berkeley: University of California School of Information Management and Systems. Retrieved May 30, 2006, from http://www.sims.berkeley.edu/research/projects/how-much-info-2003/

Talja, S. (2002). Information sharing in academic communities: Types and levels of collaboration in information seeking and use. *New Review of Information Behavior Research, 3,* 143-159.

Tang, C., Xu, Z., & Dwarkadas, S. (2003). Peer-to-peer information retrieval using self-organizing semantic overlay networks. *Proceedings of ACM SIGCOMM'03,* Karlsruhe, Germany.

Tang, R., & Solomon, P. (1998). Toward an understanding of the dynamics of relevance judgment: An analysis of one person's search behavior. *Information Processing and Management, 34*(2/3), 237-256.

Tang, T., & McCalla, G. (2005). Smart ecommendation for an evolving e-learning system: Architecture and experiment. *International Journal on E-Learning, 4*(1), 105-129.

Taylor, R. (1968). Question-negotiation and information seeking in libraries. *College and Research Libraries, 29*(3), 178-194.

Tempich, C., Staab, S., & Wranik, A. (2004). REMINDIN': Semantic query routing in peer-to-peer networks based on social metaphors. *Proceedings of the 13th International World Wide Web Conference,* New York.

Ternier, S., Olmedilla, D., & Duval, E. (2005). *Peer-to-peer versus federated search: Towards more interoperable learning object repositories. In P.* Kommers & G. Richards (Eds.), (pp. 1421-1428).

Terveen, L., McMackin, J., Amento, B., & Hill, W. (2002). Specifying preferences based on user history. *Proceedings of the Conference on Human Factors in Computing Systems* (CHI'02). Minneapolis, MN.

Thelwall, M. (2006). Interpreting social science link analysis research: A theoretical framework. *Journal of the American Society for Information Science and Technology, 57,* 60-68.

Thelwall, M., & Harries, G. (2004). Do the Web sites of higher rated scholars have significantly more online impact? *Journal of the American Society for Information Science and Technology, 55,* 149-159.

Thelwall, M., & Vaughan, M. (2004). A fair history of the Web? Examining country balance in the Internet Archive. *Library & Information Science Research, 26,* 162-176.

Thelwall, M., & Wilkinson, D. (2004). Finding similar academic Web sites with links, bibliometric coupling and colinks. *Information Processing and Management, 40,* 515-526.

Thelwall, M., Vaughan, L., & Björneborn, L. (2005). Webometrics. *Annual Review of Information Science and Technology, 39,* 81-135.

Thelwall. M. (2004). *Link analysis: An information science approach.* Amsterdam: Elsevier.

Theng, Y.L., Mohd-Nasir, N., Buchanan, G., Fields, B., Thimbleby, H.W., & Cassidy, N. (2001). Dynamic digital libraries for children. *Proceedings of the Joint Conference on Digital Libraries* (JCDL) (pp. 406-415).

Tijssen, R., Buter, R.K., & van Leeuwen, Th.N. (2000). Technological relevance of science: An assessment of citation linkages between patents and research papers. *Scientometrics, 47,* 389-412.

Tkatchenko, M. (2005). *Combining reputation and collaborative filtering systems.* Retrieved September 1, 2006, from http://www.cs.ubc.ca/~kevinlb/teaching/cs532a%20-%202005/Class%20projects/Maria.pdf

Torres, R., McNee, S.M., Abel, M., Konstan, J.A., & Riedl, J. (2004). Enhancing digital libraries with TechLens+. *Proceedings of the 4th ACM/IEEE Joint Conference on Digital Libraries* (JCDL 2004) (pp. 228-236).

Travers, J., & Milgram, S. (1969). An experimental study of the small world problem. *Sociometry, 32,* 425-443.

Twidale, M., & Nichols, D. (1998). Designing interfaces to support collaboration in information retrieval. *Interacting with Computers, 10*(2), 177-193.

Tzikopoulos, A., Manouselis, N., & Vuorikari, R. (2007). An overview of learning object repositories. In P. Northrup (Ed.), *Learning objects for instruction: Design and evaluation.* Hershey, PA: Idea Group.

UMBC. (n.d.). What is KQML? Retrieved January 28, 2006, from http://www.cs.umbc.edu/kqml/whats-kqml.html

Upstill, T., Craswell, N., & Hawking, D. (2003). Query-independent evidence in home page finding. *ACM Transactions on Information Systems, 21*(3), 286-313.

Vakkari, P. (1999). Task complexity, problem structure and information actions: Integrating studies on information seeking and retrieval. *Information Processing & Management, 35*(6), 819-837.

Vakkari, P. (2000, July 24-28). Relevance and contributing information types of searched documents in task performance. In N.J. Belkin, P. Ingwersen, & M.-K. Leong (Eds.), *Proceedings of the 23rd Annual International ACM SIGIR Conference on Research and Development in Information Retrieval* (vol. 34, pp. 2-9), Athens, Greece. New York: ACM Press.

Vakkari, P. (2003). Task-based information seeking. In B. Cronin (Ed.), *Annual review of information science and technology* (vol. 37, pp. 413-464). Medford, NJ: Information Today.

Vakkari, P., & Hakala, N. (2000). Changes in relevance criteria and problem stages in task performance. *Journal of Documentation, 56*(5), 540-562.

Van Assche, F., & Vuorikari, R. (2006). A framework for quality of learning resources. In U. Ehlers & J.M. Pawlowski (Eds.), *European handbook for quality and standardization in e-learning.* Berlin: Springer-Verlag, 443-456.

van de Wijngaert, L. (1999, August 13-15). A policy capturing study of media choice: The effect information [sic] of needs and user characteristics on media choice. In T.D. Wilson & D.K. Allen (Eds.), *Information Behavior: Proceedings of the 2nd International Conference on Research in Information Needs, Seeking and Use in Different Contexts* (pp. 463-478). Sheffield, UK: Taylor Graham.

Van Impe, S., & Rousseau, R. (2006). Web-to-print citations and the humanities. *Information - Wissenschaft und Praxis, 57,* 422- 426.

Van Rijsbergen, C.J. (1979). *Information retrieval* (2nd ed.). Butterworths.

Vance, D.M. (1997, August). Information, knowledge and wisdom: The epistemic hierarchy and computer-based information system. In B. Perkins & I. Vessey (Eds.), *Proceedings of the 3rd Americas Conference on Information Systems,* Indianapolis, IN.

VanFossen, L. (2005). *Top specialty search engines list.* Retrieved May 28, 2006, from http://www.cameraontheroad.com/index.php?p=196

Vaughan, L., & Shaw, D. (2003). Bibliographic and Web citations: What is the difference? *Journal of the American Society for Information Science and Technology, 54,* 1313-1322.

Vaughan, L., & Shaw, D. (2005). Web citation data for impact assessment: A comparison of four science disciplines. *Journal of the American Society for Information Science and Technology, 56,* 1075-1087.

Vaughan, L., & Thelwall, M. (2004). Search engine coverage bias: Evidence and possible causes. *Information Processing and Management, 40,* 693-707.

Vicente, K.J. (1999). *Cognitive work analysis: Towards safe, productive and healthy computer-based work.* Mahwah, NJ: Lawrence Erlbaum.

Vlassis, N. (2003). A concise introduction to multiagent systems and distributed AI. Retrieved January 14, 2006, from http://staff.science.uva.nl/~vlassis/cimasdai/

Voss, A., Nakata, K., & Juhnke, M. (2000). Concept indexes: Sharing knowledge from documents. In M. Divitini, T. Brasethvik, & D. Schwartz (Eds.), *Internet-based organizational memory and knowledge management* (pp. 123-146). Hershey, PA: Idea Group.

Wagner, C.S., & Leydesdorff, L. (2005). Network structure, self-organization, and the growth of international collaboration in science. *Research Policy, 34,* 1608-1618.

Walker, A., Recker, M., Lawless, K., & Wiley, D. (2004). Collaborative information filtering: A review and an educational application. *International Journal of Artificial Intelligence and Education, 14,* 1-26.

Wang, J., Pouwelse, J., Lagendijk, R.L., & Reinders, M.J.T. (2006, April 23-27). Distributed collaborative filtering for peer-to-peer file sharing systems. *Proceedings of the 21st Annual ACM Symposium on Applied Computing (SAC'06),* Dijon, France.

Wang, P., & Soergel, D. (1998). A cognitive model of document use during a research project. Study 1. Document selection. *Journal of the American Society for Information Science, 49*(2), 115-133.

Wang, Y., & Kitsuregawa, M. (2001). Link based clustering of Web search results. In C. Claramunt, W. Winiwarter, Y. Kambayashi & Y. Zhang (Eds.), *Proceedings of the 2nd International Conference on Web Information Systems Engineering* (vol. 1, p. 115). Washington, DC: IEEE Computer Society.

Wasserman, S., & Faust, K. (1994). *Social network analysis: Methods and applications.* New York: Cambridge University Press.

Waterhouse, S. (2001). *JXTA search: Distributed search for distributed networks*. Santa Clara, CA: Sun Microsystems.

Watts, D., & Strogatz, S. (1998). Collective dynamics of "small-world" networks. *Nature, 393*, 440-442.

Watts, D.J. (1999). *Small worlds*. Princeton, NJ: Princeton University Press.

Wayne, L. (2004, January). Quality metadata. *Proceedings of the 2004 ESRI Federal User Conference*, Washington, DC.

Webdesign. (2005). How to write Web cookies. Retrieved March 20, 2006, from http://Webdesign.about.com/b/a/136789.htm

Webdesign. (n.d.). Cookies: HTTP cookies—Web cookies. Retrieved January 25, 2006, from http://Webdesign.about.com/od/cookies

Webopedia. (n.d.). Do cookies compromise security? Retrieved January 1, 2006, from http://www.Webopedia.com/DidYouKnow/Internet/2002/Cookies.asp

Wellman, B. (1997). An electronic group is virtually a social network. In S. Kiesler (Ed.), *Culture of the Internet* (pp. 179-205). Mahwah, NJ: Lawrence Erlbaum.

Wellman, B. (2001). Physical place and cyberplace: The rise of personalized networking. *International Journal of Urban and Regional Research, 25*(2), 227-252.

Wellman, B. (Ed.). (1999). *Networks in the global village*. Boulder, CO: Westview Press.

Wen, J.R., Nie, J.Y., & Zhang, H.J. (2001). Query clustering using content words and user feedback. In W.B. Croft, D.J. Harper, D.H. Kraft, & J. Zobel (Eds.), *Proceedings of the 24th Annual International ACM SIGIR Conference on Research and Development in Information Retrieval* (pp. 442-443). New York: ACM Press.

Wenger, E. (1998). *Communities of practice: Learning, meaning and identity*. Cambridge: Cambridge University Press.

Wenger, E. (1998). *Communities of practice: Learning, meaning and identity*. Cambridge: Cambridge University Press.

Wenger, E., & Snyder, W.M. (2000). Communities of practice: The organizational frontier. *Harvard Business Review*, (January-February), 139-145.

Wenger, E., McDermott, R.A., & Snyder, W. (2002). *Cultivating communities of practice: A guide to managing knowledge*. Boston: Harvard Business School Press.

Westerveld, T., Kraaij, W., & Hiemstra, D. (2001) Retrieving Web pages using content, links, URLs and anchors. In E.M. Vorhees & D.K. Harman (Eds.), *Proceedings of the 10th Text Retrieval Conference* (TREC-10) (pp. 663-672). Gaithersburg, MD: National Institute of Standards and Technology.

White, H.D. (2000). Toward ego-centered citation analysis. In B. Cronin & H.B. Atkins (Eds.), *The Web of knowledge; a festschrift in honor of Eugene Garfield* (pp. 475-496). Medford, NJ: Information Today.

White, H.D. (2001). Authors as citers over time. *Journal of the American Society for Information Science and Technology, 52*, 87-108.

White, H.D. (2003). Pathfinder networks and author cocitation analysis: A remapping of paradigmatic information scientists. *Journal of the American Society for Information Science and Technology, 54*, 423-434.

White, H.D., & Griffith, B. (1981). Author cocitation: A literature measure of intellectual structure. *Journal of the American Society for Information Science, 32*, 163-171.

White, H.D., & McCain, K. (1998). Visualizing a discipline: An author cocitation analysis of information science, 1972-1995. *Journal of the American Society for Information Science, 49*, 327-355.

White, H.D., Wellman, B., & Nazer, N. (2004). Does citation reflect social structure? Longitudinal evidence from the "Globenet" interdisciplinary research group. *Journal of the American Society for Information Science and Technology, 55*, 111-126.

Wikipedia. (n.d.). Collaborative filtering. Retrieved March 3, 2006, from http://en.wikipedia.org/wiki/Collaborative_filtering

Wiley, D. (Ed.). (2002). *The instructional use of learning objects*. Bloomington. IN: AECT. Retrieved August 10, 2005, from *http://reusability.org/read/*

Willett, P. (1988). Recent trends in hierarchic document clustering: A critical review. *Information Processing and Management, 24*(5).

Willy, C. (2001, April 17). Web site personalization. Retrieved May 31, 2005, from http://www-128.ibm.com/developerworks/Websphere/library/techarticles/hipods/personalize.html

Wilson, C.S. (1999). Informetrics. *Annual Review of Information Science and Technology, 34*, 107-247.

Wilson, T.D. (1999). Models in information behavior research. *Journal of Documentation, 55*(3), 249-270.

Winner, L. (1989). *The whale and the reactor: A search for limits in an age of high technology.* Chicago: University of Chicago Press.

Winograd, T., & Flores, F. (1987). *Understanding computers and cognition: A new foundation for design.* Reading, MA: Addison-Wesley.

Witten, I.H., Boddie, S.J., Bainbridge, D., & McNab, R.J. (2000). Greenstone: A comprehensive open-source digital library software system. *Proceedings of the ACM Conference on Digital Libraries* (pp. 113-121).

Wolf, J.L., Squillante, M.S., Yu, P.S., Sethuraman, J., & Ozsen, L. (2002). Optimal crawling strategies for Web search engines. *Proceedings of the 11th International Conference on the World Wide Web* (pp. 136-147), Honolulu, HI.

Wooldridge, M. (2002). An introduction to multiagent system. Chichester, UK: John Wiley & Sons.

World Wide Web Consortium. (n.d.). *PICS-specification.* Retrieved August 10, 2005, from *http://www.w3c. org/PICS*

Wu, X., Zhang, L., & Yu, Y. (2006, May 23-26). Exploring social annotations for the semantic Web. *Proceedings of the 15th International World Wide Web Conference* (WWW 2006), Edinburgh, Scotland.

Wu, Y., Pan, Y., Zhang, Y., Ma, Z., Pang, J., Guo, H., Xu, B., & Yang, Z. (2004). China Scientific and Technical Papers and Citations (CSTPC): History, impact and outlook. *Scientometrics, 60,* 385-394.

Xie, H. (2000). Shifts of interactive intentions and information seeking strategies in interactive information retrieval. *Journal of the American Society for Information Science, 51*(9), 841-857.

Yamada, T. (2004, May). Role of metadata in quality assurance of multi-country statistical data in the case of UNIDO industrial statistics. *Proceedings of the Conference on Data Quality for International Organizations,* Germany.

Yang, B., & Garcia-Molina, H. (2002). Improving search in peer-to-peer networks. *Proceedings of the 22nd International Conference on Distributed Computing Systems* (ICDCS'02), Vienna, Austria.

Yang, Y., & Liu, X. (1999). A re-examination of text categorization methods. *Proceedings of SIGIR-99, the 22nd ACM International Conference on Research and Development in Information Retrieval* (pp. 42-49).

Yeates, S., Witten, I.H., & Bainbridge, D. (2001). Tag insertion complexity. *Proceedings of the Data Compression Conference* (pp. 243-252).

Yeung, C., Tung, P.F., & Yen, J. (1998). A multi-agent based tourism kiosk on Internet. *Proceedings of the 31st Annual Hawaii International Conference on System Sciences* (vol. 4, p. 452).

Yin, L.C., Kretschmer, H., Hanneman, R.A., & Liu, Z.Y. (2006). Connection and stratification in research collaboration: An analysis of the COLLNET network. *Information Processing & Management, 42,* 1599-1613.

Yu, K., Wen, Z., Xu, X., & Ester, M. (2001). Feature weighting and instance selection for collaborative filtering. *Proceedings of the 2nd International Workshop on Management of Information on the Web—Web Data and Text Mining* (MIW'01) (pp. 285-290).

Yu, K., Xu, X., Tao, J., Ester, M., & Kriegel, H.P. (2002). Instance selection techniques for memory-based collaborative filtering. *Proceedings of the 2nd SIAM International Conference on Data Mining* (SDM'02). Retrieved February 21, 2006, from *http://citeseer.ist. psu.edu/yu02instance.html*

Zamir, O., & Etzioni, O. (1998). Web document clustering: A feasibility demonstration. *Proceedings of the 19th International ACM SIGIR Conference on Research and Development in Information Retrieval* (SIGIR'98) (pp. 46-54).

Zamir, O., & Etzioni, O. (1999). Grouper: A dynamic clustering interface to Web search results. *Computer Networks,* 1361-1374.

Zamir, O., Etzioni, O., Madani, O., & Karp, R.M. (1997). Fast and intuitive clustering of Web documents. In D. Heckerman, H. Mannila, D. Pregibon, & R. Uthurusamy (Eds.), *Proceedings of the 3rd International Conference on Knowledge Discovery and Data Mining* (KDD'97) (pp. 287-290). Menlo Park, CA: AAAI Press.

Zaragoza, H., Craswell, N., Taylor, M., Saria, S., & Robertson, S. (2004). Microsoft Cambridge and TREC-13: Web and HARD tracks. In E.M. Vorhees & L.P. Buckland (Eds.), *Proceedings of the 13th Text Retrieval Conference* (TREC-13). Gaithersburg, MD: National Institute of Standards and Technology.

Zeng, C., Xing, C.X., & Zhou, L.Z. (2003). Similarity measure and instance selection for collaborative filtering. *Proceedings of the 12th International Conference on the World Wide Web* (WWW'03) (pp. 652-658), Budapest, Hungary.

Zerubavel, E. (1993). Horizons: On the sociomental foundations of relevance. *Social Research, 60*(2), 397-413.

Zhang, X. (2002). Collaborative relevance judgment: A group consensus method for evaluating user search performance. *Journal of the American Society for Information Science and Technology, 53*(3), 220-231.

Zhao, H., Meng, W., Wu, Z., Raghavan, V., & Yu, C. (2005, May 10-14). Fully automatic wrapper generation for search engines. *Proceedings of the 14th International World Wide Web Conference Committee* (IW3C2) (pp. 66-75), Chiba, Japan.

Zhao, Y., & Karypis, G. (2003). Prediction of contact maps using support vector machines. In H. Jamil, & V. Magalooikonomou (Eds.), *Proceedings of the 3rd IEEE Symposium on Bioinformatics and Bioengineering* (pp. 26-33). Washington, DC: IEEE Computer Society.

Ziegler, C.N. (2005). *Towards decentralized recommender systems.* PhD Thesis, Albert-Ludwigs-Universität Freiburg, Germany.

Ziegler, C.N., & Lausen, G. (2004). Spreading activation models for trust propagation. *Proceedings of the IEEE International Conference on E-Technology, E-Commerce and E-Service* (EEE04), Taipei, Taiwan.

Zuccala, A. (2006). Modeling the invisible college. *Journal of the American Society for Information Science and Technology, 57,* 152-168.

Zuccala, A. (2006). Author cocitation analysis is to intellectual structure as Web cocitation analysis is to…? *Journal of the American Society for Information Science and Technology, 57,* 1486-1501.

About the Contributors

Dion Hoe-Lian Goh earned his PhD in computer science and is an associate professor of information studies, Wee Kim Wee School of Communication and Information at Nanyang Technological University, Singapore. He is also director of the school's Master of Science in Information Systems program. His research areas are in the areas of information retrieval, digital libraries, text mining, use of information technology in education, and user interfaces.

Schubert Foo is professor and associate chair of the Wee Kim Wee School of Communication & Information at Nanyang Technological University, Singapore. He received his BSc (Hons.), MBA, and PhD from the University of Strathclyde, UK. He is a chartered engineer, chartered IT professional, fellow of the Institution of Mechanical Engineers, and fellow of the British Computer Society. He is a board member of the National Archives of Singapore and the National Library Board. He has published more than 160 publications in the areas of multimedia technology, Internet technology, multilingual information retrieval, digital libraries, and knowledge management. He is a member of the Editorial Advisory Board of the *Journal of Information Science, Journal of Information and Knowledge Management, International Yearbook of Library and Information Management,* among others. He co-edited a book *Design and Usability of Digital Libraries: Case Studies in the Asia Pacific* with Yin-Leng Theng in 2006.

* * *

Naresh Kumar Agarwal is a PhD candidate and teaching assistant in the Department of Information Systems, School of Computing, National University of Singapore. His work has been accepted for publication in the *Journal of the American Society for Information Science and Technology* (JASIST) and in conferences such as the International Conference on Human-Computer Interaction and the Information Resources Management Association Conference. His research interests include information searching and retrieval from the user/behavioral perspective, information management, and knowledge management. Mr. Agarwal serves as a board member of the APRU Doctoral Students Network.

Ruj Akavipat is a PhD student in the Computer Science Department at Indiana University, USA. He earned a master's degree in computer science from Southern Illinois University Carbondale and is a member of the anti-phishing group at Indiana University. His research interests include artificial intelligence, computer security, distributed systems, and information retrieval systems.

Theresa Dirndorfer Anderson's research explores the relationship between people and emerging technologies. She has a particular interest in examining ways information systems and institutional policies might better support creative and analytic activities. Her research builds on her PhD thesis ("Understandings of Relevance and Topic as They Evolve in the Scholarly Research Process") to focus on human decision processes, information retrieval interactions, and e-scholarship. In 2005 her thesis was awarded the 1st Annual Emerald/EFMD Outstanding Doctoral Research Award (Information Science category). She designs and delivers courses (postgraduate and undergraduate) in information retrieval and organization, as well as in social informatics.

George Buchanan is a lecturer in the Future Interaction Technology Laboratory at the University of Wales, Swansea. He has published extensively in the fields of digital library and mobile interaction design. In 2004 he won the ACM Ted Nelson award for research carried out during his PhD, which he completed in 2005. Dr. Buchanan is a visiting researcher at the New Zealand Digital Library project at the University of Waikato, and collaborates with a number of industrial researchers, including Microsoft Research, Cambridge, UK, and Nokia, Finland.

Richard Butterworth is a senior lecturer in computer science at Middlesex University, UK, with a research interest in the usability of digital library systems and the information seeking and retrieval behavior of non-academic researchers. He was awarded a PhD in 1997 from Loughborough University. He also worked at Senate House Library, University of London as the project technical liaison officer for the Accessing our Archival and Manuscript Heritage project, developing the Helpers site described in this book, and he also developed a digital library site for the Vaughan Williams Memorial Library.

Antonella Carbonaro is an associate professor of computer science at the University of Bologna, Italy. She received the Italian Laurea degree in Computer Science from the University of Bologna in 1992. In 1997 she finished her PhD studies at the University of Ancona on the topic of artificial intelligent systems. From 1997 to 1999 she received a research fellowship focused on artificial intelligence. Her current research interests concern personalization and content-based services for data and knowledge mining, and the personalized learning environment.

Armin B. Cremers is a full professor of computer science and chair of the Department of Computer Science III at the University of Bonn. Prior to this position he was a full professor at the University of Dortmund and an assistant professor at the University of Southern California. He holds a PhD in mathematics from the University of Karlsruhe, Germany. His scientific research is in the areas of database and information systems, autonomous mobile robots, and artificial intelligence. Presently, he serves as dean of the School of Mathematics and Science.

Erik Duval is a professor in the research unit on hypermedia and databases in the Computer Science Department of the Katholieke Universiteit Leuven, Belgium. His research interests have long focused on the application of information and communication technology in education and training, currently his interest being in metadata in a wide sense, learning object metadata in particular, and how they enable finding rather than searching in an open, global learning infrastructure based on open standards.

Moreover, human-computer interaction in a learning or digital repository context has drawn his attention, so that we can "hide everything but the benefits." Professor Duval serves as president of the ARIADNE Foundation and as technical editor for the standard on Learning Object Metadata (LOM).

Rodolfo Ferrini received the Laurea degree in computer science from the University of Bologna, Italy. He is a PhD student in the Department of Computer Science of the University of Bologna. His current research interests include natural language processing and knowledge representation in the semantic Web.

Melanie Gnasa is a post-doctoral researcher in the Department of Computer Science III at the University of Bonn. She studied computer science and computational linguistics at the University of Koblenz-Landau. In 2006, she finished her dissertation "Congenial Web Search—Conceptual Framework for Personalized, Collaborative, and Social Peer-to-Peer Retrieval." Her research interests are in several areas of information retrieval, including personalized and collaborative Web retrieval, as well as peer-to-peer information retrieval.

Claudia Hess received her diploma in information systems from Bamberg University, Germany, in 2004. Currently, she is a research assistant at the Laboratory for Semantic Information Technology at Bamberg University. In her PhD studies, which are jointly supervised at Bamberg University and University Paris 11, France, she is interested in the integration of social relationship data, above all trust relationships, into recommendation and ranking technology.

Annika Hinze is a senior lecturer and head of the information systems and databases research group at the University of Waikato, New Zealand. She has an established portfolio of research across the spectrum of information systems, specializing in event-based communication. In 2006, Dr. Hinze won the Australian Computer Society award for her work on event-based tourist information systems. Her interests include a strong commitment to the full participation and recognition of women in computer science, and she has founded and organized the Computing Women Congress, the pan-Pacific conference series for females of all ages in IT.

Sebastian Marius Kirsch is a graduate of Rheinische Friedrich-Wilhelms-Universität Bonn, Germany, where he studied computer science and computational linguistics. His research focuses on algorithms for information retrieval in social media. He is currently employed by Google Ireland, Dublin.

Nikolaos Korfiatis is a PhD student in the Department of Informatics at the Copenhagen Business School, Denmark. He is currently pursuing his PhD in the area of recommender systems, with a research emphasis on the applications from behavioral economics and social network theory into the design of more effective recommender systems. He obtained a BSc in information systems from Athens University of Economics and Business, Greece, in 2004 and an MSc in engineering of interactive systems from the Royal Institute of Technology, Sweden, in 2006.

Chu Keong Lee is a lecturer in the Division of Information Studies, Wee Kim Wee School of Communication and Information, Nanyang Technological University, Singapore. His research areas are knowledge sharing, social network analysis, and scientometrics.

Brendan Luyt is an assistant professor in the Division of Information Studies, Wee Kim Wee School of Communication and Information, Nanyang Technological University, Singapore. His research interests lie in the exploration of the social and policy landscape of information access.

Ana Gabriela Maguitman is an adjunct professor in the Computer Science and Engineering Department at the Universidad Nacional del Sur, Argentina, and a researcher at the National Scientific and Technical Research Council (CONICET), Argentina. Before joining the Universidad Nacional del Sur, she was a postdoctoral fellow in the School of Informatics at Indiana University, USA. She earned a master's degree in computer science from the Universidad Nacional del Sur in 1997 and a PhD in computer science from Indiana University in 2004. Between 2000 and 2004 she was a research assistant for the NASA-funded project, "Integrated Intelligent Support for Knowledge Capture, Refinement and Sharing." She was a CONICET fellow from 1996 to 1999 and a Fulbright-FOMEC fellow from 1999 to 2001. She is pursuing research in the areas of knowledge capture, recommendation systems, context-based search, and Web mining.

Nikos Manouselis is a researcher at the Informatics Laboratory of the Agricultural University of Athens. He has a diploma in electronics and computer engineering, a master's degree in operational research, as well as a master's degree in electronics and computer engineering from the Technical University of Crete, Greece. Mr. Manouselis was previously affiliated with the Informatics & Telematics Institute of the Center for Research & Technology, Greece, as well as the Decision Support Systems Laboratory and the Multimedia Systems & Applications Laboratory of the Technical University of Crete, Greece. His research interests involve the design, development, and evaluation of electronic services, and their applications.

Konstantinos Markellos, an electrical and computer engineer, is a researcher in the Department of Computer Engineering and Informatics at the University of Patras. He obtained his diploma from the Department of Electrical and Computer Engineering (1999) and his MSc on "Hardware and Software Integrated Systems" (2003) from the Department of Computer Engineering and Informatics. Today, he is a PhD candidate in the latter department. His research interests lie in the area of Internet technologies and especially electronic commerce, and he has published several research papers in national and international journal and conferences.

Penelope Markellou is a computer engineer and researcher in the Department of Computer Engineering and Informatics at the University of Patras. She obtained her PhD in "Techniques and Systems for Knowledge Management in the Web" (2005) and her MSc in "Usability Models for E-Commerce Systems and Applications" (2000) from the University of Patras. Her research interests focus on algorithms, techniques, and approaches for the design and development of usable e-applications including e-commerce, e-learning, e-government, and business intelligence. She has published several research papers in national and international journals and conferences, and is co-author of two books and eight book chapters.

Soe Yu Maw is an assistant lecturer at the Government of Computer College, Taunggyi, and also a PhD candidate at the University of Computer Studies, Yangon, Myanmar. Her research efforts focus on agent technology, personalization, information retrieval, and information extraction. She received a bachelor's and master's degrees in computer science from the University of Computer Studies, Mandalay.

Daniel Memmi has a double training in linguistics and computer science. He earned an MA in linguistics from the University of Chicago, a PhD in linguistics from the University of Paris-VII, and a PhD in computer science from the University of Paris-Sud. He was a researcher in computer science with CNRS in Paris and Grenoble from 1980 to 2004. He has since been associate professor of computer science at the Université du Québec à Montréal, Canada. Throughout his career, he has worked mostly on natural language processing and expert systems, using both symbolic and connectionist techniques. His present interests include text analysis, collaborative information retrieval, and social networks.

Filippo Menczer is an associate professor of informatics and computer science, an adjunct associate professor of physics, and a member of the cognitive science program at Indiana University, USA. He holds a Laurea in physics from the University of Rome and a PhD in computer science and cognitive science from the University of California, San Diego. Dr. Menczer has been the recipient of Fulbright, Rotary Foundation, and NATO fellowships, and is a fellow-at-large of the Santa Fe Institute. His research is supported by a Career Award from the National Science Foundation which focuses on Web, text, and data mining; Web intelligence; distributed information systems; social Web search; adaptive intelligent agents; complex systems and networks; and artificial life.

Aristotelis Mertis graduated from the Computer Engineering and Informatics Department of the University of Patras. His current research area is personalization techniques in e-commerce applications.

Ioanna Mousourouli is a graduate computer engineer from the Computer Engineering and Informatics Department of the University of Patras. She currently is a postgraduate student of computer science. Her research areas are personalization and recommendation techniques in e-business and e-learning systems, information retrieval techniques, and Web usage mining techniques in adapting content and structure.

Myo-Myo Naing is an associate professor at the University of Computer Studies, Yangon, Myanmar. Her research interests include information extraction, machine learning, semantic Web annotation, and multi-agent systems. She received her bachelor's and master's degrees in computer science from the University of Computer Studies, Yangon, and her PhD in computer engineering from the Nanyang Technological University, Singapore.

Keiichi Nakata is associate professor of social informatics and dean of the School of Information Technology at the International University, Germany. He holds a BEng and an MEng from the University of Tokyo, and a PhD in artificial intelligence from the University of Edinburgh. He has held academic posts in the UK and has been a member of the CSCW Research Group at GMD in Germany. Prior to his current appointment, he was associate professor in cognitive systems engineering at the University of Tokyo. His research interests include collaborative and cognitive systems, social informatics, human-computer interaction, and knowledge sharing.

Angeliki Panayiotaki obtained her diploma in computer engineering and informatics from the University of Patras in 1996 and her MSc in "Advanced Information Systems" from the University of Athens in 2000. She is currently working as a researcher (PhD student) at the Computer Engineering and Informatics Department of the University of Patras, and also at the General Secretariat for Information Systems of the Hellenic Ministry of Economy and Finance. Her research interests focus on personalization, Web mining, and interoperability techniques applied in the e-commerce, e-government, and e-health domains. She has published several research papers in international and national conferences.

Danny C.C. Poo graduated from the University of Manchester Institute of Science and Technology, UK. Currently, he is associate professor and assistant dean in the School of Computing, National University of Singapore. Dr. Poo has extensive experience and publications in the area of software engineering, information management, and knowledge management. His current research areas include effective search strategies, relevance ranking/feedback, metadata, taxonomy generation, knowledge management portals, and object-oriented software engineering. Dr. Poo serves on the Steering Committee of the Asia Pacific Software Engineering Conference and is the author of five books on Java/Java EE technologies.

Khasfariyati Razikin is a project officer in the Division of Information Studies, Wee Kim Wee School of Communication and Information, Nanyang Technological University, Singapore. Her research interests lie in information retrieval, natural language processing, and machine learning.

Ronald Rousseau is an associate professor in the Department of Industrial Sciences and Technology, Association Katholieke Universiteit Leuven, Germany, where he teaches mathematics to engineering students. He also teaches a course on knowledge representation at the Antwerp University School for Information and Library Science. He is a Derek de Solla Price awardee (2001) and co-writer of the book *Introduction to Informetrics* (1990). Other awards and achievements include: Prize of the Belgian Academy of Science (1979), Honorary Professorship Henan Normal University (2001), and guest professor of the Library (school) of the Chinese Academy of Science (2003). He has published more than 100 articles in journals indexed by Thomson Scientific.

Christoph Schlieder is professor and chair of computing in the cultural sciences since 2002 at Bamberg University, Germany. He holds a PhD and a Habilitation degree in computer science, both from the University of Hamburg. Before coming to Bamberg, he was professor of computer science at the University of Bremen where he headed the Artificial Intelligence Research Group. His primary research interests lie in developing and applying methods from semantic information processing to problems from the cultural sciences. Application areas of his research work include GIS and mobile assistance technologies as well as digital archives.

Ray Chandrani Sinha is pursuing her PhD in the Division of Information Studies, Wee Kim Wee School of Communication and Information, Nanyang Technological University, Singapore. She also obtained her master's degree in information studies from the same school. Her research interests include mobile applications, context-aware computing in mobile computing environments, information retrieval, and data mining.

Miguel-Ángel Sicilia earned an MSc in computer science from the Pontifical University of Salamanca, Spain, in 1996 and a PhD from the Carlos III University in 2003. He worked as a software architect in e-commerce consulting firms, being part of the development team of a Web personalization framework at Intelligent Software Components (iSOCO). From 2002 to 2003 he worked as a full-time lecturer at the Carlos III University, after which he joined the University of Alcalá. His research interests are driven by the activities of the Information Engineering Research Unit, which he directs.

Amrish Singh is a software developer who is always searching for new and innovative ways to simplify the complexities of business software. He earned a BSc in information technology from the International University in Germany in 2004, and is currently working at SAP's Research and Breakthrough Innovation department, at its headquarters in Germany. Mr. Singh's interests are in Web services, the semantic Web, machine learning, and human-computer interaction; he has been working with computers for as long as he can remember.

Klaus Stein obtained an Informatics (CS) diploma in 1998 and a doctoral (PhD) degree in 2003 from the Munich University of Technology, Germany in the field of spatial cognition. He currently works on computer-mediated communication processes (COM) at the Laboratory for Semantic Information Technology at Bamberg University, Germany.

Athanasios Tsakalidis obtained his Diploma in Mathematics from the University of Thessaloniki, Greece (1973), his Diploma in Computer Science (1981) and his PhD (1983) from the University of Saarland, Saarbuecken, Germany. His is currently a Full Professor in the Department of Computer Engineering and Informatics, University of Patras and the R&D Coordinator of the Research Academic Computer Technology Institute (RACTI). His research interests include data structures, graph algorithms, computational geometry, expert systems, medical informatics, databases, multimedia, information retrieval, and bioinformatics. He has published several research papers in national and international journals and conferences and is co-author of the "Handbook of Theoretical Computer Science" and other book chapters.

Riina Vuorikari currently pursues her PhD in the Katholieke Universiteit Leuven, Belgium, at the department of computer Science. Her main research focuses on Social Information Retrieval, such as social bookmarking and tagging, and how it can enhance the discovery and reuse of learning resources within a repository of learning resources. Additionally, she works in European Schoolnet (EUN) where, since 2000, she has been dealing with issues related to digital learning resources, quality, repositories and various aspects of semantic and technical interoperability within a network of European educational authorities. She has a Master's degree in Education from University of Joensuu in Finland, and a postgraduate degree in Hypermedia from Paris 8, France.

Nyein Chan Soe Win is a graduate of the Master's in Information Studies program at Nanyang Technological University, Singapore.

Markus Won is a business analyst at Deutsche Post World Net. Prior to this position, he was employed by Conet AG as an IT consultant in the field of business travel. He studied computer science at the University of Bonn, Germany. He earned a PhD in the Department of Computer Science III at the University of Bonn, where he was also employed as a junior researcher. His research topics are computer-supported cooperative work, human-computer interaction, and requirements engineering.

Le-Shin Wu is a PhD student in the Department of Computer Science at Indiana University, USA. He holds an MS in civil engineering from the National Central University, Taiwan, and an MS in computer science from Indiana University. Since 2003, he has been a research assistant in the Computer Science Department and the Center for Cell and Virus Theory at Indiana University. His research interests include databases, distributed information retrieval systems, Web mining, machine learning, and Web service.

Index

Symbols

6Search (6S) 155

A

abundance problem 144
algorithm 115
archive description standards 73
authority-based retrieval 134

B

backlinks 110
blogs 135
bookmarking 9

C

centrality 117
centrality, actor degree 117
centrality, betweenness 118, 143
centrality, closeness / distance 117
centrality, contributor degree 128
centralized search engines 155
citation analysis 252
citation linking 252
classification, document 57
classification, hierarchical 57
clustering, K-means algorithm 36
clustering, query algorithm 34
clustering, query approach 33
clusters, query measuring 38
collaborative classification 47–66
collaborative classification, as a social process 49
collaborative classification, of concepts 49

collaborative indexing 47
collaborative querying 31–46
collaborative search 7
collaborative source, dynamic 14
collaborative source, static 14
combinator module 165
communication module 165
computer-supported collaborative work (CSCW) 72
Concept Index 56
conceptual framework 230
content-based approach 31
cookies 297
criteria 96
cues 1

D

data analysis 322
data gatherer 4
denial of service (DoS) attack 159
digital learning resources 90
digital library (DL) technology 209
disintermediation 69
document reference network 109

E

E-Shop 323
ego density 117
environment 96
ethics 179
ethnographic exploration 230
evaluation approaches (EAs) 91
evaluation results 96
extended K-means algorithm 35